Y0-BRW-703

Contemporary Cultures and Societies of Latin America

Random House / New York

CONTEMPORARY CULTURES AND SOCIETIES OF LATIN AMERICA

A Reader in the Social Anthropology of Middle and South America and the Caribbean

EDITED, WITH INTRODUCTIONS AND NOTES, BY

Dwight B. Heath

BROWN UNIVERSITY

and

Richard N. Adams

UNIVERSITY OF TEXAS

FIRST PRINTING

Library of Congress Catalog Card Number: 65-17443

MANUFACTURED IN THE UNITED STATES OF AMERICA BY
The Haddon Craftsmen, Scranton, Pa.

Design by Tere LoPrete

Preface

The recent resurgence of Latin American studies programs reflects the increasing importance, to governments and individuals, of understanding the peoples and societies of that area. This book attempts to combine outstanding descriptions of fundamental aspects of Latin American life with the insights of social scientists concerning the dynamics of important processes.

It is unlikely that anyone could in a single volume satisfy the diversity of interests that characterize students of Latin America—anthropologists, sociologists, political scientists, geographers, historians, missionaries, government administrators and technicians, and others. And although the student in each of these fields has a distinctive focus, each also finds himself heavily dependent on the work of colleagues in related fields. The present volume is not designed to be all things to all these men. Although its scope is broad, in subject matter as well as area, it has a specifically social anthropological emphasis. Anthropologists pioneered in the study of society and culture in Latin America. Their focus, dictated by earlier interests in the discipline, has been on the rural and more primitive or underdeveloped aspects of society. In recent years, Latin America has been increasingly studied by economists, sociologists, and political scientists. In this volume, therefore, explicit recognition is given to contributions from these fields, as illustrated by the work of Hill, Mosk, Germani, Goldrich, and others.

The substantive bias of anthropology has led to a relative weakness in the literature with respect to many aspects of modern society. We have made some attempt in this book to correct this weakness, but to do so from the point of view of anthropological interests. So it is that, although "the city" is an object of increasing interest to students, we have no specific papers on "cities." Rather, we have included a series of papers, such as those by Lewis, Mangin, Leeds, Strickon, and Germani, that concern certain aspects of social relations that are manifested in the city. Similarly, we have included papers that concern traits found in city and country alike, such as those by Simmons, Gillin, Wagley (on race), De Azevedo, Wolf, and Beals, as well as the general descriptions in the first section.

We have refrained, insofar as possible, from giving in to a strong temptation to pay more attention to matters of current political importance, but have, instead, chosen to emphasize matters of more general and enduring concern to social scientists. Therefore, specific events are treated more as illustrative of processes than as historically critical in themselves. This is not to say that social scientists have been unaware of or unconcerned about crucial problems; a number of the papers in this book deal with topics that are important to political understanding, notably those by Germani, Goldrich, Wolf, Wagley, Gillin, Kunkel, and Leeds.

Although we have little to say about tribal peoples who tend to remain politically and economically isolated from participation in their nations, emphasis on the rural side of life remains. This is appropriate not only in that it reflects a traditional anthropological bias, but also because the focus of life in Latin America is, in fact, still primarily rural. Only four major countries have populations that are over 50 per cent urban: Argentina, Chile, Cuba, and Venezuela. Therefore, important papers on land and agriculture are included, since these subjects are still more representative of Latin American economic life than is the occupational complex of the nonagrarian sector. In short, a number of general processes are illustrated, with specific examples from throughout Latin America.

At the outset, it was hoped that some kind of regional balance could be maintained in the selection of papers. Our thinking was in terms of Middle America, the Andes, southern South America, Brazil, and the Caribbean (including the Guianas). If the twenty-odd papers that explicitly deal with specific areas are set against the relative populations of these regions, we find that Middle America and the Andes are over-represented, whereas Brazil, the Caribbean, and southern South

America have been somewhat slighted. This ratio, however, reflects the amount of work done in these areas, as well as the editors' competence and confidence in the material.

Although on some topics we could find no suitable papers, there are obviously more good papers than we could use in this compilation. The basis for selection involved a complex combination of factors, including overall area distribution of the articles, overlap in subject matter between papers, accessibility of the original, and so forth, all in relation to a realistic limitation on the length of the book. Arbitrarily, some papers of considerable importance have been omitted simply because they are readily available in other form—notably in the Bobbs-Merrill Reprint Series in the Social Sciences, or in Olen E. Leonard and Charles P. Loomis, eds., *Readings in Latin American Social Organization and Institutions* (East Lansing, Michigan State College Press, 1953). These collections should be consulted for further outstanding readings on the subjects dealt with here. Of the 28 articles, two were prepared expressly for this volume (Goldrich, Leeds), and four appear here for the first time in translation (De Azevedo; Hill, Silva, and Hill; Germani; Vázquez). The last two translations are the only articles that have been slightly abridged; all others are reprinted with only minor editorial revision.

The Introductions are purposely brief, intended only to set the papers in historical and intellectual context. Each introductory essay is followed by a list of References Cited and a bibliography of Further Readings that serves as a guide to other selected readings on the subject. At the end of the volume is a general bibliography.

The editors are indebted to a number of people for their suggestions, both as to specific items and emphasis. Charles Wagley, Elman Service, and Anthony Leeds are primary among these; responsibility for the final product is entirely ours, however. Editing the book was a joint effort. As is evident, each of the editors prepared certain of the introductory sections and topical bibliographies. Helen Travis, Mary van den Bergh, and Jo Enna Reece of the Institute of Latin American Studies staff at the University of Texas devoted many hours to helping prepare portions of the manuscript for press, as did Anna M. Cooper, Robert N. Lynch, and Ann N. Welsh, at Brown University. A special note of thanks is due to Mrs. Leonore C. Hauck of Random House for seeing the manuscript through press.

We are also grateful to the authors who kindly gave permission for us to reprint their papers—especially to those whose papers had to be omitted in later stages, owing to space problems—and to the publishers who kindly gave reprint permissions.

Believing that a volume such as this represents essentially a collective effort, we have chosen to forego any profits, and all royalties will be turned back to further research in Latin America, through Human Relations Research, Ltd. and the Institute of Latin American Studies, University of Texas.

DWIGHT B. HEATH,
Providence, Rhode Island

RICHARD N. ADAMS
Austin, Texas

Contents

LAND, AGRICULTURE, AND ECONOMICS

SOCIAL ORGANIZATION

VIEWS OF THE WORLD

THE DELINEATION OF CULTURAL ENTITIES IN LATIN AMERICA

Introduction

RICHARD N. ADAMS

The papers in this section have been selected with an eye to both the more traditional interests in social organization and some newer areas of investigation. The study of social organization in Latin America has been marked neither by comprehensiveness nor by stunning discoveries. It has, however, been the scene of a continuing development of understanding about contemporary society that is perhaps equal to, if somewhat different from, that obtained elsewhere in the world. In some respects, it has been overdominated by a concern with problems at the community level, and is only now beginning to examine with care events on a larger scale.

This essay touches on six kinds of structures that are particularly important in Latin America, together with the processes that characterize them in the current world. Four of these are of comparable order: community and nationalization; class sectors and mobility; family, friendship, and laterality; and power structures and centralization. The first and sixth, however, are of a different order. The first concerns demographic processes and their consequences in the mobility and organization of the society; the sixth—the region, reform, and revolution—is the complex result and concomitant of the processes earlier described. In addition to the four central topics, there is also that of economic development and its social consequences. This is omitted in the present discussion since upon which it is based. The rest of the papers are directed at different regions of Latin America, and each takes a rather different conceptual framework in the effort. The Service paper doubles as a later critique of the Redfieldian notions, as well as a view into Paraguayan town life. Núñez del Prado's paper is an introductory description, and Wagley's paper still provides a good general introduction to the areas of Brazil, although both Brazil and ways of thinking about nations have changed somewhat since the paper's first appearance.

The rest of this introductory section is devoted to a brief review of thinking about Latin American peoples and cultures as it has developed in social anthropology and allied fields. It is not possible to provide a real history here; rather, we review a number of general complexes of thought and interest that have been particularly important.

For purposes of discussion, we will deal with nine complexes of interests, theories, and contributors: *indigenismo*, historicism, the Great Dichotomy, psycho-cultural study, rural sociology, evolution and ecology, applied anthropology, structural studies, and classification.

Indigenismo

Although most modern social anthropological field research in Latin America has been initiated or carried out by foreigners, particularly North Americans, a great deal of the work has been dominated in both obvious and subtle ways by *indigenismo* and local nationalism. There are two major reasons for this: the fact that local students were motivated by these concerns led their foreign mentors to pay more attention to them than they might otherwise have done; and the intellectual-theoretical sterility of American historicism, already revealed by the attacks of Malinowski and Radcliffe-Brown, made some North Americans particularly receptive to a more meaningful framework. Margaret Park Redfield, in commenting on the papers of her husband, Robert Redfield, notes how his interest in Mexico was specifically influenced by Manuel Gamio, a leading *indigenista*.*

Indigenismo as an intellectual trend, however, found its major development and continuity in Latin America. Even among the growing group of North Americans who directed their attention to the problems of Indians in the United States, many, such as Oliver La Farge, Edward Spicer, Michael Pijoan, Emma Reh, and Sol Tax, had direct experience

* Margaret Park Redfield, in an editorial introductory note in *Human Nature and the Study of Society: The Papers of Robert Redfield*, Chicago, University of Chicago Press, 1962, p. 145.

in the field with Latin American Indian populations. The Latin experiences and ideas had more influence on the northerners than the reverse. But the rather logical line of development of Latin American *indigenismo* that produced a revolutionary doctrine and that finally led to its being encompassed by a broader nationalism was blocked in North America by the fact that the vast political majority was totally disinterested in the Indian's welfare, and by no stretch of the imagination could the Indian be held responsible for the major problems that faced the nation as a whole. In contrast, Middle American and Andean Indians were a visible part of a great national backwardness.

Indigenismo, for better or worse, was more talk than action. Further, relatively few *indigenistas* contributed greatly to building knowledge of the local societies. Certain of them were, however, of special importance, and their work has made a real mark on the development of social science in the area. Of specific note, and by way of illustration, mention may be made of Manuel Gamio, Hildebrando Castro Pozo, Luis Valcarcel, and Moisés Sáenz, although many others played important roles.

Gamio was one of the very few Latin American scholars who worked directly with Franz Boas and carried some of the objectivity that so affected that scholar's other students. Gamio, however, was immersed in the Mexican Revolution and was in a position to play a real role in Mexican political development. In this role he combined an understanding of the importance of objective observation of social events with a strong nationalistic motivation. In the same period that Gamio was carrying out the work that led to his monumental *La población del Valle de Teotihuacán* (1922), a Peruvian, Hildebrando Castro Pozo, was visiting numerous villages and towns of his country's highlands. The product of Castro Pozo's observations, *Nuestra comunidad indígena* (1924), served, over the years, to educate some of his countrymen about the contemporary Indian. From the more general point of view, perhaps the most influential early contributor to the interest in the Indian was Moisés Sáenz, who visited Indian populations in both the Andean countries and Middle America. His books had perhaps the widest influence among intellectuals and students. Although *indigenistas* did not produce scholarly products in any proportion to their numbers, the fact that the major individuals with interest in the contemporary Indian were *indigenistas* contributed to their continued influence on social anthropologists. With the end of World War II, *indigenismo* became indistinguishable from the more general and broader nationalism that was coming to dominate the world scene. The older activists were dead or becoming politicians or academicians; younger heads were either turning to international socialism or communism as their guide or to direct-action programs of development.

Historicism

Until the early 1930's, the guiding framework of North American anthropologists in Latin America was that known as *American historicism.* Led by Franz Boas and his early students, the few trained North American anthropologists who ventured south of the border were either interested primarily in prehistory or else looked at contemporary peoples with the idea of searching out the historical origins of the traits they observed. Elsie Clews Parsons' work in Mitla and Otavalo was ethnography by an acute and sympathetic observer, but the major interest beyond sheer description was an attempt to pigeonhole traits. Melville Herskovits studied Negro populations in the Antilles and stimulated such interest that Gonzalo Aguirre Beltrán studied Negroes in Mexico and a number of Brazilians followed the same path in Brazil.

In general, the younger students trained in the historical tradition turned to a variety of theoretical concerns. George Foster's study tended to focus on the Tarascan area and Ralph Beals did a series of general ethnographic works. John Rowe in the Andes and Isabel Kelly in Mexico were principally interested in archaeological problems, but turned their attention to ethnographic and social anthropological studies on many occasions. In general, individuals trained in the historical tradition developed in Latin American studies, as elsewhere in anthropology, a variety of theoretical interests, little marked by a single tradition.

The Great Dichotomy

The first set of North Americans to come into Latin America in a continuing scholarly operation were those of the Carnegie Institution of Washington program in Middle America. Under this program, Robert Redfield and his colleagues initiated work in Yucatan, and somewhat later Sol Tax went to Guatemala. Redfield brought to Central America an intellectual bent as much influenced by Chicago sociology as by American historicism. Further, he was directly stimulated by Manuel Gamio's *indigenista* concerns. He looked less to history than to current social organization, and more to the changes under way among the Indians than to their past. His first study, *Tepoztlán* (1930), showed nascent interest in social change, and when he arrived in Yucatan, he had gone so far as to define the focus of his work as "Under what circumstances do secularization and individualism arise?" In 1933, Redfield presented to the American Anthropological Association the paper "Culture Changes in Yucatan." We have chosen to initiate the present volume with this selection because in it Redfield not only outlines the substantive findings that led to the volume *The Folk Culture of Yucatan*

(1941), but also states clearly the intellectual position that marked his work.

Robert Redfield has been the most influential North American in Latin American social anthropology. Not only through his direct contacts, such as Alfonso Villa Rojas, Calixta Guiteras-Holmes, Antonio Goubaud, and Juan de Dios Rosales, but also through students in the United States and Mexico, his influence reached into the Andes and Brazil. He introduced into the social anthropology of the region a major theoretical position, the great dichotomy between the past and the present. This general intellectual framework had first been felt in American sociology through the work of Tönnies and Durkheim, and in anthropology stemmed back to Henry Maine. What Redfield did during the 1930's was to take what had been a set of general models and elaborate on them to fit the materials that he and his co-workers found in Yucatan. Redfield's theory, fathered by European scholarship, was mothered by Yucatan field work.

In subsequent years, the folk-urban or folk-city distinction was to dominate the intellectual processes of students and to become a reference point even for antagonistic field workers. It was not until the 1950's that criticism of the theory, coupled with adequate case material and alternative theoretical positions, began to make themselves felt. The number of papers on the subject in the late 1940's and early 1950's finally reached such a point that Sol Tax, then editor of the *American Anthropologist,* announced at an annual business meeting of the American Anthropological Association that he simply would not accept any more articles on the subject.

The heuristic value of Redfield's work is to be witnessed by the contributions of his critics. Sol Tax (see pp. 487–502) showed how the ideological concomitants of the dichotomy did not follow Redfield's thesis when applied to Guatemala. Oscar Lewis traced urban migrants from Tepoztlán and demonstrated that many of the features that Redfield claimed to be characteristic of the urban end of his folk-urban continuum were not borne out in fact. The families did not break down and close ties were kept with home. Lewis' interest in these urban folk led to his *Five Families* (1959) and *The Children of Sanchez* (1961), the two bestselling volumes to come out of Latin American anthropology. Sidney Mintz (1953) challenged Redfield on the issue that his entire scheme failed to take account of a major portion of the Latin rural population, the wage laborer on the large plantations, that is, the rural proletariat. In terms of understanding development, the omission of this population, which accounted for a great portion of the national income of the Latin American nations, was crucial. The Services (in an article included in this section) pointed out that rural peoples did not hang on to older traits through some intrinsic attachment, but, in many cases, simply because poverty made the city traits unavailable to them. And Howard Cline (1945) indicated that the tribal end of Redfield's continuum was less a closed tribal community than an armed camp created by the Yucatan War of the Castes.

Psycho-Cultural Study

The fact that Redfield's work was so widely read tended to obscure the pursuit of another interest in Latin American studies. Concern with the psychological bases of culture, the hallmark of Yale's Institute of Human Relations and implicit in the work of Harvard's Clyde Kluckhohn, led John Gillin, Harry Tschopik, and Allan Holmberg to focus on psychological problems and to use psychological concepts in their analyses of cultural events. Tschopik's sudden and early death took from the field one of its most stimulating and picturesque younger members; their interest in psychology led both Gillin and Holmberg into a concern with modern culture that was even more consonant with the concern of the *indigenistas*.

Gillin's *The Culture of Security in San Carlos* (1951), a study of an eastern Guatemalan town, in which the general psychological orientation of the Ladino (i.e., the Guatemalan mestizo national population) is contrasted with the Indian, was the first and is still one of the few field studies of its kind. It led him subsequently to attempt broader statements about Latin American value orientations in general, as can be seen in his article in this volume.

Rural Sociology

An independent development occurred during World War II when the U. S. Department of Agriculture underwrote a series of rural sociological studies of some selected Latin American countries. Directly and indirectly related to this program were the work of Carl Taylor in Argentina, Nathan Whetten in Mexico and Guatemala, Olen Leonard in Bolivia and Ecuador, Charles Loomis in Peru, Lowry Nelson in Cuba, T. Lynn Smith in Brazil and Colombia, and George W. Hill in Venezuela. All these men produced useful works (examples of which are cited in the Bibliography, pp. 556–74) and many were influential in the development of interest among Latin American students in this kind of study. The Institute of Agricultural Sciences at Turrialba, Costa Rica, later served as a center for such work under the encouragement of Loomis and others. Among the students of these men are Orlando Fals-Borda of Colombia, Manuel Alers-Montalvo, and Antonio Arce. Intellectual developments in rural sociology have remained separate from those in social anthropology, but the materials of the former field have consistently been of value in our understanding of the rural components of the Latin American societies.

Other branches of sociology have, with few exceptions, developed more recently their interests in Latin America. The work of Kingsley Davis in demography, Gino Germani in Argentine social development, Gilberto Freyre in Brazilian social history, and Lucio Mendieta y Núñez and Donald Pierson have been important influences in this field of study.

Evolution and Ecology

Following the death of Boas, Columbia University gradually became the center of a set of interests that might have made the old scholar wince. In the middle 1940's, Julian Steward came to Columbia, bringing two kinds of experience of central importance to Latin American social anthropology. First, as editor of the *Handbook of South American Indians* (1946–59) he was in touch, perhaps more than any other single individual, with the range of scholars and scholarship that marked anthropological studies in Latin America. Second, he had been the first director of the Institute of Social Anthropology, an organization set up during the war to send North American anthropologists (and kindred scholars) to Latin America to do research and train Latins in modern social anthropology. Within that program, a number of people who were to become leading scholars found early experience. The effect of the Institute of Social Anthropology personnel was very great. George Foster, Donald Brand, and Isabel Kelly in Mexico and Donald Pierson and Kalervo Oberg in Brazil were all involved in training students. Harry Tschopik, John Gillin, John Rowe, Allan Holmberg, George Kubler and Ozzie Simmons carried on similar work in Peru. In Colombia, John Rowe and Charles Erasmus worked, and elsewhere, the geographer Webster McBryde. Among the Latins who involved themselves in anthropological work were Jorge Muelle, Gabriel Escobar, Oscar Núñez del Prado, José Matos Mar, and Roberto and Virginia Pineda.

At Columbia, Steward turned immediately toward conceptual and theoretical problems of the discipline. In addition to attempting problems much broader than those of Latin America, he tried to form evolutionary statements in accord with materials then current. It is too early for agreement as to whether Steward successfully formulated useful notions on evolution, but there is no doubt that his concern with this broader area provided the training ground for students who were to contribute significantly to Latin American social anthropology.

The Puerto Rican project started by Steward and involving a large number of both Columbia and Puerto Rican students introduced evolutionary and adaptive theory into Latin American social anthropology.

Elman Service, Eric Wolf, Sidney Mintz, and many others either contributed to this general group or were participants in it.

Important advances were being made by other scholars during this period. Charles Wagley, following work in Brazil and Guatemala, was the guiding spirit of a number of students in Brazil, an area in which few North American scholars had worked. Marvin Harris and Anthony Leeds are among the most productive scholars to have come out of this program. George Foster, who replaced Steward as head of the Institute of Social Anthropology, began exploring the Spanish background of New World cultures, and continued his Mexican work. Foster's *Culture and Conquest* (1960) brought this material for the first time within the focus of American scholars. Foster proposed that the Iberians brought with them a highly selected culture, and that this found its niche in the New World. Subsequent Iberian and other European innovations were not of such consequence. His thesis is essentially an adaptive one, and continues the development of this important theoretical direction.

Applied Anthropology

The *indigenistas*' constant demands became more widely circulated through the establishment of the Inter-American Indian Institute and the work of Juan Comas and Alfonso Caso in Mexico and Luis Valcarcel in Peru. Anthropologists working in Latin America increasingly found themselves on the margins of serious practical, and often political, work. The Mexican National Indian Institute was occupying the services of the country's best trained anthropologists, including Gonzalo Aguirre Beltrán, Julio de la Fuente, Alfonso Villa Rojas, and Ricardo Pozas. When the Institute of Social Anthropology was stopped by the United States Government in early 1951, Foster found an immediate home for most of his remaining staff in the programs of the Institute of Inter-American Affairs, the first technical aid agency of the government working in Latin America. Through these programs Ozzie Simmons continued work in Peru and Chile; Charles Erasmus in Colombia, Ecuador, Chile, and Haiti; Isabel Kelly in Mexico, Bolivia, and finally in Pakistan; Kalervo Oberg in Brazil and the Guianas. Somewhat later, Richard Schadel worked in similar programs in Peru, Haiti, Venezuela, and elsewhere; the present writer carried on work with the Institute of Nutrition of Central America and Panama.

Independent of these efforts, Allan Holmberg of Cornell University initiated a program of research and development on the Hacienda Vicos in Peru in conjunction with the Peruvian National Indigenist Institute. Although long underfinanced, this program served as a most important training ground for Peruvian and Cornell anthropologists and had a telling effect nationally on the status of the Indian.

The work of these applied anthropologists was responsible for the issuing of both ethnographic materials and papers concerned with contemporary action programs. The restrictions placed on their work by bureaucratic structures and political realities often left something to be desired, but essentially they were concerned with providing transitional changes within the structure of their society. They were criticized for this both by those who preferred to see nothing done and by those who preferred to see a complete social turnover.

Structural Studies

During the 1950's the Caribbean became the scene of important work by the Institute of Social and Economic Studies of the University College of the West Indies. Various English-trained anthropologists, including Michael G. Smith and Raymond T. Smith, together with an increasing number of staff members and students from Columbia University's program "Study of Man in the Tropics," concentrated on social and economic structure in this region. Working with them was the geographer David Lowenthal. This Caribbean focus did more than merely call attention to an area little studied since the earlier work of Herskovits. It served both to introduce the structural interests of British social anthropology and to call attention to the concept of cultural pluralism. Work in the Caribbean led to an increase in ethnographic work and to the further exploration of the structural bases of pluralistic societies.

Classification and Conceptualization

By the middle 1950's, intensive social anthropological studies had reached every major country of Latin America except Chile, Argentina, and Uruguay. An inevitable and desirable consequence was the attempt to compare the structures and forms of the various areas and to make some sort of classification of the cultures and societies of Latin America. Aside from the implicit categorizations of the Great Dichotomy, the first major attempts at classification appeared in a 1955 issue of the *American Anthropologist*. Elman Service suggested a new general classification of the major regions, modifying Gillin's more general "mestizo" culture concept; Eric Wolf provided an imporant first approximation of classifying communities in terms of their structural arrangements; Kalervo Oberg refined the possibilities of evolutionary sequence in developmental complexities for the culture history of the entire lowland region; and Charles Wagley and Marvin Harris (in an article that is included in this section) presented a typology of the kinds of subcultures that were to be found in Latin America. It was clear from the work of the two preceding decades that whereas the Great Dichotomy could continue to serve as an heuristic device, it could never again be mistaken for a classificatory one. In the following year, the present writer (Adams, 1956) attempted a classification of the entire population of Central America on the basis that classification was of specific populations and specific kinds of relationships. This effort suggested that it was possible to include all the peoples in a single classification if both varieties of relationships and cultural tradition were included.

These attempts at classification could, at best, be mere conveniences for the individual to arrange in his mind the societies of the region. While they were being formulated, other more pressing problems were being explored. The paper by Wolf on complex societies pointed the way to uniting a sophisticated ecological approach with understanding of changing structure. And the work of Michael G. Smith (1960) on pluralism, although far from widely accepted, reintroduced some basic features of Malinowskian institutions to further our understanding of the ways different societies combine into distinctive political entities

The decade of the 1930's was the serious beginning of social anthropological work in Latin America; initial theoretical outlines were set forth and first field uses were made of them. During the 1940's field activities spread from an occasional community into the Andes, Brazil, and the Caribbean. The 1950's saw the emergence of the theoretical reformulations derived from the work of the 1940's, and set the intellectual scene for the following period. Social anthropology in Latin America today has arrived at the point where most major countries have at least a core of trained professionals. National interests and national problems are directing its development locally, just as such interests did in the work of the United States at an earlier period. The social anthropologists of the United States, and a few from Europe, continue to explore numerous phases of the scene. But the work is now truly international and its development will certainly be irregular.

REFERENCES CITED

Adams, Richard N.
1956 "Cultural Components of Central America," *American Anthropologist* 58:5:881–907.

Castro Pozo, Hildebrando
1924 *Nuestra comunidad indígena,* El Lucero, Lima.

Cline, Howard

1945 "Remarks on a Selected Bibliography of the Caste War and Allied Topics," in A. Villa, *The Maya of East Central Quintana Roo*, pp. 165–173, Carnegie Institution of Washington, Publication 559.

Foster, George M.

1960 *Culture and Conquest: America's Spanish Heritage*, Viking Fund Publication in Anthropology 27, New York.

Gamio, Manuel

1922 *La población del Valle de Teotihuacán*, Dirección de Talleres Gráficos, Mexico.

Gillin, John

1951 *The Culture of Security in San Carlos*, Middle American Research Institute Publication 16, Tulane University, New Orleans.

Lewis, Oscar

1959 *Five Families: Mexican Case Studies in the Culture of Poverty*, New York, Basic Books.

1961 *The Children of Sanchez*, New York, Random House.

Mintz, Sidney

1953 "The Folk-Urban Continuum and the Rural Proletarian Community," *American Journal of Sociology* 59:2:136–143.

Oberg, Kalervo

1955 "Types of Social Structure among the Lowland Tribes of South and Central America," *American Anthropologist* 57:3:472–487.

Redfield, Robert

1930 *Tepoztlán: A Mexican Village*, Chicago, University of Chicago Press.

1941 *The Folk Culture of Yucatan*, Chicago, University of Chicago Press.

Service, Elman R.

1955 "Indian-European Relations in Colonial Latin America," *American Anthropologist* 57:3:411–425.

Smith, Michael G.

1960 "Social and Cultural Pluralism," in V. Rubin and D. Keur, eds., *Social and Cultural Pluralism in the Caribbean*, Annals of the New York Academy of Sciences 83:5:763–777.

Steward, Julian H., ed.

1946–59 *Handbook of South American Indians*, Washington, D.C. Bureau of American Ethnology, Bulletin 143, Smithsonian Institution, 7 vols.

Wolf, Eric R.

1955 "Types of Latin American Peasantry: A Preliminary Discussion," *American Anthropologist* 57:3:452–471.

FURTHER READINGS

Indigenismo

Aguirre Beltrán, Gonzalo
1955 *Programas de salud en la situación intercultural,* Instituto Indigenista Interamericano, Mexico.

Caso, Alfonso
1958 *Indigenismo,* Colección Culturas Indígenas, Mexico.

Comas, Juan
1953 *Ensayos sobre indigenismo,* Instituto Indigenista Interamericano, Mexico.

Mariategui, José Carlos
1928 *7 ensayos de interpretación de la peruana* (primera edición), Biblioteca "Amauta," Lima.

Sáenz, Moisés
1933 *Sobre el indio peruano y su incorporación al medio nacional,* Secretario de Educación Pública, Mexico.

Salz, Beate R.
1944 "Indianismo," *Social Research* 11:4:441–469.

Historicism

Beals, Ralph L.
1952 "Notes on Acculturation," in Sol Tax, ed., *Heritage of Conquest,* pp. 225–233, Glencoe, Ill., Free Press.

Brand, Donald
1951 *Quiroga: A Mexican Municipio,* Smithsonian Institution, Institute of Social Anthropology, Publication 11, Washington, D.C.

Foster, George M.
1951 "Report on an Ethnological Reconnaissance of Spain," *American Anthropologist* 53:3:311–325

Kelly, Isabel and Angel Palerm
1952 *The Tajin Totonac, Part I: History, Subsistence, Shelter and Technology,* Smithsonian Institution, Institute of Social Anthropology, Publication 13, Washington, D.C.

The Great Dichotomy

Adams, Richard N.
1962 "The Community in Latin America: A Changing Myth," *The Centennial Review* 6:3:409–434.

Cámara, Fernando
1952 "Religious and Political Organization," in Sol Tax, ed., *Heritage of Conquest*, pp. 142–173, Glencoe, Ill., Free Press.

De la Fuente, Julio
1949 *Yalalag, una villa zapoteca serrana,* Museo Nacional de Antropología, Serie Científica, no. 1, Mexico.

Guiteras-Holmes, Calixta
1961 *Perils of the Soul: The World View of a Tzotzil Indian,* Glencoe, Ill., Free Press.

Miner, Horace
1952 "The Folk–Urban Continuum," *American Sociological Review* 17:5:529–537.

Redfield, Robert
1947 "The Folk Society," *American Journal of Sociology* 52:2:293–308.

Villa Rojas, Alfonso
1945 *The Maya of East Central Quintano Roo,* Carnegie Institution of Washington, Publication 559, Washington, D.C.

Psychology and Cultures

Billig, Otto, John Gillin, and William Davidson
1947–48 "Aspects of Personality and Culture in a Guatemalan Community: Ethnological and Rorschach Approaches," *Journal of Personality* 16:1 and 2:153–178, 328–368.

Fillol, Thomas
1961 *Social Factors in Economic Development: The Argentine Case,* Cambridge, Mass., M.I.T. Press.

Foster, George M., *et al.*
1960–61 "Interpersonal Relations in Peasant Society," *Human Organization* 19:2:174–184.

Holmberg, Allan R.
1950 *Nomads of the Long Bow: The Siriono of Eastern Bolivia,* Smithsonian Institution, Institute of Social Anthropology, Publication 10, Washington, D.C.

Rotondo, Humberto, *et al.*
1960 *Estudios sobre personalidad básica en mestizos,* Departamento de Higiene Mental, Ministerio de Salud Pública, Lima.

Sayres, William C.
1956 "Disorientation and Status Change," *Southwestern Journal of Anthropology,* 12:1:79–86.

Wolf, K. L.
1952 "Growing Up and Its Price in Three Puerto Rican Subcultures," *Psychiatry* 15:401–433.

Evolution and Ecology

Mintz, Sidney W.
1953 "The Culture History of a Puerto Rican Sugar Cane Planta-

tion, 1876–1949," *Hispanic American Historical Review* 33:2:224–251.

Palerm, Angel and Eric R. Wolf
1957 "Ecological Potential and Cultural Development," in *Studies in Human Ecology*, Pan American Union, Washington, D.C.

Wolf, Eric R.
1953 "La formación de la nación," *Ciencias Sociales* 4:20:50–93; 4:21:98–143; 4:22:146–191.

Applied Anthropology

Aguirre Beltrán, Gonzalo
1957 *El proceso de aculturación*, Colección de Problemas Científicos y Filosóficos, Mexico.

Bonfil Batalla, Guillermo
1962 *Diagnóstico sobre el hambre en Sudzal, Yucatan*, Instituto Nacional de Antropología e Historia, Mexico

Erasmus, Charles J.
1954 "An Anthropologist Views Technical Assistance," *The Scientific Monthly* 78:3:147–158.

Foster, George M.
1962 *Traditional Cultures: And the Impact of Technological Change*, New York, Harper.

Holmberg, Allan R.
1960 "The Research-and-Development Approach to Change: Participant Intervention in the Field," in R. Adams and J. Preiss, eds., *Human Organization Research*, pp. 76–89, Homewood, Ill., Dorsey Press.

Holmberg, Allan R. and Henry F. Dobyns
1962 "The Process of Accelerating Community Change," *Human Organization* 21:2:107–124.

Rubio Orbe, Gonzalo
1957 *Promociones indígenas en América*, Quito, Editoral Casa de la Cultura Ecuatoriana.

Classification

Beals, Ralph L.
1961 "Community Typologies in Latin America," *Anthropological Linguistics* 3:1:8–16.

Murdock, George P.
1951 *Outline of South American Cultures*, Behavior Science Outlines, Vol. 2, New Haven, Conn., Human Relations Area Files.

Culture Changes in Yucatan

ROBERT REDFIELD

I

In studying any culture known to be derived historically from two markedly different sources—as for example any of the cultures of the present Indian-Spanish populations of Mexico and Central America—one's interest is inevitably engaged in an attempt to analyze the culture into its two principal historical components. The investigator seeks to assign each element of present-day custom to a Spanish or to an Indian origin. This familiar problem has attracted Dr. Asael Hansen, Mrs. Hansen, Mr. Alfonso Villa, Mrs. Redfield, and myself in the course of ethnological work which we are now carrying on among the Maya of Yucatan on behalf of Carnegie Institution of Washington. Of course it turns out that some elements of the contemporary Yucatecan culture are easily to be identified with Spanish or with Indian influence, while others are refractory to this historical analysis.

Where elements of culture are definitely known from Europe, and where they are also not characteristic of American Indian cultures, they

Reprinted from *American Anthropologist*, 1934, XXXVI, 57–69, by permission of the author's literary executrix and publisher. This paper was presented June 22, 1933, at the joint meeting of Section H of the American Association for the Advancement of Science and of the American Anthropological Association. It recently appeared in *Human Nature and the Study of Society: The Papers of Robert Redfield*, Vol. I, edited by Margaret Park Redfield (Chicago: The University of Chicago Press, 1962).

are without difficulty regarded as importations from Spain. In Yucatan such elements, to mention only examples, are oranges, ordinary domestic fowl, cattle, rice, saffron and other Old World condiments, trousers, the seven-day week, the novena, crossing oneself, the idea of incubus and succubus, and possibly also the ghoul and the witch's familiar, the notion of the evil eye, purgatory, and probably judgment of the soul after death. Other traits are not known to characterize sixteenth-century Europe, and are either actually reported for the ancient Maya by the first white invaders or else are known to be characteristic of other American Indian cultures. In Yucatan such elements, which must of course be regarded as indigenous and pre-Columbian, are most of the agricultural techniques centering about maize; the firedrill; the loincloth and the sandal; the hammock (although its use may not have become general in Yucatan until after the Conquest); the notion that eclipses are caused by an animal that is devouring the sun or the moon, and that should the luminary fail to reappear the household furnishings would revolt against their masters and devour them; the idea of four cardinal directions associated with rain-, sky-, and maize-deities and with colors; multiple rain-gods, associated with clouds, the east, lightning and thunder, the cenotes, gourd rattles and calabashes, and objects of special cult involving ritual breads and oriented altars; the ritual breads themselves, made of maize and squash seed and baked in an earth oven; bee-deities, the objects of a special cult; deer-gods (who bear almost the same name as the patrons of hunters mentioned by Landa); bark beer as a ceremonial drink; offerings of turkeys, ritually killed, especially as offered at regular four-year intervals; and divination by casting grains of corn.

Other elements, as for example many techniques of house construction, are equally safely, though more circumstantially, assigned to an Indian origin. These elements are not affirmatively recorded for the ancient Maya; but they are harmonious with Indian cultures, and are difficult to imagine in a European setting. Such a trait is the ceremony whereby at an age of three or four months certain objects connected with the future activities of the child are placed in the child's hand and it is for the first time set astride the hip. A ritual not very different is reported for the ancient Aztecs.

Other traits, however, do not readily yield to this sorting process into one of two pigeonholes. Many elements in the culture of present-day Yucatan have both ancient Indian and European parallels, and could be attributed to either source, or to both. Shall we say that the custom of making religious pilgrimages to distant shrines is an Indian or a European custom in Yucatan today, when the historians tell us that both Indians and Europeans have long made such pilgrimages? Are the patron *santos* of present-day Maya villages the descendants of the local saints of the Mediterranean World, or are they translations of pagan patron gods? We can probably say that they are both, but that is about all we can say, lacking information as to just what was in the minds of the sixteenth-century Maya before and during the period of Catholization. The number thirteen which plays an important part in the present-day Maya rituals, is almost surely derived from indigenous culture, just as three and seven, which go together in the Catholic prayer context, are probably European. But what of nine, which now is a magical and sacred number in a wide variety of ritual contexts? We can only point out that the ancient Maya had nine gods of the underworld as they had thirteen sky-gods, and also that the Catholic novena was introduced by the missionaries and is still generally practiced.

I have been interested in the first-fruit ceremony performed throughout Yucatan when the maize is ripe. In the remoter villages this ceremony involves the offering in the cornfield of thirteen ears of maize to pagan gods, while Maya prayers are recited by a shaman-priest. But as the observer moves nearer and nearer the city, this ceremony takes on, little by little, more and more of the elements of a medieval harvest-home until at last it does not look at all Indian; the account of it reads like a page from Chambers' Book of Days. At what point does this ceremony cease to be Indian in origin and become Spanish?

Or consider the custom of bleeding for illness. This treatment, accompanied by cupping, is performed in Yucatan much as an old-time European barber would do it; and no doubt the Spanish conquerors were familiar with it. But the shaman-priest who bleeds his patients in the villages often uses a rattlesnake's fang as his instrument, and when he prescribes bloodletting to his patient because the sick man's ailment has been caused by his failure to offer the maize-gods the ritual they expect, it begins to suggest the penance by bloodshed of the ancient Maya.

With respect to the historical origins of some of the most fundamental complexes of contemporary Maya practice and belief, I find myself unable to make any statement. Among such I may mention the basic twofold category of "hot" and "cold" into which are divided foods, medicines, lands and people; the ceremonial planting of a ceiba pole to which the bulls are tied in the festal bullfight; the dance with a decorated pig's head and a decorated pole; and the far-reaching and important concept of evil winds, named, specialized and semi-personified, that are thought to cause most illnesses. Many of these special problems are, however, capable of solution. One needs a familiarity with Spanish folk cultures, and a thorough study of early sources on Maya culture at the time of the Conquest.

The student experienced in Indian but not in European cultures tends to attribute to Indian origins elements of culture that are actually at least in part Spanish. Sometimes the reasons are apparently very good. The Maya today predict the weather for the coming year by observing the weather on each of the first twelve days of January, then check this observation by reading the next twelve days as corresponding to the months in reverse order, and further check it by dividing the last six days into halves, and the last day into hours. This custom—first reported, I believe, by Starr—has been regarded by writers on the Maya as aboriginal, probably because it was known only from the Maya area, and because Landa says the priests, in the second month of the Maya year, opened their books and read the prognostications of that year. But the identical custom, under a Spanish name, has turned up in regions far from Maya influence, and where Indian influence of any sort is small or nonexistent—in Santo Domingo, in Venezuela, and in Costa Rica. So the likelihood that the custom is native to the Maya is much reduced. In historical inquiries of this sort often a very small change in facts will bring about a diametric reversal of conclusion.

These remarks will serve to suggest some of the reasons why those of us who are studying the contemporary Maya of Yucatan are disposed to turn from this problem of historical analysis to a problem of another sort, which I will soon state. In the first place these historical problems, as has just been indicated, are incapable of solution from a consideration of the contemporary Maya culture alone, but wait upon study of sources as to the pre-Columbian Maya, and upon knowledge of Indian and of European folk cultures. In the second place, some cannot be solved at all; or rather, the question, Indian or Spanish? cannot be asked in these cases; for some customs are probably both Indian and Spanish. In fact, some are probably neither Indian nor Spanish, in the sense that neither sixteenth-century culture exhibited the custom now characterizing the present-day peoples. Thus there is today an important belief, many years ago described by Brinton, in the supernatural character of the clay images, incense burners and other pottery artifacts made by the ancients and encountered by the present-day people. These beings, the alux, are regarded as mischievous spirits, and are propitiated in certain ceremonies. Although it is conceivable that European ideas of fairies and goblins have influenced the development of this complex of ideas and practices, it is also quite possible that this is a parallel development, or degeneration, of god to goblin, that has taken place in Yucatan with the systematic destruction of the pagan religion by the priests.

Indeed, ultimately no Yucatecan culture element, whether originating in Europe or in America, turns out to be the same today as it was in 1519. We may say that the rain-gods, bearing the same name (*chaacs*) and many of the same attributes, are the same rain-gods of the ancients. But today they are captained by Saint Michael, they ride on horseback, and so riding are plainly confused with the horsemen of the apocalypse.

We may observe the shaman-priest, sacrificing a turkey which is held by wings and feet by four men designated so to act, under the name "Chacs," and recall how closely this picture conforms with Landa's account of the mode of human sacrifice performed by the Mayas of his time. But we cannot say that the connotations of meaning of the present-day act correspond at all closely with what went on in the minds of the actors in the ancient drama.

The present-day culture is a closely integrated body of elements derived from Spanish and from Indian sources, and all entirely remade and redefined in terms of one another. Nothing is entirely Indian, nothing is entirely Spanish. The ritual offering to the rain- and maize-gods incorporates the forms of a Catholic communion, but the chalice is a calabash and the sacramental wine is the bark beer of the ancients. The books of Chilam Balam tell us that anciently there was an important cult centering around the *Plumeria* flower (*nicte*), but today that flower, instead of being used in the rituals predominately pagan, as we might expect, is the appropriate adornment of Catholic altars and the suitable offering to the saints.

And in the third place—to return to the considerations which check the historical analyst—these problems, even if solved, do not easily lead into larger problems. If we are to distinguish science from history in that the former seeks always to reduce phenomena to general categories of wider and wider scope, then these problems do not readily lend themselves to science. We may be able to assign the day count which I just cited to the Spanish heritage, but having done so we are not in a position to compare this fact with another like it and erect a generalization on that base. Facts of this sort tend to remain discrete and noncomparable; the scholarly effort comes to rest when the assignment to the one heritage or the other has been made. To use these facts in making generalizations we would have to know a great deal, probably more than we can ever know, as to what—for example—happened when the weather-prognostication custom was imported to the ancient Mayas, and as to what their culture at the time was like.

II

The type of historical analysis which I have just been illustrating, if it can be taken as the sum of its details, amounts to a study of an instance of acculturation: the cross-modification and fusion of Indian and Spanish cultures. But as such it is a study of a series of events four hundred years after their occurrence, of events that took place in a period forever beyond direct observation and poorly documented by historians. The ancient Maya culture is known only very sketchily; the recovery of sixteenth- and seventeenth-century Spanish culture is a special problem; and just what took place when the two met is to be known only in so far as written records, as yet not collected, reveal it to us, or as a series of dubious historical inferences from consideration of the culture of the present time.

In view of these difficulties it is natural that an interest in culture changes should find lodgment, in Yucatan, in changes nearer at hand and more subject to direct observation. My associates and I have found such a problem in the study of the changes taking place in the Yucatecan folk culture—this integrated and unified mode of life which has been made of both Indian and Spanish elements and which characterizes the hinterland villages of the peninsula of Yucatan today. Beginning with this culture as a point of departure, we find it unnecessary to commit ourselves to assertions as to the precise ways in which Spanish and Indian elements contributed to make it up; our concern is with what has recently taken place in this culture and is currently taking place in it under influences exerted by increasing mobility and communication. The culture changes of the peninsula have, of course, always taken place as a result of contact and communication, but thus broadly stated they are not changes that ceased when the Spanish influences diminished, or that were most marked in the sixteenth century; on the contrary they become increasingly effective with the spread of what we call "civilization"—that is, schools, roads and economic exploitation. These changes are happening under one's eyes.

The procedure which we have adopted to study these changes is the simultaneous comparative observation of several Yucatecan communities that have been affected by modern influences in varying degrees. We have selected three or four communities and ranged them in the order represented by the degrees to which these modern influences have impinged upon them. This we are able to do with assurance, because of the simplicity of the situation in the peninsula with reference to contact and communication. The peninsula is a single geographic region: a forested limestone plain. The rainfall increases as one goes southeastward until it is so great that human habitation is difficult. Merida, the capital city, is located in the northwest corner of the peninsula. This is the center of contact and of influences political, social, and cultural. From this point the roads and railroads move outward, becoming, in the southeast, trails through the bush. These trails, as one continues to move southeastward, become less frequent and less traveled, until one reaches the isolation of central Quintana Roo, where the Indians are visited only by the *chiclero* and the occasional traveling merchant.

We have begun studies in three communities. Mentioned in this same order of increasing remoteness, these are: first, the city of Merida itself; second, a community on the southeasternmost branch of the railroad, and third, a village some thirty miles in the bush to the south of the second community. This last community, which I shall speak of as "the village," is inhabited by persons of nearly pure Maya blood and with Maya surnames; there has been a school in the community for a dozen years; it is not yet, but is likely soon to be, in communication by wagon road with the rest of Yucatan. The second community, which I shall refer to as "the town," includes many persons with much white blood; about half the inhabitants bear Spanish surnames, and speak Spanish along with Maya; the community has had a school for many generations; and it is the seat of a central municipal government, a judicial district, a federal school district, and a newspaper correspondent. We hope also to add a fourth, and most isolated community: a village of the still tribally organized Indians of Quintana Roo. Mr. Villa has made four or five trips among these villages, but the work done there is still insufficient to permit me to include this fourth type of community in the summary comparison which I am about to make.

This comparison is underlain by a fundamental assumption: that by means of it we shall be able to outline a process of culture change, that we shall be able to indicate what is taking place in the folk culture under influences from the city and from the world outside of Yucatan. It will readily occur to one that this problem could be studied in at least two other ways. One might select a single community and observe what happened to it over a period of time during which it was exposed to these influences. But obviously this procedure would require a number of years. Or one might again take a single community and make two (or more) studies of its culture: one, of its contemporary mode of life, and another, of its mode of life a generation or two ago, as reported to the investigator from the memory of the older inhabitants. These two cultures could then be compared. We have in fact made some use of this latter procedure. For reasons which I shall try to make apparent, it is not necessary for us to assume that the life of the village we are studying represents an earlier stage in the development of what we now find in the town, and indeed this is not in detail the case; but as a matter of fact we have frequently found the old people in the town recalling from their childhood customs and features of social organization which are today characteristic of the village. That is to say, one can go back either in time or in space, one can delve into memory or retreat into the bush, and reach the same set of facts. One example will illustrate this. Today in the city a young man, even of a lower-class family, selects his own wife and himself makes request of the girl's father for permission to marry her.[1] It is remembered, however, that the boy's father and mother used to make this formal request. In the town the latter practice is general, although the actual selection of partners is made by the young people themselves. The older people look back, with some regret, to the days when older people arranged the marriages, selecting husbands for their daughters and wives for their sons. Coming to the village, we find that there marriages are in fact parentally arranged and controlled, the girl having nothing to say in the matter, and the boy very little. The coming-to-ask-for-the-girl's-hand is a solemn and highly formalized piece of ritual, in which the boy and the girl have no part. Finally, it is only a few years in this village since the custom disappeared whereby after the betrothal the boy served his parents-in-law in their house for a year before marriage. And Mr. Villa's information from Quintana Roo indicates that this last custom is still general there. At this point we are in effect back in the early sixteenth century, for this last-mentioned mode of marriage is substantially the same as that described for the ancient Maya by Bishop Landa.

The comparison of these three communities—city, town, and village—can therefore be expressed in terms of a process of transition. I think of this process as a shift from one type of society, which the most isolated village represents, toward another type, illustrated by the Yucatecan capital city but even better by our more mobile northern cities. But the process is also, as I have just indicated, in large measure an actual historical process, in that the sequential changes made manifest by the comparison are actual events that have taken place in the chronological development of certain members of the series. In the summary statement of some points of this comparison immediately to follow, the description may be understood in either way: as an account of a general trend in social or cultural type as Western civilization has entered Yucatan, or as a somewhat schematic recapitulation of the cultural history of any town in eastern Yucatan that began as an isolated homogeneous village and became progressively modified by contact with the city and the wider economy and society.

Beginning, then, with more general and obvious differences, I will say that as one moves from the village through the town to the city one finds the communities increasingly mobile and heterogeneous. The increasing heterogeneity is not merely a function of the size of the community, for there are remote villages that are five times as large as the town we have been studying, but are much more homogeneous. By this I mean that the mental world of one individual is much like that of any other; or, to put the same thing in other words, objects and acts have much the same meaning to everyone. Correspondingly, the division of labor becomes more complex; in the village every man is an agriculturalist and performs the necessary domestic tasks to supply himself with what he needs, while town and city are increasingly constituted of interdependent specialists. Such specialists as exist in the village are chiefly "sacred specialists"—midwives, shamans, and reciters of ritual prayers—who perform their functions as matters of prerogative and public duty. But as one goes to town and city the proportion of secular specialists increases; their functions are discharged as matters of livelihood, and their fees, instead of being nominal or traditional, are dependent upon the fluctuations of free economic competition. Communal labor, which is a powerful instrument in maintaining the solidarity of the village community, breaks down with the introduction first of money substitute, for personal labor, and then with the development of hired and prison labor. Lending of money, at first without interest, becomes subject to exorbitant interest rates; land comes to be regarded as subject to individual sale and then as security for debt; and later banking begins. In the village, estates are maintained intact until the death of the surviving spouse, even if the children and grandchildren are married; this is an aspect of the unity of the extended domestic family group. But moving to the town and then to the city, one finds distribution of a deceased man's property among the children and the widow more and more common; and testamentary disposition of property becomes familiar.

This same cityward progression sees the gradual breakdown of a familial organization in which the essential features are the subordination of women to men, and of young people to older people, and the responsibility of the individual to his kindred on both sides and of them to him. Marriage ceases to be an arrangement of two groups of kin to become connubially united and to provide for the adult security of two young people just leaving adolescence, and becomes gradually an enterprise of youth and maiden in which the elders are less concerned and little influential. The sometimes elaborate and always religious rituals in support of marriage decrease in complexity and solemnity and at last disappear: the solemn asking for the hand of the bride; the ceremonious delivery of the bride-price with the admonishment of the marriage intermediary; the ceremony after the wedding wherein the bride formally acknowledges her subservience to her parents-in-law, the groom acknowledges his respectful relation to his parents-in-law, and the two sets of parents-in-law pledge their new relation to each other and their obligation to the sponsors of the wedding.

Similarly, the godparental and *compadre* relationships, which in the village parallel and support the parental and parent-in-law relationships, become less important as institutions of control. With the development of class- and wealth-differences, godparents come to be selected for practical or prestige advantage, and as the *compadres* are no longer on the same social level, the reciprocity of the relationship is broken down. The requesting-the-godparent-to-act ceases to be a religious ritual, and becomes perfunctory; and the ceremony of hand washing whereby the parent acknowledges his obligation to his *compadre* disappears. At the same time, because of the disparity in mental worlds between the generations, young people cease to show respect for their godparents, and the latter are less and less expected to intervene in the control of the godchild's conduct.

One of the most striking changes is the diminishing importance of religious belief and ritual. This applies as well to those elements which are of European Catholic origin as to those which are pagan. In the villages practical acts and needs are closely supported by sacred sanctions. Ritual is an immediate expression of an anxiety or a need, and as all men are similarly interested and engaged, this need is often general throughout the community. But in the town and in the city, there are the very Catholic and the less Catholic, as well as Protestants and skeptics; and there are men in the community—few in the town and many in the city —who are not agriculturalists, and for whom therefore the anxieties of sowing and drought are not acute. This topic is of course a very long and involved one; I can only mention a few of the conspicuous differences. The novena, for example—the Spanish or Latin prayer recited before the effigy of the saint or the symbol of the cross—is in the village a spontaneous individual or familial utterance of prayer: a man and his wife organize a novena when their child is sick, or their crop is threatened, or in gratitude for the recovery of the one or the safety of the other. But in the town the annual name-day novena becomes the dominant type, and its performance no longer is an expression of religious mood. It is a social occasion, with a religious flavor, performed, as much as anything, to maintain prestige. And in the city the novena tends to disappear entirely. Furthermore, in the town and in the city men take less and less part in religious activity, whereas in the village they lead.

In the village the solidarity of the local community is expressed in the paramount importance of the village *santo*; other saints are of small consequence. But in the town the patron suffers from competition with individual patrons, and with miraculous *santos* of other communities; and this individuation of the gods is still further developed in the city, where the patron saint of the community almost completely disappears. In town as in village the pagan gods of the cornfield are the objects of worship, for the townsman is, generally speaking, a farmer, as is the villager. In the city these deities are largely gone, except in the peripheral communities where agriculture is still practiced. But village and town exhibit notable differences. In the village the agricultural rites are acts of piety; in the town they are acts of safeguard. They become less the direct responses to crisis, and more matters of traditional performance. In the village the forms are still full of meaning; the layman understands and follows what the shaman-priest says and does. In the towns this is less true. The shaman-priest is not a member of the town-community; he is brought in from a village, and the symbolism of what he does is less understood. It is simply an act of prudence to have him perform his ceremonies: otherwise the crop might fail. In a word, this functionary becomes less of a priest and more of a magician.

The same fact can be approached from a consideration of the pagan gods themselves. In the village these are close at hand, plainly defined, and worshiped in ritual of apparent symbolism. In the town they are more remote; and their individual differences are blurred. The lesser deities—those of the bees, deer, and cattle—disappear entirely, while the rain-gods lose their definite attributes and become confused with the guardians of the *milpa* and the forest. In the villages the mischievous goblin embodied in the ancient clay effigy—the alux—is fairly well kept distinct from the true gods; but in the town the alux becomes a principal recipient of offerings made in the fields. The effect of this is to reduce what was a true prayer to a being defined in terms of the awesome and the benign, to the mere humoring of a mischievous sprite. The villager and the townsman carry corn gruel to the fields in acts that have the same external appearance, but the townsman's act comes to have about the same meaning as the putting out of a pan of milk for the brownie by a Scotch rustic. In the city, finally, all these beings are hardly more than eery characters in folk tales told to amuse or frighten.

The same diminution of the religious element is to be observed in the changes that take place in the ideas as to the causation of diseases. In the village a man's sickness is most often brought about by his failure to perform the expected rituals; illness, in other words, is commonly the proof of a lapse from piety; physical well-being is an aspect of moral well-being. But in the town sickness too becomes secularized. Fidelity to ritual is not emphasized as insurance against sickness. Both villager and townsman believe in evil winds as a principal factor in disease, but the villager, constantly instructed and admonished by the shaman-priest, is apt to regard these winds as the punitive aspect of deity, while the townsman thinks of them as operating of their own malevolence, or as encountering the stricken one by mere accident.

We have been struck, in studying this matter of disease and its causation, by the apparent increase of black magic as a cause of sickness and death as one moves away from the village toward the city. This is a matter requiring more investigation to confirm, for our information is drawn from a single village, which may not be typical. But unless further facts change the conclusions, it will appear that sorcery is commoner in the town than in the village, and commoner in the city than in the town. Certainly Dr. Hansen's materials from Merida indicate a development of black magic much greater than that shown by our materials from the village. Tentatively we suggest that this situation is to be explained by two kinds of reasons. One, a historical explanation, points to the diffusion of West Indian magic, largely medieval European in origin and perhaps partly African, into the city, to which come many Cubans. The other explanation might be spoken of as sociological; this would regard the increase of sorcery in the city as an adaptation to the greater insecurity and instability of life in the city among a people still partly illiterate and primitive in habit of thought. In the city the familial and neighborhood controls are broken; one does not know one's neighbor; and the authority of ritual and religious belief is largely removed.

Each one of the topics to which I have referred in this summary invites further study, and I have not mentioned all that have presented themselves to us. There are interesting changes in the body of folk tales and myths. The progressive secularization of the annual fiesta is a matter adapted to detailed investigation, for the rituals are many and well defined, and the local variants are so numerous that it is possible to describe with some fullness the transition of a sacred ritual to a social entertainment—the change from prayer to party.

The transition which has been sketched in the foregoing paragraphs I conceive, I repeat, as a shift from one type of society, illustrated by the isolated primitive or peasant village, toward another type most nearly realized in our northern cities. In other words this particular historical change that has taken place and is taking place in one particular place, Yucatan, need not be regarded as a unique series of events. It can be compared with the effect of white civilization upon peripheral peoples in other parts of the world, and it can be compared with the gradual civilization of Europe as known to us from history.

The trend of this paper can therefore be summarized by asserting two advantages which inhere in the mode of defining a study of culture change which has been developed in the consideration of our materials. In the first place, the simultaneous study of communities enjoying the same fundamental basic culture but exposed in different degrees to outside influences allows the study of culture change directly—the data are under immediate observation—and without the necessity of waiting until the lapse of time has brought about marked changes in a single community. And in the second place, the changes observed can be compared with others like it so as to lead the student into scientific generalizations.

This comparison requires, of course, a terminology which will eliminate what is peculiar to one time and place and will emphasize what is alike in spite of these temporal and local differences. A review of the specific changes which I have mentioned for Yucatan will indicate the direction to be taken by this generalizing terminology. The one type of society, approached in the village, is a relatively immobile society, culturally homogeneous, in which the ways of life form a single web of interrelated meanings. This culture is closely adjusted to its local milieu. Relationships are personal, and the important institutional controls are familial. The sanctions which control conduct are prevailingly sacred, piety is emphasized, and custom has the force of moral rule. Ritual is highly developed, and expresses vividly the wishes and fears of the people. On the other hand, as one leaves the village and moves through the town to the city, one goes toward a contrasting type of society. This society is much more mobile, and culturally heterogeneous. The ways of life are less closely interrelated; group habits exist more in terms each of itself, and do not to the same degree evoke a body of closely associated and definatory acts and meanings. These ways of life rest upon, but are not of, their natural environment. Relationships are increasingly impersonal, and formal institutions qualify the acts of the individual. The familial organization is much reduced in importance as an instrument of control. Life is secularized; economic advantage and valuation have penetrated the social body; and the individual acts from constraint or convenience rather than from deep moral conviction. Religious belief and action are much reduced; the individual can no longer express himself in the comfortable grooves of sacred ritual.

I have found it convenient to speak of the former type of society as Culture, and the latter type as Civilization. If this terminology be adopted, the study we are engaged upon is one of deculturalization, rather than of acculturalization. But as there are objections, at least those of usage, to denying the term "culture" to the life-ways of the city man, it may be more acceptable to describe this study as that of the change from folk culture to city culture.

NOTE

1. It is still considered proper for a meeting to take place between the parents of the boy and those of the girl, but usually everything, even the date of the wedding, has been determined by the young couple before this.

Analysis of Complex Contemporary Societies: Culture Patterns of Puerto Rico

JULIAN STEWARD

This essay will deal primarily with the culture patterns or life-ways of certain classes or segments of the Puerto Rican people, with special attention to how the processes of industrialization have modified a predominantly agrarian population. The term "industrialization" used in connection with rural people refers rather broadly not only to their involvement in a system of cash crop production and of consumption of mass manufactured commodities, but also, at least in the Western world, to the development of political democracy, an augmented role of the state in controlling and directing change and in providing services to its people, religious freedom, and other patterns which have accompanied technological progress and the growth of economic free enterprise.

Reprinted from *The Theory of Culture Change,* Urbana, University of Illinois Press, 1955, Chapter 12, by permission of the author and publisher. The present chapter is a résumé [of the volume *The People of Puerto Rico,* subsequently published (1956) by University of Illinois Press] that was written not only by the present author but by those who did the field research in Puerto Rico: Robert A. Manners, Sidney Mintz, Elena Padilla, Raymond L. Scheele, and Eric Wolf. The author wishes his co-workers to share full credit and responsibility for the analyses herein offered. The whole chapter is a republication of an article by the same name which first appeared in "Puerto Rico: A Study in Democratic Development," Millard Hansen and Henry Wells, eds., *The Annals of the American Academy of Political and Social Science,* 1953, CCLXXXV, 95–103.

In Puerto Rico, industrialization has produced certain general trends which provide a kind of common denominator to all classes of people. These trends began during the nineteenth century, but they were greatly accelerated during the twentieth century after the island came under United States sovereignty. Industrialization in Puerto Rico today is developing rapidly, and it involves not only general tendencies but certain economic patterns, a political ideology, a legal and governmental system, and other features specific to the United States.

Urban Changes

All segments of the Puerto Rican population have been influenced by industrialization, but the town and urban centers have responded most uniformly. Urbanization, itself a major trend, has entailed a number of characteristic changes. Not only do towns become much larger and comprise an ever greater percentage of the total population, but their functions and internal composition are being altered. The local communities mediate the national institutions to the countryside by serving as centers for marketing, wholesaling, retail trade, and credit; for governmental administration and for education, farm extension, health, and other public services; for the servicing and building trades and the transportational workers; for local political parties and labor unions; for religious and recreational functions; and for the distribution of certain media of mass communication.

While these new urban functions tend to create greater similarity between towns, they also differentiate the population within each town into special segments, classes, or sociocultural groups: wealthy commercial and professional personnel; civil servants, transportational workers, and servicing and building trades groups; and skilled and unskilled laborers. Most characteristic of these are the new middle classes of varied occupation and income. They represent a new trend, a new set of values which ascribes major importance to the symbols of personal achievement and wealth. Upward mobility in the socioeconomic hierarchy becomes a crucial goal; and individual effort, thrift, education, and utilization of governmental services and opportunities become means to the goal.

Rural Changes

The rural population also is affected by these industrial trends. Cash crops or wage labor provides money with which to purchase desired items in the rising tide of manufactured goods offered by the town merchants, and to maintain a standard of living that carries prestige. The farm population is acquiring a cash-oriented value system, which is supplanting the older rationale of personal relations and services. The traditional patterns of labor exchange between small farmers, of personal favors and perquisites between landowners and laborers, and of kinship and ritual kinship duties and obligations are disappearing or being seriously modified.

However, the sociocultural groups created in the rural areas by industrialization are less uniform than those in the urban centers. Each rural region has a distinctive environment and therefore particular crop potentials. In each region the productive arrangement—the kind of crop, mechanization in field production or in processing, land tenure, capitalization and credit, and the nature of labor and of owner-worker relations—has created distinctive subcultures among the people involved. The present article is primarily concerned with the subcultures of the rural workers.

Puerto Rican Culture and Subcultures

In order to understand the cultural patterns of contemporary Puerto Rico, it is necessary to view the processes of industrialization against the background of the cultural tradition of the island. For four centuries the culture was essentially Hispanic, both in its national institutions and in its folk aspects. Early in the island's history there were probably important subcultural differences between landowners, ecclesiastical and lay officials, craftsmen, merchants, subsistence farmers, and other groups. For an undetermined period there were probably also differences between ethnic groups—Indians native to Puerto Rico and from the continent, Africans, and Europeans of various origins and classes. But true ethnic minorities are not now important. The Hispanic heritage, however, was the basis of Puerto Rican culture and subcultures, and, despite the effects of industrial trends, many features of the tradition survive today: the Spanish language, certain familial patterns, religious practices, forms of recreation, food habits, and others.

Today, the Puerto Rican subcultures, or special regional and class groups, represent distinctive interactions between the Hispanic patterns, the local productive arrangements, the effects of industrialization, and the specific influence of Americanization. The subcultures are many and varied. Only certain of the more important types were selected for analysis: a representative *municipio* of the small farmers of subsistence crops and tobacco in the mountains, the so-called *jíbaro*, who are in the tradition of the isolated and independent farmers of the island; the growers of coffee, both landlords and workers, who are of interest because they exemplify the traditional Hispanic paternalistic pattern of two closely interrelated classes; the sugar-cane workers on a corporate plantation and on a government-owned, profit-sharing plantation, both groups of whom comprise a rural proletariat; and the insular upper class, which consists of a few hundred families who live in San Juan, the capital, who represent United States commercial enterprises, and who are by far the most Americanized of any segment of the population.

In spite of these subcultural differences there is an overall Puerto Rican culture, in that the Hispanic heritage provides a common background, the processes of industrialization are creating insular-wide trends, and most of the Puerto Rican people feel a sense of common origin and destiny. But the cultural common denominator can be overemphasized. The following pages will be concerned with the more important subcultures which have emerged from Puerto Rico's complex historical background.

The Small Farmers

The mountain farmers who grow their own foods as well as a cash crop of tobacco are of interest not only because they are numerically important but because they exemplify the adaptation of a formerly self-sufficient, isolated, and independent folk society to the demands of modern industrialization. During much of its history, Puerto Rico was somewhat distinctive among Spanish possessions in lacking important mineral wealth and in having little access to markets for such crops as it could grow. Until the nineteenth century the country was underpopulated, and there was ample opportunity for squatter farmers of Indian, Negro, and white ancestry to clear lands in the interior where they lived in comparative self-sufficiency and isolation from the state, the church, and the currents of world economy.

During the last century, however, world trends began to reach these farmers. Improved communications drew them more into the orbit of national affairs. The lure of manufactured goods stimulated their desire for cash, which they obtained primarily through growing tobacco. Tobacco can be grown at little risk, it can be rotated with other crops on small plots, and it requires no expensive field or processing machinery. Moderate credit facilities will carry the producer over a year. Neither losses nor profits can be great. Owing to market restrictions, Puerto Rican tobacco production has not run to large plantations. It is the small farmer's source of cash income, whether he be landowner or sharecropper.

Our study of a tobacco *municipio* shows that certain changes have accompanied the introduction of the cash crop. As the people still grow their own food, subsistence is not so vital a problem as it is in the monocrop sugar area, where all food must be purchased from wages. But cash goals have led to individualization of landownership, and, since population has increased beyond the agricultural resources, farms tend to be divided among heirs to the extent that individual holdings are often insufficient to support the family. This individualization of landownership has been a major factor in disrupting the extended family. Duties and obligations to the extended kin group have become secondary to responsibility for the immediate family.

The trends in land use and landownership have reduced the functional household and familial unit to the nuclear family. The somewhat patrilineal and patrilocal traditional Hispanic family has been modified in that residence and affiliation tend to follow lines of property, which may be inherited on either side of the family. The nature of the marital union, moreover, is affected by economic and social considerations. Where property or social status is involved, marriage is usually religious or civil; where neither counts, it tends to be consensual.

These tobacco farmers have a new value orientation based on monetary standards and the importance of individual effort. It is known that upward mobility in the socioeconomic scheme can be achieved, and the people are eager to take advantage of all aids: education, farm extension services, health facilities, and the like. Simultaneously, interfamily relations based on labor exchange and other services lacking a monetary standard have declined. The goal of upward mobility has been facilitated by the constant fragmentation of landholdings, for it is possible for a thrifty and successful small farmer or sharecropper to purchase small parcels of land. Although few persons can acquire great wealth, there is considerable opportunity for upward as well as downward mobility in the socioeconomic hierarchy.

SOCIAL, POLITICAL, RELIGIOUS FEATURES

The socioeconomic mobility in the tobacco region has influenced social relations. Class lines cannot be sharp, even though there are differences in wealth and corresponding differences in social participation, recreation, standard of living, and other features. Comparative equality is manifest in various ways, including the nature of the *compadrazgo. Compadres* (co-parents, that is, godparents of one's children) are selected from among one's economic superiors and inferiors as well as among one's equals.

Political ideology of the tobacco farmers is consistent with other aspects of their culture. They are independent in their political as well as economic and social attitudes. Since they are actual or potential landowners, they stand to gain less than the proletariat of the sugar areas from a political program designed to benefit landless workers. The greatly expanded governmental services have been to their advantage, and they have utilized them perhaps more than any other rural group. But in the 1948 election, a much larger portion of the tobacco farmers than of any other rural group voted for the rather militant *Independentistas* rather than for the dominant Popular Democratic party which has stood for rural and social reform.

The small mountain farmers are traditionally and nominally Catholic, but Protestant sects have begun to penetrate the area. It is perhaps too early to appraise this trend, but a factor which appears to favor the new faiths is the ideal of individual initiative and the concept of individual responsibility—the "Protestant ethic," which is part and parcel of the new socioeconomic trends. Another aspect of religious change is that the Catholic festivals, although still observed, have assumed a recreational rather than religious character.

The Coffee Hacienda Culture

The coffee haciendas are of interest less because they involve large numbers of persons today than because they still exemplify in many ways a typically Hispanic pattern which once characterized much of the sugar area as well as the coffee area. The earlier pattern has been perpetuated through several factors.

First, coffee cannot be the poor man's cash crop, for it requires a fairly large capital outlay. Unlike tobacco, which can be grown on plots of any size and during brief periods, coffee requires a fairly large acreage in order to justify the processing equipment; and, since it does not bear for several years after planting, the owner must have resources to carry him over. There are a few small and medium coffee farms, but the tendency is toward large holdings which are worked by peasants or landless laborers. Because needed capitalization for coffee production has increased, coffee haciendas tend to become fewer and larger.

Second, since coffee production can be carried on profitably in isolated areas which lack improved roads and communications, the farm population tends to remain socially and culturally isolated from the urban centers. Public services, political ideologies, and the effects of media of mass communication have been slow to reach the coffee workers.

OWNER-WORKER RELATIONS

The productive arrangements of the large haciendas set the framework for the survival of the traditional culture. The owners are largely Spaniards, often third or fourth generation, and they constitute a well-defined upper class of highly educated and sophisticated persons who maintain close ties with the town. The laborers, both peasants and landless workers, are mostly native Puerto Ricans. The relationship between owner and worker is typically paternalistic, personal, face to face, and variable, as compared with the impersonal wage-based and legalized relationship in sugar production. Between owner and laborer there is a mutual dependency, a system of personal understandings and perquisites. The laborer is paid in wages, but since work is seasonal he is also granted favors in lieu of wages, such as a subsistence plot on which to grow foods, or the chance to burn charcoal on shares. The owner takes a personal interest in him, advising him in his affairs and looking to his welfare. In return, the worker renders unpaid services to his landlord and may even supply daughters as servants in the landlord's household.

The culture of the workers and peasants reflects the isolation and traditionalism perpetuated by the productive arrangement. The family is strongly paternalistic. The father manages its property and income, directs the labor of all its members, including the children, who usually perform useful tasks, and dictates the social behavior and marriages of his offspring.

Solidarity and reciprocity within the working class are manifest in many traditional ways. There is labor exchange based on reciprocity rather than on monetary standards; there is visiting and participation in socioreligious events; there is choice of *compadres*; and there is intermarriage.

Between owners and workers, relations are reciprocal but unequal. They include the system of favors and services already mentioned. The workers seek *compadres* among the owners in order to strengthen their position, but the reverse is not true. They look to the owners for leadership in political as well as economic and social affairs. They are not yet sufficiently sophisticated to recognize the program of the Popular Democratic party as their own. They have too little economic opportunity to place value on individual effort, too little access to and use for education to recognize it as a means of upward mobility, and too little chance to utilize governmental services to feel that these are vital to them. They depend upon their landlord rather than upon unions, political parties, or the government.

RELIGION

The coffee workers are perhaps the most thoroughly Catholic of all farm people, but their Catholicism is not wholly orthodox. Partly because of limited contact with the church and the priests, the religion tends to center in a cult of saints. Formal church rites and priestly administrations are secondary to a system of household and village saints which constitute the principal supernatural functionaries. These saints receive prayers and supplications, and if they fail to respond they may be punished. At the same time, certain church rites such as baptism sanction *compadre* relationships and hence have great sociological importance. Moreover, the many religious festivals provide a traditional form of recreation, in contrast to other regions, where social dancing and sports have become popular.

Sugar Plantation Cultures

The sugar regions of Puerto Rico exhibit the most pronounced effects of industrialization upon the rural cultures. Since sugar is produced competitively for an outside market, it is necessary that the most modernized methods be used in field production and processing. The mills cost a half million dollars or more, and in order for them to operate at maximum efficiency, cane from a vast acreage must be fed into them. Sugar, therefore, tends to be monocrop, and subsistence farming, which is so vital to the rural people of other areas, is virtually eliminated.

Earlier in Puerto Rican history, when sugar plantations had ox-driven mills and simple steam boilers, they were family owned. At one time they depended partly upon slave labor; later upon free labor. The productive and social arrangement was the family hacienda type. As technology advanced and the necessary capital outlay increased, there became fewer and larger mills and plantations. Less opulent families, which could not afford mills, contracted to have their cane ground at the large plants. On the arid south coast, however, where cattle ranching had prevailed and where irrigation projects were essential to sugar expansion, the costs were best met by corporate credit. Meanwhile, through its program of land reform, the government finally bought up many production units and made them into profit-sharing mills and plantations.

THE CORPORATE SUGAR PLANTATION

The corporate community on the south coast consists almost entirely of a very homogeneous group of workers who have a considerable Negro admixture, having descended in part from slaves. There is no upper class today, for the private owners have sold out and moved away. Their economic functions have been taken over by a handful of managers representing the American corporation. The middle classes of the community are small, for many of the services they would normally perform are carried out by the corporation.

The working class differs profoundly from that of the tobacco and coffee regions. It consists entirely of wage earners, whose employment is seasonal and whose income is barely adequate for survival. There are no subsistence plots, and there is no system of personal favors between owner and worker, as on the family hacienda. The workers even have difficulty finding dwellings. They live in clusters of houses on small plots on some of the older hacienda centers, along public highways, and on the beach.

There is remarkable similarity among all members of this class, since opportunities for advancement are absent, and the position of everyone is fixed by a uniform system of wages and agreements. The ideal of self-improvement which characterizes the tobacco farmers is absent. Escape from the fixed socioeconomic status can be achieved only through out-migration or through winning a stake in illegal gambling or bootlegging, both of which would be regarded by the highland people as unwarranted risks rather than as opportunities.

The sugar workers place little value on individual initiative. Their hope is not to achieve upward mobility through education, thrift, or effort, for the job hierarchy holds no place for them. Instead, they seek common goals through the collective means of the labor union, which not only is used to bargain with management but which is a political instrument that lends mass support to the Popular Democratic party in its legislative struggle for improvement of wages, hours, and working conditions.

In the typical labor-class family, all members who are old enough work for wages, which gives a measure of independence to each individual. Since neither property nor considerations of religious orthodoxy are important, marriage unions are likely consensual. Because divorce is frequent and children generally remain with the mother, the family has a matrilineal and matriarchal character. The *Compadrazgo* has proliferated among the sugar workers, and a person may have thirty to forty *compadres*. *Compadres* are always chosen within the working class, however, for the American managerial staff will have no part in such arrangements. Ritual kinship, therefore, instead of binding together members of different socioeconomic classes as in the tobacco and coffee areas, serves as a surrogate for extended kin ties and as a means of furthering the security of the individual within his class.

The homogeneity and solidarity of the working group is also expressed to some extent in religion. Here more than anywhere else on the island, evangelical sects of Protestantism have made considerable progress. This seemingly reflects in part the traditional association of orthodox Catholicism with the ruling upper-class whites, and in part the need for a common emotional outlet which such religions frequently provide insecure groups. Despite the large Negro element in this community, no religious beliefs or practices of unquestioned African provenience were found.

THE PROFIT-SHARING SUGAR PLANTATION

The culture patterns and the attitudes of the workers on the government-owned, profit-sharing sugar plantations are very similar to those of the corporation employees. The workers do not have a sense of proprietorship and participation in plant affairs, because they do not manage the plant. In fact, they speak of it as "the corporation." The line of authority from worker to mill runs a devious course. The worker belongs to a union and supports the Popular Democratic party through the local organization. The party controls the government, which in turn appoints the plantation managers. The workers bargain directly with the managers through their union.

Two features distinguish the profit-sharing plantations from the corporate ones, but these have made little difference in the lives of the workers. First, the workers receive proportional benefits, but this provision has been counterbalanced by the need to spread work as widely as possible, so the labor force is several times as large as it need be, and individual income is very low. Second, subsistence plots have been provided the workers, but since little value is attached to owning land and growing one's own food, the people turn during the "dead" season to activities which yield cash, and make slight use of their plots.

Fixed essentially in a proletariat class, the workers constitute a fairly homogeneous sociocultural group. The processes of industrialization have not affected them as deeply as on the corporate plantation, for they were fairly recently on family haciendas, and the older patterns survive in slight degree. But the nature of the family, life goals, economic activity and union organization, and political attitudes are substantially the same as under the corporation.

The greatest difference between government and corporation workers is in religion. The saint cult survives in some strength among the former, and there is considerable fear of witchcraft. A plausible explanation of witchcraft is that the general insecurity of the people has led them to channel hostility toward competitors—in this case especially migrants from the highlands seeking jobs—into a fear of supernatural measures rather than to express it overtly.

The Upper Class

The Puerto Rican upper class is limited to a few hundred families which are distinguished by their wealth, their social prominence, and their extreme Americanization. Their income is usually over $10,000 a year. Most of them are engaged in commerce, especially as representatives of United States business firms, although some also derive income from the land. Unlike the wealthy agrarian families, such as the coffee growers, the primary economic allegiance of these families to the United States has been a major factor in their Americanization.

The necessity of carrying out business activities on American terms has profoundly affected the lives of the upper-class people. Children are indoctrinated at an early age in the status and role they will assume. They become accustomed to luxurious housing, automobiles, servants, and other evidences of a very high standard of living. They are educated in American social customs and business practices. Many of them are sent to the United States for their high-school education and most of them for college education, which is taken in the business and professional fields. As adults, they are largely business executives.

Cultural characteristics of the Hispanic heritage are rapidly disappearing among upper-class families. They are bilingual, but it can hardly be said that they are bicultural. The nuclear family of man, wife, and children is acquiring independence of the extended kin ties, just as it is in the United States. There is a great love of children, but the number of children has decreased despite prevalent Catholicism which disapproves of birth control.

These families must deal with Puerto Ricans in their business activities, and consequently they understand Puerto Rican behavior. But to a large extent they force their own terms upon business associates and thus become an acculturating influence.

In their relationship to one another, the upper-class families constitute a strong in-group which moves in restricted circles. They belong to highly exclusive social clubs, and their patterns of visiting and entertainment involve only their equals. Social and recreational activities have assumed a predominantly American character. Political attitudes are conservative. The upper class has been opposed to the program of the Popular Democratic party, but since the latter seems to have moderated its social reform program, most of the class has supported it. These classes may also be described as conservative in religion, in that Catholic orthodoxy continues to characterize them.

Some Conclusions

The acculturation of the upper-class families has resulted not only from the general processes of industrialization but also from conscious borrowing of the patterns of upper-class business families of the United States. These Puerto Rican families, however, have played only a minor role in acculturating other local groups. They have, no doubt, strongly influenced the lower echelons of the business classes with whom they have direct contact, but their subculture presupposes an economic basis and opportunities which are absent among the workers, the peasants, and the small farmers.

The tobacco farmers and the sugar workers are similar in many respects to their counterparts in the United States, but the similarities are less the result of borrowing (these groups have had little contact with one another) than of the industrial trends which have introduced national institutions of a North American type into Puerto Rico. Many North American culture elements, such as manufactured goods, clothes, sports, and motion pictures, have also spread very widely in Puerto Rico, but they have been incorporated in local subcultures which are patterned quite differently.

This article has emphasized the subcultural differences, the distinctive life-ways, found among certain segments of the rural population, rather than the common denominator of Puerto Rican culture. There is, of course, much that all Puerto Ricans share. All groups speak Spanish, and they have in common something of the Hispanic tradition of familial patterns, the Catholic religion, the *compadrazgo*, music, dancing, and recreation. They were all once under Spanish political, economic, and religious domination, and they have been under United States sovereignty for a half century.

The new goals, values, and patterns created by industrialization have been mediated specifically by the United States, but they would undoubtedly have been much the same under any other sovereignty. They have set up new currents of political, social, economic, and religious activity. Fundamental and rapid change is always disturbing. Most Puerto Ricans quite understandably react to some degree against these trends; that is, they exhibit evidences of insecurity. Some are openly antagonistic to the United States, which they hold responsible for what is happening to them. If Puerto Rico can be said to manifest nationalism, however, it is a form of cultural rather than overtly political nationalism. It is the spontaneous and inevitable reaction of all segments of the population to profound changes brought about by a set of institutions which has been imposed upon them from the outside.

A Typology of Latin American Subcultures

CHARLES WAGLEY
and
MARVIN HARRIS

I

One of the most perplexing problems in the study of complex national or regional cultures such as those of Latin America is the diversity of pattern and institution which they contain. There are a series of institutions, values, and modes of behavior which constitute throughout Latin America a "cultural common denominator" and which distinguish Latin American culture from other major culture spheres of the Western world (cf. Gillin 1947b and Wagley 1948). But the "common denominator" of modern Latin America does not consist simply of those institutions, values, and behavior patterns held in common by most of the Latin American population. Regular cultural differences within the complex and heterogeneous national societies must also be considered. A conceptual framework based on these differences is much needed to provide a context for the extant data and to guide future research. This is especially true with respect to the numerous anthropological community studies, whose contribution to our knowledge of a national culture is often lessened by an inadequate definition of just what variety of the national culture is being considered—or, in other words, what segment of the diverse population they treat. The purpose of the

Reprinted from *American Anthropologist*, 1955, LVII, 428–451, by permission of the authors and publisher.

present article is to suggest a taxonomic system of subcultures which we hope will have operational utility throughout Latin America.

This attempt to provide a classificatory system for ordering cultural data on Latin America is obviously not unique. As we shall discuss in more detail below, Redfield (1941), by implication at least, distinguished four types of communities for Yucatan, although only the folk and urban types were emphasized. Steward (1953) and his associates in the Puerto Rican project isolated a series of significant Puerto Rican subcultures for study.[1] And recently, there has been published a series of articles, dealing mainly with Latin America, aimed at refining and extending Redfield's folk-urban concepts. Most of these discussions of Redfield's classification and most attempts to develop a sociocultural taxonomic system have dealt with varieties of whole local communities treated as whole societies. This is to be expected from a discipline whose traditional research methods involved prolonged, sedentary, and intimate contact with a restricted locale and the analysis of local sociocultural wholes. But it is apparent that many of the communities studied in Latin America by anthropologists have an internal heterogeneity of culture pattern depending upon class differences, differences between rural and urban residents of the same community, and other factors, too numerous to list. It is therefore often difficult to classify the culture of a whole local community as "folk culture" or as "urban culture"—or as "Indian," "mestizo," or "Creole." The present taxonomy of subcultures attempts to distinguish between culture and society and to take into account not only the differences among communities but also internal cultural heterogeneity within communities.

We distinguish nine significant Latin American subculture types. They are called "subcultures" because they are variations of a larger cultural tradition and represent the way of life of significant segments of the Latin American population. They are called "types" because their content differs according to the environment, history, and distinctive local traditions of the nation or subregion in which they are found. Thus, the subculture types we have called "Peasant" differ in content in the western countries of Central and South America, with their strong American Indian tradition, from the same type as found in the West Indies and lowland Brazil, which have felt strong African influences. Yet it seems to us that Peasant subcultures throughout Latin America share certain basic features which makes it possible to include them in the same typological category.

At least in a preliminary fashion, the following subculture types would seem to be useful for ordering the universe of Latin American cultural materials: (1) *Tribal Indian*, comprising the cultures of the few remaining aboriginal peoples; (2) *Modern Indian*, resulting from the fusion of aboriginal and, in the main, sixteenth- and seventeenth-century

Iberian institutions and culture patterns; (3) *Peasant,* carried by the relatively isolated horticultural peoples of Latin America (and frequently by the lower classes of small isolated towns), who are called variously *mestizos, cholos, ladinos, caboclos,* or other local terms; (4) *Engenho Plantation,* the subculture of the workers on family-owned estates; (5) *Usina Plantation,* the way of life on the large modern corporation-owned agricultural establishments; (6) *Town,* the way of life of the middle- and upper-class inhabitants of the numerous settlements serving as administrative, market, and religious centers throughout Latin America; (7) *Metropolitan Upper Class,* characteristic of the highest socioeconomic strata in the large cities and of the owners of plantations; (8) *Metropolitan Middle Class,* characteristic of an emerging group of big-city professional and white-collar workers and owners of medium-size business, and (9) *Urban Proletariat,* characteristic of a mass of unskilled and semiskilled industrial and menial workers in the larger cities.

Undoubtedly there are many other important Latin American subcultural types, and it is hoped that the present taxonomy will be refined and extended—or that it will stimulate others to formulate a more useful system.

II

(1) TRIBAL INDIAN TYPES

In 1500, when the Europeans came to that part of the New World which is now Latin America, the natives of the lowlands (except for certain parts of the circum-Caribbean) lacked true tribal or political organization. There were innumerable "tribes" made up of villages or bands united only by a common language, common custom, and the consciousness of forming "a people" as against all outsiders. The power of chiefs seldom extended beyond one or more villages or bands; and the "tribes," sometimes even the villages or bands of the same tribe, were generally at war with one another. The population was sparse in aboriginal times, and disease, slavery, and European warfare against these highly divided groups rapidly led to the decimation and extinction of the native peoples in many localities. Nowadays, only an insignificant few of these tribal groups persist in localities such as the Chaco, the headwaters of the Amazon tributaries, and on isolated reservations and mission stations. Such tribesmen constitute an insignificant segment of the modern Latin American population, and as long as they retain their aboriginal cultures and their identity as tribesmen they are, in reality, carriers of distinct cultures within the geographic boundaries of Latin America and not subcultures of modern Latin America. However, the process of acculturation now taking place among these tribal groups does pertain to the study of Latin American culture, and, as Foster recently pointed out in his discussion of the folk culture concept, it is important to distinguish between tribal cultures and the mixed rural cultures of Latin America (1953:162).

(2) MODERN INDIAN TYPES

The Indians of the highland regions of Latin America must be included in any study of modern Latin American culture. Although their way of life differs strikingly from that of the nationals of the countries in which they live, they share many patterns and institutions, mainly of European origin, with the other inhabitants, and numerically they are an important segment of the population. Unlike the lowlands, the highland region was inhabited by a dense aboriginal population organized into native states. After the initial shock of armed conquest and disease, these peoples were brought under the control of the Spanish colonials. Through mechanisms such as the *encomienda, repartimiento, mita,* and other forms of forced labor, they were made to work for their conquerors and were integrated into colonial society. Missionaries taught them Catholicism and, in many cases, they were concentrated into Spanish-type villages and a European form of community organization was forced upon them. They borrowed freely from the European culture of the sixteenth and seventeenth centuries—a culture which in many respects contained as many "folk" features as their own. By at least the beginning of the eighteenth century, a new culture had taken form among these peoples out of the fusion of aboriginal and colonial Spanish patterns. This culture persists today, unchanged in its main outlines, and constitutes an important variant of national patterns in many highland countries.

Modern Indians generally speak an aboriginal language, although they may also be bilingual. Some of them work in mines, on coffee *fincas,* or on large haciendas, but most characteristically they are horticulturalists planting native American crops, although many European plants have also been adopted. Despite the tendency to individualize landholdings which began in the nineteenth century, among many Modern Indian groups the community is still the landholding unit. Community cohesion generally persists at a high level despite the encroaching power of the national states. Indian *alcaldes, regidores,* and other officials are often maintained alongside the national bureaucracy. While the Modern Indian is nominally Catholic, it is characteristic that a large segment of aboriginal belief has been fused with Catholic ideology. In addition, Catholic saints are endowed with local characteristics and powers. The Indians of each community generally think of themselves as ethnic units separate from other Indian groups and from the nationals of the country in which they reside; they are the people of Santiago Chimaltenango, of Chamula or of Chucuito, rather than Guatemalans or Peruvians. Frequently they wear a distinctive costume which identifies them as Indians of a particular *pueblo*, and it is characteristic for the Indians of each community to be endogamous.

Numerous examples of this subcultural type have been studied in Latin America by anthropologists. The Indians of Santiago Chimaltenango (Wagley 1942, 1950), of Chichicastenango (Bunzel 1952), of Panajachel (Tax 1953), of Quintana Roo, Yucatan (Villa 1945), of Kauri (Mishkin 1946) and of Chucuito in Peru (Tschopik 1951), to mention but a few, are carriers of Modern Indian-type subcultures. Yet, as noted above, few of these communities contain only carriers of the Modern Indian subculture type. In most of these communities, there are also a few non-Indians, carriers of a Peasant-type subculture, who form an integral part of community life. Any full community study must treat not only the two subcultures of these communities but also the "castelike" relationship between them. As Gillin has written, "Each group [Ladino and Indian] has culture patterns more or less exclusive to itself, but the two castes are part of a reciprocal pattern which characterizes the community as a whole" (1951:11). Too often our community studies have treated Modern Indian subcultures as if they were isolated tribal groups.

(3) PEASANT TYPES

Throughout Latin America, the people who inhabit rural farms and the numerous small and isolated agricultural villages have a way of life which is analogous in many respects to that of peasants in other parts of the world. Latin American peasants may be physically American Indians, Negroes or Europeans, or mixtures of these racial stocks. They are the people who are called *mestizos* (Mexico and other countries), *ladinos* (Guatemala), *cholos* (Peru), or *caboclos, tabareus, caipiras,* and *matutos* (Brazil). In some respects, their way of life is similar to that of the Modern Indian. They are generally horticulturalists using essentially the same "slash-and-burn" techniques of farming as the Modern Indians, and they frequently depend primarily upon native plants such as maize, manioc, and potatoes. As stated earlier, Peasant-type subcultures are strongly flavored with aboriginal traits in some areas, as for example in the Amazon Valley, where native shamanism is an integral part of peasant religion. In other areas, such as the West Indies and the Guianas, African traits persist in varying degrees among the Peasant subcultures just as American Indian traits do elsewhere. But everywhere Peasant-type subcultures are characterized by a predominance of archaic European patterns, which survive alongside the American Indian or African patterns and which are slowly giving way to new national patterns and institutions. Unlike the Modern Indians, Peasants generally consider themselves to be nationals of the country in which they reside. Although they tend to be regional in their loyalties and to have but a vague idea of what it means to be a member of a nation, national patterns and institutions play a larger role in Peasant than in Modern Indian subcultures. Peasant subculture economies are closely tied in with regional and national economies. There is fairly extensive participation in commercial transactions through the medium of markets, to which Peasant farmers regularly go to sell their surplus for cash. Peasants maintain accounts at stores and trading posts from which they receive goods of nation-wide circulation such as kerosene, steel tools, cloth, thread, and sewing machines.

Peasants characteristically speak the national language (i.e., Spanish or Portuguese), although sometimes an aboriginal tongue (e.g., the Tarascan of the Michoacan mestizos), or, as in Haiti, a *créole*, is spoken. Peasants participate to some extent in political life, voting if there are elections and if they have the franchise. Catholicism in Peasant subcultures tends to be more orthodox than that of the Modern Indian. Peasants share national fashions, values and aspirations, although in all of these they are generally "behind the times" since they tend to be isolated from the centers of diffusion. Thus young men may play soccer if it is the national sport, as it is in Brazil. Peasants often celebrate national holidays and perhaps know something of their national heroes. Literacy is valued as an aid in social and economic improvement. Nowadays, Peasants tend to dress after the style of the city as soon as such styles are known and when people can afford them. Because such people are generally poor, illiterate, and isolated, they have little in the way of modern technological facilities such as electric lights, motor-driven vehicles, and modern housing.

Again, it is not difficult to cite examples of this type of Latin American subculture which have been studied by anthropologists. Both Modern Indian and Peasant-type subcultures tend to be carried by relatively small and simply organized social units which thus lend themselves to investigation by the traditional field techniques of ethnology. The rural agriculturalists living in the environs of Moche in Peru (Gillin 1947a), those of the community of Tzintzuntzan in Mexico (Foster 1948), those of Cruz das Almas in southern Brazil (Pierson 1951), those of Itá in the Brazilian Amazon (Wagley 1953), and those of Marbial Valley in Haiti (Métraux 1951) are carriers of subcultures which correspond to the Peasant type. The Small Farmer subculture of Puerto Rico would also seem to correspond to this category (Steward 1953; Manners 1950).

But it must be emphasized that most of the communities mentioned above also contain people who are not peasants, not even rural, but townsmen with urban aspirations and urban patterns of behavior. The subculture of these people will be considered below as the Town type. Due to the tendency to regard "folk culture" as a way of life characteristic of a type of community, the folk subcultures (or in our terms, Peasant subcultures) of such communities have often been emphasized to the exclusion of the nonfolk elements. The restudy of Redfield's Tepoztlán by Lewis (1951) is an example of how the concept of a homogeneous folk community needs to be qualified in view of the internal heterogeneity of cultural patterns found in rural communities.

The fact probably is that the carriers of Peasant-type subcultures live everywhere in communities which also contain carriers of Town-type subcultures—whose ties with national life are the intermediate bonds by which the peasant is also tied into national life. Indeed, many peasants are actually town dwellers who have their domiciles in town and their farms in the nearby area. Although settlements inhabited exclusively by people who have a homogeneous Peasant subculture are extremely common, it is a distortion to view them as isolated communities, or even as total communities. Since the Peasant subculture is distinguished from the Modern Indian precisely on the grounds of greater identification with and participation in national patterns and institutions, it is clear that a group of peasants can only be *part* of a community, and that the terms "folk society" and "folk culture" are misleading when applied to a community which actually and necessarily contains more than one subculture. It may perhaps help to clarify the matter if the communities in which peasant households, hamlets and villages occur are thought of as larger Town-Peasant communities, implying that Town and Peasant subcultures must be considered together if a proper understanding of either is to be attained. This symbiotic relationship between Peasant subcultures and Town subcultures (i.e., "folk and nonfolk") has been recently emphasized by Foster (1953:169 ff.).

(4) ENGENHO PLANTATION AND (5) USINA PLANTATION TYPES

The Europeans who settled in the Caribbean and in the lowland parts of northern South America did not find the riches in gold and silver nor the large aboriginal labor force which their contemporaries encountered in the highlands. But by the middle of the sixteenth century sugar cane had become an important commercial crop in Brazil and in parts of the West Indies. For a time, the great wealth which sugar brought to this lowland region was comparable to that derived from minerals in the highlands. From the Old World the planters brought a commercialized version of large-scale agricultural enterprise, which had its roots in sixteenth-century Europe and even earlier in the ancient Mediterranean world. In the New World this agricultural system was modified by the massive use of slave labor, by the exigencies of sugar as a commercial crop, and by the physical and social environment of the New

World colonies. The result was the New World plantation—the *hacienda*, the *finca*, the *estancia*, the *fazenda*, or whatever it happens to be called in the various countries.

Such plantations came to form veritable communities, or neighborhoods of larger communities, with their own variety of Latin American culture. Although large-scale agricultural establishments differ from one part of Latin America to another and in accordance with the crop to which they are dedicated (i.e., sugar, coffee, bananas, cotton, cacao, henequen, etc.), there are numerous social and cultural similarities among them. Furthermore, some fundamental changes in the way of life on Latin American plantations have followed essentially the same developmental process throughout the whole area, despite differences in the commercial crops.

The general characteristics of the *Engenho* Plantation subculture type may best be illustrated by reference to plantations dedicated to sugar cane, which was for centuries Latin America's most important commercial crop. Although there were local differences, sugar-cane plantations during the period of slavery seem to have followed a similar pattern throughout the area. The center of the plantation, and of the community or neighborhood which it formed, was the mansion in which the owner, his large family, and the many domestic servants lived. A chapel, which was either attached to the mansion or situated near it, served as the church for the owners and for the slave workers. Behind the mansion were the slave quarters—a street of huts. Nearby there were sheds used to store tools and equipment and to house the oxen and other animals. A storehouse, where the food and other supplies for the field hands were kept and periodically distributed, was also a common feature. Then, nearby, there was the *engenho* (Spanish *ingenio*), which was a small sugar factory containing a mill driven by hand, by animal traction, or by water power. Such plantations were generally situated on waterways which furnished easy transportation to market centers. Characteristically, the plantation settlement pattern was a concentrated one resembling that of a small village.

The number of people on such plantations was generally not large during the slave period. On the average, no more than 200 to 300 people lived on a relatively large sugar plantation, and within this small "village-like" society social relations tended to be intimate and highly personal. The members of the owner's family were tied together into a large, extended patriarchal group. Between these aristocrats and the slaves there was a stable set of relations often accompanied by personal intimacy and intense loyalty. It was, in other words, a "caste" society made up of Negro slaves and European owners in which each "caste" was conscious of the rights and obligations of the other. Leadership was provided automatically by the dominant European group, and economics, religion, and almost all aspects of life were directed and controlled by the aristocratic owner or his administrators.

The abolition of slavery, the vagaries of the international market, and finally the industrialization of sugar refining brought about important changes in the old colonial sugar plantations. However, many plantations may still be found throughout Latin America which strongly resemble the old *engenho* despite the substitution of wage labor for slavery, and other innovations. Such plantations are still owned, and often administered, by descendants of the same aristocratic slave-owning families of the nineteenth century. The workers, some of whom may actually be descendants of former slaves, show much the same dependency and loyalty toward their employers as the slaves are said to have shown for their masters. Each of these *engenho*-type plantations, with its cluster of houses and sheds and its small chapel, forms, as in the past, a small concentrated village or neighborhood (Smith 1946:396 ff.). Economic life is still focused upon monoculture, and little land or time is left for the workers to grow their own gardens. Today, the sugar factory itself is no longer a part of the *engenho*-type plantations. The *engenho*-type plantations have become, instead, suppliers of sugar cane to large mechanized sugar mills, or *usinas*, which do the processing and marketing. But in many respects the way of life on these old-style plantations has changed remarkably little since the nineteenth century.

Here again, the community unit consists of the carriers of two distinct subcultures, that of the workers and that of the owners. Although it would be tempting to make the *engenho* plantation community unit and the *Engenho* Plantation subculture coincide, the fact is that the plantation owner is generally also an urban Latin American cosmopolitan who is found in the upper strata of the principal large cities. Since early colonial times he has had both a "town house" and his place in the country, and has alternated his residence, sometimes seasonally, between one and the other. His employees, formerly his slaves or peons, including domestic servants in town as well as the workers in the country, are treated by him with characteristic patriarchal, intimate, and usually benevolent concern. To this treatment the *engenho* plantation worker responds with loyalty and attitudes of dependence. It is this dependence and allegiance to the *patrão* (boss), together with the distinctive land tenure, occupational and communal arrangements peculiar to the monoculture regime, which distinguish *Engenho* Plantation subcultures from Peasant subcultures.[2]

Throughout Latin America, a transition from the *engenho* plantation to the modern industrialized agricultural enterprise has occurred or is now taking place. We have called the newer form the *usina* plantation, from the term used for the modern industrialized sugar mill.[3] Speaking again in terms of sugar plantations, as steam-driven mills were introduced capital came to play a more important role than land. The central-power-driven *usina* could process and distribute far more efficiently than the smaller installations, and so the small plantations came more and more to depend upon the *usina* to process the cane. Gradually, great corporations have bought out the smaller properties and welded them together into large agricultural factories. There is a transitional phase, however, in which each *engenho* plantation is administered as a separate unit by employees of the corporation. During this phase much of the old way of life continues. This period of transition is one which is particularly vulnerable to social tension and economic instability. The workers have lost the security provided by the traditional *patrão*, and the new system of social welfare and social security of the national government has not as yet been extended to cover them.

Then, as industrialization progresses, it becomes more efficient to fuse these smaller properties into one large centralized commercial farm. Where this process has been completed, as in Cuba, Puerto Rico, and Brazil, the result is a type of Plantation subculture which differs profoundly from that of the old-style *engenho* plantation. The traditional pattern of intimacy and mutual dependence between the workers and their employers is replaced by a more strictly economic relationship between the workers and the administrators and officials of the corporation. The local group becomes larger as the number of workers increases and the social unit is more heterogeneous as new specialized occupations appear. The workers, without the old emotional ties to their fellows and to their employers, are more mobile than before, often leaving the plantations to seek higher wages elsewhere. The *usina* plantation is more closely integrated with national institutions and culture patterns. Labor unions are sometimes active among the workers, and social welfare legislation is enforced more often than in the *engenho* plantation. There may be electric lights, modern housing, schools, medical clinics, public health facilities, and excellent communications with the metropolitan centers. The workers on such establishments seem to have a way of life more similar to that of the growing urban-industrial proletariat of Latin America than to that of the workers on the *engenho* plantations. Mintz has recently characterized the workers on these large commercial plantations as the "Rural Proletariat" (1953a:139 ff.).

The discussion of these two types of Plantation subculture has been based on plantations involved in sugar production. Large-scale agricultural estates that grow other kinds of commercial crops for export are of course also found in Latin America. Such crops as cacao, coffee, maté tea, henequen, and cotton are also produced on large-scale, monoculture plantations. It is probable that the regime of exploitation of each different crop determines distinctive sociocultural conditions. Thus when more data become available it may be convenient to formulate a series of additional subtypes for *Engenho* and *Usina* Plantation subcultures based on crop specialties. Livestock ranches, for example, with their small number of workers, their exclusion of female laborers, and their saturation with a kind of horse complex, clearly merit treatment as a subtype.

From another point of view, the widespread occurrence of sharecropping suggests an additional sector of refinements for our categories. Sharecropping of a commercial crop as a substitute for wages can probably be subsumed under the category of *Engenho* Plantation subcultures. Relationships between the owner and his workers approach the highly personal ones characteristic of *engenho* plantations, with the employer offering assistance in a crisis and in many instances being the sole purchaser of his tenants' produce. The individual sharecropping regime, however, may act to reduce the community cohesion characteristic of nucleated wage laborers on the other *engenho*-type plantations.

For the purpose of this paper, it seems sufficient to set forth the hypothesis that at least two broad types, the *Engenho* Plantation and the *Usina* Plantation subcultures, may be found throughout Latin America. No matter what crop the plantation produces, there has been a transition from the old traditional enterprise to the modern industrialized establishment analogous to that which has taken place in sugar production. Everywhere this transition has involved a shift from a more personal and stable set of relations between the classes to a mobile, impersonal one based on economic values and urban standards. It has involved a change from a small and relatively homogeneous society to a larger and more variegated one; and it has led to a more important role for national institutions and patterns on all levels of plantation life.

It is surprising that so few examples of the Plantation subcultures of either type have been studied by anthropologists, especially in view of the obvious numerical importance of plantation workers in the Latin American population and in view of the importance of plantation production in the national economies of the Latin American nations. A study of an *Engenho* Plantation subculture has been carried out by Hutchinson as part of a community study in the Recôncavo region of Bahia in Brazil (1954).[4] A study of a government-owned sugar plantation was made by Elena Padilla Seda in Puerto Rico (1951), and on the same island Mintz studied a large sugar plantation owned and operated by a commercial corporation (1951). Loomis and Powell have studied a Costa Rica *finca* producing sugar and coffee, and have given us a comparison of a hacienda and a peasant community in rural Costa Rica (1951). A study of a community in Brazil in which there are cacao-producing plantations has been carried out by Anthony Leeds. If the present classification of Latin American subculture types serves no other purpose, it indicates that a large segment of the Latin American population—and an important variant of the culture of the area—has been relatively neglected in our field investigations.

(6) TOWN TYPES

Towns where periodic fairs are held and which serve as the administrative and religious centers for rural districts are old in Latin America. They have their roots both in the European and in the aboriginal traditions. With the improvement of transportation (especially with the use of trucks), many of these towns have become regional markets similar to the market towns that serve the rural United States. As these market centers enlarge their range of trading, the rural population no longer produces only for local consumption but comes to plant by more modern methods cash crops that are sold on the national market. The towns thus become more closely integrated with national economic and political life. Their populations increase, and new concepts and patterns are introduced from the cities. Life in these larger towns is more like that of the great urban centers by which they are more directly influenced, than like that of the surrounding countryside.

Yet in Latin America today there are still innumerable small towns serving only an immediate rural area and preserving many traditional patterns. Such towns cannot be understood without reference to the whole community of which they are the centers. For it is characteristic of Town subcultures that their "city folk" look down upon the "country people" as "hicks," and that behavior patterns, values, standards of dress, speech and etiquette differ for the upper-class townspeople as opposed to both the lower-class townspeople and to the inhabitants of the rural countryside.

As we have already indicated, such towns are part of communities which include two strongly contrasting subcultures. The contrast between the two corresponds to a marked schism in socioeconomic class status between a nonfarming, landlord, business-owning, bureaucratic, "white-collar" group and a farming, manual-laboring group. Within the town itself, there are a small number of people who are craft specialists, like shoemakers, blacksmiths, and carpenters, who are permanent residents of the town, and who do not engage in agricultural activities. From the point of view of the local upper class these people may be "hicks" just as much as the town-dwelling and country-dwelling farmers. Although these artisans themselves often regard the rural people with condescension, the fact is that they are generally more closely related (by kinship, by marriage, by social and cultural values, by economics, and by social intercourse) with the rural farmers than with the town upper class. The stigma of poverty, of illiteracy, and of manual labor is on both groups. Thus in isolated areas, town-dwelling farmers, town-dwelling artisans and laborers, and domestic servants can generally be classed as carriers of a Peasant subculture. But such people represent a gradient of contact between isolated semi-subsistence farmers and the upper-class townspeople who are carriers of Town subculture.

The life of the upper-class townsman differs radically from that of the carriers of the Peasant subcultures. The small-town upper-class "urbanite" manifests in many respects an archaic version of the ideals and patterns of the big-city cosmopolitans and the plantation gentry of bygone days. Although upper-class townspeople are often more familiar with the geography of the nearest large city than with the geography of the rural areas of the community they live in, and although they seek to emulate cosmopolitanism with respect to dress, manners, and outlook, they are often thwarted in these ambitions by the incompleteness and inaccuracy of their notions of the contemporary standards of sophistication. Thus, in most Latin American small towns, culture patterns persist which are today considered "old-fashioned" in the metropolitan cities. Courting, for example, is closely chaperoned, and it is a common sight to see a young man quietly conversing with his fiancée from the street while she looks down at him safely from the window of the house. And in the plaza there is often the *paseo*, during which the young men circulate in one direction as the young ladies go in the other.

Except in regions where there are large plantations owned by a rural gentry, upper-class townsmen control most of the political and economic power in the community. Their political life is intense, and there is great competition for the support of lower-class peasant electors. Upper-class social life frequently revolves around clubs which sponsor dances and other forms of entertainment from which the peasants are excluded. Upper-class Catholicism is more orthodox in Town subcultures than in Modern Indian and Peasant subcultures. More emphasis is placed upon church-going and on formal sacraments as against household saints and unorthodox cults. Where deviations from Catholic tradition occur, they are apt to take the form of Protestantism or spiritualism. Upper-class townsmen have radios, receive mail, magazines, newspapers, and send their children to be educated in big-city high schools and colleges. They own fashionable clothing and often have servants to cook, wash, carry water, and take care of their house for them.

The existence of Town subcultures in isolated communities furnishes the key to the problem of the relationship of Peasant subcultures to lines of national political and economic integration. Local standards are set and maintained by this sociocultural segment, and it is through the upper class of the town that changes emanating from national legislation and metropolitan influences must filter before reaching the peasant stratum (cf. Foster 1953:169 ff.).

Many studies of local variations of Town subcultures have been made in Latin America by anthropologists as part of the study of communities which also include Peasant or even Modern Indian subcultures. But frequently, in such studies, it is difficult to know which data pertain to the Town subculture as distinguished from the subculture of the community's rural population. The town of Cunha in São Paulo, Brazil (Willems 1947), and the town of Moche in Peru (Gillin 1947a)—as against the rural peasants of both communities—seem to have subcultures of this type. Two community studies recently carried out in Brazil, namely, Monte Serrat in the arid northeast (Zimmerman 1952) and Minas Velhas in the central mountain region (Harris 1953), both distinguish between the Town and Peasant subcultures. In general, however, anthropologists have tended to emphasize the Latin American peasants or Modern Indians. A large portion of the population in countries such as Argentina, Uruguay, Paraguay, Brazil, Chile, and Colombia live in small towns. Not until we know more about the way of life distinctive of these small urban centers will our knowledge of Latin American culture be anything more than relatively superficial. It is not, in our opinion, the so-called mestizo or Creole patterns (i.e., in our terms, Peasant subcultures) which, as Gillin maintains (1947b), are the emergent culture patterns of Latin America. Rather, the predominant trend in contemporary Latin America would seem to be toward Town subcultures which are closely identified with the urbanized and industrialized world.

(7) METROPOLITAN UPPER CLASS, (8) METROPOLITAN MIDDLE CLASS, AND (9) URBAN PROLETARIAT TYPES

Little research has been carried out, either by sociologists or by anthropologists, on the modern Latin American city. As far as anthropology is concerned, such cities pose a difficult problem in research methodology, since the traditional field methods are best applied to relatively small populations and relatively homogeneous societies. The problem of class differences in the Latin American urban centers presents one of the most pressing and difficult challenges to students of Latin American culture. There is a critical lack of information about socioeconomic stratification as well as about the basic subcultural differences which attend the various levels. Accordingly in this paper we can do little more than speculate about the subcultures to be found in the great metropolitan centers of Latin America.

It is quite clear to all who have visited Latin America that while the metropolitan centers share much with cities throughout the Western world, they have their own peculiar characteristics. Caplow has pointed out two distinctive features of Latin American cities (1952:255):

> . . . those traits which are common to metropolitan cultures everywhere in the modern world are most concentrated in groups of high status,

whence they are diffused rather raggedly down through the social system of each community; second, that there is more cultural variation within the Latin American city than within most cities of the United States or Europe.

These two differences between the cities of Latin America and those of the United States and Europe explain why the population of the Latin American city often seems, in a sense, to be smaller than the census data indicate. For the number of people who participate effectively in city life (i.e., buy newspapers, attend the cinema, have electric lights and telephone service, and so forth) is exceedingly small as compared with the actual population. The largest proportion of the population lives, in one sense, outside the stream of city life, differing little in many respects from inhabitants of rural areas; as a matter of fact, a large number of these Latin American city dwellers have but recently migrated from the rural zones.

The people of the metropolitan upper class attempt to maintain, as far as possible, the traditional patterns and ideals of an aristocratic landed gentry. It is this group which participates in and generally dominates local and national politics. Its members are absentee landlords, high-level government employees and officials, owners of industry and large commercial enterprises, and many well-to-do doctors, lawyers, and other professionals. No matter whether such people are the actual descendants of the landed gentry of the nineteenth century or descendants of immigrants or others who have recently achieved wealth and position, they tend to adopt many of the ideal patterns of nineteenth-century agrarian society. There is an emphasis among them upon widely extended kinship ties which is strongly reminiscent of nineteenth-century aristocratic society. They have a disdain for manual labor and admiration for courtly manners, and a love of luxury. But, at the same time, it is this group in Latin America that permits its daughters to have "dates" and allows them to enter the professions, thus breaking the old traditional patterns of highly chaperoned courtship and the confinement of women to purely domestic realms. At least the better educated and the wealthier members of this group are in close touch with Europe and the United States. Until the last two decades, it was France to which they looked for innovations, and French tended to be their second language. Recently, however, the United States has come to supplant France in this respect, and English has become the preferred foreign language. Hence the metropolitan upper class tends both to preserve old traditional forms and to be the innovator, accepting new forms from abroad, diffusing them down to the lower class of the city, outward to the people of the towns, and ultimately to the peasants and to the workers on plantations. To a large extent, therefore, many of the ideal patterns common to the other Latin American subcultures derive from Metropolitan Upper Class patterns.

Studies specifically pertaining to the subculture of the Metropolitan Upper Class have not been carried out by anthropologists except for one by Raymond Scheele, which was part of the Puerto Rican Project directed by Steward (1950:139–40; 1953:102; 1956). To date most of our information comes from data acquired by anthropologists and others during their casual relations with Latin Americans of this group, and from what Latin Americans write about themselves. It is suggested that the ethnographic method should be used in the study of representative local segments of the Latin American upper class. Until this is done, much of what we say about this important segment of Latin American culture will remain entirely hypothetical.

Even less of a concrete nature is known about the Metropolitan Middle Class and Urban Proletariat subcultures. The middle class in the large cities of Latin America is made up of a rapidly increasing group of first-generation professionals and of white-collar workers in business and government. Most observers tend to agree that this middle class maintains standards of material consumption and prestige closely patterned after those of the metropolitan upper class. Its members place a high value on freedom from manual labor and in matters of housing, clothing, and etiquette consciously strive to reduce the gap between themselves and their wealthier models. The presence in the cities of a vast substratum of marginal wage earners, constantly replenished by rural emigration, permits the metropolitan middle class to employ domestic servants and to avoid the stigma of menial labor. But there is intense competition for white-collar positions, and salaries are often insufficient to maintain leisure-class standards in other respects. One result noted by many observers has been the multiplication of the number of jobs held by each middle-class wage earner. Some high-school teachers in Rio de Janeiro, for example, teach in as many as five or six different schools and have to rush from one place to the next with split-second precision in order to arrive at their classes on time. Caught between low incomes and high standards of consumption modeled after those of the upper class, the middle class is forced to devote a large part of its income to items of high display value such as fashionable apartments, stylish clothing, and greatly overpriced automobiles. Thus, in contrast to the middle classes of other world areas, the Latin American metropolitan middle class appears not to have developed an emphasis on savings nor as yet to have distinctive "middle class ideology."

Although the urban proletariat is numerically the dominant segment of the metropolitan centers, it is the least well known of all. The phenomenal growth of Latin American urban centers in the last generation, mainly as a result of migration from rural zones, indicates that a large percentage of the urban proletariat may actually be carriers of Peasant, Plantation, or Town subcultures. A recent study by Lewis of migrants from Tepoztlán to Mexico City (1952) indicates that their ideological culture remains basically unchanged despite the urban setting. Only empirical research will answer the question whether there is a type of Latin American subculture distinctive of the urban proletariat and different from the subcultures of small towns and rural areas.

III

Whether or not the present typology of subcultures will be of any value in controlling variations and differences in the complexity of Latin American culture, and whether it will provide a useful frame of reference for research, depends on its operational utility in concrete situations. Its final usefulness over such a large area as Latin America as a whole will, of course, depend upon considerably more research and upon whether or not the available data can be ordered meaningfully within this framework. But an illustration of the use of this typology in a specific research project may indicate its possible value in the study of complex modern cultures. The research in question was carried out in the state of Bahia in Brazil in 1950–51 and comprised the study of three communities, each in a different ecological zone of the state. The communities studied were: Vila Recôncavo, in the sugar-planting area near the coast; Minas Velhas, an old mining center in the central mountain zone; and Monte Serrat, a community in the arid semi-desert of the northeast.[5] An analysis of the subcultures present in these communities and in the state of Bahia seemed to be most meaningful in describing this sociocultural diversity.

Not all subculture types outlined in this paper will, of course, be present in any particular area of Latin America. In the state of Bahia, the indigenous population was quickly exterminated or assimilated. Thus, the subculture types called Tribal Indian and Modern Indian are not present. But throughout the state there are numerous rural agriculturalists, many of whom are descendants of Indians, whose subculture is of the type identified above as Peasant. Throughout the state there are also small towns which are essentially trading and administrative centers with Town subcultures. The coast of Bahia, especially around the Bay of Todos os Santos, where it is known as the Recôncavo, was one of the earliest sites of sugar plantations in Latin America. Here are found both the old-style *engenho*-type and the new *usina*-type sugar plantations. And finally, in the city of Salvador, the capital and largest metropolitan center of the state, there is a culturally conservative urban upper class preserving many old Brazilian traditions, as well as a large metropolitan proletariat.

Each of the communities in which field research was carried out contains at least two subcultures. The old mining town of Minas Velhas is a trading, manufacturing, and administrative center for a larger community encompassing a number of satellite villages inhabited by simple peasant farmers. Monte Serrat contains these same two subcultures: a religious, administrative, and trading town which is visited periodically by the surrounding scattered peasant population. The third community, Vila Recôncavo, contains a town which is inhabited by traders, government employees, a group of fishermen, a few artisans, manual laborers, and a variety of marginal wage earners. It also contains in the rural zone a series of *engenho*-type plantations, a small *usina* which still administers its various plantations as separate units (in transition between the *engenho*-type and *usina*-type plantations), and a number of metropolitan upper-class families, owners of plantations and of the *usina,* who participate in community life. The other Metropolitan subcultures (Middle Class and Urban Proletariat) are found in the city of Salvador but were not studied by this research project.[6] Thus, of the major subculture types found within the state of Bahia, four are represented in the communities of research.

Despite differences deriving from the degree of isolation, from different environments and different local historical circumstances, there are many crucial similarities in the Town subcultures of Monte Serrat, Minas Velhas, and Vila Recôncavo, on the one hand, and in the Peasant subcultures of these same communities, on the other hand. Likewise, there are crucial differences between these subcultures of each community as well as between these subcultures and the Plantation and Metropolitan Upper Class subcultures of Vila Recôncavo. The broad sociocultural differences between subcultures of different type in the Bahia area conform to the criteria upon which this taxonomy of Latin American subcultures had been based and have therefore been described above. But a specific illustration may help to clarify how such a typology can be used to explore additional categories of patterned behavior.

During the period of field work general elections were held throughout Brazil. There was considerable regularity in the communities being studied in regard to political behavior during the campaigns and during the election.

(*a*) *Peasant subcultures:* There was little or no interest in the elections among the peasant segment of population in both Minas Velhas and Monte Serrat. On election day in Monte Serrat, political parties sent trucks out to the rural zones to bring peasants to town to vote. The day was treated as an outing by peasants who came to town with their families dressed in their best clothes. They were served free meals by the political party which claimed their vote and whose truck had transported them to town. They voted according to the dictates of an influential townsman, motivated by personal loyalty and economic bonds (i.e., debts) rather than by strong political feelings or beliefs. Similar behavior was reported also for the peasants in Minas Velhas as well as for other communities with Peasant type subcultures in which more casual observations were made during the political campaign and the elections.

(*b*) *Town subcultures:* The political campaign in both Minas Velhas and Monte Serrat (communities with Peasant and Town subcultures) was intense among the townspeople, yet their interest was focused upon local and state rather than national issues. In both Minas Velhas and Monte Serrat, the townspeople were split by allegiances to opposing political parties. In Monte Serrat each of the principal bars was frequented by men belonging to but one political party and anyone known to have any sympathy for the opposing party would not dare enter the bar of the other. Two public address systems blared forth each day competing with each other in sheer volume and in political promises and accusations. Practically all conversation revolved around the coming elections. In both Minas Velhas and Monte Serrat almost everyone had something at stake; municipal, state and federal employees were anxious for their jobs, and commercial men and artisans stood to gain favors from being on the winning side. Even the parish priests were intensely active in the campaign and their sermons were not free of political propaganda. During the campaign, normal social life (i.e., visiting among families, dances, and the like) was almost entirely suspended. Election day was a tense and active occasion for the townspeople, most of whom were busy attempting to influence the peasant voter until he actually walked into the polls. Short visits during this period to other Bahian communities made it clear that this intense political activity was typical of Town subculture political behavior.

In the third community which contained a Town subculture, namely Vila Recôncavo, the political behavior of the town dwellers was deviant from that described above as typical for Town subcultures. In Vila Recôncavo, the political scene was dominated by metropolitan upper-class families. The local candidate for mayor was a member of one of these families rather than of the town upper class as in the two communities described above. Because of the powerful personal and economic hold which this landed gentry exerted on local affairs, the townspeople were not able to organize an effective opposition and the candidate ran virtually unopposed. The townspeople (i.e., commercial men, bureaucrats, artisans, etc.) put on a weak imitation of the political campaign which took place in Minas Velhas and Monte Serrat, but it was a foregone conclusion that the party of the metropolitan upper class (i.e., landed gentry) would win. Thus, in regions or areas, such as the Recôncavo of Bahia State, where the town is overshadowed by the surrounding plantations and the communities dominated by a landed gentry, the criteria of intense political activity for Town-type subcultures will be regularly absent.

(c) *Engenho Plantation subcultures:* As stated above, the community of Vila Recôncavo contained family-owned, *engenho*-type sugar plantations. During the political campaigns of 1950 little was heard about politics from the workers on these plantations. When the question was asked as to how they might vote, they were apt to answer, "I don't know, I haven't found out how the *patrão* will vote," or, "With the *patrão*, Senhor." For them, election day was a day without work when those who were literate (i.e., able to sign their names) went to town to vote as did the plantation owners. Such behavior seemed to be typical of workers on *engenho* plantations throughout the state of Bahia.

(d) *Usina Plantation subcultures:* Although as stated above there was not a large *usina* plantation in any of the communities studied intensively in the Bahia area, we were able to observe political behavior in nearby highly industrialized sugar plantations. Simply from the messages painted on walls in red and black paint at night urging the election of one candidate or another (especially of left-wing groups) and from the numerous political posters, it was obvious that political activity was intense among the *usina* workers. Far from voting with the administrators, these workers on large industrialized plantations supported the opposing political party. Labor unions exerted considerable influence and in general the workers were much interested in politics. Furthermore, since much of their political education came from national organizations such as labor unions and Vargas' Brazilian Labor Party (Partido Trabalhista Brasileiro), their interest focused more on national elections than local and state elections.

(e) *Metropolitan Upper Class subcultures:* Representatives of the upper class were present in only one of the communities studied, Vila Recôncavo. For this group, political activity on a high level is characteristic and traditional. Most individuals in this class had friends or relatives to whom success or failure at the polls was of the utmost importance. Cousins of important families in Vila Recôncavo were candidates for federal deputy, while one of the candidates for governor was a lifelong friend of most of the members of the same families. In Salvador large, united families from this group were pitted against each other for political control of the state and city. But, as stated above, in Vila Recôncavo, since the metropolitan upper-class families have intermarried, they presented in a sense a united front. Thus, the outcome of the election in Vila Recôncavo was easily predicted.

(f) *Metropolitan Middle Class* and (g) *Urban Proletariat subcultures:* Little can be said regarding the political behavior of these groups during the 1950 campaigns and elections. It was obvious that political reactions of both groups were emotional and intense but large-scale quantitative techniques would be necessary to study the political behavior of this large mass of people.[7]

A great number of subcultural differences and similarities which are valid for the area studied might also be pointed out. Material culture, technology, concepts of the cause and cure of disease, work patterns, occupational specialization, settlement patterns, housing, etiquette, speech habits, social ranking, and many other items are variable within the communities but constant within the subcultures of the area. Even the use made of tobacco is regular according to subculture type rather than community: peasant women smoke pipes, town women do not smoke, while metropolitan upper-class women smoke cigarettes. Thus a typology of subcultures is an indispensable tool for relating the community to its larger sociocultural context. Such a typology not only lends order to research materials and directs attention to the need for additional comparative data, but it also provides a basis for predicting with reasonable accuracy the reactions of certain segments of the population to new social stimuli. It is therefore of utility for both theoretical and applied purposes.

IV

Through a comparison of four Yucatan communities—Tusik, a "tribal" village of Quintana Roo; Chan Kom, a "peasant" community; Dzitas, a town on the railroad; and the city of Merida—Redfield concluded in his *The Folk Culture of Yucatan* (1941:339):

> . . . the peasant village as compared with the tribal village, the town as compared with the peasant village, or the city as compared with the town is less isolated, is more heterogeneous; is characterized by a more complex division of labor; has a more completely developed money economy; has professional specialists who are more secular and less sacred; has kinship and godparental institutions that are less well organized and less effective in social control; is correspondingly more dependent on impersonally acting institutions of control, is less religious, with respect to both beliefs and practices of Catholic origin as well as those of Indian origin; exhibits less tendency to regard sickness as resulting from a breach of moral or merely customary rule; allows a greater freedom of action and choice to the individual; and . . . shows a greater emphasis upon black magic as an ascribed cause of sickness.

Except as these differences relate to the regional culture of Yucatan they are also implied in the present taxonomy of subcultures, and it should be noted that six of the subculture types discussed above are carried by the local societies or by segments of the societies studied by Redfield in

Yucatan. Thus, Merida would presumably contain subcultures of all three Metropolitan types. Dzitas seems to have both a Town and a Peasant type of subculture. Chan Kom, in our terms, would be a community with a Peasant subculture and Dzitas would be representative of our Modern Indian subculture. Although neglected by Redfield, Plantation subculture types are also present in the henequen-producing areas of Yucatan (Mintz 1953b:138). Tribal Indian subcultures, as defined above, are no longer present in the peninsula. Thus the present classification is clearly related to Redfield's folk–urban gradient. A fundamental difference exists, however. If the present taxonomy were to be used as the basis of a study of the urban–folk continuum in Latin America, the lines in the gradient would have to consist not of whole communities but of segments of whole communities. In this way one of the most serious defects in the use of the "folk culture" concept can be circumvented, for, as Lewis has shown for Tepoztlán (1951), the homogeneity of a rural community with respect to its folk characteristics is easily overemphasized when it is the whole local society which is the subject of characterization.

Redfield was primarily interested in culture change, especially the effects of modern urbanization upon "folk culture" and the resulting "disorganization of the culture, secularization, and individualization," to use his well-known terms. The primary purpose of the present taxonomy is not to analyze the direction and effects of culture change but to establish categories which may help to orient many additional problems. Many of the subculture types we have been describing are more or less stable features of the Latin American scene. Although individual settlements or large segments of their populations may change rapidly from carriers of one subculture type to another (e.g., "Indians" become "mestizos") and while new subculture types have appeared, most of these subculture types have been part of the cultural scene of Latin America since the sixteenth century. They have changed in culture content and in their relative importance to the wider cultural scene, but they have constantly maintained their distinctiveness as variations of Latin American culture and their essential relationship to one another.

Soon after 1500, when the distinctive culture of Latin America began to take form, at least Modern Indian, Peasant, Town, *Engenho* Plantation, and Metropolitan Upper Class types were already present in the New World. The European conquerors brought with them a strong tradition of urbanism. In their European homelands there were cities, towns, and peasant villages. Large agrarian estates, similar in some ways to the New World plantations, were also present. Furthermore, as is well known, the native civilizations of America also had their cities, their market centers, and their villages and hamlets. The Europeans transplanted to the New World a culture which was already characterized by a number of subcultures analogous to those described for modern Latin

America, but in the New World they were modified in content and in the form of interaction between them.

The Spanish and Portuguese (also the other nationals who controlled more limited areas of Latin America) who were given land grants, *encomiendas*, or other economic rights in the New World soon established a colonial aristocracy with its traditions derived from the feudal aristocratic patterns of their homeland. In the region of native American civilization, these colonial aristocrats supplanted the native ruling class, and in lowland Latin America they came to dominate the segmented tribal groups and became the owners of African slaves. Although only small numbers of European peasants came to the New World to work the land as they had done in Europe, a few did come, transposing their way of life almost intact. Before long, however, a distinctive Latin American Peasant subculture took form as the various tribal groups of the lowland region came under the influence of missionaries and colonial governments, lost their identity as autochthonous peoples and borrowed or had forced upon them European culture patterns. Under the impact of Spanish rule, the Indians of the highland regions acquired numerous Spanish culture patterns which fused with aboriginal patterns to form the subculture type called herein Modern Indian. The content of each of these subculture types differed, of course, from that of today, but those of 1600 were the historical antecedents of the contemporary types.

The transition of populations from one subculture type to another still goes on. The Tenetehara, a Tupí-speaking tribe of northern Brazil, for example, still have a culture which is essentially aboriginal and distinct from the culture of the Brazilian nation within the borders of which they happen to live. But the Tenetehara are slowly adopting Brazilian culture patterns; they are being brought into the orbit of the Brazilian commercial system through the sale of palm nuts and the increasing necessity to purchase imported and manufactured supplies (Wagley and Galvão 1949). The Tenetehara might now be classed as a Modern Indian subculture and, as the process of acculturation continues, they will lose their identity as "distinct people" and their culture will be transformed into that of a Peasant subculture of modern Brazil. Likewise, in Ecuador, Guatemala, Mexico, Peru, and other countries where there are large numbers of people living by Modern Indian subculture patterns, there is a noted trend for such Indians to adopt Peasant patterns (i.e., mestizo, Ladino, or *cholo* patterns) and to lose their identity as Indians. In many localities of Latin America both Indians and peasants are still being drawn upon as plantation workers, especially as communal forms of land tenure break down and as commercial agricultural enterprises expand their holdings. In other localities, many isolated areas inhabited by peasants are being connected with national markets by roads and other means of communication, and towns are taking form where a small local market place once existed. Under similar impulses, small towns are growing in size and in complexity to become veritable cities. And, as noted earlier, there is a continuing trend for family-owned *engenho*-type plantations to be welded into large industrialized *usina*-type plantations.

All Latin American subcultures are certainly changing under urban and industrial influences, and yet the differences between some of them may remain great for many years to come. The content of Peasant and Metropolitan subcultures in Europe has in both cases changed profoundly during the last five hundred years, but the differences between city folk and peasants in almost any European nation are still striking. In the future, certain subcultures may diminish in importance or entirely disappear as the people who carry them adopt other culture patterns. Tribal Indian subculture types will probably disappear well within the next hundred years, and *Engenho* Plantation types are becoming extinct with at least equal rapidity. Modern Indian types, on the other hand, especially where enlightened policies of government assistance prevail, are likely to endure for much longer. Barring wide political upheaval, Peasant, Town, *Usina* Plantation, and Metropolitan Upper Class subculture types also appear to have long futures ahead of them, while the Metropolitan Middle Class and Urban Proletariat types are just now beginning to emerge.

The changes in content which all these subculture types are undergoing are adequately embraced by the folk-urban transition suggested by Redfield. But any such picture of progressive urbanization must take into account the possibility that as the subculture types change toward greater urbanization, most of them do not merge in content, but remain as distinctly defined as ever within the national context. This is true because throughout all the stages of the urbanization of a nation, the city subcultures are not static but rather continue to be the innovators of most of the new features. Furthermore, although the rural-urban concept provides us with excellent hypotheses for the general direction of diffusion of new cultural items on a national scale, it does not prepare us for the problem of fundamental structural changes such as the emergence of new subcultures or the realignment of power. To describe the structure of a complex nation and the changes it is undergoing we need a taxonomy of parts such as that which has been tentatively developed in this paper. The emergence of new and the extinction of old sociocultural segments is an aspect of cultural change which the student of complex national cultures cannot afford to neglect.

NOTES

1. Our proposed taxonomy of Latin American subculture types and our general approach to the concept of national subcultures owe much to Julian Steward and his associates in the Puerto Rican project. The relationship between several of our subculture types and those distinguished in Puerto Rico will be indicated below.

2. Our *Engenho* Plantation types seems to correspond to the Coffee Hacienda subculture of Puerto Rico (cf. Steward 1953:98–100; Wolf 1951).

3. In tracing the development of a Puerto Rican sugar plantation, Mintz has distinguished three historical periods or types of sugar-cane plantations: the "slave-and-*agregado*," the "family-type hacienda," and the "corporate land-and-factory combine" (1953b). The first corresponds to our *engenho* plantation during slavery, the second to our *engenho* plantation after slavery, and the third to our *usina* plantation.

4. Hutchinson's study and the other studies carried out in Bahia State in Brazil which are cited below were part of the State of Bahia–Columbia University Research Program during which four community studies were carried out. Some of the data which made possible the distinction between the *engenho* plantation and the *usina* plantation were provided by Dr. Hutchinson.

5. A fourth community study was carried out later in southern Bahia State by Anthony Leeds, but sufficient data are not yet available to be used here.

6. A study of a working-class district is now being carried out by Thales de Azevedo of the University of Bahia, as a follow-up on our research.

7. This observation is based upon questionnaires devoted to family size and cohesiveness answered by upper-class urban residents in Salvador. It is confirmed by the data on the Metropolitan Upper Class families of Vila Recôncavo.

REFERENCES CITED

Bunzel, Ruth
1952 *Chichicastenango: A Guatemalan Village,* Seattle, University of Washington Press.

Caplow, Theodore

1952 "The Modern Latin American City," in *Acculturation in the Americas,* Sol Tax, ed., pp. 255–260, Proceedings of the XXIX International Congress of Americanists, Chicago, University of Chicago Press.

Foster, George M.

1948 *Empire's Children: The People of Tzintzuntzan,* Smithsonian Institution, Institute of Social Anthropology Publication 6, Washington, D.C.

1953 "What Is Folk Culture?" *American Anthropologist* 55:159–173, Menasha.

Gillin, John

1947a *Moche: A Peruvian Coastal Community,* Smithsonian Institution, Institute of Social Anthropology Publication 3, Washington, D. C.

1947b "Modern Latin American Culture," *Social Forces* 25:3:243–248, Baltimore.

1951 *The Culture of Security in San Carlos: A Study of a Guatemalan Community of Indians and Ladinos,* New Orleans, Tulane University, Middle American Research Institute Publication 16.

Harris, Marvin

1953 *Minas Velhas: A Study of Urbanism in the Mountains of Eastern Brazil,* Ph.D. dissertation, Columbia University, New York. Ann Arbor, Mich., University Microfilm.

Hutchinson, Harry

1954 *Vila Recôncavo: A Brazilian Sugar-Cane Plantation Community,* Ph.D. dissertation, Columbia University, New York. Ann Arbor, Mich., University Microfilm.

La Farge, Oliver

1940 "Maya Ethnology: The Sequence of Cultures," in *The Maya and Their Neighbors,* pp. 281–291, New York, Appleton-Century Co.

Lewis, Oscar

1951 *Life in a Mexican Village: Tepoztlán Restudied,* Urbana, University of Illinois Press.

1952 "Urbanization without Breakdown: A Case Study," *The Scientific Monthy* 75:31–41.

Loomis, Charles P. and Reed M. Powell

1951 "Class Status in Rural Costa Rica: A Peasant Community Compared with a Hacienda Community," in *Materiales para el Estudio de la Clase Media en la América Latina,* Vol. 5, Washington, D.C., Pan American Union.

Manners, Robert

1950 *Culture and Agriculture in an Eastern Highland Community of Puerto Rico,* Ph.D. dissertation, Columbia University, New York. Ann Arbor, Mich., University Microfilm.

Métraux, Alfred
1951 *Making a Living in the Marbial Valley (Haiti)*, Paris UNESCO.

Mintz, Sidney W.
1951 *Cañamelar: The Contemporary Culture of a Rural Puerto Rican Proletariat*, Ph.D. dissertation, Columbia University, New York. Ann Arbor, Mich., University Microfilm.
1953a "The Folk–Urban Continuum and the Rural Proletarian Community," *American Journal of Sociology* 59:2:136–143.
1953b "The Culture History of a Puerto Rican Sugar Cane Plantation, 1876–1949," *Hispanic American Historical Review* 33:2:224–251, Duke University Press.

Mishkin, Bernard
1946 "The Contemporary Quechua," in *Handbook of South American Indians*, Julian Steward, ed., Vol, II, 411–470, Smithsonian Institution, Bureau of American Ethnology Bulletin 143, Washington, D.C.

Padilla Seda, Elena
1951 *Nocora: An Agrarian Reform Sugar Community in Puerto Rico*, Ph.D. dissertation, Columbia University, New York. Ann Arbor, Mich., University Microfilm.

Pierson, Donald
1951 *Cruz das Almas: A Brazilian Village*, Smithsonian Institution, Institute of Social Anthropology Publication 12, Washington, D. C.

Redfield, Robert
1941 *The Folk Culture of Yucatan*, Chicago, University of Chicago Press.

Smith, T. Lynn
1946 *Brazil: People and Institutions*, Baton Rouge, Louisiana State University Press.

Steward, Julian
1950 *Area Research: Theory and Practice*, Social Science Research Council Bulletin 63, New York.
1953 "Culture Patterns of Puerto Rico," *Annals of the American Academy of Political and Social Science*, January, pp. 95–102, Philadelphia.
1956 *The People of Puerto Rico*, University of Illinois Press, Urbana.

Tax, Sol
1953 *Penny Capitalism: A Guatemalan Indian Economy*, Smithsonian Institution, Institute of Social Anthropology Publication 16, Washington, D. C.

Tschopik, Harry
1951 *The Aymara of Chucuito, Peru: I, Magic*, American Museum of Natural History Anthropological Paper, Vol. 44, Pt. 2, New York

Villa Rojas, Alfonso

1945 *The Maya of East Central Quintana Roo*, Carnegie Institution of Washington Publication 559, Washington, D. C.

Wagley, Charles

1942 *The Economics of a Guatemalan Village,* American Anthropological Association Memoir 58, Menasha.

1948 "Regionalism and Cultural Unity in Brazil," *Social Forces* 26:457–464, Baltimore.

1950 *Social and Religious Life of a Guatemalan Village,* American Anthropological Association Memoir 71, Menasha.

1953 *Amazon Town: A Study of Man in the Tropics,* New York, Macmillan.

Wagley, Charles and Eduardo Galvão

1949 *The Tenetehara Indians of Brazil,* New York, Columbia University Press.

Willems, Emilio

1947 *Cunha: tradição e transição em uma cultura rural do Brasil,* São Paulo, Secretaria da Agricultura do Estado de São Paulo.

Wolf, Eric

1951 *Culture Change and Culture Stability in a Puerto Rican Coffee Community,* Ph.D. dissertation, Columbia University, New York. Cambridge, Eagle Enterprises.

Zimmerman, Ben

1952 "Race Relations in the Arid Sertão," in *Race and Class in Rural Brazil,* Charles Wagley, ed., pp. 82–115, Paris, UNESCO.

General Remarks on Rural Paraguay

ELMAN R.
and
HELEN S. SERVICE

Latin America presents a bewildering variety of geographic conditions, differing racial strains in the populations, variations in cultural mixture, class differences, and great contrasts between rural backwardness and modern urban sophistication. Accepting these differences, which often are manifested within one locality or nation, there is nevertheless a common distinctiveness which sets off the area as a whole from Anglo-America. Probably most responsible for this difference is the fact that, so far, the great industrial revolution of modern times has affected most of Latin America relatively little. Many habits, attitudes, sentiments, and also structural aspects of Latin America's social, economic, and political organization remain old Spanish and fundamentally agrarian. In other words, in Latin America in general, we find a stronger survival of a relatively homogeneous, European-derived colonial culture than in Anglo-America, where there remains very little which is reminiscent of the sixteenth century. A nation like Paraguay is much more like southern Ireland than it is like the United States of America. And in many important respects it is more like any of the "underdeveloped" nations of the world than it is like the complex, highly industrialized

Reprinted from *Tobatí: Paraguayan Town,* Chicago, University of Chicago Press, 1954, Chapter 20, by permission of the authors and publisher.

nations with whom these are associated in a relation of dependency with respect to international economics (if not to politics).

If one thinks of differences among the various Latin American nations today, one of the factors useful in assessing these differences is again the degree of survival of an earlier agricultural economy. Some nations have participated more fully than others in commercial and industrial development, which is the basic cause of the modifications of the older cultural patterns. Paraguay, without question, remains strikingly "old-fashioned" in this sense, isolated as it has been from most modern economic trends.[1]

Paraguay has been consistently described by historians, however, as not only having preserved more colonial patterns than other Latin American nations but also as having been profoundly influenced by the culture of the native Guaraní Indians. H. G. Warren recently summed up the current view by concluding that "the Guaranís practically overwhelmed the Europeans racially and had a profound cultural effect upon them."[2] Anthropologists, too, have been led to accept Paraguay as the only area in Latin America where the culture of unfederated, stateless, seminomadic forest Indians had been mixed with Spanish colonial traits and finally synthesized as a national culture.[3]

Paraguay's colonial culture was in some ways distinctive in Latin America, but our investigations into the history of its consolidation show that its character was due to certain historical and circumstantial factors rather than to the survival of Guaraní culture. The colonial culture, in short, was not similar to that of Meso-America and the Andean region, where certain Indian influences remain, but was more like that of the Río de la Plata area of Argentina, Uruguay, and even interior southern Brazil, where the Indian was culturally relatively unimportant—this in spite of the fact that biologically and linguistically the aboriginal heritage is stronger in Paraguay than it is in these adjacent countries.

Despite the slowness of change since the colonial period, we find that in rural Paraguay today there are virtually no Guaraní culture traits surviving, other than language. There are, to be sure, certain native foods and perhaps a few culinary customs still in existence, but native items of this sort survived everywhere to some extent, even in North America. There is no Guaraní art, music, or dance, today, of course, because the aboriginal culture was not highly developed in such matters, nor was there an arts-and-crafts technology of much utility or interest to the Europeans. But a careful analysis of even such things as mythology, folklore, superstitions, and folk medicine failed to reveal anything of certain Guaraní origin. In fact, most of the common Paraguayan customs of this order can be quite easily traced to Europe or to a later general Latin American provenience.

As tests of this generalization, we might mention again a few categories of traits which, in the areas of strong aboriginal influence, have been seen as derived from, or affected somehow by, Indian culture and which would be of the sort most likely to retain some evidence of a Guaraní heritage. One prominent cultural feature of this sort in Latin America is the institution of *compadrazgo*. In Moche, Peru, for example, not all the rites are related to Roman Catholic ritual, but some, according to John Gillin, "bear marks of being derived from an aboriginal or 'pagan' context." Thus, in addition to the relations established at baptism, confirmation, and marriage, *compadrazgo* may be established at rites of haircutting, ear-piercing, and nail-cutting.[4] In Mexico and Guatemala, too, certain aspects of *compadrazgo* are seen as influenced by aboriginal culture.[5] But in Paraguay the institution is purely Roman Catholic in all its ritual, and the crisis occasions themselves are solely those of the church—baptism, confirmation, and marriage. Paraguayan *compadrazgo* is more similar to the southern Brazilian version[6] than it is to the kinds practiced in areas where aboriginal influence has been strong.

Personal names, especially surnames, might be expected to reveal something of the aboriginal heritage, particularly in a country where the retention of the language is so strong. The complete census of the town revealed no Guaraní names, however, and, of the many collected in the rural areas, none were discovered except one, "Arepocó," which may or may not be Guaraní. The kinship terminological categories were Spanish even in the most remote rural areas, and, where actual Guaraní terms for these categories were retained, they were equivalent to Spanish usage, except in distinguishing older from younger siblings, which is, of course, of functional utility in any agrarian context. It is also worthy of note that certain Guaraní terms for kinship categories which were crucial in aboriginal Guaraní usage are now lost.[7]

Guaraní culture should also have influenced folk medicine, but here, too, we find no certain evidence, and, in fact, some traits which are considered aboriginal in other areas are missing here. The idea of psychosomatic causation (*susto*) arising from social situations like sibling rivalry or jealousy and anger, which is so common in Mexico, Guatemala, and Peru, seems completely foreign to Paraguay. The greatest folk-medicinal emphasis in Paraguay has to do with powers residing in various herbs. A few of the plant species used may be peculiar to Paraguay, but the conception is typically European. And, as a matter of fact, most of the actual recipes have long been in use in rural Uruguay and Argentina.

Some culture traits which are in some measure Indian are found in Paraguay, but they are part of the colonial culture complex which spread all over Spanish America and even to Spain itself. They cannot be said to be peculiarly Guaraní or Paraguayan. Some of these are the mortar and pestle, the poncho, adobe bricks, the reed mat, and straw roofs.[8] Maté drinking was certainly early in the La Plata area, but it is not known whether or not it was borrowed from the aborigines.

In sum, we find little that is Indian in Paraguayan rural culture. To be sure, we had suspected on the basis of the documentary study of the colonial history that the Guaraní cultural component had been overemphasized in the later literature, but we were rather surprised to find so little of Guaraní origin. Another unexpected feature in rural Paraguay is that the people are not so Indian in physical appearance as we had expected. The prevalent anthropological conception in North America is that Paraguay should be rated as practically 100 per cent mestizo, with the Caucasian element in the mixture comparatively smaller than the Indian.[9] Our general observations led us to a different opinion as to the relative weight of the Indian and European components. Most of the population is mixed to some degree, it would seem, but we feel that it is the Indian element which is comparatively small. Our impression is supported by an earlier one reported by Emma Reh, who worked among Indians in the southwestern United States and in Mexico. On the basis of two years of intimate study of Paraguayan rural people, she observed: "In Paraguay although the lower class is somewhat darker than the upper, and country people somewhat browner than those of the city, few true Indian types are to be found. The 'native' coming out of the thatched hut in the country area and speaking *Guaraní* may be blond and blue-eyed."[10]

Considering the history of Paraguay, it would certainly be unexpected if the purely Indian component were very large in the present population. The nucleus of the nation developed during the first hundred years of the colony in the vicinity of Asunción. The growing population consisted largely of mestizos who were products of the original Spaniards and their Guaraní concubines. But the *encomienda* villages of pure Guaraní (the *mitayo* villages) never were large and by 1620 had largely become mixed villages or had disappeared. It is possible that, at that time, although the population was almost entirely mixed, the genetic predominance favored the Indian element. But from then on, Indian groups were not being incorporated into the nation. Few additions of any sort, Indian or European, were made to the population during the remainder of the colonial period, but those few seem to have been European. And it should be remembered that the Paraguayan population has always been small and relatively concentrated; it would not require many immigrants to make their influence felt. J. P. and W. P. Robertson described the people of Asunción in 1811–12 as follows: "The great bulk of the population was of a breed between Spaniards and Indians, so attenuated as regards any appearance of the latter caste, as to give the natives the air and appearance of descendants from Europeans."[11] Since 1870, Spaniards, Italians, and Argentines have mixed with the population, considerably reducing the Indian genetic proportion, especially in the towns.

It seems to be the nearly universal use of the Guaraní language in

Paraguay which has misled writers to exaggerate the proportion of the Guaraní genetic strain and to assume that indigenous culture has had an important effect. This retention of the language is, certainly, unusual. In Bolivia, Peru, Ecuador, Mexico, and Middle America much of the population is pure Indian, and some still speak an Indian language; but many large groups of them do not. In Paraguay virtually the whole population speaks Guaraní, but few or none are purely Indian genetically. The historical concomitance of race and language is broken in one direction in the former areas and in the opposite way in Paraguay.

It is distinctive of Paraguay that the native language is in use not only among the peasantry but also among the middle and upper classes as well. As we have noted, however, the native middle and upper classes are very small. Possibly the use of Guaraní among them is due in some part to certain features of Paraguayan history, which included the concubinage of Guaraní women and the relative autonomy from Spain and later the defeat and devastation caused by the War of the Triple Alliance and the subsequent continuity of isolation and backwardness. The nation's lack of economic development and its low status compared with Argentina and Brazil probably have also had the effect of supercharging nationalistic emotions. Paraguayans in general, and the middle and upper classes in particular, remain intensely nationalistic, and much of this emotion seems to be concentrated in feelings about their language.

We should like to emphasize, however, that the influence of a native population on an emergent colonial culture cannot be measured simply by enumeration of the surviving indigenous traits. The many indirect functional consequences, especially economic ones, which set apart the areas of strong Indian influence from other regions are much more important. Some aspects of the cultures of rural Meso-America and the Andes are distinctive in their retention of particular indigenous culture traits, to be sure, and in blending certain Indian and Spanish traits. But there are also very striking differences in social and economic patterns which distinguish southern South America from "mestizo America," and these are directly and indirectly related to the presence of a large settled labor force in the latter areas.

Spanish colonization in southern South America was more truly a settlement, in the literal sense of the term, than the colonization in the regions where exploitation of large sedentary Indian populations was possible, where the Spaniards remained a leisured ruling class, distinct and foreign from the exploited population. In the south the *encomienda* and the *repartimiento* of Indians were of little economic importance. The scarcity of Indians and the lack of mineral wealth reduced the Spanish colonists to a subsistence way of life, and the few Indians they were able to control were most typically *yanaconas*,[12] household drudges and concubines, rather than a truly economically productive labor force. To some extent the Indians left their imprint on the physical characteristics of the developing population and on the household economy. Their role in the larger economy was so unimportant, however, that the agricultural hacienda never was possible. Also, in contrast to certain other regions, such as the Spanish West Indies and the coastal portions of Brazil, Venezuela, and Colombia, no plantation system based on either local or imported labor was ever developed.

Mestizos and Creoles were all poor, and, as modified class divisions arose, they were not associated with racial or cultural distinctions—Hispanicized mixed-breeds could be found at any level of the society. The true Indians who were still tribally organized lived in the hinterlands, wandering and raiding. Even the missionized Guaraní of the Alto Paraná region largely retreated to the forests after the Jesuits were expelled in 1767. There never were any sizeable groups of "republican Indians"—Spanish-acculturated Indian groups who had lost the old tribal organization yet had not become fully involved in the national life.

As a matter of fact, Paraguay has never had a complete tribe-to-city continuum of the sort so often found in the Andes and in Meso-America. In those regions one may place communities along a scale of national-cultural participation ranging from isolated tribal societies through republican Indian communities, peasant villages, and market towns to the urban center. Within the boundaries of Paraguay there are tribal Indians, chiefly in the Chaco wilderness and scattered thinly in the great forests of northeastern Paraguay, but there are no intermediate stages between tribal life and full involvement in Paraguayan national culture. Those Indians are not *becoming* Paraguayans; they are only retreating or becoming extinct. Paraguayans are culturally integrated in the fullest sense of nationalization; the state has not had the problem of assimilating tribally organized groups since the early days of the colonization. The quickly formed small nucleus of the nation developed into the modern nation through internal population growth. Cultural differences in the nation today are the differences between social classes and economic occupations of the sort implicit in the purely European cultural organization. The nation is "backward" from the point of view of modern international commercial and industrial development; it is essentially a peasant society. But from the point of view of internal cultural unity it is very advanced.

There are many other functional consequences related to the lack of a productive Indian labor force in southern South America. One is conscious especially of three of these which have made for important cultural distinctiveness in the colonial heritage. They are (1) lack of Spanish capital investment in the region after the original exploration and the consequent lack of continuing Spanish control; (2) the lack of interest and influence on the part of the official church; and (3), perhaps most striking of all, the failure of southern South America, until quite recently, to develop planned towns and agricultural haciendas.

Spanish Crown control by various kinds of administrators was never strong in southern South America. Creole revolts (*comunero* revolts) against Spanish authority occurred successfully very early in the colonial period. The region of La Plata was virtually self-governing from the beginning, and general Spanish economic and political influence became steadily less effective.[13] The official church, too, was a more important governing force in the Andean and Meso-American regions than in the La Plata territory. The church in the latter area was never strong politically or influential culturally, and it is not to this day. There were no extensive campaigns against "idolatry," for there were no native state religions competing with Catholicism, and the Holy Inquisition touched the La Plata people hardly at all. Except for the isolated mission area, neither church nor state created large planned towns (*reducciones*) of Indians which lasted long enough to be of consequence. The agriculturalists were more or less scattered, according to their convenience. The towns grew up slowly and naturally and tended to be made up of individual houses on large plots of ground, except on the central plaza. In the Andean and Meso-American areas a striking feature of the colonial history was the continuing influence of the farsighted and meticulously planned policy of the Spanish administration. Southern South America, on the other hand, had a more nearly autonomous, unplanned local growth and adaptation to circumstances.

Today a representative Paraguayan rural area such as Tobatí seems very much like other relatively isolated agricultural zones in Argentina, Uruguay, and southern Brazil. The basic occupation is subsistence agriculture, and the majority of the people live on their somewhat scattered *chacras*. There is only a slight tendency toward congregation of the peasants into hamlets. Villages and towns are business and administrative centers almost exclusively and account for only a small proportion of the population. There are enough differences between town and country, however, both in regard to presence or absence of particular traits and in emphasis of shared traits, that the distinctions may be considered subcultural.

The peasant families tend to be larger, and family ties are considered more important, than in town, but in actuality the family members tend to be scattered and disunited, and the functional unit is normally the nuclear family rather than the extended family. The only large effective families are those of the wealthiest townsmen. The town middle class tends to have a small effective family. A wealthy townsman has many *compadres*, but he is often on the giving, not the receiving, end of the relationship. The town middle-class people have few *compadres*, and the relations tend to be reciprocal. The town poor and the peasants have few *compadres* and seek to acquire some of them from among the wealthy in order to be the recipients of aid. With respect to marriage, the peasants place a high value on it but rarely can achieve that kind of social eminence. A civil marriage is not valued at all. The townsman of upper social standing is often married in the church, and the remaining townsmen are more likely than are the peasants to have a civil marriage.

Peasants are not interested in politics, but townsmen are inclined to intense factionalism and are more likely to have their economic interests involved in personal political loyalties. Townsmen are more orthodox with respect to religious beliefs, and the women, at least, attend church for social reasons. Peasants may be more devout, or more credulous, but participation is more often limited to saints' cults and profane "games." In many other matters, such as etiquette, folk versus modern beliefs, and use of language, the peasants practice older forms of behavior. Other trait differences are purely technological.

We feel that it would be inaccurate, or at least a misplacing of emphasis, however, to think of the subcultural differences between peasants and townsmen as being due to the peasants' isolation or lack of communication, although in a sense, of course, sophistication does grow with communication. It could be said that certain traits of international, or modern, culture come to the capital city first. These may pass from the city to the towns and thence to the peasant. The peasant receives them last, if at all, because he is more isolated. But most of these modern items are such trivial things as fads in dress style, ephemeral popular songs, and various gadgets.

The most basic traits which characterize the peasant's subculture are functionally a part of his way of life and are most typically those which are related to agrarian self-sufficiency, as opposed to commercialism. More ideological traits, such as knowledge of and faith in modern medicine, and formal education pertain more to town life than they do to peasant life because more townsmen have money to pay for such services and thus are enabled to learn of their value. These differences, as well as those in general values and aspirations, are best seen as merely the subjective aspects of occupational and wealth distinctions between peasants and townsmen. We cannot regard the peasant's way of life as being due to his isolation or to his ignorance of other ways. There is very little of importance in the townsman's culture that the peasant is not acquainted with, for the two have been in close contact for a long, long time. But the peasant cannot aspire to participate in this culture. He is forced to continue to live by the customs which work for him under the particular economic circumstances that he is unable to change. There seems to be little likelihood that even the unusual commerical boom now occurring in Tobatí because of the road building will be of enough consequence to affect the peasants. The road is changing the town in certain obvious ways, but commercial townsmen participate more fully in the resulting economic advances than the peasants do.

Paraguay is relatively removed from the major world economic influences, so that the general economic expansion has not had all the effects that can be seen in some other Latin American countries; but the few changes in Tobatí are suggestive of the influence of increased market participation. In general, most of the townsmen are merely sellers, rather than investors in productive enterprises, except for the medieval-like "cottage industries"—household handicraft producers typified in Tobatí by the brickmaking families. The few enterprises of the modern sort are the small cash-crop rice plantations. The opening of a truck route to Caacupé and Asunción has had the effect of stimulating the development of these plantations and, derivatively, of stimulating business in the town.

If prosperity is maintained and trucking increased, one might expect a continuing increase in the number of stores and distributing enterprises, added prosperity for some of them, and a correlated increase in the town population. Such an increase would create an added demand for farm produce, so we might expect to see two kinds of demographic changes in the rural areas. First, the rural population of the *partido* might increase as peasants previously outside the town's economic orbit are drawn into it; produce from *compañías* which lie between Tobatí and other towns could then be marketed more advantageously in Tobatí. Second, the nomadism of subsistence agriculturalists should diminish as the sale of produce becomes more profitable and as credit facilities increase. With added capital, some of the peasants, at least, might be able to improve their agricultural technology and take more interest in permanent ownership of a plot of land.

In town the most striking effect of the recent prosperity is an increase in wealth differences. Townsmen profit much more directly from commerce than do peasants, of course, but among townsmen, those who are already established in business profit more greatly than do the others. The growing wealth differences are obviously being translated into an increased gulf in status between the *sociedad* and those just below them. Another manifestation of added wealth is the emphasis on new bungalow-style houses. An increase in prosperity anywhere seems always to give an impetus to the building trades, but in Paraguay they provide an especially sensitive index, for people (rightly) have no faith in the stability of their currency and hasten to put any spare cash into permanent assets. There is not much profit in agricultural land, nor does ownership of it have the connotation of security that it has in other parts of Latin America; hence cash is more readily put into buildings.

The recent improvements in communication are clearly correlated with the relative prosperity of various towns; the normal Paraguayan view is that roads are directly responsible for economic progress. Each town within the nation needs communication with Asunción in order to compete with other towns. At bottom, therefore, Tobatí is progressing only relatively to other towns and, in a sense, at their expense. Ultimately, of course, it is foreign markets that Paraguayans need as a nation, if all the towns are to prosper. It seems unlikely, actually, that the changes which are incipient in Tobatí will actually reach fulfillment. The present boom is highly artificial and only local, because Tobatí beat neighboring towns to the road building.

Another characteristic of the increase in prosperity in Tobatí is the highly speculative nature of the use of capital. We found the beginning of capital investment in equipment and in the hiring of labor exemplified most importantly and most typically in the several small rice plantations. We have preferred to call these entrepreneurs "farmers," to distinguish them from peasants. The peasant is an independent producer looking mainly to his subsistence needs. Thus he grows a round of diversified crops each year regardless of market conditions. The farmer, who is also an independent producer (even if he has borrowed his capital), produces mainly or entirely for the market in order to acquire money, and, according to the logic of commercial competition, he tends to become increasingly a specialist and thus ever more dependent on the market. The farmer, therefore, must have confidence in a stable and secure market, *or* he must have sufficient capital to risk a gamble if the market is not stable. It seems that the great predominance of peasant agriculture over farming in Paraguay is basically due to that very lack of a secure market, for the few farmers whom we encountered were essentially specialists gambling their capital on supplying a crop which was temporarily in great demand. Consequently, these entrepreneurs are farmers of a special sort, essentially speculators who are often involved in other commercial enterprises, such as cattle ranching, as well.

Farmers of the classic North American type, market-oriented, independent landholders who are not primarily speculators, depend on market stability for diversified cash cropping. They have been typically the strong support of the conservative middle-class political forms. But no such farmers exist in Paraguay. And the only interest in politics is the direct one of immediate reward; this interest tends to be speculative, just as it is in the realm of economic investment. The purposes of the Paraguayan farmers are akin to those of the more important capitalists of the city. In any country whose foreign trade is based on an undiversified, purely extractive economy, as is pre-eminently the case with Paraguay, the economic fortunes of the nation's capitalists fluctuate wildly. The rapid boom-and-bust cycles imbue all of them with a speculative philosophy. All this is in some measure typical of any Latin American nation, but Paraguay seemed to us an extreme case. The increase in farming, then, is an increase in the amount of speculative investment by town businessmen. It seems unlikely that many peasants could become farmers under such circumstances.

The Paraguayan peasant society clearly deviates from certain of the expectations suggested by several anthropological studies of Latin American communities. We wish to mention one especially striking feature which was unexpected. In contrast to the considerable degree of family communalism so often attributed to rural Latin America, we found the Paraguayan rural family to be nucleated and unstable, the extended family to be nonfunctional economically and consequently unimportant in much of general social life. Production and exchange were highly individualized, although not depersonalized, as they might be in an urban-commercial milieu. And the land-tenure pattern of the Paraguayan peasants seemed anomalous in important respects. Land tenure is in so many ways closely related to other aspects of rural social and economic life and is so revealing of the general economic predicament of the nation that it deserves further discussion here.

Paraguayan peasants are typically very poor in terms of money income, producing little for the market and purchasing little from it. Also, the majority hold no title to the land they occupy. It is usually asserted, in studies of other "underdeveloped" areas of the world, that the economic problems of low productivity and extreme rural poverty are closely related to land scarcity and absentee landlordism. But, in contrast, Paraguay is a relatively underpopulated country. More than any other Latin American nation, Paraguay has striven to encourage immigration, feeling that its poverty must be related to the low population density. And the political and economic problem of absentee landlordism, which has occasioned bitterness in some parts of Latin America, has not been of major consequence in Paraguay, especially since 1870, when most of the landholders lost their estates. About the only large landholders today are cattle ranchers, and their holdings are campo which would not ordinarily be used for agriculture.

To say that over three fourths of the Paraguayan agriculturalists are landless is not to say the same thing that might be implied in a similar statement about other countries. The Paraguayan is often landless only in the sense that he holds no legal title to his plot; he usually has access to more land than he can cultivate with his primitive equipment. His problem is basically that of the whole nation; he is virtually without a market for his products and consequently is without capital. The internal market for agricultural produce is very small, as there are no large cities and the percentage of the nonagricultural population is the smallest in our hemisphere, except for Haiti. The foreign market is almost nonexistent, partly because the only egress is via the Argentine-dominated

Paraguay River, where shipping costs are enormous. The cycle of sale of crops for cash, in order to invest in equipment or more land, in order to increase production for more profit, never received the necessary impetus to get it started and never can, until a sufficient market exists. For the Paraguayan peasant to hold title to the plot he occupies confers no economic benefit and might be actually a liability, in the sense that it would tend to tie him to increasingly less productive land, when, by moving, he could find a more fertile location.

A typical Paraguayan rural area such as Tobatí is not excessively primitive or poor, however, as compared with isolated rural areas in other Latin American countries. What is striking is the fact that the whole nation is more backward than most other Latin American nations. Poverty-stricken peasants are found in all these countries, but Paraguay is more overwhelmingly "peasant" in its general culture. The poverty of the rural agriculturalists clearly cannot be considered a "land problem," basically, but rather has to do with the situation of the whole country in its economic relations with the rest of the world. The *nation* of Paraguay is poor, and the plight of the peasant is merely the rural reflection of that fact. Such slogans as "Land for the landless" and "Break up the *latifundios*" have no meaning in Paraguay, and, in fact, we can think of no local political solution of any sort which could improve the peasants' condition permanently.

In most of Latin America there is a tendency for the governments to intervene bureaucratically in various enterprises and also to undertake or underwrite certain kinds of industries and many public works. But also, because of the general one-sidedness of foreign trade, the dependence on foreign capital, and the lack of internal savings, the governments tend to lack control over their currency and are thus especially prone to have extreme fiscal difficulties. In this matter, too, Paraguay has exaggerated problems.[14] The government, acting as a source of capital, cannot maintain projects which are undertaken for internal improvement, even when they are supported initially by foreign aid. Roads, schools, credit facilities, and public works in general are grandiose in plan but lag far behind in execution or fail completely.

Piecemeal economic aid of the sort offered by loans and technical assistance programs sponsored by the United States of America may lead to improvements in parts of the economy or at least may benefit certain individuals. Some advances in Paraguay are noticeable; farmers have been aided by loans and technical advice, interest has been stirred in a refurbished public health program, road building has been stimulated by the influence of the partly completed asphalt Central Highway, and the intellectuals have become enthusiastic about the educational exchange fellowships. But the nation itself does not have the means to maintain the improvements now initiated, much less to continue further development. The roads built with foreign capital are falling into disrepair. Equipment is scarce, materials are expensive, and political turnovers often result in the abandoning of projects or at least in changes in their trained personnel. We feel that, while the foreign aids have resulted in notable achievements, they must be regarded as merely alleviations of certain symptoms of the economic problem, no more curative of a desperate illness than is aspirin.

In short, we view the immediate future of Paraguay with profound pessimism. Only a few natives benefit even indirectly from the extraction of natural resources, and such rewards are likely to be ephemeral. The agrarian bulk of the population in Paraguay will remain peasants until their produce can be sold in the external market or internally to a larger proportion of nonagriculturalists who are producing something else for the external market. We cannot see any possibility for a successful Paraguayan bootstrap operation.

Paraguay has been a true nation in the political sense for a long time now, but its internal economy is still basically garden subsistence. The majority of the Paraguayan people, as individuals, are economically independent. They are not bound as serfs or tenants in a hacienda or plantation system, and only a few are employed sporadically as wage-workers in extractive industries, in ranching, or in shipping. Paraguay's limited external economy is completely extractive, consisting almost entirely of the sale of a few raw materials. Nearly all these enterprises are foreign-owned. This modest economy, as a source of foreign exchange, is typically or even exaggeratedly a case of what is usually called "economic dependence." It is also an economy which cannot build on itself and become self-sufficient as a political entity, for Paraguay is not a natural economic unit in terms of what is required for modern industrialization and diversification of production. Paraguay seems destined to remain subordinate with respect to its relations with other nations. Perhaps in an economic and political union of Latin American states Paraguay might contribute and share as a specialized region in a larger functional unit. But this is the idlest daydream from the point of view of living Paraguayans. It is sad not to be able to end on a note of hope, but what may sound like pessimism and hopelessness in this case seems to us to be actually realism.

NOTES

1. Of the South American republics, Paraguay had (in 1938) by far the least amount of exports—$8,000,000—and the least imports—$8,100,000. This was only 0.4 per cent of total Latin American exports and 0.5 per cent of imports (see George Wythe, *An Outline of Latin American Economic Development*, New York, 1946, p. 250, Table 13).

2. Harris G. Warren, *Paraguay: An Informal History*, Norman, University of Oklahoma Press, 1949, p. 33.

3. Both Ralph Beals and John Gillin have included Paraguay with the Andean and Mexican "*indio*" and "mestizo" areas of Latin America in recent publications. See Ralph L. Beals, "Social Stratification in Latin America," *American Journal of Sociology*, 1953, LVIII, 329; and John Gillin, "Mestizo America," in Ralph Linton, ed., *Most of the World*, New York, Columbia University Press, 1949, p. 161.

4. John Gillin, *Moche: A Peruvian Coastal Community*, Smithsonian Institution, Institute of Social Anthropology, Publication 3, Washington, D.C., 1947, p. 105.

5. Francisco Rojas Gonzales, "La Institución del compadrazgo entre las indígenas de México," *Revista mexicana de sociología*, 1943, V, 201–214; Benjamin D. Paul, "Ritual Kinship, with Special Reference to Godparenthood in Middle America," unpublished Ph.D. thesis, University of Chicago, 1942; Robert Redfield and Alfonso Villa Rojas, *Chan Kom: A Maya Village*, Carnegie Institution of Washington Publication 448, Washington, D.C., 1934, pp. 373–374; Elsie Clews Parsons, *Mitla: Town of the Souls*, Chicago, University of Chicago Press, 1936, pp. 525–526; Sol Tax, ed., *Heritage of Conquest*, Glencoe, Ill., Free Press, 1952, pp. 111–112.

6. See Emilio Willems, *Cunha: tradição e transição em uma cultura rural do Brasil*, São Paulo, 1947; Emilio Willems and Gioconda Mussolini, *Buzios Island: A Caicara Community in Southern Brazil*, American Ethnological Society Monograph 20, Washington, D.C.; Emilio Willems, "Caboclo Cultures of Southern Brazil," in Sol Tax, ed., *Acculturation in the Americas: Proceedings and Selected Papers of the XXIX Congress of Americanists*, Chicago, 1952, pp. 231–243; Donald Pierson, *Cruz das Almas: A Brazilian Village*, Smithsonian Institution, Institute of Social Anthropology, Publication 12, Washington, D.C., 1951, pp. 142–143.

7. The Guaraní had a "Dakota" system. Parallel cousins were lumped with siblings and cross-cousins distinguished. Similar distinctions occurred in the parents' generation.

8. Most of these items apparently had an independent origin in the Old World as well, but it seems likely that their widespread use in the New World in colonial times was due to their earlier use by the Indians.

9. John Gillin, "Mestizo America," p. 161.

10. *Paraguayan Rural Life: Survey of Food Problems*, Washington, D.C., Institute of Inter-American Affairs, Food Supply Division, 1946, p. 8.

11. *Four Years in Paraguay*, 2 vols., Philadelphia, 1838, I, 187. This comment is perhaps somewhat overdrawn. Even the modern population characteristically shows some traces of Indian mixture.

12. Usually called *originarios* in Paraguay.

13. As an illustration of this point, we may note that Spanish shipping to the La Plata region was actually prohibited by the Crown during the colonial period. All the Spanish trade was directed to the Caribbean because of the much greater wealth from Mexico and Peru and in order to muster force against the English raids on the shipping.

14. For example, all Latin American countries have been struggling with inflation in recent years, especially with respect to dollar exchange, but Paraguay's inflation is phenomenal. The Paraguayan peso, which had been the basic monetary unit, became so worthless a few years ago that the guarani was created as a 100-peso unit. The *New York Times* on January 7, 1953 (p. 74), reported that the free exchange rate was 60 guaranis—6,000 pesos—to a dollar, and still rising!

Aspects of Group Relations in a Complex Society: Mexico

ERIC R. WOLF

I

Starting from simple beginnings in the twenties, anthropologists have grown increasingly sophisticated about the relationship of nation and community. First, they studied the community in its own terms, taking but little account of its larger matrix. Later, they began to describe "outside factors" which affected the life of the local group under study. Recently they have come to recognize that nations or "systems of the higher level do not consist merely of more numerous and diversified parts," and that it is therefore "methodologically incorrect to treat each part as though it were an independent whole in itself" (Steward 1950:107). Communities are "modified and acquire new characteristics because of their functional dependence upon a new and larger system" (*ibid.* 111). The present paper is concerned with a continuation of this anthropological discussion in terms of Mexican material.

Reprinted from *American Anthropologist,* 1956, LVIII, 1065–1078, by permission of the author and publisher. A first draft of this paper was prepared while the author was Research Associate of the Project for Research on Cross-Cultural Regularities, directed by Julian Steward at the University of Illinois, Urbana, Illinois. Parts of it were read before a meeting of the Central States Anthropological Society at Bloomington, Indiana, on May 6, 1955. The author is indebted for helpful criticisms to Julian Steward, to Oscar Lewis of the University of Illinois, and to Sidney Mintz of Yale University.

The dependence of communities on a larger system has affected them in two ways. On the one hand, whole communities have come to play specialized parts within the larger whole. On the other, special functions pertaining to the whole have become the tasks of special groups within communities. These groups Steward calls horizontal sociocultural segments. I shall simply call them nation-oriented groups. They are usually found in more than one community and follow ways of life different from those of their community-oriented fellow villagers. They are often the agents of the great national institutions which reach down into the community, and form "the bones, nerves and sinews running through the total society, binding it together, and affecting it at every point" (*ibid.* 115). Communities which form parts of a complex society can thus be viewed no longer as self-contained and integrated systems in their own right. It is more appropriate to view them as the local termini of a web of group relations which extend through intermediate levels from the level of the community to that of the nation. In the community itself, these relationships may be wholly tangential to each other.

Forced to understand the community in terms of forces impinging on it from the outside, we have also found it necessary to gain a better understanding of national-level institutions. Yet to date most anthropologists have hesitated to commit themselves to such a study, even when they have become half convinced that such a step would be desirable. National institutions seem so complex that even a small measure of competence in their operations seems to require full-time specialization. We have therefore left their description and analysis to specialists in other disciplines. Yet the specialists in law, politics, or economics have themselves discovered that anthropologists can be of almost as much use to them as they can be to the anthropologist. For they have become increasingly aware that the legal, political or other systems to which they devote their attention are not closed systems either, but possess social and cultural dimensions which cannot be understood in purely institutional terms. They have discovered that they must pay attention to shifting group relationships and interests if their studies are to reflect this other dimension of institutional "reality." This is hardly surprising if we consider that institutions are ultimately but cultural patterns for group relationships. Their complex forms allow groups to relate themselves to each other in the multiple processes of conflict and accommodation which must characterize any complex society. They furnish the forms through which some nation-oriented groups may manipulate other nation-oriented or community-oriented groups. The complex apparatus of such institutions is indeed a subject for specialists, but anthropologists may properly attempt to assess some of their functions.

If the communities of a complex system such as Mexico represent but the local termini of group relationships which go beyond the community level, we cannot hope to construct a model of how the larger society operates by simply adding more community studies. Mexico—or any complex system—is more than the arithmetic sum of its constituent communities. It is also more than the sum of its national-level institutions, or the sum of all the communities and national-level institutions taken together. From the point of view of this paper, it is rather the web of group relationships which connect localities and national-level institutions. The focus of study is not communities or institutions, but groups of people.

In dealing with the group relationships of a complex society, we cannot neglect to underline the fact that the exercise of power by some people over others enters into all of them, on all levels of integration. Certain economic and political relationships are crucial to the functioning of any complex society. No matter what other functions such a society may contain or elaborate, it must both produce surpluses and exercise power to transfer a part of these surpluses from the producing communities to people other than the producers. No matter what combination of cultural forms such a society may utilize, it must also wield power to limit the autonomy of its constituent communities and to interfere in their affairs. This means that all interpersonal and intergroup relationships of such a society must at some point conform to the dictates of economic or political power. Let it be said again, however, that these dictates of power are but aspects of group relationships, mediated in this case through the forms of an economic or political apparatus.

Finally, we must be aware that a web of group relationships implies a historical dimension. Group relationships involve conflict and accommodation, integration and disintegration, processes which take place over time. And just as Mexico in its synchronic aspect is a web of group relationships with termini in both communities and national-level institutions, so it is also more in its diachronic aspect than a sum of the histories of these termini. Local histories are important, as are the histories of national-level institutions, but they are not enough. They are but local or institutional manifestations of group relations in continuous change.

In this paper, then, we shall deal with the relations of community-oriented and nation-oriented groups which characterize Mexico as a whole. We shall emphasize the economic and political aspects of these relationships, and we shall stress their historical dimension, their present as a rearrangement of their past, and their past as a determinant of their present.

II

From the beginning of Spanish rule in Mexico, we confront a society riven by group conflicts for economic and political control. The Spanish

Crown sought to limit the economic and political autonomy of the military entrepreneurs who had conquered the country in its name. It hoped to convert the conquistadores into town dwellers, not directly involved in the process of production on the community level but dependent rather on carefully graded handouts by the Crown. They were to have no roots in local communities, but to depend directly on a group of officials operating at the level of the nation. The strategic cultural form selected for this purpose was the *encomienda*, in which the recipient received rights to a specified amount of Indian tribute and services, but was not permitted to organize his own labor force nor to settle in Indian towns. Both control of Indian labor and the allocation of tribute payments were to remain in the hands of royal bureaucrats (Simpson 1950: esp. 123, 144; Zavala 1940).

To this end, the Crown encouraged the organization of the Indian population into compact communities with self-rule over their own affairs, subject to supervision and interference at the hands of royal officials (Zavala and Miranda 1954:75–79). Many of the cultural forms of this community organization are pre-Hispanic in origin, but they were generally repatterned and charged with new functions. We must remember that the Indian sector of society underwent a serious reduction in social complexity during the sixteenth and seventeenth centuries. The Indians lost some of their best lands and water supply, as well as the larger part of their population. As a result of this social cataclysm, as well as of government policy, the repatterned Indian community emerged as something qualitatively new: a corporate organization of a local group inhabited by peasants (Wolf 1955a:456–461). Each community was granted a legal charter and communal lands (Zavala and Miranda 1954:70); equipped with a communal treasury (*ibid.* 87–88; Chávez Orozco 1943:23–24) and administrative center (Zavala and Miranda 1954:80–82); and connected with one of the newly established churches. It was charged with the autonomous enforcement of social control, and with the payment of dues (*ibid.* 82).

Thus equipped to function in terms of their own resources, these communities became in the centuries after the Conquest veritable redoubts of cultural homeostasis. Communal jurisdiction over land, obligations to expend surplus funds in religious ceremonies, negative attitudes toward personal display of wealth and self-assertion, strong defenses against deviant behavior, all served to emphasize social and cultural homogeneity and to reduce tendencies toward the development of internal class differences and heterogeneity in behavior and interests. The taboo on sales of land to outsiders and the tendency toward endogamy made it difficult for outsiders to gain footholds in these villages (Redfield and Tax 1952; Wolf 1955a:457–461).

At the same time, the Crown failed in its attempt to change the

Spanish conquerors into passive dependents of royal favors (Miranda 1947). Supported by large retinues of clients (such as *criados, deudos, allegados, paniaguados,* cf. Chevalier 1952:33–38), the colonists increasingly wrested control of the crucial economic and political relationships from the hands of the royal bureaucracy. Most significantly, they developed their own labor force, in contravention of royal command and independently of the Indian communities. They bought Indian and Negro slaves; they attracted to their embryonic enterprises poor whites who had come off second best in the distribution of conquered riches; and they furnished asylum to Indians who were willing to pay the price of acculturation and personal obligation to a Spanish entrepreneur for freedom from the increasingly narrow life of the encysting Indian communities. By the end of the eighteenth century, the colonist enterprises had achieved substantial independence of the Crown in most economic, political, legal, and even military matters. Power thus passed from the hands of the Crown into the hands of local rulers who interposed themselves effectively between nation and community. Effective power to enforce political and economic decisions contrary to the interest of these power holders was not returned to the national level until the victory of the Mexican Revolution of 1910 (Wolf 1955b:193–195).

Alongside the Indian villages and the entrepreneurial communities located near haciendas, mines, or mills, there developed loosely structured settlements of casual farmers and workers, middlemen and "*lumpen*-proletarians" who had no legal place in the colonial order. Colonial records tended to ignore them except when they came into overt conflict with the law. Their symbol in Mexican literature is *El Periquillo Sarmiento*, the man who lives by his wits (cf. Yañez 1945:60–94). "Conceived in violence and without joy, born into the world in sorrow" (Fernando Benítez 1947:47), the very marginality of their origins and social position forced them to develop patterns of behavior adapted to a life unstructured by formal law. They were thus well fitted to take charge of the crucial economic and political relationships of the society at a time when social and cultural change began to break down the barriers between statuses and put a premium on individuals and groups able to rise above their traditional stations through manipulation of social ties and improvisation upon them.

The transfer of power from the national level to the intermediate power holders, and the abolition of laws protecting the Indian communities—both accomplished when Mexico gained its independence from Spain (Chávez Orozco 1943:35–47)—produced a new constellation of relationships among Indian communities, colonist entrepreneurs, and "marginals." The colonists' enterprises, and chief among them the hacienda, began to encroach more and more heavily on the Indian communities. At the same time, the Indian communities increasingly faced the twin threats of internal differentiation and of invasion from the outside by the "marginals" of colonial times.

Despite the transcendent importance of the hacienda in Mexican life, anthropologists have paid little attention to this cultural form. To date we do not have a single anthropological or sociological study of a Mexican hacienda or hacienda community. Recent historical research has shown that the hacienda is not an offspring of the *encomienda* (Zavala 1940; 1944). The *encomienda* always remained a form of royal control. The hacienda, however, proved admirably adapted to the purposes of the colonists who strove for greater autonomy. Unlike the *encomienda*, it granted direct ownership of land to a manager-owner, and permitted direct control of a resident labor force. From the beginning, it served commercial ends (Bazant 1950). Its principal function was to convert community-oriented peasants into a disciplined labor force able to produce cash crops for a supra-community market. The social relationships through which this was accomplished involved a series of voluntary or forced transactions in which the worker abdicated much personal autonomy in exchange for heightened social and economic security.

Many observers have stressed the voracity of the hacienda for land and labor. Its appetite for these two factors of production was great indeed, and yet ultimately limited by its very structure. First, the hacienda always lacked capital. It thus tended to farm only the best land (Gruening 1928:134; Tannenbaum 1929:121–122), and relied heavily on the traditional technology of its labor force (Simpson 1937: 490). Hacienda owners also curtailed production in order to raise land rent and prices, and to keep down wages (Gama 1931:21). Thus "Mexico has been a land of large estates, but not a nation of large-scale agriculture" (Martínez de Alba, quoted in Simpson 1937:490). Second, the hacienda was always limited by available demand (Chávez Orozco 1950:19), which in a country with a largely self-sufficient population was always small. What the hacienda owner lacked in capital, however, he made up in the exercise of power over people. He tended to "monopolize land that he might monopolize labor" (Gruening 1928:134). But here again the hacienda encountered limits to its expansion. Even with intensive farming of its core lands and lavish use of gardeners and torch bearers, it reached a point where its mechanisms of control could no longer cope with the surplus of population nominally under its domination. At this point the haciendas ceased to grow, allowing Indian communities like Tepoztlán (Lewis 1951:xxv) or the Sierra and Lake Tarascan villages (West 1948:17) to survive on their fringes. Most hacienda workers did not live on the haciendas; they were generally residents of nearby communities who had lost their land, and exchanged their labor for the right to farm a subsistence plot on hacienda lands (Aguirre and Pozas 1954:202–203). Similarly, only in the arid and sparsely populated North did large haciendas predominate. In the heavily populated central region, Mexico's core area, large haciendas were the exception and the "medium-size" hacienda of about 3,000 ha. was the norm (*ibid.* 201; also Simpson 1937:489).

I should even go so far as to assert that once the haciendas reached the apex of their growth within a given area, they began to add to the defensive capacity of the corporately organized communities of Indian peasantry rather than to detract from it. Their major innovation lay in the field of labor organization and not in the field of technology. Their tenants continued to farm substantial land areas by traditional means (Aguirre and Pozas 1954:201; Whetten 1948:105) and the hacienda did not generally interfere in village affairs except when these came into conflict with its interests. The very threat of a hacienda's presence unified the villagers on its fringes in ways which would have been impossible in its absence. A hacienda owner also resented outside interference with "his" Indians, whether these lived inside or outside his property, and outsiders were allowed to operate in the communities only "by his leave." He thus often acted as a buffer between the Indian communities and nation-oriented groups, a role similar to that played by the hacienda owner in the northern highlands of Peru (Mangin 1955). Periodic work on the haciendas further provided the villagers with opportunities, however small, to maintain aspects of their lives which required small outlays of cash and goods, such as their festive patterns, and thus tended to preserve traditional cultural forms and functions which might otherwise have fallen into disuse (Aguirre and Pozas 1954:221; Wolf 1953:161).

Where corporate peasant communities were ultimately able to establish relations of hostile symbiosis with the haciendas, they confronted other pressures toward dissolution. These pressures came both from within and without the villages, and aimed at the abolition of communal jurisdiction over land. They sought to replace communal jurisdiction with private property in land, that is, to convert village land into a commodity. Like any commodity, land was to become an object to be bought, sold, and used not according to the common understandings of community-oriented groups, but according to the interests of nation-oriented groups outside the community. In some corporate communities outsiders were able to become landowners by buying land or taking land as security on unpaid loans, e.g., in the Tarascan area (Carrasco 1952:17). Typically, these outsiders belonged to the strata of the population which during colonial times had occupied a marginal position, but which exerted increased pressure for wealth, mobility and social recognition during the nineteenth century. Unable to break the monopoly which the haciendas exercised over the best land, they followed the line of least resistance and established beachheads in the Indian communities (Molina Enríquez 1909:53). They were aided in their endeavors by laws designed to break up the holdings of so-called corporations, which included the lands of the Church and the communal holdings of the Indians.

But even where outsiders were barred from acquiring village lands, the best land of the communities tended to pass into private ownership, this time of members of the community itself (Gama 1931:10–11). Important in this change seems to have been the spread of plow culture and oxen which required some capital investment, coupled with the development of wage labor on such holdings and increasing production for a supra-community market. As Oscar Lewis has so well shown for Tepoztlán, once private ownership in land allied to plow culture is established in at least part of the community, the community tends to differentiate into a series of social groups, with different technologies, patterns of work, interests, and thus with different supra-community relationships (Lewis 1951:129–157). This tendency has proceeded at different rates in different parts of Mexico. It has not yet run its course where land constitutes a poor investment risk, or where a favorable man–land ratio makes private property in land nonfunctional, as among the Popoluca of Sayula in Veracruz (Guiteras-Holmes 1952:37–40). Elsewhere it was complete at the end of the nineteenth century.

The Mexican Revolution of 1910 destroyed both the cultural form of the hacienda and the social relationships which were mediated through it. It did so in part because the hacienda was a self-limiting economic system, incapable of further expansion. It did so in part because the hacienda prevented the geographic mobility of a large part of Mexico's population. The end of debt bondage, for example, has permitted or forced large numbers of people to leave their local communities and to seek new opportunities elsewhere. It did so, finally, because the hacienda blocked the channels of social and cultural mobility and communication from nation to community, and tended to atomize the power of the central government. By destroying its power, the Revolution reopened channels of relationship from the communities to the national level, and permitted new circulation of individuals and groups through the various levels (Iturriaga 1951:66).

The new power holders have moved upwards mainly through political channels, and the major means of consolidating and obtaining power on the regional and national level in Mexico today appear to be political. Moreover—and due perhaps in part to the lack of capital in the Mexican economy as a whole—political advantages are necessary to obtain economic advantages. Both economic and political interests must aim at the establishment of monopolistic positions within defined areas of crucial economic and political relationships. Thus political and economic power seekers tend to meet in alliances and cliques on all levels of the society.

The main formal organization through which their interests are mediated is the government party, the Revolutionary Institutional Party or, as someone has said, "the Revolution as an institution" (Lee 1954:300). This party contains not only groups formally defined as political, but also occupational and other special-interest groups. It is a political holding company representing different group interests (Scott 1955:4). Its major function is to establish channels of communication and mobility from the local community to the central power group at the helm of the government. Individuals who can gain control of the local termini of these channels can now rise to positions of power in the national economy or political machine.

Some of the prerequisites for this new mobility are purely economic. The possession of some wealth, or access to sources of wealth, is important; more important, however, is the ability to adopt the proper patterns of public behavior. These are the patterns of behavior developed by the "marginal" groups of colonial times which have now become the ideal behavior patterns of the nation-oriented person. An individual who seeks power and recognition outside his local community must shape his behavior to fit these new expectations. He must learn to operate in an arena of continuously changing friendships and alliances, which form and dissolve with the appearance or disappearance of new economic or political opportunities. In other words, he must learn to function in terms which characterize any complex stratified society in which individuals can improve their status through the judicious manipulation of social ties. However, this manipulative behavior is always patterned culturally—and patterned differently in Mexico than in the United States or India. He must therefore learn also the cultural forms in which this manipulative behavior is couched. Individuals who are able to operate both in terms of community-oriented and nation-oriented expectations then tend to be selected out for mobility. They become the economic and political "brokers" of nation-community relations, a function which carries its own rewards.

The rise of such politician-entrepreneurs, however, has of necessity produced new problems for the central power. The Spanish Crown had to cope with the ever-growing autonomy of the colonists; the central government of the Republic must similarly check the propensity of political power seekers to free themselves of government control by cornering economic advantages. Once wealthy in their own right, these nation-community "brokers" would soon be independent of government favors and rewards. The Crown placed a check on the colonists by balancing their localized power over bailiwicks with the concentrated power of a corps of royal officials in charge of the corporate Indian communities. Similarly, the government of the Republic must seek to balance the community-derived power of its political "brokers" with the power of other power holders. In modern Mexico, these competing power holders are the leaders of the labor unions—especially of the labor unions in the nationalized industries—and of the *ejidos*, the groups in local communities who have received land grants in accordance with the agrarian laws growing out of the 1910 Revolution.

Leaving aside a discussion of the labor unions due to limitations of time and personal knowledge, I should like to underline the importance of the *ejido* grants as a nation-wide institution. They now include more than 30 per cent of the people in Mexican localities with a population below 10,000 (Whetten 1948:186). A few of these, located in well-irrigated and highly capitalized areas, have proved an economic as well as a political success (*ibid.* 215). The remainder, however, must be regarded as political instruments rather than as economic ones. They are political assets because they have brought under government control large numbers of people who depend ultimately on the government for their livelihood. Agrarian reform has, however, produced social and political changes without concomitant changes in the technological order; the redistribution of land alone can neither change the technology nor supply needed credit (Aguirre and Pozas 1954:207–208; Pozas 1952:316).

At the same time, the Revolution has intensified the tendencies toward further internal differentiation of statuses and interests in the communities, and thus served to reduce their capacity to resist outside impact and pressure. It has mobilized the potentially nation-oriented members of the community, the men with enough land or capital to raise cash crops and operate stores, the men whose position and personality allow them to accept the new patterns of nation-oriented behavior. Yet often enough the attendant show of business and busy-ness tends to obscure the fact that most of the inhabitants of such communities either lack access to new opportunities or are unable to take advantage of such opportunities when offered. Lacking adequate resources in land, water, technical knowledge, and contacts in the market, the majority also lack the instruments which can transform use values into marketable commodities. At the same time, their inability to speak Spanish and their failure to understand the cues for the new patterns of nation-oriented behavior isolate them from the channels of communication between community and nation. Under these circumstances they must cling to the traditional "rejection pattern" of their ancestors, because their narrow economic base sets limits to the introduction of new cultural alternatives. These are all too often nonfunctional for them. The production of sufficient maize for subsistence purposes remains their major goal in life. In their case, the granting of *ejidos* tended to lend support to their accustomed way of life and reinforced their attachment to their traditional heritage.

Confronted by these contrasts between the mobile and the traditional, the nation-oriented and the community-oriented, village life is riven by contradictions and conflicts, conflicts not only between class groups but also between individuals, families, or entire neighborhoods. Such a community will inevitably differentiate into a number of unstable groups with different orientations and interests.

III

This paper has dealt with the principal ways in which social groups arranged and rearranged themselves in conflict and accommodation along the major economic and political axes of Mexican society. Each rearrangement produced a changed configuration in the relationship of community-oriented and nation-oriented groups. During the first period of post-Columbian Mexican history, political power was concentrated on the national level in the hands of royal officials. Royal officials and colonist entrepreneurs struggled with each other for control of the labor supply located in the Indian communities. In this struggle, the royal officials helped to organize the Indian peasantry into corporate communities which proved strongly resilient to outside change. During the second period, the colonist entrepreneurs—and especially the owners of haciendas—threw off royal control and established autonomous local enclaves, centered on their enterprises. With the fusion of political and economic power in the hands of these intermediate power holders, the national government was rendered impotent and the Indian peasant groups became satellites of the entrepreneurial complex. At the same time, their corporate communal organization was increasingly weakened by internal differentiation and the inroads of outsiders. During the third period, the entrepreneurial complexes standing between community and nation were swept away by the agrarian revolution and power again returned to a central government. Political means are once more applied to check the transformation of power seekers from the local communities into independent entrepreneurs. Among the groups used in exercising such restraint are the agriculturists, organized in *ejidos* which allow the government direct access to the people of the local communities.

Throughout this analysis, we have been concerned with the bonds which unite different groups on different levels of the larger society, rather than with the internal organization of communities and national-level institutions. Such a shift in emphasis seems increasingly necessary as our traditional models of communities and national institutions become obsolete. Barring such a shift, anthropologists will have to abdicate their new-found interest in complex societies. The social-psychological aspects of life in local groups, as opposed to the cultural aspects, have long been explored by sociologists. The study of formal law, politics, or economics is better carried out by specialists in these fields than by anthropologists doubling as part-time experts. Yet the hallmark of anthropology has always been its holistic approach, an approach which is increasingly needed in an age of ever-increasing specialization. This paper constitutes an argument that we can achieve greater synthesis in the study of complex societies by focusing our attention on the relationships between different groups operating on different levels of the society, rather than on any one of its isolated segments.

Such an approach will necessarily lead us to ask some new questions and to reconsider some answers to old questions. We may raise two such questions regarding the material presented in the present paper. First, can we make any generalizations about the ways in which groups in Mexico interrelate with each other over time, as compared to those which unite groups in another society, such as Italy or Japan, for example? We hardly possess the necessary information to answer such a question at this point, but one can indicate the direction which a possible answer might take. Let me point to one salient characteristic of Mexican group relationships which appears from the foregoing analysis: the tendency of new group relationships to contribute to the preservation of traditional cultural forms. The Crown reorganized the Indian communities; they became strongholds of the traditional way of life. The haciendas transformed the Indian peasants into part-time laborers; their wages stabilized their traditional prestige economy. The Revolution of 1910 opened the channels of opportunity to the nation-oriented; it reinforced the community orientation of the immobile. It would indeed seem that in Mexico "the old periods never disappear completely and all wounds, even the oldest, continue to bleed to this day" (Paz 1947:11). This "contemporaneity of the noncontemporaneous" is responsible for the "common-sense" view of many superficial observers that in Mexico "no problems are ever solved," and "reforms always produce results opposite to those intended." It has undoubtedly affected Mexican political development (Wolf 1953:160–165). It may be responsible for the violence which has often accompanied even minor ruptures in these symbiotic patterns. And one may well ask the question whether both processes of accommodation or conflict in Mexico have not acquired certain patterned forms as a result of repeated cyclical returns to hostile symbiosis in group relationships.

Such considerations once again raise the thorny problems presented by the national character approach. Much discussion of this concept has turned on the question of whether all nationals conform to a common pattern of behavior and ideals. This view has been subjected to much justified criticism. We should remember, however, that most national character studies have emphasized the study of ideal norms, constructed on the basis of verbal statements by informants, rather than the study of real behavior through participant observation. The result has been, I think, to confuse cultural form and function. It seems possible to define "national character" operationally as those cultural forms or mechanisms which groups involved in the same overall web of relationships can use in their formal and informal dealings with each other. Such a view need not imply that all nationals think or behave alike, nor that the forms used may not serve different functions in different social contexts. Such common forms must exist if communication between the different constituent groups of a complex society are to be established and maintained. I have pointed out that in modern Mexico the behavior patterns of certain groups in the past have become the expected forms of behavior of nation-oriented individuals. These cultural forms of communication as found in Mexico are manifestly different from those found in other societies (see especially Carrión 1952:70–90; Paz 1947: 29–45). Their study by linguists and students of kinesics (Birdwhistell 1951) would do much to establish their direct relevance to the study of complex societies.

A second consideration which derives from the analysis presented in this paper concerns the groups of people who mediate between community-oriented groups in communities and nation-oriented groups which operate primarily through national institutions. We have encountered several such groups in this paper. In post-Columbian Mexico, these mediating functions were first carried out by the leaders of Indian corporate communities and royal officials. Later, these tasks fell into the hands of the local entrepreneurs, such as the owners of haciendas. After the Revolution of 1910, they passed into the hands of nation-oriented individuals from the local communities who have established ties with the national level, and who serve as "brokers" between community-oriented and nation-oriented groups.

The study of these "brokers" will prove increasingly rewarding, as anthropologists shift their attention from the internal organization of communities to the manner of their integration into larger systems. For they stand guard over the crucial junctures or synapses of relationships which connect the local system to the larger whole. Their basic function is to relate community-oriented individuals who want to stabilize or improve their life chances, but who lack economic security and political connections, with nation-oriented individuals who operate primarily in terms of the complex cultural forms standardized as national institutions, but whose success in these operations depends on the size and strength of their personal following. These functions are of course expressed through cultural forms or mechanisms which will differ from culture to culture. Examples of these are Chinese *kan-ch'ing* (Fried 1953), Japanese *oyabun-kobun* (Ishino 1953), Latin American *compadrazgo* (Mintz and Wolf 1950).

Special studies of such "broker" groups can also provide unusual insight into the functions of a complex system through a study of its dysfunctions. The position of these "brokers" is an "exposed" one, since,

Janus-like, they face in two directions at once. They must serve some of the interests of groups operating on both the community and the national level, and they must cope with the conflicts raised by the collision of these interests. They cannot settle them, since by doing so they would abolish their own usefulness to others. Thus they often act as buffers between groups, maintaining the tensions which provide the dynamic of their actions. The relation of the hacienda owner to his satellite Indians, the role of the modern politician-broker to his community-oriented followers, may properly be viewed in this light. These would have no raison d'être but for the tensions between community-oriented groups and nation-oriented groups. Yet they must also maintain a grip on these tensions, lest conflict get out of hand and better mediators take their place. Fallers (1955) has demonstrated how much can be learned about the workings of complex systems by studying the "predicament" of one of its "brokers," the Soga chief. We shall learn much from similar studies elsewhere.

Summary

This paper has argued that students of complex societies must proceed from a study of communities or national institutions to a study of the ties between social groups operating on all levels of a society. It then attempted to view Mexico in this light. Emphasis on the external ties between groups rather than on the internal organization of each alone led to renewed questions as to whether these ties were mediated through common cultural forms, and to a discussion of "broker" groups which mediate between different levels of integration of the same society.

REFERENCES CITED

Aguirre Beltrán, Gonzalo and Ricardo Pozas Arciniegas
1954 "Instituciones indígenas en el México actual," in Caso *et al.*, pp. 171–272.

Bazant, Jan
1950 "Feudalismo y capitalismo en la historia económica de México," *Trimestre Económico* 17:81–98.

Benítez, Francisco
1947 "México, la tela de Penélope," *Cuadernos Americanos* 6:44–60.

Birdwhistell, Ray L.
1951 *Kinesics*, Washington, D.C., Foreign Service Institute, U.S. Department of State.

Carrasco, Pedro
1952 *Tarascan Folk Religion: An Analysis of Economic, Social, and Religious Interactions,* Middle American Research Institute Publication 17:1–64, New Orleans, Tulane University.

Carrión, Jorge
1952 "Mito y magia del mexicano," *México y lo mexicano* 3, México, D. F., Porrúa y Obregón.

Caso, Alfonso *et al.*
1954 *Métodos y resultados de la política indigenista en México,* Memorias del Instituto Nacional Indigenista 6, México, D. F.

Chávez Orozco, Luis
1943 *Las instituciones democráticas de los indígenas Mexicanos en la época colonial,* Ediciones del Instituto Indigenista Interamericano, México, D. F.
1950 "La irrigación en México: ensayo histórico," *Problemas Agrícolas e Industriales de México* 2:11–31.

Chevalier, François
1952 *La formation des grands domaines aux Mexique: terre et société aux XVIe–XVIIe Siècles,* Travaux et Mémoires de l'Institut d'Ethnologie 56, Paris.

Fallers, Lloyd
1955 "The Predicament of the Modern African Chief: An Instance from Uganda, *American Anthropologist* 57:290–305.

Fried, Morton H.
1953 *Fabric of Chinese Society,* New York, Praeger.

Gama, Valentin
1931 *La propiedad en México—la reforma agraria,* México, D. F., Empresa Editorial de Ingeniería y Arquitectura.

Gruening, Ernest
1928 *Mexico and Its Heritage,* New York, Century.

Guiteras-Holmes, Calixta
1952 *Sayula,* México, D. F., Sociedad Mexicana de Geografía y Estadística.

Ishino, Iwao
1953 "The *Oyabun-Kobun:* A Japanese Ritual Kinship Institution," *American Anthropologist* 55:695–707.

Iturriaga, José E.
1951 *La estructura social y cultural de México,* México, D. F., Fondo de Cultura Económica.

Lee, Eric
1954 "Can a one party system be democratic?" *Dissent* 1:299–300.

Lewis, Oscar
1951 *Life in a Mexican Village: Tepoztlán Restudied,* Urbana, University of Illinois Press.

Mangin, William
1955 "*Haciendas, Comunidades* and Strategic Acculturation in the Peruvian Sierra," paper read before the American Anthropological Association, Boston, November 18.

Mintz, Sidney W. and Eric R. Wolf
1950 "An Analysis of Ritual Co-parenthood (*Compadrazgo*)," *Southwestern Journal of Anthropology* 6:341–368.

Miranda, José
1947 "La función económica del encomendero en los orígenes del régimen colonial de Nueva España, 1525–1531," *Anales del Instituto Nacional de Anthropología e Historia* 2:421–462.

Molina Enríquez, Andrés
1909 *Los grandes problemas nacionales*, México, D. F., Imprenta de A. Carranza e Hijos.

Paz, Octavio
1947 *El laberinto de la soledad*, México, D. F., Cuadernos Americanos.

Pozas Arciniegas, Ricardo
1952 "La situation économique et financière de l'Indien Américain," *Civilisations* 2:309–329.

Redfield, Robert and Sol Tax
1952 "General Characteristics of Present-Day Mesoamerican Indian Society," in *Heritage of Conquest*, Sol Tax, ed., Glencoe, Ill., Free Press, pp. 31–39.

Scott, Robert E.
1955 "The Bases of Political Power in the Caribbean," lecture delivered at the University of Illinois, Urbana, January 14. (Mimeographed.)

Simpson, Eyler N.
1937 *The Ejido: Mexico's Way Out*, Chapel Hill, The University of North Carolina Press.

Simpson, Lesley Byrd
1950 *The Encomienda in New Spain: The Beginning of Spanish Mexico*, rev. ed., Berkeley, University of California Press.

Steward, Julian
1950 *Area Research: Theory and Practice*, Social Science Research Council Bulletin 63, New York.

Tannenbaum, Frank
1929 *The Mexican Agrarian Revolution*, Washington, D.C., Brookings Institution.

West, Robert C.
1948 *Cultural Geography of the Modern Tarascan Area*, Institute of Social Anthropology Publication 7, Smithsonian Institution, Washington, D.C.

Whetten, Nathan
1948 *Rural Mexico*, Chicago, University of Chicago Press.

Wolf, Eric R.
1953 "La formación de la nación: un ensayo de formulación," *Ciencias Sociales* 4:50–62, 98–111, 146–171.
1955a "Types of Latin American Peasantry: A Preliminary Discussion," *American Anthropologist* 57:452–471.
1955b *The Mexican Bajío in the Eighteenth Century: An Analysis*

of Cultural Integration, Middle American Research Institute Publication 17:177–200, New Orleans, Tulane University.

Yañez, Agustín
1945 "Fichas Mexicanas," *Jornadas* 39, México, D. F., El Colegio de México.

Zavala, Silvio
1940 *De encomiendas y propiedad territorial en algunas regiones de la América Española*, México, D. F., Robredo.
1944 "Orígenes coloniales del peonaje en México," *Trimestre Económico* 10:711–748.

Zavala, Silvio and José Miranda
1954 "Instituciones indígenas en la colonia," in Caso *et al.* pp. 29–112.

Aspects of Andean Native Life

OSCAR NÚÑEZ DEL PRADO

This paper is an anthropological report on certain aspects of native life in the mountain communities of the Andean territory occupied by Bolivia, Peru, and Ecuador. As the reader will quickly note, it consists mostly of general impressions. These impressions are the result of my experience in the native areas of Peru where I live, of observations made in the course of the International Labor Office's Andean Indian Mission survey of 1952 of which I formed a part, and of study of reports written for the Ecuadorian Institute of Anthropology and the Section of Anthropology of the University of Cuzco, Peru. I have also used the results of studies by my colleagues in the three countries of the area considered.

The descriptive and statistical data available on Andean native communities are very inadequate, and perhaps the chief virtue of a summary like the present one is that it can call attention to gaps and problems on which more work needs to be done. In the three countries visited by the Andean Indian Mission a beginning is only now being made to survey community landholdings, and it is still not possible to get many speci-

Reprinted from *Kroeber Anthropological Society Papers,* 1955, XII, 1–21, by permission of the author and publisher. This paper is a translation and abridgment by John H. Rowe of an article entitled: "Problemas antropológicos del área andina (Perú-Bolivia-Ecuador)," published in Cuzco in 1953.

fic data on concentrations of native population and the relations between it and the land. We lack measurements of cultivable and uncultivable land and have no figures on how much of the cultivable land is actually cultivated. We need data on the number of families living on large estates, the number of small landowners, etc. All we have so far are impressionistic estimates which vary considerably. Furthermore, very few anthropological studies have been made, and the handful of anthropologists who have done field work in the area have had to concentrate on small areas and have usually worked quite far apart. It is thus difficult to get a picture of local variations and to see the isolated studies in some sort of perspective.

In the following summary, I will place a certain amount of emphasis on the land question because I believe that it is a problem to which most of the others are directly or indirectly related.

Uniform and Variable Factors

The native population lives for the most part isolated from frequent contacts with the mestizos; it forms a world apart, and a very different one. This segregation may be attributed to historical, geographical, economic, or cultural factors, or to a combination of all of them; the facts are that the native population is more involved in production than in consumption and has no part in the political life of the country in which it occupies the lowest social level and usually lives under the most unfavorable conditions. In the rural areas, the native is shy, reticent, and distrustful in dealings with whites and mestizos; he is hospitable, communicative, and open with those of his own social group. It is difficult to persuade him to forget an injury, and if he has a chance to retaliate, he takes it without hesitation. On the other hand, he is loyal and affectionate as a friend, and docile and cooperative with anyone he finds he can trust. He is fond of jokes and is often ironical and biting in his criticisms. His dedication to agriculture leads him to live in the country, in communities of scattered houses, in even more scattered houses on large estates, or in towns or villages dominated by mestizos in which the natives occupy the outskirts.

We can ask first whether there is any cultural unity among the natives in the area included in the three countries with which we are concerned. The answer is yes, for although we must recognize a series of differential factors, they do not seriously affect the unity, being limited to differences in dress and house type related to climate or to certain "deviations" in habitual occupations. We will say little about dress, although it has an important function in marking the social status of individuals within the area in which they live and their degree of acculturation. Obviously, there is a general tendency for dress to be most Europeanized in the more acculturated areas, while traditional native styles are commoner in areas less affected by the acculturation process.

House type varies not only in relation to climate but also to the availability of resources. Thus, in the Lake Titicaca basin we find construction methods as different as the use of sod blocks (*tepe*, or "ch'ampa") for both walls and roof and the use of a wooden frame with a thatch or tile roof. In all cases, the floors are of earth; the interiors lack ventilation and most of them are blackened with soot from cooking fires on the floor. Dwellings commonly consist of only one or two rooms, utilized without distinction for cooking, sleeping, and raising chickens and guinea pigs. Sleeping is done on the floor or on a platform of poles or of stones and mud; bedding consists of sheepskins and a few home-woven blankets in varying stages of wear and disintegration. In Ecuador, while 52 per cent to 82 per cent of the houses are of the same simple type, it is worth noting that most of the native houses are more attractive than those of Peru and Bolivia, some even having ceilings and wooden floors. The natives bathe rarely; personal cleanliness consists in some washing about once a week. It is not uncommon for the women to wash their hair with urine because of a belief in its magical or medicinal value. In most of Ecuador standards of cleanliness are somewhat higher than in the other two countries.

Marriage is preferably within the community, and the conjugal family forms the smallest work unit, but consanguineous, affinal, and ceremonial kinship is also very important. Paternal authority is strong, and paternal kinsmen have a certain priority. Division of labor is by sex and age. Children begin to work very young, and it is not unusual to find children three or four years old in charge of a flock which they have to follow several kilometers in a day, especially if the pasturage is poor. Boys accompany their fathers to the fields where they are generally assigned a specific amount of work which they have to complete without objections or excuses; alternatively, they may be required to provide wood for fuel, irrigate a field, carry water for household use, etc. The girls go out with the domestic animals or help their mothers at spinning, weaving, and cooking, when the women are not needed to help in sowing. The women's part is to break up clods, distribute the seed, and help to cover it.

During the day, the family moves around as the work requires, dividing its time between the care of the fields and herds, repair of fences, weaving, and spinning or other handicrafts, or, in the case of tenant farmers, working for the estate. People go out at night only rarely, when participating in a fiesta; on other days, the parents discuss their problems briefly around the fire in the evening and then all go to bed. The bed itself is usually a family affair.

Social life is organized around kinship ties, whether consanguineous, affinal, or ceremonial, and usually involves patterns of cooperative labor. There is a constant interchange of rights and obligations to help in the family work which provides a certain esprit de corps in the work exchange group. Ceremonial kinship is especially important. Godparents and *compadres* are treated with special respect and deference, and it is difficult to refuse a request from them. Kinship by oath is somewhat rarer, but occurs in cases where two friends treat each other as brothers ("wawqechakuy") and establishes a closer relationship than between brothers born.

Whether segregated in the country or living near them in towns and cities, the natives' relations with whites and mestizos are strongly conditioned by barriers of fear on the one side and prejudice on the other. In the country, the relationship is that between serf and lord, and contacts are limited to the superficial ones occasioned by the rendering of service or a visit by the mestizo for reasons of his own convenience. When the native goes to live in a mestizo town or in the city, because of the loss of his land, the attraction of a good salary, or some other reason, he lives on the outskirts, crowded into miserable and filthy houses which he shares with other natives in the same condition as his own. He is merely an Indian, which means that he occupies the lowest social and economic level and is subject to strong social pressures from all sides. In many places (e.g., Paucartambo) he may be taken by any mestizo who wants his services without his wishes being consulted in the matter. The contemptuous attitude of the mestizo toward the Indian is constantly met with on all social levels. It is not uncommon to hear such remarks as: "The Indian is a dead weight, an amorphous class outside the economy; he neither produces nor consumes anything" (Ecuador); "The Indians are parasites on the country" (Bolivia); and many mestizos speak in terms of exterminating the Indians or preventing them from reproducing. In all three countries contempt for everything Indian is habitual. No one wants to belong to this class, and it is very nearly an insult to suggest to a mestizo that he has an Indian relative; the Indian himself, when he has passed to the *cholo* social class, wishes to wipe out his Indian connections or cover them up as much as possible, because he knows that society condemns the Indian to an inferior position and that even his legal rights are obstructed. He becomes ashamed of his language and even abuses his relatives who maintain their Indian status.

When the native moves to other rural areas his problems change little socially but his health is likely to be in greater danger. Such migrations are usually to lower altitudes in the tropical forest valleys where he goes to work on an estate (Quillabamba), gets a job washing gold (Quincemil), or colonizes land belonging to the government (Tambopata).

In any case, he comes to these areas without proper protection or prophylaxis and readily acquires a series of diseases to which he has no native resistance and against which he knows no way of protecting himself. Because of frequent movements back and forth between some of the highland communities and these tropical valleys, it is not uncommon to find cases of malaria and hookworm in the highlands, as the I.L.O. mission noted at Wamanruru in Puno whence there is constant emigration to Quincemil. Some of the emigrants stay permanently in the valleys, while others come back to their old homes from time to time to recoup their forces. We know little about the causes of these movements, the numbers of people involved, and the areas preferred for settlement, but such movements are frequently reported.

There appear to be regional differences in native attitudes which we can illustrate by notes on the Cuzco area in Peru, the Lake Titicaca region in Bolivia, and Otavalo in Ecuador. The description given for the Cuzco area is the most reliable, since it is based on my personal experience; my information on the other two areas is mostly second hand and comparatively superficial.

The Inca-speaking native of the Cuzco area behaves in two different ways, depending on whom he is dealing with. With mestizos, he is suspicious, silent, withdrawn, and nearly inaccessible; he offers a passive and systematic resistance. He is humble, fearful, and inattentive; reticent and evasive in his answers, indecisive in his attitudes. He suppresses and hides his emotions and rarely reveals his disagreement even when he finds himself in fundamental opposition. He is obsequious at times, but this attitude implies that he wants something very specific, that he expects an almost immediate reward. With other natives he is open, communicative, fond of practical jokes, he makes a display of his industry and is ready and willing to cooperate; he shows his feelings and states his opinions without reserve. He is fond of fiestas and enjoys himself in them. When he is drunk, he is impulsive and courageous in a fight; he bears grudges, is vengeful, astute, and often mocking. He is sober and moderate in his sex life, frugal in eating, and tranquil in daily affairs.

As a general observation, we can say that he is extremely conservative; he allows no sudden changes and is openly resistive to traits, techniques and practices different from those to which he is accustomed, at least until he has a chance to convince himself personally and objectively of the advantages he might gain from an innovation. Even so, he vacillates for a long time before deciding to accept the new practice. He has lived in a closed circle in which tradition and custom are his basic schools, and it is a nearly static circle which gives him no opportunity to grasp other possibilities or take initiative in unfamiliar matters. His accumulated knowledge is limited to the circumscribed round of relationships in his community, and his world is limited to the community, the estate, or the nearest town where he usually trades. His interests are likewise limited by these circumstances and by the possibilities which he has found in these circles. It is logical to think that initiative requires a favorable experience and innovation a previous tradition of change; as long as these conditions are not found, it is natural for us as outsiders to regard the native communities as "asleep" or "backward." Most of the native's activities consist of repeating routine behavior. His manual skill is considerable but used with a limited technology. The products of his handicrafts are elegant but little diversified, and they are made for local consumption. Textiles and pottery furnish good examples; the weaving is done on a backstrap loom and the pottery made entirely by hand. An important factor in the situation is that most of the natives speak no language but Inca and the proportion of illiterates is overwhelming. Illiteracy limits the native's sources of information to conversations in the evening or in rest periods during cooperative labor.

In the Aymara area of Lake Titicaca, the native gives an impression of greater personal security; instead of timidity, he has a rather arrogant manner, and his speech and attitudes are emphatic and peremptory. He is less shy than the Inca speaker and more quarrelsome when drunk. A clearer difference, perhaps, is his greater mobility. Although traditionally a farmer, he is less closely attached to the soil and can leave it temporarily or even permanently without regarding the fact as a catastrophe. He sometimes travels hundreds of kilometers to exchange his products and not infrequently settles down in a region far removed from his community of origin. He is skillful in trade when he devotes himself to it. Fiestas fascinate him, and he will go to great lengths to maintain his reputation as a generous spender on such occasions. His handicrafts are somewhat more diversified than those of the Inca speakers and show a certain tendency toward commercialization, although his production techniques are quite limited and he is also very conservative about changing them.

The differences we have noted seem to be the result of less strong pressures by the mestizo class in the Aymara area, providing a different social environment.

In the area around Otavalo, the studies of Professor Rubio suggest a close similarity of attitudes to those we have noted among the Inca speakers of Cuzco. He says, for example, "The Indian behaves differently with whites from the way he does in his private life . . . ; he reacts with difficulty when he is alone, but in a group he finds strength in numbers; his savings, if any, are invested in land or in animals. . . . The Indian is slow and lazy when working for whites . . . ; when he has a definite task to accomplish in a day, he is quick and efficient . . . ; his lack of foresight shows up in fiestas, for which he will spend all he has, go into debt, and sell his labor for trifling wages even though he ends in virtual slavery . . . ; his attitude is one of concentrated and latent dissimulation, and it gives him good results; in self-protection he resorts to volubility and adapts himself to the conditions imposed . . . ; he is sometimes docile to the point of humility" (Rubio 1946:262–269). On the other hand, I have noticed that he is much more accessible than the other groups with which we are comparing him; he is affable and does not show such extreme reserve and reticence toward whites. He is less conservative, more disposed to accept outside influences, and takes occasional suggestions with less difficulty.

One of his most notable characteristics is his great manual dexterity. All the Ecuadorian natives are very skillful and have developed their handicrafts into successful commercial activities, but the natives of Imbabura and especially of Otavalo are outstanding in this respect. Their success depends on their skill, for they lack adequate tools and their production is unorganized; furthermore, the market for their products is not great. Handicrafts and small industries are organized almost exclusively on a family basis, although there are also a few small factories. The market for their products is restricted by the existence of speculators who control the raw materials and often oblige the craftsmen to sell their products only to the speculator. Also, many of their products, such as ponchos, mufflers, coarse woolen yard goods, etc., are consumed by one social class only. Even when they make good quality woolens, the goods cannot compete in the market with machine-made materials. In general, the natives do not produce for the taste of the white and mestizo market. A great diversification of handicrafts is now taking place in Otavalo, and there is some talk of industrialization.

Land and Agriculture

In the three countries we are considering, the distribution of land is highly unequal. The large estates, usually occupying the most productive land, have only small portions under cultivation, while the greater part is not utilized (Cisneros 1948:151; Flores 1950:380). Alongside the large estates one finds the small properties of natives who have been pushed out onto the less productive land. The increase of the population and the division of land between children required by law have produced an excessive fractionation of native land so that in many areas native families do not have enough land to live on. In the areas studied by the I.L.O. mission, the poorest farm land was found in Bolivia and Peru; here, native life is virtually conditioned by the land problem, because of the dependence of the natives on agriculture. Even where, as occurs in some regions, the natives own large tracts of land, the yield is still inadequate because of the poor quality of the soil; this situation is common in southern Peru and Bolivia. Elsewhere in highland Peru and Ecuador, the land is more productive but the native farms are hopelessly small.

A distinction must be made between systems of landholding among the natives. Native farmers can be grouped in general into three classes in this respect: those who live in native communities (commune, " 'aynoqa," or " 'ayllu") protected by special legislation; small independent proprietors; and the tenant farmers attached to the big estates.

The community system can further be subdivided into three types: (1) a type in which the agricultural land and pastures are regarded as belonging to the community and are distributed annually among the members; (2) a type in which farm land is owned individually while the pastures and irrigation water are held for common use; and (3) a type in which all members are fully independent landowners but maintain the community organization as a means of defending their titles. In the first type, the community lands are divided into a number of sections corresponding to the number of crops in the rotation series plus the number of years a field must lie fallow after use. Thus, if the rotation series consists of potatoes, quinua, and barley and the fields must lie fallow for four years, the community lands must be divided into seven sections, as at Koqra in Puno. Each section in turn is divided into as many lots ("qallpira") as there are heads of families, and each receives a specific lot. An example will help to explain the working of this system. In a given year, all lots in one section will be planted to potatoes, all lots in another to quinua, and a third will be planted to barley. The other four are left fallow. The following year, potatoes are planted in a new section, quinua sown in the section previously devoted to potatoes, and barley in the place of the quinua. The section which had barley is now left fallow, and will be planted to potatoes after four years. In any given field, a given crop is repeated every eighth year.

In communities of class two, the common pasture and firewood resources are generally used freely by the members. In this type and in the third, the individual farmers have complete liberty to arrange whatever rotation of their crops they regard as most convenient. In all three types, irrigation is regulated by local usage depending on the availability of water.

The first type of community system has the disadvantage that the crops of a single family are scattered and correspondingly difficult to control and care for. The community needs to control a considerable area of land in order to allow part of it to lie fallow. In the second and third types, a family's land is likely to be concentrated and readily accessible.

In most of Ecuador, and in the Vilcanota and Apurimac valleys in

Peru, land is not left fallow and its productivity is regulated only by crop rotation and manuring. This practice implies that the land is of better quality.

It may be safely asserted that the natives who live under the community system enjoy a privileged position with respect to those who do not, for they are free to use their land as they think fit, live with a greater sense of security because of the legal guarantees which protect the communities, and above all have greater opportunities to work on a large scale because they can count on the cooperation of other members of the community. It is also plain that this type of collective defense has prevented the liquidation of native landownership, constantly menaced by neighboring mestizos, with whom the community is forever engaged in long and costly litigation. Frequently, the excessive fractionation of property due to growth of the community population forces many of the habitants to sell their lots to other members because they find themselves without sufficient land for subsistence. The sellers must then emigrate, often to distant regions, and become tenant or day laborers on the big estates (Rubio 1946:229–230; Núñez del Prado 1949:194).

The small native landowners who do not belong to an " 'ayllu" or commune are usually grouped in small villages, classed administratively as districts or cantons, and are at the mercy of the mestizos, who despise, exploit, molest and deceive them. They almost always lack pasture land for their animals and have to ask for the use of pasture land on some big estate, assuming in return obligations of personal service, money payments, or loan of work animals, depending on the circumstances. This type of small landowner who lacks sufficient land to support his family is an important element of the free labor force, hiring himself out to a big estate or working as a day laborer in the city or a nearby town. This supplementary work gives him an opportunity to learn some construction skills, such as working with building stone or making tiles or adobes, which enable him to earn more money. If he then decides to settle permanently in town, he becomes a member of the social class called *cholo* in Peru and Bolivia.

The tenant farmers of large estates live on estate land and are considered virtually part of the property, since the general practice is that the sale value of an estate is determined by the number of native tenants attached to it. [See Editor's Note, p. 122.]

The *huasipunguero* in Ecuador, the "sayañero" in Bolivia, and the tenant in Peru live under almost identical conditions. In payment for the farm lands and house which they receive from the estate, they owe a fixed number of days' work a week at wages which are usually far below what they could earn elsewhere. Tenant families live on the same lot for generations, chained to a series of obligations which absorb their time and energy to such an extent, in some cases, that they have little left with which to work for the support of their own families. In Ecuador, the tenant is expected to work from five to six days a week for the estate, at a minimum of eight hours a day, and he receives in wages one fifth of the going rate for free labor (Buitrón 1947: Table 19). For two to three months a year he takes his turn as *huasicama* or *cuentayo*. The *huasicama* serves the estate doing domestic service, repairing fences, looking out for the smaller animals, running errands to nearby towns, milking, etc., working from dawn to dark without a single day off, at the same rate he gets for other work for the estate. The *cuentayo* looks out for the cattle of the estate, and is fully responsible for it. There are some estates on which the management prohibits even members of the tenants' families from working off the estate where they can earn a better salary. The rule is enforced by threat of eviction (Flores 1950:380).

In Peru and Boliva, the conditions of servitude under which native tenants live are somewhat worse than in Ecuador, with more variability in Peru than in Bolivia. In Bolivia, the native receives two to three hectares of fertile soil and in return must work four days a week for the estate without pay, but he receives wages for work on the remaining days. The tenant is also allowed to plant as much of the less fertile land of the estate as he wishes, turning over one half of the harvest to the owner (United Nations 1951:94). The tenants also take turns serving as *pongos*, at tasks similar to those assigned to the *huasicama* in Ecuador, and the young women of tenant families serve the estate as *mitanis*. The *mitanis* serve for turns of seven to fifteen days, spinning, weaving, making *chicha*, cooking food for the dogs, etc., without pay. The boys similarly serve as messengers ("Iloqalla"). [See Editor's Note, p. 122.]

In Peru there is more variation. Around Cuzco, especially in Paucartambo, Anta, and Quispicanchi, the native tenant receives from half a hectare to one hectare of land from the estate and is expected to work for it from three to six days a week, depending on the season. His wages vary from 10 to 30 centavos a day (unskilled labor in the city is paid 5 soles—about twenty times as much). The tenants also serve weekly turns as *pongos*, which means that they go to live at the big house on the estate or in the owner's town house, whichever the owner prefers. On the estate, the *pongos* take care of the horses and pigs, carry firewood, milk the cows and carry the milk to nearby towns for sale, cut and carry forage for the animals, and do errands around the house. Other obligations are divided between the tenants and others laborers on the estate; these include the jobs of irrigator, " 'arariwa" (field guardian), "qollana" (foreman), and supervisor. The women do domestic service as *mitanis*, care for the chickens, and spin wool belonging to the estate, the combination varying according to the area (Morote 1951:108). On top of all this, on many estates the laborers are obliged to harvest the crops, load them on their own animals, and deliver them to the town or city designated by the owner, sometimes two or three days' journey on foot. They also serve as *propios*, private letter carriers who deliver messages for the owner on foot. On some estates, the tenants are forbidden to sell their products to anyone but the owner, and it is quite common for the owner to give his tenants pigs or chickens to take care of with the obligation of returning them at the end of a certain period with all the young they have had in the meantime.

The herding tasks are those least desired by the tenants because of the responsibilities involved. In many cases, if a sheep dies from illness or as the result of an accident, the native is supposed to bring it in, show it to the owner, give him the skin, take the meat home, and replace the dead sheep with a live one. The tenant's animals work for the estate in return for the pasturage they consume.

Conditions are distinctly better in Ancash, Junín, Ayacucho and Apurimac. In these areas, the tenants receive from one to five hectares of land and are expected to work three to four days a week for the estate at a wage of 2.50 to 3 soles. Their work for the estate is done in the fields, and they rarely have to take turns as domestic servants besides. Even where such service is given, the working conditions are much less difficult than in the south.

Landholding and the conditions under which land is held are matters of outstanding importance in native life. One of the most important measures of personal prestige is the amount of land owned, and the more land a man has the better able he is to meet social obligations which, in turn, bring him further prestige. The more land a man has, the more help he needs in cultivating it. He can expect such help from relatives, so he is inclined to be especially considerate of them. With larger harvests, he is able to serve more and better food and drinks to cooperative work parties than a man with less land would be able to do. Furthermore, he has opportunities to acquire new relatives through the pattern of ceremonial kinship, and relations with ceremonial kinsmen are even closer than those with real kinsmen. There is a belief that godchildren acquire the virtues and the luck of their godparents. Owning land is the native's dearest dream, so that, as we shall see in discussing religion, he cannot conceive of paradise without landownership. He naturally wants the good fortune of landownership for his children, and will not neglect the magical possibilities of choosing a godfather who is well provided with land. Thus, the persons who have the most land are the ones who are asked to be godfathers to most children in the community, and they thus acquire large numbers of *compadres* who respect them and are happy to join their work parties.

Land is a major factor not only in prestige but also in security. The semi-feudal situations found on the estates mean that the native tenants who cultivate estate land are virtually bound to it, without any chance of making new contacts or seeking new opportunities. In order to maintain their rights to estate land, the tenants have to put in most of their time working for the estate and their movements are severely restricted. The contrast between the opportunities of tenants and those of members of free communities can be clearly seen in the case of the community of Recuayhuanca and the neighboring estate of Vicos in the Callejón de Huaylas. Recuayhuanca is a community of small landowners, while Vicos is an estate belonging to the Charitable Foundation of Huaraz, which leases it as a whole instead of administering it directly. The traditional arrangement at Vicos before its lease was taken up by Cornell University was that the tenants owed three days' work a week to the estate and were paid wages for it. Some 90 per cent of the men of Recuayhuanca leave for the coast in the slack season to supplement their income by day labor on the coastal estates. The tenants of Vicos, on the other hand, could not make such trips because they would be immediately evicted from the estate if they did. The greater economic opportunity in Recuayhuanca gives a sense of security which is reflected in the fact that the people are better dressed and their houses are somewhat cleaner and better kept up. They own their houses, while the tenants' houses at Vicos are furnished by the estate. More of the Recuayhuanca people are bilingual and literate.

The principal and almost exclusive occupation of the native is agriculture, whether he is a tenant on an estate, a member of a community, or a small independent landowner. The labor of a tenant farmer is directed by the estate owner if the work is being done for the estate, and the tenant merely carries out plans in which he has no interest beyond fulfilling his contracted obligations or bowing to circumstances. The small independent landowner works with the cooperation of his family and requests aid on a small scale from other individuals, to whom he repays work with work. Because of the small extent of his holdings, the help of his family is usually sufficient to take care of the crops. There are, however, some independent proprietors who have managed to keep or acquire enough land so that they need extra labor, which they get through the institutions of *'ayni* and *minga,* which we will discuss in describing the work patterns of native communities.

The community (commune, "'aynoqa," or "'ayllu") is a grouping of many families which owns or controls varying amounts of land. The variation in size of holdings is particularly notable in those communities in which land is owned individually. In this type of community, the division of property among all the children, which is enforced by law, has resulted, as previously noted, in holdings so small as to be virtually useless in some cases. The only solution is for some owners to sell their lots to other members of the community, while the sellers leave to become tenant farmers on some estate or emigrate to the tropical valleys looking for jobs. The problem varies greatly from one community to another, for some control considerable areas of food land while others have far too little. A classic example of the latter extreme is "Kupir 'Ayllu" at Chinchero, some members of which have received by inheritance no more than two or three furrows of cultivable land (Núñez del Prado 1949:194). In spite of these differences, in most communities the members live in harmony and cooperate effectively with one another.

Those who possess small lots cultivate them in the same way as small independent landowners, with the help of the conjugal family or by entering into an "'ayni" relationship with consanguineous relatives or friends. "'Ayni" ("makimanachiy" in Ecuador) is the loan of work repaid by work of the same kind. Those who have more land need more help to work it, and get this help by means of a *minga* ("mink'a" in Peru, "'uyariy" in Ecuador), which consists of services given in return for food and a fiesta. The word *minga* is used in Ecuador in a different sense, to designate obligatory work done free on public works, community projects, or for an estate. This type of work is known in Peru as *faena;* both terms imply some degree of coercion.

The mechanization of agriculture has scarcely touched the highland estates, and on most of them agricultural work is done with tools and methods of colonial or ancient native origin. The same is true of farms of the natives, to whom, however, farm machinery is beginning to be demonstrated by special agricultural improvement programs under international, state, or private mission auspices (Warisata, Chuquibambilla, Watahata, etc.). In general, however, cultivation on relatively level land is done with a wooden plow to which a steel share is attached; this implement is drawn by oxen. The seed is covered with the plow during the cutting of the next furrow, and re-covered with a drag consisting of a log which is attached transversely to the plowing team in place of the plow.

On steeper land and at higher altitudes, potatoes are planted with the "chaki-taklla" (foot plow), an implement of pre-Conquest origin which consists of a shaft about 1.60 m. long with a foot rest near the lower end. The point is shod with a flat metal share to penetrate the earth. The instrument is thrust almost vertically into the earth with the foot and then pulled down like a lever to turn up a clod of earth. The men manipulate the foot plow and the women work in front of them with wooden clubs to break up the clods. Two men and a woman can plow an area 20 by 20 meters in a full day's work. Other agricultural implements consist of short-handled hoes of different sizes, forked sticks, spades, and a variety of smaller implements made by the natives of wood.

For the most part, the natives raise food crops, the crops varying in kind and importance according to the altitude and the climate. At the highest altitudes (10,000 to 13,000 feet), potatoes, *ocas*, and *ullucus* are the staple crops; cereals like maize, wheat, and barley predominate from 5000 to 10,000 feet; and at lower altitudes maize is grown with manioc, *unkucha,* and a variety of squashes.

The farmer's year begins in August or September and ends with the last harvests in May or June. The highland rainy season lasts from about December to April. Usually only a single crop is grown per season. The smallest fruits or tubers are selected from the harvest for seed, the largest ones sold, and the medium-size ones eaten. Methods of cultivation vary according to the depth of the soil and the water supply. In most cases, irrigation water is not available and crops must be grown without it. Animal manure is the only fertilizer available, and it is little used except on some estates. The manure is furnished in part by sheep belonging to the tenants, and some estate owners in Bolivia will not accept a new tenant who does not have a certain number of sheep which will produce manure for fertilizer. The manure question can then be used to keep the tenants on the land, for a landowner can refuse to allow a tenant who wishes to leave to take his sheep with him, and no other estate would accept the tenant without them.

From the point of view of land utilization, the major problem in the situation we have been describing is that the big estates, which own much of the best land, make a minimum use of it, while the native farmers, who practice an intensive cultivation, have comparatively little land to work with and what they have is often poor. At the same time, land is a major symbol of social prestige among mestizos as well as natives, and this factor causes it to be priced for sale, in some cases, at exorbitant figures which bear no relation to its productivity. Aníbal Buitrón tells me that this situation occurs in Imbabura (Ecuador), for example.

In spite of the difficulties involved, there have been some interesting recent cases in which the tenants on an estate formed a cooperative organization to purchase the whole estate for distribution in individual lots. I am thinking of the Hacienda Chunazaná in Azuay, Ecuador (Instituto Ecuatoriano de Antropología y Geografía, ms.) and the Hacienda Luemos in Apurimac, Peru. In both cases, the sale was negotiated directly between the native tenants and owners who were willing to be paid in installments. The natives made heroic efforts to raise the necessary money, selling everything that they had in order to do so, and in many cases borrowing money at very high interest to meet the later payments. The relatively defenseless condition of the natives leaves them at the mercy of mestizo speculators in situations of this kind.

Education

Informal education among the natives is given by the parents according to sex, and is supplemented by full participation in the activities of the community. During the earliest years, the mother guides the child's discipline by caresses and affection, while later it learns by imitation and personal experience in the activities appropriate to its sex. A boy learns first from his father and then from other men with whom he works. A girl learns chiefly from her mother's example and teaching, with a somewhat lesser opportunity to imitate the behavior of other adult women. Fiestas and cooperative labor give good opportunities to broaden and stimulate the children's development. Education is thus strongly traditional and especially oriented to teach the children how to work. A life close to the flocks, frequent attendance at adult fiestas, frank discussion by adults of pregnancy and birth, and the opportunities provided by life in a one-room house to be present at these events, give the children a perfectly natural introduction to everything connected with normal sex life. This perhaps is the reason why they lack the restless curiosity and concern with such matters which are so frequent in mestizo children. They have never been taught any special valuation on virginity and, at adolescence, have a certain liberty to satisfy their urges, since pre-matrimonial sex relations are permissible within limits at the proper age. They are thus well prepared for adult sex life, and prostitution is very rare. Adultery and sex crimes are even more unusual.

On the other hand, their participation in community activities and frequent dealings with adults give them an early understanding of all matters relating to the functioning of their society. It is not unusual to find children of seven or eight years of age who can give very exact and detailed information about community problems, the local authorities who govern them, and even the specific duties of these authorities. Granting the difference in the scope of knowledge required, it may be said that a native man knows more of his culture than a white man does of his.

Native children almost never play. It is not that they have no desire to play, nor that they are "sad" or "melancholy" as is often said, but that the values of their culture are directed toward work. The native believes that games are nothing but a preparation for indolence and hence is displeased when children play and puts pressure on them to stop it. This attitude is not the result of a concern for time wasted but rather of a traditional concept of the nature and function of playing.

Formal education for natives is generally very deficient and its results meager. The schools are provided by the state or by religious bodies and are mestizo, not native institutions. The mestizos are not particularly concerned about native education and the natives are suspicious of mestizo efforts in this direction. In all the places visited by the I.L.O. mission where there were schools, the number of literates is minimum. We found one case in which a school had been functioning for more than ten years without teaching a single person to read. Among the factors responsible for this type of situation, the following may be noted: (1) lack of understanding of rural conditions on the part of the teachers, (2) resistance on the part of the natives to sending their children to school, (3) teaching methods poorly adapted to the conditions, and (4) the language difference. Each of these factors deserves some comment.

(1) In the three countries with which we are concerned, native education is in the hands of three types of teachers: untrained ones, religious teachers, and teachers with a certificate. Untrained teachers are persons with no qualifications for the work, usually from the towns, who secure appointments through personal influence and worry about learning how to teach when they enter the schools to which they were appointed. Religious teachers are primarily interested in "saving souls" and are little concerned with matters that might be useful to the natives in this life. An exception must be made here for a few Protestant mission schools which are doing something along these lines. However, in many cases their work only increases the natives' problems since conversion produces conflicts between religious groups and division within the communities.

The training of certificated teachers takes place in two types of centers: schools for urban teachers and schools for rural teachers. Graduates of schools for urban teachers have been trained to work in a cultural situation quite different from that of the natives, but some get sent to rural schools because there are no vacancies in the urban ones. They accept these appointments as a stopgap until they can get an urban job, have no interest in their work, and take the first opportunity to get back into the kind of teaching they were trained for. There are two kinds of normal schools for rural teachers, one in the cities (the Normal Rural de Santa Rosa in Cuzco is an example) and the other in the country. The students at both types of schools are whites and mestizos of urban background. The training given in the city normal schools is highly sophisticated and bookish, with no opportunities to observe, let alone participate in, the life of the people whom they will be expected to teach in the future. They know nothing of the conditions of rural life and receive no orientation in the subject. There is a similar narrowness about the training given in the normal schools located in the country; it is mainly theoretical, with some instruction in farming practice given on the school grounds. In many cases, the student teachers see natives only when the latter come to the school to sell some of their products. Such schools are an extension of city life which is in the country but not of it. One of the few cases in which a normal school has attempted to prepare teachers for rural problems is the Centro Normal Rural of Warisata, Bolivia.

The main problem involved is the existence of marked cultural differences between the mestizos who staff the schools and the natives who are expected to attend them. The teachers are not fully aware of these differences, have not been trained to deal with them, and do not succeed in crossing the gulf which separates them from their students.

(2) The resistance of the natives to sending their children to school is notorious. There have been many cases in which it was necessary to use the police power to get the children to school. There are very good reasons for this resistance, however. In the first place, the school is a mestizo institution, as we have noted, and the natives are suspicious of it as such. In the second place, native children begin very young to contribute to family subsistence by helping in the fields or with the care of the animals, and their help can be ill-spared at home. Finally, the unsatisfactory results of existing school programs have discredited the school system. Absenteeism is somewhat less now than formerly and is commoner in the case of girls than of boys. The natives explained to me that it was because the girls were needed for herding.

(3) The greater part of the teaching methods used in the schools are ones devised for West European-type conditions and cultural values. No attempt has yet been made to study the conditions and cultural values of native life with a view to adapting teaching methods to them. An outstanding example of the problems involved is provided by the general application in the schools of the method of recreational teaching, that is, combining teaching with games. This practice conflicts directly with the native attitude toward games, which are regarded as a preparation for indolence. When parents find out that their children go to school to play games, they tend to take them out of school immediately. The experience creates antagonism in the community toward the school. In Taraco (Puno, Peru) the parents all complained to me that the teachers were teaching their children to play games and accustoming them to this type of behavior.

(4) In the regions visited by the I.L.O. mission, most of the natives speak the Inca language (Quechua), except in northern Bolivia and part of the Department of Puno in Peru where Aymara is spoken. The vast majority of the native population speaks no Spanish, and the percentage is higher among women than among men. This situation affects the schools directly, for school textbooks are uniform by law and the texts are in Spanish. Native parents are generally interested in having their children learn Spanish as a measure of protection or to better their social position, but it is difficult to find school time for this subject

in a school system in which the rules were devised for children who know Spanish to begin with.

Religion

It is not possible to classify native religion as wholly Christian or wholly pagan. Catholic worship coexists with a series of practices and beliefs which constitute perhaps the strongest and most influential part of native spiritual life. The native's supernatural world is populated by spirits of the earth, of the mountains, of springs, of animals, and of plants, and he dedicates to them a series of practices directed sometimes toward warding off their powers and sometimes to making them propitious. These practices are often confused or mixed with Catholic ideas and rites, but certain distinctions can nevertheless be made. Life on this earth is more closely linked with natural forces and the spirits which govern them. The success of the harvest depends in large part on the offerings which have been made to the earth, on the farmer's relation with the "'awki" and the "'apu" (mountain spirits), and on whether or not the winds, the hail, and the frost are favorably inclined toward him. Health and sickness depend in large part on springs, rocks, and trees, and on unknown beings provided with evil spirits. On the other hand, there is a second aspect of native spiritual life which revolves around Catholic worship and which is concerned with social relations and their expression in the fiesta, and with life after death. Both types of religious behavior have their own specialists. Those of the world of native spirits are the "paqo," the "'altu-misayoq," and the *brujo* (witch), followed by a school of curers and herbalists or people who "know" certain practices (Morote 1951:156; Rubio 1946:309; Núñez del Prado 1952:8). The world of Catholic worship is directed by the Catholic priest and the sacristan.

Beliefs and practices relating to agriculture and health include propitiatory rites for the crops, prayers for rain, exorcism of frost, hail, and evil winds, the etiology of diseases, and their diagnosis and treatment. A great variety of causes of illness are recognized. The patient himself may even have caused the illness by some action, and he may in some cases be the source of his cure, when for example he is treated with his own urine or a woman is treated with menstrual fluid.

These concepts of the forces of nature play a very important role in native life, and it is worth-while commenting in greater detail on curing practices and their function. The "paqo," "'altu-misayoq," or *brujo* is a person of great prestige in society, feared because of the supernatural source of his powers. Persons who have been struck by lightning without being killed, for example, thereby acquire supernatural powers. The "paqo" has the power to summon the mountain spirits "'awki" and

" 'apu" and ask them to punish someone with sickness, cure someone, or carry off his soul so that he will go on living without it. His power is enormous and he belongs to the highest rank of curers. His reputation often extends over wide areas and his fees are high. He is generally consulted only in the most serious cases, and his treatment is of a magical nature. Less dangerous illnesses are diagnosed and treated by a less awe-inspiring person, the "maych'a" or curer. His diagnoses nearly always contain a magical element, for he makes them by finding out first the symptoms and the possible causes of sickness and then choosing between the causes by divination. For divining, he may use coca leaves or grains of maize, or boil the patient's urine with certain salts, or rub the patient with a guinea pig and then cut it open and look for organs affected by the patient's illness. His treatment is based on herbal and other medicines, and follows the principle of the hot and cold classification of medicines and diseases, according to which a "hot" remedy is given for a "cold" disease and vice versa (Morote 1951:123). The medicines are administered as liquids to be drunk, poultices, etc., usually with prayers and invocations, and clearly require faith on the part of the patient. These curers have great prestige among the natives. In both Peru and Ecuador, the curers claim that there is a difference in the effectiveness of their medicines as applied to natives or mestizos, and that the bodies of the two groups react differently to them. It is widely believed that what is good for the white man will harm the Indian and vice versa.

The elaborate and highly rationalized system of native medicine just described naturally provides resistance to Western medicine and public health measures. Nevertheless, campaigns in which the objective utility of vaccination and DDT were successfully demonstrated have brought about the acceptance of both these measures by the natives to such an extent that they request the treatment in some cases.

The aspect of native religion most closely connected with Catholic worship is that relating to the future life. Heaven is conceived of as a fertile region of productive land and abundant irrigation water where people work and have abundant harvests. God lives there in a special place, surrounded by the saints who are his relatives. Hell is a land of fire. A person's destination in the other life is determined by his conduct in this life and the contributions he has made for the support of the Catholic cult. God or the saints can also send punishments and grant rewards on earth. The natives believe in God and the saints and frequently invoke them together with the " 'apu" and " 'awki."

People seek to establish relationships to God and the saints through the Catholic Church, and these relationships are expressed in fiestas which are occasions of pleasure and provide relief from the troubles of everyday life. The fiesta is organized in the name of a saint by a person who accepts the responsibility of making the arrangements and paying the expenses. This responsibility is called a *cargo* (obligation), *alferazgo*, or *mayordomía* in different parts of the Andean area, and it is a fixed point of reference by which a person's social position is determined. No one who has been designated by the community to undertake a *cargo* would dare to refuse, for to do so would entail a sort of moral death and absolute renunciation of all chances of gaining community respect. No excuse whatever would save him from the condemnation and ill will of his neighbors. As Professor Rubio says, "An Indian is not considered a man among his fellows until he has sponsored at least one fiesta. The epithet '*Mana cargu yallishca*' (one who has held no *cargo*) is not only the worst insult that can be offered among them but implies a sort of dishonesty" (Rubio 1946:299). *Cargos* are expensive, and often the person designated has to spend all that he has, sell his animals and land, mortgage them, or emigrate for a year or more to some other region where wages are high in order to earn enough to pay for it. Families in this situation often move for a time to the tropical valleys, the gold washings, or the mines to earn money for a fiesta and come home with malaria or tuberculosis acquired under difficult work conditions in an unfamiliar climate. Even after the *cargo* is paid for, the family faces a long struggle to recover its former economic position—and then very likely is designated for another *cargo*.

It should be noted that men very rarely volunteer for a *cargo*. In most cases a man is chosen against his will and persuaded to accept it when he is drunk. Social pressure then keeps him from backing out. Both Church and State have laws against forcing an unwilling man to accept a *cargo*, but social pressure is a very difficult phenomenon to control by legislation. Furthermore, many mestizos have a financial interest in the fiestas, and hence in the *cargo* system which pays for them, so that the system is not entirely unrelated to the picture of exploitation which we drew in discussing land and agriculture.

Several important aspects of native life, such as local government and military service, have not been covered in this review, but enough has been said to indicate the importance of considering the social and economic relationships between natives and mestizos in any study in which either group is the main focus of interest. The problems are important ones, and they will not go away simply because we ignore them.

TRANSLATOR'S NOTE

The translator has made a few changes and brief additions necessitated by the process of abridgment and by the differences in background between an English-speaking and an Andean Spanish-speaking public; these changes are based on conversations with the author.

The term "native" is used throughout to translate *indígena* in the original. In some contexts, the author is using this term in deliberate contrast to *indio* (Indian) which, in the Cuzco area, is now used almost exclusively as a social-class term.

Words in quotation marks are written in the Inca alphabet (Rowe, 1950); other non-English words are italicized. Some of them are Spanish, others Inca or Aymara or a mixture of Spanish and Inca elements. These words are given in their commonest Spanish spelling. [J.H.R.]

EDITOR'S NOTE

The Andean nations, like the rest of Latin America, are undergoing rapid change in reaction to a variety of social forces. This is reflected in the fact that some of the patterns described in this article are being displaced, notably those of land tenure and agricultural labor relations. The centuries-old social order is being transformed—in a self-consciously revolutionary manner in Bolivia; more gradually in Peru and Ecuador—and it is still too early to discern what may become the most significant new patterns. [D.B.H.]

REFERENCES CITED

Buitrón, Aníbal and Buitrón, Barbara Salisbury
1947 *El campesino de la provincia de Pichincha,* Quito, Instituto Nacional de Previsión, Departamento de Propaganda.

Cisneros Cisneros, César
1948 *Demografía y estadística sobre el indio ecuatoriano,* Quito, Talleres Gráficos Nacionales.

Flores, Edmundo

1950 "El problema agrario del Perú," *Trimestre Económico* 17:3:-355–395, Mexico.

Instituto Ecuatoriano de Antropología y Geografía

1952 *Chunazaná: informe del Instituto Ecuatoriano de Antropología y Geografía,* Quito. (Manuscript.)

Morote Best, Efraín

1951 "La vivienda campesina en Sallaq: con un panorama de la cultura total," *Tradición* 2:3:96–193, Cuzco.

Núñez del Prado, Oscar

1949 "Chinchero; un pueblo andino del sur (algunos aspectos)," *Revista Universitaria* 38:97:177–230, Cuzco.

1952 *La vida y la muerte en Chinchero,* Cuzco, Talleres Gráficos "La Económica."

1953 "Problemas antropológicas del área andina (Perú-Bolivia-Ecuador)," *Revista Universitaria* 42:104:272–320, Cuzco.

Rowe, John H.

1950 "Sound Patterns in Three Inca Dialects," *International Journal of American Linguistics* 16:3:137–148, Baltimore.

Rubio Orbe, Gonzalo

1946 *Nuestros indios (estudio geográfico, histórico y social de los indios ecuatorianos, especialmente aplicado a la provincia de Imbabura),* Quito, Imprenta de la Universidad, 1947.

United Nations

1951 *Report of the United Nations Mission of Technical Assistance to Bolivia,* United Nations Technical Assistance Administration, ST/TAA/K/Bolivia/1, New York.

Regionalism and Cultural Unity in Brazil

CHARLES WAGLEY

For both practical and theoretical reasons there is an increasing interest among social scientists in the study of the contemporary cultures of foreign nations and areas of the world. The so-called "area study" aims to present an integrated picture of the culture pattern of an area or nation rather than a series of unrelated studies dealing with single aspects of that culture. The anthropologist, with experience in dealing with primitive societies as integrated culture patterns, has much to contribute. But while for the Trobriand Islanders one man—the anthropologist—attempted to be at once the economist, the linguist, the sociologist, the historian, the student of literature, the study of modern complex civilizations calls for the cooperation and collaboration of specialists in several disciplines of the social sciences and the humanities toward a unified goal. Furthermore, there does not seem to be any widely accepted concept of the geographic and cultural units to be studied. Should one study Latin America, Brazil, or a single valley in Brazil? A taxonomic classification of the major forms of world cultures and their special varieties would provide a framework for further analysis and objective study.

Reprinted from *Social Forces,* 1948, XXVI, 457–464, by permission of the author and publisher.

Recently, Dr. John Gillin in an article in *Social Forces* has presented a very useful concept of a modern Latin American culture,[1] with common patterns and values distinguishing it from other varieties of Western culture. The institutions, culture elements, and values which unify modern Latin American culture are, according to Dr. Gillin, mainly Iberian, and are derived from a common Spanish heritage and common experience under Spanish colonial rule. This modern Latin American (or "Creole") culture, although found throughout Central and South America, has many areal, regional, and local forms due to great differences in natural environment and in the influence of various indigenous cultures. Although Dr. Gillin deals primarily with Spanish American countries, many of the elements he describes in Latin American culture apply to Brazil despite its Portuguese heritage. Yet, Brazil must be thought of, in the writer's opinion, as a unique and important variant of Latin American culture. Furthermore, because Brazil as a nation and as a cultural unit is so large, there are important regional forms of Brazilian culture to be taken into account. The present article is an attempt to classify Brazil into various regional subcultures and to relate the national culture to modern Latin American culture in general.

Throughout the immense area of modern Brazil (3,286,170 square miles), over a third of the land surface of South America, people share a set of basic culture patterns, in the main inherited from Portugal, but strongly flavored with African and American Indian elements. With the exception of a few unassimilated Europeans and a relatively few forest Indians, all people in Brazil (41,065,083 inhabitants) speak one language—Portuguese. Unlike the neighboring highland countries such as Peru and Bolivia, Brazil does not contain peoples who speak distinct languages (e.g., Spanish and Aymara in Bolivia) and who have distinct cultures (e.g., Spanish and Spanish-Indian). As compared with other great political units of the world such as China, India, and the U.S.S.R., Brazil is a country with a homogeneous national culture.

Yet, both native and foreign writers on Brazil constantly refer to the various regions of Brazil and are impressed with cultural diversity from one part of this country to another. In Brazil, the man in the street has stereotyped ideas as to the personality structure and behavior patterns of his fellow citizens from various parts of the country. The "Paulista" from the state of São Paulo is thought to be an energetic, efficient business man. The "Gaucho" from Rio Grande do Sul in the extreme South is a cowboy with rather crude manners. The "Carioca," the inhabitant of Rio de Janeiro, is sly and urbane, and the "Cearense" from the northeastern state of Ceará is a keen commercial man and a wandering exile, driven out of his beloved homeland by drought. Such stereotypes have some basis in fact. Different ecological conditions and different historical factors, combined with poor communications between one part of this huge country and another, have produced rather clear-cut regions of Brazil, each with its characteristic version of Brazilian national culture.

Most social scientists who are interested in Brazilian problems recognize regional differences, but only recently has the problem been approached with intensive and objective research methods. Each student of Brazil tends to divide the country on the basis of the major interest of his own field of specialization. That is, a geographer, an economist, an historian, an agronomist, tend to see the map of Brazil somewhat differently. Yet most of them agree on the main outlines of the principal regions, and their differences are due chiefly to the criteria they use in defining regions and to the confusion of state boundaries with subcultural areas. Based on a combination of criteria such as climate, surface features, racial composition of the population, historical past, and modern cultural patterns and institutions, it seems to the writer that modern Brazil may be tentatively divided into six major regions: the Amazon Valley, the Northeast Coast, the arid Northeast, the extreme South, the industrial Middle States, and finally the "Wild West" Frontier.

The Amazon Valley is a tropical, humid, low area covered for the most part by thick, monotonous forest, although grassy plains and occasional ranges of hills do occur. The great river system formed by the Amazon and its tributaries has provided man with an easy mode of transportation, and the majority of the Amazon people live along the water routes. The tropical forest provides the characteristic economic activities of the region—the collecting of forest products (Brazil nuts, rubber, palm nuts, hardwoods, *timbó* vine, etc.). The Amazon population has a strong American Indian component, and the Indian has contributed more to the culture of the Amazon region than to any other part of Brazil. Only a few Negro slaves were imported into the region, and the basic population of the Valley consists of Portuguese and Indian mixtures.[2] The culture of rural inhabitants is strongly flavored by American Indian culture patterns. Until the nineteenth century, *lingua geral*, a modified form of the aboriginal Tupí-Guaraní tongue, was the most commonly spoken language of the area. Amazon agricultural techniques, folk beliefs, and folklore are basically American Indian patterns. Medicine men who cure the sick by sucking and massaging practice in small Amazon towns, and Amazon folktales tell of Zurupari, a forest demon who was formerly an Indian supernatural. The Amazon region is characterized by a distinctive ecology, a pronounced residue of Indian culture patterns in the modern culture, and a strong American Indian element in the population.

To the south and east of the Amazon basin lies the arid *sertão* of Brazil. It is a region of scrub forest, cactus, and low thorny bushes.

There are low mesas and a few mountain ranges. Periodic droughts occurring each eight to fifteen years are recorded as far back as 1710–11, and during each of these droughts thousands of people die and additional thousands are forced to migrate to other regions of Brazil. The typical economic pursuit of the region is grazing. Agriculture is only profitable in a few oases where there is a steady water supply and irrigation produces magnificent yields. The typical *sertanejo*, as the rural inhabitants of this region are called, is a cowboy, and his leather garb used to protect him from the thorny bushes is characteristic of the arid Northeast. The northeastern rural inhabitant shows strong indications of his American Indian ancestry, for it was not profitable to bring Negro slaves into this region, and the Portuguese landowners used Indians to care for their herds. This region is famous for religious fanatics and for numerous outlaw bands. The fanatic religious movement led by Antonio Conselheiro, described by Euclides da Cunha in the Brazilian classic *Os sertões*,[3] occurred in this region and has been repeated on a minor scale several times since. Bandit bands, such as that of *Lampeão* (The Lamp), were common in the region until a few years back. Despite the ravages of drought, the arid Northeast is still one of the most densely populated areas of Brazil (14.1 per square kilometer for Ceará as compared with 4.9 per square kilometer for Brazil as a whole). Despite the strength of American Indian elements in the population, the Indian has not influenced the culture of the arid Northeast to the degree that it has the Amazon. The culture patterns of this region are basically Iberian but strongly marked by the necessity of adapting human life to a hostile and inhospitable environment.

The Northeast Coast region somewhat south of the so-called bulge on the Brazilian coastline contrasts violently with both the arid *sertão* and the humid Amazon. This strip of coast, with a regular rainfall and a fertile red soil, was the scene of a rich sugar economy during the seventeenth and eighteenth centuries. Profits from sugar attracted wealthy families from Portugal, and the need for labor was solved by the importation of slaves from Africa. The Negroid element is therefore stronger in the modern population of the Northeast Coast than in any other portion of the country. And, as one might expect, African culture elements are more numerous in the modern culture of the Northeast Coast than elsewhere in Brazil. Such typical foods as *vatapá* (dendê oil, peanuts, rice flour, fish, shrimp, and various spices) and *acarajé* (beans fried in dendê oil) were adopted from African slaves. The *macumba* or *candomblé*, the religious cult of African origin which corresponds to the Haitian *vodun*, is found in great strength in this region. The folklore of the region is a mixture of African and Iberian tales for the most part. Culture patterns derived from Africa as well as the traditions inherited from the aristocratic plantation system distinguish this region from the rest of the country. This is the region described by Gilberto Freyre in his *Casa grande e senzala*.[4] Although the plantations of the Northeast Coast have long since lost their preeminence as sugar producers, plantation-type agriculture is still the characteristic economic activity of the region. Sugar, cacao, tobacco, fruits, and castor beans are grown.

The three southernmost states of Brazil, namely Paraná, Santa Catarina, and Rio Grande do Sul, are temperate in climate in contrast to the semi-tropical and tropical climate of the rest of Brazil. The southern portion of the region is *pampa*, the great rolling prairie which extends into Uruguay and Argentina. The Brazilian *pampa*, like the *pampa* across the border to the south, is an area of grazing. The Gaucho, the Brazilian cowboy of the *pampa*, shares with his counterpart in Uruguay and Argentina many culture patterns such as the *bola*, the wide breeches cut something like plus fours, a colorful poncho, a wide hat, the habit of drinking maté tea in a gourd vessel through a tube, a meat diet, and a life on horseback. In the states of Paraná and Santa Catarina, the *pampa* fades into great stretches of pine forest very different from the rain forests somewhat to the north. These pine forests cover rich fertile soil and the region has attracted a large number of settlers from Europe (Germany, Poland, Italy, Switzerland, etc.). There are almost one million people in southern Brazil of German descent, and some 500,000 Poles and their descendants. These Europeans, especially the Germans, have resisted assimilation tenaciously and their influence upon the culture of the region has been profound. Farming techniques, crops, language, and house types, to mention only a few culture traits, show this European influence. The extreme South, therefore, is characterized by two varieties of Brazilian culture—the recent European and the Luso-Brazilian Gaucho. The two groups have combined to create in the South the most energetic and dynamic region of the country.

The Middle States of São Paulo, Minas Gerais, Rio de Janeiro, and part of Espirito Santo, form a region which today might well be called industrial Brazil. Within this region are found the two great cities of the country, Rio de Janeiro, with almost 2,000,000 inhabitants, and the city of São Paulo, with more than 1,300,000 inhabitants. Most of Brazil's motor roads and railways, most of its heavy industry, most of its modern universities, research laboratories, trade schools, and cultural institutions, and most of its commercial farming are found in this part of Brazil. It is this region of Brazil where modern Western technology has been introduced most successfully and from which modern Western culture diffuses to the rest of the country.

Industrialization and a modern system of communication have in recent years smothered old cultural differences. Formerly, this region contained three distinct local traditions, which have not yet been forgotten by Brazilians. The state of Rio de Janeiro, during the colonial epoch, was developed by sugar planters who brought numerous slaves, and the colonial system of Rio de Janeiro was similar to that of the Northeast Coast. In contrast, the state of São Paulo was the home of the adventurous *bandeirantes,* who penetrated into the interior of South America during the sixteenth and seventeenth centuries in search of gold and slaves. São Paulo was the center of the rich coffee industry in the late nineteenth and early twentieth centuries, and wealth from coffee attracted immigrants from abroad and from other Brazilian regions. São Paulo today is the richest Brazilian state and the center of Brazilian financial and industrial life. The state of Minas Gerais owes its importance in the colonial period to the discovery of rich mineral deposits in the seventeenth century. Gold made this state the richest portion of Brazil for a time and an important political center of colonial Brazil. Residues of these differences in historical development are still retained in the rural areas of these Middle States, but for the most part they have given way nowadays to a standardized Brazilian version of modern machine culture.

West of these industrial Middle States, in the heart of South America, in the states of Goias and Mato Grosso, lies a great modern frontier. The territory between the Xingu and Tapajos rivers in Mato Grosso is only partially explored. It is inhabited only by a few tribes of Indians who are among the few remaining untouched savages of the world. Other areas of this great frontier "Far West" are already partially settled, and the social conditions usually associated with the frontier are present. Law and order are loosely organized; there are well-known bad men with several killings to their credit, and citizens in small towns go about armed. Prospectors and placer miners constantly explore the hinterlands, and boom towns grow up over night when they make an important find. The Far West at this particular time in its history is a region only inasmuch as it reflects a dynamic frontier culture. The population is drawn from all regions of Brazil and contains Europeans, Negroes, Indians, and mixtures of every conceivable degree of these three elements. Much of the Far West is good farming and grazing land, and Brazil has under way a movement called "The March of the West" to attract Brazilians from the Coast into this undeveloped region.

Within each of these six Brazilian regions, differences exist in contemporary culture as between socioeconomic classes and between urban and rural groups. In each region, with the exception of the Far West frontier, there are large cities, and in these cities the upper classes, at least, live in a manner which differs only slightly from their counterparts in Rio de Janeiro and São Paulo. Yet each of these urban centers reflects strongly the region of which it is the economic and cultural center. The basic economic activity of the region provides a major industry for the city. The population of the city has approximately the same racial components as the region. A large proportion of the population of the city, many of whom originated in the surrounding rural areas, share the current folk culture of the region. Porto Alegre, for example, the largest city of the extreme South, has meat packing as an important industry, and there are a large number of Germans in the population. Belem, the major center of the Amazon region, is the export center of forest products, and the population of Belem is basically Iberian-Indian mixtures, as it is throughout the entire Amazon.

These six regions, as indicated in their bare outlines, present, to my mind, specialized versions of a Brazilian national culture. Despite such marked differences from one region of Brazil to another, however, there seems to me to be a general framework of cultural uniformity, which characterizes Brazil as a nation and as a distinct cultural area apart from the other national and regional cultures of the Western Hemisphere and from European cultures in general. As Gilberto Freyre says in his *Brazil: An Interpretation*,[5] there is over all Brazil a "healthy minimum of cultural basic uniformity" which is composed for the most part of Portuguese, therefore of European, culture patterns and values. Although American Indian influences are strong in one part of the country, African influences in another, and recent European influences in still another, it was the Portuguese who were the governors and, in a broad sense, the creators, of Brazil as a nation. Portuguese settlers formed an important component of the Brazilian people from the Amazon Valley in the North to the *pampa* in the extreme South. The Portuguese in a sense might be thought of as forming the common denominator of all Brazil.

Because so many of its basic patterns and values derive from Portugal, Brazil therefore shares many common culture traits and institutions with all so-called Latin cultures. As Dr. Gillin has pointed out, Latin American culture is Roman Catholic in religion, and this Catholicism is Iberian in its emphasis on the cult of the saints, public fiestas, monastic orders, and religious brotherhoods. "Ideologically this culture (of modern Latin America) is humanistic rather than puritanical . . . and intellectually it is characterized by logic and dialectics rather than empiricism and pragmatics."[6] In Latin America the family is an exceptionally strong and solid unit. There is a strong double standard of sexual morality. There is a wide extension of kinship terms, and patterns of ceremonial kinship (godparenthood) are used for greater social solidarity. Latin American towns are built with a plaza plan in contrast to our Main Street plan, and their houses are generally placed flush in the street with no front yard. Latin American patterns of law and legal procedure follow Roman Law as developed by the Code Napoléon rather than Anglo-American patterns which we know. These and many other cultural institutions and elements are common to all Latin American cultures, and, in a sense, are characteristic of Brazil.

Yet, the national culture of Brazil is clearly distinguishable from other Latin cultures. It differs not only in specific institutions and formal patterns peculiar to itself, but in the singularly Brazilian interpretation given to features which are held in common with other Latin cultures. The result is a different culture configuration, a different way of life and a different way of looking at the world.

Such differences in form and in meaning of culture patterns result from ecology, from the Portuguese variety of Iberian culture, from the aboriginal American Indian cultures encountered in the area, from the strong influences from Africa, and from the unique fusion of all these elements in the historical development of the country. The aboriginal people of Brazil, although few in number when compared to those of West Coast South America, had a culture especially adapted to the semi-tropical and tropical environment. They had an influence on the culture of Brazil out of keeping with their small numbers. The Portuguese suffered less from religious fervor than their Spanish neighbors and they were, and still are, famous for their lack of racial prejudice. The large number of African slaves (estimated at over 3,300,000 from 1600–1900) gave a special tone to Brazilian culture. As the only Portuguese colony in America, Brazil was isolated through a strict mercantile policy from the other American colonies and its historical development differed from that of the Spanish American countries. Brazil was first an Empire, then a Republic, and the class structure of the Empire with its native nobility, the "Barons of the Empire," was unique in America. The mother country, Portugal, was a minor nation in the nineteenth century and as soon as Brazil gained political freedom, it looked down on Portugal and turned to France, even more than did other Latin American countries, as a center of cultural influence.

Most apparent of the cultural features which distinguish Brazil from the other countries and culture areas of America is language. Not only is Brazil the only country in the Western Hemisphere in which the people speak Portuguese, but Brazilian Portuguese is quite different from that spoken in Portugal. Brazilian Portuguese has such a different intonation and vocabulary from the language of Portugal that there is never any doubt which language is being spoken. Brazilian Portuguese has developed so many local expressions and has borrowed so many terms, foreign to the mother tongue, from native languages (both American Indian and African) as well as from other European languages, that a recent arrival from Lisbon would have about the same trouble understanding what is said in a Brazilian café as an Englishman in an American fraternity house.

With difference in language, both from English, Spanish, and

Portuguese of Portugal, goes a multitude of subtle cultural differences reflected by language such as modes of address, concepts of beauty, and expressions of values and attitudes. The Brazilian expression of endearment, *minha nega* (literally, "my Negress"), used sometimes by a white man to his white wife reflects the peculiar Brazilian memories of warm personal relations with Negroes as nursemaids and as personal servants.[7] The *é mato* (literally, "it is forest") used to express superabundance of anything can only be understood in terms of the overabundant forests in Brazil.

Although race mixture is a common phenomenon in most Latin American countries, nowhere in the Western Hemisphere has race mixture taken place to the extent it has in Brazil. The Brazilian attitude toward race is one of the characteristic traits of the national culture. Although Brazilians are not without certain racial prejudice, as is shown by the claim of some Brazilian whites that they feel a revulsion from the *catinga do preto* (smell of the Negro), in general one finds that in Brazil less emphasis is placed on color as a symbol of superiority or inferiority than elsewhere in Latin America. Even the caste system of colonial times with its numerous slaves and its plantation aristocracy seems to have been tempered by the Brazilian lack of racial antagonism. During the Empire, men of slave ancestry and low birth rose to high positions in the Brazilian aristocracy and monarchical system. There were mulatto barons and viscounts during the Empire, and the Crown Princess herself is said to have made a point of dancing with André Rebouças, a noted engineer and a dark mulatto, when she noticed that a lady had refused him a dance, presumably because of his color.

In all Latin American cultures there is an emphasis on family ties, but in Brazil it might be almost said that there is a cult of the family. Although present-day conditions with smaller houses, apartments, and industrial life have brought profound changes in the Brazilian family, it is still a relatively large and decidedly intimate group. The social life of many Brazilians is carried on predominantly with relatives. There are birthday parties, baptisms, weddings, and family gatherings. The group of relatives is remarkably large; kinship terms are applied to individuals for whom kinship would have been forgotten in other countries. A father's first or second cousin may be called "Uncle" and his children may be "cousins." The spouse of a distant "cousin" is often called "cousin." Beyond any possible kinship connection, solidarity is assured in Brazil by the godparent relationship (*padrinho*, *madrinha*, and *afilhado*) which is set up at baptism, at confirmation, and at marriage. It is common in Brazil at marriage for each participant to invite one man and one woman to act as godparents at the religious ceremony and a different pair for each in the civil ceremony. The couple thus garners eight new godparents at marriage. In Brazil "cousins" and godparents are used to facilitate official and commercial relations; small favors and special considerations may be asked of a *parente* (relative) or of a *padrinho* (godfather). This extraordinary extension of the terms of relationship and the use of these ceremonial relationships to extend family ties is considered *muito Brasileiro* (very Brazilian) by Brazilians themselves.

Brazilian foods and food habits differ from those of the surrounding Latin American cultures. Although each of the various regions of Brazil is famous for special dishes, such as the Afro-Brazilian dishes of Bahia and *churrasco* (a barbecue) of Rio Grande do Sul, over most of the entire country *farinha* (manioc flour), black beans, rice, dried beef (*charque*), and coffee form the basis of meals. *Goiabada* (guava paste) and *marmelada* (quince paste) with a piece of cheese are desserts known in every part of Brazil. Except in the maté-drinking area of South Brazil, nothing is more typically Brazilian than the small cups of black coffee, the *cafézinho,* served several times a day in Brazilian homes and offices. Spain and Spanish American countries are famous for their late dinners. In Brazil, breakfast is coffee and milk with a piece of bread or manioc cake *(beijú),* lunch is traditionally at 10:30 to 11:00 A.M. and dinner at about 5:00 P.M. followed by a light supper before retiring. In Brazilian cities, these traditional hours for meals have been modified by the necessities of modern commercial and industrial life in the direction of the meal hours of Paris or New York.

Numerous other culture patterns differentiate Brazil from the rest of Latin America. The Carnival period before Lent, although it is celebrated in most Catholic countries, is the most important festival of the year to Brazilians, overshadowing both patriotic and religious holidays. The zeal with which the Brazilian people lose themselves in dancing and music for four days and the manner of celebrating Carnival are not found elsewhere. The music they sing and the style of dancing is uniquely Brazilian. The music and the dance which is known abroad by the generic term of *samba* (in Brazil there are local terms and local varieties) is quite distinct from the Argentine tango, Cuban rumba, Mexican folk music, and North American jazz. Other festivals, such as *São João* (on June 24th), are celebrated in Brazil in a specifically Brazilian manner. On the great Brazilian plantations, St. John's day was the equivalent of Christmas on the southern plantations of the United States during colonial times.[8] There were great dances in the *Casa grande* and in the slave quarters the Negroes danced their *sambas* around large bonfires. There were special foods, songs, and music for the occasion. Even nowadays Brazilians celebrate the Eve of St. John by building large bonfires, roasting sweet potatoes, sending up paper balloons, and setting off fireworks.

Brazilian folklore with its complex of *bichos*—such as *quibungo,* of

African origin, a horrid creature half human and half animal which swallows children through a hole in his back, *saciPererê*, a little Negro with one leg who pursues travelers, and *pé de garrafa*, the man with a sharpened leg who lures men into the forest—is a fusion of American, African, and Iberian folklore elements. It is now a truly Brazilian folklore, no longer similar to any of the ingredients.

Although Brazilian domestic architecture resembles in a general way that of other Latin American countries, the *patio* is replaced by a backyard-like *quintal*; and the internal arrangement of the Brazilian house, with its small room for visitors and its emphasis on the dining room, which serves the family for intimate living, is somewhat different from the typical Spanish American dwelling. In northern Brazil, the Brazilian-type hammock is a common fixture in any house. These, and many other cultural traits too numerous to describe here, are distinctive aspects of Brazilian culture.

Finally, there seems to be a series of distinctively Brazilian "psychological" traits, if we may accept the impressions of travelers and of students of Brazil, which set off Brazilians from other Latin Americans. Brazilians are said to be more overt and more voluble than the comparatively taciturn Argentinian; they are less proud and less worried about losing face than the Spanish American. Yet, many writers, both native and foreign, mention a certain sadness, a softness, and a melancholy about the Brazilian. "In a radiant land lives a sad people," is the opening line of Paulo Prado's famous interpretative work on Brazil.[9] This is another side of the Brazilian personality. Both Paulo Prado and Gilberto Freyre describe the excess of sensuality and the great love for luxury of Brazilians, and Freyre writes of a "gentleman complex," that is, an inclination toward white-collar work and the professions and a distaste for physical labor, as a personality trait of Brazilians inherited from colonial feudalism.[10] With these traits go a desire to "get rich quick" and a love of gambling. The economic history of the country is made up of a series of speculative booms and almost all Brazilians gamble in some form—either in the *jogo do bicho* (a sort of numbers racket), or in the federal or state lotteries, or, until recently, in one of the luxurious casinos.

The Brazilian monarchical system, Brazilian democracy, and Brazilian dictatorship were unlike similar forms of government as they existed in Europe or even in neighboring countries. The recent dictatorship, despite its aping of European patterns, never became a harsh system with strict control over the people. Jokes about the dictator, complaints and discussions of the lack of freedom of expression, and rumors of growing opposition were discussed openly in cafés and salons. When the dictator was finally overthrown, it was a typical bloodless Brazilian revolution. Brazilians give a uniquely Brazilian twist to institutions and concepts which they share with the Western world. As one student of colonial art remarked: "In Brazil, even Christ hangs comfortably on the cross."

The foregoing sketch of the regions of Brazil and of a few of the culture complexes which unify Brazil is necessarily tentative and brief. It is presented as a framework to be tested by future interdisciplinary research using objective methods. On a tentative basis, however, the writer finds that modern Brazil contains six distinct regions, namely, the Amazon, the arid Northeast, the Northeast Coast, the industrial Middle States, the extreme South, and the Far West frontier. Each of these regions is characerized by a particular ecology, a major economic activity, an emphasis on one of the three racial stocks which form the Brazilian population, and a distinctive modern folk culture. In such regions as the extreme South and the industrial Middle States, more than one historical tradition has been present, but modern tendencies seem to have welded these older traditions into a single region. To be specific, in the seventeenth and eighteenth centuries, the states of Minas Gerais, São Paulo, and Rio de Janeiro each must have constituted a distinctive Brazilian region, but modern technology with its rapid communications and transportation is breaking down these old local differences. At least two of the regions described (i.e., the Amazon and the arid Northeast) are characterized in terms of population by the strength of the Indian component, but a violent contrast in ecological conditions clearly distinguishes the regions one from the other and assures differences in their cultural adjustments.

These regional differences in Brazil are local varieties of a national culture. As a nation, Brazil has had a unique historical development. The Indian, the African Negro, and the Portuguese have each contributed to modern Brazilian culture and the resulting configuration sets off Brazil from the other Latin American countries and the Anglo-American countries of this hemisphere. Even the Latin institutions and culture forms which it shares with the other Latin American countries have been given different connotations and meanings in Brazilian culture. Brazil is a distinctive and important "culture area" of modern Latin America, and within Brazil there are important regional differences in the Brazilian culture pattern. These facts must be taken into account in forming policies for Latin America as a whole or specifically for Brazil.

NOTES

1. "Modern Latin American Culture," *Social Forces*, 1947, XXV, 243–248. In another publication he calls it "Creole Culture" *(Moche: A Peru-*

vian Coastal Community, Smithsonian Institution, Institute of Social Anthropology Publication 3, 1947, pp. 151–154).

2. In 1852, it was estimated that whites made up only 8.5 per cent, Negro slaves 2.3 per cent, and Mestiços (probably Negro-white mixtures) 4.9 per cent of the total Amazon population. The rest were American Indians. (V. Correa Filho, "Devassamento e ocupaçao da Amazonia Brasiliera," *Revista Brasiliera de Geografia,* 1942, IV, 283.) Since that time there has been an influx of people from the arid Northeast who are themselves mixtures for the most part.

3. English translation entitled *Rebellion in the Backlands,* translated by Samuel Putnam, Chicago, University of Chicago Press, 1944.

4. Translated into English by Samuel Putnam, *The Masters and the Slaves,* New York, A. Knopf, 1946.

5. New York, A. Knopf, 1945, p. 75.

6. Gillin, *op. cit.,* pp. 243–248.

7. Freyre, *The Masters and the Slaves,* p. 418.

8. Freyre, *Brazil: An Interpretation,* p. 57.

9. *O Retrato do Brasil,* 5a. ed., São Paulo, Edit. Brasiliense Ltda., 1944, p. 11.

10. Freyre, *Brazil: An Interpretation,* pp. 62–63.

LAND, AGRICULTURE, AND ECONOMICS

Introduction

DWIGHT B. HEATH

Latin America is an area of extremes, in natural and social features. Topographic, climatological, and other factors combine to create a wide variety of ecological niches that have been exploited by man in different ways throughout history and prehistory. The importance of economics in Latin America is clear both in theoretic terms and in the view of the people themselves.

Anthropologists tend to think of economic behavior as comprising all that people do and think about making a living, that is, ideas and activities concerning production and exchange. A few anthropologists (e.g., Goodfellow, Herskovits, LeClair) appear to have felt quite comfortable using concepts, categories, and definitions from classical economics and applying them in new and different contexts among non-Western peoples. Others (e.g., Polanyi *et al.*, Firth, Dalton) have clearly felt that the analytical categories developed in Western cultures cannot be applied to primitive economies.

Anthropologists' early and continued interest in economic studies in Latin America has resulted in the collection of more detailed data, slightly greater development of theory, and much more work in the applied field than is typical in other major world areas. It has also demonstrated that the approaches of anthropology and economics are by no means contradictory, or even particularly difficult to reconcile, as is illustrated in this section by Mosk's article. In general, the anthropologist tends to take a microscopic view, intensively analyzing limited local situations. Illustrative of this tendency in Latin America are studies of regional markets (e.g., Malinowski and De la Fuente [1957], McBryde [1933]); of specific communities (e.g., Wagley [1941], Foster [1942], Tax [1953]); or even of individual households (e.g., Nash [1961]). Another approach is to deal with particular economic institutions (for example, slavery, Aguirre Beltrán [1944]; land tenure, Carroll [1962]; plantations, Pan American Union [1959], Thompson [1957]). By contrast, the economist more often deals with macroscopic patterns, such as balance of payments, total national production of major commodities, taxation, and so forth (e.g., Gordon [1950], Wythe [1949], International Bank for Reconstruction and Development). These approaches are clearly complementary, and a number of studies demonstrate how fruitfully they can be integrated (e.g., Le Beau [1956], Glade and Anderson [1963]).

The papers in this section reflect some of the dominant themes in Latin American economy, as well as providing a sample of the kinds of studies that have been made.

Mosk's succinct synthesis of data from Guatemala was a pioneering effort in relating the minutiae of anthropological community studies to broader economic systems. In the past decade, this has become one of the principal foci of concern of such careful investigators as Erasmus, Nash, Kunkel, Salz, and others, and a number of international organizations now conduct research in conjunction with their programs of technical and economic assistance. The article by Erasmus is one of a very few studies available on the phenomenon of reciprocal labor, a widespread aspect of Latin American culture in which the interrelation of social organization and other aspects of life is dramatically illustrated. The degree of integration of the economic system with other behavioral systems is well demonstrated by just those changes Erasmus describes in accounting for the progressive disappearance of reciprocal farm labor.

Greenfield's study of land tenure and transmission in Barbados is a nice demonstration of the interrelation of what Redfield called "the great tradition" and "the little tradition," and also shows the importance of historical perspective in the analysis of economic patterns. In discussing detailed data on specific regions of Venezuela, Hill, Silva, and Hill briefly summarize some of the important institutions of colonial Latin America and illustrate the social and economic implications of various types of land tenure and use in a situation marked by the classic combined problems of *latifundismo* and *minifundismo*.

A study of Jamaican marketing, by Mintz, relates the system of distribution to the system of production and sets economic behavior in the context of other kinds of values. Kaplan's analysis of the impact of mechanization in a Mexican craft community is an excellent example of how findings in a local and specialized context can suggest general principles for economic development.

In order to set these papers in perspective, I will briefly review the development of studies under four broad rubrics: land and agriculture, wealth and power, systems of exchange, and economic development.

Land and Agriculture

The agricultural sector employs at least 50 per cent of the labor force in half of the Latin American republics. A significant portion of these people are engaged in subsistence farming and participate only slightly in the economic and political life of the nation. This group includes independent small-scale farmers as well as tenants on haciendas where archaic methods of production persist, depending on massed labor rather than mechanization, or other capital inversion. Agriculture in such contexts is qualitatively as well as quantitatively distinct from commercial farming; the latter involves different kinds of social relationships as well as production of more (and often different) crops. The hacienda, or uncapitalized latifundium, is often a feudal estate with unsalaried tenants in some variant of the *colono* system of labor (cf. Schulman [1955], International Labor Office [1957]). By contrast, the plantation is highly capitalized, producing for world market, employing wage labor. This fruitful distinction has been well made by Wolf and Mintz [1957].

There is an abundant literature on agricultural methods, and detailed data are available in virtually every ethnographic account or community study. In fact, some of the earliest systematic studies of Latin American communities were conducted under the auspices of the U. S. Department of Agriculture, and the interests of rural sociology predominate in characterizations of national patterns prepared by the same authors (Hill, Leonard, Loomis, Nelson, Smith, and Whetten).

The specifics of the annual round, motor habits, tools, and so forth, are clearly important in understanding the life of the local people, but beyond this, some social scientists have attempted to describe and analyze the relation of agriculture to other aspects of the economy at the national and even international levels (e.g., Le Beau [1956] in Guatemala; Hill, Silva, and Hill in Venezuela [1960]).

Furthermore, anthropological studies of agriculture in Latin America have sometimes yielded new insights that challenge long-standing assumptions. Examples of this are Lewis' demonstration of the significantly greater productivity of hoe cultivation over plow cultivation, and Carneiro's careful contradiction of many myths concerning slash-and-burn agriculture.

Since the overwhelming majority of the population depends for its livelihood on working the land, it is little wonder that these people have developed complex and varied systems of thinking and acting with relation to it.

The supposed persistence of some pre-Columbian patterns of man-land relations has long been a focus of attention for Latin American sociologists and social philosophers (e.g., Castro Pozo), and has led to the myth of community, criticized by Adams [1962]. Several European institutions were transplanted to the New World, where they underwent peculiar adaptations to local situations, and have persisted for centuries in modified form. Scholars who have contributed to our understanding of these patterns include Weeks, Ots Capdequí, and others. For a long time, contemporary patterns of land tenure were not systematically studied, but were the subject of novels of social protest in the *indigenista* school (e.g., Alegría [1941], Icaza [1934]).

Until recent years, students of land tenure tended to sketch general national or regional patterns (e.g., McBride in Bolivia [1921], Chile [1936], and Mexico [1923]; Martínez [1939] in Colombia). An increasing number of detailed local studies indicate the range of variation around the norm, and deal with attitudes and values of the rural populace, as well as with national laws (e.g., Borde and Gongora [1956], Romney [1959], Heath [1965]).

In studies of land tenure, anthropologists tend to introduce historical perspective somewhat more systematically than in their analyses of some other aspects of culture. This is appropriate to an understanding of how contemporary patterns came to be, and sometimes reveals new insights that could not be gained by synchronic study alone, as in Greenfield's paper in this section. Because of the jural and political importance of land in European cultures, it is a recurrent subject throughout historical sources—published and unpublished, official and unofficial.

Many of the most important values attached to land have no immediate relevance to its productive capacity, however. In a predominantly agricultural economy, the distribution of wealth is determined largely by control over land, and power and prestige usually accrue to wealthy landowners. Virtually all Latin American countries have long been characterized as dual societies, composed of a small elite who appear to exert economic and political dominance over the ineffectual majority of the populace. Not only do these few seem to control most of the wealth; they often effectively dominate regions and even nations, and enjoy privileges denied the majority.

The dual problems of *latifundismo* (concentration of vast areas in the hands of a few) and *minifundismo* (excessive fragmentation of plots among the great majority) are universal in Latin America except in those nations that have undergone thoroughgoing social revolution (Mexico,

Bolivia, and Cuba). The actual degree of concentration of landownership is reflected in the fact that, throughout Latin America, almost 90 per cent of the cultivated land is owned by less than 10 per cent of the landholders, whereas more than 70 per cent of the landowners control less than 4 per cent of the land (Carroll [1961]).

The successes and shortcomings of existing land reform programs indicate clearly that reallocation of land is not enough to markedly increase agricultural production for market; in fact, reallocation often seems to have had the opposite effect. Most analysts agree that maximum economic impact can come only from a sweeping agrarian reform which includes credit facilities for small farmers, improvement of agricultural techniques, development of transportation and processing facilities, and so forth. Such programs are extremely costly and difficult to administer, and so are understandably rare. But however much the national economy may suffer, land reform is often sought as a prerequisite to social reform.

The idea of land reform as crucial in Latin American social reform is by no means limited to Marxists. Certainly the United Nations, United States, and Alliance for Progress have all been outspoken in support of such a view (see, e.g., U.N., Department of Economic Affairs [1951], International Labor Office [1953], U. S. Agency for International Development [1961], Inter-American Economic and Social Council [1961]). Agreement on the principle is widespread, but there is no consensus on how to achieve it. Most North Americans tend to speak in terms of gradual social reform and evolution, whereas some Latin Americans do not hesitate to suggest that actual revolution may well be necessary.

There is one major obstacle to the enactment of economic reforms such as those enjoined by the Alliance for Progress, which include land reform, increase of taxes on income, property and inheritance, and so forth. The problem can be simply stated, but its resolution is not easy; those who control the legislative process are precisely those who would suffer the greatest immediate loss, so that enactment of such reforms would appear to be an exceptionally altruistic act. Among those who consider violent revolution a realistic, even imminent alternative, however, such philanthropy can be interpreted as a good investment. This view is not, however, widespread among those who now enjoy political and economic dominance. The writings of Delgado, Flores, and others cannot be dismissed as merely polemic; not only do they reflect an increasingly widespread and powerful current of thought among Latin Americans, but their interpretation fits the stark historical and social realities of the area. There appears to be strong and growing pressure for major realignment of the distribution of wealth and power, by whatever means may be effective.

Wealth and Power

We have already discussed the stereotype of dual societies in Latin America, with wealth and power concentrated in the hands of a small oligarchy who control most of the land. Although Beals (pp. 342–60) is also correct in identifying a middle sector that is growing in numbers, wealth, and influence (cf. Johnson [1958]), it is still true that landed oligarchies often enjoy an effective monopoly on education, voting, large-scale commerce, and other important activities, while the majority are, at best, second-class citizens, and often serfs in a feudalistic social order.

The distinction between the "power-prestige sector" and the "work-wealth sector" formulated by Adams in the Introduction that follows seems both valid and appropriate in many areas. The fact that wealth and power are not precisely correlated is indicated, as Adams notes, in the recent and progressive growth of a middle sector whose control over wealth has not provided easy access to power and prestige. It can also be seen in the Latin American equivalent of "genteel poverty," which seems to be widespread although it has rarely been noted in the literature. Many of the rural gentry are not wealthy—in terms of liquid capital—even in relation to merchants in nearby villages. Their apparent wealth is often in symbols which have only local currency, such as control over unused land, access to laborers, personal leisure, and so forth. Such people seem wealthy because peasants are obliged to work for them where monopolization of land offers no feasible alternative. A surfeit of labor is then one kind of conspicuous consumption appropriate to landlords who cannot afford hard goods, and *hacendados* may live well in terms of the local patterns, even though they command no negotiable assets that would allow them to "sell out" and move anywhere else. This pattern seems particularly characteristic of haciendas, and is illustrated in the papers by Strickon and the Services.

Systems of Exchange

One of the most striking features of Latin American economies is the widespread use of money by those people who retain their indigenous languages, dress, and other customs. Although we sometimes speak of peasants operating at a subsistence level, complete self-sufficiency is rare and fast disappearing. Furthermore, the geographic mobility of Latin American peasants is often appreciable, whether they are in quest of seasonal wage-work or on marketing trips. The isolated peasant is at one with the self-sufficient peasant—mythical, except in a few very limited areas. A variety of systems of exchange are operative throughout Latin America. A brief review of some of these indicates the degree to which economic activities are integrated with other kinds of interaction.

Ecological variation is one of the reasons for marked regional specialization, as where differences in elevation make for different agricultural systems within the radius of a few miles. But custom is also operative, for example, in fairly uniform areas where virtually each village specializes in a particular crop, craft, or service, and communities are interdependent, as in highland Guatemala (McBryde [1947]), Bolivia (Bowman [1910]), or parts of Mexico (West [1948]). Within such networks, special importance attaches to the market, which, in this sense, is a distributive mechanism rather than a place. In fact, one widespread pattern is to have a cyclical market which meets in various towns on particular days (Silverman [1959]). Concerning markets and marketing, as is true of many aspects of culture, descriptions including community studies are available in many ethnographic monographs. Meticulous quantitative analysis is rare, however, even among those who have paid particular attention to the subject, such as Mintz, Malinowski and De la Fuente, and Tax.

Another important system of exchange is the civil-religious hierarchy which is found in many Indian communities. It is generally expected that each adult male will progress through a series of offices (*cargos*), and the mandatory sponsorship of initiation parties from time to time serves to dissipate accumulated wealth. A number of fairly detailed studies suggest that this is an effective means of economic leveling within a closed community (cf. Carrasco [1952], Wolf [1957], Bunzel [1952], and others).

The analysis of reciprocal labor by Erasmus reflects another kind of economic stabilizer which is effective where the group is limited and social sanctions carry considerable weight, in the "closed corporate community" characterized by Wolf [1957]. There is no real fallacy in such a group's "making a living by taking in each other's laundry." Although such a system may appear unworkable at any given time, it is perfectly suitable when one views it as redistributive system over the period of a year or more. A significant characterization of the ways in which such local communities relate to national institutions, offered herein by Wolf, has applicability far beyond Mexico.

Another important aspect of Latin American economics is the flow of wealth among individual nations. It is beyond the scope of our discussion to analyze such factors as monoculture, inflation, export of capital rather than inversion, and other aspects of large-scale economic systems, but it seems important to note that they are widespread features of immediate relevance in evaluating problems and prospects for economic development.

Economic Development

Primary among the domestic and international concerns of virtually every Latin American country is economic development. Agriculture and mining have long predominated, perpetuating an extractive "colonial" type of economy in which high returns were favored over long-range investment. Industrialization has gained real importance in only a few countries since World War II. An early general assessment of problems and prospects for economic development in Latin America remains basically sound (Hanson [1951]).

Values and attitudes in Latin America have long been cited by North Americans as major obstacles to greater efficiency, the imposition of stricter direction on labor, and so forth, whereas lack of domestic capital has been especially lamented by national critics. Although we do not understand the process very well, we have seen enough examples of abrupt and enthusiastic adoption of commercial-industrial values to seriously question the importance of the stereotypical cavalier-picaresque laissez-faire outlook as impeding development, and the regular flight of large amounts of capital to Europe and the United States is well known. Kaplan's paper, in this section, is very much to the point in this connection.

Increasing experiments in nationalization of major industries provide a discouraging climate for private capitalization (in Bolivia, Brazil, and Peru, for example). In a sort of vicious circle, widespread poverty limits the market for manufactured goods, so that new kinds of employment develop only slowly, and the rapid growth of population aggravates unemployment with its associated poverty. Demographic pressures and reactions to them are briefly characterized by Adams below; suffice it to say at this point that the population explosion is progressing in Latin America at a rate greater than that anywhere else in the world, so that few nations there—even those that are relatively highly industrialized—do not have a lower per capita income now than they did a decade ago.

Large-scale migration to cities (often called "urbanization") is another major trend in Latin America today, and although it is related to both industrialization and population growth, it must not be considered congruent with either (cf. Hauser [1962]). Two papers by Mangin, included in this book, investigate the reasons for and means of such migration; another by Lewis reveals significant continuities between urban and rural dwellers. Migration from densely populated regions to sparsely populated frontiers is only beginning, but may progress rapidly in Colombia, Bolivia, Ecuador, and Mexico, among others.

Throughout the 1950's and 1960's, technical and economic assistance from abroad have loomed large in the economies of many Latin American nations. In this connection many North American anthropologists have been involved in "action programs" which require the application of their skills, insights, and knowledge to the solution of practical problems. A diagnostic review of successes and shortcomings is offered by Foster [1962]; a general theory of culture was developed by Erasmus [1961] on the basis of his extensive work throughout Latin America and a searching evaluation of continuity and change in part of Sonora, Mexico. Despite the fact that the impact of foreign aid has often been disappointing to enthusiastic proponents, it has offered a fruitful field for the study of the dynamics of cultural change.

Domestic and international economic problems are characteristic of all Latin America. Dissatisfaction over the unequal distribution of wealth and power is finding increased expression among the people, and the slow rate of economic growth is frustrating to officials. These problems are fundamental to understanding the social ferment that characterizes the area today.

REFERENCES CITED

Adams, Richard N.
1962 "The Community in Latin America: A Changing Myth," *The Centennial Review* 6:3:409–434.

Aguirre Beltrán, Gonzalo
1944 "The Slave Trade in Mexico," *Hispanic American Historical Review* 24:412–431.

Alegría, Ciro
1941 *El mundo es ancho y ajeno*, Santiago, Ediciones Ercilla.

Borde, Jean and Mario Gongora
1956 *Evolución de la propiedad rural en el Valle de Puangue*, 2 vols., Instituto de Sociología, Universidad de Chile, Santiago.

Bowman, Isaiah
1910 "Trade Routes in the Economic Geography of Bolivia," *Bulletin of American Geographical Society* 42:22–37, 90–104, 180–192.

Bunzel, Ruth
1952 *Chichicastenango: A Guatemalan Village*, American Ethnological Society Monograph 22, Seattle.

Carrasco, Pedro
1952 *Tarascan Folk Religion: An Analysis of Economic, Social, and Religious Interactions*, pp. 1–64, Middle American Research Institute Publication 17, Tulane University, New Orleans.

Carroll, Thomas F.
1961 "The Land Reform Issue in Latin America," in A. O. Hirschman, ed., *Latin American Issues: Essays and Comments*, pp. 161–201, Twentieth Century Fund, New York.
1962 *Land Tenure and Land Reform in Latin America: A Selective Annotated Bibliography* (preliminary version), Inter-American Development Bank, Washington, D.C.

Erasmus, Charles J.
1961 *Man Takes Control: Cultural Development and American Aid*, Minneapolis, University of Minnesota Press.

Foster, George M.
1942 *A Primitive Mexican Economy*, American Ethnological Society Monograph 5, New York.
1962 *Traditional Cultures: And the Impact of Technological Change*, New York, Harper & Row.

Glade, William P., Jr. and Charles W. Anderson
1963 *The Political Economy of Mexico*, Madison, University of Wisconsin Press.

Gordon, Wendell
1950 *The Economy of Latin America*, New York, Columbia University Press.

Hanson, Simon G.
1951 *Economic Development in Latin America*, Washington, D.C., Inter-American Affairs Press.

Hauser, Philip M., ed.
1962 *Urbanization in Latin America*, New York, UNESCO.

Heath, Dwight B.
1963 "Successes and Shortcomings of Agrarian Reform in Bolivia," *Land Tenure Center Discussion Paper* 2:16–23, University of Wisconsin, Madison.

Heath, Dwight B., *et al.*
1965 *Land Reform and Social Revolution in Bolivia*, Madison, University of Wisconsin Press.

Hill, George W., José A. Silva M., and Ruth Oliver de Hill
1960 *La vida rural en Venezuela*, Ministerio de Agricultura y Cría, Caracas.

Icaza, Jorge
1934 *Huasipungo*, Quito, Imprento Nacional.

Inter-American Economic and Social Council at the Ministerial Level
1961 "The Charter of Punta del Este: Establishing an Alliance for Progress within the Framework of Operation Pan America," in *Alliance for Progress: Official Documents*, Pan American Union, Washington, D.C.

International Bank for Reconstruction and Development
(A series of monographs on the economies of individual Latin American countries), Baltimore, Johns Hopkins University Press.

International Labor Office
1953 *Indigenous Peoples,* Geneva.
1957 *The Landless Farmer in Latin America,* Geneva.

Johnson, John J.
1958 *Political Change in Latin America: The Emergence of the Middle Sectors,* Stanford, Calif., Stanford University Press.

Le Beau, Francis
1956 "Economía agrícola," in J. Arriola, ed., *Integración social en Guatemala,* Publicación del Seminario de Integración Social Guatemalteca 3:267–312, Guatemala.

McBride, George M.
1921 *The Agrarian Indian Communities of Highland Bolivia,* American Geographical Society Research Series 5, New York.
1923 *Land Systems of Mexico,* American Geographical Society Research Series 12, New York.
1936 *Chile: Land and Society,* American Geographical Society Research Series 19, New York.

McBryde, F. Webster
1933 *Sololá: A Guatemalan Town and Cakchiquel Market,* Middle American Institute Research Series Publication 5, Tulane University, New Orleans.
1947 *Cultural and Historical Geography of Southwest Guatemala,* Smithsonian Institution, Institute of Social Anthropology Publication 4, Washington, D.C.

Malinowski, Bronislaw and Julio de la Fuente
1957 "La economía de un sistema de mercados en México," *Acta Antropológica,* Epoca 2., Mexico.

Martínez, Marco A.
1939 *Régimen de tierras en Colombia,* 2 vols., Talleres Gráficos, Bogotá.

Nash, Manning
1961 "The Social Context of Economic Choice in a Small Society," *Man,* Article 219, pp. 186–191.

Pan American Union
1959 *Plantation Systems of the New World,* Social Science Monograph 7, Washington, D.C.

Romney, D. H.
1959 *Land in British Honduras,* 2 vols., Her Majesty's Stationery Office, London.

Schulman, Sam
1955 "The *Colono* System in Latin America," *Rural Sociology* 20:1: 34–40.

Silverman, Sydel
1959 "Some Cultural Correlates of the Cyclical Market," in V. Ray, ed., *Intermediate Societies, Social Mobility, and Communication,* pp. 31–36, American Ethnological Society Proceedings, Seattle.

Tax, Sol
1953 *Penny Capitalism:* A *Guatemalan Indian Economy,* Smithsonian Institution, Institute of Social Anthropology Publication 16, Washington, D.C.
Thompson, Edgar T., comp.
1957 *The Plantation:* A *Bibliography,* Pan American Union Social Science Monograph 4, Washington, D.C.
United Nations, Department of Economic Affairs
1951 *Land Reform: Defects in Agrarian Structure as Obstacles to Economic Development,* New York.
United States Agency for International Development
1961 *Latin American USOM's Seminar on Agrarian Reform,* International Cooperation Administration, Washington, D.C.
Wagley, Charles
1941 *Economics of a Guatemalan Village,* American Anthropological Association Memoir 58.
West, Robert C.
1948 *Cultural Geography of the Modern Tarascan Area,* Smithsonian Institution, Institute of Social Anthropology Publication 7, Washington, D.C.
Wolf, Eric R.
1957 "Closed Corporate Peasant Communities in Mesoamerica and Central Java," *Southwestern Journal of Anthropology* 13:1–18.
Wolf, Eric R. and Sidney W. Mintz
1957 "Haciendas and Plantations in Middle America and the Antilles," *Social and Economic Studies* 6:3:380–412.
Wythe, George
1949 *Industry in Latin America,* New York, Columbia University Press.

FURTHER READINGS

Land and Agriculture

Carneiro, Robert L.
1961 "Slash-and-Burn Cultivation among the Kuikuru and Its Implications for Cultural Development in the Amazon Basin," in J. Wilbert, ed., *The Evolution of Horticultural Systems in Native South America: Causes and Consequences,* Sociedad de Ciencias Naturales La Salle, Caracas.
Castro Pozo, Hildebrando
1924 *Nuestra comunidad indígena,* El Lucero, Lima.
Delgado, Oscar
1963 "Revolución, reforma, y conservatismo como tipos de políticas

agrarias en Latino América," *Revista de la Universidad Libre* 4:15:3–41.

Fals-Borda, Orlando
1955 *Peasant Society in the Colombian Andes: A Sociological Study of Saucío*, Gainesville, University of Floida Press.

Flores, Edmundo
1961 *Tratado de economía agrícola*, Fondo de Cultura Económica, Mexico.

Ford, Thomas R.
1955 *Man and Land in Peru*, Gainesville, University of Florida Press.

James, Preston E.
1960 "Man-Land Relations in the Caribbean Area," in V. Rubin, ed., *Caribbean Studies: A Symposium*, pp. 14–20, Seattle, University of Washington Press.

Leonard, Olen E.
1952 *Bolivia: Land, Peoples, and Institutions*, Washington, D.C., Scarecrow Press.

Lewis, Oscar
1951 "Agricultural Systems," in *Life in a Mexican Village: Tepoztlán Restudied*, pp. 129–157, Urbana, University of Illinois Press.

Loomis, Charles P., *et al.*
1953 *Turrialba: Social Systems and Social Change*, Glencoe, Ill., Free Press.

Métraux, Alfred, *et al.*
1951 *Making a Living in the Marbial Valley (Haiti)*, UNESCO Occasional Paper in Education 10, Paris.

Nelson, Lowry
1950 *Rural Cuba*, Minneapolis, University of Minnesota Press.

Ots Capdequí, J. M.
1959 *España en América: el régimen de tierras en la época colonial*, Fondo de Cultura Económica, Mexico.

Saunders, John V. D.
1961 "Man–Land Relations in Ecuador," *Rural Sociology* 26:1:57–69.

Silva Herzog, Jesús, ed.
1961 *La cuestión de la tierra*, 4 vols., Instituto Mexicano de Investigaciones Económicas, Mexico.

Smith, T. Lynn
1954 *Brazil: People and Institutions*, rev. ed., Baton Rouge, Louisiana State University Press.

Taylor, Carl
1948 *Rural Life in Argentina*, Baton Rouge, Louisiana State University Press.

Weeks, David
1947 "European Antecedents of Land Tenures and Agrarian Organization of Hispanic America," *Journal of Land and Public Utilities Economics* 13:60–75.

1947 "The Agrarian System of the Spanish American Colonies," *Journal of Land and Public Utilities Economics* 13:158–168.

Wealth and Power

Benham, Frederic C. and H. A. Holley
1959 *A Short Introduction to the Economy of Latin America,* Oxford, Oxford University Press.

Cochran, Thomas C. and Ruben E. Reina
1962 *Entrepreneurship in Argentine Culture,* Philadelphia, University of Pennsylvania Press.

Heath, Dwight B.
1959 "Land Tenure and Social Organization: An Ethnohistorical Study from the Bolivian Oriente," *Inter-American Economic Affairs* 13:4:46–66.

Poblete Troncoso, Moisés and Ben G. Burnett
1960 *The Rise of the Latin American Labor Movement,* Bookman Associates, New York.

Tannenbaum, Frank
1929 *The Mexican Agrarian Revolution,* Brookings Institution, Washington, D.C.

Vázquez, Mario C.
1963 *Hacienda, peonaje y servidumbre en los Andes peruanos,* Lima, Editorial Estudios Andinos.

Whetten, Nathan
1948 *Rural Mexico,* Chicago, University of Chicago Press.
1961 *Guatemala: The Land and the People,* New Haven, Yale University Press.

Wolf, Eric R.
1955 "Types of Latin American Peasantry: A Preliminary Discussion," *American Anthropologist* 57:3:452–471.

Systems of Exchange

Mintz, Sidney W.
1959 "Internal Market Systems as Mechanisms of Social Articulation," in V. Ray, ed., *Intermediate Societies, Social Mobility, and Communication,* American Ethnological Society Proceedings, Seattle, pp. 20–30.

Economic Development

Cook, Robert C., *et al.*
1962 "Latin America and Population Growth," *Population Bulletin* 18:6.

De Vries, Egbert and José Medina Echavarría, eds.
1963 *Social Aspects of Economic Development in Latin America,* 2 vols., UNESCO, Paris.

Dobyns, Henry F. and Mario C. Vázquez, eds.
1963 *Migración e integración en el Perú,* Lima, Editorial Estudios Andinos.

Fillol, Thomas
1961 *Social Factors in Economic Development: The Argentine Case,* M.I.T. Press, Cambridge, Mass.

Gibbons, William J.
1961 "Growth Trends in Latin American Populations," *American Catholic Sociological Review* 22:99–123.

Glick, Philip M.
1957 *The Administration of Technical Assistance: Growth in the Americas,* University of Chicago Press, Chicago.

Nash, Manning
1957 "The Multiple Society in Economic Development: Mexico and Guatemala," *American Anthropologist* 59:5:825–833.

Salz, Beate R.
1955 *The Human Element in Industrialization: A Hypothetical Case Study of Ecuadorian Indians,* American Anthropological Association Memoir 85.

Smith, T. Lynn
1961 *Latin American Population Studies,* University of Florida, Social Science Monograph 8, Gainesville.

Tax, Sol
1957 "Changing Consumption Patterns in Indian Guatemala," *Economic Development and Cultural Change* 5:2:147–158.

Whyte, William F. and Allan R. Holmberg, eds.
1956 "Human Problems of U.S. Enterprise in Latin America," special issue of *Human Organization* 15:3.

Indigenous Economy in Latin America

SANFORD A. MOSK

No one can complain nowadays that the underdeveloped countries are being neglected by academic and other writers, in view of the mounting volume of articles, papers, reports and books dealing with such countries and their problems. However, if we take the literature on Latin America as an example, it is obvious that certain kinds of questions are being studied with care while others are receiving hardly any attention at all. The field of Latin American economics is developing unevenly. As a general proposition, major efforts are being devoted to the study of problems which can be treated by conventional economic analysis—such as balance of payments difficulties, terms of trade, and inflation. These are important issues. They should be studied and discussed widely, but it is unfortunate that other issues are not receiving a like amount of attention. Comparable efforts need to be put into the study of neglected problems that are also vital to Latin American countries as they attempt to move toward new levels of economic development.

I

In the hope of stimulating discussion of one of these neglected problems, I believe it is useful to raise some questions, and suggest some

Reprinted from *Inter-American Economic Affairs*, 1954, VIII, 3–25, by permission of the author's literary executrix and the publisher.

tentative ideas, about "indigenous" economies in Latin America. This phenomenon goes by a variety of terms, such as indigenous, subsistence, regional, nonmonetary, pre-capitalistic, and noncapitalistic, to mention some of the more common ones. Different writers describe it in different ways. They differ, too, in the emphasis assigned to individual features. A general model can, however, be constructed, consisting of the following principal elements: a high degree of self-sufficiency; limited production for the market; transactions based on custom and tradition, rather than on market forces; little response to gainful incentives; insulation from fluctuations in the national ("money," "commercial") economy of the country concerned, including, of course, the fluctuations originating in international conditions.

The situation thus described is most important in Latin America in the countries with large Indian populations, such as Mexico, Guatemala, Ecuador, Peru and Bolivia, but it is found in one degree or another in virtually every country of the region. It is not, of course, a phenomenon peculiar to Latin America. It is widely distributed throughout the underdeveloped areas of the world. Special attention has been paid to it in Southeast Asia, and writers like Boeke and Furnivall have given currency to the term "dual economy" (or "plural economy") to denote the coexistence of an indigenous and a money economy in the countries of that region.

The model referred to above of an indigenous economy in Latin America may or may not be a good one. What needs to be emphasized, first of all, is that we really do not know. By "we," I mean Latin Americans, as well as outside observers. It is a striking fact that most Latin American economists have little knowledge of the indigenous economies of their own countries. If their lack of knowledge about this question is lamentable, their lack of interest is even more so. They seem to regard an indigenous economy as a separate, airtight compartment. They are troubled by it, and they are impatient with it, but they do not consider it to be a main preoccupation in economic development. This attitude is unfortunate, especially in those countries where the indigenous economy involves a relatively large percentage of the population, since in such countries bringing about changes in the indigenous economy should be considered a central problem in the economic development of the nation as a whole.

If we accept for the moment the generalized list of features suggested above for the indigenous economy of a given country, there are two principal questions that have to be answered about each condition, namely, (1) the degree to which the condition prevails, and (2) to what extent the condition has been undergoing change. We cannot, of course, expect statistical answers to all these questions; some of them are clearly of a nonquantitative character. Even those which lend themselves to quantitative treatment can probably only be estimated in a rough way in the beginning. It is the beginning which is urgently needed. Once that is achieved, we can count on experience to act as a guide to the refinement of techniques of investigation and the development of working hypotheses for further study.

Anyone who has had even slight contact with an indigenous economy realizes the difficulties of making the kind of studies suggested here. Source materials, about which more will be said below, are both fugitive and fragmentary. In many cases, new field work has to be done, even for a preliminary study, and field work is time-consuming as well as costly. Where Indian groups are involved, the problem of communication is a complex one. The difference in language is itself a serious obstacle in getting information. To this must be added the heritage of history, going back to the days of European conquest, which often makes the Indian hostile to the non-Indian and fearful that the gathering of information will be used against him in taxation or in other ways, such as forced labor. Even where a good spirit of cooperation prevails, obtaining reasonably accurate economic material is handicapped by the lack of written records and by variations in the units of measurement employed. This list of difficulties does not purport to be complete, but is merely intended to illustrate the kinds of problems encountered in this field of research.

The materials already available on the indigenous economies of Latin America are found principally in the works of anthropologists, sociologists and cultural geographers. Anthropological research is the major source. It must, however, be recognized that anthropological research has typically been directed toward answering other kinds of questions than those which concern us from the standpoint of economic development. The anthropologist's interest in a people is a comprehensive one; he is generally concerned with all aspects of their mental and material culture, thus making it difficult to deal with any one aspect in detail. Furthermore, the anthropologist is likely to have a strong bent toward reconstructing the "original" nature of a culture—which in Latin America usually means trying to find out what it was like in pre-Columbian times. In dealing with change, his goal is the past, not the present or the tendency toward the future. Unavoidably, therefore, his attention is deflected from recent and contemporary changes which might be going on in an indigenous economy. For the same reasons, he is more interested in earlier relations between European colonizers and indigenous groups than in contemporary relations between an indigenous economy and the national economy with which it is in contact.

Lest there be some misunderstanding, I hasten to add that these comments are not intended to be a criticism of the work done by anthropologists in Latin America. Anthropology, like any other discipline, has had its own central problems. There is no reason to expect anthropologists to drop those problems in order to make a special contribution to the study of economic development. There are, however, signs that anthropologists are beginning to ask new questions in connection with their research—questions which have a special bearing on problems of economic development. This is an encouraging trend. We may hope that other social sciences will keep up with anthropology in this respect.

II

As a means of suggesting the kind of preliminary studies that might be done on the basis of materials already available, an effort can be made to analyze the indigenous economy of the highland region of Guatemala, where the bulk of the country's Indian population is living. There is perhaps more evidence available on this indigenous economy than any other in Latin America, owing to the special interests of Sol Tax, the anthropologist who has done extensive work in that area, and to the studies of Webster McBryde in cultural geography. In the section which follows, I have drawn heavily on the writings of Tax and McBryde, and I have also made use of a good deal of material found in the publications of Oliver La Farge and Charles Wagley. When I was in Guatemala, I had the benefit of numerous discussions with Richard Adams, who has for several years been doing fruitful work in applied anthropology in Guatemala and other parts of Central America.[1] These are the principal sources from which I have drawn conclusions about the nature and functioning of the indigenous economy of highland Guatemala.

Self-Sufficiency

Much economic effort in highland Guatemala goes into production for subsistence. Nevertheless, self-sufficiency is rare, even in the basic foodstuffs consumed, such as corn. This is true of communities (*municipios*) as well as of individual families. In his survey of evidence on forty *municipios* in the heart of the Guatemalan highlands, Tax found that only a few of them grew enough corn to satisfy their own needs.[2] Wagley records a similar impression for a different part of the highland area, farther to the north.[3] Corn is, of course, the mainstay of the diet throughout this whole region; according to McBryde, corn represents possibly as much as 80 per cent of the food consumed there.[4]

This lack of self-sufficiency in foodstuffs finds its counterpart in other particles of general consumption. The prevailing picture is, therefore, one of economic specialization—specialization both among individuals and among communities. Specialization occurs in agricultural production, in handicrafts, in trade, and, in a somewhat different form, in wage labor.

In agriculture, the principal lines of specialization are found in the production of corn, wheat, vegetables, and sheep. Some communities specialize in more than one type of agricultural production. Totonicapán, for example, is noted for wheat as well as sheep. In handicrafts, community specialization is found in pottery, furniture, mats, rope, blankets, and grinding stones, to mention only a few of the main ones as illustrations. A complete list would have to be much longer. In trade, specialization is more common on an individual basis than on a community level, but there are some communities, such as Santiago Atitlán and Chichicastenango, where it is very important. The specialist in trade is usually also a specialist in transport, since the bulk of the stuff is hauled on the human back.

Specialization naturally gives rise to trade, and a highly active commercial life is an outstanding characteristic of the indigenous economy of highland Guatemala. The pattern of trade is an intricate one within the highland area, and also between the highlands and the lowlands on the Pacific side, as McBryde has shown in the map he prepared of Indian markets and trade routes in southwest Guatemala.[5] The pattern is, however, a regular one, involving well-defined markets and channels of traffic. In certain communities a principal market is held once, or perhaps twice, a week, and at such times vendors come to the market from all over the region. Such a vendor is a specialist in what can properly be called long-distance trade. He buys as well as sells and when the market day draws to a close he sets off for the next market center on his itinerary, perhaps one or two days' travel away. The travel is done mostly on foot, and the merchandise is typically carried in a wooden frame (*cacaste*) on the back, aided by a tumpline at the forehead. Following a regular route and schedule, the professional trader spends most of his time on the road.

To guard against a misunderstanding, it should be pointed out that the professional traders are not the only ones who bring goods to a market. Local producers offer articles for sale in the community market, and sometimes a producer will himself carry goods to a distant market and offer them for sale. In that case he is a part-time trader. Whether part-time or full-time, the merchant is a prominent and vital factor in the indigenous economy as a whole. When McBryde made a study of the market of Sololá in 1932 he found in the market place vendors from eighteen towns beside Sololá itself.[6] Judging from additional material on the same survey published subsequently, McBryde calculated that only about one fourth of the vendors in the market place at Sololá were local residents.[7]

Specialization and markets apparently have a long history in the highlands of Guatemala, going back to pre-Columbian times. Frans Blom some years ago assembled some evidence on this question from early Spanish accounts, in a suggestive paper on "Commerce, Trade and Monetary Units of the Maya."[8] Other writers have more recently placed great emphasis on pre-Columbian commerce in the region, although it is not clear whether they have drawn inferences exclusively from Blom's pioneering paper on whether they have encountered additional evidence. Robert Redfield, in an article on the "Primitive Merchants of Guatemala," has written: "The market is an institution that was native to Guatemala before the white man came, and probably the system of distribution there is much as it was in ancient times."[9] Sol Tax, specifically expressing agreement with Redfield, has written in similar vein.[10] McBryde has gone so far as to venture the opinion that commerce was more important to the Indians of the Guatemalan highlands in pre-Columbian times than it is at present.[11] Since we are concerned here with the present and recent past, it is not possible to explore further this intriguing question of the nature of the pre-Columbian economy.

Nor is it possible, within the scope of this article, to deal in a comprehensive way with changes that took place in colonial times and in the period since Guatemala became an independent country. It is interesting, however, to call attention to a few changes of recent or fairly recent vintage, which suggest a tendency toward lesser self-sufficiency in this indigenous economy.

One is the decline of hand spinning of cotton yarn. This decline has been noted in the last generation, at least. The practice has not died out entirely, but it has become rare, and in some communities hand spinning is unknown nowadays. When Lila O'Neale was carrying out her field studies of highland textiles in 1936, she observed that the practice of hand spinning was "fast disappearing under the impact of available commercial yarns."[12] The use of primitive spindles was becoming confined largely to giving additional twist to factory-spun yarn, or to uniting two plies of such yarn for increased size. La Farge and Byers also noted a decline in hand spinning of cotton thread in Jacaltenango when they were doing field work in that community in 1927.[13]

In a subsequent study of another community, Santa Eulalia, La Farge observed that the women had abandoned two of their earlier crafts—namely, weaving cotton materials and making pottery.[14] His field work in this community was carried out in 1932, and he noted that these changes were recent ones. Pottery, he states, was still being made as late as 1927. He is less specific about the weaving of cotton cloth, but he gives the clear impression that the change had been going on rapidly in the years prior to the time he made his survey.

La Farge explains the dying out of these two crafts, as well as other changes in the material culture of Santa Eulalia, as the result of expanded seasonal employment in coffee *fincas*. Both consuming habits and the composition of local production, he found, had been undergoing changes under the influence of the larger cash income derived by the community from outside employment. The number and variety of local products had been reduced, and a parallel expansion had taken place in the consumption of "imports"—that is, articles obtained from other communities in the indigenous economy, and factory-made goods produced in Guatemala or abroad. The growing use of factory products was especially noteworthy in clothing and kitchen utensils. La Farge makes some further observations about the effects of the Depression on the consumption of "imports," which will be referred to below, where this question is taken up. But the main point is that the gaining of cash income from labor in the coffee *fincas* had brought about changes in the local economy, making it less self-sufficient and more interdependent than it had been in an earlier day.

La Farge's explanation for the decline in weaving and pottery making in Santa Eulalia may well serve also to explain the decline in hand spinning of cotton yarn generally throughout the highland area. Miss O'Neale, because her research interests centered in other problems, did not undertake to explore this question systematically. She merely records the fact that informants often told her that "the preliminaries to spinning *cuestan*,"[15] in the sense that they require time and patience, and cause weariness. This fragment of evidence is obviously not conclusive, but it is suggestive. Surely it is possible to interpret it to mean that they dropped the more tedious processes when the gaining of cash income made it feasible to satisfy their needs for cotton yarn by purchase rather than by handiwork.

Apart from his special study of Santa Eulalia, La Farge has emphasized the role of coffee production in bringing about changes in indigenous life in the highland area as a whole.[16] Evidence is admittedly meager, but I believe that this emphasis is sound. It suggests, moreover, that the bent of change since the latter part of the nineteenth century has been toward lessening self-sufficiency and toward increasing specialization in production and in services. The process has not been uniform in all parts of the area, and it has probably not gone on evenly through time. Measured by standards of the Western world, it has been slow, and nowhere in the area can it be said to have run its full course. It is, nevertheless, significant that the process is under way and that it has an appreciable historical depth and momentum.

Custom in Economic Transactions

Lack of information makes it difficult to appraise the exact role of custom and tradition in this indigenous economy, as contrasted with the free play of market forces. There is, of course, no doubt that custom is more important than it is in the industrialized nations. It is, however, by no means the dominant influence, and in some communities of highland Guatemala it may even be of negligible significance.

Probably the strongest statement on this question has been made by Tax in connection with his study of economic life in the community of Panajachel.[17] To convey the full flavor of his conviction that custom and tradition play a minor role in this economy, I believe that a somewhat lengthy quotation is justified. The paragraph quoted below is found in his discussion of interferences with the free play of market forces in Panajachel.

> The third class of interferences are those which customs, institutions, and beliefs impose on the "free play" of supply and demand. These are, I think, remarkably few and unimportant. There are a few beliefs that perhaps impede the most efficient production, such as that lumber and corn are to be cut and harvested only in certain phases of the moon. There are some sentiments impeding the most economic allocation of time and resources; for example, in Panajachel it is felt that every housewife should have chickens, even if they do not "pay." There are social considerations that prevent land, for example, from being treated absolutely as a commodity, though in Panajachel it is nearly that. But on the whole, one is hard put to find clear examples of any "cultural" interferences with economic behavior; even those just mentioned are equivocal. The difficulty here is the methodological one of having to document a negative statement. As one examines the materials contained in this monograph, it becomes clear that "cultural interference" is largely absent; but there is a possible exaggeration involved in the very bookkeeping method that is employed. All I am able to say is that in working out the economy of Panajachel I rarely came across anything not quickly reducible to economic terms. Customs, beliefs, sentiments and institutions seem, where they are not divorced from, to be rather *affected by*, than affecting, economic behavior.[18]

Better knowledge, particularly of relative price changes, might require some qualification of such a statement. There are some indications that certain prices have a traditional flavor, but the difficulties of getting comprehensive price information have impeded the gathering of satisfactory evidence on this question. Such a qualification, however, would only be a matter of degree. The main point would stand—namely, that economic transactions in Panajachel are not fixed by social customs, but rather depend upon monetary calculations and market forces.

What is true of Panajachel is apparently broadly true of the highland area as a whole, although it might not apply equally to all communities. Business behavior seems to be set apart from other aspects of living, in which custom and traditional rituals play a central role. Thus, La Farge and Byers set down the following observation about Jacaltenango: "Above all else, these Indians are conservative, and cling to their old customs with great tenacity, although their conservatism does not interfere where matters of business are concerned. . . . Any trifle may be turned into a business venture. . . ."[19]

As one would expect from what has been said above, barter transactions are not common in the indigenous economy of the Guatemala highlands. Some barter has been observed in one part of the region, near the Mexican border,[20] but it is exceptional in the heart of the highland country. Tax and Redfield have emphasized the exceptional nature of barter in this area, and McBryde has stated that he saw no barter transactions in the important market center of Sololá.[21] Tax has also suggested that barter was much more common a generation or two ago.[22] This observation is interesting, since it implies a trend analogous to the increase in specialization which was referred to above.

Another indication of the importance of market forces is the intense interest which the highland Indians show in prices. There appears to be disagreement among anthropologists who have studied in the area as to whether Indians as a general practice bargain among themselves or whether they only bargain when they are dealing with Ladinos (non-Indians). Their keen interest in prices is, however, not a matter of dispute. Even casual contacts, such as I myself have had with Indians in the Guatemala highlands, show an impressive consciousness about prices. It is not considered impolite to ask about the price of something another person has bought; indeed, it seems to be customary to do so during the course of a conversation.

Response to Gainful Incentives

Much that has been said above carries the implication that the Indians of highland Guatemala respond readily to the incentive to make a gain. This is true, in a meaningful sense. In making this statement, there is of course no intention to suggest that motivations in economic affairs are identical with those which prompt action in our own society. Fundamental motivations, about which we know little in any event, may or may not be similar. Nor are the ways of responding identical. They are undoubtedly not as far-reaching. Nevertheless, the available evidence indicates that gainful incentives are extremely important in this indigenous society, and that personal relations are greatly influenced by monetary considerations.

In this connection, it is interesting first of all to call attention to the practice of paying for services performed by other members of the same community. Evidence is limited in scope, but the practice in some important communities, at any rate, is to pay for such services, usually in cash, even when the services are provided by kinfolks other than those of the same household. Revealing illustrations are found in house construction, agricultural labor and ritualistic ceremonies.

HOUSE CONSTRUCTION

In Panajachel, Tax found that houses are constructed by the owner and members of his household, with the assistance of hired labor for specialized occupations, if necessary. The kinds of specialists whose services are hired are adobe makers, masons and carpenters. They work on a commercial basis. There is no system of neighborly help or communal labor.[23] In Chichicastenango, according to Redfield, the arrangements for house construction are similar to those of Panajachel.[24] Tax reports, however, in another study, that the social aspects of house construction vary among the *municipios* which, like Panajachel, border on Lake Atitlán.[25] In Santiago Atitlán, assistants are hired at regular day-labor rates, whereas in Santa Catarina Palopó the men who help build a house receive only food for their efforts. La Farge also found different practices in the two communities he studied. In one, Santa Eulalia, neighbors were hired to help in building a new house.[26] But in the other, Jacaltenango, houses were built by community help, and no cash payments were involved. Food was provided for those who worked, but more in the fashion of a ritualistic ceremony than a payment for services rendered.[27]

Lack of evidence makes it impossible to know which system is most common in the area as a whole—whether it is the commercial approach of Panajachel, or the community-help system of Jacaltenango, or perhaps some arrangement of an intermediate character. Also, there may be some correlation with the extent and nature of other economic activities and opportunities, or the differences may be explained by local custom and tradition. It would be interesting to have comprehensive information on this question, and for certain purposes it would, of course, be essential to do so. For our purpose, however, it is a significant fact that even in a few key communities of the Guatemala highlands the construction of dwellings is carried out as a commercial proposition rather than as a project of neighborly cooperation.

AGRICULTURAL LABOR

It is common in the Guatemala highlands for some people to gain their livelihood wholly or in part by farm work. Some of this work consists of seasonal labor in the coffee *fincas*, a topic which we shall deal with later, when outside connections are discussed. At the moment, our interest centers in the farm work performed for other Indians of the same community, or neighboring communities.

The most specific information on this question is contained in Tax's study of Panajachel.[28] Such labor is typically done by those who do not have land, or who have inadequate amounts of land, and the arrangements by which they work are varied in nature. It is the rule, however, that the person working receives compensation for his services in cash, or in food, or in some combination of the two. Payment in kind is simply another form of cash payment, since the cash value of the food is ordinarily taken into account in determining the wage. Only among members of the same household is field work done without specific compensation. As soon as a different household is involved, payment is expected, as shown by the following quotation from Tax:

> Within a family (the group with a common kitchen, that is) work is communally done. The land is worked in common and one member of the family does not pay another to work, say, on a piece he happens to be especially interested in. But such a communal attitude stops with the simple family, the economic household. When a father and son, or siblings, live separately, they may work together, but the one whose land is being worked still invariably (according to all informants, observations, and cases) pay the other at prevailing cash rates. The impoverished son of a wealthy man, for example, frequently works as a farm hand for his father as if they were not related.[29]

In contrast, there is evidence that a system of work exchange, or work cooperation, is in vogue in some places. Whether this system is more typical of the whole highland area than the commercialized system of Panajachel is a question which cannot be answered on the basis of present knowledge. It is, however, probably safe to assume that Panajachel is not unique in this respect, and that a substantial fraction of the farm work done for others in the area represents a response to a monetary incentive rather than a cooperative sharing of a total work load.

RITUALISTIC CEREMONIES

Persons engaging in such ceremonies are often paid for their services. This is true not only of shamans performing rites for individuals, but also of musicians participating in community ceremonies in their own towns. These occupations are usually carried out on a part-time basis, but they are thought of as specialized activities for which payment is made in cash, as well as in food and liquor. It is interesting, too, to observe that dance masks and costumes used in community ceremonies all over Guatemala are commonly rented from a few suppliers located in Totonicapán and Chichicastenango, and that the rental fee is usually paid by the individual participant rather than by the community.

The broad impression conveyed by the illustrations offered above is well summarized in Tax's statement: "The Indian is perhaps above all else an entrepreneur, a business man, always looking for new means of turning a penny."[30] Again, referring specifically to the Indians of Panajachel, Tax says that he hardly knows a man "who is not interested in new ways of making money, who does not have, typically, an iron or two in the fire, and who does not make his living partly as a business enterpriser."[31]

The pursuit of gain is followed freely because the accumulation of wealth is considered socially acceptable. It is true that certain social responsibilities are normally attached to wealth, but the practice of accumulating wealth is considered desirable for individual as well as community ends. Tax has written most fully about this question,[32] but we also have Wagley's judgment about the people of Santiago Chimaltenango that "there are few . . . who do not strive to accumulate wealth and add to their heritage."[33] Both writers also report that people are keenly aware of wealth differences among individuals and families.

Tax has written a paragraph which sums up so well the drift of this discussion on response to gainful incentives that I believe it should be quoted here. The flavor and strength of his opinion can only be conveyed in his own words.

> It is frequently said of Indians in Guatemala, sometimes as a reason for not improving their work conditions and wages, that if they earn enough money for the week in 3 days, they will not work the rest of the week. I doubt if this is true on an important scale anywhere in the country, but as applied to Panajachel, nothing seems further from the truth than this dictum which implies that the Indians work for bare necessities alone and have no desire to improve their way of life, or attain the security that wealth (especially in land) gives, or accumulate something for their children. I think that enough evidence has been presented to make my assertion credible. The Indians already live above a subsistence level (by their standards); they are certainly working for the luxury of meat as well as corn, for their church as well as for their food. I have never heard of a poor Indian ever refusing to work for another (when sober and capable of work) if he had nothing to do for himself and if the work and wage offered were reasonable by local standards. If a plantation owner should try to contract labor to go to the lowlands, he might get a contrary impression; but he would be in error because of ignorance of the fact that there *is* enough work in Panajachel where the climate and health conditions are more favorable and where the Indians have their families and friends. Furthermore, it has been seen that the Indians do strive for wealth and that there is strong motivation toward greater land holdings, a desire to have more for themselves and their children.[34]

Indigenous Economy and National Economy

The broad picture developed in the preceding sections of this article is that of a commercialized regional economy among the indigenous people of highland Guatemala. We have dealt mainly with features of an intra-regional character. Now it is necessary to examine the connections between the regional economy and the national economy of the country, in an effort to learn whether the regional economy is affected by fluctuations in the national economy, or whether it is essentially insulated from such fluctuations.

One main connection with the national economy is found in the seasonal labor which highland Indians perform in the coffee *fincas* at lower elevations. This practice of working outside the region during part of the year is more typical of some communities than of others, but it is common throughout the whole area. Although some individuals and communities have other sources of income outside the region, there is little doubt that work in the coffee *fincas* is the principal means by which money comes into the highland region as a whole. This link with the national economy, it should be observed, is also a link with the international economy, since most of the Guatemalan coffee is produced for export.

The other principal connection with the national economy of Guatemala, and with the international economy as well, is found in the consumption of articles produced outside the regional highland economy. There is, of course, considerable variation in this respect among individuals and communities. Nevertheless, evidence from scattered places suggests that consumption of such commodities has become an important element in the standard of living of the highland Indians as a group. Because this condition is apt to be underestimated—certainly it can be said that economists in Guatemala underestimate it—it is fruitful to offer some illustrations.

Prominent among the items bought from the outside nowadays are cotton yarn and cotton cloth. Attention has already been called to the decline in household spinning of cotton yarn. The yarn used in household weaving of cotton cloth is mostly purchased; it comes from the factory at Cantel in Guatemala, or is imported from the United States, England or one of the other industrialized nations. Much cotton cloth is also purchased rather than made in the household. Many highland women, especially in certain communities, no longer weave the cloth for their blouses (*huipiles*) but instead they buy the heavy cotton material produced at Cantel, and confine themselves to sewing and embroidering the garment. As regards men's clothing, much of the material used in making garments is produced in the highland area itself, but there is some evidence that factory-made cloth has become increasingly used.[35] The communities on the periphery of the highland region near Guatemala City have gone farthest in this respect. Five studies of communities in this area showed that the men bought ready-made clothing in all cases, with the minor exception of the belts worn in one community.[36]

Metal articles are also important among the articles purchased from the outside. I have already referred to the growing use of factory-made kitchen utensils in Santa Eulalia, as reported by La Farge; and McBryde, writing more generally of the highland region, notes that earthenware dishes and cups "are giving way rapidly to bright-colored imported enamel ware."[37] The metal articles of most general use are the hoe and the machete. The ax, another "import," is also employed, but much less frequently than the machete. The hoe is the basic implement used in tilling the soil. The machete is used for clearing fields prior to planting, for gathering firewood, and for a variety of other purposes. Judging from fragments of evidence gathered by the Instituto Indigenista Nacional in the community studies referred to above, the Indian farmers have to buy a new hoe every year, or every other year. There is less uniformity in the replacement rate of the machete, but four to five years seems to be a reasonable estimate of the length of time between new purchases.

Among the other articles bought by the highland Indians from the outside, special mention deserves to be made of matches, and the beads used by women for decorative purposes, both of which are imported from abroad. Liquor is another item of significance, in view of the high consumption connected with ritualistic ceremonies of all sorts. Illegal distilling is apparently not unknown in the highland area, but there is no doubt that large amounts of *aguardiente* are bought from the established distilleries of Guatemala. Fireworks, another article of widespread use in rituals and fiestas, are bought from the outside as well as produced locally. Patent medicines should also be mentioned, although they are not used nearly as much as the local remedies administered by *curanderos*. Food products are brought in from the low country; some of these are commodities that are scarcely produced in the highlands, while others supplement local production in off seasons or in periods of poor harvests. Sugar, coffee, and vegetables are prominent in this traffic, and in some years substantial amounts of corn are transported from the lowlands for sale in highland markets.

Labor and "imports" represent the two principal connections between the indigenous economy of the highland region and the national economy of Guatemala. In addition, the region gets money from the outside by the sale of certain farm produce, such as the onions and other truck crops raised in Panajachel, and a variety of fabricated articles, including items made especially for the tourist trade. The latter are interesting because they indicate another response to a business opportunity which has developed in recent years.[38] A complete list of miscellaneous products sold to the outside would be quite long, but the aggregate income derived from such sources probably falls well short of the total earnings derived from wage labor in the coffee *fincas*.

What has been said above about connections with the national economy suggests that the indigenous economy is not isolated from national and international economic fluctuations, but is rather affected by them. How important is the effect? Is it significant to the Indians who make up the indigenous economy, or is it merely a marginal circumstance in their livelihood? Economists in Guatemala are inclined to take the latter viewpoint, but I believe that they are not correct in doing so. Moreover, I think it is proper to discount the judgment of Guatemalan economists on this question because of the cultural gap which exists between them, as Ladinos, and the Indian population of the country. This gap is wide and deep. There is no doubt that the Indian is culturally isolated from the Ladino, and probably this very cultural isolation leads the Ladino to exaggerate the economic isolation of the Indian.

At best only fragmentary evidence can be cited. La Farge did his field work in Santa Eulalia in 1932, when the world was suffering intensely from Depression conditions, and he recorded some effects of the Depression which were called to his attention. The use of Japanese silk blouses by the women had been curtailed, and a parallel decline had taken place in the use of European-type clothing by the men of the community.[39] It is interesting, too, that La Farge picked up the opinion from several people that hard times would bring about a revival of pottery making, a craft which, as we have already noted, had been abandoned in the preceding years of good times. Cash, which earlier had been abundant in Santa Eulalia, was very scarce in 1932, owing to a reduction in the earnings obtained from labor in the coffee *fincas*, and standards of living had suffered a setback.

Tax, who was already carrying out field work in Guatemala in the post-Depression days of the 1930's, has also noted that the indigenous population suffered when the price of coffee fell during the slump.[40] In addition, Tax has pointed out that in the villages around Lake Atitlán the elders frowned on cutting down expenditures for religious ceremonies, so that the burden of carrying on the *servicios*, as they are called, became a heavy one. Even such expenditures had apparently become geared to the prosperity conditions of the preceding years. Ultimately, too, they responded to the effects of the Depression, and in some communities at any rate they were scaled down to correspond with Depression conditions.[41]

To appreciate fully the effects of the Depression, we would, of course, have to know a good deal about relative price changes in the economy of highland Guatemala. Statistical information is lacking, but there is every reason to believe, as Tax concluded from his observations in Panajachel,[42] that such changes have taken place. In this connection, it is interesting to call attention to an observation made by Wisdom in his study of the Chorti Indians, even though this Indian group is not located in the highland region itself, but rather in eastern Guatemala near the boundary with Honduras. The economy of the Chorti is much less commercialized than that of the highland region, and Wisdom found that traditional prices were common in transactions between one Indian and another. Bargaining was not the standard practice. Nevertheless, Wisdom observed that during times of Depression they did engage in haggling over prices,[43] a fact which suggests that even traditional price relations were affected by depressed circumstances in the national economy.

In concluding this discussion of relations between the indigenous economy of the highlands and the national economy of Guatemala, it is well to emphasize that the question involved is one of comforts and conveniences rather than basic subsistence, although that, too, may be involved in some years when crops are poor in the highland country. But obviously comforts and conveniences are an integral part of the standard of living of these people, even though they may seem meager to outsiders. The highland people are in my opinion already substantially tied to the national economy, and thus to international fluctuations as well. Granted, the whole question needs to be studied carefully, and much more evidence has to be assembled before a firm judgment can be arrived at. Meanwhile, I think it is a serious mistake for Guatemalan economists to assume, as they are wont to do, that the indigenous economy of the highland region is a separate compartment which for practical purposes can be regarded as isolated from the national economy of the country. It is dangerous to assume that the cultural wall between Indian and Ladino has an exact counterpart in economic affairs.

III

The material reviewed in the preceding section indicates that the indigenous economy of highland Guatemala possesses the following main characteristics: Production is directed toward the market, rather than toward individual and family consumption; productive effort is specialized, by communities as well as by individuals; a vigorous and complex trade is carried on throughout the region; transactions are based on market forces, rather than custom and tradition; there is an active response to gainful incentives; the regional economy is significantly tied to the national economy of Guatemala, and to international economic conditions as well.

Furthermore, the evidence indicates that these characteristics have been becoming more fully developed since the latter part of the nineteenth century, owing to the elaboration of the coffee economy of Guatemala. No one can say whether the rate of change is fast or slow. The direction of change, however, seems clear, and it suggests that the people of highland Guatemala are being further prepared for full participation in the national economy of the country. It may be that only a short distance needs to be traveled to bring about economic integration of the highland peoeple. At any rate the remaining distance is probably much shorter than students of Guatemalan economic affairs are inclined to believe.

The observations just made about highland Guatemala are not, of course, intended to apply to other indigenous economies of Latin America. An identical spirit of commercialism may not be found in any other. Nevertheless, it may well be true that many of them have more in common with highland Guatemala than with the "model" of an indigenous economy set forth near the beginning of this article. Obviously, we have here a large field for investigation—one which is of the utmost importance for some of the Latin American countries. It is, moreover, a field to which contributions can be made by scholars from different disciplines, such as anthropology, cultural geography, sociology, economics, and history, although they do not have to work in teams. Indeed, it is probably best if they do not. They must, however, be willing to address themselves to questions which are at the moment unconventional in their respective disciplines. In this field, the central questions are found on the margins among disciplines. Thus far, anthropologists have shown the greatest response to the opening up of such new lines of inquiry. Surely some economists, and others, can afford to meet them half way. Unless they do so, it is difficult to see how a whole range of significant Latin American economic problems can be properly understood and evaluated.

NOTES

1. Adams has set forth some of his ideas in *Introducción a la antropología aplicada*, Seminario de Integracion Social Guatemalteca, Pub. 13, Guatemala, 1964, N.D.

2. Sol Tax, "The Municipios of the Midwestern Highlands of Guatemala," *American Anthropologist*, 1937, XXXIX, 438.

3. Charles Wagley, *The Economics of a Guatemalan Village*, American Anthropological Association Memoir 58, 1942, p. 21.

4. F. Webster McBryde, *Cultural and Historical Geography of South-*

west Guatemala, Smithsonian Institution, Institute of Social Anthropology Publication 4, Washington, 1947, p. 128.

5. *Ibid.*, Map 19.

6. F. Webster McBryde, *Sololá*, Tulane University, Middle American Research Institute Publication 5, New Orleans, 1933, p. 112.

7. McBryde, *Cultural and Historical Geography of Southwest Guatemala*, p. 104.

8. New Orleans, Tulane University, Middle American Research Institute Publication 4, 1932, pp. 531–556.

9. *Quarterly Journal of Inter-American Relations*, 1939, I, 48.

10. Tax, "World View and Social Relations in Guatemala," *American Anthropologist*, 1941, XLIII, 35.

11. McBryde, *Sololá*, p. 110.

12. Lila M. O'Neale, *Textiles of Highland Guatemala*, Carnegie Institution of Washington Publication 567, Washington, 1945, p. 7.

13. Oliver La Farge and Douglas Byers, *The Year Bearer's People*, New Orleans, Tulane University, Middle American Research Institute Publication 3, 1931, p. 51.

14. Oliver La Farge, *Santa Eulalia*, Chicago, University of Chicago Press, 1947, pp. 5, 36.

15. O'Neale, p. 5.

16. See La Farge's paper, "Maya Ethnology: The Sequence of Cultures," in *The Maya and Their Neighbors*, New York, Appleton-Century Co., 1940, pp. 281–291. In his tentative list of post-Conquest cultural sequences in the Maya highlands, he has a separate classification for the period since 1880—namely, Recent Indian II—when coffee production became important.

17. Sol Tax, *Penny Capitalism: A Guatemalan Indian Economy*, Smithsonian Institution, Institute of Social Anthropology Publication 16, 1953.

18. *Ibid.*, p. 16.

19. La Farge and Byers, p. 17. For comments of a more general character on the highland area, see Tax, "World View and Social Relations in Guatemala," pp. 27–42.

20. See McBryde, *Cultural and Historical Geography of Southwest Guatemala*, p. 84. Wagley, p. 22, notes specific instances of barter trading in Santiago Chimaltenango.

21. McBryde, *Sololá*, p. 123.

22. See his paper on "Economy and Technology" for the Viking Fund Seminar on Middle American Ethnology: Sol Tax, ed., *Heritage of Conquest*, Glencoe, Free Press, 1952, p. 54.

23. Tax, *Penny Capitalism*, p. 145.

24. Redfield, "Primitive Merchants of Guatemala," *op. cit.*, p. 51.

25. Tax, "The Towns of Lake Atitlán," Microfilm Collection of Manuscripts on Middle American Cultural Anthropology, no. 13, Chicago, University of Chicago Libraries, 1946, pp. 10–11.

26. La Farge, *Santa Eulalia*, p. 31.

27. This is an inference which I have drawn from La Farge's discussion in *The Year Bearer's People*, p. 40.

28. Tax, *Penny Capitalism*, pp. 98–105.

29. *Ibid.*, pp. 103–104.
30. *Ibid.*, p. 12.
31. *Ibid.*, p. 18.
32. *Ibid.*, pp. 18–19, 186–207.
33. Wagley, p. 76.
34. Tax, pp. 204–205.
35. See O'Neale, p. 188.
36. Publicaciones Especiales del Instituto Indigenista Nacional: no. 2, Chuarrancho; no. 4, Chinautla; no. 5, Parramos; no. 7, Santa Catarina Barahona; no. 9, San Bartolomé Milpas Altas. All these studies have appeared only in mimeographed form.
37. *Cultural and Historical Geography of Southwest Guatemala,* p. 47.
38. See Tax's comments in *Heritage of Conquest,* p. 59, and "World View and Social Relations in Guatemala," *op. cit.*, p. 35.
39. La Farge, *Santa Eulalia,* pp. 5, 29.
40. Tax, "La economía regional de los indígenas de Guatemala," *Boletín del Instituto Indigenista Nacional,* 1947, II, 171.
41. Tax, *Heritage of Conquest,* p. 58.
42. Tax, *Penny Capitalism,* p. 138.
43. Charles Wisdom, *The Chorti Indians of Guatemala,* Chicago, University of Chicago Press, 1940, p. 32. Wisdom's work was carried out during the years 1931–33.

The Occurrence and Disappearance of Reciprocal Farm Labor in Latin America

CHARLES J. ERASMUS

Throughout the world the employment of wage labor is replacing or has already replaced older reciprocal forms of farm labor by which families in need of extra help either exchanged an equal number of days' work with their neighbors or entertained work parties of neighbors with feasts and drinking bouts. Causal explanations of the occurrence and disappearance of reciprocal farm labor are the concern of this paper. My treatment of this subject has two major objectives: first, to examine the breakdown of reciprocal labor as one aspect of a larger process—the individualization of society, and second, to perform this examination in the form of a culture structure analysis.

For my purposes here a "process" will be defined as a sequence of culture changes involving some degree of spatial recurrence or regularity by virtue of similar causes. Although this study has been stimulated in part by the developmental implications of Redfield's folk–urban con-

Reprinted from *Southwestern Journal of Anthropology*, 1956, XII, 444–469, by permission of the author and publisher. Minor changes by the author include revision of title from the original "Culture Structure and Process: The Occurrence and Disappearance of Reciprocal Farm Labor." For helpful criticism during the preparation of this paper, the author is grateful to John H. Rowe, George M. Foster, Kenneth E. Bock, and Julian H. Steward. A synoptic version of this study was read during the 1954 American Anthropological Association meetings at Detroit.

tinuum, my treatment of process in this instance will conform more to what Redfield[1] would call an "analytic" or "scientific" study rather than to the "holistic" approach he seems to prefer. Furthermore, it will focus on cross-cultural explanations of change rather than on the description of the equilibrium structures of social organisms. In this respect it follows in the structure-developmental tradition rather than that of structure-functionalism and might therefore be called a study of the structure of cultural causality. Motivational, limitative, and cognitive causes form the three fundamental categories of culture structure and will constitute the three headings under which I shall discuss causes of the occurrence and disappearance of reciprocal farm labor.

My interest in reciprocal farm labor began during a mission in Haiti as an applied anthropologist in 1952. Although many local social planners looked upon the Haitian *combite* as a practice on which to base cooperative self-help projects, its disintegration everywhere seemed to correlate with the very socioeconomic changes which the planners were endeavoring to accelerate. As applied assignments took me about western South America over the next two years, data on reciprocal farm labor were gathered opportunistically during free moments for some seventy different locations in Colombia, Ecuador, Peru, and Chile. This paper, then, is based largely on my data from western South America although frequent reference will be made to comparative material from other parts of the world. Since a detailed presentation of my field data is available elsewhere,[2] the emphasis here will be on interpretation. I shall begin, however, with a brief introduction to the two forms of labor reciprocity with which this paper is concerned.

Festive and Exchange Forms of Labor Reciprocity

In western South America a distinction is commonly made between two forms of reciprocal farm labor which I shall refer to as "festive" and "exchange" labor. The festive form is known by several names such as *convite* (Colombia and Ecuador), *minga* (southwestern Colombia and highland Ecuador), *minga bailada* (north coast of Ecuador), and *mingaco* (Chile). Names such as *ayni* (Peru), *cambio de mano* (Colombia), and *vuelta mano* (Chile) indicate the exchange form. The distinction made between these two types of labor is not peculiar to this area, however, for they coexist in many parts of the world. Provinse,[3] for example, describes identical forms for the Siang Dyaks which he calls "feast" and "exchange" labor, terms we have borrowed almost intact. There seems to be no evidence for considering either form as older than or pre-conditional to the other; both are found together among primitive and rural peoples. Although exchange labor survives among poorer farmers in most of rural western South America, festive labor has become comparatively infrequent. Nearly everywhere, however, the disappearance of either or both forms has been so recent that older people clearly remember their practice.

The distinctions made between exchange and festive labor generally concern the degree of obligation to reciprocate labor as well as the quantity and quality of the food and/or drink served the workers. In the first case the obligation to reciprocate is very strong and any food or drink provided are usually considered ordinary fare. A day's labor is expected in return for each day given; and if one is unable to meet an obligation due to sickness etc., he must send someone in his place. According to prior arrangements, those exchanging work may feed one another in turn, take their own food with them to the fields, or return home for lunch. At festive labor parties the host wines and/or dines his worker-guests in extraordinary fashion, and his obligation to reciprocate their labor is not only weaker but in most cases obviated. In case of illness, for example, he would certainly be under no obligation to send a replacement. In western South America the two categories are not always mutually exclusive on the basis of these criteria. Reciprocity, particularly among close relatives, may be very strong in some festive forms as is the case at house construction work parties in the Jauja Valley of Peru and around Otavalo, Ecuador. In general, however, festivities usually exempt the host from reciprocating the labor of at least some if not all of his guests.

In comparing the above data with that found in the literature on other areas, one is faced with the usual problem of unequal reporting. Writers do not always discuss the obligations of reciprocity or the quality of food, but in general the same correlation appears to hold true—labor reciprocity is weaker in the presence of festivities. Again, however, some cases do occur in which a high degree of reciprocity co-occurs with festivities as in house building at Yalalag, Mexico,[4] and Suye Mura, Japan,[5] and in agricultural labor among the Mexican Mixteca,[6] the Gonave Islanders,[7] and the South African Pondo.[8]

While most exchange labor groups in western South America and other parts of the world contain less than ten individuals, festive work groups usually run well over ten and sometimes into the hundreds. One of the largest reported occurred among the Pennsylvania Amish.[9] Both types of work party are made up of relatives and/or neighbors; kinship, friendship, and proximity tend to overlap in the rural societies which practice reciprocal labor. The distance between residences of exchange group members is inclined to be greater when they share farm equipment since the convenience of workable combinations may outweigh other considerations. This is illustrated by the Tonga of British Central Africa[10] and by Michigan farmers.[11] A significant aspect of work groups is their tendency to be composed of members of the same ethnic units.

In western South America Indians, whites, and Negroes usually have separate work groups, and Kimball[12] reports a similar cleavage between Michigan farmers of Polish ancestry and those of old American stock.

Women generally prepare the food for work parties and may reciprocate labor among themselves for this purpose. Men do not usually exchange labor with women unless women traditionally perform some special collaborative task, as in the case of Quechua women who turn over the clods hoed up by the men, or unless the task is performed with equal facility by both sexes as in the case of rice transplanting at Suye Mura.[13]

Seldom mentioned in the literature[14] but widespread in western South America is the practice of mixing exchange and hired labor. Thus, the labor force at a man's disposal on a given day may consist of men whose labor he has agreed to repay with his own at a later time as well as men whose labor he has agreed to pay for in cash. It is for this reason that the food which the host may give his exchange laborers is so frequently said to be the same ordinary fare given hired labor; all eat together.

Ideally the labor reciprocated in an exchange agreement does not have to be for the same tasks. One man who helps another weed his field may, for example, request help in repairing his roof as repayment. The amount of time—usually a day for a day—rather than the job is the important consideration. In practice, however, exchange usually results in a rotation of services during phases of the farming cycle so that like tasks as well as equal amounts of time are exchanged. When inequalities in size of landholdings result in inequalities of labor needs, the difference is usually compensated for in western South America by the practice of mixing hired and exchange labor and sometimes by sponsoring festive work parties. Around Otavalo, Ecuador, payments in produce may compensate for inequalities; Wagley[15] mentions a similar phenomenon for Guatemala.

Exchange and festive work parties differ from one another in their organization largely as a result of the differences in degree of labor reciprocity. Exchange labor occurs among social equals whose work-group membership tends to be repetitive as a consequence of obligatory reciprocity. Such groups may have a semi-permanent character when work is rotated among members at certain periods of the farming cycle. This is particularly true when rotation of services is associated with the pooling of equipment or machinery as in the case of some Araucanian plowing partnerships. Although sanctions are quite informal, in the case of exchange labor they are extremely effective; the quantity and quality of work given is the measure of its return.

Since obligations of reciprocity are much weaker in the festive form and the size of work parties much larger, attendance tends to vary with each affair. However, when the host's status is the same or close to that of his guests, sanctions are again largely informal. The host may personally direct the work or may designate certain individuals to supervise different groups working simultaneously. Sometimes, as in Chile or at Haitian *combites*,[16] the host appoints an intermediary to act as communication link between him and his worker-guests. Such an intermediary may carry the host's orders and complaints to the workers and the workers' grievances to the host. This practice helps resolve any conflict in the host's dual role as festive host and work boss. That such a custom is not incompatible with exchange labor is indicated by its occurrence at the exchange hoeing parties of Bulgarian women.[17] As in the case of exchange labor those invested with authority at informal festive labor parties are usually individuals whose superior skill is recognized by the group.

Where the disparity of status between host and workers at festive labor parties is so great that little or no labor reciprocity is involved on the part of the host, control tends to be enforced from outside the labor group. Work foremen hired by the landowner tend to represent his interests exclusively. Individual workers may even be rewarded preferentially during the festivities to increase work incentives as in the case of Haitian *combites*.[18] Festivities clearly become a form of repayment in these instances. In hacienda or "feudal" situations where landowners control their labor through the ability to withhold perquisites, such as the use of subsistence plots, pasture land, firewood, and roads, attendance at "festive" work parties becomes almost mandatory and the composition of the work groups may be quite fixed. This tends to be the case, for example, around Otavalo, Ecuador, and Cuzco, Peru, and apparently was also true of thirteenth-century England.[19]

In some cases exchange labor groups may form into permanent or semi-permanent organizations. Two well-known examples affiliated with age grading are the West African *dokpwe*[20] and the Sema-Naga "gangs."[21] While in both cases the groups apparently work in turn for the families represented by their membership, they may also work for individuals who reward them with festivities in lieu of labor reciprocation. Similarly in Haiti permanent and semi-permanent exchange labor groups worked for each member in turn and for wealthier individuals outside the labor-reciprocating membership who either hired them as a group for wages or enticed them with the promise of festivities.[22] These seemingly "mixed" cases in which the same individuals perform exchange and festive labor illustrate the differences between the two forms; for while labor reciprocity is strictly obligatory among the exchange membership, beneficiaries of festive work performed by such exchange labor organizations are usually outside the labor-reciprocating membership.

I encountered only one example of a "permanent" exchange labor organization in western South America and that one in a Negro village on the Cayapas River of Ecuador. The group or "committee" worked consecutively for each member in turn and any member had the right to sell his "turn" to another member or an outsider. If the work of the committee was hired out of turn through the "president," the money went into a treasury to pay for week-end parties. According to local accounts the committee had been "invented" by the president. Although no other similar case was encountered during my stay on the Cayapas, my visit to the area was too brief for me to establish the authenticity of this claim to my complete satisfaction.

Although a competitive spirit may exist even among exchange workers, organized competition is much more characteristic of festive work parties at which there are more people and at which an atmosphere of sociability prevails. Where found in western South America such competition seems to be among individuals. However, in Haiti[23] and Africa[24] organized competition at agricultural chores may take place between or among groups of workers, a practice which would appear to be associated with large work parties. The host of a festive labor party often provides music and dancing after the work, a common but not universal phenomenon in western South America and elsewhere. Moreover, festive labor tends to occur on holidays and exchange labor on regular workdays. Music during work is not a general characteristic of reciprocal labor in western South America as it is in some parts of the world such as in Haiti,[25] West Africa,[26] among the Sema Naga,[27] and in Bulgaria.[28]

Motivation

Although human motivations are a necessary cause of culture, they never provide a sufficient explanation. They put the locus of culture in man himself, but they do not determine the forms of expression nor the degrees of energy which they may activate. Forms and energy of culture at any given time and place are further determined by limitative and cognitive causes. We shall begin, however, by considering some of the more probable motives underlying the occurrence and disappearance of exchange and festive labor.

The motivation to survive is perhaps the most obvious. In cases such as that cited by Fei and Chang[29] for Yunnan, China, where one family alone cannot take care of enough land during the busy season of rice transplanting to maintain itself for the rest of the year, labor exchange during periods of peak labor load may clearly be a matter of survival. It may be assumed for the moment that the labor performed by such a reciprocal work party is no greater than the sum of its parts, in other words that the work done by five men in one day could be done in five days by any one of them, discounting differences in skill. Evidence to support this view has been provided by Foster's[30] quantitative analysis of exchange labor among the Mexican Popoluca. The motivation for group work in such cases is to do in one day a job which cannot wait five.

There is considerable evidence, however, that natives in some parts of the world are motivated to seek labor exchanges because they *feel* that more is accomplished together than alone. This feeling, expressed to me by some Araucanians, has been recorded for example by Malinowski[31] for the Trobriands and by Hogbin[32] for Wogeo and New Guinea. Although Malinowski was uncertain of the validity of native opinion on this point, Hogbin gathered some quantitative though inconclusive data which tended to confirm it. While it does not indicate that a group of five men would necessarily accomplish more in one day than one man *could* accomplish in five days working alone, Hogbin's material does indicate that in a group situation the desire for social approbation may offset procrastination to the extent that an individual may be more likely to approximate his true work potential under those conditions. Again, the underlying motivation on the part of the host may be to meet a need for an accelerated work schedule.

However, a survival or "efficiency" motivation does not underlie reciprocal labor everywhere. For example, in comparing the Heiban and Otoro of Central Sudan, Nadel[33] found that group labor would be just as useful in planting as in seeding or clearing in that it would enable "the cultivator to . . . ease his crowded time table." But while the Heiban use group labor for planting, the Otoro do not. Nadel concludes that "The restriction of group labour to certain specified activities seems largely a matter of convention." Writers on many different areas have pointed out the social nature of reciprocal labor, though almost always with reference to the festive form. In such cases the sponsoring of work parties would seem to be motivated largely by the desire for prestige obtained through conspicuous giving. In western South America the host of a festive work party was invariably esteemed for the quantity and quality of the food and/or drink he provided his worker guests. Men took pride in the size of their work parties, and where the practice still exists or has recently disappeared, informants were unanimous in stating that the size of festive work parties was in direct proportion to the known generosity of the host.

As noted previously, the same basic motivations may take innumerable forms; thus we find the same motivations underlying the disappearance of reciprocal labor as underlie its occurrence. The survival problem of peak labor loads may motivate the employment of wage labor as well as participation in work exchanges. Similarly, the desire for social approbation which may motivate the host of a festive work party to conspicuous giving may equally motivate an employer to expend much of the surplus produced by his hired labor on individual forms of conspicuous consumption.

Since participants in labor exchange alternate as workers and hosts, their motivations are likely to be similar. In the case of festive labor, Willems[34] distinguishes between immediate and delayed reciprocity, the festive aspect being an immediate short-term form of reciprocity or reward while the labor itself constitutes a more delayed form. To the extent that festive labor is not reciprocal, the immediate reward of festive enjoyment becomes the only reward, and it may not provide the same quality of motivation for host and workers as when each reciprocates with his own labor. The same is true of a monetary reward, and we shall have more to say on this point later. Now we turn to limitative causes of the different forms of agricultural labor which motivations activate.

Limitation

The limiting causes of any given culture behavior are conditions which increase the probability of its occurrence, a causal relationship posited where possible from cross-cultural regularities. Such a relationship implies potentiality as well as limitation. Limiting causes are of two major kinds: noncultural (biological and environmental) and cultural. Cultural limitations may belong either to the realm of specialized culture (culture which cumulates through the division of labor—primarily technology and knowledge) or to the realm of nonspecialized culture (marriage, art, religion, etc.).[35] The latter limitations are frequently "limitations of possibilities," such as limitations in the possible variations of marriage forms,[36] kinship terms,[37] corpse disposal,[38] and games.[39] Before discussing the major limiting causes of the occurrence and disappearance of reciprocal farm labor, we shall illustrate the types of limitation by considering their relationship to some of the secondary or derived aspects of reciprocal labor previously described.

A biological limitation, for example, operates through the sex division of labor to decrease the probability of labor exchanges between the sexes and to increase the frequency with which women are assigned the task of preparing the food at festive work parties. Similarly, the advantage of working to rhythm on some jobs requiring coordination is related to physical and biological limitations predisposing toward the cross-cultural recurrence of work performed in time to music. According to Firth,[40] Tikopian work parties sing while carrying canoe trunks to the coast, for the rhythm "helps to set the pace for the activity and indicates appropriate pauses." Rhythm may even help in coordinating the muscular movements of a single individual. A recent study of the "extensive rhythmical movements"—called a "jig"—performed by soap wrappers in a British perfume factory showed a significant positive correlation between the "jig" and the efficiency of the workers.[41]

An example in the nonspecialized sphere illustrating the limitation of possibilities is the correlation between group competition and festive labor. Only festive work parties are usually of sufficient size to permit group competition. Similarly, the probability of a cross-cultural recurrence of worker-host intermediaries is enhanced by the limitation of possibilities in the basic structure of interpersonal relations—in this case the potential conflict between host-guest sentiment and boss-worker authority. A limitation of possibilities is also inherent in the rotational nature of exchange labor and increases the probability of the occurrence of exchange labor groups with repetitive and semi-permanent membership.

Given the tendency for a repetitive rotation of exchange labor and given the incipient development of local entrepreneurs who have specialized in management to the extent that they no longer exchange their own labor for the labor they require (a limitation of specialized culture), the resemblance between the "permanent" exchange labor organization encountered among the Cayapas River Negroes and similar organizations in Haiti and Africa does not necessarily establish diffusion or African origin. In the Haitian forms,[42] as well as in the Cayapas example, permanent exchange work groups which also sell their labor to outsiders grow out of the more informal exchange labor relationships on which they are patterned. The Cayapas members had long been in the habit of exchanging labor among themselves and were individuals of equal status with landholdings of about the same size.

TIME AND WEIGHT

In this section we shall appraise the noncultural limiting causes of reciprocal labor and their modification through the technological addition of extra-human sources of energy. We shall consider here the two major types of jobs performed by reciprocal farm labor: those which must be done faster than one man can do them and those which exceed the strength of a single man.

Jobs of the second category tend to be construction tasks requiring heavy lifting, such as putting house beams into place. Unlike the seasonal chores of agriculture, construction tasks are usually more infrequent in family life, and their very infrequency would seem to help to explain why they are so much more often associated with festive rather than exchange labor. Labor reciprocity in the case of chores involving a low frequency of recurrence is more likely to be delayed, and in such cases the festivities provide an immediate reward to reinforce worker motivation.

Urgency is the principal physical limitation in reciprocal farm labor.

Some writers speak of "heavy" agricultural tasks such as land clearing in virgin forests, but these jobs can be performed by one man if he burns and cuts the larger trees into manageable sizes. However, the work would be detrimentally delayed by such tactics. Hall[43] states the problem clearly in describing agricultural practices on Gonave Island, Haiti: "The problem of clearing thirty or more acres [the amount Hall deemed necessary to support a family] of tropical vegetation is impossible for one man. By the time he is ready to plant, the first acres cleared will be brush-covered again. The planting, too, of such an area could scarcely be completed in the time necessitated by weather conditions." In the case of food processing tasks, the problem of urgency may become one of ubiquity. As in sugarmaking among the Chorti, several individuals—although none of them specialists in the sense that their jobs require specialized skills—may be necessary to perform simultaneous functions.[44]

Urgent tasks may be classified into two general categories: predictable and unpredictable. The latter are usually the result of a delay in farm work caused by some unexpected circumstance, such as illness in the family, irregular rains, occupancy of a farm late in the season, and enforced absence from the farm. Unpredictable urgent tasks are less frequent than predictable ones, and they, like heavy tasks, tend to be more closely associated with festive labor and its immediate rewards. Convenience is another reason for the association since exchange labor is more difficult to arrange in unpredictable cases. In the event of a delay, those with whom one might normally exchange labor may have finished their seasonal chores and no longer have need for the reciprocal benefits of labor exchange. Moreover, since an emergency task may require a considerable number of helpers at once, the inconvenience of contracting a large labor debt might well outweigh the expense of sponsoring a festive work party. Exchange labor, however, does not seem to be any more closely associated with tasks of predictable urgency than does festive labor. Festive work parties can be planned as readily as labor exchanges.

Predictable urgent tasks conform to seasonal peak labor loads and consist of such chores as clearing before the rains come or before the weeds can grow back, weeding before the crop is choked, and harvesting or processing before crop spoilage can occur. The seasonal nature of these predictable peak labor loads raises the question of how farmers in the same area can exchange labor if they all need each other's help at the same time. For most of western South America the answer is simple—the seasons allow enough leeway that operations on neighboring farms are by no means simultaneous. In the tropics the flexibility of work schedules may be very great. On the Cayapas River, for example, land is cleared for the planting of bananas at any time of the year. In China, however, the dates of planting may be deliberately staggered by those exchanging labor,[45] and in Haiti the members of Congo Societies even diversified their crops to avoid conflicts in working schedules.[46] In the highlands of western South America the climatic changes may be great enough within short distances that neighbors frequently have slightly different planting and harvesting seasons. Where irrigation is practiced, as at La Victoria, Peru, the rotation of irrigation periods may result in different individual cropping schedules. Conflict is also reduced in the case of festive work parties by the custom of holding them on Sundays and holidays.

Since limitations of time and weight are predisposing factors in the occurrence of reciprocal labor, it is not surprising to find that technological changes which supplement men's strength and speed modify reciprocal labor patterns and decrease their incidence. Even the elementary change from stone to metal tools may have considerable effect on the size of reciprocal labor parties. On the island of Wogeo, for example, land clearing was once performed by groups of fifteen or twenty men, but today with the use of steel implements reciprocal labor groups seldom consist of more than five or six.[47] In Japan mutual aid groups have been decreasing in size since the war partly as a result of the increased use of farm machinery.[48] Similar reductions in the size of reciprocal labor groups as a result of the introduction of machinery have been noted for Ireland[49] and the United States.[50]

As indicated previously, exchange labor groups may become more permanent and the interpersonal relationships more formalized when equipment is shared or jointly owned. Plowing partnerships, for example, occur today among the Tonga[51] and Lovedu[52] of Africa and the Araucanians of Chile. In Michigan, Kimball[53] found that the old harvesting and threshing rings had been practically abandoned since the appearance of the combine and had been replaced by labor-exchanging silo-filling groups or "companies" which share ownership of the silo-filling machine. In all such cases there seems to be a shift of "emphasis"—as the Kriges[54] note for the Lovedu—from the "sharing of services" to "the sharing of tools." The persistence of exchange labor groups with this change of emphasis is related to the scale or level of farm operations as Kimball[55] has shown. Although the maintenance and depreciation costs of equipment may be out of proportion to a farm's productivity at a given level of operation, through joint ownership or equipment pools the costs may be readily absorbed by the combined productivity of several such farms. On a larger scale of commercial operations the same costs may be borne by a single farm.

In addition to modifying reciprocal labor, machinery has eliminated it in many places, as in the case of the Michigan harvesting and threshing "rings." Likewise in Chile the *mingaco* has been steadily disappearing with the greater use of harvesting and threshing machinery. And on some haciendas near Otavalo, Ecuador, tractors now perform the plowing that *minga* workers once did by hand. For most of western South America, however, modification and disappearance of reciprocal labor have taken place without significant corresponding changes in the farmers' technology. Obviously, then, if technological alterations in the limitations of weight and time do not alone account for the disappearance of reciprocal labor it becomes much less probable that these limitations suffice to explain its occurrence.

LAND AND DURABLE GOODS

In this section we shall be concerned primarily with the social nature of reciprocal labor and therefore almost exclusively with the festive form. We indicated earlier that a desire for social approbation might serve equally well as a motivation for both conspicuous giving and individual conspicuous consumption. A shift from the first form of expression to the second seems to correlate with the disappearance of festive labor insofar as the festive form serves as a vehicle for conspicuous giving. Conditions which increase the probability of this change are its limiting causes. Two which shall concern us here are the abundance of land and the abundance of durable goods. We shall also see how these causes are reflected in the three most common reasons which people in western South America give for abandoning festive labor in favor of wage labor: (1) the poor quality of festive work, (2) its high cost, and (3) the difficulty of controlling worker-guests.

Festive labor, as previously noted, does not necessarily involve the same high degree of labor reciprocity that characterizes the exchange form; and where the obligations of labor reciprocity are weak, the status disparity between host and guests is likely to be strong. Exchange labor tends to occur among social equals, and even where there are differences in wealth it prevails among social equals at the poorer end of the scale. Thus, today in western South America we find the practice of exchange labor still widespread among small farmers and sharecroppers while their wealthier neighbors prefer to hire or feast their labor. Similar findings have been reported for Brazil,[56] Haiti,[57] Dahomey,[58] the Yako,[59] the Yoruba,[60] the Trobriands,[61] the Siang Dyaks,[62] Japan,[63] and China.[64] Festive labor cuts across differences in wealth and status but predominantly in one direction, for work benefits generally go in the direction of higher status and festive rewards in the direction of lower status.

It is not surprising that exchange rather than festive labor should appear to be more closely related to a survival level of existence, for festivities are obviously favored by a surplus of production above the immediate needs of the sponsoring household. Where festive labor is reciprocated among equals most of the economic units within the groups are capable of producing a surplus. Such a condition would seem to be met by a land–population ratio sufficient to permit an extensive and often shifting type of cultivation. Where festive labor still occurs among equals in western South America such a condition prevails. Thus, we find the practice in Colombia among land clearers[65] near the Atlantic Coast, land clearers near Playarrica (Caldas), Antioqueño colonists near Pueblorrico (Caldas), Negroes and Chamí around Tadó (Choco), the Negroes of coastal Nariño, and in Ecuador among the Cayapas River Negroes.

As Conklin[66] has recently pointed out, the relative efficiency of shifting cultivation can be determined "only by taking into account the total yield per unit of labor, not per unit of area." However, only so long as land is plentiful can yield per unit of labor suffice as a measure of efficiency. When land becomes scarce, a change in attitudes toward farming techniques will be made more probable by the need to increase yield per unit of area. A case in point is the Caldas coffee belt around Pereira, Cartago, and Armenia where older informants claimed that festive labor was still a common practice at the turn of the century. This was a period of colonization, and cultivation was extensive rather than intensive. It did not matter in those days, said informants, if the work of festive labor parties was imperfect, for more than enough was planted and harvested. But after population pressure on the land increased, farmers had to give more attention to the quality of their work and have now come to disdain that of festive labor. According to our informants, the quality of festive work parties did not deteriorate; it was always "poor" by present standards.

The attitudes of Caldas farmers toward festive labor are widespread. Criticisms of the quality of festive work parties in western South America always include either crop damage (during weeding or hoeing) or unevenness of work (in clearing, plowing, planting, weeding, and harvesting). In south central Chile the expression "This looks like *mingaco* [festive] work" is used to indicate disapproval of a job poorly done.

The limitation of perishable capital, a characteristic of pre-specialized society, is another crucial factor in the occurrence and disappearance of festive labor. In a primitive economy where capital is largely food surplus and therefore relatively perishable, the advantage gained by the host of a work party through the festive labor of others will depend considerably on his reputation for generosity. Those who give more labor than they receive, allocate to the beneficiary the right to entertain them with the product of their own labor. The primitive "entrepreneur" is largely a prestige entrepreneur whose temporary advantage is made possible only so long as others willingly give him more labor than they expect to receive in return.

The limitation of perishable capital results in what Polanyi[67] referred to as "redistribution," a behavior of nonliterate people which in his opinion was "not primarily associated with economics." An excellent example of redistribution is provided by Schapera[68] in depicting the South African chief as a kind of tribal banker who could accumulate wealth through the festive labor of his subjects but who would be abandoned if he failed to distribute it in behalf of the tribe. In the Solomon Islands, Hogbin[69] writes that "a mere accumulation of valuables is never sufficient for a person to establish himself in a position of authority; he must give away wealth the whole time." Even though the Islanders sometimes grumble when they have to interrupt their own labors to work in the gardens of their chief, they recognize that "It is to their advantage to do so; they all share in the chief's wealth, partake of his feasts, and live under his protection." Although most Tarahumara[70] "are on the same economic level" those with greater wealth and prestige are those who give "better fiestas, with more food and drink."

As Firth[71] has pointed out for Tikopia, one of the principal limitations "upon individual greed and acquisitiveness" in a primitive society is "the lack of the means for individual economic assertion, the low level of material culture and the limited range of possible satisfactions." However, "The introduction of European material goods has provided new expressions for the desire for individual wealth." Similarly, "In Nuba economy," writes Nadel,[72] "which is largely a subsistence economy with hardly any provisions for long-time storage, the economic effect of an expansion of food-crop cultivation through group labour is limited; it produces only a short-lived surplus or, at the most, a stationary economic advantage. But the 'entrepreneur' who can once afford to enlist group labour for the cultivation of a 'cash crop' like cotton secures an increased return of permanent value, which will progressively add to his working capital in the modern sense of the word." And as Watson[73] has noted for the Cayuá of Brazil, "Trade goods . . . present a problem of distribution quite different from that of jointly produced food. The bulk of trade goods, like their aboriginal equivalents, pots, articles of clothing, implements, and so forth, are matters of individual concern. These items could not easily, like food, be distributed and consumed jointly. . . ."

As a primitive society becomes increasingly dependent upon the outside for articles of a more durable and less distributive quality, it becomes increasingly probable that conspicuous consumption will find satisfaction in acquisitiveness rather than in giving. The conspicuous giving pattern, largely limited by the perishable capital of the primitive society, tends to give way to more individualized patterns of conspicuous consumption as the use of money and the specialization of production proceed toward the expansion of durable forms of goods.

The second widespread criticism of festive labor in western South America concerns its relatively high cost in comparison with that of wage labor. A customary complaint is that food costs have become so inflated over what they were twenty years ago that feasting is now more expensive than hiring. However, the problem of relatively higher food prices is unquestionably related to the tendency for farmers in some rapidly commercializing areas to become increasingly dependent on markets for much of their food. In the Caldas coffee belt of Colombia, for example, farmers are planting so much of their land in coffee that they no longer have the surplus of subsistence crops they claim was once general. Much of the food for a festive work party would now have to be purchased and at such high prices that the cost would be considered excessive.

Among the Negro population along the Cayapas River of Ecuador we find another case where "costs" are being computed to the disadvantage of festive labor. A miniature banana boom has recently come to the peasant population of the Cayapas as a result of which many small entrepreneurs have moved up river from the coast. The latter do not sponsor festive work parties because they claim the expense would be too great. As they point out, local Negroes spend four or five days in the forest shooting meat prior to a work party, grow their own plantains and other foodstuffs, and not only grow their own sugar cane but also make their own rum. Cash is no problem when all the materials for a feast are at the farmer's disposal; but for the individual who would have to purchase them, the cash expenditure would exceed the cost of hiring labor, and all the time and work that must be expended in such preparations are deemed a nuisance by the entrepreneur. However, at the time of our visit even the local Negroes were beginning to "figure the cost." As more of them turned to the planting of bananas for market, their participation in festive labor practices was diminishing.

Similar complaints about the high costs of festive labor are reported for Brazil,[74] Mexico,[75] Haiti,[76] West Africa,[77] South Africa,[78] British Central Africa,[79] nineteenth-century New England,[80] and thirteenth-century England.[81] However, as Nadel[82] points out, "a cost is high only measured on the profit it can realize." Commercial farming and individualized patterns of conspicuous consumption entail a measure of profit quite different from subsistence-oriented farming and conspicuous giving. In the first case costs are measured on profits in durable consumption goods and in the second case on the temporary ability to be a generous host. The more individualistic form of conspicuous consumption tends to replace the redistributive form with increasing involvement in a money economy. However, the effects of this change on festive labor are not only reflected in the attitudes of wealthier individuals whose affluence would make them more likely hosts but also in the attitudes of those who would come as guests. In place of a festive reward the peasants of western South America have come to prefer a monetary payment and the ability, which it facilitates, to make their own choice from a wider selection of rewards. This brings us to the third reason for which festive labor is now widely condemned in western South America, the difficulty of controlling worker-guests.

Guests are said to attend festive work parties with the attitude that they are doing the host a favor, an attitude which farmers do not now consider conducive to the type of control which they prefer to exercise and which they feel can be better obtained through wage labor. The same complaint has been recorded for Brazil,[83] Haiti,[84] and South Africa.[85] In all these cases a local subsistence-oriented economy in which the host of festive work parties derived prestige from the number of his guests and his reputation for conspicuous giving has been superseded by a money economy in which the entrepreneur can establish a permanent advantage and a prestigeful consumption pattern independently of any personal and sentiment-invested redistribution relationship with his labor force. Festivities which are now a final as well as an immediate reward are increasingly considered a repayment and one which can be compared in money terms not only with the wage value of the same work but with the growing selection of durable consumption articles into which those wages can be converted.

Where festive labor has persisted longest in western South America despite the intrusion of a money economy, it has done so as an inter-class phenomenon without any labor reciprocity. The motivation of the workers in such cases is that of survival, since their attendance at "festive" work parties may be a necessary condition for receiving the feudal perquisites on which their existence depends. Such is the case, for example, on haciendas around Otavalo, Ecuador, and Cuzco, Peru. According to Homans,[86] even on the English manor festive work parties were "the longest preserved of all work services. Freeholders rendered them when they rendered no other services; villeins still rendered them when all their other services had been commuted." What was valuable, says Homans, "was not so much the work itself as the circumstance that it could be mobilized at once." From the standpoint of the landowner, the persistence of the festive work party in these instances is motivated by a need for an adequate labor supply at periods of peak labor requirements, not by a desire to give conspicuously.

Despite the presence of money, the hacienda, like the feudal manor, tends more toward a conservative tradition of self-sufficiency than toward entrepreneurial commercialization. Leisure and the consumption of labor are conspicuous and individualistic on the part of the landlord class. But cash may actually be scarce, and if so, wages will tend to be low. This condition can lead to the somewhat circular incrimination that occurs around Otavalo and Cuzco where many hacienda owners claim that the indolent Indians are not interested in working for wages and the Indians in turn claim that the hacienda owners do not pay enough to interest them. Consequently, the Indian prefers to exchange his labor for food or for the use of a piece of land. Furthermore, to control its labor supply the hacienda class employs whatever means it can to monopolize local land resources and to keep workers from developing the new felt needs that arouse dissatisfactions. Although Polanyi,[87] following Thurnwald, considers such feudal-like conditions redistributive, he points out that the system can "become predominantly political" in stratified societies as compared to more homogeneous primitive groups.

The occurrence of the exchange form is also limited by the availability of land, particularly where the size of landholdings is reduced through fragmentation by equal inheritance. In general, western South America is not an overpopulated area, but conditions of *minifundio* do occur in highlands, frequently among Indian populations bordering haciendas. In some communities close to Otavalo, Ecuador, for example, plots are too small either to maintain the family or to require extra-familial assistance at periods of peak labor load. In some overpopulated areas of the world, disguised rural unemployment may conceivably reduce the occurrence of labor exchange by providing those who require outside help with a ready market of laborers in need of a food or monetary—rather than a labor—repayment. At the time of his visit to Haiti, Hall[88] called Gonave Island "still a frontier" where "land is to be had in plenty." Exchange work societies were still prevalent in Hall's day, but by the time of Métraux's[89] visit they were disappearing on the overpopulated mainland. Only three work socieities still survived at Marbial and these were made up of small groups of poor peasants who sold their labor to landlords able to buy it. He also found a growing class of wageworkers composed of peasants who had inherited land too small in area to support them or who were landless. Similarly, Pierson[90] writes of a decrease in reciprocal work exchanges in a Brazilian village resulting from the subdivision of land through inheritance.

SPECIALIZATION AND THE USE OF MONEY

Effects of labor diversification were considered both under "Time and Weight" and "Land and Durable Goods." By means of specialization man has developed a technology which adds other sources of energy to his own and with it a great variety of consumption and capital goods. We have seen how both these circumstances become limiting causes for the disappearance of reciprocal labor. This section is directly concerned with limitations of labor diversification and their relation to the use of money, a subject particularly relevant to the disappearance of the exchange form.

Although exchange labor is outlasting the festive form nearly everywhere in western South America, it too is being replaced by the payment of a monetary wage. Unlike its festive counterpart, labor exchange is considered superior to wage labor both for its high quality workmanship and its low cost. As noted previously, sanctions, though informal, are strong in the exchange form since participants know that the quality and quantity of effort expended on a neighbor's chores will be the measure of their return. Moreover, when the workers agree to provide their own food, none of them is involved in any expense or cash outlay when it becomes his turn to be the labor beneficiary. Considering the high opinion in which exchange labor is universally held in these respects, why then should it be abandoned for wage labor? The answer would seem to lie in the common objection to it in western South America—inconvenience.

Actually, labor obtained by exchange is not free; it must be returned in an amount equal to that received. To work out exchange arrangements at a time when extra help is needed is not always easy, for others must be found who are willing and able to exchange. In addition, adjustments may be necessary to balance inequalities resulting from differences in size of landholdings. Similar assertions of inconvenience have also been recorded for Brazil,[91] Haiti,[92] South Africa,[93] Japan,[94] and the United States.[95]

The inconvenience to which we refer reflects changes in the behavioral forms of basic motivations, changes made increasingly probable by the use of money. Let us take the case of an individual possessing special skills. Earlier we noted that social recognition was ascribed to an individual of special ability by placing him in charge of a work party. However, when a recognized specialist such as a carpenter is employed at work parties in western South America, he usually receives some remuneration over and above that of festive or labor reciprocity. Perhaps the most outstanding characteristic of reciprocal labor is the unspecialized nature of the work performed. The use of money, on the other hand, facilitates increased reward and social recognition for special skills by facilitating the division of labor. To understand the way in which money facilitates this change, we can begin with a case of incipient specialization in a pre-money society, the case of the East African Hehe.[96] If a man required a spear, a stool or a pot, etc., he went to the appropriate artisan taking twice the amount of raw materials required, and during the manufacture of the product he either assisted the artisan or cultivated his fields. Thus, unskilled labor was exchanged for the product of specialized skill. The "profit" to the artisan lay in the accumulation of raw materials from which he made gifts for the chief, who might respond with gifts of cattle. In this case we can see that political control had become sufficiently centralized that the surplus production controlled by the chief could be redistributed to support a somewhat cumbersome system of labor diversification.

In Inca civilization, where political control was much more centralized, the unskilled labor of the population was taxed to cultivate state lands, the produce from which supported, among other things, skilled craftsmen who manufactured consumption goods exclusively for the emperor. The latter in turn redistributed the consumption manufactures among the nobility.[97] The "divine households" of early Mesopotamian civilization apparently followed a similar pattern of specialization, and, as Childe[98] has indicated, the development of crafts under such conditions would be limited largely to the market comprised by the favored class.

It seems highly improbable that anything approaching the present high degree of labor diversification would have been possible without the development of a money economy, for the latter provides the most convenient type of immediate reward for special skills—one which facilitates delayed reciprocity in differential form. The laborer or craftsman who is paid in money, the commodity of commodities, has more freedom to choose his own reward at his own convenience. The development of special skills is not hampered by direct exchanges between primary producers or by direct exchanges of skilled for unskilled labor. Nor is its expansion necessarily restricted to a small number of consumers who are privileged to occupy a controlling position in a class-stratified society and who reciprocate by means of perquisites.

Another example of the way in which the use of money reduces "inconvenience" and leads to the disappearance of work exchanges concerns the change from a primitive "entrepreneurial" pattern of conspicuous giving to the more modern individualistic form. About 1949, exporters began promoting the production of bananas among the Negro population living along the Cayapas River of coastal Ecuador. Since then, bananas have become the major crop along the river. Although subsistence agriculture was general before, the people had long ago acquired a taste for outside goods and had long been participants to some degree in a money economy. They were readily able to measure the satisfaction of their own wants in terms of an external demand for bananas. Consequently they quickly entered into new and more impersonal relationships entailing greater internal consumption of external commodities and greater regional specialization in production for extra-local consumption. Men who not long before had spoken with pride of the number of guests who attended their festive work parties now hired their labor and spoke with equal pride of the value of their useless but prestigeful wrist watches. As they themselves expressed it, "We have new aspirations."

Some individuals under the stimulus of these aspirations began quite early to expand their holdings, and as a result their labor needs soon outgrew their neighbors'. Although these entrepreneurs began by exchanging labor, they found that as their operations grew larger and the management of their own enterprises took more of their time, it became increasingly necessary to hire replacements to fulfill their exchange obligations. At this point, they said, it became easier to pay directly for their own labor needs and circumvent the inconvenience of being dependent upon the convenience of others. These entrepreneurs had, in effect, become specialists in management, and their management functions had become too time-consuming to justify continuing the performance of unskilled labor in order to maintain labor reciprocities. This process has occurred repeatedly throughout western South America where roads and expanding markets have led to increasing specialization in the production of cash crops. Cases suggesting similar circumstances have been reported for Mexico,[99] Haiti,[100] Nigeria,[101] the Nuba,[102] the Baganda,[103] the Tonga,[104] the Lovedu,[105] and the United States.[106]

The greater convenience of hiring labor is also illustrated in certain cases where subsistence and cash cropping are combined. At Fredonia, Antioquia, and San Lorenzo, Caldas, both in important Colombian coffee areas, the principal commercial crop, coffee, is produced by small farmers who also grow most of their own food requirements. Exchange labor is common at both places for all chores except harvesting, for the same neighbors who exchange labor at other times of the year pay cash for each other's help at harvest time. Money is prevalent only at this season and farmers find it preferable to pay for labor rather than work out labor exchanges complicated by differences in labor needs, the mixing of local and migratory labor and the urgency of the situation. A similar case was encountered along the lower course of the Cañete River of coastal Peru where cotton has been an important cash crop since the first World War. Here again farmers who exchange their labor for such chores as weeding during the rest of the year find it more convenient to hire each other's labor at harvest time when money is prevalent.

The hiring of local labor as a means of automatically adjusting for inequalities and thereby eliminating inconveniences in the arranging of exchanges is not limited only to payments of a money wage. Around Otavalo, Ecuador, for example, harvest workers are often paid in kind. Similarly, at Santiago, Guatemala, Wagley[107] found that farmers "are willing to pay their many harvest helpers, because their family will in turn work several times at the harvests of others, and thus regain the maize paid out from their own fields. To a rich man who tills large tracts of land and needs many laborers, it makes little difference whether his family can work to regain the wages." However, the greater flexibility of a money system employing investment and credit becomes clear when we consider the case of tobacco sharecroppers in the immediate vicinity of Bucaramanga, Colombia. Here, peasant sharecroppers with a standard of living no higher than that in the preceding cases are able to hire labor as they need it throughout the year. The land they farm is owned by tobacco companies willing to extend credit to insure production of the valuable crop. By contrast, tobacco growers and tobacco sharecroppers at Socorro, San Gil, Pinchote, and Los Santos, who do not have the same access to credit as those near the city of Bucaramanga, still rely heavily on labor exchange.[108]

Lack of cash is a principal factor in the survival of exchange labor within a money economy. This is certainly true of western South America and would seem to be true elsewhere as well. Fei and Chang[109] specifically mention it for China. Labor shortages may be another reason for the persistence of exchange labor within a money economy, for in some areas it may not be possible to obtain sufficient labor even for wage payments. For example, in some parts of the Colombian coffee belt which are more inaccessible and therefore off the migratory labor routes, farmers still exchange their permanent hired men. Apparently in pre-Civil War days in the southern United States slave owners also pooled their labor resources when it was necessary.[110] Where it persists in a money economy, exchange labor—like festive labor—tends to result primarily from the need to meet peak labor loads rather than from social considerations. Unlike festive labor, however, it tends to persist as an intra-class (horizontal) phenomenon at the lower end of the social scale.

Cognition

Cognition is that aspect of cultural causality which is most peculiar to it. It includes all those countless judgments and frequency interpretations which lead to the sharing and cumulation of knowledge. However, much of the personal character of cognition, which is more likely to be prominent in the study of an event, is put aside in the study of process. This section will deal with only one aspect of the problem, the relation of cognition of reciprocity and individualization as generalized from our study of labor. The process of individualization, as reflected in the changing quality of reciprocity, will be divided into three general categories or culture "types": (1) the centripetal personal, (2) the centrifugal impersonal, and (3) the centripetal impersonal.

The centripetal personal type is directly redistributive in character. Knowledge is largely an outgrowth of primary experience—direct interaction with the human and nonhuman environment. Interpersonal contacts are highly repetitive and marked by an empathy based on direct and personal reciprocities. Thus, the farmer who practices exchange labor is more likely to call on those who owe him work or with whom he has established ties of sentiment through similar exchanges in the past. Among these individuals each knows that the quality of work he gives will be considered the measure of its return; thus, sanction and empathy are conjoined. The farmer's choice of helpers is affected by what we may call the *past bias* of close personal contacts and their mutual obligations and understandings, an influence which tends to be centripetal within small groups. A strong centripetal type of interaction may even accompany the differential reciprocities of a hacienda situation especially where a *patrón-peón* system of sentiments is involved. As we have seen, however, under hacienda or feudal-like conditions where cash is scarce, festivities may constitute an immediate reward divorced from conspicuous giving and in some cases even from sentiment. In such instances a centripetal pattern of unequal reciprocities may be maintained in a class-stratified rural society through political controls and land monopolies despite strong underlying centrifugal tendencies (resulting from the "demonstration effect" of greater social mobility and higher living standards in the surrounding money economy).

Just as the centripetal personal type of situation suggests the "gemeinschaft," "folk," "tradition-directed" or "closed" society so the centrifugal impersonal type suggests the "inner-directed" character and the "urban," "rural proletariat," "gesellschaft," "open," and "acquisitive" society. As specialization and the use of money facilitate delayed reciprocity in differential form, past bias comes into conflict with *present bias*—the dictates of individual convenience affected by changing forms of conspicuous consumption and operating within limits set by the impersonal state rather than by the personal conjunction of empathy and sanction through direct reciprocity. Increase in specialization, durable goods, and the use of money do not reduce the opportunities for achieving social approbation; they make possible alternative means of achieving it. Instead of being limited to highly personal reciprocities tending to equalize differences in material advantage, social approbation may be achieved through a conspicuous consumption pattern more individualistic than the giving pattern but offering the successful individual the added enjoyment of a greater abundance of consumption goods. Cognitive recognition of this added advantage is evident in the weighing of relative costs in so many parts of the world, a method of comparison facilitated by a common quantitative frame of monetary value reference.

For the farmer who hires his labor, the choice of a helper becomes a free one to the extent that it is no longer biased by previous commitments and sentiments but only by the availability of potential helpers at the moment of choice. Thus the way is open for centrifugal interaction even to the degree of impersonality inherent in the employment of migratory labor. This type of impersonal relationship in expanded modern form has often been held to involve a cultural "lag" in which growth in knowledge of the material world and of its technological manipulation has outstripped knowledge of human social behavior. In our opinion the culture-lag hypothesis is a totally unnecessary attempt on the part of some social scientists to justify their own existence. Only through advanced specialization and considerable harnessing of non-human sources of energy did the freeing of man power make specialization in the form of social science a probability. The centrifugal impersonal situation was an essential step in the development of knowledge leading to what may be a new centripetal impersonal type of human relations.

The existence today of governmental agencies for technical and financial aid to "underdeveloped" areas, which provided the author with the opportunity to collect information on reciprocal labor, also provides an illustration of this new third type of human relations at the international level. Through increasing knowledge and the development of communication facilities, a growing realization that the fortunes of all peoples are bound together would seem to contain a *future bias*. As the fund of knowledge increases, there appears to be a growing willingness on the part of those populations with more probable knowledge to assist those which possess less even though the limitations of a lower level of knowledge do not always enable the recipients to experience immediately the same degree of impersonal empathy toward their benefactors.

The impersonalization of empathy and its detachment from the mutual sanctions of past bias are illustrated by the strong health orientation of much of the assistance to pre-industrial areas. The somewhat anachronistic effect in many overpopulated countries of increasing population pressures and economic problems by alleviating the immediate evidences of human suffering is in part a result of the highly specialized culture of the foreign benefactors. Although the peoples of pre-industrial areas may feel the same deep sense of personal loss on the death of a loved one as do the latter, their high death and morbidity rates make a difference in their *expectations* as compared to those in the highly specialized societies where the increasing probability of knowledge has lowered the death and morbidity rates. For the participant of highly specialized society this difference in expectations results in shock on contact with living conditions in underdeveloped areas and strengthens the impersonal empathy of future bias provided him by his greater knowledge. However, his actions to reduce unnecessary suffering are the product of a knowledge much greater than that of the beneficiaries whose actions determine their high birth rates and who add thereby an even greater challenge to his cognitive abilities.

Thus, the centripetal impersonal type refers to human relation situations in which expectations stemming from probable knowledge facilitate the occurrence of a form of empathy independent of the highly repetitive personal contacts of direct experience and past bias. Developments in knowledge and technology seem to make increasingly possible a conjoining of the differential and impersonal quality of centrifugal impersonal reciprocity with the cohesive and unifying empathy of the centripetal personal type.

NOTES

1. Robert Redfield, *The Little Community*, Chicago, 1955, pp. 11, 16.

2. Charles J. Erasmus, *Reciprocal Labor: A Study of Its Occurrence and Disappearance among Farming Peoples in Latin America*, unpublished Ph.D. dissertation, Library of the University of California at Berkeley, 1955, microfilm.

3. John H. Provinse, "Cooperative Ricefield Cultivation Among the Siang Dyaks of Central Borneo," *American Anthropologist*, 1937, XXXIX, 87.

4. Julio de la Fuente, *Yalalag: una villa zapoteca serrana*, Museo Nacional de Antropología, Serie Científica, no. 1, Mexico, 1949, pp. 121–123.

5. John F. Embree, *Suye Mura, a Japanese Village*, Chicago, 1939, p. 125.

6. Alejandro Marroquin, *Tlaxiaco, una cuidad mercado*, Edición Mimeográfica no. 4 del Instituto Nacional Indigenista, Mexico, 1954, p. 35.

7. Robert B. Hall, "The Société Congo of the Ile à Gonave," *American Anthropologist*, 1929, XXXI, 692.

8. Monica Hunter, *Reaction to Conquest: Effects of Contact with Europeans on the Pondo of South Africa*, London, 1936, pp. 88–89.

9. Walter M. Kollmorgen, *The Old Order Amish of Lancaster County, Pennsylvania*, Rural Life Studies, no. 4, United States Department of Agriculture, Bureau of Agricultural Economics, Washington, D.C., 1942, p. 56.

10. Elizabeth Colson, "The Plateau Tonga of Northern Rhodesia," in *Seven Tribes of British Central Africa*, E. Colson and M. Gluckman, eds., London, 1951, p. 106.

11. Solon T. Kimball, "Rural Social Organization and Co-operative Labor," *American Journal of Sociology*, 1949, LV, p. 45.

12. *Ibid.*

13. Embree, *op. cit.*, pp. 134–135.

14. George M. Foster, *A Primitive Mexican Economy*, American Ethnological Society Monograph 5, New York, 1942, pp. 33, 35; Embree, *op. cit.*, p. 136; Kimball, *op. cit.*, p. 42.

15. Charles Wagley, *The Economics of a Guatemalan Village*, American Anthropological Association Memoir 58, 1941, p. 43.

16. Hall, *op. cit.*, p. 698.

17. Irwin T. Sanders, *Balkan Village*, Lexington, Kentucky, 1949, p. 46.

18. Melville J. Herskovits, *Life in a Haitian Valley*, New York, 1937, pp. 70–73.

19. George C. Homans, *English Villagers of the Thirteenth Century*, Cambridge, 1941, p. 260.

20. Melville J. Herskovits, *Dahomey*, New York, 1938, vol. 1, pp. 63–73.

21. J. H. Hutton, *The Sema Nagas*, London, 1921, p. 153.

22. Hall, *op. cit.*, pp. 693, 696; Alfred Métraux, *Making a Living in the*

Marbial Valley (Haiti), UNESCO Occasional Papers in Education, Paris, 1951, pp. 85, 74.

23. Herskovits, *Life in a Haitian Valley*, p. 73; Métraux, *op. cit.*, p. 72.

24. Herskovits, *Dahomey*, pp. 73–74; C. K. Meek, A *Sudanese Kingdom: An Ethnographical Study of the Juken-speaking Peoples of Nigeria*, London, 1931, p. 405; S. F. Nadel, A *Black Byzantium, the Kingdom of Nupe in Nigeria*, London, 1942, p. 243; Jomo Kenyatta, *Facing Mount Kenya, the Tribal Life of the Gikuyu*, London, 1938, p. 59.

25. Herskovits, *Life in a Haitian Valley*, p. 71; Hall, *op. cit.*, p. 696.

26. Nadel, *op. cit.*, p. 248; Herskovits, *Dahomey*, pp. 65, 73.

27. Hutton, *op. cit.*, p. 154.

28. Sanders, *op. cit.*, p. 47.

29. Hsiao-tun Fei and Chih-i Chang, *Earthbound China*, Chicago, 1945, pp. 35–36.

30. Foster, *op. cit.*, p. 35.

31. B. Malinowski, *Coral Gardens and Their Magic*, New York, 1935, p. 157.

32. H. Ian Hogbin, "Tillage and Collection, a New Guinea Economy," *Oceania*, 1938–39, IX 291–296; also *Transformation Scene: The Changing Culture of a New Guinea Village*, London, 1951, p. 63.

33. S. F. Nadel, *The Nuba: An Anthropological Study of the Hill Tribes in Kordofan*, London, 1947, p. 54.

34. Emilio Willems, *Cunha: tradicão e transicão em uma cultura rural do Brasil*, São Paulo, 1947, p. 35.

35. For a similar dichotomy see Richard Thurnwald, *Economics in Primitive Communities*, London, 1932, pp. 286–287, and Harvey Moore, "Cumulation and Cultural Processes," *American Anthropologist*, 1954, LVI, 347–357 (p. 349).

36. Thurnwald, *op. cit.*, p. 287.

37. George P. Murdock, *Social Structure*, New York, 1949, pp. 115–116.

38. George P. Murdock, "The Common Denominator of Cultures," in *Science of Man in the World Crisis*, Ralph Linton, ed., New York, 1945, 123–142.

39. Charles J. Erasmus, "Patolli, Pachisi, and the Limitation of Possibilities," *Southwestern Journal of Anthropology*, 1950, VI, 369–387.

40. Raymond Firth, *Primitive Polynesian Economy*, London, 1939, p. 118.

41. P. C. Wason, "Soap Wrappers' 'Jig,'" *British Journal of Industrial Medicine*, 1954, XI, 279–283.

42. Métraux, *op. cit.*, p. 73.

43. Hall, *op. cit.*, p. 621.

44. Charles Wisdom, *The Chorti Indians of Guatemala*, Chicago, 1940, p. 243.

45. Fei and Chang, *op. cit.*, p. 36.

46. Hall, *op. cit.*, p. 691.

47. Hogbin, "Tillage and Collection, a New Guinea Economy," pp. 145, 297.

48. Arthur F. Raper and others, *The Japanese Village in Transition*, Report no. 136 of Public Opinion and Sociological Research Division of Civil

Information and Education Section, Tokyo, General Headquarters, Supreme Commander for the Allied Forces, 1950, p. 198.

49. Conrad M. Arensberg and Solon T. Kimball, *Family and Community in Ireland,* Cambridge, 1940, p. 74.

50. Earl H. Bell, *Sublette, Kansas,* Rural Life Studies, no. 2, United States Department of of Agriculture, Bureau of Agricultural Economics, Washington, D.C., 1942, p. 74.

51. Colson, *op. cit.*, p. 107.

52. E. Jensen Krige and J. D. Krige, *The Realm of a Rain-Queen:* A *Study of the Pattern of Lovedu Society,* London, 1943, pp. 55–56.

53. Kimball, "Rural Social Organization and Co-operative Labor," p. 44.

54. Krige and Krige, *op. cit.*

55. Kimball, *op. cit.*, p. 47.

56. Emilio Willems, "Caboclo Cultures of Southern Brazil," in *Acculturation in the Americas,* Sol Tax, ed., Chicago, 1952, p. 234; also, *Cunha,* p. 36.

57. Herskovits, *Life in a Haitian Valley,* pp. 70–71; Métraux, *op. cit.*, pp. 72, 77, 86.

58. Herskovits, *Dahomey,* p. 72.

59. Daryll Forde, "Land and Labour in a Cross River Village, Southern Nigeria," *Geographical Journal,* 1937, XC, 40, London.

60. William R. Bascom, "Acculturation among Gullah Negroes," *American Anthropologist,* 1941, XLIII, 44.

61. B. Malinowski, *Argonauts of the Western Pacific,* London, 1922, p. 161; also *Coral Gardens and Their Magic,* p. 157.

62. Provinse, *op. cit.*, pp. 86–87.

63. Embree, *op. cit.*, pp. 134–135.

64. Morton H. Fried, *Fabric of Chinese Society,* New York, 1953, p. 117.

65. People having three years' use-rights to virgin land cleared on large estates with the understanding that the land is to be left planted in pasture grass upon the expiration of the three-year period.

66. Harold C. Conklin, "An Ethnoecological Approach to Shifting Agriculture," *Transactions,* New York Academy of Sciences, 1954, XVII, 141.

67. Karl Polanyi, *The Great Transformation,* New York, 1944, pp. 47–52.

68. I. Schapera, "Economic Changes in South African Native Life," *Africa,* 1928, I, 170–188, London.

69. H. Ian Hogbin, *Experiments in Civilization,* London, 1939, p. 73.

70. Wendell C. Bennett and Robert M. Zingg, *The Tarahumara, an Indian Tribe of Northern Mexico,* Chicago, 1935, pp. 193–194, 328.

71. Firth, *op. cit.*, p. 364.

72. Nadel, *The Nuba,* p. 56.

73. James B. Watson, *Cayuá Culture Change,* American Anthropological Association Memoir 73, 1952, p. 108.

74. Donald Pierson, *Cruz das Almas:* A *Brazilian Village,* Smithsonian Institution, Institute of Social Anthropology Publication 12, Washington, D.C., 1951, p. 70.

75. De la Fuente, *op. cit.*, p. 123.

76. Métraux, *op. cit.*, pp. 70–71, 74, 86.

77. Nadel, A *Black Byzantium,* p. 251.

78. Krige and Krige, *op. cit.*, p. 60.
79. Colson, *op. cit.*, p. 105.
80. Rowland E. Robinson, *Danvis Folks*, Boston, 1894, p. 117.
81. Homans, *op. cit.*, p. 261.
82. Nadel, *op. cit.*, p. 251.
83. Pierson, *op. cit.*, p. 71.
84. Métraux, *op. cit.*, p. 69.
85. Krige and Krige, *op. cit.*, p. 54.
86. Homans, *op. cit.*, p. 261.
87. Polanyi, *op. cit.*, p. 52.
88. Hall, *op. cit.*, p. 691.
89. Métraux, *op. cit.*, pp. 74, 86.
90. Pierson, *op. cit.*, p. 70.
91. *Ibid.*, p. 71; Octavio Da Costa, *The Negro in Northern Brazil*, American Ethnological Society Monograph 15, New York, 1948, p. 24.
92. Métraux, *op. cit.*, p. 86.
93. Krige and Krige, *op. cit.*, p. 42.
94. Embree, *op. cit.*, p. 306.
95. Bell, *op. cit.*, pp. 73–74; Kimball, *op. cit.*, p. 47.
96. G. Gordon Brown and Bruce Hutt, *Anthropology in Action*, London, 1935, p. 151.
97. John H. Rowe, "Inca Culture at the Time of the Spanish Conquest," in Julian Steward, ed., *Handbook of Indians of South America*, Bureau of American Ethnology Bulletin 143, vol. 2, 1947, pp. 265–268.
98. V. Gordon Childe, *What Happened in History*, New York, Penguin Books, 1946, pp. 88–92.
99. Foster, *op. cit.*, p. 38.
100. Charles J. Erasmus, "Agricultural Changes in Haiti: Patterns of Resistance and Acceptance," *Human Organization*, 1952, XI, 25–26, New York.
101. Daryll Forde and Richenda Scott, *The Native Economies of Nigeria*, London, 1946, pp. 87, 252.
102. Nadel, *The Nuba*, pp. 56–57.
103. Lucy P. Mair, *An African People in the Twentieth Century*, London, 1934, pp. 126–127.
104. Colson, *op. cit.*, p. 101.
105. Krige and Krige, *op. cit.*, pp. 54–56.
106. Kimball, *op. cit.*, p. 43.
107. Wagley, *op. cit.*, p. 43.
108. Roberto Pineda, *El Tabaco en Santander*, Departamento Técnico de la Seguridad Social Campesina, Ministerio del Trabajo, no. 2, Bogotá, 1955, pp. 72–76.
109. Fei and Chang, *op. cit.*, p. 64.
110. Herman C. Nixon, *Possum Trot*, Norman, Oklahoma, 1941, p. 27; Bascom, *op. cit.*, p. 45.

Land Tenure and Transmission in Rural Barbados

SIDNEY M. GREENFIELD

M. G. Smith began a recent article describing the system of land tenure and transmission practiced by the peasant section on the island of Carriacou with the following paragraph:

> Two highly distinctive systems of land tenure are to be found side by side in many British Caribbean societies. One system is defined by statute and common law, and guides official policy in relation to land. The other system, which has recently been described for Jamaica by Miss Edith Clarke, is of customary and traditional character which neither observes the forms nor directly invites the sanctions of law. These differing systems of tenure are normally practiced by different sections, and for holdings of disparate value (Smith 1956:103).

For both Carriacou and Jamaica, then, we now have descriptions of a traditional system of land tenure by which peasants customarily transmit their holdings—either informally or by bequest—to both legitimate and

Reprinted from *Anthropological Quarterly*, 1960, XXXIII, 165–176, by permission of the author and publisher. An earlier draft of this paper was presented at the annual meeting of the American Anthropological Association, Mexico City, December, 1959. The research upon which it is based was conducted in 1956–57 and was supported by fellowships from the Social Science Research Council and the Research Institute for the Study of Man.

illegitimate children. "According to customary belief and practice family land passes to 'all the family' or 'all the children' and may be used jointly by a group of kindred who subscribe towards the 'tax money' " (Clarke 1953:83). On both islands these holdings are considered inalienable and reserved for the use of *all* children—existent and potential. Both Clarke and Smith maintain that this system is not in conformity with the legal pattern. They differ, however, in that according to Clarke, "The peasant theory of land tenure . . . [reflects] . . . West African principles . . ." (*ibid.*:87) while Smith sees it as a functional adaptation to the social structure of Carriacou (Smith 1956:138; 1957:42).

In this paper I shall discuss the system of land tenure, use and transmission found among the rural folk of the island of Barbados. I shall show that they also believe in and practice—at least in part—a traditional system of land tenure that is similar to the family land concept of the Jamaicans and Carriacouans. I shall demonstrate, however, that when its historical emergence is examined, this system of tenure is found not only to be in complete harmony with the law, but is actually based upon it. The present system of family land—which is dependent upon a form of transmission called "seed-to-seed inheritance"—will be shown to have been an application by the rural folk of certain principles of the English common law of an earlier period. This pattern was also employed by the upper classes in both Barbados and England. The rural landholders, we shall see, adapted this upper class pattern in order to protect themselves and their offspring, under the law, from a series of restrictions—called the "located labor system"—imposed upon the laboring classes by the legislature in the years following emancipation.

The English common law of real property, however, was consolidated and modified during the second decade of the twentieth century. In its revised form, when applied in Barbados, the law no longer sanctioned "seed-to-seed" inheritance. The system of family land itself—which once provided the Barbadian villager with a legal means of escape from "located labor"—no longer invites the sanctions of law. The new judicial principles, however, have spread slowly to the rural areas since its inhabitants only learn of changes in the law by hearing them from judges in court. Local custom, not fully aware of the new code with respect to land, still provides sanctions for the old beliefs and associated behaviors.

Barbados is a relatively flat, small, pear shaped island, 21 miles long and 14 miles wide situated at the eastern rim of the Lesser Antilles. It contains approximately 166 square miles or 106,470 acres. This land area supported an estimated population of 230,000—increasing at a rate of 2 per cent per year—at the time of this study. The island's density of almost 1,400 persons per square mile is the highest in the Caribbean and, for an area of tropical agriculture, one of the highest in the world (Lowenthal 1957).

The economy of the island is based almost exclusively on one crop—sugar—which, with its by-products, accounted for more than 95 per cent of Barbardos' exports and 45 per cent of the gross domestic product in the period 1951–55 (Statistical Service 1956). The importance of sugar to the overpopulated colony is made vivid in the conclusions reached by the architects of Barbados' Ten Year Development plan in 1946. "In the long run," they declared, "everything brings us back to sugar; sugar is the life blood of the island!" (1946:11).

Almost all of the arable land is planted with sugar cane. The crop is grown both on large plantations—which control 76,000 acres of land, of which 54,000 are arable—and by "peasants"[1] who hold approximately 18,000 acres, 14,500 of which are estimated as arable (Foster 1956:1). A survey conducted in 1946 revealed that peasant land was divided into more than 27,000 holdings that concerned an estimated 125,000 persons—65 per cent of the population recorded in the last census (Halcrow and Cave 1947:2). For information about the system of land tenure and transmission practiced by these numerous peasants—who are so dependent on the land—we shall turn to the data collected in the rural village of Enterprise Hall in the years 1956–57.

Enterprise Hall is a small village of a little over one hundred acres, located in the Parish of St. George near the center of the island. In 1956–57, approximately one hundred years after its establishment, it contained 630 inhabitants who occupied 135 dwellings. The one hundred some-odd acres of land were distributed in 187 holdings ranging in size from one eighth of an acre to one piece that was five and one-fourth acres. The average size of each holding is one half acre. Rights of ownership and use of the land are held by both village residents and outsiders—a term which includes both occupants of other villagers or plantation tenantries and people living outside the island.

Two conflicting sets of attitudes were held by the villages with respect to land tenure. The first, and traditional belief, is that land should be left to and shared by all children—without reference to birth order and legitimacy. The peasants say that "the old people" bequeathed their land in this way; and since they were wise, their example should be followed. This ideal, however, is often neglected in practice. The modern tendency toward individual ownership and freedom to alienate the land—which at times leaves some members of the family landless—is in conflict with the older theory and often produces disharmony, and at times, open hostility among kin. The villagers rationalize their peasant behavior by saying "if people lived lovin'," as they were assumed to have done in the "old'n days" they all could share. But since others are selfish, they too must be selfish.

Most villagers do not have title deeds to their holdings. The few who do, either have purchased the property in the recent past, or have obtained title in court under the Statute of Limitations—according to which an individual can obtain title to land after possession for ten years without paying rent. Since the fees associated with obtaining title under the Statute of Limitations are beyond the means of most peasant proprietors, even those who know that they have a legitimate claim to land usually do not exercise it—unless they wish to sell the land. Most proprietors, however, are unaware of the Statute of Limitations.

In the eyes of the villagers there are two major categories of land—"buy ground" and "rent ground." The term "buy ground" is generally applied to all holdings that are owned—in any form of tenure—as compared with land that is rented. In its more specific usage, however, "buy ground" refers to land that has been either purchased by the proprietor, or inherited—"free and clear"—from the purchaser. The villagers believe that this land is individually "owned" by the proprietor and can be sold, bequeathed or given away according to his wishes.

The second type of "buy ground" is referred to as "family land." It differs from individually owned land in that it is believed to be inalienable and to belong to all members of the family. The villagers regard "family land" as subject to the claims and interests of several generations of kin who may be scattered over many parts of the earth. They see the proprietor as the trustee for the kinship group. In addition, they adhere to the firm belief that this type of land should not be sold without agreement by all members of the family. In most cases the property was left by the family founder—either informally or in a written document—to all his descendants. The phrase "seed-to-seed inheritance" is used to describe the form of transmission that is the basis of this type of tenure. In recent years some of the land in this category has been subdivided and parceled out to all of the recognized claimants. In spite of the subdivision, however, the land has retained the essential qualities of family land since each proprietor believes that he has only the right to till the land and reap the profits from it during his lifetime; at his death it must pass on to his seed.

"Rent ground" is also divided into two types. The first is land that is rented from the plantations. In the past the tenant on this land was greatly restricted as to his geographical and occupational mobility. Since the war, however, the restrictions have been lifted and, today, the renting party's responsibilities to the plantation are not significantly different from those of any rent paying tenant in the western world.

The second type of "rent ground" is a product of the family land system. If some of the members of a family do not wish to press their claims to the family property at present, but are afraid that their kinsman in possession will attempt to take title under the Statute of Limitations, they insist that he either sell the land and divide the proceeds or rent it to himself or to a third party. Since selling, in addition to being unprofitable to the occupant, means alienation out of the family, the land is never sold. Renting, which keeps "ownership" within the family even though an "outsider" is in possession, is the usual choice. Renting is also a solution when there is a dispute over land "owned" by a family, some of whom are not on the island. Here the proprietor usually holds the property in trust for his absent kinsmen. Where the latter desire to safeguard their interests against the occupant's invoking the Statute of Limitations, they require him to pay rent, or to turn the land over to a tenant.

We see then, that the Barbadian villagers have a traditional system of land tenure and transmission similar to that practiced in Jamaica and Carriacou. According to tradition, the land is considered inalienable and the peasants leave their holdings to all their children or all the family. Since this practice is opposed to contemporary legal theory and invariably leads to conflict and family disharmony at times of transmission—"it causes humbug and murderation" according to the villagers—we shall now turn to the historical emergence of the system of "family land" and "seed-to-seed" inheritance to see how it developed.

At emancipation in 1834 more than 82,000 former slaves were given freedom in Barbados. The fruits of liberty, however, were not to be tasted by the vast majority. The colony was densely populated and fully cultivated. There were neither mountains nor jungles to give refuge to the freedmen. Most of them had little alternative but to remain as wage laborers on the same plantations they formerly served as slaves. Here they remained in possession of their houses and allotments, paying no rent, but giving labor in lieu thereof, usually five days per week at a rate some 20 to 30 per cent below the prevailing market rate (Hamilton 1956:4). Their even limited mobility, however, soon showed itself to be at odds with the wishes of the planters, especially when agricultural workers left the estates of their traditional settlement to work elsewhere for higher wages. To strengthen their bargaining position in the newly created labor market, the planters turned to the legislature.

In the decade following emancipation, several laws that became the basis of the "located labor system" were enacted that set strict limitations on the occupational and physical mobility of the laboring classes. The laws—aimed directly at the agricultural workers—stipulated that as a condition of renting—either "working allotments" or "housespots"—the tenant was required to give the estate a certain number of days labor at a fixed wage varying from one sixth to one third below the current market price. Furthermore, the tenant was obliged to perform the service required by the landlord who was sole judge of the rights of each party (*ibid.*:4).

Land, which was both scarce and expensive in the densely populated colony, was the cornerstone of the new legislation. Consequently, its ownership—which provided the only means of escape from "located labor"—was even more coveted by the laborers. The price of the small supply soon soared. In spite of this, however, the number of landowners increased. By 1859, the number of small proprietors with less than five acres of land had increased from 780 in 1840 (Schomburgk 1848:153) to more than 3,500 (Sewell 1859:39).

Most of the holdings of the growing class of small proprietors had formerly been parts of large plantations. The land, therefore, was distributed throughout the island in clusters, or "villages." One such village was Enterprise Hall. At the end of the eighteenth century it had been a small, family-owned plantation. In a will dated 1816 it had been bequeathed by its owner to his grandson who departed from the island soon after emancipation. The 102¾ acres were purchased then by a solicitor for £3,500 and, after being surveyed and subdivided, they were put up for sale in the early 1850's. The selling price varied—by as much £50 per acre—but averaged £70 per acre. The purchase was usually made on terms. Half the total price was given as a down payment and the remainder plus interest in several installments. Possession was taken at the time of the down payment. Until 1891, Barbadian law, like English law, did not require registration of title. Consequently, only a handful of the original purchasers recorded their deeds.

The settlement pattern was one of dispersed "farmsteads," much the same as it is today. Houses were placed as close to the road as possible and almost surrounded by growing crops. The system of farming was also similar to that practiced today. The land was divided in half, one part planted in cane, the other again divided, one part in yams and/or potatoes in preparation for cane and the other, "thrown out" of cane, to roots and fodder. In this way the land was cropped with sugar cane to be reaped in alternate years while the other half produced food and fodder[2] (for details see Skeete 1930:2–8; Halcrow and Cave 1947:21–27).

The proprietors of these small holdings were not bound to the plantations as "located laborers." They were free to seek more remunerative and prestigeful employment elsewhere. Most of the men became artisans, trained as masons, carpenters, blacksmiths, wheelwrights, saddlers, and factory specialists. Since their work required them to travel to distant parts of the island, they had little time—or inclination—to till their land themselves. Tillage, consequently, was left to the hired hands who worked under the supervision of the village women.

From the beginning the land was secondary to a man's job as a source of income. Its primary value was that it freed its owner from the restrictions of the located labor system. Realizing this, the village founders were careful to make sure that their children would retain an interest in the land at their death—and with it continued freedom and opportunities for mobility. To accomplish this, they employed a legal technique borrowed from the local upper class who, in turn, had taken it from the English upper class. In order to keep their property within the family the English landowners would make a "settlement," under which future generations were left a limited, or "entailed" interest in the family "estate." Under the provisions of the settlement the land became inalienable, or perpetually retained within the family.

As Cheshire states:

> The desire of the upper classes to order the future destiny of their land and to prevent it from being sold out of the family, which has been a feature of English social life for many centuries, requires attention. . . . The inclination of a fee simple owner . . . is to make what is called a *settlement* by which he retains the benefit of ownership during his own life, but withholds the entire ownership in the shape of the fee simple from his descendants for as long as possible by reducing them, one after another, to the position of mere limited owners (1958:69).

"Settlements in one form or another," he continues, "have been common since . . . the early thirteenth century . . ." (*ibid.*:69). The evolution of the form, however, "was complete towards the end of the seventeenth century" (*ibid.*:71).

The English doctrine of "estates" is ideally adapted to the objectives of the settlement. "English law has never applied the conception of ownership to land" (*ibid.*:27), though the person in whom its seisin (possession) is vested is entitled to proprietary rights in respect of it. English law has created an abstract entity called an "estate" which is interposed between the land and the owner. In the eyes of the law, the estate is owned, transferred and transmitted, not the land. Therefore, under the settlement, each descendant inherited restricted or limited rights in an estate. In this way both the theoretical and practical ownership of the land became inalienable within a designated class of heirs of the person creating the settlement.

Under common law, settlements entailing interests in land could be made by deed or will. In either case, the creator of the entailment, by his choice, could limit future interests in his property to a certain class of heirs. He could choose the heirs of his body, the heirs of his marriage, the heirs of his wife's body, or any other class of heirs he preferred. The significant feature of the settlement then, is that it transfers an inalienable and perpetual interest in an estate to a class of heirs that is selected by the person creating the settlement.

The founding fathers of Enterprise Hall used the settlement to entail the interests of "all their descendants," thereby insuring all of their future generations an interest in their property and with it a refuge from the plantations and the located labor system. The descendants of those who did not protect their offspring in this way, soon returned to the unenviable status of located laborer.

The elders of Enterprise Hall invariably created settlements by leaving a will at their death. Many of these documents were quite detailed and specific. Some individuals went so far as to create different classes of heirs to share in each of their several parcels of land. In general, however, all of the documents shared certain basic features. There are two main provisions found in almost all of the dispositions that are basic to understanding both the legal principles upon which they were based and the contemporary pattern of family land. First, *all* children—male and female, legitimate and illegitimate—were almost always included amongst the beneficiaries. Second, and more important, the document invariably contained a clause that read as follows: "I . . . (name of testator) . . . bequeath to . . . (name of *all* children) . . . *and their seed forever* . . ." followed by an enumeration of the property in question. This terminology—commonly referred to as the "seed-to-seed" clause—had several important legal implications. One was that it begged the question of legitimacy of issue. The class of heirs selected was the seed of the body. Thus the intent of the testator not to restrict interest to legitimate issue was established in law. In addition, the land became factually and legally inalienable and perpetually retained within the family as long as there were issue. Each generation also inherited no more than a life interest in the estate. Each member of the family obtained the rights and privileges associated with ownership but never actual ownership. By applying the principles of the settlement the village founders were able to maintain their descendants perpetually above the status of located laborer.

We must point out that there were ways of evading the limitations of entailing settlements (see Cheshire 1958:167–169). Several embittered informants reported cases of heirs with only a life interest in an estate "going to court" and "obtaining papers." The land was then sold and the seed of the village founder subsequently forced back to the plantation tenantries and the restrictions of located laborer. These cases, however, were statistically infrequent.

Though testamentary disposition was the general rule, several cases were brought to the author's attention in which the original purchaser died intestate. According to the law, the oldest legitimate son could have claimed the entire property, limited by the "dower" or life interest of the lawful widow. In practice, however, very few "legal heirs" pressed their claims in court. In most cases the land was simply divided amongst all the children in much the same manner as it would have been if the purchaser had left it in strict settlement to all his seeds.

Though all children usually inherited an interest in the family property, there was informal agreement that once a son purchased land of his own or a daughter married a property owner, they and their heirs would not press their claims to the family land since they no longer needed the protection it offered. In the event that they lost their rights in this other land they could then reassert their claims to the family land.

Family land based upon seed-to-seed inheritance was established in Barbados in the second half of the nineteenth century. Subsequent changes, however, both in sociological conditions and in the legal system served to modify both the attitudes of the villagers toward the land—particularly family land—and to alter its legal status. We must pause, however, to emphasize that the concept of family land had its roots in the common law of the time and was a functional adjustment—with legal sanction—to a situation that existed on the island for almost one hundred years. The end of the located labor system, plus the legal changes that followed the statutory consolidation of the English real property laws in 1925, which were later applied in Barbados, may have changed the legal status of family land and seed-to-seed inheritance, but they did not change the fact that this traditional set of beliefs emerged within the island as a response—recognized by law—to a set of legally imposed social restrictions.

One of the main objectives of the legislature of 1925 was ". . . to render the sale of land as rapid and simple a matter as the sale of goods or of shares" (Cheshire 1958:5). To accomplish this, the ability of landowners to entail the interests of their heirs was restricted—by formalizing the rulings against perpetuities. The intestacy law was also changed so that all real estate of the intestate was to be sold and the money divided amongst the heirs. One effect of the 1925 legislation, then, was to end the legal status of family land. Under the new law, wills granting a perpetual interest in land to all future descendants were no longer binding. Now the persons in possession of the land, or their parents, if named in the will, had outright ownership. Where the parent died without making further provisions for the next generation the land would be sold and the money given to the heirs—if the case was brought to court. Most villagers, however, knew little of the statutory changes. For many years they believed that the old rules were still binding. Consequently, they followed the traditional pattern established by their ancestors. It was only when they went to court with land disputes that they learned of the new regulations.

Both legal and social conditions in Barbados have changed in the past half century. This does not, however, give us the right to disregard the antecedent cultural patterns. The understanding of an aspect of culture such as a land tenure system requires both diachronic as well as functional analysis. The examination of the historical conditions associated with the emergence of the family land system in Barbados gives us no reason to suspect that the peasant theory of land tenure is derived from a cultural tradition other than the one in which it is found. There is, therefore, no need to look for an external source in explaining peasant attitudes and beliefs about land that are not in conformity with contemporary legal theory. I agree with Clarke that "... few laymen in any country fully understand the intricacies of their own legal system" (1953:86). I see no reason, however, to assume that English and social tradition was incomprehensible to the peasant of the British West Indies (*ibid.*:86). If anything, this paper suggests the opposite.

NOTES

1. The term "peasant" is used in Barbados to refer to a proprietor with less than ten acres of land. The term is used here in that sense only.
2. In recent years, however, with new varieties of cane that produce excellent ratoons for several years, little land is ever "thrown out." An additional cane crop, therefore, can be harvested from the section that was formerly "thrown out" before it is prepared again for planting new cane.

REFERENCES CITED

Cheshire, Geoffry
1958 *The Modern Law of Real Property*, London, Butterworth and and Co., Ltd.

Clarke, Edith
1953 "Land Tenure and the Family in Four Communities in Jamaica," *Social and Economic Studies* 1:81–118.

Foster, G. B.
1956 *The Yield of Sugar Cane in Barbados in 1956*, Bulletin No. 24 of the Department of Science and Agriculture, Bridgetown, Barbados.

Halcrow, M. and J. M. Cave
1947 *Peasant Agriculture in Barbados*, Bulletin No. 11 of the Department of Science and Agriculture, Bridgetown, Barbados.

Hamilton, Bruce
1956 *Barbados and the Confederation Question 1871–1885*, London, Crown Agents for Oversea Governments and Administrations.

Lowenthal, David
1957 "The Population of Barbados," *Social and Economic Studies* 6:445–501.

Schomburgk, Sir Robert
1848 *The History of Barbados*, London, Longman, Brown, Green and Longman.

Sewell, William G.
1859 *The Ordeal of Free Labor in the British West Indies*, New York, Harper.

Skeete, C. C.
1930 *The Condition of Peasant Agriculture in Barbados*, The Department of Science and Agriculture, Bridgetown, Barbados.

Smith, M. G.
1956 "The Transformation of Land Rights by Transmission in Carriacou," *Social and Economic Studies* 5:103–138.
1957 "The African Heritage in the Caribbean," in *Caribbean Studies: A Symposium*, Vera Rubin, ed., Jamaica, Institute of Social and Economic Research.

Statistical Service of Barbados
1956 *Abstract of Statistics No. 1.*

A Ten Year Development Plan for Barbados, 1946–56, Bridgetown, The Advocate Co., Ltd.

Patterns of Land Tenancy and Their Social Repercussions

GEORGE W. HILL,
JOSÉ A. SILVA M.,
and
RUTH OLIVER DE HILL

Land, the basis of agricultural and livestock production, has no real value in itself, but depends for its worth on the use that man has made of it, either to raise grain and food or to extract minerals. The social value of land is also determined by its use, and its abundance or scarcity are additional factors in assessing its worth.

Two principal systems of tenancy, owning and renting, have been created for the management and use of land in agricultural and livestock enterprises. Although each could be subdivided, they can, nonetheless, be included under the general heading of land tenancy, which is the theme of this [selection].

In Venezuela, as in other Latin American countries, there is an interesting history of the ownership, distribution and use of lands. The basic patterns of land tenancy in the New World, some of which are still in practice today, were determined, to a great extent, by the methods used by the first explorers in their search for gold and in the production of the necessary foods for subsistence. A brief review of a few of the more developed of those first patterns will be useful in interpreting the present

Translated from "Patrones de tenencia de tierras y sus repercusiones sociales," Chapter 2 of *La vida rural en Venezuela, Revista de Sanidad y Asistencia Social,* 1960, XXIV, 1–2, 24–52, by permission of the authors. Translated by Nicole L. Hunt.

situation. The patterns of land tenancy in Spanish America had their beginnings in Hispaniola (today the Dominican Republic and Haiti) and Cuba. Regarding Cuba, one sociologist says:

> . . . it is clear from the writings of Columbus that . . . whatever labor or toil was necessary in the new country (whether it were digging in search of gold or establishing a food supply) was certainly not to be performed by Spaniards. There is apparent in his records the assumption that the people they were to meet at the journey's end would become subordinate to the will of the Spaniards. Forced labor on the part of the natives—if not actual slavery—was a foregone conclusion.[1]

Forced labor of the Indians was used in gathering the little gold that could be found in the Antilles and in searching for new sources of supply. Tributes to the overlords were established, and finally, in order to increase operations and colonize new lands, it became necessary for Columbus to make an agreement in Hispaniola with a Francisco Roldán which would "establish a system of exploitation that became the basis of the social institutions of New Spain. This was the system of *repartimientos,* later known as *encomiendas.*"[2]

The etymology of these terms indicates their meaning. The first refers to the concession and distribution of lands by the Crowns of Spain and Portugal to leaders of royal expeditions, colonizers, and founders of cities in the New World. Pope Alexander VI, in the papal bulls of the third and fourth of May 1493, divided the newly discovered lands between the Crowns of Spain and Portugal, and consequently only these countries could cede lands.

The monarchs of these two European powers accepted not only the division of the lands, as specified in those edicts, but also took on the obligation of converting to Catholicism the Indians who inhabited them. In order to comply with this religious obligation the Spanish Crown commended or entrusted the natives to their favorite subjects. In other words, whoever received a *repartimiento,* or concession of land, accepted the obligation of the *encomienda* and became responsible for the security and spiritual welfare of the Indians.

The dangers inherent in the system of *encomiendas* have been described by the historian Lesley Byrd Simpson in the following words:

> They (the monarchs) were, in fact, spiritual viceroys of the Holy See. With this assumption by the civil government of the religious mission it soon found itself between the devil of papal displeasure and the deep sea of economic necessity. On the one hand the government undertook to see that the natives were protected and made Christians; on the other, it was bound to favor the multitude of Spaniards who had gone to the Indies in the hope of some material reward, while the needs of the poverty-stricken Crown could not be lost sight of . . .[3]

Unfortunately the spiritual motives of the *encomienda* were never carried out in good faith by the colonists, who misused their royal privileges to their own best advantage and instituted the practice of slavery. The abuses of the newly created landed aristocracy finally became so infamous that the representatives of the Church interceded to abolish the *encomienda* system. The practice of conceding *encomiendas* ended in Venezuela in 1637 with the creation of the Catholic Missions, which were entrusted then with the care of the natives. There are differing opinions among investigators regarding the exact time of the initiation of the *encomienda* and the *repartimiento* in the New World, some contending that they originated under the administration of Ovando from 1502 to 1509. Most agree, however, that the system had its precedents in the period of the reconquest of Spain, when the Catholic kings gave concessions of lands as spoils to their captains.[4]

The Venezuelan historian Tomás Polanco Martínez attributes to a German company, Alfinger, de Bartolomé Welser and Company, of Santo Domingo, the introduction of the system of *repartimientos* in Venezuela, and says:

> It was actually Alfinger (Ehinger, as the name appears in German) and his German successors who initiated the distribution of lands, a privilege that, as is known, was granted to all those who in the name of the Crown exercised civil authority in the Americas. But it is to the first Spanish mandates that we owe the true point of departure of our history of territorial ownership.[5]

The economist A. Arellano Moreno believes that we find in this dual distribution of lands and Indians on the part of the Crown the origin of large landholdings and the latifundia which typify parts of the nation today. He writes:

> We find here the beginnings of the rural aristocracy in Latin America and of the latifundia and vast landholdings of history. Many sold their lands, some, like the Church, kept theirs, and others who were not satisfied acquired greater holdings. The economic value of landholdings thus gave rise to disputes not only of a commercial, but of a social and political nature as well, as evidenced by some of the great lawsuits of history.[6]

In the Antilles, under the *encomienda* system, the native population disappeared in less than one generation because of overwork, malnutrition, and illness.[7] In Venezuela the tragedy of Cuba, Haiti, and Santo Domingo was not repeated, for there was a greater expanse of territory, a larger native population, and an external source of manual labor constituted by the Negro slaves from Africa.

The most interesting factor about this new source of manual labor, for the purposes of this study, is that it demonstrates the contempt of rural aristocracy for the working of the land, and emphasizes the extremes to which they went in order that others might do the labor.

Simpson, an American historian, in his analysis of the *encomienda* system, describes the first English colonists who settled in the southern region of the United States. They too, apparently, belonged to the social class that despised manual labor.[8]

The Venezuelan historian Polanco Martínez writes as follows:

> In Venezuela, as was true in the Indies, the African native was a highly desirable investment and played a substantial role in the late formation of the economy. They were the solution to the problem of work, that ticklish question which had plagued the Peninsular settlers since the first days of the conquest, when either their noble bearing or the hazards of war did not permit them to work, and they were forced to rely on the exploitation of the uncouth and puny native in order to survive. The hardiness of the Negroes, whose black skin was impenetrable to the rays of the sun, was as precious as pearls to them.[9]

On the heels of the *encomienda,* and while slavery was at its peak in the eighteenth century, the *jornaleros* (day laborers), *aparceros* (sharecroppers), and *arrendatarios* (renters) began to appear. Some of the plantation owners, owing to the high price of slaves and the expense of their upkeep, found that it was more economical to employ day laborers than it was to use slave labor. At the same time, due to the fact that the seasonal nature of some of the agricultural operations demanded the employment of many laborers for short periods of time, some of the large landowners began distributing part of their lands among their laborers, giving them the right to work their portion as their own in exchange for a certain part of the harvest. Other owners required payment for the use of small plots which were worked by the sharecroppers or *conuqueros* (very small-scale farmers), thus providing most of the vegetables and fruit for the community.

Polanco Martínez commented on the addition of these new systems of land tenancy, which evolved at the same time that these first patterns were established in the New World, with the following words:

> It was then that the owners of the large areas of arable land began to cede to the laborer small plots in tenancy, thus allowing them to work the land on their own, and giving rise to the system known as *alquileres de pisos* that still exists today. In this way, the small farmer not only earned his own subsistence but provided for the needs of the community.[10]

We have superficially reviewed the historical factors most important in relation to the establishment and development of the system of land tenancy that prevails in this country today. The purpose of this historical review is to emphasize that the present system of tenancy has roots in Venezuela's cultural background and therefore is not susceptible to rapid change. To go deeper into this problem would be to depart from the purposes of this study, so we shall therefore take up the discussion of the present system of tenancy, keeping in mind that it has not been rapidly devised but has evolved as an integral part of the culture of the Venezuelans.

Patterns of Land Tenancy According to the Census of 1950

In terms of national totals, according to the statistical figures contained in Table 1, 41.3 per cent of the farms and livestock enterprises of the country were operated by the owners, whereas the next most numerous group, 35.8 per cent of the total, was composed of occupants. The renters composed 14.3 per cent and the sharecroppers 6.3 per cent.

It is in regional aspects, however, that the patterns of tenancy are most interesting. For example, in the Andes, the proportion of owners and sharecroppers was the highest in the nation, with 68.8 and 11.4 per cent respectively. The occupants formed 8.5 per cent and the renters only 8.1 per cent. Even though the sharecroppers formed only 11.4 per cent of all the farms of the Andes, that region alone had close to 40 per cent of the total number of sharecroppers of the country. In no other region is the sharecropper system practiced with such frequency as in the Andes.

In marked contrast to the Andes, the Central region, composed of the states of Aragua, Carabobo and Miranda, has a higher proportion of renters than any other group. They formed 38.6 per cent of the total whereas the owners represented only 19.1 per cent and the occupants approximately the same percentage, or 15.5 per cent.

In the Falcón-Lara depression the owners and occupants formed almost the total number of farmers and herdsmen of the region, or 53.7 per cent and 33.5 per cent respectively. The same was true in the Western region, represented by the state of Sucre. Owners and occupants formed 84.7 per cent of all the farmers. Of these, 41.2 per cent were owners and 43.5 per cent were occupants.

The situation in the Plains was unique and different from that in the rest of the regions. In the four plains states of Apure, Barinas, Cojedes and Guárico, the type of tenancy most prevalent, according to the Census of 1950, was that of occupancy, which formed 62.6 per cent of all the systems of land development. Only 20.9 per cent of the total were owners and 15.5 per cent were renters.

The fact that occupants form 35.8 per cent of all the farmers and herdsmen of the nation should be of interest in relation to problems of

TABLE 1

Distribution of Farming and Livestock Units According to Type of Tenancy, 1950*

Federal entities	Land tenancy					
	Owner	*Renter*	*Sharecropper*	*Occupant*	*Other*	*Totals*
Venezuela Total	102,817	35,587	15,624	88,994	5,716	248,738
Distrito Federal	484	814	260	882	70	2,510
Anzoátegui	1,506	1,077	254	8,594	78	11,509
Apure	605	855	9	3,065	12	4,546
Aragua	1,463	3,619	780	3,152	57	9,071
Barinas	1,341	647	13	5,632	76	7,709
Bolívar	1,371	37	89	4,927	17	6,441
Carabobo	1,313	3,557	340	1,093	170	6,473
Cojedes	610	1,615	453	2,211	65	4,956
Falcón	11,601	366	568	5,011	128	17,674
Guárico	2,959	1,022	397	5,752	156	9,386
Lara	8,595	1,767	1,686	7,597	327	19,972
Mérida	14,602	686	2,030	1,655	1,134	20,107
Miranda	3,750	5,438	937	6,828	184	17,137
Monagas	3,530	924	138	6,119	40	10,751
Nueva Esparta	1,568	123	404	281	72	2,448
Portuguesa	2,036	4,061	681	3,717	472	10,967
Sucre	8,859	1,801	1,010	9,355	484	21,509
Táchira	19,931	1,197	1,723	2,549	1,017	26,417
Trujillo	10,941	3,433	2,823	1,444	905	19,546
Yaracuy	2,773	2,192	924	5,144	152	11,185
Zulia	3,814	330	91	1,867	11	6,143
T. F. Amazonas	1	—	—	103	5	109
T. F. Delta Amacuro	63	26	14	2,013	54	2,170
Islas Federales	1	—	—	—	3	4

*Source: *Resultados Preliminares del Censo Agropecuario*, 1950, Ministerio de Fomento, Dirección General de Estadística y Censos Nacionales, Table 2, Caracas, 1952.

rural well-being. Generally speaking the occupant has little economic and social security and owns no property to call his own. This explains why he may have no interest in conserving the fertility of the soil, to say nothing of improving it. These are problems that should be recognized by specialists in erosion and in mineral and soil conservation. More serious, however, are the problems of "social erosion" created when large numbers of the rural population have no legal rights to the land from which they earn a living. Their social status in the community is uncertain. They cannot participate completely in their social institutions nor do they have the feeling of belonging to them, for they are constantly subject to being ousted by the owner—be this an individual, the municipality or the state. Their status not only relegates them to an asocial position but tends to make them belligerent and antisocial as well. These people are excluded by the laws of the country, all of which favor legal tenure, and as a consequence they learn to distrust and frequently defy them.

TABLE 2

ESTIMATE OF THE DISTRIBUTION OF THE LAND DEVELOPMENT UNITS ACCORDING TO TYPES OF TENANCY*

Types of tenancy	*Number of farms*	*Per cent*
Total	397,823	100.00
Owner	100,000	25.14
Renter	94,600	23.78
Sharecropper	9,200	2.31
Other types**	194,023	48.77

* Source: *Encuesta Agropecuaria Nacional*, 1956, Ministerio de Agricultura y Cría, Dirección Planificación Agropecuaria, Table 1, p. 10, Caracas, 1957.

** Includes various combinations of the first three types.

In the Encuesta Agropecuaria Nacional (National Agricultural and Livestock Survey) of 1956, as seen above, the Ministry of Agriculture estimates the total of land development units at 398,000 in contrast to the 249,000 reported in the Census of 1950. No explanation accompanies the ministry's publication to indicate whether this greater number is due to an actual increase in the number of units of development in the six-year period, or whether it was due to a more complete estimate than that of the census. Our experience leads us to accept the latter explanation for this difference. Table 2 shows that whereas the absolute number of owners was calculated to be the same as that reported by the Census of 1950 (Table 1), 100,000 or 103,000 respectively, the percentage estimated for 1956 decreased from 41.3 per cent of the total in 1950 to 25.14 per cent in 1956. The number of renters doubled by increasing from 14.3 per cent in 1950 to 23.78 per cent, according to the estimates of 1956. The ministry's estimates included only 9,000 sharecroppers in 1956, in comparison with 16,000 shown in the Census in 1950.

The *Survey* of the ministry does not specifically report the number of occupants but lists them in a category of "other types" that comprise 194,000 units, or 49 per cent of the total, and double the number of any other group. Since the classification is so indefinite, we can only conclude that it contains at least the 88,994 occupants reported by the Census of 1950 and perhaps more in the same category.

Table 3 shows the distribution of the exploitation units according to size. It can be seen that 51 per cent of all the units of the nation were

TABLE 3

DISTRIBUTION OF LAND DEVELOPMENT UNITS ACCORDING TO SIZE, 1950*

	Units of development		*Area of development in hectares*	
Hectare groups	*Number*	*Per cent*	*Number*	*Per cent*
Total	248,738	100.00	22,774,585	100.00
Less than 1	18,231	7.33	7,270	0.03
1 to 5	109,179	43.90	255,650	1.12
5 to 10	41,261	16.59	271,463	1.20
10 to 20	26,949	10.84	352,086	1.55
20 to 50	18,470	7.43	539,005	2.37
50 to 100	6,905	2.77	457,282	2.01
100 to 200	4,142	1.66	352,042	2.34
200 to 500	3,469	1.39	1,007,080	4.43
500 to 1,000	1,843	0.74	1,210,961	5.32
1,000 to 2,500	1,644	0.66	2,399,434	10.55
More than 2,500	1,821	0.73	15,557,871	68.40
No information	14,821	5.96	154,440	0.68

* Source: Armando Tamayo, *Land Tenure Problems and the Agrarian Reform Program in Venezuela*, M.A. Thesis, University of Wisconsin, Library archives, Madison, Wisconsin, 1952, according to the unpublished figures of the Census of 1950.

of less than 5 hectares, and that these comprise only 1 per cent of the 23 million hectares occupied by the farms and pastures of all the nation.

On the other hand, it can be seen that only 6 per cent of the 248,738 units are over 100 hectares, and that this small percentage comprises 91 per cent of the area, or more than 20 million of a total of 22,774,585 hectares under development in 1950. This contrast in the distribution—at opposing ends of the scale—speaks eloquently of the dual organization of the agriculture and livestock enterprises of the nation, characterized on the one hand by the minute fragmentation under which the majority of the farmers of the country live and on the other by the immense estates or latifundia which comprise the rest of the land. It would be interesting to compare the size of the developments, as they are given in the preceding table, to the tenure status of those who work the land, but unfortunately the necessary data for such a comparative analysis have not yet been published by the census.

The Encuesta Agropecuaria Nacional conducted by the Ministry of Agriculture in 1956, to which we have referred, provides information about differences among the exploitation units, which are interesting when compared to those reported by the census. The figures of the ministry increase the percentage of small units to 67 per cent from the 51 per cent shown by the Census of 1950, whereas the figure of the percentage of the large landholdings is approximately the same as that quoted by the census. The census reports 6 per cent, while the survey lists this group of owners as just over 5 per cent. These differences between the two sources of information might well be expected by those acquainted with the problems involved in compiling a census. Due to the fact that many of the data of the census were obtained from informed officials and private individuals in the capitals of municipalities and districts, these "informed" sources undoubtedly forgot thousands of small plots and listed only the large landowners and cattle raisers of the region. The data of the ministry's study are presented in Table 4.

TABLE 4

ESTIMATED DISTRIBUTION OF EXPLOITATION UNITS ACCORDING TO SIZE*

	Units in exploitation	
Hectare groups	*Number*	*Per cent*
Total	397,823	100.00
Less than 1	54,166	13.62
1 to 5	212,121	53.32
5 to 10	54,503	13.70
10 to 20	29,273	7.36
20 to 50	18,785	4.72
50 to 100	8,297	2.09
100 to 200	5,517	1.39
200 to 500	5,307	1.33
500 to 1,000	3,095	0.78
1,000 to 2,500	2,822	0.70
2,500 to 10,000	3,432	0.86
More than 10,000	505	0.13

* Source: *Encuesta Agropecuaria Nacional,* 1956, Ministerio de Agricultura y Cría, Table 2, p. 11, Caracas, 1957.

Land Tenancy and Related Factors in Venezuela Today

The rest of this chapter will be concerned primarily with the presentation of the data collected by us in a study of five agricultural regions of the country; a) Sucre; b) Falcón and Lara; c) Aragua and Carabobo; d) Apure, Barinas, Cojedes, and Guárico; e) Mérida, Táchira, and Trujillo. In this way we hope to show, in a more concise and specific way than is possible with the limited data of the National Census, the present situation among the different types of tenancy.

TABLE 5

SIZE OF OPERATION (EXPLOITATION) ACCORDING TO LAND TENANCY

Land tenancy	*Total*	*Number of hectares per operation* 0–0.9	1–4.9	5–9.9	10–19.9	20–49.9	50–99.9	100 and more
Owner	100%	12.6	43.7	13.9	8.0	9.2	4.3	7.3
Lessee	100%	16.1	54.8	22.6	3.7	3.7	0.0	0.0
Sharecropper	100%	20.7	38.0	17.2	10.3	10.4	3.4	0.0
Other	100%	23.3	46.6	13.7	6.8	5.5	1.3	2.6

SOME GENERAL CONSIDERATIONS RELATED TO THE STUDY

The specific purpose of this study was to determine, as accurately as possible, how the agricultural families of Venezuela live, by an analysis of their agricultural enterprises in five different regions. In each region one community was selected as being "typical" and as being devoted to general agriculture, as opposed to the cultivation of a particular product. This is not a study of the large landholders who cultivate corn, sugar cane, rice, cacao, coffee, or any other of the principal products or who raise cattle. The problems of these economic and social segments, as well as their contributions to the maintenance of the economy, are well known, for they form well-organized and articulate groups. Our study is concerned with discovering the agricultural and cattle-raising activities of those farmers who make their living *on* and *from* their small farms. Such units of development rarely exceed 10 hectares, and their median size is 2 or 3 hectares each. Our interest in small-scale farmers is based on the fact that they comprise three fourths of all the farming families of the country, as was shown in the discussion of Tables

3 and 4. Also, regardless of the fact that they represent 170,000 to 200,000 rural families, the scientific programs of investigation and of government credit have rarely been conceived with their well-being in mind. The majority of the programs have been concerned primarily with the quantitative production of a few units rather than the producing masses that constitute the majority of the rural population of Venezuela.

Random choice was used, so far as possible, in selecting the families in each community that were chosen for the study. Since no office has a detailed archive, list or map of the farmers of a given area and since every "community" was in effect a municipality with its center of population, its isolated farmhouses, and its own boundaries, we had to depend on community leaders and on other informed persons to determine the composition of the sample. Wherever there existed an office of the Ministerio de Agricultura y Cría in the municipality, its personnel helped us in the preparation of the sample. The cooperation of the civil officers of the municipality, the municipal council, the rural doctors, the parish priests and the local businessmen were vital in helping to orient us in the community. Using the combined information from these sources, we sent interviewers to visit the families of all the populated parts of the municipality. Insofar as possible, we included families of different neighborhoods of the municipality and interviewed approximately 15 per cent of its families. The sample obtained by this method was distributed according to the place of residence, as shown in Table 6.

TABLE 6

RESIDENCE OF FAMILIES INTERVIEWED, ACCORDING TO LAND TENANCY

	Residence		
Land tenancy	*In the village*	*Outside the village*	*Total*
Owner	45	106	151
Lessee	13	18	31
Sharecropper	4	25	29
Other	10	72	82
Wage laborer	4	7	11
Total	76	228	304

Those who are familiar with the social structure and demographic patterns of the rural areas of the country will understand the distribution of the families that were visited. The pattern was quite uniform throughout the municipalities with a small proportion of the agricultural families living in the center of the municipality and a far greater number scattered in the outlying farms and their respective boundaries. In the municipalities of the sample, 25 per cent of the families lived in the centers of population or capitals, and 75 per cent in other parts of the municipality. Depending on the availability of highways or roads, jeeps were used for transportation in the majority of cases, but when it was necessary we traveled by mule and sometimes found it necessary to walk. Insofar as possible, the samples were taken in proportion to the number of residential units in the municipality.

Among the families of the sample, 50 per cent classified themselves as owners, 10 per cent as renters, 9 per cent as sharecroppers, and 27 per cent as "others" for they did not belong to any of the other groups. Some of this last group worked unappropriated plots or waste land, others occupied communal lands, and so forth, but in no cases were they the owners, nor did they pay rent for the use of the land. This group corresponds to the category of "occupants," which comprises 35 per cent of the total, as reported in the Census of 1950 and as classified by the Office of the Census.

As there was no way to verify the reports of the majority of those who classified themselves as owners, and due to the fact that a large number of that group appeared to have all the characteristics of those belonging in the "others" group, we believe that a large number of those who called themselves proprietors actually belonged in the classification "others," but we have no means of determining the number.

Of the families visited, 4 per cent were classified as laborers, that is to say they had no lands, nor did they cultivate any for their own benefit, but worked by the day. The census did not classify these persons in any of the tenancy groups, but we believe they should be included, for they represent a significant portion of the rural families whose lives depend on work with agriculture or livestock.

Ownership, whether real or supposed, was the most common form of tenancy in almost all the regions studied, comprising approximately three fifths of the farmers, except in the West where it was two fifths, and in the Plains where it was practically nonexistent.

Sharecropping (*aparcería*) was the system that was extensively practiced in the Andes, where it formed 34 per cent of the total. In the Falcón-Lara depression and in the Plains, this system was not found at all. In the Central region we found less than 5 per cent and in the West, less than 6 per cent.

In the Falcón-Lara depression, 27 per cent of the families were of indefinite status, that is, they occupied unappropriated or waste lands, and others had taken what land they could find unoccupied and claimed it by "squatter's rights." In this region 9 per cent of the families were day laborers. Only one case was found in which money was paid as rent.

In the Central region, due perhaps to its being close to the largest center of consumption in the country and to the high cost of land, we found that in comparison with the other regions the rental system was more prevalent, constituting 18 per cent. Occupants comprised 20 per cent and there was only one case of sharecropping.

In the Western region, ownership was the predominant system, forming 43 per cent of the total, whereas the "others" formed 35 per cent. In the Plains region, however, the "others" constituted the greatest part of the total, 87.5 per cent. Some occupied communal lands and others used private property.

The regions of greatest insecurity in terms of land tenancy were the Plains, the West, and the Falcón-Lara depression.

SIZE OF THE ENTERPRISES

Table 7 shows the size of the units of development among the various types of tenancy. It can be seen that 17.8 per cent of those who worked the land had plots of less than 1.0 hectare, and 44.9 per cent worked from 1.0 to 4.9 hectares. In other words, 62.7 per cent of all the farmers had less than 5.0 hectares at the time of this study, and it should be kept in mind that 4.1 per cent were workers without lands.

Since the Office of the Census has not published data regarding the size of the enterprises on a regional basis, the only comparisons possible will be with the country as a whole. In Table 7 we present data from the Census of 1950, together with that of the Encuesta Agropecuaria Nacional of 1956 of the Ministry of Agriculture, and it will be seen that the distributions are similar to those found among the families interviewed for this study.

There were found, among the families studied, some regional differences in the size of the farms. In the Andes, 20.5 per cent of the farms were of less than 1.0 hectare whereas 51.8 per cent of the total were of between 1.0 and 4.9 hectares. In other words, 72.3 per cent of the total number of farms in this region were of an area of less than 5.0 hectares. In the Falcón-Lara depression 12.3 per cent of the families had less than 1.0 hectare, and 42.9 per cent had from 1 to 4.9 hectares, forming a total of 55.2 per cent of the farms which were of less than 5.0 hectares. In the Central region 21.1 per cent cultivated units of less than 1.0 hectare and 38.1 per cent of the farms were between 1.0 and 4.9 hectares; thus in this region 59.2 per cent can be classified as being of less than 5.0 hectares. The concentration of small farms was heavy in the West and in the Plains. In the former, 14.8 per cent of the farms were of less than one hectare, whereas 55.5 per cent of the total were of less than 5 hectares. The percentages in the community of the Plains were 12.5 and 62.5 respectively.

In regard to status of tenancy, whereas 56.3 per cent of the owners had farms of less than 5 hectares, the remaining 43.7 per cent had larger farms. Among those of the group classified as "others," composed principally of occupants, 69.91 per cent had farms of less than 5 hectares and 70.9 per cent of the renters had units of development of the same

TABLE 7

NUMBER OF HECTARES EXPLOITED BY FAMILIES STUDIED, AND COMPARATIVE CENSUS DATA

		Number of hectares per operation						
	Total	0–0.9	1–4.9	5–9.9	10–19.9	20–49.9	50–99	100 *and more*
Operated by families studied	100.0%	17.8	44.9	14.7	7.2	7.5	3.7	4.1
In accordance with Census of 1950	100.0%	7.3	43.9	16.6	10.8	7.4	2.8	5.1*
In accordance with survey of Ministry of Agriculture, 1956	100.0%	13.6	53.3	13.7	7.4	4.7	2.1	5.2

* No information on 6 per cent of the cases.

size. Among the sharecroppers, 58.7 per cent had units of less than 5 hectares each. Table 5 shows this in detail.

PRINCIPAL PRODUCTS

Table 8 presents data concerning the principal crops and livestock that are produced on the farms that were visited. As was explained above, since our sample was chosen to represent areas devoted predominantly to general agriculture, the majority of the farms raised a variety of products and sometimes a few cattle or goats. These formed 51 per cent of all the farms, and we have classified them under the well-known Venezuelan term *conuco*, or "garden patch." The types of products found on the *conucos* depended, naturally, on the region. In the Falcón-Lara depression, for example, there was invariably some sisal and perhaps some *cocuy*, as these were the most important crops of the region, together with yucca, maize, and carrots. In the Andes, the sisal was replaced by garden vegetables and perhaps by small quantities of potatoes and wheat, but in other respects operations were similar. In the Western zone the *conuqueros* had small quantities of

TABLE 8

SIZE OF OPERATION ACCORDING TO CROP OR PRINCIPAL PRODUCT

Crop or principal product	*Size of operation*							
	–1	1–4	5–9	10–19	20–49	50–99	100 *and more*	*Total*
Potatoes	2		1	2	1			6
Onions	1	2	3	1	1	1	1	10
Sugar cane		3	3	1	4			11
Coffee		3	1		2	2	4	12
Oranges	2	9	1					12
Tobacco		3	1	1				5
Goats	5	3		1	1	1		11
Cattle		1				1		2
Other	2	1	1					4
Vegetables	2	6	2		3			13
Mixed crop		8	11	12	10	6	7	54
Conuco	38	92	19	2				151
Total	52	131	43	20	22	11	12	291

coffee in addition to the base crops already mentioned, and in the Plains some sugar cane was grown.

As we said at the beginning of this study, the small farmer tried to raise a little of each of his basic necessities so as to provide for his own subsistence, and occasionally he was able to devote some of his land to the raising of products that could be sold for cash in his region. Essentially, however, he did not produce for the market. This was left to those who concentrated their efforts in the raising of one, two, or three crops that were best adapted to the conditions of the soil and the climate of the different regions, and who produced in sufficient quantities to sell their products at market.

In Table 8 it can be seen that the *conuco* is a small unit, almost always of less than 5 hectares and often of less than one. We found that 80 per cent of the *conucos* were of less than 5 hectares in area and 25 per cent of less than one hectare.

Another notable characteristic was the prevalence of farmers who raised several crops. That is, their operations were devoted to two or three commercial crops, all of which were apparently of equal importance in the organization of the farm. Thus they are classified under the general heading of "multiple crop farms." We wish again to remind our readers that the samples for the study were chosen so as to avoid the well-known areas of the country where single crop agricultural organizations prevailed: that is, regions in which great quantities of rice, corn, cotton, sugar, coffee, sesame, and other principal products were produced. However, since those products could be produced in all the areas, we find that the most industrious and ambitious farmers augmented their total production by raising several crops. Table 8 shows that, on the average, the size of the farms was larger among those dedicated to the raising of one crop, and, as would be expected, much larger than the *conucos*.

The relatively large number of farms raising vegetables is due to the type of agriculture found in the Andes. All but one of the farmers who raised vegetables lived in this region. Goat raising and the production of sisal and onions were mostly found in the Falcón-Lara depression. A few years ago this region was devoted exclusively to the raising of sisal, *cocuy*, and goats, but governmental restrictions imposed on goat raising have caused drastic changes in the agricultural organization of this semi-arid zone. Not long ago the region had agricultural enterprises with thousands of head of goats, and hundreds of the small farmers used the arid vegetation of the hills to graze their herds of 25 to 35 head. Today they have almost disappeared. The river valleys are devoted to the production of onions, which are cultivated by the Spanish immigrants who have moved to this region since the mid-1950's. Since the production of onions requires a great deal of manual labor, the families who previously made their living from their small goat herds now find seasonal work in the onion farms. From the standpoint of soil conservation the prohibitions on the raising of goats are justified. However, unless something is done to give these families alternate working possibilities, or they are vocationally trained in skills that will enable them to find work outside of this zone, there will inevitably follow discontent and hardship.

Another factor contributing to the discontent in this semiarid region has been the disappearance of the *cocuy* industry. Until the middle of the 1930's the community had 32 stills in operation, and it is estimated that they provided work to about 200 families in the different phases of the industry. The loss of work that resulted from the closing down of nearly all the stills is clearly visible to whoever visits the community.

All the production of oranges is concentrated in the Central region, whereas potatoes are grown mostly in the Andes and in the Central region. Potatoes were at one time the primary source of income in the Western community, but pestilences and potato blights have made it necessary to abandon completely the production of this crop. The people speak sadly of the days when they were the "principal producers of potatoes" in the country, and now this lucrative activity has had to give way to the production of sugar cane. They also complain that they have not been able to find a variety of sugar cane adapted to the region, with the result that the quality and yield are hardly adequate. Potato farming made it possible for even the smallest farmers to participate in the production of a marketable product, but now the poverty of the region is attributed to the loss of that crop and the necessity of having to depend on work in the haciendas or in the sugar cane and coffee plantations.

On the river banks of the Plains region, the principal crops of the small farms were sugar cane and a variety of bananas, but, as happened in the West, there was a universal complaint about the "plague" that had almost destroyed the crops. The principal complaint was the sickness called by them *hereque*. Almost all the bananas are lost, causing tremendous repercussions in individual income since this is the principal crop of the region.

WAYS IN WHICH THE WORK IS DONE

The majority of the families visited depended on their own brawn and the most rudimentary of tools to do the necessary farm work. To be exact, 66 per cent of all the farms had only the simplest of tools: a pick, a shovel, and a machete. Another 25 per cent owned oxen for plowing and cultivating, and the remaining 9 per cent had tractors. These data are presented in detail in Table 9.

It is obvious that in some cases the factors determining the way in which the work was done were not purely economic. All the teams of oxen, for example, with the exception of two, were found among the farmers of the Andes. Some of the determining factors are the type of soil, the preference of the farmers, and the size of the farms, but we

TABLE 9

Ways in Which Work Is Done, According to Land Tenancy

Land tenancy	Ways in which work is done		
	Tractors	*Team of oxen*	*By hand*
Owner	18	42	91
Lessee	4	3	24
Sharecropper	1	25	3
Other	3	3	76
Total	26	73	194

can also suppose that cultural factors are of some influence, since oxen have been used by the Andean peasants since the first days of the colonies. For the most part, the tractors were in the hands of the owners, and were most common in the Central region and among the onion farmers of the Falcón-Lara depression. Only one tractor was found among the farmers of the Andes, and another one in the West.

Table 10 shows the relation between the size of the farms and the type of tools used in their cultivation. As would be expected, none of the very small units of development—those of less than one hectare—had tractors. Some were found in units of up to 9.9 hectares, especially among the onion growers, but 65 per cent of the total number were

TABLE 10

Ways in Which Work Is Done, According to Size of Operation

Ways in which work is done	*Size of operation*							
	0–0.9	*1–4.9*	*5–9.9*	*10–29.9*	*30–49.9*	*50–99.9*	*100 and more*	*No inf.*
With tractor	0	4	5	5	1	1	10	0
With team of oxen	13	30	13	12	4	1	0	0
By hand	40	97	25	11	9	7	2	3
Total	53	131	43	28	14	9	12	3

found in developments of more than 10 hectares in area. In those farms that used only manual labor, 70 per cent were of less than 5 hectares each. The few other informants who reported having only manual tools were those who raised cattle or goats, and the greater part of their lands were natural pasture lands. Oxen were used in the smaller farms and in those of medium size, for 18 per cent of the oxen were found in farms of less than one hectare, another 41 per cent in farms of from 1.0 to 4.9 hectares and the other 41 per cent on farms of 5.0 hectares and larger. In the Andes, oxen are invariably used for work in the small units, though this may often involve paying rent for them to the more fortunate neighbors who own them.

GROSS ANNUAL INCOME

In Table 11 the gross annual income of the agricultural enterprises is indicated according to the "status" or type of tenancy and the size of the farm. Expressed in *bolivars*,* this gross income was calculated by asking the farmer the amount of land in production, the crops that he had and his estimate of the previous year's yield. Using figures supplied by the Office of Agricultural Planning of the Ministry of Agriculture on the average yields of the different crops and the prices, we calculated the gross income of those farmers who were able to give sufficient information about their operations. Although we admit that these figures are estimates, we believe them to be fairly accurate.

According to these estimates, 19.5 per cent of all the families in the study who gave information about the earning power of their farms had a gross income of less than Bs. 400.00 per year. Another 13.1 per cent earned from Bs. 400.00 to Bs. 799.00, and 13.6 per cent stated that their agricultural endeavors only provided them the necessities of the family and nothing for sale. In other words, 46.2 per cent of the families who gave information about their earnings had incomes that ranged from zero to a maximum of Bs. 799.00. A third (33.5 per cent) of the families earned Bs. 800.00 to Bs. 5,000.00 per year, leaving only 20.3 per cent of the total who had incomes of more than Bs. 6,000.00 per year.

Agricultural income in the various tenancy groups tends to be bimodal; that is, among the owners we found groups with the highest and the lowest incomes. This distribution is due to the definition of "owner" as discussed earlier, but we believe that many heads of families who classified themselves as owners were actually occupants or laborers and should have appeared in the "others" classification. The distribution was closer to being bimodal among the renters and the sharecroppers, while the great majority of the "others" come within the lowest levels of income, or produced only for home consumption.

Since a great percentage (56.3 per cent) of the owners operated farms of less than 5.0 hectares, their gross incomes were more closely related to the type of agricultural enterprise they operated or the kind of crop they raised than to their status of tenancy. Table 12 demonstrates this, for we can see that the higher gross incomes were found generally on

---

* In 1960, 3.35 bolivars equaled one U.S. dollar.—EDITORS' NOTE.

TABLE 11

ESTIMATED GROSS INCOME ACCORDING TO LAND TENANCY AND SIZE OF OPERATION

Level of gross annual income, Bs.	Owner (hectare)							Lessee (hectare)						
	–1	1–4	5–9	10–19	20–49	50–99	100*	–1	1–4	5–9	10–19	20–49	50–99	100*
0–399	8	12	2		1			4	4					
400–799	2	14	5						3	1				
800–1,199		6		1					2					
1,200–1,599		4	4	1					1	1				
1,600–1,999		2	1			1			1					
2,000–2,399		3			3	1			1	1				
2,400–2,799	1	5												
2,800–3,199		2							2					
3,200–3,599	1	1	1											
3,600–3,999				1					1					
4,000–4,399		2							1					
4,400–4,799	1	1		1										
4,800–5,199				1	1	1								
5,200–5,599	1	1												
5,600–5,999														
6,000 and more		1	7	6	8	6	10			3	1	1		
Consumption	5	9						1						
No inf.		3	1	1	1				1	1				
Total	19	66	21	12	14	9	10	5	17	7	1	1		

* No information was obtained regarding size of operation in cases classified as other, and those with an income between Bs. 5,600–5,999.

TABLE 11 *(Continued)*

ESTIMATED GROSS INCOME ACCORDING TO LAND TENANCY AND SIZE OF OPERATION

Level of gross annual income, Bs	*Sharecropper (hectare)*							*Other (hectare)*							*Total*
	–1	1–4	5–9	10–19	20–49	50–99	100	–1	1–4	5–9	10–19	20–49	50–99	100	
0–399	4	4	1					8	5	1	1				55
400–799	1	3						1	4	2					30
800–1,199		2			1				3	1					16
1,200–1,599			2						2						15
1,600–1,999															5
2,000–2,399									4	1					14
2,400–2,799	1		1						2			1			11
2,800–3,199									2	1			1		8
3,200–3,599									1	1		1			6
3,600–3,999															2
4,000–4,399									2		1				6
4,400–4,799												1			4
4,800–5,199										1				1	5
5,200–5,599															2
5,600–5,999															0
6,000 and more		1		2	2	1			3		3				55
Consumption		1	1	1				12	7	1					38
No inf.								1	2	1		1		1	14
Total	6	11	5	3	3	1		22	37	10	5	4	1	2	292

TABLE 12

CROP OR PRINCIPAL PRODUCT ACCORDING TO LEVEL OF GROSS ANNUAL INCOME OF OPERATION

Level of gross annual income, Bs.	Product or main crop												
	Potatoes	*Onions*	*Other*	*Sugar cane*	*Vege-tables*	*Coffee*	*Oranges*	*Goats*	*Tobacco*	*Cattle*	*Conuco*	*Mixed Products*	*Total*
0–399	2	1	2		3		2	5			41		56
400–799				1	2	1					32		36
800–1,199		1			2		3		1		9		16
1,200–1,599						1	1				8	5	15
1,600–1,999				1			1			1	2		5
2,000–2,399	1							1	2		8	2	14
2,400–2,799					3		1				6	1	11
2,800–3,199				1		1					4	2	8
3,200–3,599				1			1				2	2	6
3,600–3,999					1							1	2
4,000–4,399					1	1	1					3	6
4,400–4,799							1			1		2	4
4,800–5,199								1				4	5
5,200–5,599											1	1	2
5,600–5,999													0
6,000 and more	3	7		6	1	8			1			29	55*
Consumption			1					4			33		38
No inf.		1	1	1			1		1		5	2	12
Total	6	10	4	11	13	12	12	11	5	2	151	54	291

* One case included in the Bs. 6,000 and more category in Table 11 was transferred to category of Bs. 0–399.

farms that had only one main crop in large quantities—onions, potatoes, coffee, or sugar cane—or on farms that had these same crops or others as part of their multiple crop enterprises. Contrastingly, however, it was in the *conucos* that the greatest number of families of low income were found. Among the *conuqueros*, 21.8 per cent produced only for their own subsistence, another 34.4 per cent produced up to Bs. 800.00 during a year. In the *conucos* the peasants try to hold body and soul together by raising infinitesimal amounts of whatever the soil will produce, but the yield is very low, as shown by the statistics on income.

The eleven day-laborers who are not included in the foregoing analysis reported receiving salaries that ranged from a minimum of Bs. 5.00 for an eleven-hour day of work (six cases) to Bs. 12.00. One of the informants earned Bs. 6.00, others Bs. 7.00 and one Bs. 12.00.

Women and children who work ten hours a day in the onion fields earn Bs. 3.00 for their work. The reader should bear in mind that agricultural workers are not protected by social security, nor do they receive any of the social guarantees that protect the urban or industrial worker, such as overtime wages, vacations, advance notice of termination of employment, etc. They receive no medical benefits in their employment, but depend exclusively on the rural doctors in their area, if there are any. To summarize, the quantities mentioned in the previous paragraph represent the total earnings, and with this amount they must supply all their needs.

To conclude the discussion of the income of the agricultural families included in this study, we should repeat that our tables and the discussion of the data contained in them refer to *gross* income, and not to net income. That is, we have not taken into account any of the expenditures of the family in running their farms. Whatever expenditures that had to be made for the land, machines, rent, buying of animals, seed, insecticides, fertilizers, etc., as well as the value of the part of the harvest that had to be given to the owners by the sharecroppers, all had to be paid from the gross amount that we have quoted. It is obvious, therefore, that the vast majority of these families had very little money, if any, to spend on the lives of their families, and inevitably we found many families in the most miserable of living conditions. Cleanliness, minimal education, medical services, and participation in social and religious activities require levels of income far above those of these families.

We must conclude, therefore, that all the families who show incomes of less than Bs. 6,000.00 per year (and these include 80 per cent) must be classified as living in extreme poverty. If we take into consideration the average size of the families who live on these farms and the number of workers that each family needs to attain the income shown, we expose the problem of poverty in its appalling reality.

In those cases in which income was greater than Bs. 6,000.00, as shown in our table, it ranged from Bs. 20,000.00 to more than Bs. 100,000.00, with the largest number of cases grouped between Bs. 30,000.00 and Bs. 60,000.00. The intervals chosen for the table, from Bs. 400.00 to Bs. 5,000.00, were chosen to best represent the situation among the majority of the small farmers.

AGRICULTURAL CREDIT

Table 13 demonstrates the use that agricultural families, excluding day-laborers, have made of agricultural credit. Except for a very few cases, the practice of using bank credit to help in agricultural operations was entirely unknown. Among the 151 owners, only 3.3 per cent had used this kind of credit for buying land, while another 13.2 per cent had borrowed money to improve their farms in other ways. Only 7 per cent of the sharecroppers and 12.8 per cent of the renters had used agricultural credit to improve their farms. Only one of those families had ever used that type of credit to improve his home. Considering the group as a whole, 88.1 per cent had never used credit in any form in the operation of their farms.

TABLE 13

PURPOSES FOR WHICH BANK CREDITS WERE USED BY THE FAMILIES

Land tenancy	*Purpose of credit used*				
	Purchase of land	*Improvement of farm*	*Improvement of home*	*No credit used*	*Total*
Owner	3.3	13.2	0.0	82.8	100.0%
Lessee	0.0	12.8	0.0	87.2	100.0%
Sharecropper	0.0	7.0	3.5	89.5	100.0%
Other	1.2	1.2	0.0	97.6	100.0%

Considering these data, it is not surprising to find that only 2.0 per cent of the families answered affirmatively when we asked them if they believed that the facilities for agricultural credit in their community were adequate for the farmers' necessities. The remaining 98 per cent either did not know about the use of credit or answered our question negatively. The farming families with incomes as low as those we have described have nowhere to go for credit except to the local usurers, if there are any, who charge exorbitant rates of interest. The requirements for eligibility for a loan from the Banco Agrícola y Pecuario deny them the use of credit facilities.

NOTES

1. See Lowry Nelson, *Rural Cuba,* Minneapolis, University of Minnesota Press, 1950, p. 80.

2. S. E. Morison, *Admiral of the Ocean Sea,* Boston, Little, Brown & Co., 1942, p. 567. See also David Weeks, "The Agrarian System of the Spanish American Colonies," *Journal of Land and Public Utility Economics,* Madison, Wis., February, 1947, 153–168.

3. Lesley Byrd Simpson, *The Encomienda in New Spain,* Berkeley, University of California Press, 1929, p. 19.

4. See Robert Chamberlain, "Castilian Backgrounds of the Repartimiento-Encomienda," in *Contributions to American Anthropology and History,* Carnegie Institution of Washington Publication 509, Vol. 5, Art. 25, as cited by Lowry Nelson, *op. cit.,* p. 80.

5. Tomás Polanco Martínez, *Esbozo sobre historia económica venezolana, primera etapa: "La Colonia,"* 1498–1810, Caracas, Editorial Ancora, 1950, p. 43.

6. A. Arellano Moreno, *Orígenes de la economía venezolana,* Mexico, Imprenta Nuevo Mundo, 1947, p. 124.

7. See Ramiro Guerra y Sánchez, *Manual de historia de Cuba,* Havana, Cultural, S.A., 1938, p. 44.

8. Lesley Byrd Simpson, *op. cit.,* p. 25.

9. *Ibid.,* p. 59.

10. *Ibid.,* p. 123. The term *aparcero* refers to all systems in which the farmers are partners to the owners of the lands. The system in general has several regional variations in Venezuela, and, depending on these, the practice is called *pisatería, medianería,* or other similar terms. In this study *medianero* and *aparcero* are used interchangeably. [In the present translation these terms have been rendered as "sharecropper."—EDITORS' NOTE.]

The Jamaican Internal Marketing Pattern: Some Notes and Hypotheses

SIDNEY W. MINTZ

Even the most casual visitor to Jamaica cannot fail to take notice of the internal marketing system by which almost all perishable vegetable foods, and many other locally produced goods, are conveyed from the primary producer to the ultimate consumer. This system is very old in Jamaica; although the writer could find no reference to it during the Spanish period, descriptions of markets and of marketing appear frequently in works on Jamaica written in the eighteenth and nineteenth centuries. While present-day marketing probably differs somewhat from the marketing typical of pre-emancipation Jamaica, the pattern fundamentally seems to have remained unchanged. The particular character of Jamaican marketing is rooted in the island's past—a past shaped by a system of slavery under which the slaves had to produce their own foodstuffs. The sugar estates traditionally required their slaves to produce the greater part of their own food on land allotted from the upland slopes or from unused scrub portions of the property (Lopez 1948: 289–290; Olivier

Reprinted from *Social and Economic Studies,* 1955, IV, 95–103, by permission of the author and publisher. Data for the present paper were collected during the summers of 1952 and 1954, while the writer was serving as field director of Yale University's Inter-disciplinary Training Program. The writer is indebted to that Program, and to the Ford and Carnegie Foundations, which financed it, for the opportunity to collect the data. Many persons in Jamaica made valuable suggestions regarding the materials presented here. Especially helpful were Mr. W. D. Burrowes, Mrs. Ella Campbell, Mr. David Edwards, and Dr. M. G. Smith.

1936: 108, 158). Slaves were permitted to do as they pleased with any surplus they produced, and quite a few apparently were able to accumulate considerable sums of money through their independent production and marketing operations (Gardner 1874: 181, 390; Olivier 1936: 73–74). Important conventions concerning the slave's rights to his own produce, and to the financial rewards of the sale of this produce, developed over time, and appear to have been respected as a matter of course by the planters.[1] A slave, cultivating foodstuffs for himself and his family, could produce more than the family consumed, making an exchangeable surplus available to be funneled into the marketing system. Some slaves, in turn, were thus freed from food production and could use their free time for craft specialization, producing goods to be sold at market, and using the proceeds to buy necessary foodstuffs. Basket-makers, pannier makers, leatherworkers, woodworkers, and other artisans, for instance, who worked at their crafts or at other jobs for their masters during the week, were enabled by the market system to exchange the products of their skills for foods and other necessary goods (Gardner 1874). The marketing system thus facilitated a wider division of labor within the slave group. Marketing also provided the slave with an opportunity to obtain foods or other products which came from different regions of the island and might not have been obtainable in his home region. Markets also enabled slaves to congregate with a certain amount of freedom in centers where news could be exchanged as well as goods, and where respite from the plantation regimen could be enjoyed. Although the missionaries objected vigorously to the fact that markets were held on Sunday (Bickell 1825:66, 204), it was there that many slaves received their first direct exposure to Christian teaching.[2]

There is ample reason to suppose that the market system in Jamaica had important African antecedents. The vast majority of Jamaican slaves came from West Africa, where markets were highly developed,[3] and where women were predominantly the marketers—as they are in Jamaica today. However, the Jamaican pattern could develop and persist only because the slave, and later the freeman, had access both to land and to a marketing institution so that he could produce and exchange foodstuffs and craft articles.[4]

Perhaps the first significant point to be made about Jamaican internal marketing, in terms of its present character, is that it is carried on largely by women rather than men. Historical accounts lend some support to the idea that this has long been the case;[5] at the same time, men appear to have predominated, although not to the exclusion of women, in the agricultural work. The pattern of women as marketers and men as cultivators on the subsistence plots remained consistent both before and after slavery, and this division of labor has probably persisted because there has been no reason for it to change. To what degree marketing and small-scale agriculture were the two sides of the sexual division of labor within the slave family when the estate was not exacting the family's labor, is not clear. In this connection, it is interesting to note that "divorce"—that is, the termination of common-law unions in the slavery period—was consummated by tearing in two the "cotta," or head cloth, which supports the market woman's basket of produce (Gardner 1874: 182; Philippo 1843: 218–219). This may have signified the breaking in two of a symmetrical economic relationship between male cultivator and female marketer.

Marketing is conducted in Jamaica today almost exclusively through the use of money, rather than by barter. Barter, to the writer's knowledge, is very rare,[6] and probably was infrequent even in the early periods once some currency had filtered down into the slave group through the selling of goods or the performance of special services for the free members of the society. The presence of a highly standardized medium of exchange, which serves in nearly all marketing transactions, is perhaps the second significant diagnostic feature of the Jamaican internal marketing system. This highly standardized medium of exchange—money—makes it possible for a marketer to exchange her goods completely a dozen times in the course of a pre-market night, and for a single item of produce to be passed from hand to hand perhaps a like number of times before reaching the ultimate consumer. Such a process increases the time spent in handling the goods involved, and may increase their cost, since every handler expects to receive some reward for her part in the exchange process. From the point of view of the ultimate consumer, who must pay the difference between the original price of the goods and their final selling price, this is an inefficient process. It possesses certain very important advantages, however. Prices for the consumer naturally respond to variations in supply. In this sense, the consumer benefits rather than loses when a large number of middlemen are involved in supplying him, since miscalculations may lead to a glut which is immediately followed by a sharp drop in consumer prices. Unevenness of supply of a given product may depend on seasonal variation and on available transport; but it is also dependent in good measure on the very nature of the whole productive and marketing system in which thousands of small-scale producers and middlemen are involved. The fact that the internal marketing operations in Jamaica are carried on by great numbers of individual entrepreneurs, in many thousands of individual and discrete steps, is the third extremely important point to note in interpreting the system.

To understand the connection between Jamaican internal marketing and other aspects of Jamaican culture, several other characteristics of the marketing system must now be enumerated. The fourth characteristic is the fact that goods for internal marketing are hardly ever trucked without carrying those who buy and sell them. The trucker of produce is almost always a trucker of marketers as well. This is important in considering the amount of human energy and time invested in the distributive process, and in evaluating the efficiency of distribution. The fifth characteristic is the tendency for sellers to operate on a very small scale, buying and selling small quantities of produce which represent a small capital investment. This capital is usually borrowed, at least initially, either from the market woman's husband or, more commonly perhaps, from a small business man who usually charges an exorbitant rate of interest. The sixth characteristic of Jamaican internal marketing follows from this: the profit margin for such marketing transactions is extremely small. These points, common knowledge to most Jamaicans, are among the essential characteristics of Jamaican internal marketing; inherent in them are important advantages and disadvantages for the primary producer, the ultimate consumer, and for all those who take part in the movement of goods or who hold property in those goods.

The individuals who act as middlemen in the marketing process—who sometimes produce a portion of what they sell and perhaps consume some of what they buy, but who serve mainly as transporters of produce, sharing the risks of buying and reselling largely perishable goods in variable supply—are known as "marketers," "vendors," "speculators," or "higglers" in Jamaica. "Higgler" is probably the term most commonly used and tends to be applied indiscriminately to people filling roles at every step in the marketing process. In addition to those characteristics mentioned earlier, such as a small stock, transactions in cash, etc., which typify the higgler, there is one final feature to be mentioned—she usually (though by no means always) carries a diversified stock of produce, so as to avoid being caught in the glut of a single item. This is the seventh and last diagnostic characteristic of Jamaican internal marketing to be mentioned here.

The observations thus far are intended to describe some features of the marketing system without reference to other aspects of Jamaican culture. But there is agreement among students of human behavior that apparently unrelated features of culture often are so interwoven into a web or network that they are dependent on one another, and that changes in one feature are likely to lead to completely unanticipated changes in the other. The remainder of the present paper purports to suggest that certain relationships exist between the internal marketing system and the system of agriculture, the pattern of land tenure, the structure of the rural family, and other aspects of Jamaican life, such that changes introduced into the marketing system without reference to these other aspects of the culture might result in unforeseen and far-reaching consequences.

First of all, it is hypothesized here that the Jamaican marketing system, as described above, and the Jamaican pattern of small-farm cultivation are wedded not only historically, but functionally and psychologically as well, and that changes in either of these parts of Jamaican culture would almost certainly result in changes in the other. Had it not been for the pattern of subsistence-plot cultivation under slavery, and the perpetuation of it by the growth of a rural peasantry after emancipation (Lopez 1948; Paget 1945), the Jamaican economy would have taken on a very different character. The production of a per capita agricultural surplus within the internal economy under slavery facilitated and made advantageous the development of a strong marketing pattern, which probably rested on the foundations of the African cultural heritage of the slaves. After emancipation, the market system proved to be of great value to the small-scale cultivator who, by means of it, was provided with access to the cash he needed to supply himself with those items that could not be produced locally. This situation still obtains. Like the higgler, the small-scale cultivator's capital fund is minimal, his production very small, and his margin of profit narrow. He depends heavily on the higgler, who helps him to transform at least part of the products of his labor into cash. This interdependence between higglers and small-scale cultivators, between marketing and small-scale agriculture, has never been broken, and may be even stronger today than it was a century ago. The owners of the tremendous number of small farms which are at present maintained in Jamaica must depend on the sale of at least part of their produce for obtaining cash. And while the owner-cultivator of half an acre may be unwilling to invest the time and energy necessary to go to market to sell his handful of yams and cocoes, he is quite happy to sell them to the market woman who scours the neighborhood to buy just such odd handfuls of resaleable goods. The same small-scale farmer is unwilling to put his entire half acre into corn or escallions or any other single crop for fear of a seasonal glut, when all he had produced might have to be sold at a loss, if sold at all; he prefers to diversify his tiny farm in order to reduce the risk involved in the production of any one item. It will be noted immediately that the small-scale farmer distributes risk in production by crop diversification, just as the higgler distributes risk in distribution by carrying a selection of items. The market woman who buys from the small-scale farmer is sensitive to the very same dangers her supplier faces. However, the same diversification which reduces risk in both production and distribution increases the complexity of both. Some have argued that if the Jamaican small-scale farmer were willing to put his entire half acre into a single crop and then sell the harvest to a wholesaler, the agricultural and marketing processes would be made much more efficient. But to this argument both small-scale farmer and higgler are likely to respond: "Efficient—for whom?" On a number of occasions when small-scale farmers have put all their land into a single crop, they have lost everything. The small-scale farmer cannot afford to put all his resources into the production of a single item, the market for which is not guaranteed. Given the demand situation, and the marketing system by which all internally consumed crops are handled, the man who farms on a small scale in Jamaica must diversify; given the diversified farming on this minuscule scale, the marketing will tend to remain as it is.

The higgler provides the essential link between producer and consumer in the whole process of local distribution, because no one, at least in present-day Jamaica, is willing to take her place. So long as farmers sell their surplus in the form of several hands of bananas, a handful of ackees, a few breadfruit, half a dozen eggs, and so forth, truckers who, in some countries, serve the consumers' needs by buying wholesale in the countryside and selling wholesale to retail stores or jobbers cannot supplant the higgler in Jamaica. No trucker can profitably tour the Jamaican countryside buying on the scale of higgler operations. It would take him several days to acquire a load of often highly perishable goods, since he would have to purchase these goods in tiny quantities. Moreover, with no wholesale outlet for them, he would have to unload his stock through individual resale of similarly tiny quantities. The higgler, on the other hand, is able to carry on her business profitably on such a small scale because her capital outlay is very small and she is willing to work on an extremely low margin of profit. She is willing to do this because higgling is one of the very few ways in which she is able to convert her labor into a cash reward, however small. In the course of her transactions, the higgler makes a very significant contribution, not usually recognized, to the functioning of Jamaican society. While she is engaged in providing the consumer with needed produce and the small-scale producer with an access to market, she pays a very high rate for services. Thus, she contributes up to a third or more of her gross income to the trucker (the number of trucks engaged in carrying higglers and their goods to and from markets is considerable: twenty trucks is not an unusual number to see at one of the busy country markets, and there are eighty-seven such markets in Jamaica); she frequently pays as much as 5 per cent or more interest for *three days' use* of capital borrowed from the butcher or shopkeeper who finances her business; and the market itself may collect 5 per cent of the estimated selling value of her load in addition to other fees, in return for letting her sell.

If it be true that small-scale farming and the particular kinds of marketing arrangements that exist in Jamaica are closely related, it may be useful to consider briefly the nature of consumer demand in the island, since Jamaican production and distribution are naturally linked to the kinds of demand situations which Jamaican consumers create. Certain sectors of consumer demand seem to be relatively stable, for instance that of the suburban buyers of Cross Roads, St. Andrew, or the staff of the University College at Mona, St. Andrew. But these are relatively circumscribed consumer groups, composed of buyers with assured incomes and fairly fixed buying habits. The broad base of the consumer group consists of individuals with irregular incomes who, because of this, the writer would hypothesize, manifest irregular demand for goods. In the sectors of the buying public where demand is regular and assured, it may be possible to eliminate the market woman (and to some extent, the markets as well), and to establish greengrocers on the American or British model, exactly because consumer demand in these sectors of the economy is sufficiently stable to encourage businessmen at every stage of the production and distribution process—cultivation, trucking, wholesaling, and retailing—to risk investment.[7] But the irregularity of demand among the majority of Jamaican consumers would appear to preclude any overall replacement of the present marketing system with a different one.[8] Thus it would appear that small-scale agricultural production is functionally related to the prevalent marketing arrangements, and that in turn both are related to the demand situation. The writer has restricted himself mainly to the first two components of the total system—production and marketing—because the connection between them is fairly clear. In the Jamaican situation they are interdependent and reinforce each other. Yet it is conceivable that a market system like that found in Jamaica today might be maintained in another society where peasant farms are of a much larger average size; contrariwise, a small-scale farming pattern such as Jamaica's might be maintained in conjunction with a very different form of marketing system. The writer would not hold that the two adaptations are inseparable, nor that any change in one is certain to destroy the other; he would suggest, however, that before any serious changes be made in either pattern, serious thought be given to what the results might be for the other.

From the point of view of the small-scale cultivator, it is sensible to maintain an "uneconomic" farm, because to own land in Jamaica has a very special meaning, and being independent on the land is a value of deep significance to the Jamaican peasant. One can reason that the very small farms are frequently wasteful from the agronomic, conservation, and economic points of view. Much the same may be said of the market woman and her scale of operations. She, too, operates an "uneconomic" and wasteful business. But she, too, is maintaining her independence. Many market women have told the writer in describing their fellows that "one week she gains and the next she loses, but she'd rather be a higgler and make a shilling than work in someone's house." In a country where over 70,000 adults, most of them women, are employed as domestics (Cumper 1949), where labor is relatively plentiful, where average incomes are low, where there is no social barrier to lower-class women working, and where the only economic alternative to marketing is domestic labor, it is easy to see why many women choose to be higglers

Mention has been made of the division of labor between men and women which historically and functionally seems to parallel that between cultivation and marketing, although by no means strictly so. This division of labor, which characterizes rural lower-class peasant society as a whole in Jamaica, is replicated in thousands of individual families. The higgler wife or "partner" provides an outlet for some of her cultivator husband's foodstuffs. At the same time, higgling provides a woman with a largely separate economic activity in which the husband does not exert a great deal of control. The significance of the marketing pattern in affecting the husband-wife relationship in thousands of Jamaican families is likely to be considerable. How the wife's independent or quasi-independent role as marketer and contributor to the total family income may influence conceptions of authority, equality, dignity, and other basic value-concepts within the family seems to be virtually unexplored. The writer would hold that an intimate functional relationship obtains between the marketing system and the patterned sexual roles evaluated by the Jamaican peasant people themselves as permissible and desirable. That there are basic Jamaican peasant values involved in being a higgler and hence "independent," in having a source of income largely separate from that of one's mate—these are hypotheses and require substantiation. The more basic hypothesis that small-scale farming and the present system of Jamaican internal marketing neatly sustain one another also requires substantiation, and can be proved or disproved only by careful field study. Studies on these problems could help to throw light on one of the most fundamental institutions of Jamaican culture.

NOTES

1. Cf., for instance, Edwards (1793): "I do not believe that an instance can be produced of a master's interfering with his Negroes in their *peculium* thus acquired [from the sale of produce]. They are permitted also to dispose at their deaths of what little property they possess; and even to bequeath their grounds or gardens to such of their fellow-slaves as they think proper. These principles are so well-established that whenever it is found convenient for the owner to exchange the Negro grounds for other lands, the Negroes must be satisfied, in money or otherwise, before the exchange takes place. It is universally the practice."

2. Of particular interest is the story of James Finlayson, a slave, said to have returned from his marketing at Falmouth one Sunday, deeply moved by the rebuke of a minister for breaking the Sabbath, who later became a leading figure in the spread of the Baptist faith in St. Ann parish. Cf. Henderson, (1931).

3. The bibliography on West African marketing is a rapidly growing one. For two brief but useful analyses, cf. Herskovits (1952) and Nadel (1951).

4. The slaves were permitted to maintain or to rework the African traditions of marketing and to derive significant advantages from doing this, although they were severely punished for attempting to perpetuate certain other features of the ancestral cultures, such as those connected with personal magical power, funerary practices, the use of drums as part of religio-political activity, etc. It is quite clear why they were encouraged to keep subsistence plots, but further historical research is needed before the writer can attempt to explain why they were allowed to build up an elaborate and lucrative marketing system for themselves. Da Costa Eduardo's contention that "Negroes in parts of the New World have preserved religious survivals and orientations more carefully than economic, social or artistic aspects of African culture . . ." because these are ". . . more important life values, which are obviously culturally determined . . ." and accordingly, ". . . less subject to change than others having less moment" Da Costa Eduardo (1948) is not supported by the evidence from Jamaican history. Rather it would seem that the Negro slave preserved those parts of his ancestral culture which he was *permitted* to retain, and that this in turn depended primarily on the needs of the plantation system, and on the power of the planter to exact conformance.

5. Cf. for instance, Bickell (1825), Bigelow (1851), Sturge and Harvey (1838), and especially Livingstone (1900). Livingstone writes of the market women " . . . they appear unconscious of any hardship in the arrangement which transfers to them so large a part of the burden of life. It gives to them a certain power, apart from sex, over the men, which in the circumstances is perhaps essential." The implications of this comment are touched upon later in this paper.

6. Mr. David Edwards informed the writer that in a highland market of the Upper Yallahs Valley, Portland "higglers" barter tree crops like coconuts and breadfruit for ground crops, such as escallion.

7. In confirmation of a statement made by Mr. W. D. Burrowes to the writer a modern greengrocer's (part of a general food store) has now been opened in the Cross Roads section of St. Andrew.

8. It has been noted by Mr. E. Seaga (in an article in the *Daily Gleaner*, of February 18, 1954) that in one portion of the consumer market—the north coast hotel trade—the higgler and the small-scale farmer have been virtually cut out of the economic picture. In the present writer's view, this is the result of the development of a relatively fixed demand situation. It would seem that the emergence of fixed demand eliminates the higgler and the small-scale farmer, by encouraging larger-scale entrepreneurs to enter the production and distribution picture. When a market for substantial quantities of agricultural products is assured, the trucker-wholesaler and the large-scale farmer are willing to invest in supplying that market. The competitive advantage which accrues to the large-scale farmer and the trucker-wholesaler in the fixed demand situation, as opposed to the small-scale farmer and the higgler, rests in the fact that, for obvious reasons, a greengrocer or a hotel owner will prefer to buy twenty sacks of potatoes from one trucker-wholesaler or large-scale farmer, rather than one sack each from twenty higglers or twenty individual small-scale farmers.

REFERENCES CITED

Bickell, R.
1825 *The West Indies As They Are*, London, Hatchard, p. 204.
Bigelow, J.
1851 *Jamaica in 1850*, London, George Putnam, p. 117.
Cumper, G. E.
1949 "Social Structure of Jamaica," *Caribbean Affairs*, Extra-Mural Department, University College of the West Indies, Jamaica, p. 55.
Da Costa Eduardo, Octavio
1948 *The Negro in Northern Brazil*, American Ethnological Society Monograph 15, p. 2.
Edwards, Bryan
1793 *The History, Civil and Commercial, of the British Colonies in the West Indies*, London, John Stockdale, p. 133.
Gardner, W. J.
1874 *A History of Jamaica*, London, Elliot Stock.
Henderson, G. E.
1931 *Goodness and Mercy*, Kingston, The Gleaner Co., Ltd., pp. 5–7.
Herskovits, M. J.
1952 *Economic Anthropology*, New York, Knopf.
Livingstone, W. P.
1900 *Black Jamaica*, London, Sampson, Low, Marston and Co., p. 220.
Lopez, A.
1948 "Land and Labour to 1900," *Jamaican Historical Review* 1:3.
Nadel, S. F.
1951 *A Black Byzantium: The Kingdom of the Nupe in Nigeria*, rev. ed., London, Oxford University Press, pp. 314–340.
Olivier, Sydney
1936 *Jamaica, the Blessed Island*, London, Faber and Faber.
Paget, H.
1945 "The Free Village System in Jamaica," *Jamaican Historical Review* 1:1.
Phillippo, James M.
1843 *Jamaica, Its Past and Present State*, London, John Snow.
Sturge, Joseph and Thomas Harvey
1838 *The West Indies in 1837*, London, Hamilton Adams and Co., pp. 176–177.

Mechanization in Paracho: A Craft Community

BERNICE A. KAPLAN

Nature of the Craft Community

Paracho is located in the high sierra of the state of Michoacán. The county (*municipio*) of which Paracho is the county seat is 332 square kilometers and is largely agricultural. The town of Paracho has over one third of the county's population, but only about a twentieth of the land. The attitudes of the residents of neighboring villages toward land ownership make it impossible for the town of Paracho to acquire more public land and difficult for its residents to acquire or cultivate land elsewhere within the county. The town, with an estimated population in 1952 of approximately 4,500, consists of 817 households interspersed with gardens and small plots, all contained in an area of about one square kilometer. There is a genuine insufficiency of agricultural land in Paracho, for there are only fifty-four men living in the town who have enough land to be fully occupied with farming, and virtually all foodstuffs must be brought in from elsewhere.

Manufacturing and trading have characterized the community since its settlement at its present location some four centuries ago. Through the centuries the items manufactured and the organization of trading

Reprinted from *Alpha Kappa Deltan*, 1960, XXX, 59–65, by permission of the author and publisher.

have been modified as new methods have been introduced—now by a returning trader, now by a new family coming from afar to settle, now by migrant laborers returning from sojourns in far-off places. Paracho is a community receptive to technological change, and, as a result, there appears to have been a minimum of unfavorable social consequences resulting from the most recent series of innovations (chiefly since 1940) as I observed them in the period from 1948 to 1953.

I was interested in the changes which occur in a community where modernization stems from local initiative and the investment of local capital. I wished also to learn something about what happens when changes grow out of local experience and represent a continuation of the old tradition. In Paracho economic expansion was effected through local investment in machinery for the continued manufacture of regional specialties. It is one thing to state that investments represent local savings and native capital, but another to understand how, once this community accumulated funds, it was impelled to invest them in local manufacture rather than solely in land and animals.

There are several factors which favor the accumulation of funds and their investment in productive enterprises. Among these are facilities for rapid transportation and communication, a source of cheap power, a money and business orientation of economic activity, a willingness to experiment with new ideas coupled with a desire to "do things better," and contacts with people and markets beyond the local region. Some factors may be peculiar only to Paracho: land poverty which led most inhabitants to be concerned with manufacture or distributive activities, and the presence in the town of a large number of individuals who, while out of the country as temporary migrant laborers, accumulated monetary reserves.

These characteristics describe the conditions in one of a number of possible situations which make for satisfactory technological development. In such cases change develops within the existing sociocultural framework, and radical breaks with expected norms of behavior are few. Thus, in such situations the traditional values of social life (close family relations, face-to-face personal relations with many people, importance of religious sanctions for social activities, etc.) may be expected to persist. While the traditional values will come to be interpreted differently over the generations, inter-generational conflict will be minimized since the changes will not be abrupt. Such indeed was the case in Paracho.

Here, for several reasons, the introduction of mechanization and the innovation of a wage system met with little resistance. In the first place, throughout its history Paracho has always been a business and trading community, and the community has always rewarded participants in these activities with a respected social status. Secondly, many members of the present population had had experience with wage labor before its introduction into Paracho and consequently were prepared for the change. Furthermore, the introduction of machinery brought with it no change in the manufacturing skills required in the new type of work; these have largely remained the same in the change-over from handicraft to machine manufacture. Finally, the introduction of the new techniques was local and marked by no outside interference.

The Historical Development of the Town

Throughout the Tarascan region it has long been a tradition for each town to specialize in the manufacture of certain items, which were then traded to other towns manufacturing other items. It is said locally that it was the Bishop Vasco de Quiroga who, in the sixteenth century, instituted this practice of craft specialization by towns to bring about trade through the region. Actually, however, such differentiation of activities goes back to pre-Conquest times, as examination of early chronicles shows.[1]

In one important way, however, Paracho differs from many of the communities in the Tarascan region which also have their particular specializations. In other communities the specialization is secondary to farming as a means of providing for the economic needs of the community. There are nonagricultural specialists in these towns, it is true, but most money income in these places derives from the sale of grown produce, and it is the aspiration of most of the people in these communities to increase their landholdings or buy farm machinery (which they would use and rent out to others) rather than to invest their savings in other sorts of business enterprises. Paracho, from the first, has been literally land poor. The first Parachoans, living on a site several kilometers from the present location, are believed locally not to have been Tarascans at all, but a group of nomadic people known as Tecos. It is said that the Tecos were relative newcomers in their previous location, having lived at Paracho *viejo* (old Paracho) one hundred years or less, when a Spanish edict moved all people in mountain communities onto the plains. According to local tradition, at this time the four towns of Aranza, Ahuiran, Quinceo, and Pomacuarán all bordered on each other and had frequent boundary disputes. The Spanish priest serving these communities is said to have suggested that each town lend a small parcel of land to the people from Paracho *viejo* "who have no land of their own" and in this way bring to an end the land disputes between the several towns. The suggestion was followed and so the community of Paracho was founded in its present location. Bitter and sometimes violent boundary disputes persist to the present day, but they now concern each of the aforementioned communities and Paracho. In any case, the landholdings of Paracho have remained constricted for the last three hundred years.

Today the town lands—both agricultural and forest—extend beyond the inhabited area about one or two kilometers to both north and south and one and a half kilometers to the east and west. Altogether, of 1,779 male workers, only 132 are farmers and farm laborers. A few others make charcoal, collect turpentine, or cut firewood or lumber.

Markets and Commercial Travel

Whether because of its location, approximately central to all Tarascan towns and hence a natural trading spot, or because its inhabitants began trading through the region soon after settlement, Paracho came to have an important weekly market. Most towns in the region have weekly markets, but some of them serve only to meet the immediate needs of the local community, whereas others are important exchange points for all the goods of the region. Paracho's market fits into this latter category. The basic pattern of economic organization in Paracho was thus set from early days. According to West, "Since colonial times Paracho has been the largest Indian commercial center of the Sierra."[2] An exchange of products from the cold, temperate, and hot lands occurs here, as it has in the past, every Sunday.

Exchange is also conducted outside the region by a variety of tradesmen. Before the coming of the highway in 1940, *huacaleros* (porters in business for themselves, who carried their loads on their backs) and *arrieros* (men usually in the employ of others who transported goods by donkeys) took the products of the town and the immediate region for sale in distant places. Coming back to Paracho they brought with them raw cotton, machetes, salt, wool, fish, and other products for which there was a local demand. Today both *huacaleros* and *arrieros* have virtually disappeared; only one or two families continue to take items to more isolated regions by mule train. Nevertheless, with the highway, trading relations have expanded greatly, both in the area reached by Paracho-made goods and in the quantity of goods sold. Traveling merchants still carry locally made items to fiesta fairs and regional markets, but today they travel by bus or train and hence can make more trips in a year and dispose of more goods.

The Organization of Work in Contemporary Paracho

Since the turn of the century local men have worked hand-driven lathes to make various turned objects of wood (e.g., rosaries, chocolate beaters, chessmen, candlesticks, chair legs, tops and other toys), and even long before 1900 the town was known for its guitars, violins, and other stringed instruments, as well as for its handmade wooden furniture. Until 1941 electric machinery was almost unknown in the town. The boarding school for Tarascan-speaking children and the movie house had small generators for electricity and there were one or two gasoline-driven corn mills. Generally, however, craft work was done manually. In 1941 the federal government built an electric power line between the cities of Zamora and Uruapan which went through, and provided service for, the town of Paracho. This new source of power made increased production of wooden objects possible, and, with this greater production, a wider market developed.

It is not surprising, in a town such as this, to find that the organization of marketing of the locally made products is well developed. There is a relationship in Paracho between the techniques of production and the methods of marketing employed by the several classes of manufacturers. *There is a decreasing choice in the methods of distribution of goods with increasing technological advancement of the method of manufacture and the organization of work.* Those who work alone have three means by which they can sell their products: they can sell directly to the consumer either through a shop attached to their place of work or by taking the goods themselves to the nearby markets or to regional fiesta fairs; they can arrange with a traveling tradesman to take all or part of their goods to the distant markets for them; or they can deal (either under contract or not) with the local entrepreneurs who, in turn, deal with city distributors. Many townspeople with individually owned and operated craft establishments use all three methods of selling their products—depending on whether they need cash immediately or can afford to have funds tied up in unsold merchandise until they have enough goods to go on a trip or to commission another to take their goods for them. The net gain, per item sold, decreases as one's direct relation with the ultimate consumer diminishes—so that only those in greatest poverty will sell by preference to the large local stores owned by the major entrepreneurs. Where several men work in a mechanized workshop (usually one employer working together with anywhere from one to five shopworkers)[3] the first alternative mentioned above usually no longer is possible. Employers, who are the owners of the shops, prefer to continue at their manufacture rather than peddling their goods through the region. Marketing cooperatives do not exist, and the owner of the small workshop usually does not distribute his own goods, except in those instances where he has city customers for his products. In this situation the methods of manufacturing are more efficient and the volume increased, but the alternatives for distribution are reduced to two.

In some instances workers in small shops are not employed by the shop owner at all, but rent work space from him. Such workers must supply their own wood and, except for the difference in technique employed in the manufacture of the finished product, they have the essential status of craftsmen and market their goods as do craftsmen. In other instances a shopworker, in the employ of another, may wish to invest some money in a small supply of wood for his own use—either to supplement the wood supply of his employer or to take a preliminary step toward establishing himself in business. The owners of small shops usually will permit this extra use of their machinery by workers. The product, in such instances, belongs to the worker but he usually sells it to the owner. In the larger shops this arrangement does not occur.

In the large shops (eight to thirty workers) the employees are completely divorced from the distribution of the goods they produce, and they never buy any wood for their own use. The owners of these shops usually make use of only one of the three alternatives—that of dealing directly with the urban distributor. The owner thus receives an order from a businessman elsewhere in the nation or in a foreign country, supervises the work of the artisans who produce and deliver the finished products to him, and passes them on to his client. Not only do the choices available for distribution of goods diminish with the increasing efficiency of production, but so also does the worker's freedom in terms of the number of items of each type which he will produce.

The worker's freedom of choice concerning how much of each item he will make is governed by two other factors besides the boss's orders on hand: the supply of raw materials available and the boss's ability to purchase the necessary materials. It is not unusual for a small owner to close shop for several months while he works elsewhere (usually in the United States as a contract laborer) to get enough money to buy wood for his workers and for himself. Workers prefer, of course, to be employed where there is an assured supply of wood, but this is not always possible and newcomers to the town or to the trade may have to start work in a small shop where the wood supply may fluctuate.

Despite incipient shortage of raw materials, production is expanding in Paracho. Whereas in 1947 there were twenty-two motorized wood-turning establishments, there were thirty-seven in 1952. Of those in the current work force, three times as many were employed in these shops in 1952 as in 1947. Some of these new workers came to the shops from crafts at which they previously had worked at home on hand-operated wood-turning lathes. Others chose shopwork as their first adult job, while still others entered shopwork from noncraft occupations which were less remunerative. Still others in search of work came to Paracho from communities where opportunities for employment, usually in agriculture, are more restricted and wages are lower.

Some Effects of Mechanization

In addition to the obvious changes in the organization of the work force and, to some extent also, in the standard of living, caused by the coming of motorized lathes for wood-turning and machines in the carpentry shops, other aspects of life in Paracho have also been intensified. One outstanding example has been the growing interest in education. Experience in the outside world, coupled with the mechanization of the town (which has brought about increased competition for the good positions available), has made most parents acutely aware of the advantages of education. It is not unusual to hear parents explain, "I want my child to have things which I cannot have, and it is only with education that this will be possible." The striving for upward mobility in this community, seen in the emphasis on education as well as in the industriousness and progressiveness of the working population, has had an important bearing on the local developments which have occurred. It is believed locally that with greater education one can get a better job and thus increase one's level of living, and it is in this way that status may be acquired in the community.

The main focus of people's attention in the cultural realm, however, is for more and better schools so their children "can be better educated and will have an easier time making their way in the world." This interest in education in the community is not solely verbal, for many of the teachers who have had experience teaching in other towns and villages in the Republic remarked on it to us. Such teachers are unanimous in agreeing that there is greater eagerness for schooling in Paracho than in the other towns where they have taught. "In the other towns," said one of these teachers, "the teachers have to go about knocking on doors for two to three weeks after classes have begun for the year in order to get the parents to enroll and send their children. But here, no. Here on registration day the parents and their children are all milling around the registration desk calling 'take mine, take mine' so the rolls are always filled up long before the first day is over."

One measure of the improved standard of living which already has come to the village is to be seen in the increasingly large number of children who are remaining in primary school to be graduated from the sixth grade. In 1937 there were ten graduates from the sixth grade. In 1951 this number had increased to fifty. In 1952 the secondary school was opened with sixty-two students registered in the first two of three years of classes. Age ranges from fifteen to twenty-two years. Students from the nearby towns of Aranza and Cherán (seven and fifteen minutes away by bus) commute daily, and one from Chilchota (about one hour away by bus) boards in Paracho during the week and goes home only on week-ends. There are approximately an equal number of boys and girls. That even such a small number of young adults can be spared from economic activity is one indication of the increased income level of the community; in earlier years such time spent in school would have been considered beyond their families' means. Children of wealthier parents have always gone away from the town to attend a *colegio* (private equivalent of the public secondary school), but for the most part the children now in the local secondary school are from families unable to afford the additional expense of high tuition fees and boarding expenses. In Paracho tuition is only 50 pesos a year, considerably less than the cost of sending a child away to school. The students now in the secondary school represent, thus, a new group entering the realm of higher education.

Conclusions

It is appropriate to ask whether there have been no social disruptions resulting from the economic changes of the last decade. So far as I am aware there have been none. This is not to say that there are no social problems existent in the community, for most certainly there are. Both minor and major crimes occur, but there were, for example, only half as many homicides in the *municipio* between 1945 and 1949 as there had been from 1940 through 1944.[4] There are cases of family friction and family disruption, but not more in 1952 than there were in 1948. There are also instances of psychological imbalance. Furthermore, economic inequalities between the several occupational groups do exist. These problems, however, tend to be general social problems, not necessarily peculiar to communities undergoing mechanization and consequent industrialization. Some problems which mechanization might have been expected to initiate have not occurred: for example, the breakdown of the extended family, a diminished importance of ritual kinship, and disruptions in traditional living arrangements resulting from either a changing population make-up of the community or from permanent emigration. Besides the specifically social problems there are other potential difficulties: depletion of the wood supply is one; overpopulation is another; and the continued centralization of economic control in the hands of a few people is, in a social rather than an economic sense, another.

In conclusion, our study of Paracho suggests the existence of a type situation in which the problems of social adjustment to a new economic system are minimal. In such a situation innovations are introduced to the local community by its own members on their own initiative, and these innovations elaborate already existing institutions. Although the end results of social organization under industrialism will probably be similar to occurrences elsewhere (heterogeneity of the population, secularism, a class-organized society), changes in communities of the sort here reported upon will permit modification from the earlier, more closely knit society to a more modern social organization without marked discontinuities and social chaos.

NOTES

1. Robert C. West, *Cultural Geography of the Modern Tarascan Region*, Smithsonian Institution, Institute of Social Anthropology, Publication 7, 1948, p. 56.

2. *Ibid.*, p. 71.

3. In the present context a *shopworker* is a wage earner employed by one who owns machines. The shopworker uses the machinery in the production of the items he makes. A *craftsman* is one who is self-employed and manufactures items without the benefit of mechanized apparatus. In a few instances the owner of a motor is the only one in his shop engaged in production, or perhaps has only dependent sons working for him. Here the work situation parallels that of the craft worker, but the addition of the mechanized mode of manufacture justifies grouping the few individuals in this category into the class of owners, although not that of employers.

4. Gonzalo Aguirre Beltrán, *Problemas de la población de la cuenca del Tepalcatepec*, Mexico, Instituto Nacional Indigenista, Memorias del Instituto Nacional Indigenista, 1952, III, p. 281. (1940–44: 39 homicides; 1945–49: 19 homicides.)

SOCIAL ORGANIZATION

Introduction

RICHARD N. ADAMS

The papers in this section have been selected with an eye to both the more traditional interests in social organization and some newer areas of investigation. The study of social organization in Latin America has been marked neither by comprehensiveness nor by stunning discoveries. It has, however, been the scene of a continuing development of understanding about contemporary society that is perhaps equal to, if somewhat different from, that obtained elsewhere in the world. In some respects, it has been overdominated by a concern with problems at the community level, and is only now beginning to examine with care events on a larger scale.

This essay touches on six kinds of structures that are particularly important in Latin America, together with the processes that characterize them in the current world. Four of these are of comparable order: community and nationalization; class sectors and mobility; family, friendship, and laterality; and power structures and centralization. The first and sixth, however, are of a different order. The first concerns demographic processes and their consequences in the mobility and organization of the society; the sixth—the region, reform, and revolution—is the complex result and concomitant of the processes earlier described. In addition to the four central topics, there is also that of economic development and its social consequences. This is omitted in the present discussion since it forms a major topic in the Introduction to the previous section.

Finally, the reader should be warned that this Introduction does not attempt to tie in a neat bundle all the facts and interpretations of the papers here reproduced. Our level of understanding of Latin American social organization is, to put it charitably, extremely loose and unsatisfactory; it would be misleading to leave the reader with a sense of confidence as to his comprehension.

Demographic Structure, Migration, and Urbanization

The cardinal fact about the peoples of Latin America is that they are growing rapidly in numbers. Estimates for the region as a whole place the growth rate at about 2.75 per cent (for period 1950–61), and certain regions are expanding much more rapidly than this. Middle American countries (in 1958–61) had rates varying from 4.4 per cent in Costa Rica to 2.7 per cent in Panama (United Nations [1962]).

This growth is principally the result of improvements in public health and environmental sanitation. The birth rate in provincial Latin America has for centuries been adjusted to a fairly high death rate. The steady growth that was recorded after the middle of the eighteenth century was probably due to the fact that the populations took some centuries to adapt to the ways of the New World under conquest. As with peasant and pre-industrial peoples everywhere, an anticipated high death rate was to be offset by an even higher birth rate. Even minimal efforts at disease prevention and sanitation, under these circumstances, lead to a sharp decline in the death rate. Today, Latin America is experiencing the consequences of this development.

The specific consequences of this population growth for social organization are manifold, and only a few of them may be mentioned here. A rapidly growing population has what demographers refer to as a broad-based age pyramid; the ratio of children and young people to mature and old is very high. Thus, there are relatively fewer economic producers, and relatively more consumers. Were there to be no change in the output of producers, per capita production for the total population would decline. This, obviously, has consequences for the distribution of income and, hence, social ranking contingent upon wealth, as well as for problems of economic development.

The fact that different segments of the population manifest different growth rates also has ramifications. The child–woman ratio* in rural areas is considerably higher than in provincial cities; the ratio in provincial cities is higher than the ratio in capital cities. The lack of major

* $\frac{\text{Children between 0–4 years}}{\text{Women 15–44 years}} \times 1000.$

changes in rural production technology results in many rural areas reaching the maximum population they can support. The forced sloughing off of people in every generation leads to the internal migration that is so characteristic of Latin America today.

The real questions arise when we begin to ask where this population is moving to. Fundamentally, movement is in three directions: to the cities, to areas of rural wage labor, and to frontier or unoccupied regions where subsistence and market-oriented agriculture is continued. Each of these movements is contributing to fundamental changes in the social face of Latin America.

Even though the fertility ratio of urbanites is considerably less than that of rural peoples, the great migration to urban centers is causing an urban growth far surpassing that in most of the rural regions. The most apparent result of this movement is the expanding "shack towns" to be found in almost all the major capitals and larger provincial cities of the area. Brazilian *favelas,* Chilean *callampas,* Peruvian *barriadas,* Guatemalan *colonias,* or whatever they may be called, are growing and budding off with increasing numbers of provincial people. There is little question that economic necessity is the prime mover, but the choice of the city over the other alternatives seems to lie in considerable part in the known availability of educational facilities in the city and the belief that jobs are more available there. The papers by Lewis, Mangin, and Strickon which follow examine various aspects and features of this movement. The Strickon paper also looks at intra-rural movements.

Not only the lower class comes to the cities; the upper sectors of provincial populations have long had central urban connections, and the availability of both jobs and education acts even more forcefully on people in search of mobility. It is in part through this group that recognition of the nation as a centralized and culturally common whole penetrates to the furthest reaches of the rural and provincial areas.

Migration to areas of rural wage labor has long been familiar to many Latin American peasant peoples. Many regions witness seasonal migrations of labor to supplement their subsistence crop production in areas of restricted land resources. Latin America has experienced periods of hacienda and plantation expansion, and during these periods there has been pressure for wage labor. Today the demand for wage labor is increasingly affected by population pressure; at the same time, the entrepreneurial interests are leading to some expansion of large-scale agriculture. There seems to be a real difference, however, between a really convinced rural proletariat and the peasant who moves with some ease between private agriculture and wage labor. Seasonal migrations usually leave a residue, and some who have been involved in wage labor will return after years to take up subsistence agriculture again. What determines such decisions is not understood.

Migration to open and frontier areas is another alternative for agrarian populations, and is having some peculiar social consequences. While the Indian population of Guatemala, Mexico, and the Andean countries is declining in proportion to the total population, in some instances the expansive migration of these peoples is actually increasing the geographical area of their occupation. The Quechua have been moving out of the Andean highlands into the *montaña* and *yungas* for some centuries, and more recently the Alta Verapaz population of Guatemala has been expanding into the Peten region. Of greater significance, of course, is that, whether Indian or mestizo, most of these migrants are subsistence agriculturalists and take into the new regions the same relatively primitive technology that produced so little at home. The peasant society, therefore, is perpetuated even though it is increasingly influenced by attitudes and aspirations characteristic of the upper urban sector.

The consequence of migrations to rural wage labor and urban situations is a vast incrementation of the proletarian population of the countries. Depending upon local access to and knowledge of the prestige symbols of the nation, this incrementation either restricts or opens up the possibility of mobility. In either case, a wider multiplicity of occupations and of geographical alternatives of work-places becomes an increasing reality for a growing segment of the population. It must not be thought in this regard that urbanization is a simple product of industrialization; it has, since shortly after the invention of agriculture, been one of the answers to an overexpanding rural population. Today, however, the process is vastly complicated and augumented by simultaneous industrialization.

Community and Nationalization

The community, in one sense or another, has occupied an inordinate amount of space in studies of Latin American social organization. Robert Redfield, who as much as anyone else set the interest in motion, found the subject so suggestive that he devoted an entire volume to it (Redfield [1955]; see also Cline [1952], Adams [1962]). One reason the "community" has received so much attention is that the term has been used not to refer to a delimited set of social relations, but rather to all the relations that were found in a particular community. The so-called "community" studies in American anthropology have not focused on community structure, but rather have used the community as a locale in which a variety of relations could be examined, including family, friendship, class, etc. In this sense the community is really a kind of theater in which many other kinds of relations are acted out. And, as in a play, these other relations are severely restricted by the shape and other characteristics of the stage.

I have found it convenient, in trying to distinguish a structure that is peculiarly that of the community, to use the following definition: *a community is the minimal set of relationships established by the residential contiguity of a set of individuals, where (1) the group thus formed and the territory established by the contiguity of residence bear the same name; (2) the group so formed forms one of a set of such groups which, collectively, form a macro-group that is also defined in terms of the residential contiguity of its members and by the fact that the membership and the territory bear the same name.* The term, in this sense, then, is restricted to that set of relationships that is territorially identified and named; it need not be confused with all the other relationships that occupy the same territorial locale.

In much of the literature, of course, characteristics are ascribed to the community which, in fact, do not pertain to this relational set but to other relations that simply are being carried on within this territory. Thus, the peasants of an area, a large, extended family, the Indians in a bi-ethnic town, or a particular political organization do not form communities, but may account for all kinds of collective activity that is described in a "community study."

It is very important to see this structure as being a minimal structure within a maximal structure. The community is identified in part by virtue of being one of a set of communities, and these, in turn, are collectively recognized as being part of a whole. In monolingual Indian areas, this whole is usually the region. In most of Latin America's communities, however, the whole is the nation-state. Also, because the community is defined in terms of territorial contiguity, it should not be confused with the order of nationally defined administrative units, such as *municipios, distritos, cantones,* etc. These very frequently are congruent with a community, but it is more common for a given administrative unit to have within it more than one community. By the same token, the region within which a community lies should not be confused with the national middle-level administrative entities, such as departments, states, or provinces.

The relationship of the minimal, or community, unit to the maximal, or national, unit is that of an inferior entity in a power structure and a party that can never be inferior (although it may, from time to time, be brought on a par with the community). Today, the community contrasts with the nation (rather than with the state or the region) because the nation is the maximal unit in most instances.

The process of "nationalization" involves, among other things, a fundamental change in the nature of communities. Communities within a state structure—especially an agrarian state, as many Latin American countries have been—face an entirely different social environment from those involved in the economic and political penetrations central to national development. Many features of agrarian state communities persist in Latin America because that area continues in great part to be agrarian. On the other hand, characteristics of developing nationalism are also there, because this process is ubiquitous.

Unquestionably, the most important set of relationships in the nationalization of the community consists of the many ways in which it is linked to the cities and to activities at the national level. Under a state system, communities essentially stood as agrarian suppliers to the cities and towns, tribute payers wherever possible, and human reservoirs for labor needed in public works, the army, workshops, or for large agrarian establishments. Under these kinds of relations, the particular culture of a community or a region was of little concern so long as the differences did not inhibit the integration of the producing communities with the state. In fact, differences were advantageous, since culturally distinctive populations found it more difficult to mount a political revolution to unseat the incumbent rulers.

Nationalization, however, requires many things contrary to a state organization. It requires ability to communicate to the diverse regions, to introduce the populations to participation in the political process. It involves the economic development of the regions such that the nation as a whole can grow richer; as an inherent part of this, it requires a greatly increased economic interdependence between the growing industrial centers, so that they have a growing market for their products, and the population's increasing its supplies to the national market rather than the local community.

The city, under a state system, was much as Sjoberg [1960] has described it. It was an administrative and marketing center, but it seldom accounted for more than 10 per cent of the total population of the country, and there was seldom more than one major city. Relations between provincial peoples and the city were, and in considerable part continue to be, marked by a maintenance of rural patterns of thought and rurally set relational systems. The picture painted by Oscar Lewis [1959, 1961] represents neither all urban patterns nor all Latin patterns, but it does identify an important phase of rural-urban relations that went almost unnoticed by social scientists until Lewis undertook his pioneering work. The maintenance of relations through the multitudinous voluntary associations, such as are described by Mangin in this section and the straightforward extension of rural relations into the major industrial urban centers, as is described by Strickon, indicate the importance of rural patterns in a society that is still not nationalized in all its aspects.

Important changes that occur in the community as the center begins to dominate include the position of the local leaders and informal judges. As national leaders and national power grow, the local boss or *cacique,* who may be crucial to effective articulation of a community or region under a state system, is replaced by political workers operating in close contact with the national level. The administration of justice in regional traditions often simply ignored long-standing and complicated national statutes. Even more important has been the intentional institutionalization at the regional and local levels of new power centers to compete with the older community leaders. The *ejidal* organizations of Mexico were established in part to establish political control, just as the distribution of land also had this as a central part of its purpose.

The development of the community in Latin America is a part of national development. It is important that a sufficient number of communities be brought into a productive relationship to the nation. Community development, however, requires tremendous inputs from outside, and except for the relatively few areas where large private installations are being set up, the government must supply these or arrange that they come through technical aid or some other source. A community seldom has more to offer than it is already manifesting. It needs new technologies, new skills, new ideas, as well as straightforward material and cash inputs for development. Communities can do a certain amount by themselves, but they can never, by themselves, raise themselves materially much beyond the general economic and cultural level of the region of which they are a part, unless they go outside the region for help.

The relationship that holds between the various kinds of communities within a region is an important factor in their organization. It is very common for small farmer communities to be scattered in the marginal hinterlands of larger-scale agrarian enterprises. Although at some time the larger enterprises attempt to dominate and even consume these smaller communities, they more often allow them to occupy the less valuable lands so that they may provide crucial reservoirs of labor and food for resident labor on the larger enterprises. Labor for a plantation is always crucial, and to have a supply to take care of seasonal needs is most valuable. Also, as plantations have increasingly concentrated on large-scale production, and less and less devoted land of their own to food crop production, the food supply from surrounding areas has grown in importance.

In the general structure of a state, communities take on characteristics of their neighbors, and these in turn reflect various regional patterns. To some degree these regional distinctions always reflect some major environmental features, such as differences in altitude, location in one valley as opposed to another, occupation of a coastal region, and so on. But cultural regions also reflect events in their social history. Thus, the delineation of cultural regions, like the communities that compose them, must reflect a variety of relationships.

Many of the features that characterize specific regions are not immediately evident to casual observers. In some instances, however, a region will still retain distinctive dress and language, even though the communities therein are already involved or are fast becoming involved in the national scene. Among these regionally distinct populations are the mestizos of Tehuantepec and Yucatan in Mexico and the mestizos and Indians of the various highland interior valleys of the Central and Southern Andes, such as the Huancayo Valley in Peru and the Cochabama Valley of Bolivia. There are, in addition to these regions with clear-cut habitat distinctions, some larger segments of distinctive populations that show marked differences when carefully delineated. Whether or not the differences are evident to outside observers, they are almost always readily distinguishable to people of neighboring regions. Be they the Antioqueños of Colombia, the Guaraní-speaking nationals of Paraguay, the dwellers in the La Plata region of Argentina and Uruguay, rural northeasterners of Brazil, or *oriente* dwellers in Guatemala, they are marked by distinctive dialects, mannerisms, and tastes.

Some regional populations achieve a degree of cultural distinctiveness that places them in another class. The Indians of western Guatemala and adjacent Mexico; the East Indians of Trinidad, British Guiana, and elsewhere in the West Indies; the Japanese intensive farmers in Brazil manifest cultural and social relationships that are still more distinct than those in the regional variants previously mentioned. This distinctiveness is owing to the fact that the communities in question have maintained a cultural and social system wherein the basic institutional forms, such as family and kin organization, class structuring, internal ordering of social control and resolution of disputes, language, and numerous contingent cultural forms, differ from the more common pattern in the culture of the dominant population. This extreme situation has been referred to as pluralism (Keur and Rubin [1960]).

The pluralistic group is, essentially, in an uncomprehending social environment. It is faced with one of two alternatives: it can either succumb, giving up enough of its variant institutional forms so that it becomes acceptable (although usually in a very low social category) to the society of the dominant group; or it can set itself farther off by placing special values on its differences, taking as strong steps as possible to differentiate itself to avoid communication and intermarriage and reject interaction with the dominant group. A community that has successfully done the latter, and maintains itself as an entity, is generally referred to as a corporate community (Wolf [1955]). The development of the corporate quality cannot be had merely for the asking. It also requires the presence of some fundamental set of recognized rules in the society that permit the members of the society to regard themselves as being correct, whereas others are wrong; even more, some kind of economic input source, the nature of which does not endanger the relational structure that composes the community and is independent of outside sources, is required. It is in this last respect that the presence of community lands has been of such great importance to the corporate Indian communities of the Andes and Central America. By the careful maintenance of these lands, a community could survive economically, with its own cultural system, in the face of considerable threat and change on the outside.

The cultural bases for pluralism and corporate communities are not, however, entirely understood. The caste system of the East Indians (Niehoff [1960], and Klass [1961]) is central to the maintenance of that society, whereas in another instance, language alone has been described as the basic element (Hohenthal and McCorkle [1955]). Of importance in the present discussion, however, is that such pluralistic entities continue to occupy a place of importance in various parts of Latin America.

The disappearance of pluralism, such that the population in question becomes part of the national population even though it continues to manifest distinctive "minority" traits, is inevitable. World War II caused the Japanese and Germans, who had maintained a somewhat pluralistic society until that time, to give up that quality in large part. The passing of pluralism is merely part of the general internal acculturation that is an intrinsic part of nationalism.

Before leaving the subject of the community, it is worth noting that communities, as defined here, are almost never production organizations. Production in Latin American communities is founded on households, haciendas, and even cooperatives, but these are almost never coterminous with the community. The only role that the community has classically played that is closely related to the production process is in the matter of community lands and community work. But community lands are seldom worked collectively; they are always allotted to individual members of the community (or to households) and are worked privately. And community work is almost never devoted to productive labor, but rather to repair or construction of community properties. There are, as is well examined in Erasmus' article in the previous section, collective and exchange labor arrangements, but these are not based on the community so much as on propinquity, friendship, kinship, and, usually, class.

In view of this discussion, it should come as no surprise that no selection herein is devoted to the community. The reason is that most students have looked at the community as a place in which things happen, and not as an entity in itself. As a result, with all the work on Latin American communities, there are few specific studies of the community as it has been defined here.

Class Sectors and Mobility

An understanding of class systems in Latin America has been somewhat inhibited by the use of concepts and terms appropriate to other systems. The term "caste," for example, has been applied to the relations within a single village within a total society in which social mobility is a patent fact (Tumin [1952]). And interest in the emerging middle class has led students to comb census categories of occupation in search of some estimate of their numbers (Crevenna [1951]). Our concern here will be to provide a general picture of the structure of society insofar as it concerns mobility, status, and ranked social position.

The article by Beals in this section still provides an excellent introduction to many of the variations in the class structures of Latin America. Perhaps the major feature of our understanding of the entire structure that has emerged since the time of the writing of that article is that, even with the variations present, and even with the multiple effects of industrialization and urbanization, most specific locales can still be recognized as being divided into two major classes. The continuing importance of this dual structure has, perhaps, been somewhat obscured by the application of multiple criteria of different social scientists and by the growing complexity of the upper sector. Time has been spent in wondering whether class criteria should be cultural, occupational, economic, or something else. The crucial distinction, it turns out, is not which criteria should be used to distinguish classes, but that there are two profoundly different views of the nature of the stratification structure. One view characterizes the upper portion of the whole; the other, the lower. To avoid confusion with the multivariant uses of the term *social class,* I am going to refer to these as two sectors: the upper is the *power-prestige sector,* or prestige sector, and the lower is the *work-wealth sector,* or work sector.

In the lower sector, the general process of intra-sector mobility is to gain wealth, and the only sure way to do this is through work. The lottery, buried treasure, and luck in general are often held as possibilities, too, but upon examining peasant communities, it will be found that no matter what hopes there may be for easier ways out, it is generally recognized that money will not be had without work. In those communities that are, for whatever reason, culturally or physically isolated, work may even be a prestige attribute.

An interesting feature of recognizing the work sector concept is that it indicates that the Indian peasants, such as are described in the article by Vázquez, fit snugly within the same stratification system as do non-Indian peasants. There is a major difference, but it is not in the question of whether work and wealth provide the means and motivation or not.

The difference is that in the Indian communities of the Andes and Meso-America, the amount of wealth that can be gained by a peasant is sufficient to gain the prestige symbols of the Indian system. Thus a man of prestige in an Indian community will be a person who has carried a number of community *cargos* (public offices) successfully; and only men who work hard and get enough wealth can afford to hold these jobs. Also, in this system, the total amount of wealth is so slight that an agreeable accumulation can be dispersed merely through the process of inheritance (Wolf [1955], Goldkind [1961]).

In a non-Indian community, the same product may be expected for the same labor. The great difference between the Indian and the non-Indian peasant is that the non-Indian individual lives within a community in which the amount of wealth that can be gained by work is not sufficient to permit access to the prestige symbols of the upper sector. The annual income of a peasant or laborer earning between 10 cents and a dollar a day, with some income from his household members and even with a good crop on a large subsistence plot, can seldom reach $200 a year, and much of this will be used to pay interest rates on loans or be lost in the price fluctuation between the time of taking credit and harvesting the crop. In short, people in the work sector operate in what is essentially a manual labor-based technology, and can, with few exceptions, never expect to accumulate enough through work alone to get out of that sector. What they can do is to move about within that sector; and this movement depends upon getting together a little wealth.

The prestige sector operates on an entirely different basis. Wealth is one way to get and retain prestige symbols; however, the nature of the lateral relations of Latin society makes it not only possible, but quite common, for the individual to gain help from a multitude of friends, acquaintances, relatives, and, in many instances, from people who do not even know him but who may serve his purpose at the moment. Leeds' description of Brazilian career patterns, in this section, illustrates well how it is possible for this to occur. Moreover, even if a newcomer has wealth, he will still find it almost impossible to purchase some of the prestige symbols. The "correct" use of language (necessary, since one needs to avoid dialectic usages that mark him to be of a peasant or laboring origin) and the "correct" behavior on many different kinds of occasions are almost impossible to learn without actually participating and, in many instances, without actually growing up in the company of people who observe such occasions. Finally, kinship provides a most important set of relations through which one may expect to operate, and the lack of entrance to such networks in the prestige sector makes it extremely difficult to have a place to turn.

Thus it is that within the prestige sector, mobility is to be had through the gradual accumulation of specific prestige symbols that have as a minimal prerequisite a bearing that marks one to be of that sector. Quite obviously, any occupation having to do with manual labor is negatively valued, and thereby the entire work sector is excluded.

Power is the major means by which to gain prestige symbols. Just as work provides the surest way to wealth in the work sector, so power is the clearest way to prestige in the prestige sector. Power lies in the ability to manipulate events and people so that things turn up to your advantage. This is extremely well illustrated in the characteristics of the "*criollo* outlook" described on pp. 518–30 by Ozzie Simmons. The ability to keep "one up" on others, to show oneself to be more clever, agile, and quicker on the verbal draw, is a quality of the individual who is successfully operating in the prestige sector, but usually with little or no wealth.

In general, mobility within each of these sectors may be had through adaptation to the major means available for it, i.e., work in the lower, and power in the upper. There are special instances, however, in which additional obstacles may be set forth within a sector, inhibiting mobility within it. In those areas in which an elite of traditional wealth has maintained both a high degree of endogamy and a certain oligarchic control over either the politics or the economy, or both, it is likely that not being born to the right family effectively eliminates the upwardly mobile. In this situation, controlling groups seldom refuse all mobility, since marriages to persons of the non-elite will occur. In these instances, however, it is usually the children who are considered to belong to the group, and the non-elite parent remains something of an outsider. This kind of structure is described for Popayan, Colombia, by Whiteford [1960], and may still be found to some degree in Lima and Panama.

Much more common today, however, is the presence of a top elite that does not keep airtight protection against new members, but rather uses influence to help some in, keep others out. As in all constantly changing elite situations, the particular prestige symbols in these groups are often intentionally obscured so that they cannot be easily adopted by the unwelcome climber.

The fact that work is the only secure way of producing wealth in the lower sector does not mean that there are no prestige symbols relevant to that sector. The presence locally of the upper sector means that its symbols are available. But aside from this, the lower sector in itself will have an ordering of attributes, such as ability to converse cleverly, to play or sing beautifully, to exercise sexual prowess. These activities, however, are ends in themselves and are not used as mobility devices. The fact that wealth may be easily lost within the work sector means that these prestige symbols may offer more consistency for ranking and, therefore, be highly prized; but since they are generally based on personal skills, they provide relatively little chance for mobility.

The fact that the local upper class of rural regions generally circulates within the middle sectors of the large cities indicates that these two comprise, on a national level, part of a single sector. Both are prestige-oriented, and for both wealth is only one of a number of devices for a constant move upward. Structurally, the expansion of the middle in the whole society reflects a number of important things. First, it indicates that mobility occurs between the sectors if the individual in the lower gains wealth and uses it to gain upper-sector prestige symbols. Second, it suggests that the growing society does not prize work very highly, but, rather, is oriented toward the upper prestige system. It is probably not correct to perceive the middle as either something that has developed between the lower and the upper or as something that is a slice off each of the sectors. Rather, it is definitely an expansion of the upper sector, with structural differentiation of some attributes. Clearly below it, the work sector also continues growing, however, but now differentiating in terms of new skills, some of which are occupational. In short, what is occurring, as has been observed by various students, is an expansion of the old social structure, with many kinds of changes that seem to parallel the development in Europe and North America, but which structurally is holding the basic form it has always had. Biologically, the upper and middle help generate each other, since impecunious and inept members of one will fall somewhat, and particularly apt and ambitious members of the other may rise. But seldom will one find members of either falling into the work sector. And work sector individuals will not move out of that sector without a conscious effort.

In one sense, the middle class in Latin America is more of a process than a stable structural entity. It is the ever-growing area in which people who are going somewhere live. It is, however, much more than this, since it is also the large non-manual-laboring sector of the population that peoples the growing bureaucracies of government and business. Many of these individuals have definitely stepped aside from, or out of, the work sector, but few will ever reach the top.

Studies of how mobility occurs between the prestige and work sectors suggest that in great part the change usually requires two generations. Children of working parents in an area in which education is available do have the chance of shifting from their manual-laboring backgrounds, and the evidence is clear that the shift is regularly being made. It is also clear, however, that such mobility is more frequent in the towns and cities than in the countryside. Often there is a change from a value system in which work occupies a place of reasonable importance to one in which work, within some specific local definition, becomes a singularly important attribute to avoid.

Since in many peasant societies it is possible to maintain oneself without constant labor, it is not surprising that avoidance of work has made its appearance among people of the work sector in situations in which the wealth differential between the two sectors is not great. Aritama (Reichel-Dolmatoff [1961]) and Tobatí (Service [1954]), two of the many towns subjected to community studies, have been reported to have had an extreme attitude toward the avoidance of work; in Aritama, work is actively avoided. This exaggerated attitude does not necessarily correspond with either an inability or a real reluctance to work. Aritama workers are known elsewhere as being excellent laborers. But leisure, regarded in the prestige sector as a major symbol, is one trait that members of the work sector can afford. As often as not, it is the only visible symbol of the prestige sector they can manifest. Coupled with the unquestionable fact that no matter how much work they do, they have little likelihood of mobility, the only rational position is "to take it easy."

The simplicity in this delineation of the prestige and work sectors of Latin American society should not be allowed to obscure the internal complexity of the system in the growing cities and the fact that the system may be changing in some places. Nor, on the other hand, should the warmth of relations that may exist in some areas between individuals of the distinct sectors be allowed to cloud the fact that the sectors dominate the lives of the people living within them.

Family and Friendship Structure and Laterality

Two features of Latin American family structure have tended to give the general impression that Latin American society is dominated by vertical and hierarchical structures. One of these is the presence in upper-class families of strong cognatic ties, with the existence in some areas of what appear to be ramages. Such large, bilateral kin groups are described in the article by De Azevedo. The other is the so-called "grandmother" family or "matri-focal" family, as also described by De Azevedo for the poorest level of the population. In addition to these two features, the great social distance existing between top and bottom, the visible emphasis on family connections in the prestige sector, the importance of inherited land and wealth all combine to further the impression of vertical and hierarchical social structure.

It would be misleading to say that the above observations are incorrect. But it is certainly true that they have obscured what is probably a much more important feature of Latin social structure, and of particular importance to understanding family structure. This is the great importance of lateral relations, not only in the area between the extreme top and bottom, but within those two sections as well.

A recent study by Michael Smith [1962] provides an almost microscopic examination of a series of cases and indicates that for the British West Indies there is probably a basic family structure. A superficial comparison of many of the features he describes suggests that his assertion may hold good for much of Latin America as well, provided allowance is made for variations that must be assumed in an area so great. A cardinal feature of Smith's analysis, however, is its demonstration that West Indian families are strongly lateral in character.

If one carries this notion over to the Latin cases, it is evident that collaterally oriented relationships are equally important there. The only difference between large, upper-class bilateral kindred and smaller, lower-class kindred of the same kind is that the former can afford to keep track of larger groups, stemming back through more generations. But by the same token, as was mentioned earlier, many of these collateral branches fall down into the middle class (Hawthorn and Hawthorn in Leonard and Loomis [1953]). Although observers have been more impressed with the importance of the vertical structure than with the lateral, the importance of the latter becomes evident when one looks to the survival of the individual and the continued operation of the society.

The whole issue of mobility within the prestige sector is closely related to the collateral kinship upon which one can draw. It is a mistake to note only the hierarchical characteristic of the upper-class family and to ignore the fact that this very structure spans continuing generations of collateral relatives who remain in the prestige sector, but who at any one time may not be sharing in any great portion of the family wealth.

When we look lower in the structure, as illustrated in Leeds' article, we again see the importance of collaterality. Career mobility requires a wide range of relatives. It is not important that many of them are of modest means. Looking still farther down into the work sector, one discovers that the Argentine Creoles described by Strickon provide a superlative case of the importance of extensive collateral relations. In their articles Lewis, for Mexico, and Mangin, for Peru, provide convincing support for the idea that the general picture set forth by Strickon is to be found over much of the area. It is in this sector that Smith [1962] notes the importance of collaterality; that there are more meaningful collateral relationships, and many more of them, than there are relationships across generations.

A possible reason why this collateral structure has not been sufficiently appreciated before may be due to the anthropologist's tendency to treat family organization as if it were a separate feature of a society, to study it as if it were an independent institution. All the studies just cited in the present volume make it very clear that it is not *just* family and kin that are important laterally, but a grouping of family, kin, friends, associates, and second-degree connections extending these. The importance of friendship, of willingness to be of assistance to a person who is recommended as being a person of *confianza;* the importance of the numerous fictive kin ties established by the *compadre* system; and the importance of the dyadic relation noted and described so well by Foster [1961] all stem from the fact that they provide a highly flexible set of relationships that extend, literally, over much of one's own country and very often into many other nations.

These collateral relations take on even more importance when examined in the light of the two-sector society described earlier. Mintz and Wolf [1950] have noted that where a two-class system seems to operate, the *compadre* relations will be extended between classes. This is generally regarded as a way to provide the work-sector individual or the middle-class individual with aid from someone who is likely to be able to provide it. As has been noted by a number of studies, the so-called extension of the fictive kin has less to do with kinship than with a meaningful device to keep relations open and to keep order in the society. Mobility within the prestige sector depends greatly on the availability of these relations, especially through the gaining of and exercise of power. In the work sector, however, the lateral relations have an equally important basic role: the survival of individuals through an extensive pattern of dependency and aid.

Among the features that have received extensive comment, especially insofar as the upper and lower sectors are concerned, is a distinction of sexual activity of the man from the conjugal unit, as well as an ideal limitation of a married woman's sexual activity to the marriage relationship. Premarital chastity for women is still of some importance in the middle and upper sector, but post-marital faithfulness is generally important in all sectors. This does not mean that married women have no extra-marital sexual relations. But in most situations the man has the right to exercise sanctions over the offending woman that she seldom has over the man.

The woman's rights in this matter take different forms in the different class sectors. In the lower sectors, marriage is sometimes avoided by women as a way to keep their rights toward the men. Marriage, while important in some areas, is regarded as a means of enslavement in others. In the upper sector, a woman may always maintain close relations and dependency with her parents and siblings, and if a husband is misbehaving excessively, she simply will see little of him. In the middle sectors, the relationship may have aspects of both top and bottom. Free sexual activity may be regarded by the man as a sign of his *machismo;* on the other hand, the woman in the middle sectors has increasing educational and professional opportunities, so that she may exercise independence if she regards herself as being offended. This situation has not reached the proportions that it has in more industrialized areas, however. More important, it has not necessarily provided the woman with stronger rights within the home should she choose to remain there. The complementary situation of free sexual activity for men with strong family units is being threatened in a number of places where illegitimate children may now legally claim equal inheritance with legitimate offspring.

In some areas, but by no means all, affinal relations provide a major fracture line in the general relational system. Ill feelings and hostilities can be ascribed to one's in-laws. Where no major inheritance is involved, a woman is expected to remain the core of the household, even though the man is usually expected to be the head of the family. This is part of the much discussed relationship between a mother and her children, especially between mother and son. The Latin father is often described as not providing his son with the emotional support that is provided by the mother, and that is the subject of numerous songs and stories. The presence of this fracture line in narrow-scope relations does not mean that a person may not turn to affinal relatives for help of certain kinds, particularly insofar as mobility is involved.

Basically, the family in Latin America is bilateral, and various factors will dictate the form it will take in a local situation. The maintenance of a strong bond between siblings, however, is to be found over much of the area and in various class sectors. In some areas, this bond is so marked that it must be publicly repudiated if an individual wishes to be rid of his responsibility to these relatives. The alternative lateral relations that are open to an individual, however, may make this relation relatively inoperative.

The study of the Latin American family is in its very early stages. In a provocative book Raymond Smith [1956] proposes that the role of the husband in many Caribbean homes is directly related to his role in the occupational structure. Michael Smith [1962], in a comparative structural study holds that it answers to the mating patterns of the society, and that these, in turn, may be explained historically. The divergence of these two students, working with closely similar materials and essentially the same theoretical background, indicates how far we have to go in this study. The variety of circumstances that affect any given family situation, involving class, regional, pluralistic, and economic factors, means that a great deal of focused study will be necessary before we can begin to have confidence in our understanding of the general area.

The Power Structure and Centralization

The traditional power structure in Latin America was formed around the control of the landed resources. During the nineteenth century, extensive landholdings in Argentina steered immigrant Europeans into tenancy positions rather than into homesteading. The expanding countrymen populations of Middle America and the Andes were increasingly brought under the control of expanding and sometimes predatory owners of *latifundios*. The Church retained title to great extensions, and numerous small communities succeeded in maintaining a degree of independent action through closely guarding the titles to their lands. Politically, the long struggle between liberals and conservatives did not revolve so much around the particular philosophies as about who was to have control of the landed base of power. The conservative position held that it should remain in the hands of those who already had it: the *hacendado,* the Church, and the villagers. The liberals held that it should be shaken loose from these inactive hands and be allowed to be developed through the efforts of entrepreneurs supported by government aid. Parenthetically, as Germani has pointed out in the last article in this section, one should not confuse the liberal of the nineteenth century with the liberal of the middle twentieth century. The former was essentially concerned with free enterprise in order to achieve growth and wealth—what, today, we would call economic development. The interests of the twentieth-century liberal, such as social justice and obtaining political representation and rights for depressed segments of the population, were of very minor concern to his nineteenth-century counterpart. This kind of interest was to come later when individuals of the working sector began to have access to education and began to hear of the revolutions that were shaking the world.

The nineteenth-century liberal was nationalist. He challenged the power of the segments that controlled the land and, thereby, held control over the wealth and labor power of the country. The liberal fought the Church, succeeding in some areas in virtually eliminating it from active political influence. In Mexico and Guatemala, Church lands were removed, and repeated efforts were made, beginning with Bolívar, to break up the communally held lands of the Indian communities. Because of the liberal emphasis on putting lands into circulation, into wider production, it has sometimes been assumed that these efforts were simply devices to shift the immediate ownership. In fact, there was a more important process being enacted. The removal of these lands was a major step, after political independence from Spain, toward centralizing power in the hands of the government.

The centralization of power, a cardinal process in Latin America, has been accompanied by a shift in the basis of power. Until well into the twentieth century, the major basis of power continued to be land; in all areas land continues to be of considerable importance. The beginnings of industrialization in the late nineteenth and early twentieth centuries, the build-up of an urban population, and the expansion of the middle sector, however, added a new dimension to the power basis. Whereas control of land formerly was sufficient to control the population, an increasing segment of the population has become educated and does not live on the land. Urban lower and middle sectors do not respond to the pressures of the provincially based gentry.

A device for utilizing this population base, however, has been long in coming in Latin America. The development of trade unionism that marked European and North American industrialization was not of such crucial importance in Latin America. In part, this was simply due to the fact that industrialization was proceeding very slowly. Of greater importance, however, is the fact that the centralization of power had to contend with the regular reforming of the current holders of power so that they might maintain their own power and action independent of the government. When effective labor unionism came, it did so not as a device whereby labor battled for rights against employers under the protection of the national government, but rather as a device whereby a nationalizing government began to utilize nascent labor organizations as a device in its battle for centralization of power.

The importance of unionism—or, better, syndicalism—in Latin America is readily seen if it is remembered that among the most important syndicates have been those of middle-class employees, not those of industrial labor. Revolutionary political action has stemmed as much from this segment as from the industrial labor force. The syndicates of schoolteachers, commercial employees, and government workers have been more politically active in many instances than have those of the working trades. The Mexican government's tight surveillance of unions, Perón's outright manipulation to obtain control, and the role of the teachers' union in Guatemala under Arevalo and Arbenz have been outstanding examples of the importance of syndicalism to centralization of power. The other aspect of the picture may be seen in those cases where labor unions have been unable to develop effectively without governmental permission. Where they have tried to act in the interests of labor as against the government, they have either been shorn of all power or eliminated. Quite clearly, the process of centralization has used syndicalism, and by the same token government has not intended to permit the syndicates to become a new competing power center.

The landed basis of power, however, continues to be important over much of Latin America, and centralization faces the fact that power continues in the hands of a few people who operate essentially independently of the immediate concerns of the government. The governments have realized themselves both too weak to shake the landholding element and, at the same time, too dependent upon that element for the continuing national income of the country. In recent years, the landholders have not acted directly as politicians on the national scene (although there have been important exceptions). Political action has been left to those who could gain some measure of power by entering the political area. This has perpetuated a common interest between the older power controllers and some upwardly mobile individuals from the middle sector. As the middle sector has expanded, however, an important and growing set of individuals find themselves ideologically antagonistic to the older power structure. This antagonism may in part be ascribed to the fact that there is not enough power to go around, hence some find that fighting the power controllers for control is more promising than playing along with them; it also must, more importantly, be ascribed to the fact that power on the international level can be, in some instances, a satisfactory substitute when power at the local level is missing.

The appearance of a socialist world in the latter part of the nineteenth century, and its sudden importance and potential as evidenced by the Mexican and Russian revolutions, provided Latins who sought mobility with both an important device—revolution—and with external support. The shattering effects of World War II on the older control system, and the rapid delineation of the forces within the Cold War, made help from the outside important to those bent upon completely changing the power system. Knowledge of social manipulation, development of the skills of revolution, the availability of arms for insurgents, the dependability of outside sources all became important during the inter-war and immediate postwar periods. Not until the 1950's, however, were these finally brought together in the successful revolutions in Bolivia and Cuba.

An understanding of power structures in Latin America demands an understanding of the operation of power control and interests across the world. When a local *cacique* system in Mexico, such as that described by Friedrich [1958] begins to operate in terms of power interests beyond the nation, the nation itself must either succumb to the larger system, or it must wrest effective control from the local leaders. The process of nationalization involves not only the internal acculturation mentioned earlier, but also the effective politicization (cf. Goldrich in this section) of the population such that it answers to the interests of the nation as a whole, and not merely to the interests of some local segments.

One of the most significant continuing outside interests in Latin America is the political and economic concern of the United States. Although many North Americans are unaware and continue to be reluctant to act as witnesses, the older power structures of Latin America have generally received the tacit, and sometimes the active, support of the northern neighbor. Until World War II, the effective economic base of Latin America depended greatly upon North American consumption. The picture was always obscured, however, because the power holders of the old landed base did not seek their "cultural" sustenance from North America, but maintained strong intellectual and social liaisons with Europe. North American influence, therefore, was specifically on the maintenance of economic operations and on the maintenance of what has been called "political stability" to permit the economic operations to continue.

The North Americans played a parallel role. Although economically deeply interested and committed to Latin America, they, too, turned to Europe for their intellectual connections. The socially or politically mobile North American could not move far by indicating any particular interest in either the culture or the politics of Latin America. Just as World War II made the United States an increasingly fashionable place for upper-class Latins to visit, so it led to the development of Acapulco, Rio de Janeiro, and other Latin American tourist centers for North Americans.

The great movement in both Latin and North America to mix and intermingle their cultures on a formal basis is thus a new fashion for both, and is not occurring in a vacuum. The economic and political controls that so long tied the Latin society to North America have been loosened. Although the United States is still the dominant customer and purchaser in the Latin market, the shift of Cuba completely outside this pattern marks the beginning of the end of an old era.

Internally, one of the most important events (and not one universally cheered) has been the emergence of the military as a distinctive political entity. In the nineteenth century, military men played their political roles, and civilians often put on military garb. But with the introduction of formal training procedures in the early twentieth century by foreign military missions, there has developed in almost every country a set of professional soldiers who have little to do professionally except wield power. Just as Latin American syndicalism has been somewhat misunderstood as a worker-dominated trade-union movement, so the military has been mistakenly seen as an entity that is gradually being "nationalized," that is, brought under the control of the government (Lieuwin [1961]). It develops, instead, that the military is the first distinctive power organization to develop solely out of the middle sector. As such, it is the first major competitor to replace the land-based power groups that continue to dominate important sectors of most countries.

The development of the military in Latin America parallels the development of our own commercial and business interests in the United States. In the United States, industry and business based on industry have been a major path of mobility to power. The growing business and white-collar bureaucracies in Latin America have obviously been of importance to the middle sector, also. However, finding the prestige symbols difficult to achieve, some parts of the middle sector have attempted to organize themselves apart from the upper sector, as in the syndicates mentioned earlier. Since business and industry have not played such a strong role in Latin America, the field has been open to a segment of the middle sector that could provide access to power. The military fills these requirements, and, internally, provides the major basis for the mobilization of a middle sector.

Equally important in the rise of the military is the relationship of

Latin America with other nations. With the exception of the fabled millionaires, many businessmen in Latin America are dependent upon import-export business, either for basic materials or for consumer products. Even home-owned industries, such as textiles, steel industries, and so on, must depend upon the external market for replacement parts and for the basic production machinery. Although this picture is changing the businessman can afford to offend neither his potential market nor his major suppliers. The military, on the other hand, can use business as a weapon as much as it can use arms. And although the Latin American military is dependent upon outside suppliers for arms, the fact is that both the United States and Russia are usually ready to supply them should the government indicate continued cooperation.

Some members of the military have long recognized that the mission of the military may be to exert pressure of this kind. In spite of their training to wield power, they are also motivated citizens. There are groups of younger officers who, like other educated members of the middle class, are much concerned with the future of the country. The military life, fortunately or not, provides time for individuals to dream of themselves as leading the country. These young officers have aspirations stemming from the same conditions that produce the activists among students, lawyers, economists, and other young people. They differ in one important respect, however: they have some means whereby they might accomplish it.

It is probably a serious mistake to predict the behavior of the military simply on the basis of presumed internal composition. In the first place, most of the military bodies contain individuals ranging from one side to the other of the political spectrum. Although there is no direct evidence to support the notion, the political interests of the military collectively probably represent most of the variations in the national population, with the important exception that the military is most concerned with its own perpetuation. It is customary, when a rightist segment of military men have control, for them to send their leftist colleagues to foreign assignments or obscure posts in order to neutralize them.

In the second place, the only real threat to the military's continued position of power is the possibility that some segment of the general population will become armed, so that it can successfully contest the military's position. It is probably this possibility, rather than the particular political color of the membership, that leads the military to fear any really popular party or leader. For all its power, the military does not easily gain popular support, and the prospect of an armed peasant or mining militia, such as developed in Bolivia, is real cause for alarm.

The power structures of Latin America are still difficult to evaluate, not because they cannot be observed, but because the observers usually are so involved in their own political and power positions that their biases all but obscure the object. It is clear, however, that the older bases of power are changing, and that the direction of this change is not following that manifested in the history of the United States. The accessibility of power support from various parties to the Cold War places the military in a position of power that it has seldom had in recent Western history. In this respect, the development of the Latin American nations more closely approximates the Middle East and Southeast Asia than either Europe or the United States.

The Region, Reform, and Revolution

Just as the various structures thus far discussed are today dominated by certain kinds of change, so may Latin America as a whole be seen as a macro-structure within the social organization of the world, undergoing changes in relation to that maximum system. Each Latin American country is a nation, or an aspiring nation, within both the regional community of such nations and the world community. Within the region, however, there are probably more profound similarities among the countries than among any similar number of nations anywhere in the world. Only the Arab world provides an area of comparable similarities.

The importance of seeing Latin America as a region lies in the fact that the Latin Americans themselves are keenly aware that they have important similarities. That the countries manifest profound differences is also obvious, and it is as obviously a central part of nationalism that these differences be valued and hailed. But the fact is that many specific experiences and patterns of organization are shared, and, further, all the Latin American countries find themselves confronting much the same outside world.

The centralization of power and nationalization discussed in earlier sections pertains specifically to the internal development of nations. But it was made perfectly clear that these processes, and the nations themselves, operate in a community of like nations, and that there are problems common to most of them. Perhaps the major process that actually and potentially characterizes Latin America is the gradual change from a social structure that was initiated in the colonial period and that crystallized during the nineteenth century. This social structure is maintained internally by the power structure, and the power structure, in turn, is being profoundly affected by the increase in available power from outside the area.

The problem faced by each country is: How are the changes going to take place? The most common approach is to see the major basis of power as control of the land, and therefore, to view the question in terms of ways of reorganizing the land-control system. Oscar Delgado [1963] set forth three methods of reorganization of land control that have been sought thus far. There is no question that land control, as is well illustrated in the essays of Germani, is of major importance. As was suggested in the last section, however, there is evidence that in the past hundred years, and most especially since the end of the last century, a new form of power has taken its place—military control. Part of the process of nationalization and centralization has involved the establishment of standing armies of varying sizes, and part of the world power struggle involves keeping these armies fairly well stocked. This has both complicated and simplified the power picture. For the continuing control of power by the military is dependent not on the produce of the lands, mines, or industries of the nation, but on the derivative power to be gained from the East or the West in the Cold War. This places the military of Latin America, where it is technically prepared, in a position of power surpassed nationally only by the power of those who may control the military.

There are those who like to classify Latin American revolutions. It has long since been pointed out that there are different kinds of revolutions, and that those of Mexico and Bolivia and, most particularly, of Cuba are "social revolutions," whereas most of the other arbitrary changes in government concern changes in power holders with little fundamental change in the system. It is also possible to trace the developments in revolutionary technology, since the Mexican Revolution, showing how revolutions and attempted revolutions have provided lessons on how to and how not to try to carry out such an effort. However, little attention has been given to the importance of *coups d'état* or barracks revolts, because they have seldom brought any reforms in their trains.

It is still not out of the question that such military takeovers will result in the attempt to establish old-style *caudillos* or new-style dictators. Of much greater importance, however, is the fact that many of the recent military coups have not been led by a single individual who was priming himself for permanent control of the country, but rather were military group exercises in which part of the motivation lay in the threat to the existing military by the recent events of Bolivia and Cuba. In both those countries, part of the successful social revolution involved the elimination of the current standing army and the institution of new military forces. The role that is characteristically ascribed to the military in Brazil seems best to illustrate this position: they stand guardian over the affairs of state, and should the civilians prove incapable, they will step in, preferably only temporarily. Sometimes they prove as inept (although much stronger) than the civilians. But consistent in recent history has been their willingness to use power to take control.

As was mentioned earlier, the modern military is middle class run and lower class based. In this it provides an interesting parallel and counterpart to the socialist revolutionary organization, which is also characteristically middle class run and lower class based. Also, the military is distinguished in its mode of control from that of the past by depending upon access to force rather than direct control of the landed or industrial resources. Oddly enough, the socialist efforts follow exactly the same pattern. When once in power, of course, the military does not, usually, follow the socialist pattern, but retains an organization and general philosophy based on the past. If we look at the military as important power controllers of the future in many Latin American countries, however, it is clear that they must be able to satisfy certain increasing demands of the populations they control. Given this fact and the fact that their greatest threat stems from leftist revolutionaries, it is not surprising to find them, like the Catholic Church, looking for means of reforming both themselves and their countries, but trying to do so without permitting a completely socialistic revolution to occur. It is, unfortunately, the case that past history in Latin America has provided precious few cases of effective far-reaching reforms that were not the products of social revolutions. And the contrast between the major protagonists of the Cold War makes it increasingly difficult for the reform-minded, nonrevolutionary leader to accomplish much. He is damned by both sides—by one for too much; by the other, for too little.

Latin American countries, because of the state of the world and the state of their regional neighbors, seem to be destined in the near future to live with inadequate reforms or excessive revolutions. But with one or the other, they will increasingly have to make do. And they will have to do so increasingly under the ever-growing powerful weapons of the military, whether they are of a traditionally trained, regular military or are a newly trained revolutionary army.

REFERENCES CITED

Adams, Richard N.
1962 "The Community in Latin America: A Changing Myth," *The Centennial Review* 6:3:409–434.
Cline, Howard
1952 "Mexican Community," *Hispanic American Historical Review* 32:2:212–242.
Crevenna, Theodore, ed.
1951 *Materiales para el estudio de la clase media en la América Latina*, Pan American Union, Washington, D.C. (Mimeo).

Delgado, Oscar
1963 "Revolución, reforma, y conservatismo como tipos de políticas agrarias en Latino América," *Revista de la Universidad Libre* 4:15:3–41.

Foster, George M.
1961 "The Dyadic Contract: A Model for the Social Structure of a Mexican Peasant Village," *American Anthropologist* 63:6: 1173–1192.

Friedrich, Paul
1958 "A Tarascan Cacicazgo: Structure and Function," in V. Ray, ed., *Systems of Political Control and Bureaucracy in Human Societies*, pp. 23–39, American Ethnological Society Proceedings.

Goldkind, Victor
1961 "Sociocultural Contrasts in Rural and Urban Settlement Types in Costa Rica," *Rural Sociology* 26:4:365–380.

Hohenthal, W. D. and Thomas McCorkle
1955 "The Problem of Aboriginal Persistence," *Southwestern Journal of Anthropology* 11:3:280–300.

Keur, Dorothy L. and Vera Rubin, eds.
1960 *Social and Cultural Pluralism in the Caribbean*, Annals of the New York Academy of Sciences 83:5:761–916.

Klass, Morton
1961 *East Indians in Trinidad*, New York, Columbia University Press.

Leonard, Olen E. and Charles P. Loomis, eds.
1953 "Part VII: Status and Stratification," *Readings in Latin American Social Organization and Institutions*, pp. 183–218, East Lansing, Michigan State College Press.

Lewis, Oscar
1959 *Five Families: Mexican Case Studies in the Culture of Poverty*, New York, Basic Books.
1961 *The Children of Sanchez*, New York, Random House.

Lieuwin, Edwin
1961 "The Military: A Revolutionary Force," *The Annals of Political and Social Science* 334:30–40, Philadelphia.

Mintz, Sidney W. and Eric R. Wolf
1950 "An Analysis of Ritual Co-parenthood (Compadrazgo)," *Southwestern Journal of Anthropology* 6:341–368.

Niehoff, Arthur and Juanita Niehoff
1960 *East Indians in the West Indies*, Milwaukee Public Museum Publications in Anthropology, no. 6.

Redfield, Robert
1955 *The Little Community*, Chicago, University of Chicago Press.

Reichel-Dolmatoff, Gerardo and Alicia Reichel-Dolmatoff
1961 *The People of Aritama*, Chicago, University of Chicago Press.

Service, Elman R. and Helen S. Service
1954 *Tobatí: Paraguayan Town,* Chicago, University of Chicago Press.
Sjoberg, G.
1960 *The Preindustrial City,* Glencoe, Ill., Free Press.
Smith, M. G.
1962 *West Indian Family Structure,* Seattle, University of Washington Press.
Smith, Raymond T.
1956 *The Negro Family in British Guiana,* London and Jamaica, Routledge and Kegan Paul.
Tumin, Melvin M.
1952 *Caste in Peasant Society,* Princeton, N.J., Princeton University Press.
United Nations
1962 *Demographic Yearbook* (issued annually), New York.
Whiteford, Andrew H.
1960 *Two Cities of Latin America,* Logan Museum Publications in Anthropology, no. 9, Beloit, Wis.
Wolf, Eric R.
1955 "Types of Latin American Peasantry: A Preliminary Discussion," *American Anthropologist* 57:3:452–471.

FURTHER READINGS

Demography, Migration, and Urbanization

Bates, Margaret, ed.
1957 *The Migration of Peoples to Latin America,* Washington, D.C., Catholic University of America Press.
Beegle, J. Allan, Harold F. Goldsmith, and Charles P. Loomis
1960 "Demographic Characteristics of the United States–Mexican Border," *Rural Sociology* 35:1:107–162.
Burnight, Robert, Nathan Whetten, and B. D. Waxman
1956 "Differential Rural-Urban Fertility in Mexico," *American Sociological Review* 21:1:3–8.
Dotson, Floyd and Lillian Dotson
1956 "Urban Centralization in Mexico," *Rural Sociology* 21:1:41–49.
Hutchinson, Bertram
1963 "The Migrant Population of Urban Brazil," *América Latina* 6:2:41–72.
Instituto Interamericano de Estadística
1959 *La estructura demográfica de las naciones americanas,* Unión Panamericana, Washington.

Métraux, Alfred
1956 "Las migraciones internas de los indios aymara en el Perú contemporáneo," *Estudios antropológicos publicados en homenaje al doctor Manuel Gamio*, pp. 391–408, Mexico.

Norris, Thomas L.
1953 "A *Colono* System and Its Relation to Seasonal Labor Problems on a Costa Rican *Hacienda*," *Rural Sociology* 18:376–378.

Population Reference Bureau, Inc.
1961 "Latin America: A Decade of Decision," *Population Bulletin* 9:6:65–75.

United Nations
1954 "The Population of Central America (Including Mexico) 1950–1980," *Population Studies* no. 16, New York.
1955 "The Population of South America, 1950–1980," *Population Studies* no. 21, New York.

Wagley, Charles
1951 "Cultural Influences on Population: A Comparison of Two Tupi Tribes," *Revista do Museu Paulista* 5:95–104, São Paulo.

Waibel, Leo
1950 "European Colonization in Southern Brazil," *Geographical Review* 40:4:529–547.

Weeks, David
1946 "Bolivia's Agricultural Frontier," *Geographical Review* 36:4:546–567.

West, Robert C.
1957 *The Pacific Lowlands of Colombia*, Baton Rouge, University of Louisiana Press.

Community and Nationalization

Beals, Ralph L.
1952 "Acculturation, Economics and Social Change in an Ecuadorean Village," in Sol Tax, ed., *Acculturation in the Americas*, Chicago, University of Chicago Press.

Comhaire, Jean
1952 "The Community Concept in the Study and Government of African and Afro-American Societies," *Primitive Man* 25:41–48.

Faron, Louis C.
1960 "The Formation of Two Indigenous Communities in Coastal Peru," *American Anthropologist* 62:3:237–253.

Fujii, Yukio and T. Lynn Smith
1959 *The Acculturation of the Japanese Immigrants in Brazil*, Latin American Monograph 8, Gainesville, University of Florida Press.

Johnson, John J.
1951 "The Latin American Municipality Deteriorates," *Inter-American Economic Affairs* 5:1:24–35.

Loomis, Charles P. and John C. McKinney
1956 "Systematic Differences Between Latin American Communities of Family Farms and Large Estates," *American Journal of Sociology* 61:5:404–412.

Manners, Robert
1957 "Methods of Community Analysis in the Caribbean," in V. Rubin, ed., *Caribbean Studies: A Symposium*, pp. 80–92 (includes discussion by Conrad Arensberg), Seattle, University of Washington Press.

Nash, Manning
1958 "Political Relations in Guatemala," *Social and Economic Studies* 7:1:65–75.

Smith, M. G.
1960 "Social and Cultural Pluralism," in V. Rubin, ed., *Social and Cultural Pluralism in the Caribbean*, Annals of the New York Academy of Science 83:5:763–785 (includes discussions by Charles Wagley and Vera Rubin).

Snyder, Joan
1957 "The Changing Context of an Andean Community," in V. Ray, ed., *Cultural Stability and Cultural Change*, pp. 20–29, Proceedings of American Ethnological Society.

Tax, Sol
1937 "The Municipios of the Midwestern Highlands of Guatemala," *American Anthropologist* 39:3:423–444.

Young, Frank W. and Ruth C. Young
1960 "Social Integration and Change in Twenty-four Mexican Villages," *Economic Development and Cultural Change* 8:4:366–377.

Class Sectors and Mobility

Cochran, Thomas C.
1959 *The Puerto Rican Businessman: A Study in Cultural Change*, Philadelphia, University of Pennsylvania Press.

De Young, Maurice
1959 "Class Parameters in Haitian Society," *Journal of Inter-American Studies* 1:4:449–458.

Hammel, Eugene A.
1962 "Social Rank and Evolutionary Position in a Coastal Peruvian Village," *Southwestern Journal of Anthropology* 18:3:199–215.

Hutchinson, Harry W.
1961 "The Transformation of Brazilian Plantation Society," *Journal of Inter-American Studies* 3:2:201–212.

Mangin, William P.
1955 "Estratificación social en el Callejón de Huaylas," *Revista del Museo Nacional*, 24:174–189, Lima.
1960 "Organización social en Vicos," *Etnología y Arqueología* 1:1:24–37, Lima.

Pereira, L. C. Bresser
1962 "The Rise of the Middle Class and Middle Management in Brazil," *Journal of Inter-American Studies* 4:3:313–327.
Romano V., Octavio Ignacio
1960 "Donship in a Mexican-American Community in Texas," *American Anthropologist* 62:6:966–976.
Williamson, R. C.
1962 "Some Variables of Middle and Lower Class in Two Central American Cities," *Social Forces* 41:2:195–207.

Family, Friendship, and Lateralization

Adams, Richard N.
1960 "An Inquiry into the Nature of the Family," in G. Dole and R. Carneiro, eds., *Essays in the Science of Culture*, pp. 30–49, New York, Crowell.
Cohen, Yehudi A.
1956 "Structure and Function: Family Organization and Socialization in a Jamaican Community," *American Anthropologist* 58:4:664–686.
Deshon, Shirley
1963 "*Compadrazgo* on a Henequin Hacienda in Yucatan: A Structural Re-evaluation," *American Anthropologist* 65:3:574–583.
Hammel, Eugene A.
1961 "The Family Cycle in a Coastal Peruvian Slum and Village," *American Anthropologist* 63:5:989–1005.
Haynes, Norman S.
1954 "The Family in Mexico," *Marriage and Family Living* 16:4:369–373.
Leonard, Olen and Charles P. Loomis, eds.
1953 "Part II: Marriage and the Family" (papers by Lewis, Simpson, Frazier, Biesanz, and Smith), in *Readings in Latin American Social Organizations and Institutions*, pp. 23–52, East Lansing, Michigan State College Press.
Reina, Ruben E.
1959 "Two Patterns of Friendship in a Guatemalan Community," *American Anthropologist* 61:1:44–50.
Rubel, Arthur J.
1960 "Concepts of Disease in Mexican-American Culture," *American Anthropologist* 62:5:795–814.
Sayres, William C.
1956 "Ritual Kinship and Negative Affect," *American Sociological Review* 21:3:348–352.
Willems, Emilio
1953 "The Structure of the Brazilian Family," *Social Forces* 31:4:339–345.

Power, Centralization, Revolution, and Reform

Blanksten, George I.

1960 "The Politics of Latin America," in Gabriel A. Almond, James S. Coleman, and others, *The Politics of the Developing Areas,* pp. 455–531, Princeton, N.J., Princeton University Press.

Cosio Villegas, Daniel

1961 *Change in Latin America: The Mexican and Cuban Revolutions,* Lincoln, University of Nebraska Press.

Dissent

1962 A special issue devoted to Latin America, 9:4:313–417.

Dozer, Donald Marquand

1959 *Are We Good Neighbors? Three Decades of Inter-American Relations, 1930–1960,* Gainesville, University of Florida Press.

Draper, Theodore

1962 *Castro's Revolution: Myths and Realities,* New York, Praeger.

Gil, Federico G.

1959 "Cuatro tendencias en la política latino-americana," *Journal of Inter-American Studies* 1:4:459–476.

Kling, Merle

1961 *A Mexican Interest Group in Action,* Englewood Cliffs, N.J., Prentice-Hall.

McAlister, Lyle N.

1961 "Civil-Military Relations in Latin America," *Journal of Inter-American Studies* 3:3:341–350.

Mills, Charles Wright

1960 *Listen Yankee: The Revolution in Cuba,* New York, McGraw-Hill.

Newbold, Stokes

1957 "Receptivity to Communist Fomented Agitation in Rural Guatemala," *Economic Development and Cultural Change* 5:4:338–361.

Scott, Robert E.

1959 *Mexican Government in Transition,* Urbana, University of Illinois Press. Revised edition, 1964.

Suslow, Leo A.

1949 *Aspects of Social Reform in Guatemala, 1944–1949,* Colgate University Area Studies, Hamilton, N.Y.

Wood, Bryce

1961 *The Making of the Good Neighbor Policy,* New York, Columbia University Press.

Family, Marriage, and Divorce in Brazil

THALES DE AZEVEDO

The role of the large, patriarchal family prior to the present phase of intense urbanization and economic development is well known through historical and sociological studies of Brazilian civilization. Chroniclers, historians, demographers, natural scientists, and ordinary travelers who visited the country since the colonial period have left us information and observations about this form of family. It was Gilberto Freyre, however, who devoted special attention to the institution. In the cyclic work he dedicated to it he analyzed the patriarchal family from its origins to the most advanced stages of its decadence. His analysis is presented in a unique way in the monographs *Casa grande e senzala*, which concerns the period of the complete predominance of the sugar plantation and the apogee of rural patriarchalism; *Sobrados e mucambos*, which describes the epoch of the diversification of colonial society with the political and social growth and development of urban populations; and, finally, *Ordem e progresso*, which presents the analysis of the changes associated with the disintegration of the slave system since the *Lei do ventre livre* (Law of Free Birth) at the beginning of the

Translated from "Familia, casamento e divorcio no Brasil," *Journal of Inter-American Studies*, 1961, III, 213–237, by permission of the author and publisher. Translated by Agnes Toward.

Republic in 1889. Freyre and others called attention to the influence of that basic model on other family types still existing in Brazilian society.

The fact that many, if not the majority, of the Portuguese colonists during the early years of settlement were bachelors or married men who migrated and remained in Brazil without their families has received less attention. Those whom Freyre calls the founders and vertical[1] colonizers of the new country (the bureaucrats, the governors general and the viceroys, the brigadiers and militia captains, and, particularly, the plantation owners), brought their families with them from Portugal to their new homes on the large estates, in the fortresses, palaces, and mansions of the coastal cities. But not all the founders followed this pattern. The first governor general, sent in 1549 to unify the colony politically before the collapse of the hereditary captaincies regime, implored the king to let him return to Portugal four years after his arrival in Bahia. Besides feeling tired and ill, he had in Lisbon "an old wife" and two daughters whose separation he could no longer bear. Neither did the recipients of the captaincies established in 1534 usually have their wives and children accompany them to the lands given by the Crown. One explanation for the failure of the captaincy system is that its grantees did not want to settle the land with their families. They either went to Brazil alone, or they entrusted the administration of their grants to others. The horizontal[2] settlers, the pioneers and adventurers, young wanderers who went to discover land, penetrate jungles, ascend rivers, seize Indians, search for emeralds, diamonds, and gold and establish ranches, were, almost without exception, bachelors eager for all kinds of adventures or married men whose families were not with them. These restless and roving horizontal settlers, like all stalwart pioneers, enjoyed in the savage lands of the colony a liberty that included the completely un-Christian freedom of having many women; and the big landowners enjoyed similar privileges. Without leaving their lands they were afforded as many women as they wanted in addition to the legal wife brought from Portugal or acquired in Brazil.[3]

Documents of the period indicate that few of the thousands of Portuguese attracted by the fame of gold mines at the end of the seventeenth century went to Brazil with wives and families. Even some one hundred years later, Louis de Vilhena wrote that white servant girls coming from Portugal to serve wealthy families of Salvador were sought after as wives by settlers who rejected the general custom of concubinage with Negroes. And adventurers were not the only bachelors. As I pointed out in another study, judges, lawyers, agents of the Crown, and public employees did not take wives to Portuguese America. Nor were they able to marry there without the permission of the court, and this authorization was either delayed for years before being granted or it was never granted at all. Not a few of these educated bachelors became involved in cases of seduction and abduction because of difficulties encountered in their attempts to marry. According to some foreign chroniclers this situation, in combination with the sybaritic life of the well-to-do, resulted in cases of adultery involving women of the upper class. Wealthy fathers, on the pretext of lack of schools, sent young daughters to convents or to Portugal so that garrison officials might not marry them.[4]

The only remaining alternative for many bachelors, despite the disapproval of the Jesuits and some secular administrators, was concubinage with Indians, *mulatas,* or even Negroes. In a famous letter to the king the first superior of the Jesuits, Manoel da Nóbrega, suggested that the remedy for such a grave situation was to send "lost women" from Portugal. According to one chronicler of the period the settlers were content "to eat the food of the land and to have four women." Unlike English attempts to populate Australia, the Portuguese never sent "lost women" to Brazil. The queen of Portugal however, did choose some orphans from among those she was educating in an asylum in Lisbon to be the first legal wives of the settlers.

One possible explanation for the Brazilian tolerance of illegitimate births is the attitude of the Church which, from the colonial period, legitimized in sacramental marriages the old concubinal unions. This preceded the Portuguese government's decision, in the middle of the eighteenth century, to liberalize the legislation which forbade the marriage of whites with Negroes and even with Indians. Actually, illegitimate children, like the unions from which they came, never were viewed in Brazil with the aversion one would expect of a Christian people.

The double standard of morality that traditionally governs the relations of the sexes and their behavior—permitting ample freedom to men and rigorously guarding the virginity and purity of women—emerged in Brazil from a number of conditions. These included the value systems developed in the Iberian peninsula from contact with the Moors; moral conditions of an impoverished and underpopulated country such as Portugal was in the era of the Discoveries;[5] the moral ills of slavery; and the demographic and economic conditions that characterized the Portuguese colony.

Various explanations exist for the spread of "free unions" [i.e., those not sanctioned by civil or religious authority] in the lower classes. Among these are the general social structure of the colonial and early independence periods; relations between different social-racial levels; economic relations attendant upon production; the preponderance of males of reproductive age among whites, enslaved natives, and Negroes; and, generally, a moral and religious laxity. Possibly similar types of marriages exist also in the present-day upper classes.

The family was, undoubtedly, the matrix of Brazilian society. It was the basis of legal institutions, patriarchal paternalism, ethical realism, and of a domestic particularism in religion, politics, and business, and in art, tastes, and psychology.[6] From that fundamental *familismo* the peculiar type of "individualism"—one might better call it *privatismo* or *particularismo*—originated and persists, even today. This characteristic of Brazilians is different in its nature, procedure, and action from rationalistic and modern political individualism; it resembles Anglo-Saxon personalism more closely, being more ethical and religious, less divisive and explosive. It is certainly more affectionate and sentimental, because of the extensive and cohesive family institution from which it originates.

The structural and situational factors which have, since the Discovery, favored the existence and growth of certain institutions as departures from the patriarchal and traditional family archetype still merit attention, perhaps more than that dedicated to them here. In schematic notes such as these it is possible only to suggest such factors, hoping that some use of this knowledge will later be made.

Indispensable to the topics here delineated is a knowledge, however brief, of social stratification in Brazil. Brazil's economy was based for at least three and one-half centuries on extensive slave monoculture, with an upper class of white landowners and a large mass of native and African slaves. The society developed two social strata in which status was assigned according to nature of the occupation, noble and servile, and physical type, white and colored. This was the pattern on the sugar and coffee plantations, and gold-mining regions as well. The formation of urban nuclei, and intensive miscegenation, produced an intermediate group with no place in the traditional scheme of artisans, free workers, civil servants and businessmen. Virtually no vertical mobility was possible in such an economic system and the population divided itself *grosso modo* into two groups: the upper—made up of *brancos ricos*; and the lower—consisting of *pretos pobres*, with mestizos distributing themselves throughout these layers according to physical type and profession. Marked social change was seen in the nineteenth century, however, with the breakdown of the rural patriarchy, the social ascent of the mestizo, and the emergence of social classes.

This two-strata hierarchy is still influential in industrialized areas and predominant in the country's vast traditional regions. It could be described as two "states" in which individuals are classified in terms of family origin, prestige of occupation, level of property and income, education, and physical type. It is now changing into a regimen of social classes wherein status is acquired through economic and educational achievement, with vertical mobility and a minimum of concern for genetic background.

Currently there are three fundamental socioeconomic groups: an upper class or elite, a middle class, and a poor, or lower class. The elite generally corresponds to the old *estado* of the *brancos ricos*. It includes most European physical types, the socially "white" of the "traditional families," descendants of the rural aristocracy, big businessmen, bankers, industrialists, professionals, and public servants. The middle class, which some prefer to call the "middle sectors," embodies *brancos* in general and mestizos with nonmanual occupations and average incomes. This class identifies itself with the values, ambitions, and standards of the elite. Thus assimilated, these two strata constitute the "superior" group of the population within which occurs maximum social mobility and intermarriage. The "inferior" group coincides with the lower class—the Negroes and dark mestizos who perform manual occupations and have lower economic status.

Family types, kinship relationships, and marriage rules are closely related to the stratification scheme, as we shall see. At the present time four different family types can be found in Brazil: the "residual patriarchal" family; the nuclear, conjugal family; the *amasiados*; and the "partial family."

The first type persists in those sectors of the upper class that still derive status and prestige from the rural aristocracy of the slave-holding past. These are the descendants of the plantation owners of Pernambuco and the neighboring strips of the humid Northeast, of the Bahian Recôncavo, of the sugar- and coffee-growing state of Rio, and of the *Paulistas* "of 400 years tradition." It was among these families, still extensive and largely endogamous, that Carmelita Hutchinson[7] recently verified how powerful remain the ties of solidarity, the expectations of reciprocal help, and the system of obligations and loyalty that unite the descendants of a traditional family branch. These long networks of relatives maintain constant contact by telephone, by visits, by "family reunions," and by correspondence, neatly distinguishing the "strangers" from the relatives by many means. A member of one of these families is capable of identifying from memory some 200—perhaps as many as 500—close and distant relatives, recalling their names and histories.[8] To this numerous group of primary interaction and socialization adheres a considerable number of godchildren and godparents. In such families godparents may have the function of reinforcing blood ties; for certain the many godparents and godchildren also extend the great unity of relatives. This is especially true of those godchildren and godparents who are tenants, renters, employees, or neighbors of the farms which some families possess and use as goods inherited from ancestors. Some family "reunions"—for a wedding, a baptism, or a graduation—may gather together seventy, eighty, or one hundred relatives and a smaller proportion of friends.

These great groups do not form a residential unit, but the conjugal families that comprise them often live in the same apartment building, thus maintaining cohesiveness and facilitating contacts in large cities. Solidarity and the power regimen are structured around the oldest and most respected member of the old line, who is shown deference and is consulted when circumstances require. He symbolizes the unity of the entire group. The absolute authority of the patriarch and the unconditional submission of wife and children has not, in general, existed for some time. The dependency of newlyweds is, at best, affectionate. Endogamy is no longer the rule, although it may still be a tendency.

The predominant family type on all levels of social stratification is the nuclear, conjugal, biological family. This is particularly true in the new areas of industrialization, urbanization, and intense foreign immigration. In older areas, less changed by present developments, unity of residence rather than family structure is the solidifying and socializing institution. Even in the new urban middle class throughout the country, a new conjugal unity predominates, not as a result of disintegration of the old, extensive, patriarchal family, but of conditions created by the growth of cities, by the new division of labor, and by a different conception of individual liberty and life goals. The higher cost of personal maintenance, the commercialization of entertainment, the growing demands of ostentatious consumption (Veblen's "conspicuous consumption"), and the preoccupation with a high-level education and a secure future for their children are primary concerns of young couples. Not only do they close the walls of their homes around them, excluding relatives, but they also try to limit procreation. Contributing to this attitude are the reduced size of homes or apartments and the scarcity and rising cost of servants. In marriages in which the wife has a job, pregnancy is inconvenient and may even be ridiculed where she works, in government bureaus, commercial firms, and schools.

In the conjugal family, husband and wife share responsibilities about equally. One exception may be financial responsibility when the wife—as is true of many cases—does not have a remunerative job. Wives were traditionally the property of their husbands, signifying that the latter protected them and watched over their fidelity in a manner that included choosing amusements, limiting social contacts, and sometimes dictating religious conduct. Now a wife may try to reconcile her preferences with those of her husband, the ideal being the increasing independence of both within the traditional conception of fidelity and dedication. Thus, a growing number of married women find themselves in professional careers, in public and commercial jobs, or in teaching. It would be unjust to deny the disadvantageous position of women as provided for in the Civil Code, particularly with respect to marital infidelity and adultery. A woman may be accused of adultery—or at least of breaking marital fidelity—when she is suspected or accused of intimacy or of affectionate and pecuniary dependence upon a man other than her husband, even if this is an infrequent occurrence. By tradition, a husband is only adulterous when he maintains a mistress.

The right to dispose of her own goods is still limited for a married woman. On this issue a brief movement of revindication of women's rights, of which nothing had been said for more than twenty years, recently occurred. Groups of feminists, composed of intellectuals, professionals, and educators, had promoted the recognition of women's political rights. When the right to vote was given to women after the Revolution of 1930 the movement lost its vigor. Today very few women are interested in political posts, although many have been elected deputies, mayors, or councilwomen. Others have been named judges, and they practice law in the courts, or assume responsibilities in public service assignments, secondary teaching, or diplomacy.

Authority, disciplinary power, and economic responsibilities are distributed between the couple more or less partially, certain masculine precedence still persisting. Many young men preserve the old ideal that the wife should not work for money. The question of the wife's status, perhaps as the symbol of the regime of "states" and of classes, involves the right to a certain idleness. This causes many men to postpone marriage for years until they attain conditions permitting their wives the privilege of not taking a job outside the home.

Sons and daughters reaching twenty years of age—or as soon as they have sufficient preparation—expect to find a job that will not prejudice their studies and will permit them to pay expenses for recreation, transportation, and personal items. As their income grows and they become adults, their contribution to the general budget of the family becomes obligatory. Ordinarily the children do not leave home except to marry, unless they must move to a different city. Dependence upon the parents diminishes. Girls and boys are encouraged to decide for themselves the career they will follow, to choose their friends, and to select their activities and the hours in which they leave and return home—within, of course, somewhat conservative limits. These freedoms are not completely unrestricted, since the parents maintain their old roles of guides, advisors, and disciplinarians, especially of the daughters. Sons, from childhood, are permitted greater freedom of action and decision. In many circumstances girls are still accompanied to dances, on walks, and on trips by a member of the family, often by a younger brother.

One of the most perceptible changes in the function of the family is that of choosing mates. Formerly, the first phase of that process—the flirtation—was kept secret but developed in some manner in the home. The girl conversed discreetly with her admirer from the window, or at the door, or the garden gate. These meetings lasted months and could be extended for years until the candidate had the economic means to ask for the hand of his choice. They were concealed from the family, particularly from the father and older brothers, with the complicity of servants, a relative, or even, at a certain stage, with maternal connivance. The father should not discover or indicate that he has discovered the situation. At this point, should he consider the flirtation inconvenient he could exercise his authority directly or through the intermediation of his wife to force the end of it. Brothers considered themselves obligated to defend their sisters against bad-intentioned suitors or those so judged. It was to be expected that they might intimidate such suitors or attack them physically. The suitor was not mentioned or allowed in the home, at least not before there were signs of an "understanding" between the couple, if not an agreement meriting confidence. The suitor who insinuated himself into the home of his sweetheart would be, ipso facto, "compromising himself," that is, giving to the relationship a formal appearance which implied an irretractable promise of marriage. According to custom only the courtship resulting from the "request" and the father's "consent" had a formal character.

The engagement also lasted months or years and was strictly controlled. There were certain days for the fiancé's visits, which were received either in the family circle, or by the fiancée under direct or disguised vigilance. After having made "official" their new understanding, the couple could meet in public, usually under the same discreet vigilance. It was principally in the home that the process was carried out so that after some investigation of family, qualities, and personal antecedents, the family might "become acquainted with the suitor." Marriage was believed to be a question of luck; "marriage and shrouds are made in heaven," according to the refrain. Great care was taken in the choice of a mate—of a fiancée above all—because one chose one's wife, as with dogs, "for the race." Family origin was a factor to be carefully considered, in the belief that the virtues and conjugal defects of the woman were transmitted by inheritance or communicated just as fatally by contagion among relatives.

The pattern of flirtation and engagement has changed considerably. Small apartments, new freedom of movement of young people and the dispersion of family members as a result of labor demands, contacts outside of the family circle, and commercial entertainments give an opportunity for freer and more intimate contact between friends. The flirtation has lost almost all of its secretive character; it often becomes involved with other relationships, such as camaraderie at school, at work, in recreation, or in professional associations. The friends are much freer to circulate during the day and even at night, attending movies together, going to the beach or on excursions. As in other countries, the automobile plays an outstanding role.

In spite of these changes the choice of a mate is still very much under the control of the parents, who can even forbid plans and, when sons and daughters remain in the home, keep track of movements. As a result of persisting ties of affection, respect for parents, and deference to their preferences, however, the majority of the families' decisions may be made without serious crises or ruptures, even when there are divergences of opinion.

As I mentioned earlier, the conjugal family in the more traditional regions is tied to relatives in still vast and cohesive groups nourished by frequent visits and facilitated by limited spatial mobility. Thus the population of the older Brazilian cities constitutes a network of blood relations allied to a smaller number of spiritual relatives resulting from godparents in the urban middle-class families.

In the urban industrial centers the conjugal family has now lost many of its attributes. As in Europe, Asia, and the rest of the Americas, the school, recreation club, professional association, sports group, church, beneficent society, street gang, restaurant, café, laundry, hospital, vacation colony, night club, movies and the theatre have all encroached upon conjugal family functions. Residence in apartment buildings, as in all the civilized world, makes neighborhood relationships more formal, impersonal, and distant. The family as a result is more isolated and autonomous, its functions much reduced compared with traditional standards.

In the lower class the nuclear family has approximately the same characteristics of constitution, composition, structure, and function, although it is apparently less stable and the exterior circle of relatives and godparents much more limited. Desertion—above all, masculine desertion—seems much more frequent.

Because in the lower levels of the social structure the indices of illiteracy are higher, the effects of the slave system persist, and the economic conditions are precarious, the taboo of virginity is less obligatory and the formal sanction of the conjugal union less institutionalized. This explains the high number of *amasiados*, a kind of consensual union of relative stability. Lasting from several years to a lifetime these unions are usually accepted less as evidence of immorality and social disorganization than as a product of custom and tradition. The *amasiados* are effectively bound by the expectation of reciprocal obligations of loyalty and assistance.[9] In Brazil as in the Caribbean islands,[10] this type of union and its corresponding family are common to the poorer classes and to the colored population of cities and rural zones, principally those in which descendants of slaves are concentrated. Some idea of the frequency of these unions emerges from the fact that more than 800,000 of them were registered throughout Brazil in the 1940 demographic census.[11] The majority of illegitimate births result from such marriages. Apart from illegitimacy, the births of a considerable number of children are not recorded on civil registries because this is not a part of the tradition of lower-level groups. In one eastern town 705 infants were baptized in 1950, whereas only 276 births were registered, among them some adults, probably for requirements of social security, the electoral list, and other reasons.[12]

These figures help to indicate the correlation between the predominance of free unions and economic and educational backwardness. In 1950 in the state of Bahia, an area of concentration of slave descendants and at that time of very low economic and educational indices, many more unwed mothers were found than in Minas Gerais, Rio Grande do Sul, or São Paulo, regions of generally more intense and accelerated development. Among 1,000 women 15 years of age or older, only 297 were single in São Paulo, 342 in Minas Gerais and 348 in Rio Grande do Sul; in Bahia the figure rose to 455. In all these states, however, a considerable number of single women "had experienced the pains, if not the joys, of motherhood."[13] In fact, of each 1,000 single women in Bahia no less than 244 had had children, alive or dead; the corresponding figures were 110 for Rio Grande do Sul, 56 for Minas Gerais, and only 31 for São Paulo. But of each 1,000 women who had had children, 191 were single in Bahia, 63 in Rio Grande do Sul, 32 in Minas Gerais, and 15 in São Paulo. "The high proportion of unmarried women among those who had children in Bahia," concluded an official report, "confirms the suspicion that in that state the number of free unions is very high."

A majority of these unions certainly involve persons of the lowest levels of the population, in which are concentrated more colored persons. Actually, the highest proportions of single women exist among the Negroes in Bahia, in Pernambuco, and in the old Federal District, the city of Rio de Janeiro, Among these groups in the same areas the lowest number of married women is found. The opposite occurs in São Paulo where Negro single women are less numerous and married women of the same group much more numerous.[14]

The *amasiados* create families of variable stability. The union may last throughout the lives of the partners, or it may be very brief. Often a woman has had children previously by two or three men. Ordinarily, a man agrees that his companion may keep with her these children of previous unions; in the new home they are neither separated nor rejected, and the only discrimination is that the mother is solely responsible for them.

Couples of free unions almost always resist the temptation to be bound by legal and sacramental ties, alleging many reasons. Some say they are unable to pay the expenses of papers, judge, and priest, or the charges required by solemnization of the act. Some believe that legally united persons soon forget duties of affection and assistance toward their spouse. Many, especially women, simply lament that they haven't been lucky: "God willed it so . . . ."[15] As a consequence of regulations of social security agencies, clarification of the legal advantages of a formal union, and campaigns of religious organizations, a tendency exists toward "legalization" of many free unions in the cities. In the rural zones, one of the objectives of missions organized by the Catholic clergy is to effect "reparation marriages," that is, the sacramental, and sometimes civil, legitimization of free unions.

A variant of the type described above is the "partial family" in the state of Bahia, described by Carmelita Hutchinson.[16] It consists of homes presided over by women, often an elderly woman with one or two daughters and their children, without the presence or permanent residence of husbands or "companions." In this mother-centered family, as in the similar Jamaican family,[17] all power and responsibility fall upon the mothers. Virtually no economic or moral responsibility belongs to the fathers who never lived in the home nor had any function in it. They are but the biological fathers of some of the children; they are not the heads of the households. The woman must sustain the children by her work as a domestic servant, washerwoman, or market vendor; her job is to educate them and start them in life. In such cases the reproductive function is separated from the residential and social function, and neither authentic conjugal relations nor father-child relationships exist that are—according to Fortes—characteristic of the family. Solien[18] considers the "partial family," for such reasons, to be below the level of organization of the family.

The scarcity of studies of urban sociography is one of the reasons why in Brazil the family has been described and analyzed in a diachronic, historical perspective and, to a certain extent, from somewhat unreliable data such as the demographic censuses. The degree of unreliability results, in the first place, from variation of criteria used in the computation of persons in different "civil" or conjugal states; in the second place, the reports concern the home or residence and not the family itself. In such studies the distinction between home and family, and among the various types of homes—as suggested by Solien and supported by Linton, Clarke and others[19]—is fundamental but has not always been made in Brazil. The need for this distinction is recognized by several authors who have interested themselves in Brazilian social institutions in recent years.[20]

Data from rural community studies are the only results of first-hand investigation and analysis of the institution of the family and its function. These results indicate that except where economic and social relations stemming from the old system of extensive agriculture still predominate—as for example in the Recôncavo of Bahia—generally neither an extensive nor a residual patriarchal family exists in the rural zones. The most frequent types are the nuclear, the *amasiado,* and the matri-centric. Few cases of extensive families are recorded, although residence of three generations in the same home may be relatively frequent. The presence of guests and boarders is not exceptional; for many poor families the maintenance of an aged relative is always considered unfavorable. In spite of high value on parental ties, many persons do not wish to live with relatives. The nuclear rural family is patriarchal in the sense that greatest power is concentrated in the hands of the husband and father. Wives and daughters are more submissive and live in greater seclusion than their counterparts in big cities. The division of labor within the rural unit is also much more discriminatory. According to ideal standards, modified in reality, the areas of power and action are quite distinct, as are the roles and status of husband, father, head of the family, wife, mother, and children according to their sexes and ages. The family is poly-functional, depending little on other institutions for its functions.

Marriage sanctions vary in the rural zones according to local social class. Two examples taken from among the communities studied in recent years give sufficient indication of this. In Vila Recôncavo, Bahia, all families of the five lineages of the upper class landowners, including owners and managers of cane fields and sugar mills, were of the "residual patriarchal" type, united simultaneously by religious and civil rites. Of 18 couples in the middle class, composed of small businessmen and public employees, 15 were united by such rites and 3 were *amasiados*. Among 95 couples in the lower class of workers, fishermen, and peasants, 22 were united by the two rites, 8 by the civil only, 34 by the religious only; 23 were *amasiados* and of 8 no reliable information was obtained. The *amasiados* followed the standard characteristic of the category; one out of three was legally married to another person whom he had abandoned.

Data confirm the preponderance of the religious tie. Nineteen civil marriages and 50 religious marriages were performed in 1950. There were 90 "partial" families presided over by women in a total of 290 homes in the poorer class.[21] In the community of Itá, in Amazonia, of 15 couples "of the first class," 9 were united by both civil and religious ties, 3 by civil only, and 3 by religious only; of the 91 couples of the "second class," 22 were married in civil and religious ceremonies, 8 in civil, 38 in religious; 23 were *amasiados*. An observation by Wagley, made in that community, can be extended to include the lower-class families in other regions. Several of the religious and civil marriages were performed after some years of free union; some civil marriages also were performed years after the religious ceremonies. The validation of unions seems to obey the desire to lend greater respectability to the persons involved. One explanation given by the inhabitants of Itá, that can be generalized, concerns the many free unions. Men refuse to marry formally, by civil or religious ceremony, when they know or suspect that their companion was not a virgin at the time of the union. Important to note also is that marriage is so significant and functional in that society, that few persons older than twenty do not participate in some kind of marital alliance.[22] Several of the above observations coincide with those of Pierson in Cruz das Almas, São Paulo.[23]

In an analysis of seven studies in communities of São Paulo, Bahia, Minas Gerais, Alagoas, and Pará, Wagley concluded that the circle of relatives is quite extensive even in the rural families, although the importance of "kinfolk" varies from one social stratum to another. "In those communities to which we refer, three social levels seem to be characterized by extensive networks of relatives—the descendants of the rural aristocracy (Vila Recôncavo), the local elite (Minas Velhas, Cerrado e Retiro; Passagem Grande e Cunha); and the stable workers of subsistence culture (Itá and Cruz das Almas). The rural farm workers, the sharecroppers, the rubber gatherers and others of an unstable and precarious economic condition seem characteristically to possess fewer relatives. These same groups of the lower class, however, are often related to important kin groups (*parentelas*) in the communities in which they live." He adds, moreover, that in these communities "the ties of kinship preserve many of their principal functions of the good old days."

"The continuing importance of kinfolk in Brazilian society should not be looked upon as social or cultural backwardness, but as the continuation of a fundamental cultural value. There is ever greater proof that, in spite of the universal tendency to industrialization and urbanization, relationships and the sentiment of kinfolk must not necessarily disappear, principally in cultures such as those of Brazil, Portugal, French Canada, and others with a profound tradition of *familismo*."[24] Fernando de Azevedo, Gilberto Freyre, and Emilio Willems insist that the family is, without doubt, the central institution of Brazilian society because of its solidarity, cohesion, multiplicity of functions, and creative dynamism.[25]

The family in Brazil, as in modern-day competitive and individualistic societies, tends to restrict its size, ancient functions, and reciprocal dependence. Even though it conserves its central position among the socializing institutions as a nucleus of solidarity, the family becomes progressively more specialized, less poly-functional, and more independent of other families in the same nucleus of blood relatives. The ties that bind the members are even stronger; the authority and orienting role of the parents persist, somewhat attenuated. The paternal home is the obligatory residence of the children until marriage, since the custom of living outside the home is not generally accepted except for unusually serious reasons. A great deal of the economic interdependence of the components of the home remains. The nuclear family continues as the only, or the principal, group of primary relationships for the majority of Brazilians. They feel responsible for its survival, reputation, and stability. Many factors conspire, however, against the traditional *familismo*. In modern Brazil the way in which the conjugal union is sanctioned varies according to social class, to rural or urban zone, and to areas of unequal development. We will indicate only a few of these variations here.

During the Empire, when Church and State were united and there was an official religion, religious marriage was the only recognized form. The republican regime introduced, in the Constitution of the 24th of February, 1891, an obligatory civil wedding, since then considered by the State to be the legal tie for all purposes. Legitimate births, for example, are the result of civil marriages. In terms of the Civil Code, civil marriage consists of a monogamous and indissoluble union. The Federal Constitution states that the family has the protection of the State. The religious, sacramental marriage of the Catholic Church has persisted although it is not recognized by the State.

From the interplay of legal protection, tradition, religious sentiment, and personal convenience there has developed, since 1891, the sanction of formal marriage by simultaneous civil and religious ties, or by only one of the two. Legal and canonical recognition of the two different types of union leads to other combinations and standards complicated by informal ties already alluded to as the *amasiados* and the "partial families." Other examples similar to the latter will be indicated later on.

The concurrent union by civil and religious rites, with the solemn public celebration of two ceremonies in which that of the state customarily precedes the ecclesiastical, was derived from the ancient prescription of civil law. This custom has been universally adopted by the so-called superior group of the Brazilian population, the middle and upper social classes of the city and the country. Until very recently no one would consider a family formed in another way as a legitimate family. The few exceptions only confirm the rule. Cases of civil-union-only arising from social sanctions, such as ostracism and discrimination in the inner family life, or as a result of canonical penalties, were very few during the first two or three decades of the Republic. However, the religious ceremony persisted as the form preferred by the rural population, especially by the members of the inferior level of the middle class, the small ranchers and inhabitants of villages and cities in the rural zones, and the lower class of small farmers and employees. The same standard extended to a portion of those groups in the larger cities.

The tolerant attitude of the Church, which exercises only moderate pressure for the celebration of the sacrament, has contributed to the acceptance of the religious wedding even by unbelievers and indifferent persons. A considerable number of engaged couples are excused from confession, for example, in order to encourage the marriage, or they agree to confess only to fulfill a formality without obligating themselves to continue in the practice of the sacrament. It is very common to find persons who declare in their old age that they confessed and took communion for the last time when they married twenty years before. According to tradition, irreligious or indifferent husbands do not interfere in the religious life of their wives nor oppose, in the majority of cases, the religious education of the children. There is a tacit compromise to act in accordance with that tradition. Thus, practically all of the mentioned social classes that are not a-Catholic, or do not have any insurmountable obstacles, ordinarily recognize the social necessity of marrying before the Church, even those who are without religious or church affiliation.

The exclusively sacramental union characterizes the less informed and more conservative groups, particularly of the rural zones, for which civil marriage has no meaning because it is not a "true" marriage. Those groups, moreover, do not recognize the obligation and usefulness of state sanction since they do not have interests, due to their poverty, that require civil protection (such as recognition of the civil status of the children including rights to vote, occupy public office, perform military service, share legacies, inheritances, and other grants of immovable goods, etc.).

At least 25 per cent of the married couples are united only by the religious tie. That figure was verified in the 1940 census and remains about the same, since it rose to only 25.5 per cent in 1950. Those who have studied the matter call attention to the difficulty of interpreting the figures in view of the different interpretations of the census questions. The average figures for purely religious marriages vary, of course, from one region to another, being much higher in the poorer and more backward areas such as the Northeast, where the figure for 1950 was 51.8 per cent. In the industrial states of the South the figure was only 8.2 per cent. The other 75 per cent are civil marriages, but available figures do not indicate the proportion of marriages that are both civil and religious. Such combinations should be very high also, although for various reasons the number of purely civil marriages is apparently increasing.[26]

Another consequence of the double standard of matrimonial sanctions is bigamy. Cases are not infrequent, especially in the rural zones, in which a man from another region convinces an ignorant woman that one of the two types of marriages, either the civil or the religious, is not valid. Their marriage is, consequently, either a civil ceremony or a religious one only. This allows him to allege later that the marriage has only a relative validity, and to contract a new marriage according to the alternative rite. In the majority of cases, the single woman thus marries a man who is already married. In recent times, it has not been unusual for the deceived wife to compensate for her disgrace by marrying, in the other type of ceremony, a man who is often in the same situation. Or she throws herself into prostitution, another known effect, although one not analyzed statistically or sociologically. This state of affairs results from the mutual resistance of both State and Church to the recognition of ceremonies not their own. Such resistance is evident in the conduct of judges performing marriages who usually consider as a bachelor the candidate who has previously contracted only a religious union. Also, until 1920, the census considered "married" only those who had participated in civil ceremonies. Beginning with the 1940 census couples united only by religious ceremonies began to be counted among the "marrieds."[27] In the last three decades the Catholic hierarchy has instructed its clergy to dissuade those already married by civil ceremonies from a religious ceremony and to advise a civil wedding to those who seek the religious ceremony. As a result of efforts of the Church, of other sectors of public opinion, and the administration, a federal law was promulgated in 1937 establishing, under certain conditions, the registration and civil recognition of the religious ceremony. Only in 1941, however, was a law promulgated that the Church considered satisfactory, following upon which clergy and faithful were required to comply with its provisions. At the present time two standards are in effect; this results from the new legal situation and from the fact that the religious ceremony lends itself more to the social expression of prestige symbols. The civil ceremony is celebrated without solemnity, in the presence of witnesses and some relatives at the home of the bride or in the office of the judge. The sacramental wedding follows on the same day in the home or the church. The alternative is the solemn celebration of the religious ceremony, followed by the reading by the priest of the act that will be registered in the civil registry. Newlyweds and witnesses sign the act, which includes the mention of the legal formalities, including the authorization of the marriage judge. Both standards are characteristic of the middle and upper classes of small and large cities.

In view of the high number of exclusively religious weddings and the fact that until recently (relatively speaking) those unions were not registered as marriages because legally they could not be, it is difficult to calculate with assurance the marriage figures in Brazil. One notes that even today the majority of the marriages performed solely in the Church are not registered—as civil law permits—since they unite persons of little education in the rural zones and among the lowest economic levels of the cities. This explains, in part, why the number of weddings is low. The average number was 7.3 per 1,000 inhabitants in 1957 and it varied according to physiographic and socioeconomic region. In the poorer regions, where religious marriages predominate, the figures varied from 1.99 in Porto Velho, Federal Territory of Guaporé, up to 5.22 in Macapa, Territory of Amapá. In those areas the religious weddings rose almost 50 per cent. In the capitals of the Northeast the figures were a little higher: 7.57 for Maceió, 8.86 for Recife, and 10.29 for Fortaleza. The areas of most intense urbanization are the industrial and agricultural areas of the south.

Because of intense female migration and the probable influence of the process of secularization, concomitants of urbanization, and industrialization, our major city, the old Federal District, records very low figures. Curitiba, Paraná, had the highest figure, 12.28 per 1,000 inhabitants. In São Paulo it was 9.44 and in the city of Rio de Janeiro, 4.26.[28] The small number of weddings in the latter city is explained by the great migration of single women from neighboring states and other regions of the country. These women migrate in search of jobs in industry, in domestic service, in the bureaucracy, and in commerce. According to the demographic census of 1950, over 930,000 persons migrated to that city, of which 437,000 were males and 493,000 females. Even allowing for the higher mortality rate for men, the preponderance of females in that migration is evident.[29]

The concentration of females, above all from the lower rural classes, is a positive factor in the "partial families" and the *amasiados* in the urban zones of the entire country.[30] (See Table 1 below.)

TABLE 1

PROPORTION OF MEN PER 1,000 WOMEN IN THE URBAN, SUBURBAN AND RURAL DISTRICTS ACCORDING TO THE PHYSIOGRAPHICAL REGIONS, 1950

Physiographical region	*No. of men per 1,000 women* Districts		
	Urban	*Suburban*	*Rural*
North	889	940	1,102
Northeast	808	885	999
East	890	957	1,025
South	938	1,005	1,086
Central-West	903	978	1,093
Brazil	898	951	1,041

The low number of men in the rural districts of the Northeast and the East is related to the fact that these are regions of more intense and continual migration to the new zones of the South and even to Amazonia and the cities of that area. The greater number of men in the suburban districts of the South is explained by the development of industrial parks in the suburbs of São Paulo, Rio de Janeiro, and other cities of the region.

Since the civil marriage enforced by the Federal Constitution and the Civil Code is monogamous and indissoluble, divorce *a vinculo* does not exist. The republican regime tried to introduce it but the constitutionalists, the Church, and a large segment of public opinion opposed it. The spirit and the letter of the law of family orientation presently in force continue to be undermined by the persistent attempts of the advocates of divorce. Such efforts have intensified in the last thirty years, but the supremacy of the segment that defends society against the disorganization of the family persists.

In place of total divorce, legal separation, or divorce *a mensa et thoro*, which does not dissolve the marriage ties but releases the partners from the obligation of living together, was introduced by a law of January 24, 1890, and incorporated into the Federal Constitution of 1891 and later constitutions. That institution, designated "divorce" at the beginning and thus referred to in judicial and census reports and documents, is called *desquite*. The reasons for *desquite* according to law are, in order of importance: (1) adultery, (2) attempt to kill, (3) ill treatment or serious injury, and (4) voluntary abandonment of the home for two successive years. Mutual consent is a more recent reason introduced into law. Adultery seems to be the most frequent cause of separation and that most often invoked against women while, in the cases published, men seem to be more guilty of ill treatment and abandonment of the home, since male adultery is much more difficult to prove. Proof that a woman has had sexual relations with a man other than her husband is sufficient, according to tradition, to secure a conviction of marital infidelity. Male adultery is usually defined as the permanent and ostentatious maintenance of a mistress, since by tradition the married or single man always enjoyed considerable freedom of movement and extramarital sexual liberty.[31]

The total number of *desquites* has grown continually since its introduction. In 1890, only 21,313 were registered in the entire country; in 1950 the number had risen to 40,164. The number of *desquitados* in the 1940 census was 67,156 because of the addition of the *separados de fato*, separations which had not been legally processed, as a result of which they had previously been included in the married group.[32]

Even with this reservation in mind, one sees that the relative frequency of *desquites* has decreased in view of the fact that, while the number of persons fifteen or older of both sexes doubled since 1890, the number of marriages increased from less than four million to more than sixteen million in 1950. Since the number of *desquites* doubled and the number of marriages quadrupled, the ratio between the number of legal separations and the total population remained stable. Actually, the percentage referred to declined from 0.14 to 0.13, although for practical purposes it could be considered unaltered. If we correlate the separations with the number of marriages we find that the first declined from a percentage of 0.56 to 0.24, which really means a reduction of less than half the number registered at the beginning of the period. Figures of the Anuário Estatístico do Brasil, referring to the period from 1955 to 1957, indicate that in the latter years the number of friendly separations granted increased slowly (from 2,577 to 2,785) and was almost three times greater than the number of disputed separations. Among the latter there were two times as many cases of abandoned homes as of adultery.

While in the United States divorce is much less frequent in rural areas than in urban areas,[33] in Brazil separation is less frequent but seems to decrease more slowly in the less urbanized regions than in the large industrial cities. The phenomenon can be explained by the migration of persons of marriageable age from the less-urbanized areas to the industrial cities. In Maranhão and Bahia, two typical rural states although different types, the percentage of correlation between the number of separations and of marriages declined, respectively, from 0.60 and 0.56 to 0.10 and 0.11, while in São Paulo it descended from 0.34 to 0.30. The highest figures and the lowest relative declines were those of the city of Rio de Janeiro, with 1.34 in 1890 and 1.21 in 1950.

Table 2 contains the figures used in this discussion.[34]

The phenomenon of desertion or abandonment of the home usually passes unnoticed, in the lower classes, since it is not publicized. The publicity about separations in the upper group of the population and their registration in high political, economic, and intellectual spheres, in combination with the agitation produced by the divorce campaigns, leads to the belief in an accelerated increase in separations. The figures given here do not confirm that impression. The total increase does not keep pace with either the increase in population or in number of marriages. Still, one must note that little is known about the phenomenon, due to the lack of sociological studies.

One of the preoccupations in Brazilian society is the appearance and apparent multiplication of new types of sanctions tending to confer an appearance of morality, legitimacy, or even legality, to unions between persons legally impeded from contracting valid civil or religious marriages. Almost thirty years ago a type of union informally called a "commercial wedding" was invented. It consisted of a contract, signed by the participants in a notary's office in the presence of witnesses, which was an agreement of mutual assistance or maintenance of the woman by the man. Usually men who had married in a civil ceremony and later separated, or who were separated only "de facto" from their wives,

Marilu Pease from Monkmeyer

Jocotepec, Mexico. A little girl is given a bath in hot water that comes from the well in the village churchyard. The tilted flat rock behind her serves as a washboard for scrubbing laundry.

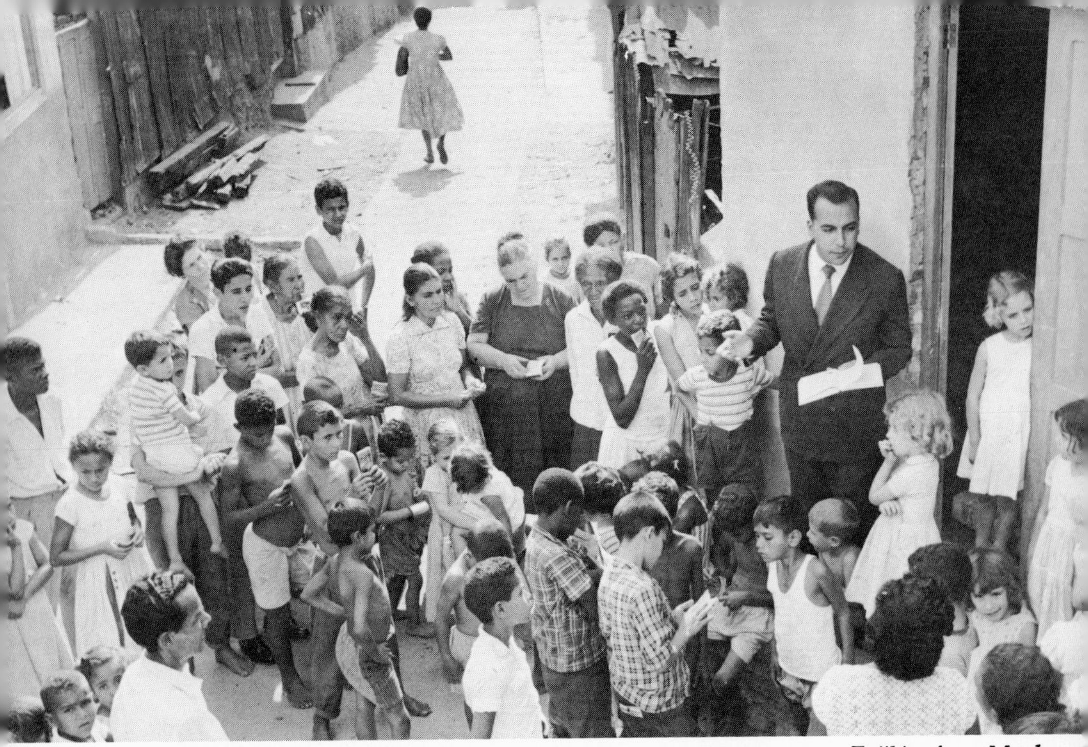

Fujihira from Monkmey

Brazil. An evangelist preaching in a *favela* (hilltop slum) in Rio de Janeiro.

Brazil. A slum in Rio de Janeiro.

A. Leeds

William Mangin

Lima, Peru. A *barriada* and the modern city.

Colombia. A pioneer woman's laundromat on the edge of the Selva forest.

Grabitzky from Monkmeyer

A. Lee

Brazil. The lake in Salvador, Bahia, is invaded by the slum.

Venezuela. Oil derricks on Lake Maracaibo.

Elizabeth Hibbs from Monkmeyer

Dwight B. Heath

Montero, Bolivia.
Winnowing Rice.

Quillacollo, Bolivia. The ox-drawn wooden plow, introduced by the Spaniards four centuries ago, is still used.

Dwight B. Heath

Henle
from Monkm

Jamaica. Cutting stone.

Bolivia. A sidewalk stall in Cochabamba offers everything from used bottles and flour sacks to new sewing machines.

Dwight B. H

A. Leeds

Brazil. A shopping area in São Paulo.

Brazil. Journalists on strike in São Paulo.

A. Leeds

Richard A

Peru. People covered with confetti and talcum powder during a carnaval fiesta in Muquiyauyo.

Guatemala. Girls at the Nimaya School in San Antonio Agua Caliente.

Tiers from Monkm

TABLE 2

NUMBER OF SEPARATIONS IN RELATION TO THE NUMBER OF MARRIAGES IN THE POPULATION 15 YEARS OR OLDER OF BOTH SEXES IN BRAZIL, IN THE CITY OF RIO DE JANEIRO, AND IN SOME STATES, BETWEEN 1890 AND 1950

Year	*Population no. 15 yrs. or more*	*No. married*	*Separated No.*	*Separated %/Pop.*	*Separated %/Married*
		Maranhão			
1890	430,854	75,743	462	0.10	0.60
1940	706,261	320,655	1,130	0.16	0.35
1950	899,871	439,573	483	0.05	0.10
		Bahia			
1890	1,919,802	420,872	2,403	0.12	0.56
1940	2,251,684	982,859	3,207	0.14	0.32
1950	2,741,473	1,273,451	1,503	0.05	0.11
		Rio de Janeiro			
1890	522,651	115,602	1,556	0.29	1.34
1940	1,228,078	560,627	9,606	0.78	1.71
1950	1,703,652	817,023	9,919	0.52	1.21
		São Paulo			
1890	1,384,753	439,827	1,524	0.11	0.34
1940	4,277,199	2,475,398	13,848	0.32	0.55
1950	5,672,788	3,349,850	10,492	0.18	0.30
		Brazil			
1890	14,333,915	3,746,869	21,313	0.14	0.56
1940	23,709,769	12,231,079	67,156	0.28	0.54
1950	30,249,423	16,371,303	40,164	0.13	0.24

The high percentages of separation in relation to the population in 1940, because of the counting of the *separados de fato* together with the legally separated, does not give an exact indication of the phenomenon of relative decrease of separations.

married single women in this manner. Women who were separated married bachelors or separated men in the same way. The lack of investigation about this institution and the little publicity about it in recent years creates the impression that it has decreased. It is not likely, however, that a phenomenon that is characteristic of the urban middle class would be decreasing.

Since these "commercial marriages" are not legally valid they give rise to a certain degree of ostracism toward the participants. In spite of this, many cases in the higher circles are ostentatiously publicized, with the intention of validating unions that would supposedly be less acceptable if they were to remain, or to begin, without any formality. In the same social spheres another type of tie is sought that might approach more closely the legal and socially consecrated ties. Since the legally separated cannot marry as long as their spouses live (since the physical separation does not imply the dissolution of the marriage bond), it is necessary to find a means of dissolving the bond in order to have a legitimate marriage.

The solution offered by certain lawyers is that of obtaining the recognition of the separation as a real divorce *a vinculo* in another country and later marrying according to the laws of that country with a person freed in the same way. Thus marriages in Uruguay or Mexico are advertised in the newspapers by certain agencies and some participants advise their friends of them by printed announcements, just as they would legal marriages. Ideally these unions require a trip to the selected country; in practice few make the trip, although some consider it important in order to give a more complete and valid appearance to the fictitious act. In fact, the agencies mentioned assume the task of carrying out the entire process "by proxy." A refinement of the formula is represented by the marriage of individuals who are ineligible to marry under Brazilian law, in countries where divorce is permitted so that they may later obtain divorces in that same country, thus making a mockery of the national laws. Advertisements, such as the following, are published in the newspapers:

> YOU CAN MARRY AND OBTAIN A DIVORCE
> outside of the country without
> traveling. All information available
> from the first agency established in
> 8 years and the only one to grant banking
> and commercial references. Information...

Because of their high cost these marriages are restricted almost entirely to the more sophisticated groups of the upper classes in the large cities. In view of the orientation of Brazilian civil law by the *jus sanguinis*, none of the foreign divorces obtained by Brazilians are recognized by Brazilian courts. For the same reason the marriages of separated persons in Uruguay, Mexico, or some other country are not recognized.

NOTES

1. EDITOR'S NOTE: See G. Freyre, *The Masters and the Slaves*, New York, Knopf, 1946, p. 16. "The terms horizontal and vertical are not here employed in the pure and restricted sociological sense that is attributed to

them in the book by Professor Pitirim Sorokin, *Social Mobility* (New York, 1927). In speaking of the vertical activity of the Pernambucans, I have reference not so much to the change of economic activity, followed by social and political changes, in accordance with Sorokin's concept, as to the regional concentration of effort in the establishment of sugar-raising and the sugar industry, the consolidation of a slave-holding and agrarian society, and the expulsion of the Dutch, who disturbed this effort and this process of forming an aristocracy."

2. EDITOR'S NOTE: G. Freyre, *The Masters and the Slaves, ibid.* "This is in contrast to the activity of the Paulistas, or rather, as Sorokin would say, the horizontal mobility of the slave-hunters and gold-seekers, the founders of the backland cattle ranches, and the missionaries. It may be noted, however, that in the special sense of Sorokin's terminology, Brazilian society was mobile in both a horizontal and a vertical direction—in the changes, at times abrupt, that occurred, especially in the south, in the position of the individual in the economic and social scale. This phenomenon is expressed by the old proverb: 'Father a tavern-keeper, son a gentleman, grandson a beggar.' The truth is that in Brazil, even where colonization was the most aristocratic in character, as in Pernambuco, the patriarchal system was never absolute, nor could it be with 'the more or less general custom of parceling out inheritances and estates,' to which Sylvio Romero alludes in a letter to E. Demolins in *Provocações e debates (Polemics and Debates)*."

3. Gilberto Freyre, *New World in the Tropics: The Culture of Modern Brazil*, New York, Knopf, 1959, p. 69.

4. Thales de Azevedo, *Povoamento da cidade do Salvador*, São Paulo, 2a edição, 1955, pp. 160–221.

5. *Ibid.*, p. 25.

6. Fernando de Azevedo, *Brazilian Culture: An Introduction to the Study of Culture in Brazil*, New York, Macmillian, 1950, p. 129; and Freyre, *op. cit.*, p. 254.

7. Carmelita Junqueira Ayres Hutchinson, "Notas preliminares ao estudo da familia no Brasil," *Anais da II Reunião Brasileira de Antropologia*, Bahia, 1957, *passim.*

8. Charles Wagley, "Formas de parentesco luso-brasileiro," Comunicação ao IV Colóquio Internacional de Estudos Luso-Brasileiros, Bahia, 1959 (inedito), *passim.*

9. René Ribeiro, "The 'Amaziado' Relationship and Other Aspects of the Family in Recife (Brazil)," *American Sociological Review*, 1945, X, *passim.*

10. Dom Basil Mathews, *Crisis of the West-Indian Family*, University College of the West Indies, 1953, *passim.*

11. IBGE, Conselho Nacional de Estatística, *Flagrantes brasileiros*, no. 15, 1959, p. 33.

12. Harry W. Hutchinson, *Village and Plantation Life in Northeastern Brazil*, Seattle, University of Washington Press, 1957, p. 272.

13. IBGE, *Estudos demográficos*, no. 158, "Indícios da frequência das uniões conjugais livres em alguns estados do Brasil." (Mimeo.)

14. *Ibid.*

15. Thales de Azevedo, *Serviçio social e problemas bahianos*, Bahia, 1944, *passim*.

16. Carmelita Hutchinson, *op. cit.*, *passim*.

17. Yehudi A. Cohen, "Family Organization and Socialization in a Jamaican Community," *American Anthropologist*, 1956, LVIII, 664.

18. Nancie L. Solien, "Household and Family in the Caribbean: Some Definitions and Concepts," *Social and Economic Research*, Jamaica, W.I., 1960, p. 105.

19. *Ibid.*, p. 103.

20. Emilio Willems, "Brazil," in Arnold M. Rose, ed., *The Institutions of Advanced Societies*, Minneapolis, 1958, p. 527; Wagley, *op. cit.*, p. 4; T. Lynn Smith, *Brazil: People and Institutions*, rev. ed., Baton Rouge, Louisiana State University Press, 1954, p. 536.

21. Harry W. Hutchinson, *op. cit.*, p. 127.

22. Charles Wagley, *Amazon Town: A Study of Man in the Tropics*, New York, Macmillan, 1953, p. 148.

23. Donald Pierson, *Cruz das Almas: A Brazilian Village*, Washington, D.C., Smithsonian Institution, Institute of Social Anthropology Publication 12, 1951.

24. Wagley, "Formas de parentesco luso-brasileiro," p. 16.

25. Azevedo, *op. cit.*, p. 129; Freyre, *New World in the Tropics*, p. 254; and Willems, "The Structure of the Brazilian Family," *Social Forces*, 1953, XXXI, 343.

26. Ovidio de Andrade, Jr., "Repartition de la population brésilienne selon l'état matrimonial," *Proceedings of the World Population Conference*, United Nations, Vol. 4, 1954, p. 548; and Germano Jardim, "La statistique par état matrimonial dans les recensements brésiliens," *Proceedings of the World Population Conference*, United Nations, Vol. 4, 1954, p. 705.

27. IBGE, *A população do Brasil: Dados censitārios 1872–1950*, 1958, p. 7.

28. IBGE, no. 15, *passim*.

29. E. Thimotheo de Barros, "As migrações interiores no Brasil," *Revista Brasileira de Estatística*, 1954, XV, 79.

30. IBGE, *Estudos de demografia*, no. 17, "Pesquisas sobre as populações urbanas e rurais do Brasil," 1954, p. 17.

31. Gordon Ireland and Jesús de Galíndez, *Divorce in the Americas*, Buffalo, 1947, p. 72.

32. Andrade, *op. cit.*, p. 542.

33. Mabel A. Elliott and Francis E. Merrill, *Social Disorganization*, New York, 1950, p. 446.

34. IBGE, no. 17, *passim*, and IBGE, *A População do Brasil*, 1958, *passim*.

The Role of Regional Associations in the Adaptation of Rural Migrants to Cities in Peru

WILLIAM P. MANGIN

In recent years the population of Lima has grown enormously. In 1946 the population of Lima-Callao was estimated at 703,216.[1] In 1956, according to the Dirección Nacional de Estadística, the figure was 1,207,250.[2] Most of this increase is due to migration from the provinces, although the birth rate in Lima is also phenomenally high.

Provincial migrants of all social and economic classes arrive in Lima and they live in many different sections of the city. Most migrants from the mountain provinces come to Lima with very little money, however, and, although many are able to live with relatives or people from the same region (henceforth called *paisanos*) for a few weeks or months, permanent housing is one of their most serious economic problems, even if the head of the family secures steady work. This problem has been virtually ignored by the government and the popular solution, arrived at not solely by migrants but through the initiative of a large

Reprinted from *Sociologus*, 1959, n.s. IX, 23–36, by permission of the author and publisher. Minor changes by author include revision of title from original "The Role of Regional Associations in the Adaptation of Rural Population in Peru." The material in this paper was presented, in an abbreviated form, at the Round Table of Anthropology, San Marcos University, January 1958. The field work on rural migrants to Lima was financed by a grant from the National Institute of Mental Health, U. S. Public Health Service, Bethesda, Md.

segment of the economically poor population of Lima, has been the creation of a ring of clandestine squatter settlements which practically border Lima on the north and east along the banks of the Rimac River and on hillsides owned by the state.

At least 120,000 people live in clandestine urbanizations or *barriadas*. These settlements are quite visible but officially ignored. Most of them lack water, sewers, streets, garbage and trash disposal, police protection, and all municipal services other than tax collection. Of these 120,000 the great majority of heads of families come from the provinces, mostly from the mountain areas.[3] The motives for their migration are socio-economic, generally, and are related to population and land pressures, extreme centralization of power, money, and government services in Lima, and the recognition of a whole series of new ideas and desires by a large segment of the provincial population coupled with the idea that these desires can be realized only in Lima. Equality of men, social mobility of the children through education, and steady wage labor (plus the idea that the good things in life can be bought with cash), are new attractive concepts, and, although mostly illusion for the migrant, they remain attractive because they are more frequently encountered in Lima than in the semi-feudal mountain provinces.

In studying the experiences of rural mountain migrants (henceforth called *serranos*) in Lima I have concentrated on two populations. Using traditional anthropological methods of observation, conversation, and participation and, later, intensive interviews with a few selected informants, I have worked, alone, with migrants from the mountains of the Department of Ancash. I worked in that area for twenty months in the years 1951–53[4] and had many friends and relatives of friends in Lima to begin the work. This aspect of the study leads to all sections of Lima and involves people in all social classes. There are over 150,000 Ancashinos in Lima so no attempt was made at sampling except seeking out people in as many different situations as possible.

The other aspect of the study involves two limited areas, one, a *barriada*, or squatter settlement on a hillside bordering Lima, with about 620 families, the other a slum section with no water, no sewers, etc., in the heart of a populous barrio (district) of Lima which has been bypassed by the city. In this study I have worked with Dr. Humberto Rotondo of the Ministry of Public Health and Dr. José Matos of San Marcos University. We have had two staffs of interviewers, made up of psychiatrists, anthropology graduate students, and social workers. We have interviewed carefully selected samples in both places using a battery of questionnaires including the Cornell Medical Index.[5] I have supplemented this by intensive work with a few good informants in both places both in and out of the samples.

In the course of the study I have been constantly reminded of the importance of two subsidiary phenomena. First, that the wholesale market area, La Parada, is a social and communication center for many *serranos*, both Indian and non-Indian. Close contact is maintained with the town of origin through the medium of the ubiquitous truck drivers who travel routes from the Lima market to some particular part of the country, usually the native region of the driver, two or three times a week. The market area features mountain music, mountain food, cheap hotels catering to mountain visitors, and it is close to a district where many *serranos* live, as well as to the most *serrano* of all the squatter settlements (henceforth called *barriadas*), a large hill called El Agustino.[6]

The second of these recurrent phenomena is the important role of the informal regional association or social club in assisting so many migrants to adjust to Lima. This article is concerned with these clubs.

There seems to be a limited amount of anthropological literature about social clubs, so it is somewhat difficult to place the Peruvian situation in regard to such clubs in cross-cultural perspective. Men's social clubs are found in many parts of the world but, impressionistically at least, it would seem that the proliferation of these clubs in Peru is extreme both in relation to the number of clubs and the intensity of the participation of the members. The tendency to form clubs is carried into many areas of activity and the formal features (i.e., rules and regulations, election of officers, regular meetings, minutes of meeting taken, etc.) are generally similar. There are professional clubs, occupational clubs, sport clubs, neighborhood clubs, music clubs, drinking clubs, pistol clubs, automobile clubs, equestrian clubs, mountain climbing clubs, etc.

The type of club dealt with in this article is the social club organized around a locality, usually the place of birth or early residence of the member. The place may be a department (the largest administrative unit in the country), a province, a district, a town, or even a barrio or parish of a town.

There are clubs in practically every town, both coastal and mountain. There are regional clubs in departmental capitals. There are *serrano* clubs in coastal cities and large haciendas. The clubs that this article concerns are *serrano* clubs in Lima. The large departmental clubs are slighted because they are of a different type from the provincial and local clubs. They draw heavily on professionals, politicians, senators, army officers, etc., who are generally quite sophisticated about Lima, and who also often belong to provincial clubs.[7]

The material presented here is based on interviews with over one hundred club members from the department of Ancash presently residing in Lima, attendance at many meetings of these clubs, participation in several fiestas given by various clubs during the 1957–59 period, and acquaintance with similar clubs in Ancash during the 1951–53 period.

This is supplemented by dozens of interviews and conversations with club members from most other departments.

To date I have been unable to arrive at a realistic figure as to the number of such clubs in Lima. Practically every town of over 1,000, and many of less, seems to have a club in Lima, and virtually every district has a club. In many cases the district and town clubs form a union at the provincial level and do certain things together. In a few cases there is relatively efficient communication and organization of clubs in Lima at the departmental level. Some of the clubs are registered with the government, meetings are held regularly, minutes taken and filed, and, during the recent dictatorship police investigators attended meetings of some clubs from known Aprista (then-outlawed opposition party) districts. There is a vast body of data on the formal organization and official business of clubs over a long period of time. Clubs often publish newspapers, provincial papers carry news of clubs, and two of the largest Lima daily papers carry columns with club notices and news. From a cursory examination of these written sources it would seem that the influx of migrants in the last ten years has not changed the character of the clubs appreciably but it has increased their influence on provincial affairs just through the increase in numbers.

Membership in these associations is both male and female, but even in clubs with many female members, the officials of the club are mostly men and most club decisions are made by men. As Little has noted in voluntary associations in West African urban areas,[8] in the city women are often in a new relationship with men. They have more economic independence and more social freedom, and in many Lima clubs, women play a much more important role than women in similar clubs in the provinces. There are cases of membership in clubs by both husband and wife, based on the wife's or wife's brother's home town, and many cases of membership in two or more clubs.

The clubs are usually recognized back in the province and quite often reflect the strengths and weaknesses of the towns and districts. When a club reaches a certain size and age, roughly between fifty to 150 members and from two to ten years, there is a tendency toward factional splitting. Sometimes these splits are based on local kinship or social-class lines, sometimes they are political, but most commonly they are associated with personality clashes within the Lima club, and the focus of the difficulty in a remarkable number of cases is the accusation of misappropriation of money by the group in power. In many cases the accusation has been true, but this type of disagreement is generally symptomatic of some older factional difference in the province. There are many contacts back and forth between Lima and the province and communication is very good.

Leadership in the club may well lead to leadership later in the town.

This is particularly true since practically all local appointments throughout the whole country are made in Lima. Officials of the clubs meet many people and play a role somewhat like that of various immigrant club leaders in the United States fifty years ago. Various political parties like their members to be club leaders and often aspirant politicians are attracted. Some of the North Coast clubs are Aprista clubs, at least one Ancash club is a communist club, but the vast majority of clubs, although often having "political" officials, are not political clubs. Club office, however, is often a form of political mobility.

The club members often defend local interests in the various government ministries and are usually in the forefront of attempts to get new schools, roads, water systems, sewers, clinics, and other public services and advantages for the town or district. Since few towns can afford full-time lobbyists in Lima, and since these things can only be done in Lima and the delays are legendary, this function of the clubs is quite important for the towns. Centralization is so extreme that to buy chalk for a school in the jungle one has to go through Lima. The feeling is also very strong, and rightly so, that any document sent to any ministry has to be followed by an agent from day to day and desk to desk or it will disappear. The club members do this job and it frequently seems that regional loyalty ("He is my *paisano*") is nearly as important as kinship and *compadrazgo*, to many ministry bureaucrats. The three considerations of kinship, *compadrazgo*, and regionalism, although nowhere mentioned in the rules and regulations of the government, are of the utmost importance in getting things accomplished at all levels in every ministry.

Within the club kinship, *compadrazgo* and friendship from the town carry over to Lima and provide security for the migrant. Possibly, also, the clubs represent a functional alternative to the *compadrazgo* system of the town. There is a feeling of obligation on the part of club members toward one another. It is also very common for compadres to be chosen from within the club. Often these are relatives or friends who might have been chosen in any case but there are also many *compadrazgo* relationships, for example an Indian worker choosing a middle-class lawyer, that would be impossible outside of the club. Provincial fiesta days also provide a focus of activity for Lima club members. Sometimes the patron saint day of the town is celebrated with a fiesta in Lima and at other times a group or sodality from the Lima club will return to the town for the fiesta. A common sight at sierra fiestas is the young man who left the mountains as an "Indian" in homespun clothes and without shoes, returning for a visit with his short jacket, necktie, dark glasses, and camera.

One of the most important aspects of the clubs is the role they play in acculturating the *serrano* to life in Lima. Few come to Lima completely naive and the club's influence is often felt before leaving the town. Clubs in the town are modeled on the Lima club and there is frequent interchange of members and many dual members as people move back and forth from Lima to the town. There are few places in Peru that escape the influence of the mass culture or national culture, or the influence of New York, Hollywood, Moscow, Peking, Buenos Aires, and Havana for that matter, but the degree of penetration varies with social class, language, isolation of town, etc. In any case, when the *serrano* arrives in Lima, even though he may have heard of Nasser, Eisenhower, Khrushchev, Haya de la Torre, and the Pope, he still has a lot to learn about how to get along in the city. Many Lima customs are learned in the clubs and unacceptable customs, or at least those marking the person as rural, Indian and *serrano*, are discouraged. The most visible traits, such as hair style, coca chewing, and the more obvious clothing differences disappear first, and in most cases men change before women. The only civilians who wear hats in Lima are Indians, upper-class women, and American Mormon missionaries. Braided hair is found only among Indians and some Europeans and Americans. It is surprising how fast migrants learn the significance of things like hats and braids, also how willing most of them are to discard them. Other less visible and more subtle differences between *serrano* and Limeño maintain themselves for generations, but the tendency is certainly toward active and voluntary change. Most of this process occurs outside of the sphere of the social club but much of it is assisted by formal and informal instruction by the club and by observation of club leaders. In at least one club a course in etiquette was offered.

Interest in the national culture is fostered in the clubs through informal discussions of politics, soccer, bullfighting, strikes, prices, scandals, etc. Some clubs subscribe to newspapers and magazines which members might not otherwise see.[9] Contact with officials of various ministries while serving on club committees also broadens the horizon of the new arrival and provides him with contacts which may prove useful. In one club representing a *comunidad indígena*, or legal Indian commune, recent arrivals who have strong Quechua accents and markedly Indian features are chosen to deal with officials of the Ministry of Work and Indian Affairs because of the belief that they expect commune residents to look and talk like Indians. This same club sends the most able talkers and the "white" members to the Ministry of Education and the Ministry of Justice because of the belief that Indians are often not allowed in the buildings and if they enter stay permanently at the end of the line. These examples are not unusual and there is a remarkable amount of cultural awareness on the part of many migrants. The experience gained in approaching officials of the bureaucracy plus the sophistication attained from contacts with people of different social status within the clubs proves quite valuable for many members. Social-class barriers, although strong, are not as strong in Lima as in the home town. Merit and accomplishment in terms of the national culture count for more and, particularly for Indians, the clubs do provide some opportunity for social mobility.

There are many material advantages to club membership. The member has access to lawyers, doctors, politicians, and businessmen that he might otherwise never meet socially and there is often a feeling of obligation on the part of the professional members. They themselves gain clients in the clubs and the political uses of the club are obvious. *Compadrazgo* again enters and, following the custom of the sierra, a low-status individual often chooses a high-status club member as *compadre*. In some cases the club members get together to work on a member's house or, if several reside in the same area, to repair a street or top an irrigation ditch. Club members call on each other for loans, help when sick, baby-sitting, and any number of simple cooperative tasks. In most of these instances the facts of kinship and *compadrazgo* and being from the same town are of more importance than being in the club, but interaction between people in these categories is facilitated by the club. Clubrooms provide a place for men to go when out of the house without spending too much money and credit is available on beer and liquor sometimes up to a month. A club, or sometimes a group of clubs, will often rent facilities such as a soccer field, a basketball or volleyball court, or hire a hall and an orchestra for a dance.

The social advantages of club membership are many. There is considerable personal security involved in associating with familiar people, even if many are disliked. Friendships and feuds (some of which seem to provide great satisfaction for participants and spectators) are carried over from the town. The strong conservative function of these clubs is also a source of security. When the acculturative pressures are too strong the club provides an opportunity to talk to *paisanos*, to play and listen to sierra music, eat sierra food and dance sierra dances at club fiestas, without feeling ashamed or anxious about the ridicule of Lima or coastal people. There is considerable preservation of sierra customs while learning how to act with outsiders and learning which customs to discard or de-emphasize.

Club fiestas provide familiar enjoyment with familiar people and, particularly in Lima, serve an important function in bringing men and women of similar background and interests together. There is a general Peruvian pattern of falsehood and trickery in the courtship relationship over marital status, age, previous parenthood, etc., so there is also a strong preference especially on the part of women for courting individuals from the same district or province, *gente conocida* (known people). Many future marital partners met at fiestas sponsored by the clubs. House servants, who make up a large part of the *serrano* population of

Lima, are often confined to their employer's house six and one-half days a week and for many of them, especially girls, the club fiesta provides one of their few amusements. When they are allowed out women generally have more freedom in Lima than in their home town. A certain amount of the same social controls do operate in Lima, however, due to the presence of friends and relatives, the prevalence of gossip, and the rapid communication between club and town.

The club fiestas and the club bar (if the club has a clubhouse and bar) provide an opportunity for men to drink and get drunk in familiar surroundings and among friends and acquaintances. In my as yet unpublished study of drinking in two mestizo towns in Ancash I noted a great deal of anxiety about getting drunk among strangers and even among friends if the friends were sober. The club situation duplicates, to a certain extent, the sierra situation, and the familiar controls and customs keep most of the participants at about the same level of drunkenness at any given time.

Participation in athletics is greatly emphasized in Peruvian culture and seems to be connected with ideas about virility, masculinity, and the need for recognition among associates, as well as with a deep-seated belief that sport is good for the health. The club provides opportunities for both men and women to play in soccer, basketball, and volleyball teams, and for those who do not play there is the enjoyment of planning tournaments, making arrangements for games, and just watching. The excitement of inter-club rivalries is intense, especially within a province, and the soccer matches are often reflections of inter-town rivalry in the sierra. Town loyalty in Lima, in many cases, seems much stronger than in the town itself. Band competitions or mass attendance at Lima folk-song theatres to cheer local provincial artists are other modes of expressing town loyalty within the club.

Club office provides recognition for individuals in the urban environment and the importance of club offices is emphasized by the club paper and the town paper, as well as by the large dailies in their provincial sections. The newspapers which some clubs publish sporadically provide sources of activity, and they, along with the town papers, maintain contact between town and residents in Lima. They are read with great interest, especially the sections dealing with town economic problems, gossip about *paisanos,* and university and professional activity of members.

So far the features of club life described have been largely integrative in nature and provide some personality security for the members. As with any complex human activity, there are many disintegrative aspects which produce insecurity and, in this particular case, many of these are the same features which provide security. The hostilities of the town and the province, inter-town, inter-parish, and class and caste conflicts, and factional or family feuds are carried over to Lima and expressed within the clubs. A reputation for good or evil in the town is carried over. The gossip and lack of privacy characteristic of the sierra town continues within the club and limits the freedom of behavior of members. The time and money demands made on professional and other economically or politically successful members become excessive at times and resentment and dependency are encouraged. If a club sponsored activity for the benefit of the town fails there is resentment in the town and within the club with the almost traditional accusations of dishonesty against the officials. Club activities often exclude women and children and take the man out of the home and involve expenditures of which the wife may not approve.[10]

Club rivalries encourage and even increase inter-town rivalries to the point where fights occur. Many customs are preserved which, for better or for worse, impede progress toward assimiliation to the national culture. In the desire to conform to new values and expectations much that is good in the mountain Indian and mestizo cultures is lost. This is often accompanied by ambivalence and anxiety which make the individual less effective. Unless two clubs form along class or caste lines, the same people tend to be in control in the club who were in control in the town. Racial and cultural prejudices operate within the club to produce more conflict than in the town because of the increased influences of democratic ideas in Lima.

A selective factor does operate, however, to emphasize the essentially integrative aspects of the clubs. In most cases, if an individual feels overly burdened by club demands he can and does quit or decrease his participation. Many form new organizations and two or even three clubs may exist from the same district. There are also a number of other associations he can join which, although not to such a great extent as the regional club, also proved substitutes for many of the relationships of rural mountain culture. Some of these were mentioned earlier, i.e., political clubs, soccer clubs, music clubs, labor unions, neighborhood associations, associations of property owners in the illegal urbanizations, etc. It must also be kept in mind that probably the majority of migrants to Lima do not associate formally to any great extent.

The following is a combination of data and comment pertaining to a club meeting. The subjects brought up are all typical of topics of interest at club meetings and this particular reunion was unusual only in the number of different things discussed. The association is the only one from a particular district in the mountains of Ancash. The town is a *comunidad indígena*,[11] or legal Indian commune, which means that there is some communal land (most of the land in the district is privately owned by either members of the *comunidad* or hacienda owners), and that the members have certain economic advantages and certain responsibilities to the Indian Institute in the Ministry of Work and Indian Affairs. The commune has weekly business with the ministry, much of which is conducted by mail. Important affairs cannot be handled by mail and club members usually represent the commune on other than routine matters. In 1940 there were 2,716 people in the district;[12] there are probably about 3,500 today. My best guess as to the number from this district in Lima is about 400 to 500, including university students. The club can count on about forty active members, some sons and nephews born in Lima, and about 200 others who will have some contact during the year, e.g., attending a fiesta or a raffle, or coming to an occasional meeting. The membership includes people from fifteen to eighty years and there are several professional men, businessmen, and politicians, but the steady active members and the officials are generally between twenty and forty years old. They are drawn mainly from workers, white-collar employees, or students. The officials are and have been either white-collar workers and students, with an occasional *obrero*,[13] and recently a woman secretary. The club formerly held meetings every week but this year the rent of the meeting room was raised from 5 to 10 soles (about $40), and they decided to meet every two weeks. The clubs of the province in which the district is located have organized a federation to which clubs from ten of the twelve districts belong. They cooperate on fiestas and they have organized a soccer league. They rent a field each Sunday and play five games starting at 11 A.M. The games are often occasions for family picnics or male drinking parties.

The meeting in question was scheduled for 8:30 P.M. I arrived at 9:30 and joined five fellows who were discussing a bank employees' strike. It was the first time I had seen them since my arm had been put in a cast, so that became the topic of conversation and they spent over fifteen minutes relating stories of medical incompetence, especially in bone setting.[14] Other people arrived and at about 10:30 the meeting began. There were nine men present at the start and four men and two women came in during the meeting.

The small attendance was attributed to weariness because of the activity involved in a fiesta that they had held five days before. The fiesta was the first order of business. The president of the club began by saying that all the fiestas of clubs from the province seem to be financial failures, that none has any money, there are too many fiestas, there are too many competing attractions, there wasn't enough publicity, etc. After several indirect answers from the president, O. B., a fast-rising employee of the Ministry of Finance who had been directing most of the questions and generally dominated the meeting, insisted upon knowing how much money was made or lost.[15] The president said they had 400 soles profit and that 1,800 soles worth of tickets were still in members' hands and he didn't know how many of those had been sold and how many would be returned. He also said it would be a long struggle to find out. The organizing committee of nine didn't work hard enough and five of them didn't even attend the fiesta. O. B. himself, the source of most of the complaining, was on the committee but he had "fever" and almost died. "My mother had to go out in the street at midnight to call two doctors," he explained. The president had to return to the town on personal business. They ordered eighty cases of beer and only sold thirty-five. "The drinkers didn't show up," said one. "Men like C. V. and L. T. didn't come," said another. (C. V. and L. T. are professional men who would have bought large quantities of beer to treat the others.) "The young fellows (*juventud*) didn't appear until 3 A.M." "We ran out of guinea pig too early," said a woman. To this O. B. said, "We should pay for a caterer. No one likes to work at his own fiesta." The fiesta was hashed over and the president let the discussion run on informally for about twenty minutes. He then read an invitation to a fiesta of all the federated clubs of the province of Aija to be held next week. Fiesta discussion concluded with general agreement that the locale of the fiesta was elegant, but since many people come to the door and look in before entering a fiesta, and in this place the orchestra and the action were too far from the door, they would look for a new place next time, and also they would consider having an orchestra which played mountain music instead of only boleros and "cha-cha-cha's."

The second item of business was a letter from the office of the Venezuelan ambassador to Peru. The club has been trying for some time to get the Venezuelan government to finance a bust of San Martín ("all that oil money") for the Plaza San Martín in the town. The ambassador said it was a great honor but due to certain political confusion in his country action would have to be postponed. This was taken as a hopeful sign by the members present.

The third matter concerned two schoolteachers in the town. Several efforts have been made by town dwellers and club members to dislodge these teachers but they have had no success. They are a man and wife from a nearby town and are considered unpleasant and incompetent by many parents and others from the town. The complaining faction has presented petitions both in Lima and in the provincial capital and they have also exhibited a practically illiterate letter from one of the teachers attacking the club. The provincial school inspector told the president of the club that he didn't think he could get them out if *all* the family heads in the town signed the petition because the wife is the sister of a congressman and a cousin of the governor of the provincial capital, and the husband is a godson of a general. The members present agreed to keep on trying.[16]

The fourth item of business was the soccer league. A brief discussion ensued about how to get more people to come to the games and what could be done about a certain town that was paying professional soccer players to represent them.[17]

The last matter concerned a petition they were going to present to the congress, with the help of a congressman, asking for the expropriation of a large number of acres of land from an hacienda in the district which they claim was stolen from the commune by the hacienda owner. There was no discussion of this during the meeting. Actually the nucleus of the active members had been planning this matter for some time and after the meeting several of them went to the president's house to discuss it some more.[18]

A very noisy meeting of the bank employees' union had been running concurrently with ours and we had to cross the back of their room to reach the street. We listened for a short time and then went out. There were about twenty members of the police riot squad outside with clubs, Sten guns and tear gas. We debated whether to stay and watch or go. O. B. said, "Nothing will happen" (he was right), so we went. It was about 12:15.

NOTES

1. Roque García Frias, "Crecimiento de la población de Lima, ciudad capital," *Estadística Peruana*, 1945, I.

2. *Boletín Estadística Peruana*, 1958, I, 65.

3. A census of barriadas was conducted in 1956 by the Institute of Ethnology of San Marcos University, under the direction of Dr. José Matos Mar. He found the total population of barriadas of Lima to be 119,886. This is about 10 per cent of the population of Lima. Of this total 46.6 per cent were born in Lima. This figure includes children. The percentage of heads of families born in Lima is only 11.7 per cent.

4. William Mangin, "Haciendas, Comunidades and Strategic Acculturation in the Peruvian Sierra," *Sociologus*, 1957, VII, 142–146; "Estratificación social en el Callejón de Huaylas," *Revista del Museo Nacional*, 1955, XXIV, 174–189, Lima.

5. Humberto Rotondo, "Morbilidad psiquiátrica en una area urbana en estado de desorganización," "Estudios de morbilidad psiquiátrica en la población urbana de Mendocita, resultados de la aplicación del indice médico de Cornell," "Estudio de la 'moral' en la Colectividad Mendocita," *Informes Técnicos*, Ministerio de Salud Pública y Asistencia Social Lima, 1958; William P. Mangin, "Conflictos culturales y salud mental," Proceedings of 2nd Latin American Congress of Mental Health, Lima, October, 1958.

6. A recent novel about life in the *barriada* El Agustino, *La tierra prome-*

tida, by Luis Felipe Angell, has caused considerable public comment in Lima, both pro and con.

7. The departmental clubs often act as coordinating agencies for the provincial and district clubs and, in some cases, the smaller clubs meet in the building of the departmental club.

8. Kenneth Little, "The Role of Voluntary Associations in West African Urbanization," *American Anthropologist,* 1957, LIX, 579–596.

9. At present in Lima there are five daily newspapers, at least twenty weekly magazines, and at least twenty other sporadic publications, mostly political.

10. The same sort of thing occurs in the mountains but my impression is that women object much more vocally in Lima, perhaps because they see the possibility for more freedom and more authority in family affairs for women in the city.

11. For a brief description of fact and fiction about legal *comunidades indígenas* see Felix Cosío, "Realidad y ficción de las comunidades indígenas," *Perú Indígena,* 1952, II, 212–216.

12. Censo Nacional de Población, Vol. 3, *Ancash,* Ministerio de Hacienda, Lima, 1940.

13. The distinction between "worker" *(obrero)* and "employee" *(empleado)* is extremely important in the Peruvian prestige system. The *empleado* is similar to the classification "white-collar worker" but somewhat more inclusive.

14. A remarkable phenomenon in Peru is the ambivalence toward medical doctors. For even the slightest illness, panic reactions are not uncommon and one notes a marked dependence on doctors, hospitals, and medicines, yet the conversation of the same individuals is studded with references to doctors as "brutes," "savages," and "thieves," who "*solamente saben cortar y cobrar*" (only know how to cut and charge).

15. O. B. is now president of the club and has to answer the questions of others.

16. The two had been appointed again for 1959.

17. The town accused of hiring professionals won the championship last year. This year they were not allowed to use outsiders so they quit the league. This has caused considerable consternation because it threatens the federation of clubs.

18. Expropriation of land by the government in favor of hacienda or commune populations in Ancash is a current political issue causing considerable comment. To date *no* land has been successfully expropriated but the example of the Cornell-Vicos project, where the government is trying to expropriate a hacienda to give it to the workers, has led to demands by other haciendas and communes that they get the same treatment. The case referred to in the text has been brought up twice in the congress and the owner of the hacienda has not answered. The club is now planning to start a lawsuit. They have had experience in the courts, having just won a seven-year suit from the police over a land dispute in a *barriada* of Lima.

Class and Kinship in Argentina

ARNOLD STRICKON

In this paper I shall describe the kinship organization of the Argentine *criollos* (classically known as the Gauchos), a rural proletariat in existence for more than 300 years, and shall compare it with the kinship structure of a group which, in addition to being the employers of the *criollo,* also constitutes part of the Argentine national elite.

In the past decade or so a growing body of description and analysis has centered on kinship structures variously labeled as bilateral (Murdock 1949), cognatic (Murdock 1960), or nonunilinear (Goodenough 1955). Prior to this recent growth of interest it was assumed, as Pehrson (1959:271) pointed out, that bilateral systems resulted in "unstructured," "amorphous," and "loosely organized" groups. Now it is becoming ever clearer that this certainly is not always the case. Rather the extension of bilateral relationships, either laterally in Ego's generation or

Reprinted from *Ethnology,* 1962, I, 500–515, by permission of the author and publisher. The field work on which this paper is based was carried out in Argentina from September, 1958, to September, 1959. It was supported by a grant from the Henry L. and Grace Doherty Foundation. The name of the local community, the *partido* in which it is located and the surrounding *partidos,* and family names have been changed. Detailed historical and field documentation will be found in Strickon (1960). The author would like to thank Dr. David Aberle and Dr. David Kaplan for their comments, criticisms, and suggestions. The responsibility for what appears is, however, his own.

vertically in his line of descent, results, at least in some cases, in groups as highly structured as those which reflect unilineal rules of descent. Goodenough (1961), in fact, seems to feel that rules of both unilinear and nonunilinear descent can be subsumed under a few all-encompassing statements.

The descriptions of bilateral kin groupings have been drawn from a wide variety of cultures ranging in complexity from primitive herdsmen (Pehrson 1959) to peoples living in modern, industrial, urban environments (Garigue 1956; Mitchell 1961). Freeman (1960:85), pointing out that "many of the world's bilateral societies are to be found in Southeast Asia and the Insular Pacific," hopes that "research in these areas . . . will provide the materials for a comparative analysis of bilateral social structures." There is no doubt that we should indeed gather such materials for comparative purposes. There are, however, other sources of comparison. It is clear that at least some hypotheses developed about cognatic systems may also be tested within advanced (i.e., pre-industrial or industrial) class-structured societies characterized by cognatic descent.

Goodenough (1955:73) and Davenport (1959:569) suggest that kindreds, on the one hand, and at least some "non-unilineal descent groups," on the other, tend to correlate, respectively, with the lack or presence of control over scarce basic resources and with the manner in which these resources are allocated. Such an hypothesis may be tested cross-culturally. However, it may also be tested within a single culture where two or more segments, classes, subcultures, or any other divisions are characterized by the same formal descent and terminological system and are also characterized by differential access to the strategic resources of that culture. It is this approach I shall follow in this paper.

Murdock (1960:5) distinguishes three categories of kin groups. The first of these are "corporate kin groups," including such groupings as families, lineages, and clans, which are almost universally corporate. "Occasional kin groups" are those which become operative only for specific occasions. "Circumscriptive kin groups," the third category, are noncorporate and never function as units; rather they serve to define the limits of various rights and obligations of their members. Murdock assigns the kindred to the second of the above kin-group categories. Following Davenport, Firth, and Goodenough he distinguishes between kindreds and other cognatic forms of kinship structure. He reserves the term "bilateral" to refer exclusively to the former.

Murdock (1960:5) rightly takes a dim view of applying the term bilateral (or any other such kin classification) to an entire society, "rather than rigorously confining [it] to types of kin groups." Nevertheless, he goes on to say that if the term is to be so applied, "it would seem appropriate to speak of a society as bilateral if it has no functionally significant descent groups, either unilineal or cognatic, and possesses only kin groups of the bilateral type such as small families and kindreds." In his ensuing discussion of the world distribution of "bilateral societies" Murdock (1960:6) explicitly includes Argentina, and implicitly all of Ibero-America. Murdock's discomfort about the characterization of whole societies is well founded, at least in the Argentine case. It is the contention of this paper that while lower-class *criollo* kinship is unequivocally bilateral, elite kinship is not.

Criollo kinship organization conforms perfectly to the eight criteria of bilateral organization advanced by Murdock (1960:6). Elite kinship organization, however, diverges from bilateral criteria in that it is not characterized by "prominence of small domestic units and absence of any form of extended family" and is marked by "functionally important descent groups, unilineal or ambilineal." The lack of such groups is characteristic, says Murdock (1960:6), of bilateral organization. For most of the other criteria which Murdock uses, information is either sparse or completely lacking on elite practice in Argentina or elsewhere in Latin America. As far as kinship terminology is concerned, although both groups operate within the framework of European bilateral terminology, there are significant differences in usage between *criollo* and elite.

I will demonstrate not only that these differences do exist between the kinship organization of *criollo* and elite, but also that these differences are functions of the differential access of these classes to Argentina's strategic resources. These resources I define as both property and effective rights of access to high-status social roles (see Sjoberg 1960).

It is not my intention here to become involved with the question of the particular terminology to be applied to various types of cognatic descent groups (Goodenough 1961; Murdock 1960; Davenport 1959). This is not to deny that such terminological questions must be settled. Rather, this paper will attempt a description and structural-functional analysis of field data relating to the problems discussed above. I shall begin with a description of the community in which the field work took place and follow this with descriptions and analyses of *criollo* and elite kinship and related institutions.

The Community Studied

The field work was done in an open-country neighborhood located about 180 miles southwest of the national capital of Buenos Aires, in the heart of the province of Buenos Aires. Argentine community organization, at least in this part of the pampas, consists of a series of overlapping open-country neighborhoods which roughly center on a *cabeza del partido*, which is about equivalent to a county seat in the American south (Arensberg 1955:1151). Each of the constituent neighborhoods, in turn, centers on a small country service village with a population of from 200 to 600 people. These villages are commonly named after the founder of their neighborhood's dominant ranch. The village which was the center of the neighborhood where the field work was done I shall call here "Eleodoro Gomez." This village has grown up in the last forty years or so around the railroad station which predated it. It lies on the railroad line which runs from Buenos Aires through the county seats of Sarmiento and O'Higgins. Eleodoro Gomez is about fifty kilometers from each of the latter two provincial cities. The population of the village and neighborhood of Eleodoro Gomez is about 2,000 people occupying a total area of about 200 square miles.

The region of Argentina within which Eleodoro Gomez is located is prime cattle country and is now, and always has been, the center of the Argentine cattle complex. Today there are two chief patterns of land use in the area. Mixed farming is carried out on small farms of 75 to 1,000 acres which are family operated by recent European immigrants or their immediate descendants. The second major land-use pattern is that of livestock grazing, which is carried out on ranches (known in Argentina as *estancias*) which range in size, within the area studied, from 1,000 to 90,000 acres. In addition to breeding and fattening cattle, sheep, and horses, the ranches also rotate their pastures by planting them to various commercial crops—chiefly wheat, maize, and sunflowers, which are the same crops as those raised by the small farmers. On the ranches, however, in contrast to small farms, agricultural operations are in the hands of local or outside contractors, using employees from outside the *estancia,* and the actual field operations are highly mechanized.

Although some livestock and farm produce, from both farms and *estancias,* is diverted to local use, the vast majority of livestock and agricultural products are sent to Argentina's industrial complex along the Río de la Plata, where they are processed and then placed on the national market or exported. Aside from meat, most local food for all classes of the population is brought in from the outside.

The *estancia* is far and away the dominant unit of land tenure. Some 217,360 acres, comprising 87 per cent of the neighborhood's acreage, are held by twenty-three *estancias,* which represent only 20 per cent of all landowning units in the neighborhood. Data on the concentration of livestock in the neighborhood were unreliable, but census figures for the *partido* of Sarmiento, in which Eleodoro Gomez is located, indicated that cattle grazed on *estancias* represent 59 per cent of all herds. The situation with respect to sheep represents an even higher degree of concentration of ranch control; one per cent of the livestock operations owned 46 per cent of the sheep.

The *estancias* are generally absentee-owned and professionally managed. The owners (*estancieros*) can be seen as a single group from the point of view of the local *criollo.* On a broader, national scale, however, a basic division within the large landowner group can be discerned.

Roughly speaking, those whose ranches fall below 5,000 acres in size derive their money in this or preceding generations from commerce, industry, or the professions. They are the children and grandchildren of Italian, Basque, recent Spanish, German, English, and Irish immigrants. In terms of the national status hierarchy they can be called a "lower-upper" class.

Those individuals and families who own or are associated with *estancias* of more than 5,000 acres represent Argentina's "upper-upper" class, the national elite. Their great wealth derives, originally, from the vast amounts of land practically given away between 1822 and 1867. In 1936 one third of the area of Buenos Aires province alone was in the hands of about a thousand people who owned 12,000 acres or more apiece. Half of this area, in turn, was in the hands of fifty families, who owned a minimum of 75,000 acres each. The names of these families are famous throughout Argentina, not only because of their wealth but also because they have traditionally held the leading positions in politics, the military, the Church, the sciences, and the arts. In this pattern they resemble elites described elsewhere in Latin America and the rest of the world (Hutchinson 1957; Whiteford 1960; Sjoberg 1960).

Since around the turn of the century the Argentine elite has expanded its interests into the industrial sector of the economy, chiefly in the areas dedicated to the processing of livestock and agricultural products. After World War I the elite began to lose its monopoly over the strategic roles in Argentine society, a process considerably hastened during the Perón regime. Although industrial interests have been growing more powerful, and despite the fact that the elite must now share its political power with groups considerably lower on the status ladder, the landed elite still clearly retains its position at the pinnacle of the Argentine status hierarchy. The kinship and related institutions of this elite group will be discussed later in this paper.

Ranking below the owners in the structure of the *estancia* are a series of managers and technicians whose social relations, and economic and political interests, are primarily with the businessmen and shopkeepers of the village of Eleodoro Gomez and the county seats and with the independent farmers of the countryside. Like the *estancieros* who do not belong to the elite, these people are the descendants of immigrants who have come to Argentina within the past eighty years. For the purposes of this paper this group need not concern us.

The Criollos

The bulk of *estancia* employees are *criollos*, the people who are most clearly marked by their command of the traditional Gaucho skills of the mounted herdsman. The group includes the cowboys and the artisans directly involved with the ranch's livestock operations: the fence and gate makers, the sheepherders, the blacksmiths, the barracks cooks, etc. In addition, *criollos* also constitute the bulk of the unskilled labor pool in the area. This latter group of *criollos* chiefly resides in villages like Eleodoro Gomez. Although many of them are the children and grandchildren of recent immigrants, their culture is clearly, in terms of content and structure, a continuation of the way of life of the traditional Argentine Gaucho (Strickon 1960).

The *criollos* constitute the backbone of the *estancia* staff. Unmarried ranch employees live in a barracks in or near the *estancia* headquarters, but the core members of the *criollo* group reside in households scattered about the ranch. The ranches are divided into administrative sections called *puestos*. Each of these is placed in charge of a section chief or *puestero*, who is responsible for overseeing the herds and equipment (but not any agricultural activities) on the 2,000 acres or more of his section. He resides on his section, together with his wife and children and possibly a few other relatives of his own and/or his wife.

Population in the countryside, outside of the village and ranch headquarters, is sparse—only about three persons per square mile. The people are organized into a series of overlapping and constantly shifting neighborhoods centered on railroad villages, such as Eleodoro Gomez, and isolated stores, bars, racetracks, and ranch headquarters. I knew of no case where one household's neighborhood affiliations coincided exactly with even its nearest neighbor's. Nuclear families constitute the most common residential unit.

The *criollos* do not own any significant amount of property. Some *puesteros* keep a few horses, sheep, pigs, and chickens, which are raised to be sold. The *criollo* owns neither his own land nor the house in which he lives. The *estancia* commonly provides the *puestero* with a house and a few acres of land, on which he may plant vegetables for his own use or as feed for his personal livestock, if any. If any use at all is made of this plot, it is usually for the latter reason; only when food prices soar does the average *puestero* plant food crops. In any event, whatever he plants is for his own use or for exchange with his relatives, and is not sold. In a few cases, especially active *criollos* with equally motivated wives earn an income from sidelines, e.g., the breaking and training of horses, which may be equal to or greater than their *estancia* wage. For most, however, the bulk of their income derives from the government-regulated wages they receive from the ranch.

The kinship terminology of the *criollo* conforms, in a sense, to the formal standard Spanish variant of the usual European bilateral type. The family name, of course, descends in the male line. Only the father's name is used; the use of the mother's maiden name following the father's is looked upon by the *criollo* as an affectation of the rich. Although the standard terminology is used, in actual practice a differential stress is laid upon collateral and affinal relationships, which contrasts with an ignorance of lineal terms beyond the second ascending and descending generations.

Two terms are characteristically used by the *criollos* in ways foreign to the other segments of the community. The first of these is the term *concuñado* (fem. *concuñada*). It literally means "co-brother-in-law" (fem. "co-sister-in-law") and refers to Ego's spouse's sibling's spouse. In *criollo* usage, however, the brothers-in-law of a *concuñado* become Ego's *concuñado* as well, and this usage is extended indefinitely. The *concuñado* relationship is chiefly of importance between men; little stress is placed upon it among women, or between women and men. The importance of this relationship between men may lead to the intervening female link being practically ignored. Thus a nephew may be boarded in the home or sent money because "he is my *concuñado's* son," apparently oblivious of the fact that he is the son of my sister-in-law (*cuñada*) as well. The second term which characterizes *criollo* usage is the word *pariente* (relative), which is technically not a kinship term at all. The word is applied to any person to whom Ego is related but to whom he cannot (or finds it difficult to) assign one of the kinship terms with which he is acquainted. It is also applied to any relative (lineal, collateral, or affinal) of a relative, thereby making him Ego's relative as well.

These two *criollo* usages provide the rationale for an ever-widening network of kinsmen. The distinction between actual and fictive kin made under the *compadrazgo* system is lost here. The fact that the *compadrazgo* has none of the functions in Eleodoro Gomez that it has in highland Middle and South America seems to be a function of a wide lateral extension of the normal kinship system. Between 1931 and 1959 a total of 1,886 baptisms were performed at the chapel in Eleodoro Gomez. In 62 per cent of these the *padrinos* were already related to one or both parents, or to each other, or both. *Compadres* are usually people of equivalent status, and, even in cases where they are not, no particular aid can be expected of them solely on the basis of the *compadre* relationship. In the year I spent in Eleodoro Gomez I heard the word *compadre* used as a term of address only once. Even in this case it was directed to a man who had been the speaker's brother-in-law long before he had been a *compadre,* and who was normally addressed either by name or as *cuñado.* The *compadrazgo,* at least in this part of Argentina, in its comparative unimportance and in the submergence of godparenthood in the extension of collateral and affinal kin, seems closer to the institution as found in Spain than to that characteristic of much of the rest of Latin America (Foster 1951:321; Pitt-Rivers 1954:107–108).

Marriage rules accord with the pattern which stresses the extension of the kindred. Incest regulations follow those of the Catholic Church.

I encountered no cousin marriages among *criollos,* although they were aware that under special conditions second and first cousins could be married. A factor of importance in a *criollo* man's choice of a marriage partner, however, is the roles held by his potential affines and his own consequent ability to extend his field of influence through a wider extension of his kindred.

Membership in a *criollo* family provides one with no claim to property; there is no significant property to claim. While the *criollo* male has no property to support his authority, many do have one lever they can use. The influence these men exert is based on the ability of senior males to distribute jobs on the *estancias* and in agricultural work parties or labor gangs. While the ranch hires its technicians and managerial staff on a presumably rational basis in terms of schooling, experience, and interviews, it depends upon personal contacts and referral by its field foremen and section chiefs, both of which positions are held by *criollos,* to hire its mounted and unskilled hands. These senior employees, in order to protect their own positions, recommend only men whose capacities they know. Invariably such men are kinsmen. Ideally, the more closely related to the foreman the applicant is, the more likely he is to get the job. In specific instances, however, the foreman or *puestero* may by-pass a close relative in favor of a *concuñado* for strategic reasons or because the former is unreliable. The *criollo* part of an *estancia* staff always consists of groups of relatives. On one *estancia,* ten of the fourteen section chiefs were related to each other by descent or marriage, and the other four were related to foremen or *puesteros* on neighboring ranches. Job hunting among *criollos* begins with conferences between the job hunter and his parents, siblings, wife, affines, and "relatives" in which they trace out the various relationships they have to key men on the ranches or labor gangs who can be approached for possible jobs.

The *criollo* kindred normally consists of direct lineals, collaterals, and affines, but it may also include *concuñados* and *parientes* on special occasions or for the specific purpose of making contacts. Like kindreds everywhere, its members assemble for weddings, wakes, parties, holidays, dances, and the like. Those who attend such gatherings may be drawn from as far as fifty miles around. These gatherings are major occasions for sounding out well-placed relatives for jobs or other favors. Members of the kindred also cooperate with each other in lending equipment and horses, in the exchange of special skills, in caring for the sick, in babysitting, and, of course, in the borrowing and lending of money.

Almost every family has some members who are living in the village or who have emigrated to the county seat or to the provincial or national capital. These migrants include men and women who, for one reason or another, have not been able to secure adequate employment in the countryside. They play a crucial role in the *criollo* network of kinship.

The *criollos* in the village of Eleodoro Gomez are either retired ranch workers or members of the area's general labor pool. The former draw small pensions and may receive additional aid from their children. The latter provide the labor for agricultural work, sheep shearing, stevedoring, etc. Most members of this group either get ranch jobs or eventually emigrate to the cities.

The village *criollos* are part of the network of kinship that ties the *criollo* community together. They take full part in the various activities which bring families together in the countryside. They also provide a base "in town" for the countryman who comes into the village for a horse race, a dance, a shopping trip, or any other reason. Often, too, they house the countryman's children while the latter are attending school in the village. The parents supply the child's food and clothing, pay the people they are living with, and also provide them with such things as meat, milk, and firewood. The child, moreover, is expected to do small (and at times large) chores for his hosts. What determines which school a country child attends is not physical proximity to his parents' home but rather in which village he has *parientes* who are willing and able to house him. I know of a few cases where children were boarded with "strangers," but such arrangements were unstable and broke up after a few months.

Migration to the cities—and in this part of the pampas this generally means Buenos Aires and its environs—is also structured by the kinship network. When a man moves to the city he generally stays with a kinsman who will also help him to find his first job. City-dwelling kinsmen likewise provide housing for visiting country relatives and *vice versa*. Money, too, is exchanged between city and country, flowing in both directions. Money from a relative, in fact, may have provided the stake which sent a *criollo* to the city in the first place. These extensions of the kindred into the cities must be renewed in each generation, since the children of the migrant tend to be sloughed off the countryman's list of relatives.

The *criollo*'s network of kinship also structures his relations to the welfare institutions of the Argentine government. From the mid-1940s to the mid-1950s, under the Perón regime, Argentina became, to the best of its economic abilities, a "welfare state." The various welfare institutions, however, have not effectively penetrated the countryside. They make contact with the public (at least in the part of Argentina under discussion) at the level of the *cabeza del partido*. Where the *criollo* contacts these institutions, however, does not depend on the *partido* in which he lives. Rather, it depends upon the "hostelry" functions (as it were) of the kindred; he makes contact with them in those county seats in which he has resident kinsmen.

The *criollo* kinship system operates within a lower-class socioeconomic matrix. The members of *criollo* groups completely lack command over the basic subsistence resources as well as access to those social roles which might provide a means of acquiring them. What is necessary for survival within such a context is access to the subordinate roles which can provide at least some degree of physical security in a world over which the *criollo* has no control. Lacking in effective industrial answers to his problems, e.g., unions or cooperatives, he depends upon his kindred to provide the necessary "insurance." By increasing the number of his kinsmen, he increases the probability that at least one of them will be in a position to be of service to him in time of need. The wide lateral extension of kin terminology reflects this need.

No *criollo* individual or family controls the significant roles of *criollo* society. The personnel occupying these roles shifts from generation to generation and from year to year on the basis of age, skills, personal qualities, and, in *criollo* eyes, pure dumb luck. As these roles are passed around over time, the membership in groups of relatives exhibits a constant state of flux; individuals are added or sloughed off, ties are strengthened or weakened. These shifting affiliations are reflected in the structure of the open-country neighborhoods themselves, with their overlapping, constantly shifting, and ill-defined boundaries. Although *criollo* kindreds do not, and cannot, represent distinct social groups (Murdock 1960:4), kinship affiliations are nevertheless a primary requisite for membership in any *criollo* grouping. The laterally extended and shifting *criollo* kindred contrasts strikingly with the strong vertical emphasis which characterizes the kinship organization of the elite.

The Elite

Wagley and Harris (1955:441) have pointed out the lack of detailed information on Latin American elites, indicating that such information as we have on them has mainly been gathered incidentally in the course of studies centering on other social groups. Scheele's study of prominent Puerto Rican families (in Steward 1956) is not concerned with an elite as defined here. Although many of these "prominent" families were originally of elite derivation, they represent today what seems to be a managerial upper class rather than a true elite. Apparently a few Puerto Rican families still cling to the vestiges of an elite way of life (Steward 1956:461). Fewer still, perhaps, actually retain some of the substance. For the vast majority, however, the critical economic and political controls over Puerto Rico are vested in governmental and private institutions which are located, not in Puerto Rico, but rather in the United States—and apparently to an even greater degree than such controls were vested in Spain during the days of Spanish colonial rule. The Puerto Rican prominent families, then, lack the controls over the island's strategic resources and social roles by which we here define elite status.

More recently Hutchinson (1957), in his study of Vila Recôncavo in northeastern Brazil, and Whiteford (1960), in his study of Popayan in Colombia, have provided us with some additional data on Latin American elites. Even in these cases, however, discussions of the elite are imbedded in wider descriptive or theoretical problems, and there is insufficient information to provide insight into the internal structuring of the elite, especially with respect to kinship.[1] In spite of the yawning gaps in our information on Latin American elites—and, for that matter, on elites in general—there is enough material, to which I shall add my own, to permit some tentative generalizations on the structure of elite kinship and to point the way for further research.

Discussions of the elite almost invariably mention that descent is a major prerequisite for elite status and that such status is perpetuated along family lines or "lineages." Parsons (1943:28–29), writing of the United States, says:

> There are important upper class elements in this country for which elite is closely bound up with the status of ancestry, hence the continuity of kinship solidarity in a—mainly patrilineal—line of descent, in "lineages." Therefore in these family elite elements the symmetry of the multilineal kinship structure [of middle class North America] is sharply skewed in the direction of a patrilineal system with a tendency to primogeniture—one in many respects resembling that historically prevalent among European aristocracies, though considerably looser. There is a tendency for this in turn to be bound up with family property, especially an ancestral home, and continuity of status in a particular local community.

Warner and Lunt, in discussing the "upper-upper class" of "Yankee City," also discuss "lineage" as a factor in elite status, but they are less struck by patrilineal tendencies. They define (Warner and Lunt 1941: 98–99) their use of "lineage" as referring to "an unbroken line of ancestors who could be traced through the father's or mother's line, or both, and who would be members of the upper class." Whiteford (1960:29–31, 45) also uses "lineage" to describe elite descent through both male and female links; he speaks of a *clase alta por abolengo*, translating *abolengo* as "lineage" where it may also be translated with the less specific meaning of "descent." Hutchinson (1957:64, 131) likewise characterizes the elite family as large, extended, and "patriarchal" with the clear implication that it represents a group which maintains some sort of control over its members.

From the point of view of current work on the analysis of cognatic kinship, the problem is whether kinship among the elite provides the structure for a series of persisting social groups. That the class as a whole represents such a group is unquestioned. The function of kinship among the elite in reinforcing common economic and political interests, as well as internal cohesiveness in the face of outsiders, has often been remarked upon (cf. Warner 1941:100–101). I do not pretend that the material to be described and analyzed in the following pages will provide definitive answers to the problems of elite kinship organization. Rather I hope it will point to the need for further research and, of more immediate importance to this paper, will reveal significant contrasts with lower-class Argentine kinship structure.

The formal kinship terminology of the elite is the same as that of the *criollo*. Where the *criollo* loses command over lineal terms beyond the second ascending and descending generations, the wealthy rancher has a firm command over them. For the wealthy, a *concuñado* is a man's wife's sibling's spouse and nothing more, and a *pariente* is a person to whom he can attach a kinship term.[2] The surname descends in the male line, but among the elite the mother's name and, for a woman, her parents' names as well as her husband's are regularly used. Such names invariably reveal affiliations to families of long-standing national or at least regional importance.

Marriage among the elite is endogamous with respect to class. Many marriages occur between second and first cousins. This requires, and presumably receives, the dispensation of the Church. The result is a generational recombination of a comparatively few family names. The economic consequences of this are obvious, in that it keeps access to the elite's property within a fairly small group of families—a pattern characteristic of at least pre-industrial elites (Sjoberg 1960:147, 149). To judge from those elite families whose land centers around Eleodoro Gomez, there seems to be a marked inclination to intermarry more with those families whose lands are located in the vicinity rather than with those whose *estancias* are more distant.

Today, as I have already indicated, the ranches are only one of many interests of the elite, but they continue to serve as major symbols of high status. The arrangement of the *estancias* over the countryside reflects the common (or at least overlapping) descent of their owners. The large *estancias* today represent subdivisions of the original founder's ranch—in the case of the community under study, the one originally owned by Eleodoro Gomez. In the first generation or so after Gomez the original ranch was subdivided among the heirs, but after that this process was slowed down by mechanisms to be discussed below. Today land maps reveal the same three or four names as the major landowners in one area, while twenty miles away a new combination of elite names appears on the land.

For each such grouping of related *estancias* there will be a single mansion, the *palacio*, usually located on the not inconsiderable remains of the ancestral ranch. The *palacio* serves as the residence for all the related people who own or have rights of access to the core ranch and the surrounding *estancia* complex, and who are resident on the ranch part time in connection with business, holidays, and vacations. Describing a similar pattern in Brazil, Hutchinson (1957:129) says that, while each individual couple maintains its own city home, "it is not unusual to find an entire apartment house in the city occupied by members of one family, each conjugal group occupying its own apartment."

In the village and open country around Eleodoro Gomez, when one refers to *La Familia* there is no ambiguity as to which family is meant. It refers to the group of people who reside in the *palacio*, in which many of them spent their early years. These same people own individually and collectively the ancestral ranch and the "related ranches" around it. In all these lands, as we shall see, they have a common interest. Finally, the same people claim descent, through ancestors of either sex, from Eleodoro Gomez.

Although some members of "The Family" in theory own their ranches outright, they are not free to dispose of them at will. "The Family" can, and does, apply pressure to prevent the sale of land by its legal owner.

Day-to-day operations of these supposedly privately owned *estancias* come under the control of a single administration, which operates them as a unit. This administration is headed in the field by a professional ranch manager. In the course of time, for reasons of efficiency and economy, the field administration may be divided up into several such units and later, perhaps, recombined once more. In any event, over the field administration(s) stands a single city administration directed by a business administrator, lawyer, or person of similar competence. This city administration supervises all the related ranches, regardless of their technical ownership and location. The Gomez city administration oversees the family's ranches, not only around Eleodoro Gomez, but also in other parts of Buenos Aires and in the provinces of Santa Fe and Córdoba as well. The city administration, in its turn, is responsible to one or two senior members of The Family who represent the family's interests directly. Such senior men are often trained (usually in the United States) in agronomy.

Under Argentine law every child has an equal claim to his parents' property, and this property must be evenly divided. In order to prevent the ultimate fragmentation of the land into economically and socially insignificant units, two methods have been adopted. The first is to defer probate of the parents' will, so that the ranch or ranches may continue to operate as a unit from which the potential heirs draw an income. Such arrangements have lasted for generations. The other alternative is legally to incorporate the *estancias* and other properties. Under either arrangement a senior member of the family (usually but not necessarily a male) sits as chairman of the board, while other members sit on the board or are, at least, stockholders. In effect, the incorporation of the family's properties provides the family with a legal, corporate identity.

Sjoberg (1960:124, 139, 178), in his discussion of pre-industrial elites, points out that recruitment into the society's strategic economic and political roles takes place "according to particularistic criteria of family or friendship ties." Preparation and training for such roles requires a great deal of money and on this basis alone separates most of the population from effective access to such positions. As indicated earlier in this paper, the group under discussion has historically filled the strategic positions in Argentine society. Beginning with Eleodoro Gomez himself, the Gomez family has played a major role in Argentine economic and political events. Among the present generation of senior Gomez males and their parents, the following positions have been held: memberships on the board of the national petroleum monopoly (Y. P. F.); presidencies, directorships, and board memberships of government and private banks; two seats on the board of Argentina's largest dairy company; one position as personal secretary to a president of Argentina; several positions as representatives to the federal legislature from the province of Buenos Aires; one judgeship; an undersecretaryship in the Ministry of Agriculture; the directorship of public works of the province of Buenos Aires; several positions as regents of universities; the post of Argentine representative to the League of Nations; and board memberships and directorships of various commercial enterprises including railroads, flour mills, and communications companies. This list is far from complete.

Although effective access to such positions is critical to the definition of the elite, it does little to clarify our specific problem of elite kin groupings. No elite family or larger kin grouping has a monopoly over any of these positions, and consequently no continuing group can crystallize around these offices. On the other hand, all elite families have a common interest in seeing that such positions are "properly" filled. Conversely, the loss by any particular elite family of its wealth and position is not necessarily critical to the survival of the class as a whole. We can accordingly discern two types of corporate interest in which the elite family and its members are involved. The first is the corporate interest of the class, which centers around the society's crucial roles. The second type of corporate interest is in the wealth which is a necessary prerequisite to admission into the larger class grouping. This corporate interest is vested in the family and any larger kin groupings that may exist. These two types of corporate interest are not, of course, exclusive; where possible, one supports and extends the other. Nevertheless, I believe it may be useful to conceptualize the two levels as distinct. One can be rich and not be elite, and one can be politically powerful and yet not elite. It is where these two levels come together, and remain together for several generations, that elite status emerges. The ancestors of the Argentine elite were not themselves elite. Our concern with elite kinship groups, then, must center on the families themselves, and not on the class as a whole.

Is there a basis for thinking that cognatic (or nonunilineal) descent groups exist among the Argentine elite? From such evidence as is available I believe there is a high degree of probability for the existence of such groups. There are groups of related people, each centering about a common residence at least in the countryside and possibly in the city as well. There are enduring estates which provide a livelihood for aggregations of related people who have common interests in such estates. The right of access to an estate is based on overlapping claims of marriage, bilateral descent from a common ancestor, and the continuity of the estate and of the groups formed around it.

To suggest the probability that elite descent groups exist, and even to indicate the presence of the necessary pre-conditions, is unfortunately not the same thing as demonstrating that they in fact do exist. The evidence on which this question can be decided will require a far more intensive study of elites than has yet been attempted in Latin America. Although the difficulty of gaining access to elites for research purposes is well known, there is a great deal of information on them in the public domain which has not been collated. A vast body of data lies untapped in *Quien es Quien,* social registers, biographies, the records of genealogical societies, birth and marriage certificates, and the records of probate courts, to mention only a few.

Whether or not the Argentine elite is characterized by some form of cognatic descent group, and if so by what kind, depends upon answers to a whole series of questions which thus far remain unanswered either for Argentina or for other parts of Latin America. Under what conditions does a man affiliate with his wife's "Family" rather than his own? When a person (male or female) "marries out" does he retain some interest in the estate of his natal "Family," or is some settlement made which terminates his claim? How are relations between "Families" structured? What is the significance of the often reported cousin marriages among the elite? Are they purely random events which could be predicted solely on the basis of the numerically small size of a group which uses bilateral terminology and practices class endogamy? Or do they reflect some pattern? What is the incidence of cousin marriage relative to total marriages? People are constantly being sloughed off from the elite "Families"; under what conditions, structural and/or economic, does this occur? These are just a few of the many questions that ethnographic field work must ask before a more detailed examination of elite kinship can be undertaken.

Conclusion

Despite the lack of detailed information on elite kinship it is clear that there are marked differences between the structure and function of the kinship systems of the *criollo* and the elite in Argentina.

In the absence of significant amounts of property which endure as units over long periods of time, birth into a particular *criollo* family does not provide an economic basis for a continuing affiliation with any particular group of kinsmen. On the other hand, the fact that jobs and assistance of various kinds depend upon some kin tie to the person who has them to dispose of makes it advantageous to extend one's kinship network as widely as possible. By so doing the *criollo* takes advantage of the opportunities provided by having relatives in a useful position at the right time. Since the personnel of the various positions is constantly changing, the network of kin affiliations must be sufficiently flexible to take advantage of changing opportunities. The uniquely *criollo* usage of the terms *concuñado* and *pariente,* the lack of command over lineal terms except for the two immediately adjacent generations, and the avoidance of cousin marriage are all functions of the adaptive advantages of the widespread lateral extension of kinship. Conversely these usages emphasize the unimportance of descent for the *criollo* in his position at the bottom of Argentina's economic, social, and political hierarchy.

The position of the elite at the other extreme of the national hierarchy likewise has its correlates in their kinship system. Their control over significant amounts of resources, especially land, and the development of legal mechanisms to conserve this property over long periods of time have provided the basis for the formation of groups formed around common residence, descent, marriage, and claims to common property. Such "lineages" have existed in some cases for well over a hundred years. To these people, lineal terms are at least as important as collateral and affinal ones. The presumably high incidence of cousin marriage serves as a means of retaining their property, at least within the confines of the class. Multiple surnames reveal affiliations to elite families on the mother's as well as the father's side. The names themselves are symbolic of claims to the society's key positions, control over which is shared with the class as a whole.

Although both operate within the same historical tradition, elite and *criollo* kinship have undergone structural and functional adaptations which reflect differing positions in the total social system. The intensive study of kinship systems which are the same in origin but which differ in class position can provide us with still another basis for comparative studies of kinship. Such studies may provide both a profounder understanding of cognatic systems and a deeper insight into the operation of the particular social systems in which these kinship systems are imbedded.

NOTES

1. The present author must himself plead guilty to this same charge.
2. Warner (1941:100) reports the upper-upper in "Yankee City" using "cousin" as a term of address to fellow members of the class when there is, in fact, no traceable relationship.

REFERENCES CITED

Arensberg, C. M.
1955 "American Communities," *American Anthropologist* 57: 1143–1160.

Davenport, W.
1959 "Nonunilinear Descent and Descent Groups," *American Anthropologist* 61:557–572.

Foster, G. M.
1951 "Report on an Ethnological Reconnaissance of Spain," *American Anthropologist* 53:311–325.

Freeman, J. D.
1960 "The Iban of Western Borneo," *Viking Fund Publications in Anthropology* 29:65–87.

Garigue, P.
1956 "French Canadian Kinship and Urban Life," *American Anthropologist* 58:1090–1101.

Goodenough, W. H.
1955 "A Problem in Malayo-Polynesian Social Organization," *American Anthropologist* 57:71–83.
1961 Review of George P. Murdock, ed., "Social Structure in Southeast Asia," *Viking Fund Publications in Anthropology*, no. 29, New York, 1960, *American Anthropologist* 63:1341–1347.

Hutchinson, Harry W.
1957 *Village and Plantation Life in Northeastern Brazil*, Seattle, University of Washington Press.

Mitchell, W. E.
1961 "Descent Groups Among New York City Jews," *Jewish Journal of Sociology* 3:121–128.

Murdock, George P.
1949 *Social Structure*, New York, Macmillan.
1960 "Cognatic Forms of Social Organization," *Viking Fund Publications in Anthropology* 29:1–14.

Parsons, T.
1943 "The Kinship System of the Contemporary United States," *American Anthropologist* 45:22–38.

Pehrson, R. N.
1954 "Bilateral Kin Groupings as a Structural Type," *University of Manila Journal of East Asian Studies* 3:199–202. (Reprinted in M. H. Fried, ed., *Readings in Anthropology*, New York, Crowell, 1959.)

Pitt-Rivers, J. A.
1954 *The People of the Sierra*, London, Criterion Books.

Sjoberg, G.
1960 *The Preindustrial City, Past and Present*, Glencoe, Ill., Free Press.

Steward, J. H., *et al.*
1956 *The People of Puerto Rico: A Study in Social Anthropology*, Urbana, University of Illinois Press.

Strickon, A.
1960 *The Grandsons of the Gauchos: A Study in Subcultural Persistence*, Ann Arbor: University Microfilms.

Wagley, Charles and Marvin Harris
1955 "A Typology of Latin American Subcultures," *American Anthropologist* 57:428–451.

Warner, W. L. and P. S. Lunt
1941 *The Social Life of a Modern Community*, New Haven, Yale University Press.

Whiteford, Andrew H.
1960 *Two Cities of Latin America: A Comparative Description of Social Classes*, Beloit, Wis., Logan Museum Publications in Anthropology, no. 9.

Social Stratification in Latin America

RALPH L. BEALS

In Portuguese America, Spanish America, and French America, although there are gross similarities in culture, institutions, social structure, and value systems, both obvious and subtle differences exist in the quality of interpersonal and intergroup relationships. Thus, while class differences are perhaps as marked in Brazil as elsewhere and many institutions are very similar to those in Spanish America, people there nevertheless often behave quite differently, and conflict situations tend to be resolved with less overt violence. In Spanish America, the accidents of history and environment have modified initially similar Spanish institutions. The relative density of native populations, the nature of aboriginal cultures, the amount and character of aboriginal social stratification, the relative number of Negroes imported, the amount and kinds of European immigration in both colonial and modern times, the location and degree of isolation of seats of power and commerce, the amount of restructuring in modern times, the character and extent of industrialization—all these factors and many more have operated to produce substantial variations.

Reprinted from *American Journal of Sociology*, 1953, LVIII, 327–339, by permission of the author and publisher.

Historical Background

Latin American societies took shape when feudal institutions and ideas were still strong in Spain and Portugal. Thus the church established in Latin America was essentially pre-Reformation in character and to a considerable degree remained insulated from changes taking place in Europe. Landholding systems tended to be of modified feudal type, with master–man or *peón–patrón* relationships and attitudes persisting into later times. Class lines were strongly drawn and tended to become in part racially defined. The basic class structure is usually defined as a dual class system with the small upper class rationalizing its hereditary position by invoking divine authority and inherent superiority. In Mexico and Peru, establishment of a feudal society was facilitated by the existence of a highly stratified native society. The Spanish initially either merged with or displaced the top stratum. Family position was validated and reinforced by wealth in the form of landed estates, mines, specie, certain professions, or power positions, but wealth alone rarely gave social status. Church, army, government bureaucracy, and the law were the respectable outlets for younger sons. Except for the pen and the sword, work with the hands was not only disparaged but virtually forbidden, certain types of work with horses and cattle making a complex and interesting exception.

A simple picture of two polar groups with a great gulf in wealth and power between them is nevertheless misleading, even of early colonial times. Within the upper class a small elite tended to monopolize power, and in some regions for as long as a century after conquest an element of the native aristocracy also survived. Similarly, the lower class was not an undifferentiated mass even when entirely Indian. Although widely separated from the upper class in prestige and wealth, certain Indian groups early identified themselves with the conquerors. Thus, as George Kubler[1] points out, in Peru the Yanacona were mainly responsible for defeating early native uprisings. Similarly, in Mexico the Indian who moved to the city quickly became Hispanicized and cast his lot with Spaniard rather than with Indian. There also seems little doubt that the managerial groups of all levels as well as a considerable variety of artisans and traders identified their interests with those of the upper class or at least considered themselves clearly apart from the lower-class mass. Thus, while from the point of view of the upper class the difference in social distance or economic position may have been indistinguishable, it was clear and significant when viewed from a lower level.

In countries with large Indian populations, such as Peru and Mexico, the early rise of large mestizo groups quickly led to a three-class system, not at all comparable to that in the United States. The distance between the upper class and the mestizo middle class may have been essentially that obtaining in a feudal two-class system. Nevertheless, the Indian or the Negro or both formed well-defined groups occupying positions inferior to the mestizo and, in some instances, to the mulatto.

Polar differences in attitude or social or economic position persist today. Thus, in the majority of countries, "family" remains one of the strongest criteria not only for social position but for sharing wealth and power. This is manifested in thousands of ways, both subtle and obvious. Great economic inequalities continue: Carolyn Campbell and Ofelia Hooper[2] point out that in Panama, a poor country with a rising middle class, the annual cash income for the rural lower class is $14 per family, as contrasted with a minimum of $5,000 per person economically active for the upper class. In many countries Indians and Negroes may be classed as nonhuman or subhuman, while mestizos are barred from the highest social and political positions. Finally, the prejudice against manual labor is tremendously powerful. In these cases the mechanical adoption of any North American model for the analysis of class or stratification leads to absurdity.

Historically and today Latin America presents strong rural-urban contrasts. Moreover, the rural pattern in most of Latin America also is markedly different from that in the United States. The vast majority of Latin American farmers live in multi-family clusters, and a substantial percentage of persons gainfully employed in agriculture today probably live in communities of 2,500 or over, which would be classed as urban in the United States. This type of settlement has strong pre-Columbian antecedents in many places and was reinforced by colonial policies. Thus the line between urban and rural is difficult to draw. Nathan Whetten points out that in the South Pacific region in Mexico 25.1 per cent of the gainfully employed population in cities of more than 10,000 are engaged in agriculture.[3] Differences in occupation are marked, as, for example, between Mexico and Brazil, where about two thirds of the population engage in agriculture, and Argentina, where only about 25 per cent are so employed.

The large city in Latin America also presents a somewhat different character from that in the United States. Urbanism in parts of Mexico, Central America, and the Andean region of South America is pre-Columbian and in many areas antedates the Christian Era. In early Spanish days, substantial pre-industrial cities existed. Centers of political administration and important trading and communication centers exercised powerful attraction for the well-to-do and for the necessary service personnel. What has been called Latin American "megalocephaly" (the disproportionate size of the city) has a long history. Industrialization, then, has not caused urbanism; rather, it has accelerated urbanization and altered the nature of urban problems.

Industrialization and the rise of new values have been accompanied by an accentuation of the rural-urban contrast in most countries. A disproportionate amount of national income has usually gone into the improvement of cities, making them increasingly desirable, in contrast with the undeveloped or unmodernized countryside. Moreover, the strong feudal class barriers have decayed much more rapidly in the city. Rural individuals or groups aspiring upward find the penetration of barriers easier in the impersonal atmosphere of the city, even though the elites may still successfully maintain their social integrity.

Regional or Type Differences in Latin America

The actual significance and functioning of the generalized processes described above are greatly modified by variable historical factors and population composition. Latin America may be divided into countries dominantly of European origin or orientation, those of heavy Indo-mestizo population, and those with heavy Negro population; and these categories are not mutually exclusive. This may be shown in outline as follows:

A. Predominantly European (or Euro-American) orientation
1. Argentina
2. Uruguay
3. Chile
4. Costa Rica
5. Santo Domingo

B. Indo-mestizo (large Indian populations or large mestizo groups with Indian way of life)
1. Paraguay
2. Bolivia
3. Peru
4. Ecuador
5. Colombia
6. Venezuela
7. Panama
8. El Salvador
9. Honduras
10. Guatemala
11. Nicaragua
12. Mexico

C. Significant Negro component in whole or in significant subregions
1. Ecuador
2. Colombia
3. Venezuela
4. Panama
5. Haiti
6. Cuba
7. Brazil

This classification is somewhat subjective and conceals significant differences. For example, in the first category, Argentina and Uruguay have virtually no Indians, and the many mestizos are almost wholly Europeanized. In addition, both have been subject to large-scale European immigration in the past century. Chile has a small percentage of distinctly Indian population, a small elite still maintaining its European orientation, and a relatively small, recent European element. The bulk of the population, including the dominant groups, is mestizo, but at all levels, except for the Indians, it is oriented to the European rather than to the Indo-mestizo way of life. Costa Rica, on the other hand, is unique in having been populated early by small farmers of Spanish origin. It has few Indians and Negroes, and class divisions are not marked. Similarly, there is a vast difference between the percentages of Indians in, say, Venezuela, and in Ecuador or Guatemala. The same is true of the Venezuelan Negro population, which is confined primarily to the coast, as compared to that in Haiti.

The countries with Indo-mestizo populations also present a variety of pictures. The Indian groups have lower status than the mestizo and present plural or parallel cultures with self-contained prestige and value systems. In some countries, such as Mexico, these plural cultures were very numerous. Moreover, the mestizo culture itself is not homogeneous. In Mexico the rural mestizo often differs little from the Indian except in identification and the lack of an internal prestige system. On the other hand, Ecuador, Peru, and Bolivia have some rural mestizo groups which are as unique and identifiable as are the Indian cultures, although sizable segments are Europe-oriented. In Mexico the mestizos not only form a non-Indian segment of the rural population and most of the urban proletariat but today dominate the power structure.

Contemporary Class Structures

In varying degree the feudal base of Latin American class structures still persists, but the usual description in polar or two-class terms is even more inadequate to describe the current situation than it was in colonial times. The most feudal of the aristocratic upper classes is still subdivided by inherited wealth, wealth in land or mining, position in the bureaucracy, or profession. Relative rank within the class, however, is still mediated by birth or family connections, and to a considerable degree entry into the elite is still conditioned primarily by family. Yet all these generalizations conceal important differences. The value placed upon land, for instance, has different meanings for the Indian who wishes enough land to grow corn by the sweat of his own brow; for the landlord, *hacendado,* or absentee owner of a vast *latifundio,* and for the efficient operator of an industrial farm.

To the degree that feudal upper-class concepts break down, conflicts or difficulties of classification arise from several sources. Formerly lowly individuals achieve great wealth or political power, while some members of the elite either enter into industry and trade, occupations of low social value in the past, or through loss of wealth no longer can maintain the minimal standards of living associated with their class. The nonpeasant group in colonial times (both rural and urban artisans, service and managerial personnel), identifying its interests with the upper class, has today been augmented by self-employed men in smaller industry and business, managerial groups, the middle bureaucracy, and skilled and white-collar workers, although in each country the membership must be differently defined. These new groups are primarily urban and are closely associated with industrialization. Except in the lower ranks they are much wealthier than the lower-class groups, and in some countries a few individuals may be wealthier than individuals of highest status. In some cases members of these groups may be recruited from the lower class; in others, membership includes or is primarily composed of impoverished former members of the upper strata. Particularly at its lower and upper fringes, members of this "middle group" (which should not be called a "middle class") are unstable and frustrated, in the one case because they cannot quite achieve "middle-class" norms in living standards; in the other, because they cannot reach the highest status. In general, the orientation of the middle-status groups is toward traditional aristocratic upper-class values, although typical bourgeois attitudes and values are found. While they strive for economic advantage and positions of power, their true goal is the difficult one of converting these into social position, for social class and economic class are far from being the same thing in Latin America. Source of wealth, family position, class-consciousness, status significance of various occupations, and the deeply intrenched dichotomy between those who work with their hands and those who do not, retain great symbolic value.

The scanty literature on social class reveals sharp disagreements as to methods, criteria, and interpretation. The majority of Latin American writers either utilize the approaches of European sociological theorists, mainly of the nineteenth century, or apply some modification of economic and occupational criteria essentially derived from more recent work in Europe and the United States. In the first case, it is usual to point out the absence of a hereditary nobility and to claim substantial bourgeois origin for the emerging middle class in the New World. In the second, classification is almost entirely based upon the status value of occupations and income, with almost no consideration of either self-identifications of groups or the nature of class value systems or attitudes. North American writers have a tendency to apply criteria and classifications derived from the United States or to place primary emphasis upon socio-psychological factors and value systems.

These varied approaches lead to sharply divergent interpretations of the existence or the character of the middle class. While some believe that the feudal two-class system persists, with a more elaborate differentiation within upper and lower classes, others insist that there is a three-class system with, in most countries, the new middle class being oriented toward old upper-class values. A third school maintains that there is a three-class system substantially similar to that of the United States.

As an example of the first position, Lowry Nelson[4] denies the existence of a middle class in Cuba, claiming that the true functional criteria are socio-psychological, to be identified by such distinctions as between manual and nonmanual workers or even between those who have servants and those who do not. He holds that the upper class consists of the managerial and clerical elements and all those descended from upper-class families, regardless of present wealth and income. Among these he recognizes an elite consisting of the very wealthy, top government officials, and those professionals who have wealth and family tradition. A given occupational group, on the other hand, such as teachers, might contain representatives of both the upper class and the lower class. A further modification is that the higher the status of an occupation the smaller the number of Negroes found in it, although apparently there is no rigid line. Nelson admits that by applying United States economic or occupational criteria a case could be made for an equivalent middle class in Cuba. He believes, however, that this does not conform to the way Cubans perceive themselves and their fellows and hence is a wholly misleading type of classification.

T. Lynn Smith[5] finds three classes in Colombia but aligns the middle class with the upper class. He states that there are few chances to rise, while the high reproduction rate of the upper class makes it impossible for all offspring to maintain the economic position associated with it. Consequently, individuals occupying what appear to be middle-class positions are descendants of the upper classes who can no longer keep up appearances and who identify themselves with the elite.

In contrast with Smith, Carlos Manuel Raggi Ageo[6] takes the middle class of Cuba for granted, remarking that Cuba is one of the countries with a large middle class. He defines it by income, education, and similar criteria but admits the absence of common middle-class sentiments or ideology. Smith's position has also been sharply challenged by Gerardo Reichel-Dolmatoff,[7] who takes particular exception to Smith's assertion that the apparent middle class in Colombia is recruited primarily from the upper class. As is typical of most writing on class in Latin America, neither author presents data for his assertions, and so we are confronted with two opposing opinions by men of considerable scholarly ability. Yet if Reichel-Dolmatoff's opinions are examined in detail, he is discovered to support some of Smith's views unawares. Smith, for example, draws much the same line as Nelson regarding views toward manual labor. Reichel-Dolmatoff protests that some upper-class members work on their haciendas; they drive their trucks and "even know how to use the machete." Such exceptions do occur in Latin America, yet the Colombian who may sometimes work on the farm will not carry a handbag across the street in the city. But a truck represents a very large investment, hence is also a symbol of prestige like a horse. As for the machete, it is necessary to know in what particular situation it is used; anyone may use a machete when hunting in the woods or riding cattle range, both "respectable" occupations under certain circumstances.

Reichel-Dolmatoff indicates that the "hard-working" middle class works with the head and not with the hands. He concludes:[8]

> Colombia is not a country dominated by a feudal system exercised by a handful of families, blue-blooded and exclusive, who dominate the illiterate mestizos. Up to a certain point this may have been true two hundred years ago. But at present Colombia is a country whose social, economic and political stability rests upon the firm and old foundation of a middle class which has its roots principally in the rural population, and which constitutes the principal force in the nation in the maintenance of democratic ideals.

The last sentence, in the light of Colombia's history of the past four years, certainly is unrealistic.

Clearly it is necessary at this point to establish a frame of reference for the discussion. I propose to adopt that of my colleague Walter Goldschmidt,[9] who suggests six bases that have been employed for class analysis:

> 1. Defined classes: culturally defined groups, in which classes have the objective reality of cultural recognition, as in the castes of India or the estates of Europe.
> 2. Cultural classes: segments having objectively divergent subcultural patterns of behavior.
> 3. Economic classes: groups having basically differentiable economic activities or differentiable relationship to the instruments of production.
> 4. Political classes: groups having differing degrees of power or authority in the affairs of the community.
> 5. Self-identified classes: groups having a unity based upon self-identification, and ranged in an hierarchical scale of prestige evaluation.
> 6. Participation classes: groups separated on the basis of participation, where social access is readily had between members but is forbidden, inhibited, or limited between groups.

Goldschmidt continues:

> If classes are to represent a system of reality in the organization of behavior, a concordance between the several bases should be formed. We suggest that a true class-organized society is one in which the hierarchy of prestige and status is divisible into groups each with its

> own social, economic, attitudinal and cultural characteristics and each having differential degrees of power in community decisions. Such groups would be socially separate and their members would readily identify. We may say that a society approaches a class system if either (a) the groups are clearly identifiable, but do not differ with respect to all the characteristics noted; or (b) the groups do differ in these characteristics, but are not sharply separated.

The foregoing makes it clear that divergences of opinion in the matter of class reflect the use of different bases for class analysis. Both Raggi Ageo and Reichel-Dolmatoff utilize primarily economic and secondarily political bases for their analyses, while Nelson uses self-identification. Smith uses mainly economic criteria but considers self-identification of primary importance for the organization of behavior and the formation of attitudes. The problems raised here are fundamental in determining whether in a given Latin American country there exists a three-class system in European or United States terms or a surviving two-class system or perhaps some third phenomenon, possible subdivisions of major-class groups being ignored for the moment.

Empirical data are inadequate for a definitive solution of the question. The following discussion emphasizes cultural definition, self-identification, and participation. Partially subjective as the analysis will be, I hope to show (1) that in some instances we are clearly dealing with three-class systems which have no relation to North American and European systems; (2) that feudal attitudes and in some cases feudal class structures persist in many countries; (3) that the term "middle class" may be used in any of its traditional European or North American senses only in those countries where economic and political criteria have become important and where the "middle class" is no longer oriented toward upper-class attitudes and goals.

The term "middle class," indeed, is not common to Latin American vocabularies except among intellectuals and the truly literate, although such terms as "upper class" and "lower class" are common. On the other hand, a host of class terms are in more current use and refer to social realities. *Gente decente, gente de razón, los ricos,* and *la clase dirigente* are more common than *clase alta,* while such terms as *mestizo, ladino, cholo, caboclo, Negro, roto, Indio, indígena, naturales,* and others convey a host of specific and readily identifiable meanings in different countries and cannot be equated with either "lower class" or "working class." In the past and to some degree in the present they represent defined classes of great social importance which can be identified in terms of the criteria of cultural behavior, economic and political activity, self-identification, and participation.

It should be noted that in colonial times the word "caste" was extensively used, and some efforts were made to define castes legally. The word is still used by a number of modern writers, for example, in George Kubler's *The Indian Caste of Peru.*[10] Although the term has some applicability in Peru, in other Indo-mestizo countries such as Mexico there is not one caste but several dozen. In such cases the Indian groups are at the lowest hierarchical level, or parallel with the lowest level of the mestizo culture. The groups are self-identified, organized by village or tribe, and have distinctive cultural, linguistic, and other social attributes, of which perhaps the most important are the existence of independent value structures and an internal prestige system based usually on individual achievement of status positions. These groups will here be called "plural cultures" rather than castes.

A set of diagrams (Tables 1–4) of four somewhat different Latin American societies illustrates the main class groupings and indicates their character. Hierarchical differences exist within each class, crudely represented by the relative vertical positions of the listed occupational groups. The lists are only illustrative and are probably not complete or verifiable. Urban and rural groups must be separated, although in all cases movement between rural and urban environments is relatively free. Horizontal movement between groups is by no means always possible, however.

In summarizing the tables, together with material in such series as the *Materiales para estudio de la clase media,* the following general statements seem possible:

1. Distinctions of significance exist between rural and urban. They are of greater importance for the lower status groups. Free movement between rural and urban is possible in most countries today but was not so free in the past except for those of relatively high status.

2. Barriers to upward mobility are great in all countries, but probably less so in Mexico than elsewhere. In particular, there are fewer obstacles to rising from middle to upper class in Mexico than in most other countries; perhaps the obstacles are greatest in Peru. Elites in the upper class tend to form a harder core of resistance than does the upper class as a whole. Upward mobility is usually easier in the city than in the country. Argentina, Chile, and Uruguay likewise seem to rank high in potentials for vertical mobility.

3. Until better tools for measurement exist, most countries can be best described by a gross three-class system, with each class containing a series of stratified groups and statuses. From the point of view of cultural behavior and self-identification, however, the feudal two-class system persists, despite the growth in most countries of economically intermediate groups. Upper-class values and attitudes toward the lower class and toward manual labor are fully accepted by most of the middle class. The upper and the middle class tend to be more alike, economi-

cally, than the middle and the lower class in some countries; in others, economic position overlaps social division.

4. Ethnic criteria for class assignment are common in the Indo-mestizo countries and in some countries with regional Negro populations, such as Venezuela and Colombia. Countries with large Negro or Negroid populations usually do not employ racial criteria overtly, although the tendency to do so seems to be increasing, for example, in Brazil, as more Negroes manage to emerge from the lower class.

TABLE 1*

BRAZIL

Rural	*Urban*
Uppermost elite tends to define self racially but ideologically opposed to discrimination in economic and political matters	
Landholders turning to industry, banking, commerce. High government officials, heads of church, army, many professional men, declining number of intellectuals	
Managerial, including some former upper-class landholders Middle bureaucracy Professionals, lower church and army officials, teachers, small landholders, storekeepers	Managerial Middle bureaucracy Storekeepers Some professionals and intellectuals Teachers Some service personnel and technicians White-collar workers
— — — — — — — — — —	— — — — — — — — — —
(Increasing breaching of barriers)	
Negro, mulatto, and mestizo with few barriers to marriage; little discrimination	
Small traders Independent small farmers Farm laborers	Petty civil servants Small shopkeepers Artisans Working-class groups
Large groups of extremely impoverished in both rural and urban settings	

* Continuous horizontal lines mean effective barriers to vertical movement; broken lines mean considerable ease of mobility.

TABLE 2

PERU

Rural	Urban
Racially defined elite: wealthy landowners, high government officials, heads of army and church, professional men of proper family, industrialists, heads of large commercial interests, some intellectuals	
(Barriers almost completely impermeable)	
Racially defined *cholo* or mestizo middle class oriented toward upper-class and elite goals:	
Hacienda managers, shopkeepers Small independent landowners Some technical, professional, church, and army personnel	Managerial; middle bureaucracy Storekeepers, some professionals and intellectuals Teachers, middle church and army personnel White-collar workers
Rural *cholos,* often with marked local cultures: Small farmers Farm workers Small-town craftsmen, nonagricultural workers, traders	*Cholos:* Small shopkeepers Working-class groups Artisans Petty civil servants Domestic service Lowest groups, often extremely impoverished
Indians—two main cultural groups locally organized Internal prestige system Independent farm villages: Villages dependent upon haciendas Rural laborers	Indian migrants from rural areas engaged in lowest-paid factory work and forming lowest ranks of army and police

TABLE 3

GUATEMALA

Rural	Urban
Large landholders, often shifting to city; high government officials; high church and army officials	
	Some intellectuals and professionals. Family of great importance

TABLE 3 *(Continued)*

GUATEMALA

Ladinos (mestizos), often impoverished, city-oriented. Landholders, but farmers only by necessity Shopkeepers, traders, local government and army officials Some managerial personnel	Middle bureaucracy Businessmen Some professionals and intellectuals Teachers White-collar workers Lower church and army officials
Indian—plural cultures: Small farmers, often renters Handicraft manufacturers, traders Own internal prestige system	Small laboring class, mainly nonindustrial: Shopkeepers Servants Indians rarely move to city; may emerge into Ladino group by moving to different village

TABLE 4

MEXICO

Rural		*Urban*
Hereditary aristocracy vanishing Few large landowners remain Domination by city businessmen and political leaders		High government officials Industrialists and businessmen Some professionals and intellectuals of wealth and/or family Heads of church and army Top managerial personnel
Storekeepers, bureaucracy, technicians and managers, teachers, lower church and army officials Small landholders		Technicians, middle bureaucracy, some professionals and intellectuals Small businessmen and industrialists Lower church and army officials White-collar workers and teachers Some skilled workers
Indian—plural cultures: Small farmers Subsistence farmers Handicraft workers Rural laborers	Indo-mestizo: Culture similar to Indian but Europe-oriented, mobility easier	Mestizo: Small shopkeepers Petty civil servants Working-class groups regularly employed Domestics

TABLE 4 *(Continued)*

MEXICO

Own internal prestige system Horizontal and vertical mobility possible but not frequent	Mestizo: Small farmers Petty officials Shopkeepers	Impoverished proletariat irregularly employed Indian in city or factory by definition becomes mestizo

5. Indo-mestizo countries present many variations, but all are marked by relatively self-contained plural cultures and societies among the Indians, who have their own internal prestige and status systems. In general the South American countries impose fairly rigid barriers to both horizontal and vertical movement out of Indian societies, although movement to cities occurs. Ecuador is perhaps the least rigid in this respect: movement from Indian cultures to urban middle-class position is difficult but not impossible. Studies are lacking, but there is considerable reason to believe that some very distinctive rural mestizo cultures are also plural societies as rigidly demarcated as are Indian cultures. It may be observed that many rural mestizos in the Andean region wear as distinctive regional or community costumes as do Indians. This is not true of Central America, Colombia, Venezuela, or Mexico. In Guatemala, parallel Indian and mestizo cultures often occupy the same town, but the mestizo (here called "Ladino") is definitely city-oriented. In Mexico, large masses of rural mestizos have substantially the same culture as many Indians but do not form distinctive plural societies, although there is a high degree of localism and regionalism.

6. The only countries where the feudal class system and, more particularly, feudal class attitudes have disappeared to any extent are the Europe-oriented countries and Mexico.

Trends and Conflicts

Traditionally, power and wealth in Latin America lay, as we have seen, with the relatively small, aristocratic upper class. Today, either this class is threatened or its values and composition have been altered. Most significant is the decline in importance of land as the most valued source of wealth through confiscation, forced sale, inability to compete with industrial-farm enterprises, or loss of labor supply to industry. Thus the introduction of the steam sugar-mill has virtually destroyed the landed aristocracy of Baía, Brazil. Land problems are everywhere of prime importance. Confiscation or purchase of large estates has occurred in Mexico and to a lesser extent in Chile and other countries. In Peru, Ecuador, and elsewhere, lack of labor or mismanagement of *latifundios* has resulted in abandonment of estates or purchase by Indian communities to some extent. In most countries, from whatever causes, the old upper class either has been impoverished to some degree or has transferred its capital to urban real estate or industrial and commercial enterprises.

The old upper class usually has held power, but within the class, conflicts have emerged whose roots are often not clear. Thus in Peru the old landholding elite has violently opposed movements arising in the lower and middle classes, yet the real threat to its power lies in industrialization, and this is in considerable part supported by the upper class itself. The present [Odria] government of Peru may be said to have come into power mainly as a reaction of the threatened landed upper class, yet ironically this very elite is still promoting industrialization without recognizing it as the real source of its destruction.

In Peru some industrialists seem to have been admitted to the upper class, although the number who did not have high family position must be few. In other countries, the new industrial and commercial classes are still barred from the upper class and are considered middle class, despite the fact that individuals often have far greater wealth and live in greater luxury than the upper class itself. In other cases, as in Brazil, the wealthiest men in industry and commerce have achieved enough power to admit them to the upper class but have not been accepted by the elite. Only in Mexico does there seem to have been a thorough reorganization of the upper class in terms of power and wealth. While an aristocratic elite still clings to its superiority, except insofar as it has entered newer fields of enterprise, it is on the whole a down-at-the-heels and nostalgic social elite with little influence on national life.

The trends thus far suggested have a bearing on the recurring problems of political stability in Latin America. If it is assumed that political upheavals arise at least in part from stresses within the social order, both the nature of the class system and its openness are of great importance. To the degree that the class system and the changes it undergoes create frustrations, anxieties, and insecurities, they also contribute to political instability and conflict.

Thus, if the upper class is threatened by emerging industrial and commercial classes or if, as in Peru and Colombia, it has outgrown the bases of its wealth, thus forcing its members into less admired economic activities, it becomes a source of instability. Either it resorts to force to retain power, or factions within it will use force to secure a larger share of power and wealth. On the other hand, the newer industrial and commercial groups will generally be oriented toward stability. But insofar as they are hampered or barred from participation in the power structure, they may be sources of instability. A frequently cited illustration is the recurring rebellion of industrial São Paulo against the domination of the older aristocracy of Rio de Janeiro.

Nor does the middle class emerge as a bulwark of political stability in Latin America, even if we accept the conventional view of its presence. Where the middle class is really an impoverished segment of the upper class, as in Colombia, or where it is completely oriented toward upper-class values which it is unable to achieve, then it is a source of instability. Where, on the other hand, the middle class is able to participate in the power structure and where the barriers to the upper class are permeable, as in Chile, the middle class may be oriented toward stability. But the stabilizing effect of the middle class is also related to its attitudes toward upward mobility in the lower classes. Where the middle class is sufficiently permeated with upper-class values to feel itself threatened by improvement of lower-class conditions, then it becomes a repressive and ultimately unsettling force.

The relation of class structures to political and social stability may be investigated by means of the following questions:

1. To what extent are new sources of wealth accorded status? Do wealthy businessmen and industrialists achieve positions in the political power structure, and are they accepted socially in all but the most select social groupings, even though they may not have an upper-class origin? The admission of new elements to the elite is a measure of the permeability of the upper-class barrier, markedly found in Chile and Mexico and to a considerable degree in Argentina and Brazil. Probably a corollary is the degree to which traditional upper-class families shift to business and industry as a basis of wealth, a shift which is notable in Brazil and to some degree in all countries with relatively advanced industrialization.

2*a*. Is the middle class recruited from descendants of upper-class families?

2*b*. Is the middle class recruited from descendants of lower-class families who achieved nonmenial and nonmanual occupations?

2*c*. Are merchants, small industrialists, farmers who cultivate their own land, technicians, and highly skilled workers and artisans of lower-class antecedents who nevertheless achieve a middle-class level of income, education, and living standard regarded as members of that group?

These questions are linked closely. If Question 2*a* is answered in the affirmative, then 2*b* will be relatively in the negative and 2*c* probably not so at all. Such a case would seem to be illustrated by Cuba and Colombia, where the class structure can be analyzed as an extended two-class system. Peru and similar countries would present a special case in which none of the three questions are important (despite the exceptions which can easily be cited), and essentially there is a three-class system defined partly racially and partly by family criteria, with very little permeability of class barriers. Where there is a true three-class system but 2*a* and 2*b* are answered in the affirmative while 2*c* is not, then the orientation of the middle class is toward upper-class standards. To a considerable degree this would be true of Brazil. The extent to which 2*c* is in the affirmative should also be some measure of shifting attitudes toward labor involving manual effort.

3. To what extent is horizontal movement relatively easy? This question is of a somewhat different order, but it is related to the permeability of class barriers. In countries with plural Indian cultures, horizontal movement between Indian societies is negligible and not significant for our purposes. Rather, the question is whether Indians can move into the mestizo or similar classes. In this respect Mexico has perhaps gone farthest, for "Indian" is defined ethnically, not racially, and by definition a person working in a factory, and usually a person living in a city, is "non-Indian," regardless of ethnic or racial origin. Moreover, Indians can move, albeit slowly, into rural mestizo classifications. In Guatemala, an anomalous situation exists, for horizontal movement is often possible for the Indian when he leaves his community; within his community, however, movement into the mestizo (here called "Ladino") group is regarded as a vertical movement and is virtually impossible. In Peru, on the other hand, it is very difficult for an Indian to move into the *cholo* class, although with increasing Indian movement to the cities this situation may change.

In countries with Negro population, horizontal movement through intermarriage, residence shifts, or occupational shifts is usually possible within the lower class. However, as Nelson has shown clearly for Cuba, there is some discrimination even within classes in more prestigeful occupations. Brazil's reputation for liberality toward Negroes rests largely on the fact that most of them are in the lowest class. More recently, with the rise of more Negroes to higher educational and economic status and increasing Negro competition for higher-status jobs, discrimination and antagonism have increased. The absence of a parallel Negro society as in the United States, for example, makes it much more difficult for a Negro in Brazil to become a doctor or a lawyer or to practice successfully if he should secure training than is the case in the United States. Some informed Brazilians declare that since World War II there has been a secret policy that Negro army officers shall not be promoted to higher rank.

Associated with these relationships are varying attitude structures and social evaluations. Or, to put it another way, they afford rough measures of both the openness of the class structure and the degree to which the feudal two-class ideologies persist or have been modified toward something resembling the ideologies characteristic of western European or United States three-class structures. Accessibility to education, the value placed upon it, and its utility as a means of social mobility will vary accordingly.

A brief look at the papers by Seri Bagu on Argentina[11] and those by Julio Vega[12] and Amanda Labarca Hubertson[13] on Chile will perhaps illustrate the points for two countries where the three-class analysis is perhaps the most applicable and where the middle class perhaps most reflects the European and United States models. Basically, all three authors place principal emphasis upon an economic classification; Bagu, for example, describes the middle class as the social group composed of persons who in the productive process carry on only intellectual and bureaucratic functions, or any activity requiring both labor and capital, or only a small capital. Vega characterizes the Chilean middle class as containing almost all the small-to-medium land proprietors, whether they farm their own land or rent; 90 per cent of the professionals; 90 per cent of the university professors; all primary, secondary, and specialized teachers; officials of the armed forces and police; two thirds of the salaried employees; proprietors of all but very small and very large business and industrial enterprises; and persons living off small invested capital.

In terms of the questions formulated above, in both countries, despite a small, often very wealthy, and exclusive elite, a considerable part of the upper class is relatively recent or gets its wealth from commerce and industry. The wealthy middle class has been influential and, especially in Chile, has held most political power in the last thirty years. Relatively few members of the middle class are decayed aristocracy: most have risen through business and industrial activities or, through education, have become employees of government or business. Self-made men of considerable wealth exist. Educational opportunities are fairly widespread, and children of lower-class families in better circumstances can obtain education and entry into the middle class. Note well, however, that in Chile even artisans with small capital and skilled workers, although economically often better off than many of the middle class, are considered lower class regardless of education or living standards. In similar circumstances, the writers under discussion and others view with alarm the proletarization of the middle class through increasing economic pressures or they approve of the narrowing of the gap between classes. That by achieving comparable living standards, education, and value systems artisans or skilled workmen might be included in the middle class is never recognized as a possibility. In other words, there is still no real break in the fundamental distinction between those who work with their hands and those who do not. It is difficult for either North Americans or Latin Americans to realize the depth of the cleavage involved. The middle-class family with two cars and no servants, the banker who washes windows in preparation for his wife's tea party, the professor in overalls wielding a shovel in his garden—all are incomprehensible in Latin America. Unless an individual occupies an impregnable social position, there are certain manual activities which may *never* be engaged in even for recreation, certain implements which must *never* be touched.

While many research problems are implicit in the preceding discussion, the following point should be made explicit—the use of strictly economic or economic and political criteria for class analysis of Latin America is the least fruitful approach.

NOTES

1. "The Quechua in the Colonial World," in Julian Steward, ed., *Handbook of South American Indians,* Bureau of American Ethnology, Bulletin 143, Washington, D.C., 1946, 331–410.
2. "The Middle Class of Panama," in *Materiales para el estudio de la clase media en la América Latina,* Publicaciones de la Oficina de Ciencias Sociales, Unión Panamericana, Washington, D.C., 1950, IV, 38–75.
3. *Rural Mexico,* Chicago, University of Chicago Press, 1948, p. 37.
4. "The Social Class Structure in Cuba," in *Materiales,* II, 45–72.
5. "The Middle Classes in Cuba," in *Materiales,* VI, 1–14.
6. "Contribución al estudio de las clases media en Cuba," in *Materiales,* II, 73–89.
7. "Notas sobre la clase media en Colombia," *Ciencias sociales,* 1952, III, 2–4.
8. *Ibid.,* p. 4.
9. "Social Class in America—a Critical Review," *American Anthropologist,* 1950, LII, 483–498.
10. *The Indian Caste of Peru, 1795 to 1940: A Population Study Based upon Tax Records and Census Reports,* Smithsonian Institution, Institute of Social Anthropology Publication 14, Washington, D.C., 1952.
11. "La clase en la Argentina," in *Materiales,* I, 34–65.
12. "La clase media en Chile," in *Materiales,* III, 60–92.
13. "Apuntes para estudiar la clase media en Chile," in *Materiales,* VI, 68–89.

Toward the Comparative Study of Politicization in Latin America

DANIEL GOLDRICH

The Perception of the Relevance of Government: The Beginning of Politicization

There has been no systematic study of the phenomenon of politicization. Frequently in commentary on contemporary Latin American politics, for example, a high level of politicization throughout these societies is assumed, whereas I believe the matter to be a critically important variable to study in the process of political change.

Logically, a political decision-making process cannot be considered to have begun, nor people to have become involved in an attempt to exercise influence, until they have perceptually entered the political arena. Before people act politically, before they formulate protests or make demands or deliberate policies, they must be at least minimally politicized. I conceive of the politicization process as a continuum ranging from lack of perception of the relevance of government to one's life, through perception of it, to active involvement in politics. This seems obvious, and yet it is tremendously significant. One of the most pro-

This paper is published for the first time in this volume. It is substantially revised from a paper prepared for the Research Seminar on Processes of Community Decision-Making and Change and Their Influence on Education, sponsored by the U.S. Office of Education at the University of Oregon, August, 1963.

foundly revolutionary developments in the culture of a less economically advanced society is the emergence of the perception among tradition-directed or long-subjugated people that government is not, *sub specie aeternitatis*, unchanging and unchangeable, but can be modified and manipulated to meet their needs.

Perhaps the most important agent of initial mass politicization, the bridging of the gap between nonperception and perception of the relevance of government, is revolution. The genesis and development of revolution is imperfectly understood,[1] but it seems clear that there is a variation in the extent of mass involvement during the earlier stages. After a revolution has succeeded, however, new channels of communication and interaction between governors and governed are frequently established. After Castro came to power in Cuba, new revolutionary organizations were created that reached into communities and levels of communities that had never before been "touched" by government. For example, administrators were sent throughout rural Cuba to organize agricultural and fishing cooperatives and state farms. For many of the people affected it was their first experience of government intervention to ameliorate their living conditions. Similarly, early urban measures such as the slashing of rents and the inception of the island's first major low-cost public housing program probably stimulated a widespread perception of the personal relevance of government among the lower classes. Other later measures such as the block internal security system must have operated in the same direction.

The Bolivian Revolution of 1952 has been evaluated in this country largely in terms of how much that government's "inefficiency" is costing the U. S. taxpayer. Its efficiency in politicizing an inert mass of Indians to assume participant roles and egalitarian norms is but dimly comprehended. As Patch has written, "Until the revolution of 1952 they were serfs. Now they vote, send their children to school, participate in political rallies, form unions, and buy Italian accordions."[2]

A similar case is the Guatemalan Revolution of 1944–54. K. H. Silvert has estimated the proportion of "national" Guatemalans as at most 10 per cent of the population, mostly resident in the capital city. But the Revolution initiated a process of politicization in the hinterlands, formerly "politically dead." Parties were organized that extended not only politics but competitive politics into the local community, local election of local officials was established, farm labor unions arose, etc. From all this came a general political awakening, the development of national consciousness, and an incipient sense of individual independence and personal dignity.[3]

A particularly important aspect of this revolution was the politicization of the younger, progressive Indians. After the anti-Communist revolution of Castillo Armas in 1954, which in the countryside quickly became a systematic counterrevolution, a number of these younger, new leaders were shot while a great many others fled.[4] This raised the important theoretical consideration of *depoliticization*. How enduring were the effects of the first revolution? What was the impact of the relatively brief terror on the newly politicized Indians? Has the reestablishment of the conservative oligarchy merely quieted the peasantry, or has the perception of the personal relevance of government actually disappeared?

While it is virtually definitional that repression or suppression can have the effect of deactivating the politically participant, it is much more difficult to imagine conditions under which people change from perception of the relevance of government to nonperception. In other words, politicization in its primary meaning of change from nonperception to perception would at first glance seem to be practically irreversible. And yet this is not at all a safe assumption. The peasant uprising in El Salvador some thirty years ago was met with wholesale massacre, and there has been no such manifestation of politicization by the peasantry since then. Extreme coercion may have deactivated or thoroughly depoliticized, and we do not know which. Furthermore, people who have hoped and waited in vain for governmental action for a long time may become cynical about the capacity of government ever to act as they wish, and such prolonged cynicism could lead to a gradual loss of the perception of the personal relevance of government. This could occur over a long period of time, across generations, or through a gradually changing process of political socialization. It must be remembered that there were a number of Indian revolts against the Spanish during the colonial period, while today it is assumed that the Indians are "traditionally" nonpoliticized.

Those interested in underdeveloped nations have made a cliché of "the revolution of rising expectations," of which an important aspect is the recognition that government can be organized and operated to meet newly recognized needs. Political-cultural revolution, however, of the kind mentioned above, is far from ubiquitous. In fact, what surprises me is its relative infrequency in circumstances that would seem likely to promote it. For example, in the cities of Latin America facilities such as housing, sewage, clinics, schools, electricity, transportation, and even water have been falling catastrophically behind population growth, yet mere politically oriented action, let alone revolution, is exceptional rather than normal among those who are objectively the most deprived. While there has been no systematic attempt to account for this, a number of separate studies made recently do indicate the manner in which certain factors retard politicization among such people as the urban mass of Latin America. A few of these studies will be briefly noted.

In extreme poverty and stress, with a continued inability to ameliorate it, people are more likely to become socially disorganized than impelled into political action as they concentrate on keeping themselves alive.[5] As Eric Hoffer has written of the abjectly poor, "When people toil from sunrise to sunset for a bare living, they nurse no grievances and dream no dreams."[6]

Very rarely, a person in such a state of misery reacts with outrage. A São Paulo *favelada* (a resident of Brazil's urban slums, the *favelas*), Carolina Maria de Jesus, somehow developed a perspective on the life she was forced to lead and wrote a diary which was published in 1960 under the title *Quarto de despejo* (Garbage Room). Frank Bonilla quotes from it as follows:

> Too tired to do her family foraging through the city's trash in search of something to eat or sell . . . [she wrote] "When I am hungry, I want to kill Janio, I want to hang Adhemar and burn Juscelino. Hardship dims the affection of the people for the politicians."[7]

But hers was an isolated protest, and her neighbors thought her diary writing was "putting on airs." When, thanks to the success of her book she moved from the *favela,* they showered her with stones, garbage, and curses.[8] Her perception of her life as affected by government and politicians (if only through their inaction), her awareness that things as they are do not have to be, did not make her a leader among a people not ready for mass political action. In the swelling *favelas* of Rio de Janeiro, where observers have imagined politicization to be high, nearly half the residents interviewed in a recent study saw nothing to be gained through political action, and less than one fifth had discussed politics heatedly with a friend in the previous six months, even though over half of them said that things had gotten worse for them in the last five years.[9] A recent Brazilian opinion survey found only the most rudimentary information or opinion on politics among the rural populace. The potential for politicization seems therefore extremely undeveloped.[10]

Another factor that may retard politicization is the sense of community developed by rural immigrants into urban areas (the rural exodus accounts for much of Latin America's recent and accelerating urban explosion); this phenomenon has been noted in both Mexico and Brazil. Oscar Lewis has found it among rural immigrants in the *vecindades* of Mexico City,[11] Richard Morse mentions the social cohesion that characterized some São Paulo proletarian neighborhoods,[12] and Bonilla writes of his Rio *favela* respondents:

> Despite the conflict, frequent aggression, exploitativeness, and insecurity of personal relationships that according to the accounts of all observers are commonplace in the *favela,* the *favelado* himself feels that he is

> part of a fairly cohesive, solidary group. It is vis-a-vis the world outside the *favela* that he feels bypassed, forgotten, and excluded.[13]

This sense of community seems to provide much security and may well retard any tendency to look to the government for the solution of daily problems.

A similar factor is the extended family and ceremonial kinship relationship. One survey indicates that a typical resident of São Paulo identifies from thirty to 500 relatives, many of whom live in the city.[14] What Morse terms the "continued vitality of the extended family" is also mentioned by Lewis as characteristic of at least some *vecindades*.[15] Other students of urbanization have similarly described the importance of kinship.[16] Since most lower-class Latin Americans have had no direct relationship with their national or local governments, it is not surprising that traditional familial relationships continue to be the major source of personal security, rather than an alien government bureaucracy whose officials are generally neither committed to assistance nor equipped to provide much of it.

In addition to this comforting sense of community and dependence on the family among rural immigrants to urban areas, Victor Alba has remarked the close relationship maintained between such immigrants and their native villages. It functions as a safety valve in times of economic pressure:

> It explains why economic crises, unemployment, etc., have less severe repercussions in Latin America than elsewhere. The worker who loses his job can return to his village without much difficulty.[17]

Some occupational factors that probably retard politicization include the very high proportion of Latin Americans who are engaged in service work and petty commercial activities such as street vending.[18] Such people tend to form an atomized labor force, and their lack of regular contact with others like themselves, plus their exceedingly long working day, probably do very little to generate an orientation toward government and politics.

Nor can it be assumed, either, that industrial employment is the locus of a politicized labor force. Most of the factory workers of Latin America are employed in handicraft types of operations or are otherwise in very small firms.[19] This kind of employment tends to maintain the traditional reliance on the boss as the protector, the *patrón*, once again in lieu of the development of a political orientation, a turning to the political process for protection or amelioration of conditions.

Strategic activities of businessmen and industrialists may also contribute to the relatively low politicization of the working class. Morse notes that São Paulo employers' groups have created social service organizations devoted to

> Resolving workers' domestic and legal problems, broadening their social horizons, giving job training, raising living standards, defending real wages—and, like the church, to subsidizing the education of promising youths to key technical and managerial positions. In its first year [one of these organizations] set up thirty-seven supply posts in São Paulo city which undersold retailers by 30 to 50 per cent and forced general price cuts in staple foods.[20]

These too may act to retard the development of political consciousness among the urban poor, but even more significant than their safety-valve function is the indirect control they exert on the future development of such consciousness. By educating "promising" lower-class youths and giving them relatively prestigious positions, the representatives of "the establishment" in São Paulo may siphon off from each generation the potential leaders of a political movement of the disadvantaged.

This resumé suggests a number of cultural, social, and economic variables that should be investigated in the search for conditions of politicization. For example, the politicization of the following contrasting groups can be compared: slum dwellers integrated into family and community and those who are isolated; new urbanites with recourse to subsistence agriculture in time of economic crisis and those who lack such recourse; people at various levels of poverty (for, as Oscar Lewis demonstrates, the culture of poverty is extremely complex, and the relationship between deprivation and political orientation is almost completely unknown); service workers, petty merchants, handicraft workers, and workers in large manufacturing plants. Furthermore, since many of these variables relate to the process of urbanization, the suggested inquiry should be carried out on a longitudinal or at least quasi-longitudinal basis. Given the relative infrequence of the perception of the personal relevance of government among the Latin American working and lower class, cases of people such as *favela* dwellers or the extremely destitute[21] who *do* exhibit this perception or more advanced states of politicization should be recognized as having great significance for theory building and for understanding the nature of the human response to deprivation, and investigated through deviant-case analysis.

Modes of Politicization

Among the minimally politicized, those who at least perceive the personal relevance of government, there are significant differences based not primarily on the quantity of politicization, but its quality. This qualitative dimension will be termed the mode of politicization. In the following, I will present some modes which seem to occur frequently in Latin America, but also elsewhere, perhaps in varying frequency, and give consideration to the conditions which give rise to the particular mode.

THE DEFENSIVE TYPE

This mode seems characteristic of citizens who are socioeconomically marginal. The defensive approach politics not to make a demand but a counter-demand. In Latin America a common catalyst of this mode of politicization is an abrupt threat to the precarious standard of living of the lower class. One such threat is the austerity program adopted by several Latin American governments in recent years as an effort to control inflation, which control is a prerequisite for getting financial assistance from some international and other foreign lending agencies. "Austerity" has frequently meant wage stabilization and increased taxes on basic consumer goods. Demands by conservative governments for belt-tightening have sometimes been resisted by a congeries of union, student groups, and "the mass" who deny the possibility of further belt-tightening under conditions already at the bare survival level. One such case, for example, contributed to the overthrow of the Velasco Ibarra government in Ecuador late in 1961. The politicization triggered by the announcement of such austerity measures seems to be quite short-lived, however. Demonstrations are made, succeed or fail rapidly and politicization of the "mass" subsides. Other such threats are plans for slum clearance or the uprooting of squatters. Despite the squalor and physical inadequacy of most of the slum areas of the major Latin American cities, they offer a great deal of security to many of their residents. Housing is at the very least inexpensive, and many find that if they build their own shacks they can avoid rent payments; often it is possible to maintain a garden plot or keep animals. Thus the kind of settlement exemplified by the *favela* provides a way station for people coming in from the country (in Lewis' term, the urban peasantry), and allows relative independence in housing for other poor residents of the metropolis. Pearse says:

> The *favela* offered to the in-migrant a means of establishing himself and his family as an unbroken unit in the shortest possible time, and with the least possible outlay, in his own house, in conditions similar and sometimes superior to those of his country home.
>
> . . . .
>
> What is significant, however, and what is overlooked constantly by the city commentators who weep over the *favelas,* is that though the house-type is "rural," the conditions of life which the *favela*-dwellers —by their illegal initiative—have secured for themselves, are rated higher by them in most respects than the conditions prevailing in the rural areas from which the great number of them have come.[22]

As suggested above, the residents of such areas frequently settle on unused land that is privately owned or acquired legally by another owner after the squatter settlement has taken place. In one such situation, squatters reacted to confrontation by the owners with sudden politicization. In a study of Panama City's *barriadas brujas* (literally, witch quarters—the shack settlements which the very poor have thrown up around the city), Gutiérrez describes a people sufficiently aware of their common problem to join together in a common effort to organize associations "to defend what they considered to be their rights." Nevertheless, the squatters' action was apparently aimed entirely at preventing owners of the property from evicting them from their shacks and adjacent lands. It never became either programmatic or oriented toward other political action.[23]

THE MARGIN-ORIENTED

This concerns the desire to arrange a special margin of economic security in one's "normal" occupational relationships. Lewis' documentation of the life of the Mexican urban poor is replete with such phenomena.[24] Similarly, there is the virtually universal "institution" of the petty *mordida*[25] (literally, the bite), in which the agent of the public bureaucracy must be paid a "consideration" to perform his official function, or to perform it in other than a routine, impersonal fashion according to statute or bureaucratic policy.

To the extent to which the poor man or the petty civil servant feels impelled to try to arrange a special margin in his human relationships, a sense of generality is impaired and may affect the whole orientation toward government and politics. If every transaction is special, politics may become a matter of private negotiation between individuals, and there can be no politics of protest, none based on planning, none aimed at a policy. Further, any general policy that threatens the whole carefully constructed system of margin through special relationships is likely to be resisted, even by those whom the policy is designed to benefit.

Margin orientation is probably promoted by the tendency of the Latin American urban poor to hold no regular job but a set of irregular jobs, or to move from job to job, as a "labor nomad."[26] If one fails to identify oneself on the basis of a rather integrated occupational role, then one may well be less likely to develop a stable orientation toward politics based on one's occupational status, a factor that would retard the development of a sense of group or class consciousness and a set of interests related to it. This has been suggested for the urban migrant from Brazil's Northeast, who sees himself as only temporarily a city dweller, a worker only until the nest egg is accumulated that will allow him to return to his rural home.[27] It matters little whether he returns home or not: with this as his orientation he will not develop a set of occupation-based demands on politics. The extent of service occupations in urban Latin America contributes to this kind of margin orientation, for the worker is wholly dependent on intermittent contacts with his patrons. Given the level of wages for the typical petty service, if he fails to develop margins in these relationships, he may well not survive.

IMMEDIATE GRATIFICATION

In the Peruvian presidential election of June, 1962, the Lima vote went neither to the *aprista* Haya de la Torre, Latin America's foremost political ideologist, nor to Fernando Belaúnde, a rising populist ideologue, but to Manuel Odría, a former dictator without a program and without any promise of the capacity to organize Peruvian government to meet ominous problems. Odría was known primarily for the public works created during his previous presidency (1948–56), and otherwise benefited from the coincidental relative prosperity of the country during those years. Since most of the urban population is extremely poor, Odría's victory in Lima suggests that ideology and abstract intellectualized reformism meant less to a large number of economically marginal citizens than tangible products of government such as a stadium or a hospital, such direct benefits as employment under the public works program (even though the program was no part of an attack on basic national problems), or than the belief that "times were good" as a result of X's presidency.

It has been noted by Lewis and others who have dealt with the culture of poverty that under pressure of deprivation slum dwellers have little ability to defer gratification, and exhibit a sense of fatalism and resignation. Thus the *favelados* are reported to respond to political campaigns with hope and relative enthusiasm, because candidates come through the *favelas* distributing food or clothing or money—it is the only time politicians exhibit any interest in these people at all.[28] But except for such infrequent occasions, living is so close to the edge of disaster that an orientation toward the future is not likely to develop. This suggests that when extreme poverty carries with it minimal politicization, the mode is one of immediacy, an alertness only to what is closely related to the needs of the moment. It suggests that the electoral process is unlikely to have meaning for the impoverished because its very nature is gradualist and abstract, and that the poor are unlikely to perceive constitutionalism as a whole as having a relation to their lives.

PERSONALISM-PATERNALISM

Personalism as a mode of politicization means reliance on personal relationships, personal guarantees in politics, rather than formal legal or contractual relationships. This is surely one of the most commonly observed characteristics of Latin American politics, though the extent of the phenomenon in Latin America as compared to the United States or other supposedly more "rational" political systems has never been empirically investigated. Personalism is so institutionalized in Latin America that in those rare instances where broad, relatively coherent programs have been enacted (for example, in Argentina under Perón or in Cuba under Grau San Martín and Prio Socarrás), they have tended to be rendered ineffective by the catastrophic waste associated with personalistic administration, characterized by graft, concessions, *botellas* (positions in the public bureaucracy filled by patronage, for which little or no instrumental work is expected), and the like.[29] The formal legal requirements of the situation tend to fall before the demands of the friend, the family, the group responsible for placing the leader in power.[30]

One type of personalist orientation toward politics is the reliance on the *patrón*.

> The patron, whether he is an estate manager or a political boss . . . , provides protection and special favors in exchange for loyalty and service. This relationship is founded upon mutual trust, not on legally defined obligations; in fact, it normally operates outside of, and to a great extent in conflict with, formally regulated social and economic (and political) structures. The benefits bestowed by the *patrón* are expected but not specifically required of him, and are looked upon as demonstrations of his generosity and magnanimity.[31]

To the extent that the culture stresses personalism and paternalism, one might also expect a focus on the specific in political orientations. These value orientations would seem to discourage a sense of political identification based on common circumstances, one form of which is class consciousness. Personalism and paternalism would likewise seem to discourage political organization based on a common conception of interest. Pearse has used the term "populism" in his description and analysis of the consequences of personalism and paternalism in urban Brazil, specifically to refer to the urban adaptation of the traditional rural dependency relationship between the lower class and the *patrão*.

> Populism does not favor the organization of common interest groups or co-operative groups, and power is usually delegated downwards rather than upwards. . . . Coming from a tradition of rural dependence . . . , the city masses still fit easily into this structure. The ordinary propertyless man feels that he is in no position to improve his lot significantly since he does not know either how to obtain his legal rights or how to operate successfully even in the lower echelons of the power and influence structures.[32]

While personalism seems from this example to characterize the relationship between the leader and a lower class following, this is not necessarily its only or even its major manifestation, for other students of Latin American culture have seen it as a characteristic primarily of the *middle* sectors,[33] and still others as a general characteristic of "traditionals" wherever they may be found in the social structure.[34] In this regard it is interesting to note that among the predominantly middle-class Cuban exiles in the United States, there are an estimated 200 "organizations" committed to particular approaches to the problem of *fidelismo*. The distribution of personalist and paternalist modes of politicization across the social structure is another major question on which research has scarcely begun. While personalism is ordinarily treated as a prohibitive barrier to the development of democracy, a more general conclusion is probably that this mode retards the institutionalization of *any* rules of the political game, so that the society is continuously thrown back on coercion as the only workable means of social control.

RADICAL EFFICACY

This mode of politicization is rarely studied, although it is critically important in political change. The radically efficacious have confidence in their ability to do "great" things, to bring about major changes, to destroy institutions or even societies and remake them in a new image. Radical efficacy seems to have been a salient characteristic of the leadership of the 26th of July movement in its struggle to overthrow the powerful Batista regime, the Castro government in its subsequent efforts to reconstruct national economic and social institutions, the Egyptian leadership in its decision to nationalize the Suez Canal, and the Cárdenas administration in its expropriation of foreign-owned petroleum industries in Mexico. Radical efficacy has come increasingly to occur in association with (or as a catalyst of) radical nationalism and social revolution, but it is also a characteristic of the (non-Black Nationalist) Negro sit-in movement in this country.

Radical efficacy seems to occur among relatively advantaged people who experience frustration. As such, the radically efficacious fall within the category identified by Crane Brinton as the stratum from which revolutionary leadership is recruited.[35] The frustration may relate to drives for wealth, status, power, or self-respect. For example, Paul Kecskemeti has noted of the leaders of the Hungarian Revolution of 1956:

> . . . revolutionary activity originated with groups who were partly privileged and partly frustrated. The writers, who were the first to rebel, had a highly privileged social and economic position, but suffered acutely from the loss of personal integrity and professional satisfaction [after the disclosure of the atrocities committed by the previous government, a government that had been systematically praised and justified

> by these men]; the students who followed suit were nurtured by the regime and could expect to rise into relatively high social brackets, but they resented regimentation and forced indoctrination.[36]

In my own work on the probable development of this mode of politicization among Panamanian students, I found the following pattern among radical nationalists:

> Though similar to the Moderates in socio-economic status and the frequency with which members of their families were involved in politics, the Nationalists' backgrounds were marginal in a few significant aspects which suggest that they may feel relatively deprived in status. Their expectation of success is high, and they seem to have a stronger motivation toward achievement than do the Moderates—radical nationalism may thus have been embraced because the success of the movement would mean the expansion of socio-economic opportunities and because the Nationalists have projected their drive for achievement onto the nation as a whole, particularly since the nation itself has also experienced relative deprivation in status in the international community.[37]

The emergence and growth of radical efficacy is extremely important, because even though the number of activists politicized in this mode is likely to be small, the symbolism they manipulate is highly dramatic and diffuse (nationalism, "Panama for the Panamanians"; equality; renunciation of weakness; the redressing of shame or humiliation, etc.), and they are capable of catalyzing major movements of political change. In Latin America and other colonial or quasi-colonial areas, radical efficacy is most likely to emerge among intellectual and student groups and, given their crucial and continuous role in educational policy making, the education system is likely to be strongly affected by it, as well as serving as the center of radical efficacious politics.[38] In Mexico, for example, the Revolution was both a cause and consequence of radical efficacy, and intellectuals politicized in this mode created the rural cultural missions designed to educate the Indian masses and thus to transform the heterogeneous congeries of traditional subsistence communities into an integrated nation. Although the relative successes and failures of the missions are hard to define and assess, the program has been immensely attractive to groups in other countries who are charged with the task of modernization. It is quite possible that the task of economic development can only be accomplished in areas such as Latin America under political conditions which generate radical efficacy, and make it possible for the radically efficacious to attain power. With the scarcity of resources, the weight of traditions of fatalism and resignation, and the entrenched opposition of the privileged and those who aspire to privilege, only the commitment of the radically efficacious and the symbolism available to them can transform such societies.

Conclusion

Clearly, the foregoing has been an unsystematic presentation of various modes of politicization. Some seem to be mutually exclusive (for example, the defensive and the radical efficacious modes), and some may well occur in a syndrome (immediate gratification, personalism, defensive). One of the next steps toward a systematic typology is an elaboration of the polar opposites of the types already presented (the demanding versus the defensive, acceptance of delayed gratification versus immediate gratification, personalism versus impersonalism, etc.). Following this, the variables implicit in the definitions of these types must be abstracted and the typology systematically reformulated. The latter will, in turn, serve as the basis for a cross-cultural research program.

In summary, then, there are two major dimensions of politicization by which political systems can be compared: the extent of politicization and the mode. For example, a comparison of U.S. and Latin American politics might show the following:

1. Minimal politicization (perception of the personal relevance of government) has been attained by a larger proportion of the citizens of the U.S. than of Latin American nations.

2. Average politicization is higher in the U.S. than in Latin American countries; there are more high participants and fewer low participants in the United States.

3. The frequency of impersonal as compared to personalistic modes of politicization is higher in the United States.

4. Though the distribution of this mode is such that the U.S. is predominantly characterized by impersonal modes and Latin American countries by personalistic ones, the ranges overlap to the point that there are substantial minorities of personalistically oriented citizens in Latin America.

5. Personalism does not vary with extent of politicization in Latin America (equal proportions of the personalistic and impersonalistic are highly politicized), but personalism varies inversely with extent of politicization in the United States.

This hypothetical summation raises some interesting questions. What proportion of its citizens must be politicized in an impersonal mode (oriented toward the rule of law) before we can characterize the polity as operating by that mode? No meaningful answer can yet be given, but it seems quite possible that even where only a relatively few citizens are politicized in this mode, if they monopolize the ranks of the highly politicized the polity may function according to the rule of law and not personalism.[39] Such a finding would accord with Stouffer's finding that the community leadership in the United States tends to value civil liberties more than the less-politicized citizens, and thus the polity functions as a relatively open society even though non-civil libertarian norms predominate in the citizenry.[40]

What factors promote impersonal modes of politicization? It is usually assumed that modern value orientations, including impersonalism and achievement orientation, etc., vary with socioeconomic development. If this is so, Argentina should exhibit a higher frequency of such modes than less economically developed Latin American countries. If this proves not to be true for Argentina[41] and yet the relationship seems generally to hold, Argentina should be analyzed as a deviant case. Why did the rule-of-law orientation fail to develop widely in its context of socioeconomic development? What special conditions account for the deviation, and what does this tell us about the general relationship? Is it possible that the impersonalistic mode did increase with economic development in nineteenth-century Argentina, but that the failure to integrate the nation politically and socially has since led to the rise of personalistic modes?

Under what conditions are personalistic modes transmuted into impersonalistic ones? Natural experimental situations abound in Latin America for this sort of inquiry. For example, the Dominican Republic changed temporarily from a situation of oligarchical regime and personalistic elite power structure to a much more democratic regime, a competitive leadership, and much greater mass participation in politics. It would have been a theoretically rather straightforward, simple endeavor to determine through survey methods the distribution of modes of politicization toward the beginning of this change, and to make new measurements after a period under the new system. Thus one might begin to analyze the effect of the change in the leadership's modes of politicization on the modes of the population-at-large.

What is the effect of class origin on the politicization of Latin American students? Where in the student body of the secondary schools and universities do we find the greatest incidence of impersonal modes of politicization? Does this mode characterize the upwardly mobile student of working-class origin, or the more established middle-class youth? This is critically important. If those who attain upward mobility are completely self-oriented and model themselves after the traditionally privileged, then they will exert no pressure toward reformation of the social system on a universalistic-achievement basis. If they do not reject their conditions of origin, they may exert some pressure for reform. What difference in this regard results from training in a classical curriculum as opposed to a more vocationally oriented one?

What happens to the defensively politicized as government changes from an emphasis on maintenance of its traditional scope (the provision of basic services to the upper social strata and control of the lower) to a focus on development through raising the general level of living? Does the government's definition of the situation of the impoverished as a state of need and its subsequent meeting of those needs lead the defensive-minded to perceive more and more needs in relation to government and produce ever-increasing demands? Does this lead to increasing support for the system or to increasing dissatisfaction, as the perception of needs outruns the capacity of the government to fulfill them?

What is the incidence of the mode of radical efficacy among the youth of the Latin American countries? Are there substantial numbers of equally highly politicized young people who exhibit other modes —for example policy orientation but not radical efficacy? What ideologies are found in association with radical efficacy? Are the radically efficacious neutralized by differences in goals, means? Does acceptance of the use of violence increase or decrease with time as the radically efficacious become increasingly frustrated? (Though the answer seems obvious, it is apparently not so simple. The long-frustrated grew increasingly violent in Algeria, but the *apristas* in Peru grew increasingly moderate. Thus other explanatory variables must be introduced.[42])

These are a few of the crucial questions in the comparative study of political systems, economic development, and cultural modernization that can be investigated through the use of the concept of politicization.

NOTES

1. See my "Toward an Estimate of the Probability of Social Revolutions in Latin America: Some Orienting Concepts and a Case Study," *The Centennial Review*, 1962, VI, 394–408.

2. Richard W. Patch, *A Note on Bolivia and Peru*, American Universities Field Staff Report, April, 1962, pp. 26–27.

3. This summary of changes is taken from John Gillin and K. H. Silvert, "Ambiguities in Guatemala," *Foreign Affairs*, 1956, XXXIV, 469–482. See also Richard N. Adams, ed., *Political Changes in Guatemalan Indian Communities*, New Orleans, Middle American Research Institute, Tulane University, 1957, and Stokes Newbold, "Receptivity to Communist Fomented Agitation in Rural Guatemala," *Economic Development and Cultural Change*, 1957, V, 361.

4. Gillin and Silvert, *op. cit.*, p. 447.

5. See the review of studies of reaction to extreme hunger, poverty, and

barbarism in James C. Davies, "Toward a Theory of Revolution," *American Sociological Review*, 1962, XXVII, 7.

6. *The True Believer*, New York, New American Library, 1958, p. 33.

7. *Rio's Favelas: The Rural Slum within the City*, American Universities Field Staff Report, August, 1961, p. 6. The three politicians named are the then-president Quadros, his predecessor in office, and an unsuccessful 1960 presidential candidate.

8. Carolina Maria de Jesus, *Child of the Dark* (translated from *Quarto de despejo* by David St. Clair), New York, New American Library, 1963, p. 14.

9. Bonilla, *op. cit.*

10. Lloyd A. Free, *Some International Implications of the Political Psychology of Brazilians*, Princeton, Institute for International Social Research, 1961, pp. 34, 48.

11. *Five Families*, New York, Science Editions, Inc., 1962, p. 63.

12. See Morse's *From Community to Metropolis: A Biography of São Paulo, Brazil*, Gainesville, University of Florida Press, 1958, p. 224.

13. *Op. cit.*, p. 12.

14. Emilio Willems, "The Structure of the Brazilian Family," *Social Forces*, 1953, XXXI, 343.

15. Lewis, *op. cit.*

16. See Gino Germani, "Inquiry into the Social Effects of Urbanization in a Working-Class Sector of Greater Buenos Aires," and Andrew Pearse, "Some Characteristics of Urbanization in the City of Rio de Janeiro," in Philip M. Hauser, ed., *Urbanization in Latin Amerca*, New York, Columbia University Press, 1961.

17. "The Latin American Style and the New Social Forces," in A. O. Hirschman, ed., *Latin American Issues: Essays and Comments*, New York, The Twentieth Century Fund, 1961, pp. 46–47. J. R. Brandão Lopes notes the same phenomenon among São Paulo factory workers. See his "Aspects of the Adjustment of Rural Migrants to Urban-Industrial Conditions in São Paulo, Brazil," in Hauser, *op. cit.*, p. 241.

18. See Harley L. Browning, "Recent Trends in Latin American Urbanization," *The Annals of the American Academy of Political and Social Science*, 1958, CCCXVI, 117.

19. Secretariat, Economic Commission for Latin America, "Creation of Employment Opportunities in Relation to Labor Supply," in Hauser, *op. cit.*, p. 120.

20. Morse, *op. cit.*, p. 213. For a description of the operation of these organizations throughout Brazil, see R. J. Alexander, *Labor Relations in Argentina, Brazil, and Chile*, New York, McGraw-Hill, 1962, pp. 104–113.

21. Examples of such groups in rural communities who have exhibited politicization are Francisco Julião's peasant leagues in northeast Brazil and some of the *paracaidistas* (literally, parachutists) in Mexico, peasants who have reacted to land hunger and abysmal poverty by moving onto others' estates and working them as their own.

22. Pearse, *op. cit.*, pp. 195–196.

23. Samuel A. Gutiérrez, *El problema de las "barriadas brujas" en la ciudad de Panamá*, Panama, Imprenta Panamá, 1961, p. 10.

24. See for example the bicycle business incident, pp. 141–142, the police's exaction from street vendors, p. 153, and Sanchez's "special arrangements" with food dealers, p. 286, Lewis, *op. cit.*

25. The *mordida* is not, of course, always petty. See the comments on it of Nathan Whetten in his *Rural Mexico*, Chicago, University of Chicago Press, 1948, pp. 545–554.

26. Morse, *op. cit.*, p. 232.

27. Brandão Lopes, *op. cit.*, pp. 236–242.

28. Carolina Maria de Jesus, *op. cit.*, *passim*.

29. This is not to suggest that all "corruption" is dysfunctional to the institutionalization of rationality in a society or polity. Two significant exceptions must be noted. To bring order out of the anarchy of the Mexican Revolution, President Alvaro Obregón had to quell the violent and unpredictable sorties engaged in by the myriads of self-styled "generals" who had arisen during the revolutionary decade of 1910–20. Obregón "slyly took all of them into the regular army and put them all on the payroll, saying that 'if a man calls himself a general, he must be one' . . ." Frank Tannenbaum, *Mexico: The Struggle for Peace and Bread*, New York, Knopf, 1950, p. 63. His liberal use of bribery dulled the clamor of any opponent who caused him much uneasiness. "To him was attributed the saying, 'No Mexican general can withstand a cannonball of 50,000 pesos.' " Howard F. Cline, *The United States and Mexico*, Cambridge, Harvard University Press, 1953, p. 196. In Uruguay, beginning in the last quarter of the nineteenth century an accommodation was reached between the dominant Colorado party and the minority, feudal-landlord-dominated Blanco party, that was based on bribery. "The precedent was thus set for a series of later agreements by which offices and money for the Blanco minority provided insurance against revolution. The great Blanco landowners were satisfied to control their own districts, and the device of bribery, to give it a blunt name, was a less costly solution for party rivalry than was civil war." Russell H. Fitzgibbon, *Uruguay: Portrait of a Democracy*, New Brunswick, Rutgers University Press, 1954, p. 23.

30. See the insightful analysis of the precedence of personalistic considerations over "efficiency" and rule of law, in Frank Tannenbaum, *Ten Keys to Latin America*, New York, Knopf, 1962, pp. 118–123.

31. Wyatt MacGaffey and Clifford R. Barnett, *Cuba*, New Haven, HRAF Press, 1962, p. 97.

32. Pearse, *op. cit.*, p. 202.

33. See for example, John Gillin, "Some Signposts for Policy," in Richard N. Adams *et al.*, *Social Change in Latin America Today*, New York, Harper, 1960, esp. pp. 28–33.

34. See the forthcoming article by Kalman H. Silvert, "National Values, Development, and Leaders and Followers."

35. *The Anatomy of Revolution*, New York, Vintage Books, 1957.

36. *The Unexpected Revolution: Social Forces in the Hungarian Uprising*, Stanford, Stanford University Press, 1961, p. 117.

37. *Radical Nationalism: The Political Orientations of Panamanian Law Students,* East Lansing, Bureau of Social and Political Research, 1962, pp. 19–20.

38. The role of Negro college students in the southern sit-ins fits this framework closely. See Ruth Searles and J. Allen Williams, Jr., "Negro College Students' Participation in Sit-ins," *Social Forces,* 1962, XL, 215–220.

39. A parallel problem in (Parsonian) social system analysis has been treated by Frank C. Nall, II. See his "Role Expectation: A Cross-cultural Study," *Rural Sociology,* 1962, XXVII, 41.

40. See Samuel Stouffer, *Communism, Conformity, and Civil Liberties,* New York, Doubleday, 1955.

41. See Silvert's "The Costs of Anti-Nationalism: Argentina," *Expectant Peoples: Nationalism and Development,* New York, Random House, 1963, pp. 347–372.

42. For an exploration into the psychology and various modes of rebellion, see Brian Crozier, *The Rebels: A Study of Post-War Insurrections,* Boston, Beacon Press, 1960.

Brazilian Careers and Social Structure: A Case History and Model

ANTHONY LEEDS

I

The research reported here is interesting not only for the data, which are novel and have a certain intrinsic fascination, but also because they confirm what was already suspected from theoretical reasoning and a few dissociated observations. I had in fact already "described" my field results before I went to the field. It will be of interest to review briefly how this came about and consider its broader implications later.

I have for some time been looking for a typology of state-organized societies which would be based on a synoptic view of the function, total structure, and trajectory of the societies rather than, as in certain previ-

This paper, a slightly shortened version of a paper published in the *American Anthropologist,* 1964, LXVI, 1321–1347, was prepared for this volume. The field work on which it is based was supported, for the writer, by the Pan American Union, Department of Social Affairs, and for his two colleagues and certain special costs by the Instituto Nacional de Estudos Pedagógicos of Brazil. The work would have been impossible without the support of Dr. Anisio Teixeira of I.N.E.P. and the Social Affairs Department, P.A.U.; without the collaboration of my two co-workers, Prof. Carolina Martuscelli Bori, Chairman, Department of Psychology, Faculdade de Filosofía, Rio Claro (São Paulo) and Prof. Nilce Mejias of the same department, and without the extensive aid and cooperation of various indispensable persons in the several cities we visited. The present version is considerably abbreviated from the presentation read before the Anthropological Society of Washington, D.C., October 16, 1962.

ous typologies, on one or a few traits or symptoms (cf. Steward 1949; Bennett, ed. 1948; Meggers, *et al.* 1956). The aim of such a typology is to permit comparisons for inquiry into regularities of developmental sequences for search for general laws of sociocultural development. Examining only unique cases prohibits generalizing from processes or mechanisms described for that case and excludes prediction.

The ideal types of state-organized societies characterize the later phases of cultural evolution, at least until the very recent present. I call these the "static-agrarian society" and "the expansive-industrial society."[1] The former is represented by such cases as Feudal Europe, pre-conquest India, the great oriental despotisms, several Near Eastern countries, possibly Haiti, and so on; the latter by today's Germany, U.S.S.R., U.S.A., England, and the like. Preceding the static-agrarian type of society is to be found the "expansive-agrarian society," all of whose examples, such as the early Mesopotamian empires, are extinct. One may hypothesize that a "static-industrial" type of society will follow the presently encountered expansive-industrial ones and one may attempt to delineate characteristics of such societies and the world in which they will be predominant (cf. Guardini 1956).

Briefly, the static-agrarian society may be described as deriving all of its fundamental resources and wealth from, and organizing its basic allocations of labor, technical equipment, and so forth, around, agriculture. Consequently, all major social features—the division of labor, management and supervision, community structure, communications, the social structure of warfare and power, the state itself—are shaped by the basic broad agrarian technology. The crops produced constitute the sources of major wealth and power.

With the given technology, agrarian and communicational, the social order is necessarily markedly structured around localities and localized communities. Therefore, face-to-face, kin, pseudo-kin, and other personal ties, often highly ritualized, appear as major organizational mechanisms of the total society.

The expansive industrial society derives its fundamental resources and wealth from and organizes all its basic allocations around industry. In the early stages of such societies, agriculture becomes subordinate to industry, economically, politically, and ideologically, and, later, itself becomes industrialized in technology and organization. All major social features are shaped by the basic technological relationships to the diverse resources necessary for industrial production, among which crops are important as non-food matériel. The fundamental ecological pattern is multiregional, tending toward global, and consequently, the societies tend to be exocentric, politically and economically; to maximize trans-local relationships at the expense of locality and community relationships; and to operate through highly organized supra-local institutions and associations. Without such necessary ties, the production-consumption system would not operate.

Maximizing trans- and supra-local institutions and associations causes these societies to expand politically and economically—the so-called growth-after-"take-off" pattern (cf. Rostow, 1960). In expansion, they display characteristic institutions of policy such as colonialism, foreign investment, foreign aid, creation of common markets, and the like.

Historically, the pristine appearance of the expansive-industrial society is an evolutionary outgrowth, through various phases, of Western feudalism. Once the pristine development has occurred, all sorts of juxtapositions with earlier societal forms may occur in acculturation situations. Thus, well or partly developed expansive-industrial societies may find themselves in varying kinds of acculturational contact with static-agrarian societies at various stages of development or with early post-static agrarian phases brought about by independent evolution.

We may, from these remarks, consider several hypotheses.[2] First, where cultures of these distinctive types are in long-term and vigorous structural contact, institutions of both will be found operating in some characteristic interlocking network. One should expect to find characteristic expansive-industrial organizational features linked with typical static-agrarian ones. One would expect to find those social and contractual-status[3] entities of industrial organization functionally related to the technology penetrating into the static-agrarian society, to be linked by characteristic "feudal" modes of interaction such as blood and affinal kin; ritual kin; friendship; man–patron, master–apprentice, *guru*–student relationships; and a variety of nonformalized interpersonal face-to-face contacts, either qualitatively or quantitatively different from the relationships found in industrial society. Examples of introduced entities include corporations, agencies, syndicates, managerial systems, vocational and professional schools, etc.

A second hypothesis relates to the transformational expansion of socioeconomic opportunities. Where two (or more) large, complex cultures, respectively at earlier and later stages of evolution, are interposed, a rapid and continuous multiplication of new economic sectors, occupations, and statuses occurs in the less-evolved societies, such as most so-called underdeveloped countries today. It follows that, in such conditions, one would expect a continual shortage of personnel for filling the emerging positions of the expanding opportunity structure, because training institutions would be absent or inadequate. Various solutions to this problem may be hypothesized:

1. The importation of personnel
2. The internal creation of new personnel more or less at haphazard, especially by self-instruction, or "autodidactism," until training is curricularized

3. The multiplication of positions held by any given individual

Personnel importation is intrinsically limited by the supply and by the cost of importation, though it may accommodate a modicum of new positions. This solution is temporary and unreliable, since it is not institutionally built into the social system itself. Most frequently, one would expect either the filling of positions by self-trained or partially self-trained persons, or the filling of a number of often diverse positions by single individuals—frequently autodidacts.

As a corollary, one would expect multiple position holding and autodidactism to be complementary, since a man in position A, in some organization, seeing an available new position B, for which no candidate exists, may train himself to fill position B. Given the nature of social links mentioned in the first hypothesis, it is to his interest to maintain connections with the first organization through his incumbency in position A, while establishing new connections through position B. Furthermore, there may actually be pressures not to leave A, since other incumbents are unavailable for that position. A second corollary is that entering into position A may be seen as a preliminary for entry into position B, or may prepare such a connection even where it is not foreseen. That is, A may serve as the springboard for leaping to B. Entry into position A may even involve the invention and creation of position A as a prelude to leaping into B.

The pilot research carried out in Brazil during June and July of 1962 was intended not only to confirm the existence of institutions described in the hypotheses, but also to get case histories to illustrate how these institutions function—how organization operates.

II

We may now turn to the research itself. During a fortnight's stay in Brazil in 1961, repeated use of the word *autodidato* began to register in my awareness, suggesting that the autodidact was an important phenomenon, as it turned out to be in other Latin American countries. It appears to be a function of the absence of what we may call curricularized training and careers so characteristic of advanced expansive-industrial societies as routes into statuses (in the general sociological sense)[4] and careers.

In asking about the Brazilian autodidact and his genesis, the phenomenon of multiple job holding, which permeates the entire Brazilian society and for certain types of which Brazilians have a word, *cabide de emprego,*[5] or "employment hanger," began to assume more and more theoretical importance.

Intuitively, the two phenomena appeared to be significantly linked, and both related to an acculturationally induced, rapidly expanding opportunity structure. In such a condition, there tend to be more positions than there are candidates. Both the autodidact and the *cabide* phenomena appeared to be functions of this situation, highly adapted to it, and of great use in the subtler operations of the society, despite many moralizing statements, especially about the *cabide* and its abuses as a system of operation.

On hypothesis, the *cabide* is a social link in a society in rapid transition from a characteristic static agrarian to a characteristic, fully developed expansive-industrial condition. As we have remarked, in the former, the links of status (in Maine's sense), such as those of kinship, pseudo-kinship (*compadresco*, vassalage), and a variety of personalized ties, are standardized, while in the latter, links of a contractual kind predominate.

In the intermediate society, where contractual links have not yet developed or become organized, the *cabide* serves both status and contractual ends, combining essential features of each in single individuals, who, in effect, maintain informal and contractual relations with themselves in different positions.

Since hypothetically, the *cabide* appears to be a major social link, the question arises as to how the *cabide* gets to be one and how, when he becomes one, he operates to tie together various organized entities in Brazilian society; entities such as bureaucratic agencies, new bits of universities, managerial structures, public services, etc., largely borrowed from the highly industrialized societies. It was to reject or confirm the hypotheses and to answer this question that the research was undertaken.

Since, however, neither the organization nor the interrelationships of the community recognized situses of the society such as the bureaucracy, the military, the Church, the business world, etc., have been adequately described for Brazil, it was necessary to develop some sort of operating model against which to assess the activities of the autodidact and the *cabide*. Teixeira's model (1962, and conversations) was useful for this. The model (cf. Fig. 1) *structurally* was compatible, by its very disjointedness, with the *cabide* phenomenon. I conceived of the *cabides*, at any one moment, as linking these oligarchies,[6] providing their internal organization, and generally weaving a network among the various above-mentioned situses of the society. At the same time, they provide the social nodes whose complex interconnections create the division between what, for convenience, we may call the "classes" and the "masses."

Here, we are chiefly concerned with the internal structure and dynamics of the classes, and more specifically with the entry into, and operations of, the higher ranks within the classes. The masses are sufficiently separate from the classes so that their internal organization

FIGURE 1

TEIXEIRA'S MODEL OF THE BRAZILIAN POWER STRUCTURE: WITH REFERENCE TO POLITICAL PRESSURE GROUPS

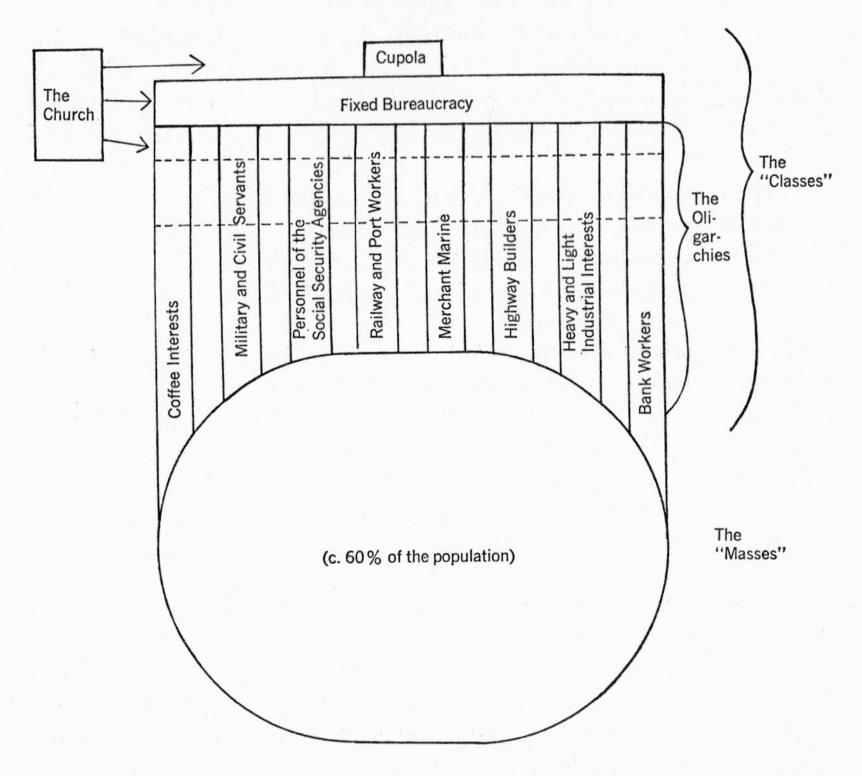

N.B. It may be noted that each column represents a pressure group or oligarchy which is described as operating on the cupola above it. It should also be noted that the *individuals, qua* individuals, who compose the oligarchies are not necessarily in the least at comparable income, prestige, or power levels: these common stratification criteria are social-structurally irrelevant here. Dotted lines represent "strata" levels within the oligarchies.

and dynamics, for the present, are irrelevant to the description of the classes. They require a separate description.[7]

III

Since the general hypotheses stated that the connections among organizations, the links among oligarchies, and the inner organization of the classes are maintained by various kinds of personal connections, and also that one would expect movement from position to position and the holding of many positions by a single incumbent, it followed that the most incisive way to discover the intimate workings of the system was to trace the histories of individuals as they moved through their careers, establishing connections and moving from organized entity to organized entity. Consequently, the primary research technique consisted of interviews with selected informants having *cabide,* and often autodidact, characteristics and representing all the major situses and oligarchies.

Several representatives from each generation were to show the increase in curricularization in any situs once such a situs has become established.

Third, given the relatively great autonomy of Brazilian provinces and states in many significant matters and their ecological, economic, and historical variety, it follows that their social structures, in themselves and as contexts for careers, would differ considerably. In fact, they might be ordered on a developmental scale so as to give a spatial representation of the development of Brazilian social organization, while careers studied in a selection of such states would reflect this developmental ordering by a corresponding increase in curricularization.

We chose the cities of São Paulo, Rio, Belo Horizonte, Recife, and Salvador as purportedly representing a series of states decreasingly developed in an industrial, financial, and political sense, or, conversely, increasingly archaic in behaviors, customs, and ideologies. We also included Brasília in our sample, since as the seat of national power, no Brazilian reality can be understood without a searching look at the *cúpola.*

In each city, we made contact with at least one, and generally more, well-informed citizens of some prominence who were prevailed upon to give us lists of the important local *cabides* with as much information as possible about each as regarded his connections. Lists of *cabides* gotten from two or more independent sources were always in substantial agreement. Thus we were able to get for each a kind of thumbnail sketch of his career and his "social genealogy." By "social genealogy" I mean a mapping of his personal connections not only through kin but also through friendships, ties of mutual obligation, and so on—a web of non-kin quite analogous to the web of kinship known from the standard ethnographic genealogy.

Whenever possible we tried to get a personal, or at least a written, introduction or to have appointments made by intermediaries who knew both us and the informant. With such contacts, cooperation never failed. Where, however, we had to present ourselves, we were often turned aside. The authority of personal introductions and of intermediaries was one of the best evidences of the significance of personal ties in Brazilian society, since it was strong enough to open doors leading to considerable intimacy even among utter strangers.

I initiated each interview by explaining what we were trying to discover and asking for the informant's cooperation. At some point in this introductory exchange, the informant invariably introduced some aspect of his own experience. We used this as an entry to move into the entire life history. An ideal interview consisted of several sessions, separated by a few days to give us time to review our notes and to formulate further questions. Some interviews had to be done in a single session. These are invariably full of lacunae.

The research team, consisting of two Brazilian psychologists and myself, was able in the six weeks to gather fifteen full interviews, several shorter ones, and one or two quite detailed career reports about certain persons from their acquaintances. Wherever possible, we tried to check respondents' data with reports from other informants who knew them and from whom we also usually got substantial additional data.

Three other sources of data provided a check on each other and on the interviews. I systematically clipped the newspapers, first, for data relating to the oligarchies and social spheres and, second, for data on careers. Unwittingly, the newspapers were useful sources for career material: career stories are very often published in most Brazilian papers.

Second, we sought informants who appeared well acquainted with the local economic, social, and political organization and the incumbent personnel. From these persons, we tried to get as much information about the local social operations as possible through cases and through reports on the behavior of the personnel concerned. This sort of information often turned out to be very rich indeed, since, for reasons to be explained below, so many of the operations become known throughout the upper circles despite their ostensible privacy—a privacy which is, in fact, always potentially, and purposively, public.

The third source of information was published material, such as studies in Brazilian politico-economic organizations; the Congressional *Diário Oficial*; analyses of bureaucratic organizations; of studies of electoral behavior; books with ulterior motives such as Niemeyer's eulogy of Jucelino Kubitschek written under guise of discussing his experiences in Brasília (1961), and magazines whose feature articles are paid for by interest groups.

IV

I present only a synopsis of our findings and discuss their implications; fuller presentation of the data must await later publication.

First, the concept and word "*cabide*" occur only in informal communication. In the course of the research, moreover, I discovered that there was a whole language, also existing only in informal communication, of the career and its structural aspects. The career and the *cabide*, however, were not the only structural units to be described in the informal discourse, familiar to everyone. I also "discovered" the *panelinha* ("little saucepan"), whose relation to careers and *cabides* no one has noted previously. For the moment, the *panelinha* may be defined as a relatively closed, completely informal primary group, held together in common interest by personal ties and including a roster of all key socio-politico-economic positions.

The fact that these social structural units which are so vital in Brazil are known only in informal discourse is itself a reflection of the lack of curricularization and formalization of the social fabric of Brazilian society. Without knowing this informal organization, one cannot understand how Brazil functions, economically or politically.[8]

Schematically, the career consists of a continual branching out into new activities—sometimes multiplications of old ones, sometimes in new situses. The main problem is to establish the first step, to create a *trampolim* or springboard, as they say. The variety of techniques for this is numerous and sometimes used singly or in combination. I mention only a few, such as notable activity in university student associations, especially in the law schools; flamboyantly joining Communist or Fascist groups; making public stands in favor of policies not in favor with the entrenched powers; marrying rich girls; being helped by one's own or one's spouse's family; being helped by one's godparents; being helped by a *pistolão* ("a friend in the right place or position to give a hand"); journalism; making a name in sports; entering into politics in lower political positions; entering into a small bureaucratic office from which upward and outward ties can be established.

The significant thing about each of these connections, as the careerist ideal-typically uses them, is that none of them is intrinsic to the career's end as such, but rather to the creation of a *nome* ("name"), the beginning of *uma promocão* ("a self-promotion"), the eliciting of *projecão* ("a presence growing in time").

As a rule, many such steps to new connections are achieved through immediate consanguineal or affinal kin connections. Plainly, large families are highly functional under such conditions and are, indeed, universally operative among the Brazilian, and the Latin American, "classes." Any one of a multitude of relatives may be in a status from which he can either provide a position for his kin-client or can persuade others, through networks of mutual obligation, to provide such positions or helping hands. The most immediate place for this sort of help, for example, is the family firm in which the parent provides loci for the early career-operations of his sons, in fact, more or less sets forth the major outlines of the career at its outset. The connections may be established through less immediate, connecting kin with nepotistic relatives of more distant degrees. The most characteristic linking relatives are parents and spouses, usually wives, the patron relative being, then, mainly an uncle or father-in-law and sometimes, by extension, a cousin. Such relationships figured in a number of our cases from quite varied fields, e.g., a politician, an industrialist-business man, a politician-real estate man, and an educator.

Still wider kin connections may be called upon occasionally, but these do not generally figure as major ties in the career trajectory. Nevertheless, even distant kin may provide a needed link, may help open a door, and in any case constitute a basis for immediate entering into relationship which is not otherwise available. Hence the importance of mapping out genealogical ties as quickly as possible and wherever practicable. A Brazilian, arriving in a community new to him, with utmost speed acquires an intricate mental map of all the significant personages of the town, both kin and non-kin, who may number into the scores or hundreds, as well as of their significant relatives in other localities. By this mapping, he has also explored for points at which he himself might be connected either by ties of consanguinity, affinity, or friendship with persons on the "genealogical" map. Kin and non-kin connecting points provide steps to advance interests or establish new relationships.

The initial moves of the career must be made known in the right places, since the young careerist may be called on to support, assist, or form alliances with others of his own age or more advanced in their careers than he. Letting the moves be known gives information about the young careerist's capacities and his connections. But the divulgations cannot be too open, because, first, one wants to have a selective response, and, second, some of the dealings are perhaps a bit shady. In short, from the beginning of the career on, there is a constant emission of cues which are intended to convey information about the state of a man's career—that is, about his positions, hence the range of his connections, the kinds of influence he possesses, the probable kinds of deals he can carry out, and also the people who can be reached through him.

It is my conviction, confirmed by the extraordinary ability, intelligence, and variegated activities of most of our informants who were not selected on these criteria, that in this whole process there is an intense selection for those persons with keener perceptions, with sharper abilities to see more meanings behind the cues, and with the energy and drive to follow up and use the information so acquired.

The mechanisms for cue emission are highly institutionalized, albeit largely informal. Perhaps the most important is journalism. The variety of techniques involved is enormous. The rector of the University of X keeps a stable of reporters in part-time employ. Through them, he can keep a daily diet of magnificent rectorship before the public, especially the politicos with whom he has extensive dealings. Most persons of considerable position can publish in a newspaper by sending in their contributions. They can contact reporters who, they know, will publish statements for or about them. They can perform some public act, a reporter's presence having been arranged. Relations of reciprocal obligation and dependence between a careerist and a reporter are not infrequent, since the reporter, too, may be advancing in his *own* career by the contact.

The newspapers present an extraordinary variety of contexts of cue emission: notices from municipalities in the interior, including the most wretched; society columns; business facts columns; the political columns; private ads. All list connections. All are suggesting new connections or advertising the potentialities and willingness of their writers or the persons written about to make new ties. Significantly, almost every career we studied showed some major connection with a newspaper. Similarly, in most, some major connection with political life or with public office provided a key. Clearly, journalism and public life are central institutions in Brazilian society and to individual Brazilians of the classes.

The *futing* ("promenading [with one's ears open]") is another technique important to information flow and making connections. The *futing* provides the opportunity for exploratory meetings which occur at coffee houses, in bookstore doorways, etc., and are cast in informal conversations about the city's social scene in such a way as covertly to emit opinions and to show knowledge and connection.

Today, TV and radio are also providing channels for cue transmission for that small portion of the personnel of the society which has access to them.

Gossip is another vital mechanism. Brazilians *listen* to gossip and store it up, in contrast to Americans whose main purpose is to project into it, pass it on, and then forget it. One case is reported of a Brazilian who even keeps a card file of gossip items and other information on a large number of people in public and private life.

Meeting in social clubs also provides a means of distributing cues which is of special significance because of its exclusiveness. The circle within which cues are to be disseminated is sharply defined and restricted.

V

The main function of cue transmission and manipulation is the maintenance of boundaries between mutually exclusive informal groupings of persons and the arrogating of prerogatives and rewards to some of these groups while denying them to others. One may look at the entire communications system as a means of diffusing only certain kinds of information in certain codings to only certain categories of people. Awareness of the codes and of the relevant kinds of information is taught by those who know them to their congeners and successors. Teaching takes place primarily in the family circle, but also in the socially proper non-kin contacts among like-minded families, as in the social clubs, cliques, and groups of friends. Access to the information which is carried in newspapers and magazines, on radio and TV, and in coffee-house gossip requires a certain minimum of resources on the part of participants. They must have been able to become literate. They must be able to buy the newspapers consistently or own a radio or TV if it is to be of continuing use. They must be able to visit the coffee shops, and so on.

Total exclusion from, or even a merely partial and highly sporadic access to, the information transmitted by these agencies renders the personnel involved virtually quite ineffective in all those operations with respect to which the cue transmission is important, that is, to all significant, organized, economic and political control, planning, and decision making. This point will become clearer below in my discussion of the *panelinha*.

It is plain that institutionalized poverty would be highly functional in the maintenance of such a system, since it automatically and effectively excludes the poor, whether totally or in significant degree, from access to cue-transmitted information. The institutionalization of poverty in Brazil includes an inflation which, especially at the lower levels, consumes virtually all wage raises given, but which, at the same time, is used by the moneyed to increase their own income. It includes a school system so constructed in various ways as to foster privilege and extrude the poor as early as possible, from the higher elementary grades, by requiring special, paid tutoring to go on (cf. Leeds 1957: Ch. 5; 1962; Teixeira 1957, 1958, 1960?). It also includes an extraordinary array of informal institutions of which the cue transmission control I have just discussed is one.

Poverty, too, entails its own outward symbols, especially dress, speech, and manners, so that its informal institutionalization easily includes differential treatment by all, both rich and poor. The techniques are legion, the consequences ineluctable.

Further, communications, more broadly defined, enter into the control of the poverty-stricken. The, in effect, institutionalized malfunctioning of virtually all Brazilian urban telephone networks (except in highly organized São Paulo) and of the so-called "Nacional" telegraph system guarantees major difficulties in organizing, both in terms of the ability to overcome problems of the spatial distribution of persons and in terms of time needed for organizing. Only the personnel of the state, politicos, and wealthier, well-connected private citizens, who have access to private or state-owned radio transmitters or to the expensive "Western" or "Radional" telegraph and telephone systems, or to rapid personal transportation, chiefly by airplane, are excepted from the slow pace of telephonic organization. Significantly, all these operate very effectively indeed on a *nation-wide* basis. In passing, it is worth pointing out that the institutionalized malfunctioning of systems of communication affects the masses of the poor totally, but it also extensively affects all the middle ranges of status and income levels of the "classes," and acts upon them, too, as a system of social control exercised by the holders of the central positions of the society.

In summary, then, cue transmission in itself, its control, the broad flow of other forms of information, the control of that flow, and all the formal and informal institutions arising from those controls create and sustain highly impermeable boundaries between two major groups—which I have called the "classes" and the "masses"—and only relatively permeable boundaries among hierarchic subgrouping in the "classes."

It must be noted that the "masses" and "classes" of such social systems as Brazil's are in quite viable functional relationship to each other. These masses are not symptoms of "disorganization" or "dysfunction" or of an "unhealthy" society. Because power, wealth, prestige, and decision making all rest with the "classes," who are vastly advantaged by them, the system tends to perpetuate itself. Furthermore, the great degree of control exercised over the masses tends to force them to look to the classes for support, thus reinforcing the system structurally and ideologically through institutions generally described as "paternalistic."

VI

Returning to the internal structure of the classes, we may examine the role of communications in leading the new careerist into significant relationships with persons of coordinate status and the kind of informally institutionalized and societally focal group into which he enters. The result of cue transmission and manipulation is an ever-widening series of connections, memberships, and positions held. Thus one twenty-six-year-old informant, who controls a social columnist by doing occasional favors for him such as paying off gambling debts or debts contracted because of women, has already become involved in a *panelinha,* has connections in Rio, and has even been made a member of various boards of directors without even being asked. That he also has specialized training in a nonacademic field is generally known and plays a role in his being selected.

The early and middle stages of the career, perhaps lasting ten to fifteen years, are characterized by multiplying the sources of support, first, so that there may be no retrogression; second, so that there be a permanent set of *trampolims*; third, so that there exist variegated sets of connections, among which, for strategic reasons, the careerist may move to advance his later career.

Perhaps our best example is a man who concurrently built a career as lawyer, academician, politician, and journalist. When defeated for political office, he had three other active sets of interests and connections to continue his *projecão,* as the Brazilians say. He had divided his academic life between native and foreign soils. When he became scandalously involved with a lady other than his wife, he found convenient temporary refuge in Europe from whence he continued his journalism. He then returned to reactivate the political pillar and to resume his academic role.

Connected with this multiplication of the sources of support is the device of surrounding oneself with a tactical corps of supporters, a kind of coterie, called in Brazil a *rotary* or *igrejinha* ("little church"). Such *igrejinhas* are especially useful if the members have journalistic or other communicational connections—as they so often do. They are carriers of information, transmitters of cues, promoters and boosters of the master careerist to whom they are attached. He reciprocates in a typical complementary relationship by using his influence to get them jobs, to advance their careers, to variegate their *bicos*[9] by mobilizing his connections, especially as a *cabide* and particularly in an upward direction.

Thus, the *igrejinha* is in fact a mutual career promotion, a web of mutual obligations, between a person with greater *projecão* or *nome* in his career, on one hand, and his supporters, on the other. Such *igrejinhas* may, if in the same domain of interests, compete for rewards of a very broad range of statuses often entirely outside the interests of the *rotary.* Such competition may be particularly sharp if the opportunity structure is not an elastic one. This seems to be especially true in the case of literary coteries. Concerning one of the most important of these in Brazil, it is reported that its central figure arranged the position of cultural attaché for one of the claque by mobilizing his own upward connections.

When a man has reached a certain point in his career, marked by the possession of desirable contacts, of a certain *nome* in his area or areas, and maybe of an *igrejinha,* he may be asked to join a *panelinha.* The asking may be explicit or may be carried out by a kind of unexplicit verbal assaying. *Panelinhas* can cover all sorts of activities, but, for our purpose, the politico-economic, rather than, say, the literary or academic, *panelinhas* are of most interest, though it must be recalled that all *panelinhas* are at least partly concerned with political ends.

The politico-economic *panelinha* characteristically consists of a customs official, an insurance man, a lawyer or two, businessmen, an accountant, a municipal, state, or federal deputy, and a banker with his bank. No formal commitment is made among these parties; no formal meetings are held. They are identifiable only by informants' reports or by the observation in various contexts over long periods of time of associative behavior among the persons involved. Often such cooperative behavior is not easily visible.

Each *panelinha* maintains its internal relations at any given level by certain very simple potential sanctions. The man who would leave a *panela* automatically would lose his connections therein. Since the *panela* in the locality is also a clique concerned with mutual protection—its members are virtually immune from the law because of the pressures which can be brought through *panela* connections—the apostate would lose his protections, unless, of course, he had already aligned himself with another *panela.* In other words, as a member of a *panela,* he both gives and receives.

The banker who leaves, loses the business and deposits of his *panela* members—and sometimes the combined assets of a *panela* may amount to eight or ten billion, or more, cruzeiros—would have difficulty finding substitutes, since most interesting prospects are already connected with some other bank. Because of the bank's dependence, it does not tend to be the predominating force of the *panela,* whose members are more or less in equivalent power status to each other.

Similarly, the deputy depends on the *panela* for his election (and his good salary)—he is their man. Yet, in turn, they depend on him because he supplies the links with the government which are so necessary to the resolution of a host of problems defined by *panela* members.

This is particularly true when there is a question of links reaching upward to the politico-administrative cupola, since every *panela* has its ties with the juridical political hierarchy up to the president, who is the keystone of the whole structure. These ties go through Rio de Janeiro, especially through Rio law firms, high Rio bureaucrats, ministry officials, federal deputies and senators, and so on, whence the ministers can be reached. The ministers make the contacts with the president where necessary, especially in such matters as may involve appointing officials or making highest-level decisions regarding the allocation of funds. In recent years, ultimate cupola decisions affecting *panelas* at lower politico-administrative levels have shifted to Brasília and will do so more rapidly hereafter.

Panelinhas, however, are not wholly in a dependent relationship with the president and other high authorities, since these, in turn, need the *panelinhas* which they have favored for return favors. This is especially true as regards local-level political support either in elections or in effecting policy decisions in state and municipal political bodies. Alienation of a *panelinha* is not good politics. The relationship between higher- and lower-level *panelinhas* is reciprocal, just as relationships within the *panelinha,* though in a different way, are reciprocal, and individual connections with groups and organizations on the part of the *cabide* are also reciprocal in their obligations and exploitations—a vast network of mutual, personalized obligation.

The state-level *panelinha* also reaches down to the lowest political level, establishing contact with the municipal *panelas* just as it does with federal-level *panelas.* Similar reciprocal relations are established here. Persons who can move in both are at an advantage, but tend to move permanently into the higher-level one, replacing the "egalitarian" reciprocal relations of a participant in the lower-level one with the hierarchical complementary relations of a participant in a higher one with respect to a lower one and with the "egalitarian" reciprocal relations of a participant in the higher-level one.

The number of *panelas* in a city or state is proportional to the level of its economic, political, or social advancement. Thus, states like Piauí and Maranhão probably have only one or two; Bahia, several; Minas, a number; São Paulo, a great many. Under an expanding opportunity structure, apparently the *panelinhas* generally do not often fight each other, especially locally. A fight which might be destructive to one *panelinha* is not joined, the losing *panelinha* preferring to attach itself to the winning one. Only for great contracts do genuine competitive battles go on, but these battles tend to be passed up the *panela* chain of command to be fought out at the highest bureaucratic, even ministerial, level.

VII

It will be seen that the *panela* is a self-maintaining group which serves a great number of ends. First, it serves to select talent of a certain kind, although it may also protect ineptitude for internal political reasons. The leading members, however, are mostly persons of great skill, indicated in such terms of admiration, almost of endearment, as *furador* ("one who worms his way in"), *cavador* ("burrower"), *absorvente* ("sops things up"), *paraquedista* ("serendipitist by intention"), etc. Inclusion by invitation gives a certain guarantee that such personnel will be brought in.

The obverse of this is that mediocre careerists tend to be excluded and all possible persons who wish to rise, to move up socially, are in effect controlled from above, even if they are already in the "classes." The control over upward mobility from the "masses" is much more severe and will be described at another time.

In brief, the *panelinha* and the *cabide* are two major structural entities (or nodes) of organization (cf. Leeds forthcoming) that, linked or not,[10] create in Brazil an almost totally impermeable boundary between the two groupings of people whom I have called the "classes" and the "masses." The term "class," in the Marxian sense, may be applied to these more or less organized groupings.

Within each of these groupings, vaguely delimited hierarchic layerings occur. The layers might perhaps best be called "strata," though they correspond to what in common American popular and sociological usage are called "classes" (cf. Bohannan 1963: Ch. 11, esp. 171–179). They arise from partial impermeabilities created by *panelinhas* and other structural entities. The boundaries between strata are not fully impermeable because of the hierarchic relationships among the *panelinhas*, because of the *igrejinhas* attached to *cabides*, and because the lower strata comprise an ever-present pool from which personnel selection from above takes place or can take place. Selection means not only taking some in, but also excluding others, and the term "partial permeability" describes this duality. The impermeability between strata is especially marked near the very bottom and at the top. These strata are by no means integrated, much less self-conscious, groups for which the Marxian term "class" would be appropriate.

In sum, Brazil displays internal stratification in at least one of its two classes; the other is just becoming known, but also appears to be stratified (cf. footnote 7; Leeds 1957: Chs. 4 and 5).

Second, the *panelinha* serves a number of economic ends. It is a capital-pooling and controlling group keeping a large part of its money in liquid form. This permits its members to lay hands on large sums of money easily by short-circuiting most of the legal restrictions and requirements and facilitates winning contracts, especially when these are being given out on bids, or making large-scale purchases or various speculations.

In various ways, the *panelinha* operates to assist its members to resist taxation by, for example, moving goods from one to another without paying turnover taxes or by introducing foreign goods as contraband or with much-reduced import taxes through the agency of their customs house members. Through their political and banking members, the *panelinha* attempts to take advantage of the government-controlled exchange rates in order to counter the inflation and to take advantage of it for the increase of capital and liquidity—and of course of personal wealth. At the same time, through the varied interests and activities of its members, a *panelinha* tries to control a very large proportion of the economic goods within the political unit in which it is operating, since control may have major political repercussions, may even be a political device, as in the recent withholding of basic foods from the urban markets with the accompanying political maneuvers at all levels.[11]

So much for the *panelinha* and its *cabide* components; we return to the career. Ideally, it should pass through a hierarchy of *panelinhas*, mainly identified with the *município*, state, and federal political levels. As a man grows in connections, activities, experience, and wealth, and contracts more vertical relationships upward and more supporters behind him, his career tends to reach into the next higher level *panelinha*. From the career point of view, he gradually universalizes or nationalizes himself (*ele se universaliza*) in the sense that his name, his influence, and his activities become geographically national in scope. That is, his *projecão* always broadens in socio-geographic range. It is made structurally firm by downward ties with various state and municipal *panelinhas*, by his *cabide* ties in several disparate types of endeavor, by his *rotary*, and by his geographically dispersed interests and activities. For example, one of our cases has his political strength in a northeastern state; his most influential associational ties and a large number of his business connections in Rio de Janeiro; his central business activities in Brasília; and a set of relatives in the national Congress and the state and municipal legislatures.

The final stage of a career is international *projecão*, but the society's positions for this are extremely limited in number, as are the highest national politico-bureaucratic positions. It is at this highest level, where the otherwise expanding opportunity structure suddenly contracts sharply, that the fiercest conflict is to be observed in Brazil.

Both national and international *projecão* are aided most significantly by access to, or control of, the means of communication and of transportation. The former aids in establishing contacts, keeping appropriate information flowing, and so on, while the latter permits the continuous maintenance of important relationships and the execution of vital maneuvers in critical, high-level competitive situations. Both together permit a relatively instantaneous control over problems needing resolution which is not at all available to the masses and only feebly so to the lower levels of the classes. In fact, the control of both of these technologies by the upper levels is one of the major mechanisms of maintaining the impermeable boundary between the classes and the masses,

FIGURE 2

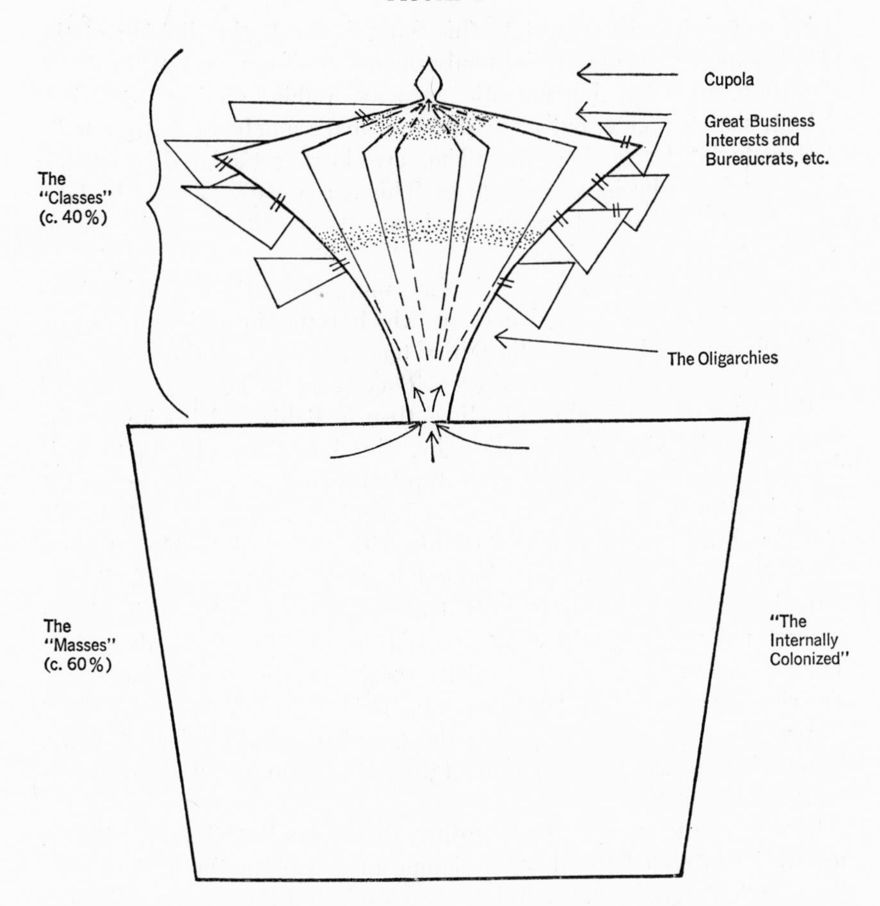

N.B. Slanting vertical lines represent expansion and contraction of the opportunity structure. Arrows represent upward mobility. Dashed lines represent indefinite or poorly defined boundaries. Dotted layers represent strata divisions. Dashed-line triangles represent rather amorphous interest groupings or categories not significantly attached to the major vested interest groupings, the "oligarchies." The symbol /=/ represents channels through which connection is made with the great oligarchies. These groupings or categories, in my present view, include such as the churches, primary and secondary teachers, self-employed professionals, some unions, some types of associations, etc.

especially, but also of the semi-permeable boundaries between the topmost and lowest strata of the classes.

VIII

A few points with respect to this synopsis. First, the division of the Brazilian politico-economy into sub-spheres or situses such as business, education, industry, bureaucratic agencies, public services, etc., has, at best, analytic value, but really does not make much sense structurally at their higher levels. They are all so very closely articulated by *cabides* whose positions lie in several situses. This is especially true in the later and "higher" phases of career development, i.e., at the higher levels of effective decision making.

Brazilian social divisions are, in fact, more along the oligarchic lines described by Teixeira, evidences of which came into the life-history materials repeatedly. The oligarchies tend to cross-cut the more conventional analytic sectors or situses. They seem to be more advanced in the states of São Paulo and Minas than in Bahia and Recife. At the highest levels within each oligarchy, the boundaries begin to fade because of the number and intensity of crossties among the personnel incumbent in the highest positions or because persons, especially highly placed politicos, enter into relationship with several oligarchies at once.

For the most part, at these highest levels, ultimate ends of all concerned are relatively uniform so that there are at present few significant generic policy cleavages at the cupola in Brazil (cf. Leeds 1964). The cleavages appear to revolve about specific policies for implementing generic policy aims and about access to control of the entire system and its rewards at the topmost point—the presidency and its dependencies. I should represent the situation of total Brazilian social organization somewhat as in Fig. 2.

Second, some comments regarding the research technique. It can readily be extended to all other significant groups in the society, e.g., the middle ranges of status and income levels and the "masses," including union presidents, skilled workers, and the like. In view of reported indicators of the existence of *panelinha*-like organization in the masses and lower levels of the "classes," research of this sort would be most revealing as to social structure, social barriers, social mobility, and the mechanisms of social organizing in and beyond any sort of locality.

In fact, the technique can, for a great many important features, be used in the qualitative description of the social systems of cities of any size—the intimate operations of the city economy and polity as well as their dependent stratification system, and so on. Indeed, the outcome of the technique is to map out a kind of kin and non-kin "genealogy" of all the significant groupings in the population of a city as well as of many of the individuals concerned, and at the same time one also describes the dynamics of social organization. It is important to note that the mapping reveals structures not usually visible and generally not accessible to observation using the ordinary categories of information gathering, such as demographic, statistical, occupational, and common stratification indicators.

IX

In conclusion, I should like to point out, first, that by route of describing the structure of careers in Brazil, it has been possible to describe several most fundamental aspects of Brazilian national social structures: social institutions which are carried out by national and locality groupings concomitantly. The description is not limited by the artificial boundaries created by the so-called community study method, or worse, by the plethora of studies of localities which are not even communities but are embedded in national social structures.

The community or locality-study method has always prevented seeing the integrating connections of the community with the larger social order by which it is so profoundly affected. Insofar as communities in national societies are social units at all, they exist in constant and active relation with the national institutions which are rarely described by anthropologists. Communities may conflict with the national institutions; coexist with them, as it were; actively participate in them; or, respecting different aspects of community life, do all of these at once in differing degrees and at different times. In the literature, the community appears, because of the method, as a kind of monad whose external dynamics and whose trajectory cannot be grasped more than obscurely. The method suggested here permits at least an approach to the analysis of both the whole and the part at the same time because they are seen as basically made up of the same social units.

Second, it can be seen that the overwhelmingly important kinds of informal organization I have described for Brazil are highly flexible under circumstances of rapid techno-economic change now being experienced, but where the existent technology of transport and communications and the rather rudimentary industrialism still create great difficulties for long-term organization over large distances. Under such conditions, the relative autonomy and geographical and social atomism of social units of all kinds are functional since they permit the units, *qua* units, to have greater ranges of response. The *panelinha,* the semi-public-semi-private autarchy, the semi-detached oligarchy, the notably autonomous states, and even sometimes municipalities, and even such bodies as the universities, the schools, and some of the churches, have a considerable flexibility because of their autonomy and atomism.

They may be contrasted with the ossified and rigid monolithic fixed bureaucracy. The flexible social units I have described here may move quickly, seize opportunities, reformulate policies, change strategies, and so on, without themselves changing much. In short, this rather atomized, loose type of organization, without a juridical foundation, is highly adaptive for societies in which a juxtaposition of their own static-agrarian past and an expansive-industrial future is occurring.

Third, hypothetically, the case described here provides a model for all similar societies. Thus, in general, one would expect Middle Eastern, Southeast Asian, some African, and other Latin American countries to conform to the model except insofar as the variable factors are more or less influential in each case.

Put another way, the various expectations deduced from the model and even the model itself are in fact predictions. The use of a model permits predictions of two kinds. First is the prediction of field situations, that is, the prior description, as it were, of what sort of sociocultural conditions one will find in an unknown sociocultural system such as, say, Yemen or Bhutan. Departure from the expected conditions would lead one to modify the theoretical principles upon which the model-construction was based, as well as to modify the model by redefining the relationships of the variables, whereas finding the expected conditions would tend to confirm both the principles, the model, and the defined relationships among the variables.

Second, the use of the model permits one to make reasonable predictions about future states of the society under consideration and even of specific events. From the model and its variable elements one may logically derive variant consequent models by describing changed relationships of the variable. Such models would constitute a range of possible trajectories and outcomes for a society under diverse conditions. Where a given outcome did not correspond to the expectations of the model constructed on the basis of variables whose values for the society are known, one would be obliged and in a position to extract new significant variables from the data, thus refining and making more powerful the theory.

Finally, it may be pointed out that the model I have been discussing has been framed mainly in terms of a juxtaposition of an already existing expansive-industrial structure with a static-agrarian one. It is incumbent upon us to ask what sort of a model we should construct for structures intermediate between the two when an expansive-industrial structure does not yet exist. This refers, of course, to the pristine development of the expansive-industrial society out of the static-agrarian. Would the model be quite different? Would it be substantially the same? Would some of the variables be extensively affected? Surely the variable of *rate* would be significantly different, since the pressure to condense the total time of transformation from one state to another is absent in the pristine sequence. Plainly, too, the variable of direct or indirect *coercion* present in the juxtaposition must needs be absent. Patently, the variable of *guidance* in transformation on the part of the acculturating body would be lacking. How do such differences affect the model? Do they suggest, for example, that the pristine development may have been more diverse, while the acculturational outcomes are likely to be relatively more like each other?

Such questions remain for future research. Answers to them might involve retrodictions of conditions that one would expect to find having happened in the pristine development (in Western Europe). For example, one might predict the occurrence, especially in the eighteenth century, of something resembling the autodidact phenomenon. Departure from the retrospective models would require modification of principles, models, and variables while discovering the conditions predicted would confirm them.

NOTES

1. These concepts were originally developed in a lecture to the School of Advanced International Studies, Johns Hopkins University (cf. Leeds 1961) and subsequently expanded in Leeds (1961, Ms; 1962, Ms).

2. These hypotheses were in part *induced* from having noted the existence of the Brazilian autodidact and the multiple position holder, discussed below. They are presented here as deduced from more general evolutionary principles, since they are intended as more general models for this "transitional" type of society. That is, on the basis of theory and the derived hypotheses, we should expect to find similar or related phenomena in other societies transitional from static-agrarian to expansive-industrial both in acculturational situations and also in the evolutionary sequence itself. The hypotheses presented below should be testable in European history in, say, the sixteenth to nineteenth centuries. If the data confirm the hypotheses, the theoretical argument is strengthened; if not, one may first investigate the consequences of asserting that the evolution of a pristine system and the acculturation between two evolutionary levels are not the same things, so that different outcomes are to be expected from each. Such figures as Michelangelo, Rubens, and Goethe, however, suggest confirmation of the hypotheses.

3. The term status, role, etc., follow the usage in Leeds (1963), pp. 73 ff., and more fully defined in the version of the paper (1963, Ms) from which the published paper was abridged.

4. The famous article by Davis and Moore (1945) deals in fact with the channels of entry and curricularization of various sorts, not with stratification at all.

5. Though the usage is not strictly correct, I shall refer to the phenomenon of multiple job holding by this term for convenience' sake. The term is used mainly for "high-level" personnel and may refer to either the person or the collection of positions he holds. Each job individually is called a *bico* ("beak, spout, nipple").

6. The Portuguese word used by Dr. Teixeira was *oligarquias* which is perhaps best translated as "vested interest groupings," since, in his conception, the entities he referred to include not only "the few" but those of "the many" who are organizationally attached to the former. Since, in contrast to the "masses," the total vested interest group numerically comprises only "a few," I shall retain the word "oligarchies." Teixeira has also used the expression "pressure groups" for these entities. (Cf. Teixeira 1962.)

7. Cate (1962, 1963, and conversations) has recently discovered an extremely complex organization of the masses in Recife, its surrounding hinterlands, and, by extension, other major cities. Similar structures were found in Maceió and Salvador, and seem indicated at least for Belém and Rio de Janeiro. The most central institution of this organization of the masses comprises the Carnaval dance organizations, such as the Escolas de Samba.

8. Indeed, any modern state society, like the United States or Germany, etc., will display analogous structures. *Panelinhas* of the type described in this paper, however, seem more restricted in number, membership, and general accessibility; seem to control much vaster resources relatively and absolutely, and much less to permeate the entire weft of society as a fundamental social form. Another way of saying this is that America is highly organized, operating more fully through jural channels, charters, contracts, and other formal devices, including schedules and curricula, than is the case in countries like Brazil. The *cabide* phenomenon in the U. S. appears mainly at the highest level of decision making, while at levels of execution or administration and of production not only is specialization present but also effectively only single-job holding. The *cabide* as a social node, a type of entity serving as a major form of social tie in the society, like the *panelinha* to which it is complementary, permeates the social order of a country like Brazil. Furthermore, the autodidact phenomenon has virtually disappeared from the United States. It is hard to think of cases. The sharp quantitative differences between societies like Brazil and those like the United States with regard to those social units, in addition to qualitative differences in their contexts, appears to me to indicate types of total societies also qualitatively quite different.

9. See footnote 5, supra.

10. There are several other nodes. Most recent, of course, has been the massive burgeoning of large-scale voluntary associations and bureaucratic agencies, but these represent an emerging trend occurring at the expense of such older and still highly important types of social nodes as the family, the inadequately described and defined unit referred to by the term "paternalism," and its special, territorially linked subclass, referred to by the term "*coronelismo*," which is presently in desuetude. Jointly all these

types of units link land, labor, capital, occupational specializations, politics, and so on, into a single dynamic system.

11. In June and July of 1962, acute shortage of all major staples was experienced in south-central Brazil, especially in the Rio area. Promises were constantly being made and ineffectual action taken to alleviate the situation, until, first, 5,000,000 sacks of rice were "discovered" "hidden" in Rio Grande do Sul, and, second, a food riot in Duque de Caxias, State of Rio de Janeiro, brought about an almost instantaneous reappearance of almost all staples in adequate supply in the stores. During the riot, all houses were damaged or broken into *except* a deputy's. The riotous mob considerately left his house untouched!

REFERENCES CITED

Bennett, W. C., ed., *et al.*

1948 *A Reappraisal of Peruvian Archeology*, Memoir 4, Society for American Archeology, Menasha, Wis.

Bohannan, P.

1963 *Social Anthropology*, New York, Holt, Rinehart and Winston.

Cate, K. R.

1962 "Final Report to the Technical Secretariat of the OAS Fellowship Program," July 15. (Typescript.)

1963 Letter to Dr. Vera Rubin, Dir., Research Institute for the Study of Man, September 11.

Davis, K. and W. E. Moore

1945 "Some Principles of Stratification," *American Sociological Review*, 10:2:242–249.

Guardini, R.

1956 *The End of the Modern World*, New York, Sheed and Ward.

Leeds, A.

1957 *Economic Cycles in Brazil: The Persistence of a Total Culture Pattern: Cacao and Other Cases*, Ph.D. Thesis, Columbia University, Ann Arbor, University Microfilms.

1961 Talk, "Cultural Patterns in 'Traditional Societies,'" to School of Advanced International Studies, Johns Hopkins University, lecture series "The United States in a Changing World Environment," Washington, D.C., October 31.

1961 "The Family in Static-Agrarian Societies and Its Transformation." (Manuscript.)

1962 "Borderlands and Elite Circulation in Latin America—Locality Power vs. Central Power Institutions," paper read at annual meeting, American Anthropological Association, Chicago, November. (Manuscript.)

1962 "Fatôres culturais em educacãe: Brasil, India, Estados Unides, União Soviética: Alguns problemas de antropologia aplicada," *Educação e Ciências Sociais*, 7:20:9–68.

1963 "The Functions of War," in J. M. Masserman, ed., *Violence and War, with Clinical Studies*, Vol. 4 of *Science and Psychoanalysis*, 4, New York, Grune and Stratton.

1963 "Toward an Analysis of the Functions of War," revised version of paper read at annual meeting, American Association for the Advancement of Science, December 1962. (Manuscript.)

1964 "Brazil and the Myth of Francisco Julião," in Maier and R. W. Weatherhead, eds., *Politics of Change in Latin America*, New York, Praeger.

In press "Some Problems in the Analysis of the Social Order," in A. Leeds, ed., *Social Structure and Mobility, with Special Reference to Latin America*, Proceedings of a seminar held in Rio de Janeiro, June, 1962, Washington, D.C., Pan American Union.

Meggers, B. J., *et al.*

1956 "Functional and Evolutionary Implications of Community Patterning," in R. Wauchope, ed., *Seminars in Archeology, 1955*, Memoir 11, Society for American Archeology, Menasha, Wis.

Niemeyer, O.

1961 *Minha experiência em Brasília*, Rio de Janeiro, Editorial Vitória.

Rostow, W. W.

1960 *The Stages of Economic Growth: A Non-Communist Manifesto*, Cambridge, Cambridge University Press.

Steward, Julian

1949 "Cultural Causality and Law: A Trial Formulation of the Development of Early Civilizations," *American Anthropologist*, 51:1:1–27.

Teixeira, A. S.

1953 *Educaçacão e um direito*, Thesis, Rio de Janeiro. (Mimeographed.)

1957 *Educaçacão nao e privilégio*, Rio de Janeiro, Jose Olympio.

1960(?) "The Brazilian School and Social Mobility." (Typescript and mimeo.)

1962 "Revolução e Educaçacão." (Mimeo.)

Changes in the Social Stratification of an Andean Hacienda

MARIO C. VÁZQUEZ V.

Physical geography divides Peru into three natural regions: the *costa* (the coast), the *sierra* (the Andean mountain range), and the *montaña* (the eastern tropical rain forest and savannah). Each is distinct from the others, not only in geography, but also in economic, social, and cultural aspects. The Andean zone presents two markedly different cultural groups: the mestizos and the Indians, and, between these two, a third group which is known as *cholo*. Each group has different values and interests, and consequently, differences in social stratification as well. Thus, whereas the criterion of social position for the mestizos is based on family lineage, occupation, or education, among the Indians the most important factor is wealth. In this study we shall attempt to describe the Vicosino criterion of social stratification before the Cornell-Peru Project, the immediate effects of the changes introduced by the project on the traditional Vicosino criterion of social stratification, the

Translated from "Cambios en estratificación social en una hacienda andina," *Perú Indígena,* 1957, VI, 4–5, 67–87. The present study is the result of the observations and investigation of the author, who was a member of the staff of the Cornell-Peru Project during three years' stay in Vicos, Marcará Ancash (1949–50; 1952–54). The author is grateful to Dr. Allan R. Holmberg, Director of the Project, and to Mrs. Joan Snyder Moore for her reading of the manuscript. Translated by Nicole Hunt.

emergence of the new *cholo* social group, and the Vicosino behavior and attitude toward this social change.

I

Vicos, a typical Andean agricultural hacienda, is situated in the Department of Ancash, Peru. It is distinguished by its semi-feudal colonial heritage whereby heads of families, in order to have the use of the lands belonging to the plantation, are obliged to give three days of work a week without pay, supplying their own plows and animals. The population is composed of 2,000 Quechua-speaking, preliterate Indians who culturally manifest the patterns of an undeveloped people.

Vicosino homesteads are scattered throughout the cultivatable area of the hacienda, along borders of the tilled land, and close to the roads and water sources. These tracts are not chosen by the *peones*, but are designated by the hacienda. Vicos is predominantly an agricultural community, but most of the inhabitants supplement this activity by raising cattle, sheep, horses, swine, and other small animals.

The Department of Sociology and Anthropology of Cornell University has had a field station in Vicos since 1952 for the study of induced cultural changes. Among the most noticeable changes introduced by the Cornell-Peru Project is the economic betterment of the Vicosinos through technological improvements in farming, and, in education, the installation of a modern school that operates under the management of eight teachers with a daily attendance of 160 students. Previously there had been only one small private elementary school, one teacher, and a daily attendance of fourteen students. There has been a change also in the traditional relationship between the *patrón* (boss) and the *peón*.

II

The mestizos, who for the most part live in urban centers, share patterns of the national culture and look upon the groups immediately inferior to them as Indians. They recognize no social differences among the Indians. Mestizos living near Vicos identify the Vicosinos as Indians, again without noticing social differences. This view derives from the fact that, among the mestizos, social classes are determined primarily by manners or by way of life, and not by strictly economic criteria, as occurs in Vicos.

An outsider's first impression on arriving in Vicos is similar to that of the mestizo's, because he encounters apparent economic equality: all the inhabitants are poor.

In their dress and in their behavior toward the stranger (we refer to the tourist and to the urban mestizo) the Vicosinos give the impression that all are poor. Excepting differences in sex and age, almost all the population dresses in a uniform style. By observing everyday dress it is difficult to differentiate rich adults from poor. Regardless of sex and age, the behavior of the Vicosinos, especially of those living in the vicinity of the highway, is that of a beggar. They usually ask gifts of the visitor. A popular phrase heard frequently is *dáme plata* (give me money). The argument used to justify this behavior, and with some basis, is poverty. But perhaps it can better be interpreted as an act of opportunism toward the outsider, whom they consider a generous and unwary type. "When the *gringos* (white foreigners) and the mestizos come to the hacienda, they give money." While not denying that a large segment of the population is poor, it is necessary to emphasize that some Vicosinos are in better economic conditions and have more security than many of the neighboring mestizos and many of the mestizo workers of the coast.

The social investigator, after a few weeks' stay in Vicos, easily perceives the presence of two economically differentiated groups: the rich and the poor. The determination of these two groups permits the identification of a third or "middle" group situated between these two polar groups. Finally, a more careful investigation leads to the definition of other subgroups, as we shall see in section V.

The foregoing suggests that wealth is the most important factor in bestowing social status in Vicos; or, to be more exact, social position is determined by the position of the individual within the local economic system. Confirmation of this requires a closer look at questions such as the following: What is the local Vicosino criterion for determining social status? Is wealth the only factor? What have been the immediate effects of the changes introduced by the Cornell-Peru Project on the traditional system of social stratification? In the following pages we shall attempt to expand on each of these questions.

III

The Vicosinos, when asked about the social differences in Vicos and about their identification with the group to which they believed they belonged (that is, when questioned in terms of class consciousness[1]), stated that wealth was the principal criterion of differentiation. "We *vicosinos* are not the same: some of us are rich and others are less rich, it depends on our inclination. Some of us are lazier than others." The principal sign of wealth consists in the number of animals that each family possesses. "In Vicos there are people who are rich because they have livestock, and others who are poor because they do not." The animals, in order of importance, are cattle, horses, and sheep.

Another criterion mentioned by a few informants is the way of life.

As we shall see below, this factor is closely bound to the foregoing criterion of economic status.

Below we shall refer to the three groups recognized by the Vicosinos as the rich, the "middles," and the poor. This study will not deal solely with those who have, gain, or spend, but rather with the social values related to the obtaining, possessing, and using of wealth.

THE RICH

This is the least numerous group, consisting of fifty-nine families. Although it can be separated into subgroups, in this section, using the Vicosino criterion, we shall consider these families as a unit, that is, "the rich."

The rich are identified by the rest of the Vicosinos as the misers of the community. "The rich are miserable people." They are the complainers (*llorones,* in its implication of "niggardliness"). "A rich *vicosino* does not help a poor one." On asking about a certain rich merchant, we received the answer, "What would *he* do to help. He'd even sell his conscience."

The rich, seemingly aware of the judgment of their countrymen, have their own explanation: "I lend money to whoever pays interest." This is confirmed by the not-so-rich: "The rich man lends money, but he doesn't give it away, though sometimes he'll treat at drinking bouts." This behavior of the rich can, perhaps, be interpreted as an act of ostentation or superiority. "Sometimes the rich think they are superior to us," a poor man observed. The son-in-law of a rich man commented, "When a poor man comes to the house of a wealthy one, the latter receives him as though he were really a lord and master."

The values of the majority of the Vicosinos are basically oriented to maintain the status quo, rejecting modern ideas or accepting them with little confidence. Contrastingly, however, the rich in the process of acculturation (four or five persons) easily accept new ideas that appear to be to their personal advantage.

The rich differ from the other groups by almost never lending their services as day laborers outside of the community. Another distinction is the frequency of the use of the system of *minkas,* a form of lending group labor. Work that requires several people, such as farming and the building of houses, is achieved by the participation of *minkas,* who are usually godchildren or relatives of the rich.

The rich dress in the same style and color as the other groups, differing only in the number of *mudas* (changes of clothing), ponchos, sandals, etc. Often their used clothing is sold or given to the poor. Their dwellings are different from those of the immediately inferior group only in their number and not in their quality. These are, with rare exceptions, almost all of the same type of structure and in the same state of repair. The diet of the rich is characterized by its quantity and variety; for example, they eat meat with some frequency, and enjoy the privilege of being able to play the role of *quelles* or *aytza-anchayki*, or the providers of meat during religious festivities.

Usually they appear to be very busy people, and in fact they are active and dynamic, consciously cultivating this behavior in order to demonstrate their superiority over other groups and to prove that they owe their riches and social position to hard work. The acculturated rich sell coca, alcohol, kerosene, sugar, cigarettes, etc., thereby trying to imitate the mestizos. They maintain commercial contact with the mestizos and the *cholos* of the neighboring villages. The mestizos and the *cholos*, in turn, try to maintain good relations with the rich, in order to buy their animals. These economic relations often lead to ties of *compadrazgo* (co-parenthood). Mestizos and *cholos* frequently serve as *padrinos* (godfathers, or sponsors) at weddings and sometimes are the godparents at baptism of the children of the rich.

Within this group there is considerable insecurity of status and preoccupation to maintain their position, especially during adulthood. The loss of status derived from wealth is justifiable in old age. It is important to point out that the loss of this status does not necessarily entail the loss of social prestige. Although it is true that wealth is one way to bring high social status, this status *per se* does not signify that the individual enjoys high social prestige, for in Vicos prestige is acquired with age and the fulfilling of certain norms and obligations of the community (Vázquez 1955: 30–31). Consequently it is not rare to find in Vicos wealthy individuals who have, nonetheless, low social prestige, or individuals of high social prestige who are not rich. This occurs with people who do not meet the conditions of prestige required by the society. For example, the rich who have extra-marital unions cannot hold positions of trust in the local political organization, for to hold such positions one must previously obtain and enjoy prestige in the Vicosino society.

THE "MIDDLES"

The Vicosinos identify approximately 128 families in this group. They are identified in the following way: An ex-mayor whose wealth had diminished by the death or sale of his steers said, "I like the rich more than the poor, but I am not rich any longer." Two other informants, when asked about their economic situation, commented, "poor, a little poor, but not very poor," and, "there are many poor people. I barely have four cows [he had had eight beeves], maybe I can place myself in the middle." Another informant added: "Here there are many people worse off than I." It depends on the number of animals that they possess.

The values of the members of the middle group are oriented toward those of the rich. There is among them much unrest and desire to acquire wealth, with the purpose, it seems, of gaining self-sufficiency or of reaching the social position of the rich. They carry out the duties of secondary importance in the local authority system. They take care to participate in the religious festivities, in the hope of gaining prestige and social rank.

In this group *minkas* are rarely used in farming activities except in the construction of dwellings or during the carrying out of religious duties. In contrast the *rantin,* one service in exchange for another, such as one day of work for another, is frequently practiced.

The dwellings of this group contrast with those of the previous group only in number. The members of this group generally possess two changes of clothing, one being better than the other. The diet is characterized by its abundance and variety during the harvest season, and by its limitation during the rest of the year.[2] In this group, deficits of production are covered by the purchasing of products by the sackful, through sale of animals in the hacienda or in the neighborhood.

The contacts with mestizos and *cholos* are frequent through employment or business. The individuals of this group generally sell an animal every two years, while the rich do so annually. Some sell coca and alcohol, a seasonal activity that is handled by the women. *Compadrazgo* relationships with the mestizos or the *cholos* are less frequent than is the case among the rich.

THE POOR

The poor constitute the most numerous group and present perhaps the most differentiation among the approximately 176 families. In spite of their poverty they try to identify themselves with the least poor. Thus for example an acceptor of the program of change [see section VI, 4] who had no beeves, a few sheep, and three pigs, tried to explain his social status in this way: "If I had been poor, the hacienda would not have allotted me any seed, and if I had been rich I would have sown more seed than I have." One old man who lived with his two single daughters and had twelve head of sheep and two pigs, with the attitude of a conformist, seemingly resigned to his present condition, said, "Happily and with the grace of God, our life [that of his family] is not as bad as that of other families, because we never lack something to eat, even if it's only *shaqui* [a watery flour porridge considered the food of the poor] . . . but then there are others who have a better life because they sow plenty and have cattle. But anyway, I'm not complaining of my lot."

A visible characteristic of the poor is the deterioration of their clothing, which is dirty and in rags. They differ from the two preceding groups in their frequent geographical movement. "Only the poor go to the coast in search of money; the rich get it by selling their animals." Most of them travel to neighboring villages where they gather on days that they do not work or when they fail to keep their obligations to the hacienda. Some go to the coast annually for one or two months. They also have the most offenses on the records of the hacienda and consequently have frequent conflicts with the administration.

The poor reject the rich man, but there is, nevertheless, frequent exchange of mutual services, for they often work as *minkas,* and in addition to their "rights" as such, accept small gifts of clothing and farm products. The attitude of the rich toward the poor is patronizing and protective so long as the poor "stay in their place," but becomes offensive and dominant if the behavior of the poor is disagreeable to them. Then the poor are called "lazy," "useless," "drunks," "irresponsibles," "thieves," and other names.

The poor become inebriated more frequently than the men of the other groups, possibly because they have more opportunities to do so. For example, every day, wherever they lend their services as day laborers, they are given as a treat their "soother" or *temple,* an alcoholic refreshment. In their work the places that sell liquor are accessible to them and they easily spend their salaries there, whereas among those of the other groups the money is in the direct control of the women. There is probably some relation between the alcoholic tendencies of the poor and their state of anxiety, for it is known that states of anxiety are produced in the course of social and cultural processes, and that the use of alcohol diminishes the tensions caused and contributes thereby to the continuation of traditional relations (Wolf 1954:271).

The majority of the poor have the reputation of "thieves" or "*raktzamaki*" (dirty hands), a name applied only to this group, although almost all Vicosinos, with few exceptions, tend to covet what is not theirs.

There are some differences between the dwellings of the poor and those of the other groups. The houses of the other groups are constructed of adobe brick on rectangular or quadrangular foundations, with tile roofs, bearing some structural resemblance to the local mestizo dwellings. The dwellings of the poor, however, are usually constructed of rocks, adobe, or sod, on a circular foundation with conical roofs of straw. This difference is related to the economy of the owners of the dwellings. The rich and the "middles," using the *minka* system, can construct their dwellings to suit their taste, whereas the poor must rely on themselves or occasionally on their relatives to build their houses. These are usually very simple and of little commercial value, for the materials used are gathered from the surrounding area and require no investment.

The diet, compared with that of the other groups, is characterized by its meagerness in quantity as well as variety. In contrast to those of the other groups, the poor have few prejudices against the mestizo foods. "If you can eat it, why shouldn't I?" is an attitude probably reflecting their frequent contacts with outsiders. The food that they lack is often obtained in neighboring towns either by day labor or by a bartering system whereby small animals such as guinea pigs and chicken are exchanged for grain. The quantity of their acquisitions is limited to one or two *arrobas* (25 to 50 lbs.), whereas the other groups acquire food by the sackful.

The poor have frequent relations with the mestizos and *cholos*, often working for several weeks during harvest season on their property and receiving board and a salary in the form of produce. This arrangement is beneficial to both: to the poor because the products are sold cheaper at the time and place of the harvest, and to the mestizo because this way he avoids having to transport his goods to the markets. The children of the poor work occasionally as servants to the mestizos or the *cholos*.

IV

According to the majority of the Vicosinos, wealth depends on "luck." They consider that success or failure is dependent first on "luck" and ultimately on "God," a concept popular in the "middle" group. They say, for example, "Wealth depends on a person's luck. It is possible for him to have many animals and live well from their sale." "Wealth depends on luck, because those who have many beeves receive a great deal of money, while those who have only a few head barely have enough money to cover expenses." Another informant of the "middle" economic group who seemed to be highly motivated to attain the status of a rich man, commented on another rich man, saying, "Z.Z. is rich, but I don't envy him. He has had more luck than I. Surely I haven't had it because God hasn't willed it so, but anyway, I'm beginning to have a few things of my own now, too."

In Vicos wealth cannot be considered of hereditary origin, for the estate of a wealthy man is usually distributed among his children, and since families are often large, the share that each receives is not great. It is not unusual, therefore, to find wealthy children of poor parents and poor children of wealthy parents.

A very few believe that wealth depends on the talents or abilities of the individual. One ambitious young man said, "The success or failure of an individual depends on himself, not on luck. God has created us all equal. If some are rich it is because they want to succeed . . . while the others (the poor) live only in the present, and, like animals, they never get anywhere." Another acculturated man said, "In Vicos there are two kinds of people: the capable and the useless. Wealth is an attribute of the former because they can work conscientiously." Before the initiation of the Cornell-Peru Project, the hacienda constituted another source of wealth for the people associated with it; as shall be described below, it provided some individuals with better opportunities to increase their well-being.

It seems then that the Vicosinos, upon reaching adulthood, have, for the most part, equal prospects for success in life, since wealth, which confers social status, is not acquired by inheritance nor is it the concomitant of education. We may suggest tentatively, then, that wealth (social status) depends on the ability of the individual to acquire and maintain it.

Social mobility from an inferior group to a superior one occurs frequently. Actually, all have the same opportunities to reach a higher status if they acquire wealth and age and have complied with the social norms of the community. There is, however, because of the possibility of rapid and unexpected loss of status, much instability among those of high social status. A privileged position can easily be altered by pestilence, theft, or other misfortune that might diminish the number of animals. Several cases are known; for example, an ex-*alcalde* (justice of the peace) tells of his poverty caused by the loss of his cattle, of which at one time he had twenty head. The loss occurred as follows: four were killed by lightning in one afternoon; four were butchered to celebrate his sons' weddings; two were given to his sons as gifts; and of the ten remaining, some were sold to meet expenses and others died from lack of care, for the sons had moved away and he could no longer tend the animals adequately himself. Finally, only 100 soles from the sale of one of his last beeves was all that remained of his fortune, and this he was saving in order to pay for his funeral expenses. Because of the devaluation of Peruvian money during the last ten years, this sum, which would have had great buying power at one time, at the time of the interview was not even enough to cover these expenses.

Concern over social status begins with marriage and the formation of a new home economically independent of paternal ties. Prior to this, the individual is a member of a nuclear family and shares the social status of his father. Depending on the number of animals that each partner contributes to the matrimony, the new family may have a status that is lower, the same as, or higher than that of their fathers.

The possession of animals and their natural increase requires much work, with the head of the family playing an important role, assisted by his wife and the other members of his family. Those who do not have any animals for breeding form their *crías* (broods) by saving and carefully managing their money. Those who have the best possibility of arriving at a position of privilege are members of large families who receive help from outside the home (from fathers and in-laws), and those whose homes are not plagued by sickness, pestilence, disgrace, or other misfortune.

We can conclude that social position for the Vicosinos, depending as it does on wealth and the possession of animals, is characterized by instability and unexpected changes that frequently result in loss of status.

V

Using the Vicosino criterion of the importance of individual economy in determining social position, we shall describe here the five social groups in Vicos in the early part of 1952.

Following is the grouping according to economic status in Vicos, based on the anthropological census of 1952:

I: Very rich	6 families
II: Rich	22 families
III: "Middles"	146 families
IV: Poor	123 families
V: Very poor	63 families
VI: Not identified	3 families
Total	363 families

This grouping was established according to the Vicosino criterion, and was based on the number of animals that each family (wife or husband) possessed, or, as occurred in some cases, by the lack of animals. As the Vicosinos themselves explained, animals constitute the only objects of real commercial value, and their sale is in the hands of the Vicosinos themselves. Owing to the system of peonage, immovable property (houses and farm lands) which in other societies constitutes a source of wealth, has only cultural or symbolic value in Vicos, for it can be sold only by the hacienda. This is not to deny, however, that the possession of cultivatable lands has some bearing on individual wealth. The rich usually do the most extensive farming, for they have yokes of oxen to work the land and use their animals both as a source of manure to fertilize the land, and as a means of transportation for their harvests. With the money they buy seed and hire *minkas*. The rich therefore are able to take full advantage of their livestock whereas the other groups cannot do so because they have very few animals or because the ones they have are not work animals.

Social inequality in Vicos, according to this hierarchy, is as follows:

I: THE VERY RICH

This group is composed of families who own more than sixteen head of cattle or the equivalent in other animals such as sheep or horses. One of the families considered to be in this group had only eight beeves but twenty-five horses and forty-five sheep. Horses have approximately the same value as beeves. Another family in this group had twelve beeves, five burros and twenty-five sheep.

The majority of the families in this group, with the exception of two, have high social prestige. In Vicos, as in other preliterate cultures, the acquisition of prestige is dependent on age and on compliance with the social norms imposed by the society (Simmons 1945:81; Vázquez 1954:30). One of the excepted families mentioned will probably soon reach a privileged position of prestige when the head of the family has come of age and has taken on some of the responsibilities of the local political administrative organization. The other one, however, in the present traditional system, will have some difficulty attaining a position of prestige, for he is a nonconformist or dissenter to the traditional Vicosino customs. This indicates that although wealth in Vicos is the principal criterion of social status, it does not always bring social prestige. This same phenomenon is described by Wheeler in the Valley View study (Wheeler 1949:95). Of the six families in this group, all but one came to their present position from a lower one. The head of the family that was mentioned as an exception said that part of his wealth had been acquired from his parents and that this was later augmented by the contribution that his wife made when they were married, and he concluded that his present success was the fruit of hard work and the careful tending of his livestock. He also gave the same reasons for his parents' wealth. One fact that was not mentioned by this informant was that his relations with the hacienda helped to maintain him in a privileged position as compared to that of other families. His grandfather and his father had been *mayorales* (overseers) of the hacienda, a position which they each held until they died. This tradition seems to be carried on by our informant, for he has held this position for thirty years and hopes his children will succeed him. One of his brothers is classified in group II (the rich) and his sister is in group IV (the poor), thus supporting the conclusion that wealth is not the result of inheritance, or if it is, it is dependent on one's ability to keep it.

The frequency of livestock sale depends on the number of animals one has. In this group, sales are not made to obtain immediate necessities, as they are in other groups, but for different reasons: the desire to replace older oxen with young blood, to avert losses, to avoid fights among the bulls, to please a friend who is buying cattle, etc. These transactions are usually beneficial to the Vicosino, and the money is put away and kept carefully, though sometimes the bills are gnawed by rats. These Vicosinos lend money with or without interest, depending on the friendliness or relationship between the lender and the borrower.

II: THE RICH

The families in this group own from eleven to fifteen beeves or their equivalent. The rich constantly rival the very rich, whom they hold in contempt and charge with having obtained their fortunes by dishonest means, in contrast to their own wealth which they consider the result of honest work and perseverance. The majority of the rich, especially those who have held important positions in the local authority system, are of high social prestige.

The rich usually sell their animals when their economic reserves from the last sale are spent. These transactions take place with approximately the same profitable results as those of the very rich. Some rich lend their services as day laborers in the neighboring towns. This is particularly the case when the wealth belongs to the wife and not to the husband.

III: THE "MIDDLES"

These constitute the most active element in Vicos. Their principal concern is to increase their animals, which usually number from six to ten. Most of them hold positions of secondary importance in the *campos* or local religious and political systems.

The sale of their animals takes place more frequently than is true in the other groups and is generally prompted by the need to meet the family's necessities, such as food, wool for clothing, misfortunes, sickness, etc. The men and frequently their sons work in the neighboring towns, especially in times of necessity or scarcity of food or during religious festivals.

IV: THE POOR

This group is made up of individuals from varied backgrounds, some with hopes of reaching a higher social position by increasing the number of their animals, and others resigned to the hardships of life. Widows and unmarried women compose about two thirds of this group.

The poor, who sow less seed than do the other groups, try to lessen the burden of their necessities by working in neighboring towns, but when the few jobs available do not meet their needs, they resort to the sale of their animals, even if they have not reached maturity. They often borrow money or obtain agricultural products on credit, promising to repay the debt with the next calf that is born, though they often cannot be sure that cow will have another calf.

V: THE VERY POOR

This unfortunate group is made up of old men, widows, orphans, etc. Both sexes and all ages lend their services to others, usually as laborers in the neighboring towns. The behavior of the very poor toward the other groups is abject as of inferior to superior.

VI

In contrast to the usual unilateral methods employed in the modernization of native groups, the Cornell-Peru Project attempted an integral program. Since modifications in only one aspect of the culture are not enough, and since the results might have negative effects on future attempts at change, it was believed that innovations should be wrought throughout the entire culture. In the education of the young Vicosino, for example, it was believed that scholastic instruction alone was not enough. In order to avoid conflicts of values between the traditional instruction received in the home and the formal education at school, and thus lessen the possibility of bringing on maladjustments in the future life of the Vicosino, it would be necessary to consider changes in the total culture.

Among the principal changes introduced by the Cornell-Peru Project are:

1. The organization of the hacienda: Weekly meetings of the *mayorales*, the administration, and the personnel of the project were instituted in order to discuss administrative matters of the hacienda and aspects of the project directly related to the Vicosinos. The *mayorales* have taken on new responsibilities in the work of the hacienda, taking the place of the mestizo workers, against whom there was some hostility. The *mando*, a weekly meeting of the day laborers to give the orders of work, is used to the ends of the Cornell-Peru Project, since it is the main avenue of contact with the Vicosinos. Free services were abolished if they exceeded the three days that were required of the *peones* and their relatives by the hacienda (as did the *mitas, tapacos, semaneros, pastores*, etc.). The earnings of the hacienda are used for the benefit of the community, as in the construction of the local school.

2. The reducing of internal conflicts between families and among the *peones*: The use of brands for cattle, horses, and donkeys was instituted, thereby avoiding such frequent thefts, embezzlements, errors, etc. Conflicts on matters of land, whose solution previously had been in the hands of the landlord or the tenant, are today referred to the *mayorales*, whose function it is to deliberate and discuss the problem during the weekly meetings, and to make their decisions in the presence of the interested parties.

3. Civic and patriotic education for adults: The Sunday drill for reserves, previously held in Marcará (capital of the district of the same name), now is held in Vicos. The reserves receive patriotic and civic education in addition to the military exercises required by law, thus preparing them to participate in the rights and responsibilities conferred upon them by the law and the constitution. Affiliated with the school there are night sessions of adult education with voluntary attendance,

and, on Sundays, classes for young men of military age, for whom attendance is obligatory.

4. Changes in the economic system: The introduction of new techniques of farming and new kinds of seeds has brought about immediate results with the increase of local production. The sale of agricultural products in the national market has replaced the traditional small local business based on the bartering system. Other effects brought about by these economic changes are obvious. The Vicosinos who have learned or increased their knowledge of carpentry or masonry are used in construction jobs in the same capacity as the mestizo technicians.

5. Installation of a modern school: In Vicos a "Pre-vocational Rural School" gives elementary education and in the future will have a full primary school program, in accordance with the Peruvian educational system, and, in addition, practical instruction in carpentry, horticulture, etc.

The school today has a double role in cultural integration, one internal and the other external. In its internal function it seems to foster better contact and interaction among the Vicosino children. This could not have happened before for reasons of topography, for the scattered homes did not allow for interaction during childhood. Only in adulthood did the Vicosinos come together in order to work in the hacienda. Now all the children, regardless of social status, parentage or place of residence, receive the same treatment and a common education. In them are the beginnings of a new consciousness that will open broader horizons in their lives. The new stimuli and responses of the individuals indicate a different kind of relationship—friendship—an orientation that is evidence of new feelings of communality.

In addition to fostering new kinds of personal relationships among the children, the school has brought about changes also among the Vicosino parents, who feel great love and affection for their children, and who confront a common problem in their education. Consequently there are now motivations causing them to think and behave toward the same ends, and awakening new aspirations for the welfare of their children. In other words, the school has created new problems and new hopes that are in turn creating new motivations for unity within the community.

In its external function of integration the school is the main vehicle for transmission of the values of the national culture, for instruction in Vicos is the same as that given all other Peruvian children. The school is now the bridge of contact between the native Vicosino culture and the Peruvian reality. In the future, the school, which now identifies itself as a mestizo institution imposed in Vicos, shall perhaps be identified as part of the community, and then the Vicosino culture will become an integral part of the national culture of Peru.

VII

What have been the immediate effects in the present social structure of Vicos of the changes introduced by the Cornell-Peru Project?

One of the immediate effects of the changes operating in Vicos we can put forth tentatively as follows: the formation of a new social segment determined not by the criterion of wealth, but by the use of certain mestizo patterns, that is to say, a new group with a mestizo orientation. Its members, notwithstanding their being called names like *leidos* (readers), *castellaneros* (speakers of Spanish), *qarakos*, etc., are being accepted by the society.

The formation of the new social group oriented toward the values of the mestizo culture undoubtedly originated before the Cornell-Peru Project. It is worth noting that before the project there were some who attempted to introduce or accept the new elements. The reaction of their fellow men can be interpreted as the "satirical sanction" of Radcliffe-Brown (1935), toward the acceptors or the sponsors of the mestizo elements. As an example, the Vicosino conduct toward discharged soldiers returning from obligatory military service after two or three years' absence was, for all purposes, to force them to reaccept the traditional Vicosino values. If they persisted in their new ideas, they were not obliged to abandon them or to leave the community, but they were deprived of certain rights, for example they were not allowed to hold any position in the local authority system. Another example is that of foreigners married to Vicosinos residing in Vicos who also are forced to become integrated in the local culture, and if they persist in keeping their own *costumbres* (customs), are given nicknames, usually depreciatory of their person.

When the Cornell-Peru Project started its program there was no obvious outward resistance. But the feeling of the majority was of indifference, which perhaps can be interpreted as expectation, for after the first year that indifferent majority gradually became acceptors. In contrast to the spectator majority, that same year a small segment demonstrated open acceptance of the program of innovation of the Cornell-Peru Project. This support was not merely verbal, but many times manifested itself in their behavior, for example, by collaboration in the building of the school, the acquisition of brands to mark their cattle, etc. The acceptors at first constituted a special segment of the community. Upon analysis it became evident that they differed from the rest in having had previous experience outside of the community, either by having lived on the coast or having relatives who lived on the coast, or by being married to an outsider. (For further information see Vázquez 1951:71). The majority of the acceptors of the changes introduced by the project seem to have found in the program an opportunity to put into practice their hopes of change or their inclinations toward the mestizo way of life. Possibly they also found the argument to defend themselves from the reproach of the traditionalists or conservatives, who were determined to maintain the status quo; they said they were only following the orders and wishes of the *patrones* (in this case the Cornell-Peru Project), who were giving the same opportunities to all Vicosinos. The majority of the acceptors can be considered integral members of the new social group in gestation, and it will undoubtedly be possible to distinguish subgroups depending on the levels of adaptation to the national culture.

The new Vicosino social group—mestizos, *cholos,* and Indians—can be classified in the regional stratification of Callejón de Huaylas as being within the group of *cholos.* Classification, according to Mangin (1954:v–29), implies at least minimal participation in the national culture and a feeling of being part of the country as well as a member of a local community.

The identification of the *cholo vicosinos* as a group is not based on the economic criterion of wealth but on terms of participation in the trends and manners of the national culture. This group includes, consequently, members of different economic levels but with a similar orientation of values.

The *cholo vicosinos,* called by the others *leidos* or *castellaneros,* actually do, in the majority of cases, know some Spanish, and this ability they use in their contacts with outsiders or when they are drunk. Their dress is characterized by the adoption of Western clothing, the use of trousers instead of the Vicosino *wara,* and the substitution of the mestizo jacket for the native jacket or *chompa.* The women tend to favor the *saco* or blouse used by the *cholo* women of Callejón de Huaylas instead of the *monillo* or native blouse. But there are many *cholos* who are difficult to distinguish by sight, and who can be identified only by carefully observing the kind of education or orientation they give to their children: if they prefer to dress their children in mestizo clothes, for example, or if they are concerned about the children's formal education. In other words, by their hopes regarding the future of their children.

It seems the formation of the new social group of the *cholo vicosino* has been aided by the following factors:

1. The success of the acceptors or participants in the early stages of the program of innovation introduced by the Cornell-Peru Project, for example in the planting of potatoes, branding of cattle, etc.

2. The course of action of the researchers, who were not merely observers but an active influence on the situation. The activities of the investigators are intimately bound up with the changes introduced by the Cornell-Peru Project in the traditional relations of *patrón* and

peón, a fact that undoubtedly encouraged the formation of a new Vicosino consciousness and inspired confidence toward outside elements.

3. The attitude and behavior of discharged soldiers and visitors to the town who expressed openly their support of the program of innovation.

4. The Vicosinos' concept of the mestizos and perhaps even their hopes of competing with them. They recognize superiority in the mestizo because he knows Spanish and uses it as a means of communication and as a source of knowledge of the Western world (technology, medicine, literature, etc.). "The *mishtis* (mestizos) are superior to us because they know how to speak Spanish." "If we [the Vicosinos] knew how to read and write Spanish we would be the same as the mestizos." "Those who know Spanish have better living conditions than the Indians of Vicos." The majority of the Vicosinos believe that if they knew Spanish they would change their way of dressing in favor of the mestizo clothes and would then enjoy the same privileges as the mestizos. The differences mentioned by the Vicosinos between the Indians and the mestizos are: clothing, knowledge of Spanish, residence in urban centers, and the color of the skin. The skin of the mestizos, they say, is lighter because they do not do farm work.

5. The school has been and still is one of the principal factors favoring the formation of the new social group in Vicos. We believe we can safely predict that the school will help to consolidate the social position of the members of this new group.

Although many Vicosinos still are reluctant to send their children to the school, they are almost all in agreement that at some time in the future their children will learn to write and speak Spanish, and that this will be to their advantage. The Vicosinos recognize the importance of Spanish as an instrument of communication and knowledge, for at present it is the principal barrier between the Indian and the mestizo and is perhaps one of the causes for the isolationism and cultural backwardness of Vicos. The following opinions support this conclusion: "I am afraid to go to other towns because I don't speak Spanish. I am ashamed not to be able to answer when I'm spoken to in Spanish." "Many make fun of us when we can't answer them, and they say 'why do you come here without knowing Spanish?' " "If I knew Spanish I wouldn't be afraid of anyone, because I would feel equal to everyone." "By knowing how to speak Spanish one has better hopes in life, for one works less and earns more." "The mestizos have more opportunities for earning money because they work more with their eyes, while we are stuck on the farms." "If I knew Spanish perhaps I would be bolder, and those who know would not humiliate me." "By knowing Spanish there are better opportunities in everything; one can travel to other places without fear and carry on business without being taken advantage of."

Since the second year of the program of the Cornell-Peru Project we have noticed a growing desire to become educated. Thus when they were asked about their hopes for their children's future the Vicosinos expressed concepts such as the following: "I can no longer learn to speak Spanish, because I am old, but I would like my children to learn, because by knowing Spanish they will understand the conversation of others." "I want my children to learn Spanish so that when they travel to any other place they will be able to earn a living." "When I am in another town, I am ashamed to be a Vicosino because I don't understand Spanish, but I am sure that my children will learn it."

VIII

If our arguments are valid, perhaps as a conclusion we might point out the following:

1. The criterion of differentiation that is socially accepted by the preliterate society of Vicos is wealth, which in turn determines the way of life. Social position, in other words, is determined by the status that the individual holds in the local economic system.

2. The Vicosinos, according to the above criterion, identify themselves as coming within one of three social strata: the rich, the "middles," and the poor.

3. One of the immediate effects of the program of innovation of the Cornell-Peru Project has been the socioeconomic betterment of the Vicosinos and the concurrent rise of new hopes. This has brought about the evolution of a new social group, determined not on the basis of wealth, but by a new orientation of values strongly resembling those of the mestizos.

4. The new Vicosino social group is the *cholo* group in the regional social classification of Callejón de Huaylas, and is based on terms of participation and behavior trends in relation to the national culture.

5. The formation of the *cholo vicosino* group or of the *leidos* (readers) or *castellaneros* (Spanish speakers) has been the result of the interplay of various factors, the school being the most important one, because it favors the consolidation of the group not only in the local culture but in the regional one as well.

NOTES

1. "Class consciousness" refers to the psychological perception of the individual of his own social position within the social class structure (Rosenberg 1953:22, 23.)

2. Regarding nutrition and diet in Vicos, see the report of Dr. Collazos C., *et al.*, 1954.

REFERENCES CITED

Collazos, Carlos *et al.*

1954 "Dietary Survey in Peru: Chacan and Vicos," *Journal of the American Dietetic Association* 30:12:1222–1230.

Mangin, William P.

1954 *The Cultural Significance of the Fiesta Complex in an Indian Hacienda in Peru*, Ph.D. dissertation, Yale University, New Haven.

Radcliffe-Brown, A. R.

1935 "Social Sanction," *The Encyclopedia of the Social Sciences* 13:531–534.

Rosenberg, Morris

1953 "Perceptual Obstacles to Class Consciousness," *Social Forces* 32:1:22–27.

Simmons, Leo W.

1945 *The Role of the Aged in Primitive Society*, New Haven, Yale University Press.

Vázquez V., Mario C.

1955 *Study of Technological Change in Vicos, Peru: Cornell-Peru Project*, M.A. Thesis, Cornell University, Ithaca.

Wheeler, Wayne

1949 *Social Stratification in a Plains Community*, Minneapolis, Minnesota.

Wolf, Eric R.

1954 "El Campesino Latinoamericano," *Ciencias Sociales* 5:30: 268–271.

Urbanization Without Breakdown: A Case Study

OSCAR LEWIS

This is a preliminary work report on a research project on urbanization in Mexico City. The research is an outgrowth and continuation of my earlier work in the village of Tepoztlán. In brief, we attempted to learn what happened to individuals and families from the village of Tepoztlán who had gone to live in Mexico City.

Before presenting some of the preliminary findings, I should like to indicate how our work is related to other studies in the same field. In the first place, it should be noted that there have been very few studies of the socio-psychological aspects of urbanization in Mexico or other Latin American countries. Urban sociology in Mexico has lagged behind developments in some of the other social sciences. The data most nearly comparable to ours are to be found in the rural-urban migration studies done by rural sociologists in the United States. These studies have been primarily concerned with the causes, the rate and direction, and the amount of migration, factors of selectivity, and occupational accommodation.

Reprinted from *The Scientific Monthly*, 1952, LXXV, 31–41, by permission of the author and publisher. Photographs have been omitted. The author is grateful to the Graduate Research Board of the University of Illinois for financial assistance on this project. The field research in Mexico City was carried out in the summer of 1951 with the aid of a group of students from the University of Illinois.

To the extent to which they have dealt with the adjustment of migrants in the city, the findings have on the whole highlighted the negative aspects, such as personal maladjustment, breakdown of family life, decline of religion, and increase of delinquency. The total picture has been one of disorganization, sometimes referred to as culture shock incident upon city living. One common theoretical explanation of these findings has been in terms of the change from the primary group environment, which is generally characterized as warm, personal, moral, and intimate, to a secondary group environment, which is described as cold, impersonal, mechanistic, nonmoral, and unfriendly.[1]

The preliminary findings of the present study of urbanization in Mexico City indicate quite different trends and suggest the possibility of urbanization without breakdown. They also suggest that some of the hitherto unquestioned sociological generalizations about urbanization may be culture-bound and in need of re-examination in the light of comparative studies of urbanization in other areas.[2] Some of our generalizations about the differences between rural and urban life also need to be re-examined. It should be recalled that direct studies of the urbanization process itself are difficult, and most studies have been indirect and inferential. Sociological generalizations about the differences between rural and urban society have been based largely on comparative statistical data on the incidence of crime in rural and urban areas, on birth, fertility, and death rates, size of family, educational opportunities, and social participation. As Ralph Beals has recently pointed out, ". . . sociologists paid much more attention to urbanism than to urbanization."[3] Moreover, we know very little about the psychological aspects of urbanization as it affects specific individuals and families.

Perhaps one of the difficulties in this field has been the inadequate methodology. There is not, to my knowledge, a single study that has followed up migrants from a rural community which had first been the subject of intensive analysis on the social, economic, political, and psychological levels. An adequate research design for the study of the socio-psychological aspects of urbanization would require a project consisting of three phases: a well-rounded study of a rural or peasant community, including intensive family and psychological studies; locating families from this community who have gone to live in the city; an intensive study of these families in the city.

The present research has attempted to conform to this design. The first phase was completed some time ago with a study of the village of Tepoztlán. The second and third phases were begun last summer in Mexico City.

The specific objectives of the research were conceived as follows: (1) to study the process of urbanization directly by analyzing the changes in custom, attitudes, and value systems of Tepoztecan individuals and families who had gone to live in Mexico City; (2) to compare family life and interpersonal relations of selected urban families of Tepoztecan origin with those of the rural community from which they had migrated; (3) to relate our findings to the more general theoretical findings and problems in the field of culture change.

The study was planned on two levels. First, we wanted to do a broad survey of all Tepoztecan families in Mexico City and obtain data for each family on such items as date of and reasons for leaving the village, size of family, kinship composition of the household, the extent of bilingualism (Spanish and Nahuatl), the general level of living, the religious life, the *compadre* system, curing practices, and the life cycle. For most of these items we had rather full data on the village of Tepoztlán; these data could therefore be used as a base line from which to analyze the nature and direction of change.

Second, we planned to do intensive studies of a few selected families representative of the different lengths of residence in the city and of different socioeconomic levels. Other variables that might become significant in the course of the study were also to be taken into consideration.

We located one hundred Tepoztecan families in Mexico City and interviewed each family at least once. Sixty-nine families were interviewed twice, and ten of these were interviewed ten times. The quantitative data in this paper are based on the sixty-nine families for which we had the fullest data. The major factor in our inability to gather more information on the remainder of the families was lack of time. On the basis of the data obtained in the one interview with each of the thirty-one families, it appears probable that our total picture would not have been appreciably changed. The fact that the sixty-nine families were distributed in many different sections of the city and that they represented distinct socioeconomic levels further insures against an inadvertently loaded sample.

The city families were located with the help of our informants in Tepoztlán, many of whom had friends and relatives in the city. But most of the families were located with the aid of officers of the now-defunct Colonia Tepozteco, an organization of Tepoztecans in Mexico City, which kept a list of the names and addresses of Tepoztecans living in the city. We have reason to believe that the one hundred families we located represent approximately 90 per cent of all Tepoztecans living in the city.

It should be noted that field work in the city is in many ways more difficult, more costly, and more time-consuming than in the village. The Tepoztecan families were scattered in twenty-two different *colonias*, or neighborhoods, extending from one end of the city to the other. Much time was lost in traveling to and from the homes, in making appointments for interviews (only one of the families had a telephone), and in establishing rapport. Often we would spend an entire morning calling on two or three families, only to find people out or otherwise unavailable. Moreover, we did not have the advantage of working through community leaders, of becoming familiar and accepted figures in the community, or of utilizing neighbors—and village gossip—as sources of information.

The earliest contacts between Mexico City and Tepoztlán probably resulted from trade. A small number of Tepoztecan merchants regularly sold their products (mainly hog plums and corn) in the Merced, Lagunilla, and Tacubaya markets. Consequently, some of the earliest migrants of whom we have record settled near these markets, and to this day there are small concentrations of Tepoztecan families around the markets.

Our study revealed that the Tepoztecan families now living in Mexico City came in three distinct periods of migration. The first was prior to the Mexican Revolution of 1910; the second was during the Revolution, from about 1910 to 1920; the third since 1920. The motives for migration and the number and quality of migrants, as well as their social composition, show interesting differences for each of these periods.

During the first period only young men left, their primary motives being to get a higher education and to seek better employment opportunities. These early migrants were generally poor young men related to the best families in the village. We located fifteen individuals who left during this period. In general these early migrants made good, economically speaking. Some became professionals and have achieved important positions in the city. Many became the intellectuals who later formed the core of the Colonia Tepozteca, which was to play such an important part in community affairs.

The second period was one of forced migration, when hundreds of Tepoztecans left the village, generally as family units, to escape the ravages of the civil war. The earliest ones to leave during this period were the *cacique* families who fled before the threat of the Zapatista revolutionaries. Later, when the village became a battleground for opposing forces, people from all social levels fled. It is estimated that by 1918 there were approximately a thousand Tepoztecans in the city, and, according to our informants, approximately 700 attended one of the early meetings preceding the formation of the Colonia Tepozteco. Most of these migrants returned to the village after peace was established. Many of those who remained were the conservative, wealthier families who had been ruined by the Revolution. About 65 per cent of the families we studied came to the city during this period.

The striking thing about migration during the third period is the relatively small number of migrants. Only 25 per cent of our families came during 1920–50. We find a wider variety of motives for migration than formerly, but the two most important seem to be improved educational and economic opportunities. During the later twenties and early thirties, however, a number of men left because of the intense political strife which flared up in the village. Again we find that the young men predominated in the exodus, but now there were also young women, who came either to attend school or to serve as domestics. In all cases during this period, the migrants came to live with relatives or *compadres*. There was apparently a sharp increase in the number of migrants to the city toward the latter part of this period, particularly after the road was built in 1936.

The figures for Tepoztecans in Mexico City are not an accurate index of the total migration from the village. This was established by a study of all the cases that have left the village since 1943. Of seventy-four cases that left, only forty-one went to live in Mexico City; the remainder went to other villages and towns. Of the forty-one in Mexico City, there were twenty-three single males, sixteen single females, and one married couple. Over 90 per cent were from two large barrios in the center of the village.

Tepoztecans in the city live in three types of housing: the *vecindad*, the apartment house, and the separate, privately owned dwelling. The *vecindad* represents some of the poorest housing conditions in the city. It consists of a series of one-story dwellings arranged around a courtyard. Often there is a communal water fountain in the center and one or two toilets for a settlement of twenty-five families. In a few cases there is piped water in each apartment. One of our families lived in a *vecindad* of 150 families—practically a small community in itself. The rentals varied from 25 to 65 pesos ($3–$8) a month. Forty-four per cent of Tepoztecan families live in *vecindades*. The dwellings are generally small, usually consisting of two rooms.

The apartment house provides much more privacy and represents a distinctly higher standard of living. Sixteen per cent of the families lived in apartment houses, at rentals ranging from 65 to 300 pesos a month. Professionals and skilled laborers live here—typical Mexican lower-middle-class families. The apartments are better constructed than the *vecindades* and have more and larger rooms.

Privately owned homes were dwellings for 28 per cent of the families. There was a wide range in the styles, size, and property value of these houses. Some were one- or two-room wooden shacks built on tiny lots on the outskirts of the city; others were modern eight- or ten-room buildings, with enclosed private gardens and patios, located in a thriving middle-class neighborhood. Home ownership is therefore not a good index of wealth or class position.

The average size of Tepoztecan households in the city was somewhat larger than in the village—5.8 as compared to about 5 (Table 1).

TABLE 1

NUMBER OF PERSONS PER HOUSE SITE, TEPOZTLÁN AND MEXICO CITY

No. of persons per house site	*Per cent of house sites, Tepoztlán*	*Per cent of house sites, Mexico City*
1–5	44.2	41
6–10	52.5	53
11 and over	3.3	6

The composition of the household shows about the same pattern as in the village except that there is a slightly higher percentage of extended families living in the city (Table 2). In contrast to Tepoztlán there were no cases of persons living alone or of unrelated families living together. There is probably greater economic pressure for families to live together in the city than in the country. In Tepoztlán, if young couples do not get along well with the in-laws and wish to live alone, they can almost always find someone who has an empty house that can be used rent-free. The same is true of old people and widows, who manage to eke out a living with garden produce and by raising chickens or pigs.

TABLE 2

KINSHIP COMPOSITION BY HOUSEHOLDS—TEPOZTLÁN, 1943, AND MEXICO CITY, 1951

Type	*Families in Mexico City (69) (per cent of all families)*	*Families in Tepoztlán (662) (per cent of all families)*
Simple biological family	66.6	70
Biological family with married children and grandchildren	17.2	13.5
Married siblings with their children	2.9	2.1
Persons living alone	0	6.7
Unrelated families living together	0	.7
Miscellaneous	13.3	7.5

We found very little evidence of family disorganization in the city.

There were no cases of abandoned mothers and children among our sixty-nine families studied nor was there a history of separation or divorce in more than a few families. Families remain strong; in fact, there is some evidence that family cohesiveness increases in the city in the face of the difficulties of city life. In Tepoztlán the extended family shows solidarity only in times of crisis or emergency. Although there is more freedom for young people in the city, the authority of parents shows little signs of weakening, and the phenomenon of rebellion against parental authority hardly exists. Nor are the second-generation children ashamed of their parents. Perhaps this can be explained by the general cultural emphasis upon respect for age, authority, and parenthood. Similarly, we found no sharp generation cleavage in values and general outlook on life.

As might be expected, the general standard of living of Tepoztecan families in Mexico City shows upward movement as compared with Tepoztlán. Thus, 78 per cent of our city families had radios as compared to about one per cent in the village; 83 per cent had clocks as compared to about 20 per cent in the village; 54 per cent had sewing machines as compared to 25 per cent in Tepoztlán; 41 per cent reported buying a newspaper with some regularity as compared to 6 per cent; three of our sixty-nine families owned cars in the city; there were no car owners at the time of our Tepoztlán study. In the city all slept in beds; in the village only 19 per cent slept in beds in 1940. However, there seemed to be more crowding in the city, especially among the poor families, than in the village. I found cases, in *vecindades*, of ten people living in one room and sharing two beds. A similar situation holds in regard to toilet facilities. All Tepoztecan families in the city had some toilet facilities, but we found cases where fifteen families shared a single toilet, and in other instances there was a semi-enclosed toilet in the kitchen. From the point of view of hygiene, it is doubtful whether this was an improvement over the orchards of Tepoztlán.

The diet of the city families is similar to that of the village except that there is greater variety, depending upon income. The city dwellers all enjoy Tepoztecan cooking and continue to make *mole* on festive occasions. They strongly prefer Tepoztecan tortillas, and many continue to prepare beans with *epazote*, as in Tepoztlán. About 80 per cent of the families continue to use the *metate* and *meclapil*, especially for preparing fiesta meals. A few buy corn and make tortillas at home; a larger number buy mill-ground corn or *masa*; a still larger number buy ready-made tortillas.

The Tepoztecan custom of having household pets continues in the city. Fifty-four per cent of the families owned a pet—dogs, cats, or pigeons, and 24 per cent owned either chickens or pigs or both. Most of these families lived in privately owned homes.

The religious life of Tepoztecans in Mexico City appears to be at least as vigorous as in Tepoztlán. Again, the evidence does not support the findings of rural sociologists in this country to the effect that there is a decline in church attendance and religious practices when farm people move to the city. In our study it is not so much a matter of becoming more or less religious, but rather of a change in the content and form of religious expression. Specifically, it is a matter of becoming more Catholic and less Indian.

In general, the city Tepoztecans follow the Roman Catholic tradition more closely. The village belief that El Tepozteco is the son of Mary is no longer held and is regarded as backward and superstitious in the city. Tepoztecans in the city tend to send their children more regularly to Sunday School to learn doctrine, to take first communion, and to attend mass. Confession is as unpopular among city Tepoztecans as in the village, but probably occurs more often.

Mexico City, as the center of the Catholic Church in Mexico, has better organized and better staffed associations, which carry on intensive programs of indoctrination. In many *vecindades* we found religious shrines, usually of the Virgin of Guadalupe, and all residents are expected to honor them as the protector of the *vecindad*, to lift the hat in passing, to cross themselves, and to partake in the collective prayers organized by some enterprising member of the *vecindad*. That social control is strong can be seen from this statement by an informant: "If one does not salute the Virgin, the janitor and all the old women of the *vecindad* begin to call one a heretic and throw dirty looks."

Such shrines are also found in some of the factories in which our informants worked. A few of our Tepoztecans who are bus drivers tell of the requirement to carry images of San Cristobal, the patron saint of their union. They also tell of religious pilgrimages organized by the unions. One Tepoztecan explained that he had never bothered about the Virgin of Guadalupe when he was in Tepoztlán, but since working in the city has gone on two union pilgrimages. This same informant, who as a child in the village had received no training in doctrine classes, had no first communion, and rarely was obliged to attend mass, now attends mass frequently, consults a priest about his economic and domestic problems, and thanks to the perseverance of Acción Católica, regularly sends his four children to Sunday School.

As another example of the increased activity of, and the greater identification with, the church is the fact that several of our city informants draped their doors with black crepe to mourn the death of a bishop of the church. In Tepoztlán it is doubtful whether the death of the Pope himself would lead to such action.

There are some differences in church organization in the city which affect participation of Tepoztecans. Unlike the village, there are no barrio *mayordomos*. Many of the tasks connected with the care of the images and the church, which in the village are assigned to members of the community or to the specific barrio, are carried out by paid church personnel in the city. Since many of these jobs were the work of men in the village, the net result is that in the city the men play much smaller roles in the religious life. Another difference is that the Tepoztecans in the city contribute less money to the church than in the village.

The system of *compadrazgo* continues to function among Tepoztecans in the city. Each Tepoztecan interviewed in Mexico City had *compadres*, godparents, and godchildren. With one or two exceptions the changes that *compadrazgo* has undergone represent an adaptation to urban life rather than a breakdown or even a weakening of the system.

A major change in *compadrazgo* in the city is the disappearance of several types of godparents known in the village—namely, the godfather of *miscoton*, godfather of the ribbon, godfather of *evangelio*, godfather of the scapulary, godfather of the Child Jesus. There is also much less use of the godfather of confirmation and the godfather of communion. The *compadrazgo* system is largely limited to the godparents of baptism and of marriage, thereby resembling the original Catholic practice as introduced by the early Spaniards and as practiced to this day in Spain.

The decline in the role of the godfather of baptism is another important change. In the city he is no longer consulted in the selection of the godparent of confirmation in the cases where this occurs. Moreover, in the city there is no *sacamisa*, thereby eliminating the role of the godparent of baptism in this ritual. The absence of the *sacamisa* is probably due to the unwillingness of the mothers to remain at home for forty days after the birth of the child, as is required in Tepoztlán. Another adaptation to city life is the delayed baptism. In Tepoztlán babies are baptized as soon as possible, often when only a few days old, almost always before three months. In Mexico City baptisms in our families did not occur for twelve to eighteen months and sometimes not for several years. This delay may be attributed in part to the lower death rate among infants born in the city and to a lessened anxiety about infant health.

Another interesting change in the city is the increased frequency with which relatives are selected as godparents. In Tepoztlán it is unusual to find relatives who are *compadres*. Most Tepoztecans consider this undesirable, for it conflicts with the basic notion of respect and social distance that should exist between *compadres*. In the city, where Tepoztecans find themselves without friends, they turn to relatives for godparents. Family ties are thereby reinforced by the ties of *compadrazgo*. But this changes the character of the *compadrazgo* relationship from a formal and ceremonial relationship to a more informal and personal one. The mode of address among *compadres* in the village is always of "*Vd.–Vd.*" In the city it is frequently merely a continuation of the form of address used prior to becoming *compadres*. Thus, in the city we find *compadres* addressing each other as "*tu–tu*," "*Vd.–tu*," and "*Vd.–Vd.*" The "*tu–tu*" is used between brothers or sisters who have become *compadres*. The "*Vd.–tu*" is used when an uncle and nephew become *compadres*. In rural Spain we found the *compadre* system to be practically identical with the urban forms in Mexico.

Still another change in the system in the city is the custom whereby a man or woman will offer to be a godparent before the child is born. In the village one always waits to be asked in a formal manner. Since it might be taken as an insult to turn down an offer of godparentage, the net effect is to reduce parental control in the matter of selection. The obligations of godparents to godchildren and of *compadres* to one another are more clearly and specifically defined in the village than in the city. In the city there is much more familiarity between *compadres*, and a *compadre* may ask for almost any kind of favor.

Many Tepoztecan families in the city still use herbs for cooking and curing. In almost all the privately owned homes and in some of the *vecindades* common herbs such as *yerba buena*, *santa maría*, and *manzanilla* are grown in gardens and flowerpots. Herbs are used to cure colds, headaches, stomach ache, toothache, and so on, much the way they are in Tepoztlán; however, city families tend to rely more upon patent medicines than do village families. Illnesses such as evil eye, *los aires*, and *muina* ("illness of anger"), for which there are no patent medicines, necessarily are cured by native herbs. In these cases it is not uncommon for city people to return to the village to be cured. It should also be noted that, when other illnesses do not respond to patent medicines or to medical treatment, the sick person may be taken to the village for rediagnosis and cure. One informant told of suffering a partial paralysis of the face and of being treated unsuccessfully by several doctors. Finally, a visitor from Tepoztlán diagnosed it as an attack of *los aires*, whereupon the patient went to the village and was promptly cured by means of appropriate herbs placed in a bag suspended around his neck. The daughter of another informant was stricken with poliomyelitis and despite hospital treatment remained paralyzed. Her father, in desperation, took her to Tepoztlán, where she was given a series of sweat baths in a *temazcal*. This treatment, according to her parent, brought about considerable improvement. Sometimes, in the hope that the local *curanderos* would "understand" the illness better, an incurably ill person may be taken from the city to the village, only to die there. Thus, not only do country people go to the city seeking cures, but the same process works the other way around.

In considering stability or change in the way of life of Tepoztecans in Mexico City it is important to realize that the ties between the city families and their relatives in the village remain strong and enduring for almost all the city families studied. They visit the village at least once a year on the occasion of the Carnaval. Many go much more often, to celebrate their own Saint's Day, to attend their barrio fiesta, a funeral, or the inauguration of a new bridge or school, to act as godparent for some child, or to celebrate a wedding anniversary, or the Day of the Dead. The ties with the village do not seem to weaken with increase in years away from it. On the contrary, some of the most ardent and nostalgic villagers are those who have been away from it the longest. Many old people expressed a desire to return to the village to die. Some men, who have been living in the city for thirty years, still think of themselves as Tepoztecans first and Mexicans second. Fifty-six per cent of the families studied owned a house in the village, and 30 per cent owned their private *milpas*.

The proximity to Tepoztlán, and the bus line which now runs to the village, facilitate visiting. The young people enjoy spending a week-end or a Sunday in their village. There is also some visiting from Tepoztlán to friends and relatives in the city.

In the past few years Tepoztecans in the city have organized a soccer team and play against the village team. The organization of a team in the city means that Tepoztecans from distant *colonias* must get together; however, the cohesiveness of Tepoztecans with their village is much greater than among themselves in the city. The Colonia Tepozteco has not been functioning for many years, having broken up because of factionalism within the organization.

In summary, this study provides further evidence that urbanization is not a simple, unitary, universally similar process, but that it assumes different forms and meanings, depending upon the prevailing historic, economic, social, and cultural conditions. Generalizations concerning urbanization must take these conditions into consideration. From our study of Tepoztecans living in Mexico City, we find that peasants in Mexico adapt to city life with far greater ease than do American farm families. There is little evidence of disorganization and breakdown,[4] of culture conflict, or of irreconcilable differences between generations; many of the trends and characteristics found among these urbanized Tepoztecans are in direct opposition to those that occur among urbanized farm families in the United States. Family life remains strong in Mexico City. Family cohesiveness and extended family ties increase in the city, fewer cases of separation and divorce occur, no cases of abandoned mothers and children, no cases of persons living alone or of unrelated families living together. Household composition is similar to village patterns except that more extended families live together in the city. There is a general rise in the standard of living in the city, but dietary patterns do not change greatly. Religious life in the city becomes more Catholic and disciplined; however, men play a smaller religious role and contribute less money to the church in the city. The system of *compadrazgo* has undergone important changes, but remains strong. Although there is a greater reliance upon doctors and patent medicines to cure illness, city Tepoztecans still use village herbal cures and in cases of severe illness sometimes return to the village to be cured. Village ties remain strong, with much visiting back and forth.

In considering possible explanations for the above findings the following factors would seem to be most relevant: (1) Mexico City has been an important political, economic, and religious center for Tepoztecans since pre-Hispanic times. The contact with an urban, albeit Indian, culture was an old pattern, and has continued throughout recent history. (2) Mexico City is much more homogeneous than most large urban centers in the United States, both in terms of the predominance of Catholicism and of the cultural backgrounds of its people. Neither Mexico City nor Mexico as a whole has had much immigration from other parts of the world. The population of Mexico City therefore has very close ties with the rural hinterlands. (3) Mexico City is essentially conservative in tradition. In Mexico most of the revolutions have begun in the country. The city has been the refuge for the well-to-do rural families whose local positions were threatened. (4) Mexico City is not as highly industrialized as many American cities and does not present the same conditions of life. (5) Mexican farmers live in well-organized villages that are more like cities and towns than like the open-country settlement pattern of American farmers. (6) Finally, Tepoztlán is close to Mexico City, not only geographically but also culturally. The similarities between the value systems of working-class and lower-middle-class families in Mexico City and those of Tepoztecans are probably much greater than those between, let us say, families from the hill country of Arkansas and working- and middle-class families from St. Louis or Detroit.

In conclusion, it must be emphasized that this study is still in its preliminary stage, and the findings are therefore tentative. The primary purpose has been to indicate a research design which might yield valid and reliable data for the understanding of the urbanization process.

It may be that Tepoztlán was not the best possible choice for this kind of study because of its proximity to Mexico City. It may also be that Tepoztlán is a special case from other points of view. Certainly we need other studies. We should have follow-up studies of migrants to the city from George Foster's Tarascan village of Tzintzuntzan, from Robert Redfield's and Villa Rojas' Maya village of Chan-Kom, from Julio de la Fuente's Zapotecan village of Yalalag, to determine to what extent the findings agree with those from Tepoztlán. It would also be important to have comparative studies of migrants to Mexico City, not from ancient and stable communities like Tepoztlán, but from plantation areas populated by poor and landless farm laborers.

NOTES

1. The tendency to view the city as the source of all evil and to idealize rural life has been corrected somewhat by the work of rural sociologists in recent years. We are no longer certain that rural society per se is nearly as Rousseauan and anxiety-free as we once thought. Studies by Mangus and his colleagues suggest just as high an incidence of psychosomatic illness among the farm population of portions of Ohio as in urban areas (see A. R. Mangus and John R. Seeley, *Mental Health Needs in a Rural and Semirural Area of Ohio,* Mimeographed Bulletin no. 1951, Columbus, Ohio State University, January, 1947). Moreover, a study by Goldhamer and Marshall suggests that there has been no increase in the psychoses (and, by inference, also in the neuroses) over the past hundred years in the state of Massachusetts, a state that has undergone considerable industrial development during this period (see Herbert Goldhamer and Andrew W. Marshall, *The Frequency of Mental Disease: Long-Term Trends and Present Status,* The Rand Corp., July, 1949).

2. Theodore Caplow's excellent article on "The Social Ecology of Guatemala City" (*Social Forces,* 1949, XXVIII, 113) suggests the provincialism of earlier sociological ideas about the nature of the city. Caplow writes, "The literature of urban geography and urban sociology has a tendency to project as universals those characteristics of urbanism with which European and American students are most familiar . . . there was until recently a tendency to ascribe to all cities characteristics which now appear to be specific to Chicago . . ." (p. 132). Caplow raises the question whether "much of the anarchic and unstable character attributed by many authorities to urban life in general is not merely a particular aspect to the urban history of the United States and Western Europe since the Renaissance" (p. 133).

3. Ralph Beals, "Urbanism, Urbanization, Acculturation," *American Anthropologist,* 1951, LIII, 5.

4. There is the possibility of other kinds of disorganization which might be manifested on a "deeper" level. In this connection it will be interesting to compare the findings of the Rorschachs given to the Tepoztecan families living in the city, with the findings on the Rorschachs from the village

of Tepoztlán. It should also be noted that our findings for Tepoztecan families in Mexico City do not mean that there is no "disorganization" in Mexico City as a whole. A comparison of the statistical indices on crime, delinquency, and divorce, between urban and rural populations in Mexico, shows a much higher incidence for urban areas (see José E. Iturriaga, *La estructura social y cultural de México,* Fondo de Cultura Económica, Mexico, 1951).

Economic Autonomy and Social Change in Mexican Villages

JOHN H. KUNKEL

The Problem

Most nonindustrialized countries are "multiple societies with plural cultures"[1] in which the majority of the population lives in relatively isolated, economically autonomous, small agricultural communities. Although there may be a few large urban centers which, together, give the semblance of a nation, the pre-industrial society today is often not a homogeneous whole, but rather an organization of diverse units which are "locally organized, subordinate societies" within a larger political unit.

Western capitalistic industrialization, defined largely in terms of the growth of secondary industry with a minimum of governmental planning and regulation, cannot develop under such conditions of social organization. The growth of industry is based on—among other prerequisites—a labor force to work in factories, a market for manufactured products, and a cash economy.[2] If a society consists of largely independent peasant communities, then the labor force, markets, and cash economy may be too small or poorly developed for the indigenous or even the imported growth of industry. If rapid economic develop-

Reprinted from *Economic Development and Cultural Change*, 1961, X, 51–63, by permission of the author and publisher.

ment is to take place on a national scale—and this is usually envisaged by those advocating industrialization—then the small, economically autonomous peasant communities whose populations constitute such an important part of the nation must be incorporated into the national network of relationships, at least in terms of the three phenomena listed above, namely labor, markets, and cash relations. That is, economic development cannot occur without a preceding or concomitant national development.

The relationship between the rise of industry and that of the nation has been recognized by a number of theorists concerned with the past and present. They not only recognize the simultaneous growth of industry and the declining autonomy of societal parts, but also treat of the social organizational changes which occur.

Schmoller, for example, in discussing the historical significance of the mercantile system in Europe, shows how economic, political, and other social changes came about simultaneously as a nation developed economically, and how the European nations became political and economic units as well as social and cultural entities:

> The essence of the [mercantile] system lies . . . in the total transformation of society and its organization, as well as of the state and its institutions, in the replacing of a local and territorial economic policy by that of the national state . . . In its innermost kernel it is nothing but state-making . . . and a national-economy making at the same time; state-making in the modern sense, which creates out of the political community an economic community.[3]

Speaking of societies generally, and not only in specific historical circumstances, Deutsch investigates the influence of communication in the process of nation making, which is inextricably tied up with economic development. Economic development brings about increased communication, which reduces internal differences and thus creates homogeneous national units whose culture and social structure become part of all communities.

> Much of the economic or technological development may force people into new and inescapable contacts with each other as workers, customers, or neighbors . . . Linguistically and culturally . . . members of each group are outsiders for the other. Yet technology and economic processes are forcing them together . . . [The] decisive factor in national assimilation . . . [is] the fundamental process of social mobilization which accompanies the growth of markets, industries, and towns, and eventually of literacy and mass communication.[4]

Wolf[5] comes to similar conclusions on the basis of his analysis of the Mexican Bajío during the eighteenth century and, on a more superficial level, of the rest of Mexico at other times, including the present. National and economic development in Mexico have been unequal. Some parts, such as the Bajío (roughly, the state of Guanajuato) have a history of economic development dating back to the seventeenth century; other sections of the nation are not even now well developed. As one stage in the development of any nation, Wolf lists internal acculturation, which is similar to Deutsch's national assimilation. In the Bajío of the seventeenth and eighteenth centuries, Indians left their villages and began to work in the mines, textile mills, and on the haciendas. They began to speak Spanish, dress like Spaniards, "ride horses like Spaniards," and, for all practical purposes, became citizens—much to the chagrin of Spaniards. Tribute, guilds, and slavery were abolished. The Indian ceased to be a member primarily of the village and became instead a member of the larger society. "Integration in the economic aspects gave rise to integration in the social and cultural aspects."[6] At the same time, textile mills in the Bajío could not develop beyond a certain point, because their markets were limited to the members of the integrated cultural and economic unit which was the Bajío; Indians outside the area had no need for factory-made textile goods.

The idea common to these approaches is that, as autonomous parts of a nation become economically integral parts of a nation, they also become part of the nation in terms of culture and social structure. Presumably, economic changes which bind the community to the nation effect changes in the social and cultural elements of the village, so that these elements become consistent with those of the nation; these changes, in turn, pave the way for the further economic development of both units. The discussion, however, is on a rather general level, and is based on little systematic analysis of villages; much of the support of these ideas derives from illustrations on the national level. There is little concern with peasant villages themselves—the social units presumably most involved in any changes connected with national development.

Redfield has studied social change within villages as they come into contact with the nation, and has arrived at the conclusion that:

> Increase of contacts, bringing about heterogeneity and disorganization of culture, constitutes one sufficient cause for secularization and individualization . . . [But] there is no single necessary cause for secularization and individualization . . . The development of important commerce and a money economy may be another such sufficient cause.[7]

From the point of view of the peasant village, rather than that of the nation, the above theories lead to the following hypothesis regarding social change in communities: as small agricultural villages come into contact with the nation—or begin to participate in the economic system of the nation—they will also begin to participate in the social and cultural systems of the nation, and their social organizations will become increasingly consistent with those of the nation.

Contact and Change

We must now determine what is meant by "contact," "communication," or "economic participation of communities" in the nation. In a recent article, the Youngs[8] have pointed out that the functional size of a community and its functional distance from the nearest (industrial) town are crucial factors in determining the economic contact which the community will have; in another article, however, the Youngs[9] indicate that this contact itself does not decide the changes which occur in village social organization. The concept "friction of space" (or functional distance) has been an important part of ecological analysis for some time, and it is useful for determining the size and location of many institutions and functions.[10] Friction of space is sociologically meaningful, because individuals and goods must overcome certain difficulties in the process of transportation. Simply equating roads (or their condition) with friction of space, functional distance, or ease of contact, however, involves the assumption that transportation routes will be used; and this assumption although tenable in an urban industrial society like the United States, is not necessarily universally applicable. The telephone, for example, is one means of communications among individuals today. Presumably, a man with a telephone and a directory is less isolated than a man who has neither. But this is not necessarily so; a man with a telephone and an address book who wishes to be alone may be more isolated in a large city than a man without these conveniences who wishes to have friends. The telephone, then, becomes a significant social phenomenon only when it is used. Similarly, the simple establishment of contact between a peasant community and another village, or a town, or a major highway, is not necessarily significant for the community. Contact is sociologically significant only if it affects individuals or the social organization of the village in some way. If it were true that contact, or low friction of space, automatically effects changes in social organization, then the solution to the problem of multiple societies would be rather simple: establish contact between isolated communities and the nation.

But the mere existence of a transportation route—be it mountain path, jungle trail, road, or highway—does not mean that villages will take advantage of it, nor that outside elements will enter the village organization. Transportation routes make it *possible* for communities to become part of the nation; but this does not mean that such communities *will* become part of the nation. Paving a road, or somehow decreasing the friction of space, may make contact and communication between village and nation easier, but it does not inevitably increase them. Examples of situations in which contact does not necessarily mean greater incorporation of the village into the nation are not hard to find.

Moore, in his study of the Atlixco area,[11] found that the more isolated of two communities furnished a greater proportion of its population as factory laborers than did the village closer to the town and with easier access to it. From the point of view of simple contact, one would expect the more accessible village to be a more integral part of the nation, more a part of the industrial society, than the more isolated one. Here the contrary was true because of the poverty and the inadequate supply of land in the more distant, less accessible village. Another instance which might be mentioned is the Yaqui village of Potam, located on a highway a few miles from Guaymas. This village, in easy contact with the nation, still retains many of its ancient customs;[12] the reason here seems to be the powerful force of tradition. The villages of Tusik and Chenalho, discussed in this study, do not permit travelers to remain more than one day; only under exceptional circumstances are strangers allowed to linger.[13] The Youngs found that contact did not necessarily bring changes in the social organization of the villages they studied.

Without disparaging the importance of the friction of space between a village and the "outside," I suggest that neither contact alone nor low friction of space is sufficient to explain the change or perseverance of social organization in peasant communities. The problem is, rather, to determine what community characteristics influence the acceptance and rejection of new elements entering from the outside.[14] On the basis of the theories and reports discussed above, we may anticipate that the economic character of the specific village itself exerts great influence on any potential changes in the social organization of peasant communities.

The Study

The hypothesis which this study will investigate is that, as small, agricultural economically autonomous villages begin to participate in the economic system of the nation, their social organization becomes consistent with that of the nation. Economic participation in the nation will be considered the independent variable, and the social organization of peasant villages will be the dependent variable.

The test of this hypothesis is based on available reports of Mexican communities investigated by anthropologists and others over the last quarter century or so. These villages are not necessarily a representative sample of Mexican communities, and the selection involves all of the biases which enter into anthropologists' choices of locations for field work. Nevertheless, these community studies must be used, since they provide the only readily available material for testing this hypothesis in the Mexican context. Of the available studies, two had to be disregarded because of the inadequate material in the accounts (the original Tepoztlán and the restudy of Chan Kom); a few additional studies could not be included because they dealt with population clusters which were not villages in the sense the others were. In all, fifteen community studies were used.[15]

Since these studies were originally made for diverse purposes—e.g., to provide training for graduate students, or to test hypotheses regarding "primitive economics"—the hypothesis must be stated in terms of variables for which data can be found in most, if not all, monographs. This procedure leads to the omission of important variables, such as the role of wealth equalization devices, and to the less than perfect operationalization of other variables; but again, the overruling consideration is that these are the only data at hand.

A village's participation in the economic system of the nation is measured by five criteria which, considered together, indicate economic autonomy. In order to minimize the scope of interpretation and error, each of the five variables is stated in terms of a dichotomy, as follows:

1. A specifically grown cash crop is regularly exported, or it is not.
2. Wage labor and cash relations are important within the village, or they are not.
3. Sufficient land to satisfy the daily needs of all villagers is not available, or it is.
4. There is significant external wage labor, or there is not.
5. Staple foodstuffs are regularly imported, or they are not.

No village is completely autonomous economically, since all, for example, import salt and metal implements. Even economically autonomous communities, then, are to be regarded as only relatively independent. A village will be considered economically dependent if a cash crop is produced in the village and exported, if there is wage labor within the village and cash plays an important part, if there is not enough land for all the villagers, if external wage labor is important for many people, and if staple foods, such as maize, are regularly imported. A village will be considered economically autonomous if no cash crop is regularly produced, if neither internal wage labor nor cash is important, if all villagers have enough land, if there is no significant wage labor outside the village, and if no staple foods are regularly imported. The communities which do not fall into these extreme categories will be placed in an intermediate group.

The consistency of a village's social organization with that of the nation is more difficult to determine, and some perhaps slightly dubious assumptions must be made. In spite of possible objections, however, we shall make an attempt at measurement, since data for Mexican villages are so meager that all possible use must be made of them. Characteristics of community social organization which are described in almost all of the monographs under discussion were used. As a result, some elements could not be considered in our analysis, although they might have been more meaningful than some of those which were actually used. The characteristics considered involved the organization of political and religious activities, kinship organization, and the role of ritual kinship. To determine whether a particular organization or element followed the national pattern or not, each characteristic was considered in terms of a dichotomy: national or non-national, on the basis of the constitution and other writings concerned with the national organization of Mexico today.[16] In the following list, the first of every pair of elements is considered national, the second non-national, i.e., peculiar to the given village and not consistent with the requirements of the nation:

1. There is no definite hierarchy of political offices, or there is one, through which all villagers are expected to pass in their lifetimes.
2. Political officials are paid, or they are not.
3. There is no definite hierarchy of religious offices, or there is, through which all men are expected to pass during their lifetimes.
4. Political and religious offices or hierarchies are separate, or they are combined and form one complex hierarchy.
5. Financial responsibility for *mayordomías* is spread among many people, or the individual or his immediate family is responsible.
6. There is no compulsory communal labor, or there is.
7. Land may be sold to anyone, or the sale of land is restricted to fellow-villagers only.
8. The extended family is relatively unimportant, or it is important.
9. Spouses choose each other, or parents determine whom their child is to marry.
10. Marriages are stable, or they may be easily broken without sanctions.
11. Ritual kinship is important, and blood relatives may not be chosen, or it is unimportant, and relatives *may* be chosen.
12. Ritual kinship is important, and usually men on a higher economic level are chosen, or it is unimportant, and men on the same economic level are usually chosen.[17]

If, in a village, all of these elements are national, the social organization of the community will be considered consistent with that of the nation; if few or none of the elements are national, then the village will be regarded as having a social organization inconsistent with that of the nation. The proportion of national elements in the social organization of a community is expressed in the form of an index derived by dividing the number of national elements by the total number of the above characteristics for which there is information in the monograph. An index of 1.00 shows, then, that all of the characteristics for which data are available are of the national type; an index of .22 indicates that barely one fifth of all the elements considered are of the national type—the social organization of the community is not consistent with that of the nation. Table 1 shows the villages arranged according to the index of national elements and the various criteria of economic autonomy.

On the basis of the five indicators of economic autonomy, the villages may be divided into three groups: (1) communities economically dependent on the outside in terms of all variables; (2) villages completely autonomous according to the indices; and (3) villages in some respects economically dependent and in others autonomous. Only Tusik and Potam smudge the pattern slightly.[18]

According to the index of national elements, the communities also fall into three categories, whose compositions are identical with the categories based on economic autonomy. The cutting points are not arbitrary, but are real breaks in the continuity of the index, indicating rather different types of social organization; the "distance" among categories is greater than that between any two elements within categories. The position of Mitla and Yalalag among the partially autonomous villages has been changed in order to indicate more clearly the pattern in the indices of economic autonomy. The reversal is probably not too serious, since the index scores are quite similar and in each village there are some aspects of social organization for which no information is available.

Table 1 supports the hypothesis that, as small, agricultural, economically autonomous communities begin to participate in the economic system of the nation, their social organization becomes consistent with that of the nation. The villages which are autonomous economically have, on the whole, a social organization which is quite inconsistent with that of the nation. On the other hand, those communities which are economically dependent on the outside have a social organization which is, on the whole, quite consistent with the nation's.

Some qualifications are immediately necessary. The hypothesized relationship holds true only for the aggregate of characteristics considered in this study; there is no apparent pattern dictating *which* elements are related to any one indicator of economic autonomy. More important, the hypothesis has been tested in an ahistorical context—necessarily, since no village under consideration here has been studied at more than one point in time. Chan Kom and Tepoztlán have been studied twice; but in each case, one study is so poor in quantifiable data that it had to be eliminated from the analysis. Furthermore, it proved impossible to ascertain systematically the specific changes which have occurred in a village in recent times, or to relate certain changes in social organization to specific changes in economic autonomy. Enough information is available, however, to support the assumption on which the whole study rests, namely, that at some time in the past, the respective social organizations of all of the villages under consideration were almost equally inconsistent with that of the nation. Unless this assumption is made, it would be possible to say, for example, that a village such as Mitla has always had a great many national-type elements in its social organization, and that, therefore, changes in economic autonomy are irrelevant in the explanation of social change. Throughout the monographs, there are spotty remarks about changes which are occurring; in all cases, these are changes in the direction of a national type of social organization.

TABLE 1

ECONOMIC AUTONOMY AND NATIONAL CHARACTERISTICS OF MEXICAN VILLAGES

		Indices of economic autonomy				
Village	*Index of national elements**	*Cash crop export*	*Internal wage labor and cash*	*Sufficient land not available*	*External wage labor*	*Staple foods imported*
Economically dependent villages						
Quiroga	1.00	x	x	x	x	x
Tepoztlán	.92	x	x	x	x	x
Dzitas	.90	x	x	x	x	x
Tzintzuntzan	.83	x	x	x	x	x
Chacaltianguis	.80	x	x	x	?	x
Partially autonomous villages						
Mitla	.64	x	x	x	x	–
Yalalag	.64	x	x	x	x	–
Cheran	.66	x	x	x	–	–
Sayula	.66	x	–	–	–	–
Soteapan	.66	x	–	–	–	–
Economically autonomous villages						
Tusik	.42	x	–	–	–	–
Chenalho	.42	–	–	–	–	–
Cancuc	.40	–	–	–	–	–
Chan Kom	.33	–	–	–	–	–
Potam	.22	–	–	–	x	–

NOTE:

"x" indicates that the phenomenon is present in the village, or that the activity is performed.

"–" indicates that the phenomenon is not present in the village, or that the activity is not performed.

* The index is arrived at by dividing the number of national elements present in a village by the total number of elements for which there is information in the monographs.

Similar comments are made about changes in the economic relations between the village and the nation. Unfortunately, it has been impossible to relate these changes in social organization and economic autonomy in any one village; for this, a longitudinal study of communities would be necessary. The assumption, however, that the respective social organizations of all the villages were at one time almost equally distinct from the present national type, although it cannot be proved with certainty, seems not at all unreasonable. Since the studies were made at various times in the last thirty years, historical circumstances cannot have had so great an influence on social change in these communities as the fact that economic autonomy has changed or remained the same.

The longitudinal studies of villages would also remove any doubts which might exist about the direction of causality. In the relationship between economic autonomy and social organization indicated in Table 1, increasing national-local consistency can be considered as a factor in reducing economic autonomy. At present, this possibility may be disregarded on the basis of evidence from the community studies, which indicates that changes in social organization occur only after economic autonomy has been lost. There are indications of on-going social organizational changes in the economically dependent villages, but little evidence of social change in autonomous communities.[19] If national-local consistency of social organization were the cause of economic dependence, the opposite—i.e., great social changes in economically autonomous villages and little change in dependent villages—would be expected. The available data force us to conclude that, at least in the communities studied, social organization is indeed the dependent variable.

It is true that most of the economically autonomous villages are small and have poor transportation facilities, whereas economically dependent villages are large and usually are located on highways of some sort. Nonetheless, the relationship between population size or contact, on the one hand, and consistency with national type of social organization, on the other, is not statistically significant. Potam, for example, has a population of 3,000, whereas Soteapan has one of 900; Potam is located on a highway, but Yalalag is not. In addition, it is difficult to judge, on the basis of the monographs, what the quality of transportation routes really is, or whether transportation routes are the cause or effect of economic dependence. When villages are ranked according to economic autonomy, however, there are no exceptions to the rule that economic dependence is related to the consistency of the social organizations of the village with that of the nation. If there were measurements of the relative importance which the various economic criteria have within any one village, it might be possible to explain the range of the index of national elements within each category of communities.

Closer examination of Table 1 reveals a pattern in the operation of the various indices of economic autonomy. It appears that the export of cash crops and the import of foodstuffs are the most important indicators of economic dependence, and that they are of approximately equal strength. Together, they may suffice to divide the communities under investigation into meaningful categories of economic autonomy, and to predict the degree of consistency with which the social organization of the community conforms to that of the nation. If more cases were available, a scale for the measurement of economic autonomy, using the elements presented here, might be constructed. Whether the indices of economic autonomy used in this study will be found fruitful in studies of different communities remains to be seen.

Discussion

Earlier, we said that contact is sociologically meaningful only if the contact situation, such as a transportation route, is used *by* the community *for* something; it now appears that the same idea can be phrased in terms of necessity. The more vitally a community depends on contact with the outside, the greater will be the changes effected by this contact. The economically autonomous village is not affected by contact—or the lack thereof—no matter how long it has existed. The economically dependent community could not exist without contact, even for a short time. The export of a cash crop and the regular import of food imply the existence of contact with the outside; but contact with the outside does not imply the export of cash crops or the import of food. Thus the export and import of important goods seem to be better criteria of "meaningful contact" than is simple contact; the role of contact in the community's life—especially in its economic life—is more important than contact itself.

The result of the study indicates at least the general nature of the answer to a question raised by the Youngs: "What are the characteristics of a community which enable it to achieve incorporation in the urban system?"[20] The greater the vital *necessity* of economic contact with the nation, the greater will be the change in social organization occasioned by the contact; and the greater a village's economic autonomy, the greater its resistance to change.

Questions about the nature of this "vital necessity" and the causes underlying it can be only briefly considered. Since the authors whose studies were used were not concerned with those aspects of community organization that are necessary for the formulation of satisfactory answers, only tentative statements can be made. An indication of what may be involved is given by Moore, who found that the poorer of two villages, in terms of quality of soil and *ejido* membership, sent a greater proportion of its labor force into the outside, industrial world.[21] A similar interpretation of the present data would hold that deterioration of the soil, population increase, or both, result in the inability of all villagers to have land available for their own needs, thus giving rise to, or increasing, poverty. The explanation of loss of economic autonomy through increasing poverty implies either the deterioration of the soil or the growth of population within a relatively short period of time. Neither of these events can be definitely demonstrated for any village; in fact, the population of some villages seems to be smaller now than in the past. None of the accounts under consideration mentions recent great changes in soil fertility, population, or poverty; on the other hand, accurate historical records of this sort are largely absent. Thus, although poverty *may* be an important aspect of the vital necessity of contact, or may make contact become more vital, the present village descriptions leave little room for this interpretation. To say that poverty is an important factor implies that the economically dependent villages are poorer than the autonomous communities, or at least were much poorer in the past. But such comparisons cannot be made on the basis of the data; no judgment of relative poverty is possible, since each author states, at least implicitly, that "his" village is simply poor and has been so for a long time.

A second, alternative approach involves the role of specialization within a village. The availability of land to all families, and the importance of internal and external wage labor, are obviously related; together, they form the economic context within which the export of specially grown cash crops and the regular import of food become more meaningful and are perhaps intensified. The availability of land for the daily needs of all families is probably important in influencing the amount of both internal and external wage labor, considered now as indicators of occupational specialization. It may be that the division of labor, which exists in every village to some extent, takes on a more vital character when it is combined with a scarcity of land and the necessary importation of food, and thus paves the way for greater national-local consistency of social organization. The index "staple foods imported" indicates the extent to which the community as a whole is involved in specialization, whereas the index "internal wage labor and the importance of cash" concerns the extent to which the division of labor has progressed within the village. The relationship between individual specialization and local-national consistency of community social organization is not perfect, however. Although within the economically autonomous villages there is, by and large, less specialization than in the dependent villages (measured in terms of the proportion of the population *not* engaged in agriculture), there are enough cases which do not fit the pattern to indicate that additional factors are operating.[22] Their identification remains a subject for further work.

The tentative conclusion about the nature and causes of the "vital necessity" of contact which engenders changes in social organization is a combination of the above two approaches. There is specialization of some sort within all villages. When specialization becomes more important—either through historical circumstances (such as in Tzintzuntzan) or through the inadequate supply of land—the alternatives for the village are either extreme poverty, or economic relations with the nation for the purpose of importing food and exporting the goods produced by specialized occupations. Specialization, land supply, poverty (or, better, the threat of great poverty), economic dependence, and historical circumstances are thus interrelated and form part of the "vital necessity" of contact. The exact nature of this interrelationship cannot be ascertained from the data in the available community studies; only through the careful historical analysis of villages can this complex relationship be spelled out more systematically.

Furthermore, apparently villages cannot choose to change or to retain their social organization, beyond a certain point of economic dependence. If they are driven by necessity to import food, and to export cash crops, then their social organization will become consistent with that of the nation. The range of the index of national elements in Table 1 indicates that economically autonomous villages seemingly have a choice regarding the acceptance or rejection of national elements; apparently there is less of a choice when the community is extremely dependent on the nation economically. The exact role of community choice in the process of social change remains to be investigated more fully; there is evidence both for the existence of choice and for the apparent lack of it under certain economic conditions.

Conclusion

If the economic role of contact in a community—or the degree of economic autonomy—determines the degree of consistency of the social organization of village and of the nation, then social change in peasant communities cannot be considered apart from economic development. The question now arises: what makes contact so vitally necessary in some villages, and not in others? On the basis of the community descriptions on which this study rests, only a tentative conclusion, subject to revision, can be drawn. Where land is plentiful and fertile, there is no economic necessity for occupational specialization, or for the export or import of goods; hence, any contact which exists may remain largely meaningless for the village. If, on the other hand, there is specialization and/or a scarcity of land, or if all needs cannot be satisfied within the community, then contact will become meaningful—and necessary. The problem of incorporating villages into the nation, then, is not solved by simply establishing contact between them; the solution involves, in all probability, either the creation of needs which cannot be met by the village and its autonomous economy, or the creation of a scarcity of land.[23] With a steadily rising population, it seems that the latter will eventually be followed by most villages. It is questionable whether new needs can be created in an economically autonomous village, since institutions and customs often reinforce each other in excluding new ideas and needs.[24]

NOTES

1. This and the following quote are from Manning Nash, "The Multiple Society in Economic Development: Mexico and Guatemala," *American Anthropologist*, 1957, LIX, 825–833.

2. See, for example, Wilbert E. Moore, *Industrial Relations and the Social Order*, New York, Macmillan, 1951.

3. Gustav Schmoller, *The Mercantile System and Its Historical Significance*, New York, Macmillan, 1895, pp. 50–51.

4. Karl W. Deutsch, *Nationalism and Social Communication*, Cambridge, Massachusetts Institute of Technology, 1953, pp. 99, 100, 162.

5. Eric R. Wolf, "La formación de la nación: un ensayo de formulación," *Ciencias Sociales*, 1953, IV, 50–62, 98–111, 146–171.

6. Eric R. Wolf, *The Mexican Bajío in the 18th Century: An Analysis of Cultural Integration*, New Orleans, Tulane University, Middle American Research Institute Publication 17, 1955, pp. 180–199.

7. Robert Redfield, *The Folk Culture of Yucatan*, Chicago, University of Chicago Press, 1941, p. 369.

8. Frank W. and Ruth C. Young, "Two Determinants of Community Reaction to Industrialization in Rural Mexico," *Economic Development and Cultural Change*, 1960, VIII, 257–264.

9. Frank W. and Ruth C. Young, "Social Integration and Change in Twenty-four Mexican Villages," *Economic Development and Cultural Change*, 1960, VIII, 366–377.

10. Amos H. Hawley, *Human Ecology*, New York, Ronald Press, 1950, pp. 236 ff.

11. Wilbert E. Moore, *Industrialization and Labor*, Ithaca, Cornell University Press, 1951, esp. Chapters 10 and 11.

12. Edward H. Spicer, *Potam: A Yaqui Village in Sonora*, American Anthropological Association, Memoir 77, 1954.

13. Eric R. Wolf has discussed the nature of static and dynamic villages generally in terms of "open" and "closed" types, each consisting of a cluster of interrelated characteristics; he does not, however, indicate any causal relations among them. See his "Closed Corporate Peasant Communities in Mesoamerica and Central Java," *Southwestern Journal of Anthropology*, 1957, XIII, 1–18.

14. It is assumed here that villages come into contact with elements which have behind them equal pressure toward acceptance.

15. The following fifteen community studies form the basis of this study: Cancuc—Calixta Guiteras-Holmes, *Informe de Cancuc,* Microfilm Collection of Manuscripts on Middle American Cultural Anthropology no. 8, University of Chicago, Chacaltianguis—Fernando Camara Barbachano, *Chacaltianguis,* Mexico, D.F., Gobierno del Estado de Vera Cruz, 1952. Chan Kom—Robert Redfield and Alfonso Villa Rojas, *Chan Kom,* Washington, D.C., Carnegie Institution of Washington, 1934. Chenalho—Calixta Guiteras-Holmes, *Informe de San Pedro Chenalho,* Microfilm Collection of Manuscripts on Middle Cultural Anthropology no. 14, University of Chicago. Cheran—Ralph L. Beals, *Cheran,* Washington, D.C., Smithsonion Institution, 1946. Dzitas—Redfield, *op. cit.* Mitla—Elsie C. Parsons, *Mitla,* Chicago, University of Chicago Press, 1936. Potam—Spicer, *op. cit.* Quiroga—Donald D. Brand, *Quiroga,* Washington, D.C., Smithsonian Institution, 1951. Sayula—Calixta Guiteras-Holmes, *Sayula,* Mexico, D.F., Sociedad Mexicana de Geografía y Estadística, 1952. Soteapan—George M. Foster, *A Primitive Mexican Economy,* New York, J. J. Augustin, 1942. Tepoztlán—Oscar Lewis, *Life in a Mexican Village,* Urbana, University of Illinois Press, 1951. Tusik—Alfonso Villa Rojas, *The Maya of East Central Quintana Roo,* Washington, D.C., Carnegie Institution of Washington, 1954. Tzintzuntzan—George M. Foster, *Empire's Children,* Washington, D.C., Smithsonian Institution, 1948. Yalalag—Julio de la Fuente, *Yalalag,* Mexico, D.F., Museo Nacional de Antropología, 1949.

16. Data for national characteristics have been drawn from, among others: Lesley Byrd Simpson, *Many Mexicos,* 3rd ed., Berkeley and Los Angeles, University of California Press, 1952; William P. Tucker, *The Mexican Government Today,* Minneapolis, University of Minnesota Press, 1957; Jorge Vera Estanol, *La Revolución Mexicana: Orígenes y Resultados,* Mexico, D.F., Editorial Porrua, 1957; and Nathan Whetten, *Rural Mexico,* Chicago, University of Chicago Press, 1948.

17. Sidney W. Mintz and Eric R. Wolf, "An Analysis of Ritual Coparenthood *(Compadrazgo),*" *Southwestern Journal of Anthropology,* 1950, VI, 341–368.

18. It should be noted that chicle is a wild crop, not specifically grown for export; perhaps, then, Tusik should not be considered as exporting a cash crop.

19. For example, a comparison of Redfield's two studies of Chan Kom reveals little change in the social organization of this village. Sayula is beginning to export more goods, but as yet the organization of the village is still that of the old days. Mitla is undergoing changes, as manifested, for instance, in the debate concerning the payment of salaries to officials. Lewis' restudy of Tepoztlán, especially pp. 427–448, indicates that the economic dependence was not the result of, but rather the cause of, cultural change.

20. Young and Young, "Social Integration and Change. . . ," *op. cit.,* p. 376.

21. Moore, *Industrialization and Labor, op. cit.,* pp. 262 ff.

22. The degree of specialization within a village, employing the extremely rough and often ambiguous data from the studies, is measured by the ratio:

$$\frac{\text{Number of adult males not engaged in agriculture}}{\text{Total population}} \times 1000$$

The larger the ratio, the smaller the proportion of villages engaged in agriculture, and thus presumably in nonspecialized occupations. The various villages have the following ratios of specialization:

Dependent villages		*Partially autonomous villages*		*Economically autonomous villages*	
Quiroga	137	Mitla	108	Tusik	4
Tepoztlán	35	Yalalag	37	Chenalho	28
Dzitas	87	Cheran	66	Cancuc	5
Tzintzuntzan	238	Sayula	?	Chan Kom	8
Chacaltianguis	73	Soteapan	2	Potam	7

23. It has often been contended that the establishment of *ejidos* has strengthened the ties of the peasant to the land and is, therefore, a factor which tends to reduce the rate of social change in rural Mexico.

24. Wolf, "Closed Corporate Peasant Communities. . . ," *op. cit.*

The Transition to a Mass Democracy in Argentina

GINO GERMANI

1. *The Argentine "Paradox" and the Problem of Its Explanation*

The political evolution of Argentina can be described as a series of stages or phases, in accordance with a scheme which in general is applicable also to the rest of Latin America. As has been shown in other works[1] this process is part of a more general change, i.e., the transition from some type of traditional structure toward some form of industrial society. In this sense the process of modification of the political structure has points in common with analogous processes occurring in the West in the early industrializing countries. Nevertheless it departs from these in greater or smaller measure depending on the peculiarity of the change within a historical context in each country, on the moment in which the transition is begun (and on the ideological and social climate prevailing at that moment at the international level), on the velocity of the transition itself, and on other factors. In the case of Argentina (and Uruguay and Chile) the transition was more similar to that of the early industrializing countries, the so-called "Western model," than was that which occurred in the other countries

Translated and abridged from "El proceso de transición a una democracia de masa en la Argentina," *Política*, 1961, XVI, 10–27, by permission of the author. Translated by Fredda Bullard.

of Latin America. Nevertheless it is precisely Argentina which presents certain paradoxical "deviations." And the profound political crisis which has affected the country for more than thirty years constitutes a veritable enigma for those studying the sociology of economic development. When the various countries of Central and South America are compared, Argentina, as is immediately recognized, appears the most "advanced" in the transition. But also in a general international comparison the position of the country is situated in a kind of "middle class" of nations, certainly much above the so-called underdeveloped countries in terms of the social "indicators."[2] An explanation of the political instability that has characterized the country has been attempted in other works, and a preliminary theory has been formulated that specifically links this instability with the transition. But causes of a general order are in no way sufficient for explaining the Argentine "paradox." This essay attempts to draw together other circumstances peculiar to the political evolution of Argentina that might clarify the origins of the present crisis. These factors are numerous, and a complete analysis is beyond the aim of this essay; but, briefly, some factors may be indicated that probably have an essential role in the political process and make the Argentine situation extremely rare, if not unique.

First is the *rapidity* of the growth of Argentine society. This involved a change of scale occurring in a short period and with a velocity unequaled among the countries in which the transition took place in a "spontaneous" manner (change not induced by planning) and along the lines of the so-called Western model. The Argentine population increased 1000 per cent in 90 years (between 1870 and 1960). Compare this with other countries of rapid growth: in the United States the population increased 400 per cent in 80 years (1870–1950); in Brazil, 600 per cent in 90 years; in Chile, 400 per cent in 110 years.

In the second place, the modernization of essential aspects of social structure also occurred with extraordinary rapidity. The dual pattern, still clearly visible around 1860–70, was succeeded by a multi-class pattern, or more highly differentiated and complex stratification (characteristic of modern societies) some thirty years later. In 1900 the middle class already represented an economic force (especially in the sense of a consumer market), as well as a political one, inasmuch as it constituted one fourth of the population. Further, its concentration in the more "developed" areas (the littoral) gave it economic and political "weight" greater than its numerical proportion. At the same time, an urban proletariat of a modern type had formed, and by the beginning of this century the country was already becoming urbanized. In 1895 more than 24 per cent of the population was living in cities of 20,000 or more inhabitants, and this proportion may be raised to 37 per cent taking as limits urban centers of 2,000 and more. These proportions correspond exactly to countries that are undergoing or have passed through the industrial revolution. Possibly fundamental is the fact that other parts of the structure remained backward. All the provinces and territories away from the littoral region remained underdeveloped in terms of land tenancy, the persistence of a traditional elite, etc. But disequilibria in development are typical of the process and are in no way peculiar to Argentina. Here the really distinctive or very uncommon element was the *rapidity* of the change.

At the same time that the class structure was being modified and the country urbanized, the social structure was becoming *secularized.* Not only physical urban concentration, but also modern modes of life were transforming the behavior of the population. A valid indicator here is the gradual decline of the birth rate, owing to the application of voluntary control, in the urban areas of the littoral—first among the middle strata and later spreading rapidly to the lower strata. This process has placed Argentina (and Uruguay) among the countries exhibiting "industrial" birth rate, although the crude birth rate represents an average between the low rates of the more modern zones and the still high rates of the provinces less affected by the change.

The third factor, the proportion of foreigners in the population, is, indeed, unique. Argentina is probably the only country in the world (except Israel and perhaps Australia) the majority of whose population remained foreign during various decades. Of course, if gross percentages are taken, the foreign proportion of the population, although one of the highest in the world, will not surpass a high of 50 per cent for the whole country and for all age groups. (In Argentina this proportion was always two to three times greater than in the United States.) But the important factor here is the proportion of foreigners in *areas and groups most significant in the life of the nation.* The proportion of foreigners among adult males in the littoral region greatly exceeded the *argentinos* for more than fifty years. As is shown subsequently there were four foreigners for each *argentino* in Buenos Aires and some six for each four in the littoral provinces, including its rural areas.

Another important factor was the sudden cessation of growth that probably occurred in the decade 1920–30 and almost contemporaneously in numerous significant aspects of the social structure. The uninterrupted demographic growth of fifty or sixty years was arrested in 1930 with the elimination of overseas immigration and the drastic reduction in the urban littoral birth rate. Economic growth experienced a similar process, and finally political evolution suffered a setback of incalculable consequences with the forced regression to a "limited participation" democracy and the systematic fraud that followed the Revolution of 1930. The effects of this growth stoppage—especially in the economy—were not clearly perceived until much later, but many indications point to this circumstance as a fundamental feature of the present situation. Obviously this arrest was a result of processes generated much earlier; but when it occurred, it became a new independent factor added to the others at that certain moment, and must, therefore, be distinguished from its own origins.

What did these four factors imply for Argentina—especially when considered as events not isolated but integrated into a system of hypothesis that accounts also for their reciprocal effects? In what manner and measure did the rapid expansion and extraordinary rate of social mobility contribute to the creation of certain features, attitudes, and expectations of the *argentinos*? In what way was this same experience differentiated within the various groups and strata composing society? How did the assimilation of that enormous mass of immigrants take place? And above all, was it assimilation, or was it, rather, syncretism, with the development of new cultural forms, in the anthropological sense? What happened and is happening to the first, second, or third generation of immigrants? What repercussions did the growth stoppage have? When and how was it perceived?

And finally in what way did these four factors—peculiar to the Argentine situation—combine with the general circumstances of development and the transition? There are other factors to be considered, such as the unequal transition between different regions of the country, the massive migration from the interior after 1930, the dependency upon dominant countries, the persistence of traditional structures and its consequences for the political and economic order, and further significant elements—all of which Argentina shares with many Latin American countries and other parts of the world. While not new, these questions have never been answered. Although it is not possible to cover them all here, a summary analysis of the political process is herein presented. [EDITOR'S NOTE: a brief discussion of three breakdowns of Argentine history is omitted here.]

2. *Independence and Failure in Establishing a National State of a Modern Type*

Independence was inspired in the ideals of 18th century rationalism and the Enlightenment. Its models were the revolutions of France and, even more, of North America. But if an independent state was constituted out of the old colony, its conversion into a modern state based on the cherished ideals failed. The reasons for this failure may be reduced to two. The first was a structural limitation to the program of reforms which the elite was able to accomplish. This limitation was rooted in the group's own position in the social structure and its nature as a social group. The democracy to which it aspired could be only a liberal democracy, in which the effective exercise of power would be restricted to this very group. Popular participation (necessary for carrying out an independence movement) was impossible in the political sphere as it was in the economic and social. This limitation on the achievement of possible reforms produced an irremedial contradiction between the proclaimed goals and effective practical policy, between ideology and concrete action.

Such a contradiction was reinforced, furthermore, by the second cause of failure: the structure of living established by colonial society and the profound ignorance of it exhibited by the intelligent elite. A glaring example is the civil wars which followed the attainment of independence. After the autocracy resisted, these were interpreted as the result of the conflict between two social classes: the small urban group of the cosmopolitan city, oriented toward Europe (civilization) and the popular masses of the interior, still submerged in colonial society (barbarism). There are three paradoxes to be emphasized in this process. The popular stratum, which submerged itself enthusiastically in the independence movement and fought for it, also represented in its way a democratic, or perhaps even more, an equalitarian beginning. The kind of human being who composed the Creole stratum did not correspond to the image of man subjected to a traditional authority, even though in most aspects of his life he was the standard-bearer of the traditional culture. Because of the peculiarities of his way of life, he was a somewhat anarchic individual: individualistic, loving his personal independence, and disposed to recognize the authority only of those who excelled in the qualities he most admired, e.g., valor and personal skill. The autocratic authority of the *caudillos* was not maintained through a *traditional legitimacy* but through its acceptance on the part of these groups of people who recognized in the leaders their own image and an exaltation of their own values. *Inorganic democracy* it was called (J. L. Romero), and it is probably an acceptable term so long as it is recognized that there also persisted all the remaining attributes of the traditional man: social and ecological isolation, ethnocentrism, religiosity (not exactly the cult religion of the cities), resistance to change, dominance of custom and traditional or "prescribed action,"[3] a subsistence economy and corresponding attitudes related to work and economic activity. Out of these characteristics of Creole man arose the first paradox: the democratic and republican solution to the institutional problem was imposed by the presence and the action of this population that could not accept the monarchical coquetries of the educated elite. But the second paradox has an exactly opposite significance: this Creole stratum started the dominion of the *caudillos*, and in particular of Rosas, and provided a place for a type of autocracy that really consisted simply in the restoration—where possible—of the colonial society and the denial of democracy in a modern sense. There is no doubt that the culture and social structure of Argentina in the years prior to 1850 were very close to the traditional pattern of the colonial period.

The third paradox may be seen in the following: The popular stratum and the *caudillos* represented the triumph of the provinces and of the interior, and an affirmation of the localism of the most limited small community; they were incapable of the ideals of the intelligent minorities of the city, of extending loyalty to what is, in a modern sense, the great national community. However, the real result of the authority exercised by Rosas and by Buenos Aires, the so-called "federal" regime, was an effective authority of *porteño* centralism, i.e., that of Buenos Aires, and ultimately facilitated the process of national organization based on a compromise between centrifugal and centripetal tendencies.

3. *Transformation of Social Structure*

The members of the generation that assumed the task of building Argentina as a modern national state were aware of the contradictions between the simple rationalism of the independentist elite and the true nature of colonial society as it was perpetuated through the first half of the 19th century by the autocracy and authority of the *caudillos*. They understood that no political reform would be possible which was not founded on radical changes in the social structure. They were "social realists," and they used the philosophic and sociological ideas of the times to understand the native, national situation, and they arrived at what can be called a true plan, a deliberate action directed toward a substantial modification of Argentine society.

TABLE 1

THE PROCESS OF URBANIZATION IN ARGENTINA: 1869–1957

Years	*Urban population (in centers of 2,000 or more inhabitants)* per cent
1869	27
1895	37
1914	53
1947	62
1957	65

The essential measures put into effect for accomplishing this proposition were three: education, foreign immigration, and economic development. In these three points may be summarized the program of the so-called "generation of 1837"—of Sarmiento, Alberdi, Echeverría, and others who formulated it and partially carried it through. But the action of the leaders in this program was no less contradictory than had been that of the earlier elite revolutionaries. They were specifically a part of what later came to be called "the oligarchy," a landholding bourgeoisie, in spite of a liberal motivation and a sincere preoccupation with transforming Argentina into a modern state. Its position in the social structure without doubt provided the main source of contradiction in its efforts toward reform.

In the immigration program the objectives were two: first, "to populate the desert," according to a well-known phrase; second, to change the social character of the population in order to give it those features considered necessary to the development of a modern nation. Fundamentally they tried to substitute for the "traditional" social form a more adequate form, the modern industrial structure. In that period this was viewed as a "racial" change and not as the effect of the transition from one social structure to another. In the parlance of the times, they were trying to "bring Europe to America," to Europeanize the interior population, considered to be the principal factor in the political instability and economic backwardness.

For this purpose it was necessary above all to "colonize," to insure the rooting to the land of the European immigrants. Although the rise of urban activities—in industry, services, etc.—was also desired, there is no doubt that immigration was correctly oriented "toward the desert." Certainly the population was radically altered, and, as is shown later, one of the features essential to the understanding of present-day Argentina is its migratory origin. The traditional social and economic structure was also transformed through the emergence of Argentina as one of the world producers of grain and meat. But the social structure of the rural regions was not changed as had been hoped. No large, strong agricultural middle class, rooted in ownership of the land, emerged. Instead of "colonization," what has been termed a colossal land speculation succeeded in increasing and reinforcing the influence of the *latifundistas*. When massive immigration began, most land accessible and adaptable to cultivation was already held by a few proprietors. In 1914, after the middle period of immigration and with foreigners composing no less than half the total active population, immigrants represented only as much as 10 per cent of the owners of landed property (Table 4). The traditional families had maintained and substantially increased the *latifundista* regime; in 1947 three fourths of the land was still concentrated in little more than 20,000 agricultural holdings, less than 6 per cent of the total.[4]

The legal pattern of land use was and continues to be land rental, or other less favorable forms, and the place of a rural middle class was occupied in large measure by renters and small proprietors, highly exposed to all the exigencies of climate and the national market. Even though some prospered, the low economic condition of the majority obliged them to move continually in search of better circumstances and subjected them to all kinds of restrictions. In still worse condition were the landless peasants, unsalaried workers exposed to seasonal labor needs, low levels of employment and low standards of living. One of the principal and undesired effects of this situation was the concentration of foreigners in the cities and an extraordinary urban growth.

Clearly massive migration and the rest of the innovations sought by the elite who directed the "national organization" from the second half of the last century meant a profound change in the country. But the social structure that arose therefrom also clearly deviated from the ideal of establishing a stable base for a democracy. One of the most consequential deviations was the unfavorable rural structure and population distribution.

To populate the desert was desired, and in a certain sense this was achieved. But the population was concentrated in the cities; and instead of reducing the disequilibrium between the underdevelopment of the interior and the development of the littoral, it was further accentuated. The consequences of this were evident by the middle of the century.

The process of urbanization in Argentina developed in two great phases: the first, 1869 to 1914, was effected by the massive European immigration; the second, corresponding approximately to the period 1930–35 to 1950–55, was sustained by massive internal migrations.[5]

The role of foreigners in the formation of Argentina's urban structure is shown very clearly in Table 2. Not only in cosmopolitan Buenos

TABLE 2

PERCENTAGE OF FOREIGNERS IN THE POPULATION ACCORDING TO THE SIZE OF THE URBAN CENTERS: 1869–1947[6]

Zone	*1869*	*1895*	*1914*	*1947*
Greater Buenos Aires	47	50	49	26
Other cities of 100,000 or more	9	34	35	15
Urban centers of 50,000 to 99,999	8	18	22	7
Urban centers of 20,000 to 49,999	12	23	26	10
Urban centers of 2,000 to 19,999	7	19	23	10
Urban centers of less than 2,000 and populations outside of urban centers	3	9	14	9

Aires, whose population was 50 per cent foreign between the years 1869 and 1914, but also in the remaining cities this proportion was exceptionally high. Also of significance is the direct correlation between population volumes and proportion of foreigners. Thus in cities of 100,000 and more inhabitants between the years 1895 and 1914 more than one third had been born abroad.

Furthermore, to this urban concentration was added another of regional type. All the large cities were situated in the littoral zone, and in general foreigners naturally located therein. Thus the metropolitan area of Buenos Aires and the provinces of the littoral always retained about 90 per cent of the immigrants. This concentration had profound effects on the social structure and the political life, particularly when combined with the expansion and transformation of the economic community. By the beginning of the present century the traditional pattern had been destroyed and replaced by forms closer to the "modern" model. Also as a result of other measures aimed at the economic development of the country—attraction of capital, construction of railroads, legal reforms—the country became a great grain and meat exporter. New demands of foreign commerce, needs of the great urban concentrations, and the increased wealth of the country gave impulse to the first industrial development. Since the last quarter of the century modern industrial activity has appeared and expanded through the country, replacing the old surviving artisan forms, and, although continuing to be centered in agriculture and livestock, already reached a respectable volume of production in the first decade of the present century. At the same time the popular strata of the old society —largely rural—are being replaced by an urban proletariat and a rapidly expanding middle class. Thus the "bipartite" traditional society (an upper stratum of the landed estate holders versus a low stratum composed of a majority of the population, with an intermediate stratum of minor importance, usually identified with the upper stratum) is replaced by a tripartite (upper, middle, and popular classes) or even multipartite system. The differentiation between classes, especially in the cities, becomes obscure, and the structure assumes the image of a continuous series of superposed ranks in which the transition from one to another becomes difficult to perceive.

The emergence of a middle-class of sufficient numerical, economic, and social importance for political influence occurred between 1869 and 1895. By the last decade of the nineteenth century it had become a group of great importance. In evaluating Table 3 it should be kept in mind that the data are concerned for the most part with an urban middle class, concentrated in the littoral zone. Its influence was greater in these areas which were playing a central role in national life. Also it is essential to take into account the qualitative changes produced by the transition from the traditional pattern to more modern forms. While the upper class, the traditional families, retained broad control in agriculture until the beginning of the century, the middle class was made up of men who promoted the new activities, small and average impresarios consolidating commercial activity and nascent industry. A smaller rural middle class, peasants of some prosperity or economic stability, was also formed. But this was a small group in comparison to the foreign immigrant masses and the rural native population. Later, particularly after 1910, the middle class owed its growth to the expansion of its "dependent" sectors: "white collar" workers, employees and functionaries, professionals and technicians of public and private bureaucracies. And this successive change in the composition of the middle class also has its political significance. From the so-called popular strata rural *peones*, people without a trade, old skilled artisans, and domestic servants are being transformed into urban workers in industry, com-

TABLE 3

MIDDLE AND POPULAR OCCUPATIONAL STRATA IN ARGENTINA: 1869–1947[7]

Occupational strata	*1869*	*1895*	*1914*	*1947*
Middle strata* (*patrones* of business, industry, agriculture, employees, professionals)	11	26	32	40
Popular strata (urban workers, rural laborers, *peones*)	89	74	68	60

* Including a small proportion (around 2 percent) of the upper class.

merce, transportation, and services, i.e., in activities accomplished in accordance with the typical relations of modern business enterprise and concentrated in the cities. The conditions are available for the rise of proletarian movements which, in the typical pattern of early stages of industrialization and urbanization, appear as movements of "social protest."

4. *End of Democracy of Limited Participation and Intervention of the Middle Class*

The political significance of these changes is well known, involving the entrance into national life of groups which were differentiated out of the old traditional strata. The implication was that a functioning democracy, particularly in its most immediate manifestation, universal suffrage, will include such recently formed classes.

Faced with this evident basis for founding a democratic state, the ruling elite did not seem disposed to share power, much less to cede it to the new groups which were being incorporated into the national life. Its goal continued to be a liberal democracy of limited participation by the upper strata of society. Although in many other respects (as already noted) its attitudes were progressive and open to greater participation in national life by the popular strata—such was its position, for example, in education—there were certain limits which were difficult or impossible to transcend in economic and political matters. In the first, it not only was unable to relinquish its monopoly of the land, but it definitely profited from advantages derived from the economic transformation, and often its development measures were oriented more toward its own class interests than toward the national interests. Politically a prolonged struggle, limited only by the amount of public opinion, was necessary for the most progressive elements of that same "oligarchy" to make possible universal suffrage and accede peacefully to the participation in power of the new social groups. The first elections with total participation of the citizenry were realized in 1916 and gave the government to men of the middle class, politically organized in the radical party that appeared three decades earlier.

This date, 1916, can probably be taken as the beginning of mass democracy and the end of limited democracy, taking into account all the reservations attendant upon fixing rigid divisions within such complex social processes. And moreover it was only the beginning of a long process, replete with contradictory alternatives, that is still in development.

The transition from a "limited" democracy to "mass" democracy in Argentina was particularly traumatic. There was, first, the paradoxical situation created by the massive immigration. During thirty or forty years persons born abroad were much more numerous than those born in the country. If one considers the effects of the double concentration—by geography and age—and the proportion of foreigners in those groups most important in political life (adults, males over 20) in the central zones of national activity (the capital and provinces of the littoral), the extraordinary fact is that this proportion reaches between 50 per cent and 70 per cent.

In terms of elections, this meant that precisely where participation in the vote could have greatest importance, between 50 per cent and 70 per cent of the inhabitants were outside its legal exercise. For example, in absolute figures, in 1895, out of 216,000 male inhabitants of the city of Buenos Aires only 42,000 were natives of Argentina (and those naturalized amounted to less than 2 per cent). In the same year in the littoral provinces (Buenos Aires, Santa Fé, Córdoba, La Pampa, Entre Ríos) of over 600,000 adult males, 287,000 would eventually have had the right to vote, as natives. If the further drastic reduction in political participation deriving from the remaining social conditions is considered, the significance of the term "limited democracy" will appear in all its plentitude.[8]

This political marginality of the majority was a constant concern to the leaders of the period, but, as is widely known, the elite maintained toward it a characteristic ambivalence. In reality the functioning of the "limited" democracy gained from this circumstance. In all probability the political effects of the appearance of the middle strata were considerably retarded by the fact of its dominant foreign composition. The failure of the popular classes to form a party capable of representing it politically was very probably due to similar reasons. It is instructive here to analyze the variable proportions of foreigners in some occupational and economic categories (Table 4).

TABLE 4

PROPORTION OF FOREIGNERS IN DIFFERENT CATEGORIES OF THE ACTIVE POPULATION: FOREIGNERS PER 100 PERSONS OCCUPIED IN EACH LISTED CATEGORY: 1895–1914[9]

Strata	*Economic and occupational categories*	*1895*	*1914*
Some sectors of the middle classes	Owners of landed property*	No data	10
	Entrepreneurs of industry	81	66
	Entrepreneurs of commerce and services	74	74
	Professionals	53	45
	Commercial employees	63	51
	Public employees	30	18
Some sectors of the popular classes	Industrial workers**	60	50
	Domestic servants	25	38
	Laborers in domestic and craft industries	18	27
Total active population		30	47

* Excluding owners in the federal capital.
** Including some employees.

As already noted, landed property remains almost totally in the hands of *argentinos*. This situation contrasts with that of commercial and industrial development. The entrepreneurs of commerce and industry, and the industrial workers are largely foreigners, and this in a proportion above the medium level existing in the total active population. Furthermore, in the popular strata the pre-industrial activities (ancient arts and crafts, domestic service) are held by a native majority, and, of course, native people predominate in the rural population, especially of the interior. The elite firmly retained control of activity in land; the middle class and proletariat were formed in the cities, founded on the massive immigration. As the children of these immigrants became active, and the extraordinary proportion of foreigners diminished, these recently formed classes began to have the possibility of a *direct* influence in political activity.

Here the word *direct* has a particular importance. Effectively these mass majorities, although marginal from the viewpoint of their electoral rights and in large part their own political interests, exercised an indirect gravitational force, although there are no studies and data which might permit it to be evaluated correctly. At the same time, the popular class nourished—as leader and as masses—the great protest movements of the first decades of the century, and the middle stratum provided the human *ambiance* most propitious for the emergence of the movement that should have represented the political expression of these groups in national life.

Thus in Argentina the step from governments of the elite, of a limited democracy, to governments of the middle class signified the incorporation of the foreign immigrant masses, or of their children, into political life. But it is probable that the peculiar composition of the population and particularly the predominance of foreigners in the protest movements of the first decades of the century implied a considerable delay in the formation of adequate political organisms of the urban proletariat that supported radicalism, the expression of the middle classes.

It was this party which governed the country for fourteen years and, until 1930, should have spoken for all the new strata in the social structure arising in the change from the traditional to the "modern." But it cannot be said that it complied with this responsibility. It in no way effectively used the power to effect those alterations in the social structure that might have assured a safer base for the functioning of democratic institutions and the participation of all social strata without limitations. It did nothing, or very little, to resolve one of the country's most basic problems, the agrarian problem. Even though until the end of this period rural conditions were significantly better than previously —the stability of the rural population was much greater, so that these years were ones of minor urban growth—the socioeconomic structure of the rural regions remained practically unchanged, since the measures adopted were totally insufficient to the magnitude of the problem. In regard to the urban proletariat the attitude of radicalism was no less ambivalent. Although numerous measures for social protection of labor were adopted, the problem was not only one of a much too moderate legislation, but also that it often had no practical application. On the other hand in spite of the climate of freedom which was enjoyed during the period, it cannot be said that the labor organizations saw much development. Legislation did not explicitly provide the unions with any legal status, although of course their activity was permitted by virtue of the general disposition of the constitution. This lack of recognition, reflecting opinion in the upper strata and openly against such organizations, increased the difficulty of their task and provided a very serious obstacle to their operating as a means of progressive incorporation of the popular strata into the political life of the nation. It is symptomatic that the radical parliaments maintained the same repressive legislation created by the "oligarchy" at the beginning of the century in the face of the first expansion of labor movements. In 1918 the radical government did not hesitate to resolve the social problem with a bloody repression of the uprisings originating in the postwar situation.

The high proportion of foreigners during the epoch of the emergence and first development of labor movements probably impeded and rendered difficult the formation of a party which might integrate them within the democratic structure of the country. On the one hand in spite of their numerical and social importance in the population, they had to remain in a marginal position within the electorate. On the other hand the foreign composition of the labor movements, together with an internationalistic ideology which in this epoch was characterizing so strongly the movements of the left, probably contributed to placing such movements in an unfavorable light precisely at the moment when the immigrant offspring was being incorporated and his identification with the new country must have been emerging with particular intensity. It is not necessary to review the undoubtedly nationalistic character (in a democratic sense) of the U.C.R. and its refined "isolationism," particularly during World War I. That which may be produced in Argentina through acquisition of national identity and transcendency of the old regional and local loyalties by means of the incorporation of the immigrant offspring continues to have a notable importance, in this and other respects.

Thus if the radical party, in spite of its popular appeal and support, was not capable of politically representing the proletariat, neither were the Socialist party and other leftist organizations—in large measure for the aforementioned reasons. Moreover the former was gradually becoming composed of middle class groups and ended by symbolizing an alternative to radicalism only for the independent electorate.

Finally the fact that large areas of the country remained in underdeveloped conditions, that the process of progressive incorporation of the inhabitants into national life was realized only in the littoral and highly urbanized zones, while the "interior" remained completely marginal, and that the same occurred in rural sections of the littoral, constituted another disturbing factor of fundamental importance for later evolution. In effect it would have been essential for the country's political equilibrium (i.e., with respect to securing a representative democracy) that the strengthening of a party of the democratic left, endowed with the support and adherence of the popular sectors, be produced in an ideologically adequate climate, i.e., within the democratic philosophical tradition of the left, such as occurred in the early industrializing countries of Europe.

5. *The Great Internal Migrations and Integration of the Popular Strata*

Such was the situation in 1930 when a repercussion of profound processes (the particular social structure of the country) and most recent events (the world-wide Depression which rudely struck Argentina's economy) produced military intervention which for the first time in many decades overthrew a constitutional government. This movement, which also was expressing the new international political climate created by the rise of fascism in Europe, fundamentally signified the return of the "oligarchy" displaced from power by the radical majority. But this "return" could not mean a reversion to the past situation and the intent to establish a type of limited democracy in which political participation would be restricted to certain classes. It was to have significance and consequences very different from the apparently analogous exclusive situation of a half century before. The principal measure employed by these groups lacking the electoral support necessary to govern was a systematic fraud, through which, without formally denying the exercise of civil rights, the exercise of these rights and their consequences in the forming of the government were effectively impeded. Freedom of the press and of association were respected, more or less, as were other rights formally sanctioned by the constitution. But the activity of the unions encountered greater and growing difficulties, and this, combined with frustration produced by the systematic manipulation of the popular will in elections, created in a majority a feeling of profound skepticism—skepticism which continued to be influenced by the general crisis of democratic ideologies during the decade of the thirties. Nor were the opposition parties, moreover, at the height of their mission just at the moment when a new stage in the country's socioeconomic development was being enacted.

In effect two convergent processes were produced in Argentina as a repercussion of the new conditions created by the world crisis of 1929: a new and decisive phase of industrialization was begun, and urbanization gained an unusual impetus with the massive migration to the cities from the interior of the country. During the decade 1936–47 the proportion of *argentinos* born in the provinces who moved to the metropolitan zone of Buenos Aires was equal to almost 40 per cent of the natural increase of these same provinces. It was an exodus en masse, by which vast layers of people from the underdeveloped zones—masses until this moment completely outside the bounds of the political life of the country—were established in the large cities and particularly in Buenos Aires.

It seemed to be a process in a certain sense comparable to that of

TABLE 5

POPULATION OF THE METROPOLITAN AREA OF BUENOS AIRES: COMPOSITION OF INTERNAL AND EXTERNAL MIGRATION: 1869–1957[10]

Years	*Total population (thousands)*	*Immigrants from abroad (% of total population)*	*Migrants from the interior (% of total population)*	*Average annual internal migration*
1869	230	47	3	
1895	783	50	8	8000
1914	2035	49	11	
1936	3430	36	12	
				83,000
1947	4720	26	29	
1957	6370	22	36	96,000

the massive overseas immigration a half century earlier, but with three great differences: first, the rhythm of the earlier was much slower, since the urban population growth lasted over at least three decades; second, the masses that exerted political pressure and led toward effective universal suffrage were not immigrants themselves (who, being foreigners, were participating only indirectly and with difficulty in political processes), but their offspring; and lastly, above all, it was a matter of a rise of the newly formed middle class, leaving a nascent urban proletariat in a subordinate situation. These large masses, transplanted in short order to the cities, transformed suddenly from rural *peones*, artisans, or persons with hardships into industrial workers, acquired a political significance without at the same time finding the institutional channels necessary for integrating themselves into the normal functioning of the democracy. The repressive policy of the governments from late in the last century until the beginning of this one, the ambivalence and relative failure of the governments of the middle class between 1916 and 1930, the severe limitations to the functioning of the democracy after that date, and the general doubts and skepticism created by all these experiences coupled with the absence of political parties capable of furnishing adequate expression to the sentiments and necessities of these masses left them in a state of "availability," making them an element inclined to be exploited through whatever happenstance might offer them some form of participation.

Meanwhile international events also were exerting pressure in a direct manner on Argentina; the expansion of nazism in Europe and its first victories during the first three years of the war precipitated reverberations. A new military intervention in 1943, this time of open totalitarian intent, interrupted the conservative experiment of "democracy limited by means of fraud." But the social structure of Argentina, particularly at this point in the process of forming an urban industrial society, and the kind of masses "available" for utilization as the human basis of a totalitarian movement, were far from lending themselves to a fascist experiment of the classic type, i.e., the Italian or German form. It was necessary to bring about extensive revisions in this system, and *peronismo*, which arose starting from the military revolution, was precisely the expression of the particular conditions created in Argentina through the accumulation of the series of factors, ancient and new, which have been summarized herein. Thus is encountered another of the paradoxes which abound in the history of the country. A movement of the fascist type set off a regime of undoubtedly totalitarian character but endowed with features very different from its European model; it was a type of authoritarianism based on the consent and support of the majority, which for the first time in sixteen years was able to express its wishes in regular elections. This fact is of singular significance, since free elections were becoming transformed into the principal if not the only symbol of democracy and constituted one of the myths most dwelled upon by the opposition democratic parties, particularly the radical, during the conservative regime.

The *peronista* regime, by its origin, the character of its leaders, and the circumstances of its emergence, was called upon to represent only an ersatz political participation of the popular classes. Although the result of a conjunction of very different forces, its fall was possible only through its intrinsic limitations. And the principal one of these was in defending itself: it should have transformed this illusory participation into a real intervention; it needed, in other words, a change of nature, to become truly an expression of the popular classes. This was impossible, and it had to fall in the face of incessant attack by groups of very different orientation and origin. But the process initiated with *peronismo*, and even much earlier with universal suffrage, has remained unfinished; and the problem of the incorporation of all social strata into national political life within a democracy functioning in an effective manner and based on the respect of political and social rights summarizes in itself the history of the present and of the immediate future in Argentina.

NOTES

1. See especially Chapters 5 and 6 of the author's work *Política y sociedad en una época de transición de la sociedad tradicional a la sociedad de masas,* Buenos Aires, Paidós, 1962.

2. This "underdeveloped" stereotype was incorporated in the image of Argentina by its inhabitants relatively recently. It contrasts with the preexisting image of a rich country, characterized by one of the highest national per capita incomes, as well as by other indices of economic and social advancement. Of course this older image was, at least in part, an ideological deformity, maintained for the support of a specific economic policy and a world-wide view of political and social organization. Those who, from opposite angles, did not share this image denounced the "dependent" character of Argentina's economy and the consequences of this dependency. But in spite of the "poor provinces" of the interior the characterization of Argentina as a socially "backward" country would not be shared even by the critics most "alienated" from the country's ruling social regime. Nevertheless, especially in the last decade, the indiscriminate usage of the category "underdevelopment" has induced many—particularly intellectuals and pseudo-intellectuals of the left (and pseudo-left) to assimilate *tout court* Argentina's case with that of the ex-colonial countries which are presently beginning the first phases of the transition in Latin America, Asia, or Africa. This image is no less deformed than the former (that of Argentina as a country completely developed economically and advanced socially, subsequently destroyed by "statist" experiments, etc.) and leads one to accept certain ideological and political orientations that are not absolutely viable for a country whose social structure is rather different from those of countries actually in initial phases of the transition. Perhaps it may be worthwhile to record some recent data. In two international typologies concerning economic and social development and based on a large number of economic, demographic, educational, sanitary, and other indicators, Argentina is in an intermediate position, closer to countries of advanced development than to the rest. In a typology prepared by the United Nations, based on a series of socioeconomic indicators relating seventy-four countries, Argentina is in the third category, on a scale of six (cf. United Nations, *Report on the World Social Situation,* New York, 1961, Chapter 3). In another work (for presentation at an international conference at Yale, September, 1963) Professor K. Deutsch places Argentina, among a total of ninety-one countries, in a second category out of a scale of five. The five categories are: Traditional Primitive Societies, Traditional Civilizations, Transitional Societies, Societies in Industrial Revolution, and Societies of High Mass Consumption; in this last category to which pertain the countries of highest

economic development there are thirteen nations, great and small (K. Deutsch, *Yale Political Program: Preliminary Report*, March 1963).

3. On the typology "prescribed action vs. elective action" see G. Germani, *op. cit.*, Chapter 2.

4. G. Germani, *Estructura social de la Argentina*, Buenos Aires, Raigal, 1955, Chapter 10.

5. G. Germani, *El proceso de urbanización en la Argentina*, Semanario sobre Urbanización en América Latina, Santiago de Chile, 1959. Mimeographed by United Nations, Economic Commission for Latin America.

6. *Ibid.*

7. Instituto de Sociología, Universidad de Buenos Aires, *Estudios sobre la estratificación social en la Argentina a base de los Censos Nacionales*, 1959. (Unpublished.)

8. The proportion of voters relative to the adult population (20 or more years old) in some presidential elections between 1910 and 1958 was as follows (until and including 1946 only the male population was considered in these computations; for 1958 the female population was also included):

Years	*Per cent of voters relative to total population 20 years and older (including foreigners)*	*Per cent of voters relative to total native argentinos only (naturalized citizens were less than 2 per cent)*
1910	9	20
1916	30	64
1928	41	77
1936	48	73
1946	56	83
1958	78	90

(The base of 20 years and older was chosen not in regard to legal arrangements but because this age was considered a departure point beyond which there exists a voting *expectancy*. Also, this procedure was used for international comparisons employing these data, in a work in preparation.)

9. G. Germani, "La asimilación de los inmigrantes en la Argentina," *Revista Interamericana de Ciencias Sociales*, 1961, I, 1–28.

10. G. Germani, *El proceso de urbanización, op. cit.*

VIEWS OF THE WORLD

Introduction

DWIGHT B. HEATH

In studying contemporary societies and cultures of Latin America, any foreign observer must be struck by differences among them, as well as by differences between any one of them and his own. It is facile to say that such differences are more apparent than real; they may, at least as often, be far more real than is immediately apparent. In fact, they often reflect very different views of the world.

The fact that there are significant differences in views of the world has come to be widely accepted in recent years, and there is increasing awareness that divergences concern not only judgments of value (what *ought* to be), but also conceptions of reality (what *is*). The following is an attempt to characterize some of the more important aspects of Latin American views of the world and to suggest their meaning for understanding and action.

Among the articles included here, that by Tax provides an excellent illustration of the ways in which world view affects interpersonal relations, both within and between societies. It is also important as an early illustration that the "folk" and "urban" ideal types of societies have limited applicability for the classification of real societies.

Gillin's characterization of ethos components of modern Latin American culture is a succinct and telling summary of some of the most critical features that distinguish that style of life from the Anglo-American. It is a tribute to Gillin's insight that this article has been widely plagiarized throughout Latin America and the consensus of magazine articles and newspaper editorials based on it seems to be grudging agreement.

Simmons describes a local Peruvian variant on the widespread urban pattern, and relates the values to different kinds of belief, behavior, and matériel in some detail. His picaresque coastal *criollo* has counterparts in some other regions, and may be a far-ranging type.

Wagley provides a broad comparative discussion of views about race, one important feature of interpersonal relations in societies that are ethnically and physically diverse. The predominance of social over biological factors in racial classification reflects their greater significance in the Latin American orientation.

Mangin's study of highland Indians who had migrated to a slum in Lima relates psychological to demographic factors, and stresses the role of an individual's world view in determining his adjustment to diverse social contexts. Like Tax's paper and Wagley's, it offers a comparison between social races.

Without attempting to summarize here the abundant and diverse descriptions and interpretations that are available concerning Latin American views of the world, it may be in order to attempt a brief classification and evaluation of types of pertinent sources, and to suggest some of the ways in which views of the world affect other aspects of culture.

For man, one of the most important aspects of the world is other men. The nature, extent, and meaning of social relationships cannot be appreciated without an understanding of a people's views about man. A basic theme throughout this volume has been the rich diversity of cultures and societies in contemporary Latin America. The reality of difference, however, should not obscure that widespread underlying unity, which derives, in large part, from the Spanish heritage. A few aspects of this unity at the level of urban culture—some views of the nature of man—are discussed by Gillin. Latin Americans and others agree on the importance of *personalismo*, *dignidad de la persona*, and *machismo* in the life of individuals, and a variety of institutions can be fruitfully interpreted as expressing these basic ethos components. Davidson has elsewhere offered a generalized outline of rural Latin American culture, which similarly rings true. Such easy characterization should not obscure the real complexity of views, which include such appositions as: easy dependence on paternalism and a high value on self-determination; strong and widespread bonds of familism and ritual kinship (*compadrazgo*) coupled with personalized individualism; high value on the dignity of the unique person in a context of fairly strict social hierarchy; a double standard of extremely contrasting morality for the sexes; strong formal emphasis on centralization of authority together with an emphasis on the adeptness of the individual; and so forth.

The marked contrast between these and surviving Indian ethos components dramatically underscores the differences between social races, which remain unlike after more than four centuries of close and sustained contact. Although "race" is used primarily or exclusively as a biological concept by most anthropologists, we can gain an understanding of intergroup relations only if we follow the usage of local peoples. In most of Latin America, we find that races are conceived as being primarily descent groups, but the salient distinguishing characteristics are often social or cultural. It is for this reason that Latin America is characterized by frequent mobility of individuals from one "racial group" to another, as when an "Indian" learns to speak Spanish, adopts Western dress, moves to town, and "becomes" a "mestizo," although townspeople retain their view that Indians are inherently inferior because of biological differences. Some authors (e.g., Tumin [1952]) have described such mobility as indicating a progressive shift from caste to class distinctions. The ideal of racial tolerance among Brazilians has become a byword throughout the world, and an abundant literature is devoted to historical as well as socio-psychological discussions suggesting that prejudice is different from, and perhaps less than that in United States, but is far from absent. The works of Freyre [1945, 1959], Pierson [1942], Wagley [1952], Wagley and Harris [1958] and others are important in this connection.

The emergence of the mestizo (or *ladino, caboclo, cholo, criollo,* etc.) as a culturally disinherited segment of the colonial society has been well described (cf. Marshall, Wolf, and others). It is these people who now predominate—numerically, politically, and economically—in most of Latin America; and it is their assertive dissatisfaction with the present distribution of wealth and power that fosters political instability far more than any action by Indians, who generally remain relatively uninvolved in national or international affairs.

The literate minority is fairly vocal, and often most articulate. An abundant literature on individual introspection, autobiography, and formal philosophy need not concern us here, but serious attempts at cultural introspection are worth noting. In the first place, it is perhaps a telling commentary on modern Latin American culture that amateur attempts at what might loosely be termed "national character study" or description of "basic personality type" should be so fashionable. Often the tone of such essays is one of breast-beating denigration of the prevailing foibles of society. In some instances, a naive combination of geographic determinism and racism provides a convenient rationalization for this supposed contemporary demoralization. According to this view, the Conquest was, in effect, a profound "psychic trauma," a second "original sin" for the conquerors and a crushing defeat for the vanquished, and it still weighs heavily on all descendants. The characterization of early twentieth-century Bolivians as "a sick people"

(Arguedas [1909]) is still accepted by many of the intelligentsia as a regrettable but unavoidable outcome of enforced miscegenation in the early colonial period. A review of Mexican character studies shows that many of them are couched in similar terms (Hewes [1954]).

One product of this defensively antagonistic portion of society is the *criollo* characterized by Simmons. A similar ideal personality type exists in eastern Bolivia, where the *cachivache* (literally, "worthless piece of junk") is idolized for his guile, verbal facility, mental agility, and general ability to "get away with" anything. Like his Peruvian counterpart, he is proudly provincial, favoring the distinctive local dance (*taquirari*) and extemporaneous composition of songs over more cosmopolitan diversions, and vaunting the local customs and dialect (Heath). In some respects, these figures are like the *charro* of Mexico and the lavishly exalted Gaucho of Argentina; perhaps they represent a widespread swashbuckling type of alternative between the traditionally aristocratic oligarch and the submissive *campesino*.

Mestizo views about the nature of man and interpersonal relations are reflected in the social structure which epitomizes the world's image of Latin America. They have been interpreted as imposing a number of obstacles: to economic development in Argentina (Fillol [1961]), to improved public administration in Bolivia (Richards [1961]), and to easy inter-American business relationships everywhere (Whyte and Holmberg [1956]). Political instability is commonplace throughout much of the area, and certainly one of the major factors impeding continuity of government is the emphasis on individuals rather than institutions. The charismatic strength of a *caudillo* or *cacique* may fit well with the value of personalism, but it is not a sound basis for administration of the complex affairs of any nation, and certainly is inadequate for international relations. In much the same way, the preference for courtesy over frankness (extending to a cavalier disregard for accuracy), the prevalence of fatalism and nonmaterial values, are sometimes difficult to reconcile with the necessities of large-scale and efficient organization. These are the kinds of things Alba [1961] had in mind when he spoke of "the Latin American style" whereby administrators perpetuate myths and seek panaceas, with little regard for empiricism.

Another aspect of personalism is paternalism, exemplified in the classic relationship of *patrón* and *peón*, employer and employee with reciprocal commitments extending far beyond "the job." In some respects, the effective politician fits this role; increasing social legislation seems aimed at making the state into a sort of *patrón*; in the interim, labor unions often function in this manner, by providing discounts on basic commodities, together with legal counsel, a modicum of social security, and so forth.

Ways of relating to other human beings are sometimes generalized and applied to inanimate objects and supernatural beings. Thus, trucks are named and treated as individuals, and people enjoy close and warm relations with their patron saints or favorite representations of the Virgin, who serve as intermediaries with God. Let us briefly consider religion and magic as aspects of life wherein world view tends to be institutionalized in some fairly standardized and visible forms. The problem of making a meaningful distinction between magic and religion need not concern us, since we can view them both as systematic views of the world which affect men's selection among alternative modes of action.

For our purposes, it is important only to note that ideological pluralism has a profound effect on the eclectic national cultures of Latin America. Fusion of different ideologies is rare, but a common outcome of contact is syncretism, the blending of forms of one system with meanings of another. A burgeoning literature on syncretism shows how European, African, Indian, and other traditions have merged to produce new emergent forms in material as well as ideological aspects of religion, art, and other symbol systems. The folk-Catholicism of Latin America includes indigenous pagan elements alongside strict doctrinal ones, and forms and meanings indistinguishably merge. The process is an old and continuing one, well documented by Wolf [1958], Madsen [1960], La Farge [1947], and others.

In areas where Negro slaves figured significantly in the population, their own patterns have become merged with indigenous patterns to produce new systems distinct from either of the original forms. Some of the more spectacular manifestations of this are surrounded with an aura of drama and mystery verging on the apocryphal, until the popular misconceptions that have grown up are even more exotic and colorful than the reality. Voodoo is only one among many such Afro-American cults with elaborate pantheons and well-developed systems of belief about which conscientious and detailed investigation by social scientists such as Hogg, Métraux, Simpson, and others, has not dispelled romantic stereotypes held by laymen.

In some respects, religion plays an important role in the economic and political aspects of life in Latin America. The Church has been a large landholder, and is often identified with the oligarchy, so that there is widespread dissatisfaction among intellectuals concerning the lack of social concern of the Catholic hierarchy. Although this has led to concern among international Catholic leaders (cf. Considine [1958]), it has not benefited Protestant missionaries, whose impact has been minimal throughout most of the area.

The widespread civil-religious hierarchy in which most ablebodied adult males are expected to occupy a series of public posts (*cargos*) and to sponsor fiestas has already been described as a religious institution which serves as an economic leveler. The public responsibilities of religious fraternities (*cofradías*) fulfill a similar purpose.

Different interpretations of reality have been thrown into sharp relief also in the realm of disease and medicine. Different views about the etiology of disease are associated with variant methods of curing, and a number of public health projects have foundered because of different views of the world (cf. Adams [1955], Sayres [1955], Wellin [1955]). Ideas of witchcraft, animal spirits, evil eye, "hot" and "cold," and related concepts are widespread even among nominal Catholics and are difficult to reconcile with the routine clinical approach of much modern medicine.

There is ample historical reason for Latin American culture to extend well north of the Rio Grande, and it is with respect to world view more than any other aspect that this has been described, as in the work of Rubel, F. Kluckhohn, and others.

One of the more fruitful approaches to understanding alien views of the world is to elicit detailed descriptions of events in the lives of perceptive native informants. A few such "life histories" are most revealing, for example those edited by Lewis [1961, 1964], Pozas [1962], and Tumin [1945].

Although virtually every ethnographic monograph, including community studies, contains some information on the predominant world view of the people, it is unusual to find social scientists who take this as a focal feature in terms of which they order other data. In Latin America, however, it is curious that some of the best-known anthropological work is of this order. The major portion of Redfield's career was devoted to this approach, and Adams has above discussed the impact of Redfield's "Great Dichotomy." With no apparent intention of provoking controversy, Redfield did so, and the efforts of other research workers to qualify his views have been extremely fruitful. Just as the folk–urban continuum brought into focus a number of significant theoretic and substantive problems that had been relatively ignored previously, his characterization of peasant ethos stimulated fuller discussion of the quality of interpersonal relations in small communities (cf. Foster [1961], Lewis [1951], and others).

One of the outstanding features of our time is the enormous and rapid expansion of cross-cultural channels of communication, interdependence, and exchange. In such a situation, an awareness of diverse views of the world is of crucial importance. In such a situation, also, we may expect some lessening of diversity, but this is an unpredictable (and usually slow) process. In sum, understanding different views of the world remains our most difficult—as well as our most important—concern in international and inter-American relations.

REFERENCES CITED

Adams, Richard N.
1955 "A Nutritional Research Program in Guatemala," in B. Paul, ed., *Health, Culture, and Community*, pp. 435–458, Russell Sage Foundation, New York.

Alba, Victor
1961 "The Latin American Style and the New Social Forces," in A. O. Hirschman, ed., *Latin American Issues: Essays and Comments*, pp. 43–51, Twentieth Century Fund, New York.

Arguedas, Alcides
1909 *Pueblo enfermo*, Barcelona, Vda. de L. Tasso.

Considine, John J.
1958 *New Horizons in Latin America*, New York, Dodd, Mead & Co.

Fillol, Thomas
1961 *Social Factors in Economic Development: The Argentine Case*, Cambridge, Mass., M.I.T. Press.

Foster, George M.
1961 "The Dyadic Contract: A Model for the Social Structure of a Mexican Peasant Village," *American Anthropologist* 63:6: 1173–1192.

Freyre, Gilberto
1945 *Brazil: An Interpretation*, New York, Knopf.
1959 *New World in the Tropics: The Culture of Modern Brazil*, New York, Knopf.

Heath, Dwight B., *et al.*
(forthcoming) *Land Reform and Social Revolution in Bolivia*, Madison, University of Wisconsin Press.

Hewes, Gordon W.
1954 "Mexicans in Search of the 'Mexican': Notes on Mexican National Character Studies," *American Journal of Economics and Sociology* 13:219–223.

La Farge, Oliver
1947 *Santa Eulalia: The Religion of a Cuchumatan Indian Town*, Chicago, University of Chicago Press.

Lewis, Oscar
1951 *Life in a Mexican Village: Tepoztlán Restudied*, Urbana, University of Illinois Press.
1961 *The Children of Sanchez*, New York, Random House.
1964 *Pedro Martínez*, New York, Random House.

Madsen, William
1960 *The Virgin's Children: Life in an Aztec Village Today*, Austin, University of Texas.

Pierson, Donald
1942 *Negroes in Brazil: A Study of Race Contact at Bahía,* Chicago, University of Chicago Press.

Pozas, Ricardo
1962 *Juan the Chamula* (translated from *Juan Pérez Jolote: biografía de un Tzotzil*), Berkeley and Los Angeles, University of California Press.

Richards, Allan R.
1961 *Administration—Bolivia and the U. S.,* Department of Government Research Publication 60, Albuquerque, University of New Mexico.

Sayres, William C.
1955 "Status Transition and Magical Fright," *América Indígena* 15:4:292–300.

Tumin, Melvin M.
1945 "Some Fragments from the Life History of a Marginal Man," *Character and Personality* 13:261–295.
1952 *Caste in a Peasant Society,* Princeton, N.J., Princeton University Press.

Wagley, Charles, ed.
1952 *Race and Class in Rural Brazil,* UNESCO, Paris.

Wagley, Charles and Marvin Harris
1958 *Minorities in the New World,* New York, Columbia University Press.

Wellin, Edward
1955 "Water Boiling in a Peruvian Town," in B. Paul, ed., *Health, Culture, and Community,* pp. 71–103, Russell Sage Foundation, New York.

Whyte, William F. and Allan R. Holmberg, eds.
1956 "Human Problems of U. S. Enterprise in Latin America," special issue of *Human Organization* 15:3.

Wolf, Eric R.
1958 "The Virgin of Guadalupe: A Mexican National Symbol," *Journal of American Folklore* 71:34–39.

FURTHER READINGS

Adams, Richard N.
1953 "A Change from Caste to Class in a Peruvian Sierra Town," *Social Forces* 31:3:238–244.
1956 *Encuesta sobre la cultura de los ladinos en Guatemala,* Seminario de Integración Social Guatemalteca Publicación 2, Guatemala.

Aramoni, Aniceto
1961 *Psiconálisis de la dinámica de un pueblo,* Universidad Nacional Autónoma de México, Mexico.

Arciniegas, Germán
1944 *The Green Continent: A Comprehensive View of Latin America by its Leading Writers,* New York, Knopf.

Billig, Otto, John Gillin, and William Davidson
1947–48 "Aspects of Personality and Culture in a Guatemalan Community: Ethnological and Rorschach Approaches," *Journal of Personality* 16:1 and 2:153–178, 328–368.

Bourricaud, François
1954 "Algunas características originales de la cultura mestiza en el Perú contemporáneo," *Revista del Museo Nacional* 23: 162–173, Lima.

Clark, Margaret
1959 *Health in Mexican-American Culture: A Community Study,* Berkeley and Los Angeles, University of California Press.

Cohen, Yehudi A.
1956 "Structure and Function: Family Organization and Socialization in a Jamaican Community," *American Anthropologist* 58:4:664–686.

Cunha, Euclides da
1944 *Rebellion in the Backlands* (translated from *Os sertões*), Chicago, University of Chicago Press.

Davidson, William
1947 "Rural Latin American Culture," *Social Forces* 25:249–252.

Edmonson, Munro S., ed.
1957 *Synoptic Studies of Mexican Culture,* Middle American Research Institute Publication 17, Tulane University, New Orleans.

Foster, George M.
1952 "Relationships Between Theoretical and Applied Anthropology: A Public Health Program Analysis," *Human Organization* 11:3:5–16.

Freyre, Gilberto
1946 *The Masters and the Slaves* (translated from *Casa grande e senzala*), New York, Knopf.

Friedrich, Paul
1958 "A Tarascan *Cacicazgo:* Structure and Function," in V. Ray, ed., *Systems of Political Control and Bureaucracy in Human Societies,* pp. 23–39, American Ethnological Society Proceedings.

Gillin, John
1947 *Moche: A Peruvian Coastal Community,* Smithsonian Institution, Institute of Social Anthropology Publication 3, Washington, D.C.
1947 "Modern Latin American Culture," *Social Forces* 25:243–248.

1951 *The Culture of Security in San Carlos*, Middle American Research Institute Publication 16, Tulane University, New Orleans.

Gomez Robleda, José
1943 *Pescadores y campesinos tarascos*, Secretaría de Educación Pública, Mexico.

Guiteras-Holmes, Calixta
1961 *Perils of the Soul: The World View of a Tzotzil Indian*, Glencoe, Ill., Free Press.

Hanke, Lewis
1935 *The First Social Experiments in America: A Study in the Development of Spanish Indian Policy in the Sixteenth Century*, Cambridge, Mass., Harvard University Press.

Hernández, José
1872 *El gaucho Martin Fierro*, C. Casavalle, Buenos Aires.

Herskovits, Melville J.
1941 *The Myth of the Negro Past*, New York, Harper.
1945 "Problem, Method, and Theory in Afro-American Studies," *Afroamérica* 1:5–24.

Hogg, Donald
1960 *The Convince Cult in Jamaica*, Yale University Publication in Anthropology 58, New Haven.

Jesús, Carolina Maria de
1962 *Child of the Dark* (translated from *Quarto de despejo* by David St. Clair), New York, Dutton.

Kelly, Isabel
1961 "Mexican Spiritualism," *Kroeber Anthropological Society Papers* 25:191–206.

Kennedy, John J.
1961 "Dichotomies in the Church," *Annals of the American Academy of Political and Social Science* 334:54–62.

Kluckhohn, Florence R.
1961 "The Spanish Americans of Atrisco," in F. Kluckhohn and F. Strodtbeck, *Variations in Value Orientation*, pp. 174–257, Evanston, Ill., Row, Peterson Co.

Leslie, Charles
1960 *Now We Are Civilized: A Study of the World View of the Zapotec Indians of Mitla, Oaxaca*, Detroit, Wayne State University Press.

Lewis, Oscar
1959 *Five Families: Mexican Case Studies in the Culture of Poverty*, New York, Basic Books.

Lobb, John
1940 "Caste and Class in Haiti," *American Journal of Sociology* 46:23–34.

Madsen, William
1955 "'Hot' and 'Cold' in the Universe of San Francisco-Tecospa, Valley of Mexico," *Journal of American Folklore* 68:123–140.

Marshall, C. E.
1939 "The Birth of the Mestizo in New Spain," *Hispanic American Historical Review* 19:161–184.

Mecham, J. Lloyd
1934 *Church and State in Latin America*, Chapel Hill, University of North Carolina Press.

Métraux, Alfred
1959 *Voodoo*, Oxford, Oxford University Press.

Mintz, Sidney W.
1960 *Worker in the Cane: A Puerto Rican Life History*, New Haven, Yale University Press.

Nash, June
1960 "Protestantism in an Indian Village in the Western Highlands of Guatemala," *Alpha Kappa Deltan* 30:1:49–53.

Parsons, Elsie Clews
1936 *Mitla: Town of the Souls*, Chicago, University of Chicago Press.

Paz, Octavio
1950 *The Labyrinth of Solitude: Life and Thought in Mexico* (translated from *El laberinto de la soledad*), New York, Grove Press.

Pike, Frederick B., ed.
1959 *Freedom and Reform in Latin America*, Notre Dame, Ind., Notre Dame University Press.

Ramos, Samuel
1934 *El perfil del hombre y de la cultura en México*, Imprenta Mundial, Mexico.

Redfield, Robert
1930 *Tepoztlán: A Mexican Village*, Chicago, University of Chicago Press.
1947 "The Folk Society," *American Journal of Sociology* 52:2:292–308.
1953 *The Primitive World and Its Transformations*, Ithaca, N.Y., Cornell University Press.
1955 *The Little Community*, Chicago, University of Chicago Press.
1956 *Peasant Society and Culture*, Chicago, University of Chicago Press.

Redfield, Robert and Alfonso Villa Rojas
1934 *Chan Kom: A Maya Village*, Carnegie Institution of Washington Publication 448, Washington, D.C. (reprinted by University of Chicago Press).

Reichel-Dolmatoff, Gerardo
1956 "Casta, clase y aculturación en una población de Colombia," *Estudios antropológicos publicados en homenaje al doctor Manuel Gamio*, pp. 435–446, Mexico.

Reichel-Dolmatoff, Gerardo and Alicia Reichel-Dolmatoff
1961 *The People of Aritama: The Cultural Personality of a Colombian Mestizo Village*, Chicago, University of Chicago Press.

Rubel, Arthur J.
1960 "Concepts of Disease in Mexican American Culture," *American Anthropologist* 62:2:795–814.

Salz, Beate R.
1944 "Indianismo," *Social Research* 11:4:441–469.

Sánchez, Luis Alberto
1960 "Texture of Life in Latin America," in D. L. B. Hamlin, ed., *The Latin Americas*, pp. 15–20, Toronto, University of Toronto Press.

Sarmiento, Domingo F.
1868 *Life in the Argentine Republic in the Days of the Tyrants* (translated from *Civilización i barbarie*), New York, Hurd and Houghton.

Sayres, William C.
1956 "Historical Perspectives in Two Mestizo Communities," *Ethnohistory* 3:2:154–162.

Seminario de Integración Social Guatemalteca
1956 *Cultura indígena de Guatemala: ensayos de antropología social*, Publicación 1, Guatemala.

Simmons, Ozzie G.
1959 "Drinking Patterns and Interpersonal Performance in a Peruvian Mestizo Community," *Quarterly Journal of Studies on Alcohol* 20:103–111.

Simpson, George Eaton
1945 "The Belief System of Haitian *Vodun*," *American Anthropologist* 47:1:35–59.

Stokes, William S.
1958 "The Drag of the Pensadores," in J. Higgins and H. Schock, eds., *Foreign Aid Re-examined*, pp. 56–89, Washington, D.C., Public Affairs Press.

Tschopik, Harry
1947 "On the Concept of Creole Culture in Peru," *New York Academy of Sciences Transactions*, Series 2, 10:252–261.
1951 *The Aymara of Chucuito, Peru, I: Magic*, American Museum of Natural History, Anthropological Paper, Vol. 44, Part 2, New York.

Valencia Cabrera, Pastor
1952 *Algo sobre apologética nacional*, Editorial Kollasuyo, La Paz.

Wagley, Charles
1950 *Social and Religious Life of a Guatemalan Village*, American Anthropological Association Memoir 71.

Willems, Emilio
1952 "Caboclo Cultures of Southern Brazil," in Sol Tax, ed., *Acculturation in the Americas*, pp. 231–243, Chicago, University of Chicago Press.

Wolf, Eric R.
1959 *Sons of the Shaking Earth*, Chicago, University of Chicago Press.

World View and Social Relations in Guatemala

SOL TAX

Two classes of people constitute virtually the entire population of the present-day Republic of Guatemala. They are the Indians and the Ladinos. The Indians are for the most part relatively full-blooded descendants of those whom the Spanish conquerors found in possession of the land in 1524. The Ladinos for the most part are mixed bloods. But the distinction is not to be drawn in terms of biological race, nor even of sociological race; for the people concerned are little inclined to attach social differences to biological origins. At least in the Western Highland region of the country, the area to which this discussion is limited, the class indices are primarily cultural and linguistic. The origin of the use of the terms Indian and Ladino with nonracial connotations is suggested by Batres Jauregui's definition of the term Ladino:

> The word . . . meant in old Spanish "the romance or new language," from which it was derived that those who spoke one or more languages besides their own were called *ladinos,* and thus the Indians who spoke *ladino* (or Castilla as they themselves call it) were called *ladinos.* The meaning of this word is now extended to all those who in these countries

Reprinted from *American Anthropologist,* 1941, XLIII, 27–42, by permission of the author and publisher.

are not Indians, or even when they are Indians, do not retain their language or customs.[1]

It appears that after the Conquest colonists were few and women among them scarce. Spanish men married Indians and an intermediate class of mestizos emerged; for a period, classes of Negroes, *zambos*, and mulattoes were also recognized.[2] But simultaneously the term Ladino came to be applied to Indians "who lived and worked in the cities as artisans"[3] and it may be surmised that such Indians had already adopted elements of Spanish culture and language. Possibly the Ladino Indians tended to marry into groups of other blood; but whatever the case, it is noteworthy that the mixed-blood classes which had been designated by race names were eventually absorbed into the Indian-Ladino classification which had from the beginning cultural rather than racial connotations. Today there is no mestizo class in Guatemala, and the term is hardly used except in its literal meaning.

The Indians today live for the most part in communities in each of which they retain ethnic identity and separateness from Ladinos expressed in a unified Indian social-political-religious system, in a body of cultural meanings and beliefs not shared by Ladinos, in a distinguishing costume pattern, and in the use of an Indian dialect. The Ladinos are the representatives of Spanish and European traditions, even though not unmixed with Indian. There is not, and apparently for a long time has not been,[4] any serious social impediment to passage from the Indian to the Ladino class. To say that despite this there occurs virtually no such passing[5] in the Western Highlands is largely another way of asserting that the Indians are not being acculturated to the Ladinos; for when an Indian adopts Spanish as his language, Ladino-style clothes, and the Ladino way of life in general, he is generally recognized as having passed into the Ladino class.

This evident lack of acculturation is not explicable in terms of physical isolation of Indians from Ladinos. It is true that Ladinos comprise less than 10 per cent of the population of the region, but they live in every part of it. They live for the most part in towns, while the Indians are to a greater extent rural. But they live in towns which are social, religious, and market centers for the Indians,[6] and as will be seen below, the contacts are continual. The towns are, moreover, linked to the capital by highways and bus lines and by telegraph and telephone, while the Ladinos of the towns often have close connections with that center of modern influences. The Indians may therefore be said to be living in continued physical contact with suburbs of modern urban civilization. To suggest some of the reasons for the lack of acculturation of the Indians to Ladino and modern Euro-American civilization, it will be necessary to turn first to the equally interesting interrelations of the Indian communities themselves.

It may be recalled that communities of typical Indians are identified with *municipios* which, while somewhat comparable to townships, are in Guatemala the important ethnic units.[7] There is much that is common to the cultures of all of the *municipios*, but there are also some rather striking differences as one passes from one to another. The Indians of a *municipio* think of themselves as a distinct group of people, biologically and socially. Each *municipio* typically has its own costume, different from those of its neighbors, and this costume is a label wherever the Indians go. Each has, moreover, a relatively exclusive set of customs and practices, including those of birth, baptism, system of naming, marriage, burial; kinship and family and household organization; and rituals of many kinds. Even in details of diet and cookery, and etiquette, as well as in house types and other material things, *municipios* often differ in greater or less detail from all of their neighbors. Each *municipio* tends to have its own economic specialties, sometimes its own economic and social values, and even its own different standard of living. Each *municipio* has a politico-religious organization independent, within limits, of any other; each has a variant of the general system of public service; each has its own saints, its own fiestas for them, and its own annual religious calendar. At the same time, all of the Indians typical of one *municipio* are strictly part of that community, wearing relatively the same costume, speaking the common dialect (different in most cases from the dialects of its neighbors), engaging in the favored economic pursuit, participating in the politico-religious organization, and having the common customs and beliefs. To be sure there are variations and non-typical individuals, but the variations are not often such as to bring a person closer to a neighboring *municipio* than to his own.

Such mutual exclusiveness exists in spite of the physical proximity of the *municipios* to each other. Towns are in some cases separated by no more than a half-hour's walk, and in one case by only a few blocks, while the lands tilled by the townspeople of two different *municipios* in many cases adjoin. Where Indians live in the country, moreover, there are many cases where neighboring families are in different *municipios*, and yet most of the differences typical of those *municipios* exist also between such neighbors.

There is, furthermore, continuous intercommunication among the *municipios*. First of all, the Indians of one often go to live in others, sometimes intermarrying (in which case the offspring are usually absorbed into the culture of the community in which they are raised), more often holding themselves somewhat aloof and forming either a separate social class or a colony apart. Such "foreign" Indians keep their old costumes, their own language, often their own trades or economic specialties, and, apparently, their own culture. Such colonies represent the closest kind of contact between *municipios* (excepting intermarriage itself) because of the social relations that inevitably grow up between the home group and the foreign groups and because the "colonial" Indians frequently visit "back home" and serve as connecting links between the *municipios* involved.

But there are other interrelations of *municipios* as well. Economic relations are most important. Specialization begets exchange of commodities which is accomplished for the most part through public markets. Most towns have regular market days on which people from far and near meet to buy and sell their own products or, as middlemen, those of others.[8] Regularly, once or twice a week or more, large numbers of Indians from diverse *municipios* come to each market to buy and sell, or often merely to enjoy the gaiety of the occasion. Usually the relations established are superficial; but often, since the same people come together repeatedly, they come to know one another by sight and by name, and learn something of the personal characteristics, language, and customs of such acquaintances. They sometimes eat and sleep together and become friends. In some important markets people from many towns regularly meet. In traveling to the market town they pass through still other places and in the course of time come to know them well and to establish personal contacts in them. At the same time, middlemen regularly visit several towns each week and establish relationships in each. Nor do merchants meet only in the markets; they also sometimes buy at homes where merchandise is grown or made, and such contacts may be repeated.

Economic relations concern not only trade, but landownership and cultivation as well. Indians of one *municipio* frequently own land in another and go to work it days or weeks at a time. Likewise, Indians of land-poor *municipios* find work in neighboring *municipios*; such laborers frequently board with their employers. It may also be noted that Indians from diverse *municipios* of the highlands meet to work and live for seasons or years at a time on plantations of the lowlands, where they are the closest of neighbors.

Government, too, brings together Indians from different *municipios*, since those who are officials in any given year frequently meet in the offices of the departmental capital to transact similar business. Also, Indians of small and out-of-the-way *municipios* pick up mail and telegrams in other towns and stay the whole day or night. Finally, religious fiestas and pilgrimages take Indians from their home towns to others where for a few days they witness dances and rituals differing in details from those of their own.

With the exception that the women of some towns rarely visit others, so that their contacts with outsiders are confined to visitors to their towns, there is hardly a man, woman, or child that I know who has not visited a dozen or more *municipios*, and who does not regularly frequent at least one or two. Some *municipios* are virtually deserted one or two days every week. Everybody travels, and travels often, for even if the Indians have nothing to buy and sell, they still enjoy going to markets and fiestas. Men, however, travel oftener and farther, as a rule, than women.

It is therefore not surprising that the Indians of one *municipio* know a great deal about the people and customs of others. The average Indian could no doubt write large fragments of the ethnography of half-a-dozen towns other than his own. Although occasionally scornful of the customs of other communities, he more frequently does not evaluate them. "That is their custom; it is all right for them," appears to be the most general attitude. To the Indians cultural differences between themselves and outsiders are as much to be expected as differences in kinds of trees. It would be inaccurate to say that the close contact and resultant knowledge on the part of one group of Indians of differences of culture among others have not resulted in some diffusion. Many cases of borrowing of crops and the techniques for growing them have been noted; when it is a matter of dollars and cents, the Indians do not ordinarily evidence conservatism; indeed, the free competition of individuals, each looking for a profitable enterprise, would discourage such conservatism. There also appears to be a fairly free interchange of folklore and remedies and the like. But it is a curious kind of interchange, one that recognizes the local nature of culture. Just as it is known that a plant that yields well in one town will not necessarily yield in another, so it is supposed that a remedy need not be universally applicable. A plant or technique or custom appears to be considered as belonging to a particular community, its people and its soil. Thus, there is a fairly strong belief in Panajachel that if a crop that grows well in one town is planted in another where it has not been grown, the "spirit" of the plant might shift its locale and the plant consequently prosper in its new habitat and fail in its old. (Hence the Indians are disturbed when Indians of another town begin to cultivate a local crop.) Somewhat similarly, merely because Indians of one town are believed able to secure fortunes from the owner of a hill or volcano does not mean that those of another can do likewise.

There may be said to be a culture trait of acceptance of cultural differences. In general the attitude required is one of neutrality—neither laudatory nor condemnatory. The Indians of one town may look down on those of another, possibly all others, but as far as I know, there are no cases of mutual acceptance of vertical status of any kind in the relations of two Indian communities. As a consequence, there is no question of the appreciation of elements of culture because of their association with a superior group. Indians of another town may be considered lazy or stupid, but as far as I know, depreciative epithets in terms of customs are not applied to them.

It is of course a relatively simple matter to explain cultural similarities in contiguous communities. We take it to be natural that culture diffuses. The great similarity of the cultures of these Indian societies, which makes it possible to draw a generalized picture of the culture of the whole region, is easily understandable when it is considered that the groups are genetically related in the first place, that influences from outside were given the opportunity to affect them all equally, and that new developments in each could easily diffuse to others. We also recognize in culture the tendency to differentiation, especially under conditions of isolation. The two opposite processes, differentiation and diffusion, account in general for the distribution of culture traits as we find them anywhere. It may appear to observers in Guatemala that the proportion of differences to similarities, in view of the lack of physical isolation, is greater than might be expected. Whether this is true or not would be difficult to judge without some study of local culture variations all over the world measured on the basis of some established index. But whether or not the Guatemalan situation should properly occasion surprise, it may supply data for the study of barriers to normal diffusion where isolation is not a factor and where the cultures involved are much alike. That is, in order to understand how culture assimilation comes about, it is of value to uncover some of the factors that prevent it.

Such factors as the relative efficiency of competing traits, differences between traits of technology, social organization, and folklore, or the compatibility of the new traits with the established culture, need hardly be discussed here. They are amply covered in the literature and are sufficiently a part of anthropological experience to permit the assumption that they are known to the reader. The observations that follow are based on such general knowledge, but they grow directly from experience in Guatemala.

In the large area of culture wherein questions of obvious efficiency are absent, a factor aside from ordinary conservatism that in Guatemala stands in the way of diffusion is the indifference that is engendered by knowledge on the part of the Indians that cultures do after all differ just as do plants or people. It would appear that just as some languages tend to adopt the foreign words that are diffused with the things or concepts for which they stand while other languages make up new words under the same circumstances, it is part of the pattern of some cultures to decline for no social or special cultural reason the adoption of new culture traits when there is no particular reason for such adoption. This happens to be a trait of the Guatemalan cultures. One of the ways in which this trait apparently works is indirect. It acts as a barrier to disorganization of the culture that is apt to result from the presence of alternative ways of customary behavior.[9] Where an individual of society

A has a culture trait *x*, he may also be aware that in society B there is a culture trait *y* that is an alternative to *x*. But for him *y* need not become an alternative mode of behavior if it is altered by the recognition that it belongs to B. So it appears to be in Guatemala. If all Guatemala should be considered one society, many of the cultural differences between the Guatemalan communities would thus be what Linton has called "Specialties," or differences of culture associated with different culturally recognized subgroups of the society. The Guatemalan communities may, however, be more fruitfully treated as separate local societies, and it may be said that as such they merely recognize in each other groups which appropriately have different cultures. By thus making "Specialties" of what would otherwise be alternatives, the attitude of culture consciousness discourages disorganization which would bring into being a fluidity in which cultural assimilation would flourish.

Another consideration involved in explaining the situation in Guatemala is that the nature of the society or culture emphasizes the impersonal character of social relations of all kinds, both within the community and between people of different communities. There is first of all, and even in the family, a commercial spirit;[10] but whether or not the development of commerce was historically responsible, today impersonality is manifest not only in economic but in political and religious life, and in family relations as well. More about this characteristic will be said later; the point here is that it allows the establishment of widespread social relations with a minimum of the kind of intimate contacts by means of which cultural items are best exchanged.

Redfield has published[11] a brief account of two institutions which exemplify mechanisms in Guatemala by which this is made possible. One of these, by which possessions are left *recomendado* with acquaintances or even strangers along the roads of commerce, is comparable to a checking service in the Union Station (except that there is no charge), and it facilitates the wide commerce without establishment of close social relations. The other, by which people ask *posada* at the homes of acquaintances or strangers when away from their home towns, is comparable to hotel service in a large city, since relations between guest and host are often no more intimate. Redfield cites a case from the Ladino community in which he lived where an Indian came several times a year to a Ladino home where "he slept in a corner of the kitchen while the women of the house continued their cooking and conversation. But these women knew almost nothing about the man; they were not even sure of his name."[12] Since merchants have regular routes, they tend to seek lodging and to leave merchandise *recomendado* in the same places repeatedly. The institutions are well established, and great impersonality characterizes their exercise.

These institutions Redfield considers mechanisms by which travelers are insulated from the deeper contact that might otherwise accompany such mobility as is found in Guatemala.[13] Thus the physical contact remains little more than physical. But they are also significant as symbols, for the reason why the social contacts do not have depth is to be found in the general culture and the structure of the society. Part of it goes back to the indifference to cultural differences; curiosity is not fanned by interest. Part of it is to be found in the general sameness of Guatemalan culture because of which many questions that might be asked visitor or host are answered without being asked; there is usually no question as to where an Indian hails from, or where he is going, or why. Part of it may be accounted for in the very frequency of such contacts, by which shoulders are rubbed with strangers every day of the week and every week of the year; if there were less physical contact of people of various communities, it is not unlikely that there would be more interchange of culture. As it is, the inter-societal relations are not unlike those of a great city in which a most general characteristic is the anonymity of the inhabitants. More will be said on that score, but it may be pointed out here that the impersonal nature of social relations that characterize the Indians may also be considered a reason why they can continue indifferent to cultural diversities, even as such indifference makes possible the impersonal plane on which the social relations are maintained.

It seems to me that the pattern of relations that exist between Indian communities and Indian cultures, and which I have now so briefly described, is a fundamental characteristic of Guatemalan Indian life. Both Redfield[14] and I[15] are inclined to the opinion, in fact, that much of it goes back to pre-Hispanic times, and that it developed with the money economy and widespread system of trade, and the wide formal political institutions, that existed in Guatemala before the Conquest. The processes of secularization and individualization that result from contact with Euro-American civilization, as Redfield has described them for Yucatan,[16] have no doubt strengthened similar tendencies already present in Guatemala. But it is not difficult to suppose that the pattern of Guatemalan Indian society served to defend it to some extent from the disorganization of culture that was another result of the contact in Yucatan. For in the first place the local Indian cultures had already built up a resistance (with the aid of their culture trait of indifference) against the acceptance of alternative patterns of behavior incompatible with those already present; in the second place, the impersonality of relations with outsiders, which could be carried to newcomers, shielded them from contacts with cultural depth; and in the third place the very similarity of their kinds of social relations to those characterizing Spain reduced the shock of the contact.

These processes are not entirely something of the past, for one can see them at work in some places in Guatemala today. There are places where Ladinos have moved into the community only relatively recently, and although the great revolution took place 400 years ago, the Indians since then were able to reorganize their lives in relative isolation until the coming of these new outsiders. One can see in a place like Chichicastenango, for example, how the Indians could take in their stride the opening of a car road, the establishment of a hotel, and the influx of thousands of tourists with avid curiosity, cameras, and most important of all, money. There was a short period from about 1932 to 1936 when there was some rebellion against the invasion of the church and market place of the town; but the tourists were rapidly fitted into the economic system as a market for textiles with no apparent effects on the fundamental culture which, after all, is patterned to make just such outward adjustments. It is seen also in places where Ladinos have lived for many generations, for here it is apparent that the attitude extended by the Indians to Indians of other communities is carried as well to the Ladinos. Ladino customs are known, but again the Indians are largely indifferent to them.

The case of Ladinos (and of course foreigners) makes significant another trait of Indian culture that has been mentioned above—the belief that culture is local, and even tied to the biology of different peoples. If an Indian is not sure that a remedy for a certain sickness will be equally effective in one community of Indians as in another, it is not difficult to see that he is also protected from conflict when he sees that Ladinos or foreigners continually do things that his culture tells him are sinful or will cause sickness or idiocy. The Ladinos can behave differently because they are different. It does not long surprise the Indians to hear that in the United States bread is preferred to tortillas, and even that there are no tortillas, in spite of the fact that they know absolutely that an Indian cannot fill up on bread no matter how much he eats. Nor does the information cause them to question the veracity of their stomachs.

Acculturation to Ladinos can therefore be described largely in the same terms as acculturation of Indian communities to each other. And indeed it seems to me that the same factors apply to what acculturational influences stem from modern civilization, if not to those resulting from the Conquest itself four centuries ago. In attempting to put the factors involved in general terms, I have had recourse to the concepts crystallized by Redfield in his interpretation of culture change in Yucatan.[17] As he generalized from his experience, he pointed out that the way of life of "primitive" peoples can be contrasted with the way of life characterizing "civilization," and especially modern urban communities, in terms of a change from a relatively immobile, homogeneous society in which relationships are personal and controls familial and characterized by a well-integrated culture adjusted to its local milieu and in which sacred sanctions and ritual are important, to one tending to have opposite characteristics. But it soon became apparent to both Redfield and myself that in Guatemala the societies studied are "small, unsophisticated, homogeneous in beliefs and practices . . . mobile, with relationships impersonal, with formal institutions dictating the acts of individuals, and with familial organization weak, with life secularized, and with individuals acting more from economic or other personal advantage than from any deep conviction or thought of social good."[18] We have been led to believe, furthermore (as I have already indicated), that this is no case of cultural lag of some elements in a process of acculturation. As Redfield put it, "The combination of commercialism and certain features of primitive life appears to be a relatively stable one. It is probable that before the Conquest the Highland Civilization had already many of these features."[19] Nor do we need to assume that Guatemala is unique in having a combination of characters that partake of the characteristics of both folk culture and civilization. West Africa, and doubtless other localities, probably supply other examples.

It seems to me that we can profitably make a distinction between two aspects of culture that will cut across Redfield's distinction. We may say that in respect to their world view the Guatemalan Indians are of the primitive type, while in respect to their kind of social relations, they are of the civilized type. By the phrase "world view" I mean of course "the mental apprehension of reality" which includes the total of knowledge and beliefs about nature and man. By the phrase "social relations" I mean to include all kinds of personal and institutionalized social, economic, political and religious relations among men. And while it is true that the mental perception of social relations enters into and is part of the world view, I mean to treat the general world view separately from the dominant kinds of social relations.

It appears justifiable to say that the world view typical of preliterate peoples is different from that typical in our Western urban society. In the first place the primitive view is quantitatively smaller and more restricted in its range; we know about them and they do not know about us; we have some acquaintance with the whole world, they of a very small portion; we are said to be more sophisticated than they. In the second place the two views differ in content. This difference, so familiar to ethnologists, is described by Boas as follows:[20]

> One of the most striking features in the thoughts of primitive people is the peculiar manner in which concepts that appear to us alike and related are separated and rearranged. . . . The whole classification of experience . . . follows entirely distinct lines (p. 198).
>
> The concepts of primitive man make it quite clear that the classes of ideas which we consider as attributes are often considered as independent objects. The best known case . . . is that of sickness. While we

consider sickness as a condition of the organism, it is believed by primitive man . . . to be an object which may enter the body. . . . Other qualities are treated in the same way. Thus the conditions of hunger, exhaustion, and similar bodily feelings are considered by certain primitive tribes as independent objects which affect the body. Even life is believed to be a material object that may become separated from the body. The luminosity of the sun is considered as an object that the sun himself may put on or lay aside.

. . . The concept of anthropomorphism seems to be one of the important categories underlying primitive thought (pp. 200–201).

This does not, of course, imply a difference in "kinds of minds" or of mental processes. The difference is strictly cultural; the world view of a people is a facet of its culture, and one of the respects in which the cultures of typical primitives differ from that of our civilization. It is not contended that the distinction is so clear-cut that a particular people or person can always be said to have either a primitive or a civilized world view; for that matter I cannot even answer the question as to which kind of world view the Chinese or the East Indians or the ancient Egyptians or Athenians have or have had. But we can safely deal in terms of such a distinction in a comparison of aboriginal Sioux Indians or Australians or Eskimoes and twentieth-century Chicago, London, or Paris.

A similar distinction can be made between the general type of social relations governing preliterate tribes and the general type present in modern civilization. Such relations in a primitive group, as Redfield has pointed out, are personal, based on kinship, and sacred, governed by informal institutions and by moral convictions. In our society, of course, the characteristic type of social relations tends to have opposite characteristics.

The world view general among the Guatemalan Indians is, as I have said, of the primitive type. Like classical "primitives," their minds are clouded with animism: sun and earth, river and hill, are anthropomorphized; animals talk; plants have emotions; it is possible for a hoe to work alone; such things as fire and maize are capable of direct punitive action. A pair of twins, a mute, and a six-toed man have special powers; a woman by her organic nature is dangerous to masculine strength; some people have such natures that with a look they bring disease to one who is "weak of blood." Animals, plants, humans alike change their natures with the phases of the moon. People can change into animals; ghosts are always abroad; the soul of a person leaves his body for hours or days while he still lives. Sorcery is a commonplace, and an important part in treatment of disease is divination and ritual.

These are not simply superstitions still left to a few old people; they are part of the life of the community, shared by old and young alike and normally taken into consideration in determining courses of action. They are premises upon which the people ordinarily reason and the considerations which shape action: you do not buy lumber that was cut in the waxing moon because you know it will rot quickly; you place the skull of a horse in the sheep corral to keep out coyotes; you do not fret at climbing a hill lest the land itself give you a terrible sickness; you try to show no fear when you meet a werewolf, lest it conquer you; you tie a woman's skirt over the horns of a bull to make him tractable; you cover the stump of a felled fruit tree lest it be ashamed before its fellows; you do what you can to avert catastrophe when a dream augurs ill; you know that barbed wire makes a superior fence because while coyotes by verbal agreement pass through other fences, they cannot strike a bargain with barbed wire that, coming from abroad, speaks a different language.

But while this complex of beliefs forming a basis of action constitutes a world view of the type we have come to expect in isolated preliterate tribes, the type of social relations of the Guatemalan Indians, as I have indicated, is of a different character. Economic relations tend to be strictly economic, without involving personal relations; money is the standard of value not only in trade but in religious rituals and in gifts prescribed by custom: a feast day, a baptism, a shamanistic rite, a funeral, or an appointment to office all require expenditures pretty well fixed and anticipated in terms of money. In matters of social control neither public opinion nor familial organization is depended upon as is the formal courthouse organization where brother may be pitted against brother or father against son. Indeed, almost all matters of religion, community welfare, and social control are taken care of by officials set apart to care for them, while the rest of the people go about their business—business usually in a literal sense because everybody individually tends toward a major interest in trading and a variety of private economic enterprises. To know these Indians outwardly—without knowing their minds, so to speak—is to know a people who, albeit on a small scale, partake of the impersonal, secular, individually free social and economic life that is the pattern of our big city. This is reflected in the mobility of the society—individuals and families rise and fall in their fortunes—as well as in the continual state of flux: for within the fixed pattern, businesses no less than styles change almost as rapidly as they do among us. People move around, go places on business and come back, or move to another town for a few years or for the rest of their lives. Life is filled with dollars-and-cents values, earning money, getting rich, legal documents, mortgaging land, borrowing, lending, witnessing, going to court, and so on. In their social, economic, political and even religious interrelations these people are in significant degree practical, matter-of-fact, mundane, and secular minded.

However interesting it may be, the case of the Guatemalan Indians is not important simply because they are neither wholly primitive nor wholly civilized. We have come to expect such a condition when a primitive tribe is in contact with modern civilization, and indeed Redfield has very good examples from Yucatan itself. The point is rather that, as has been indicated above, the situation in Guatemala is probably not attributable to such acculturation, that we suppose the Guatemalan Indian communities to be in equilibrium in their mixed character. In general the society is not changing rapidly, for although in details many alterations have occurred in the memory of living people, in respect to their kind of life and their values the old people find their young people doing what they did and would want to do. It is also well to recall again that even at the time of the arrival of the Spaniards, there were wide and complex systems of trade, government and religion, and something of a money economy.

If this supposition is correct, we have to deal with a people whose world view is of the primitive type and whose social relations are, and have been for a long time and without regard to influences of Western civilization, of the civilized type. The question immediately arises: Is such a condition anomalous? The Guatemalan situation described would have to be so considered if there were reason to believe that there is a causal relation between a civilized type of social system and a civilized kind of world view—if, specifically, it were supposed that the civilized type of social relations that developed among the Indians of Guatemala should have changed the Indians' world view from its primitive type to the civilized type. If such a causal relationship could be established, we should have to conclude that in Guatemala the world view has simply not been given time enough for its inevitable transformation—that we have only a case of long-time cultural lag. For the existence of such a causal relationship arguments may be offered, since widespread trade and governmental relations would appear to be conducive toward wider mental horizons, and since money and the development of impersonal institutions on a wide scale would seem to lead to wider contacts, cross-fertilization of new ideas, and the divorce of beliefs from restricted milieus. And indeed there seems little doubt that a study of the history of our own civilization would demonstrate that in general "advances" in mental life accompanied periods of widening integration of social and economic institutions.

Nevertheless it appears more probable that while a civilized social system is a likely necessary condition for the development of a civilized world view, it is not a sufficient condition. After all, our civilization and its history are but one case, and such factors as the development of writing and printing, and the tradition of philosophy and science that came early into our culture, make it unique. We do have at least two other cases of developments of widespread economic, political, and religious relations presumably independent of our own civilization (the reference is to West Africa and to Middle America), and in both of these cases the prevalent world view appears to have remained on a primitive level. It may of course be argued still that not enough time was given these world views to develop, but that would only bring us back to the original proposition that is supported by only one case. On the basis of present evidence it would seem easier to conclude that a civilized type of world view does not necessarily develop together with a civilized type of social relations. If that is so, of course there is nothing necessarily peculiar in what we find among the Guatemalan Indians.

It may very well be, moreover, that what is defined here as the "civilized world view" is something that developed only once in the world—in our civilization—and now of course will never be given the chance to develop independently again. I incline to that interpretation and would consider the "civilized world view" as a culture complex that has developed in our tradition. If such a thesis be acceptable, we may also treat the civilized world view as we do any other cultural invention, and we can conveniently speak of its diffusion to other peoples.

The question arises as to why, considering that the kind of social relations prevalent in Guatemala render it fertile ground for the acceptance of the civilized world view—why this invention has not diffused to the Indians of Guatemala. For generations the Indians have been in contact with urban Ladinos who share the civilized world view, while the higher officials of the government under which they live, and of their church, partake quite fully of civilized culture. Yet the Indians have proved immune, except those few who, educated in our culture, have either forgotten their education or have left the Indian community. That exception probably supplies the clue to the answer. In the nature of the culture complex with which we are dealing, no matter how fertile the ground, the seed to sprout must be given some minimum of attention; and the fact is that the education of the backward highland Indians in the fundamentals of our mental culture is all but nonexistent. It is true that the Indians are not physically isolated; but the system of impersonal relations is a form of isolation that restricts communication and borrowing. Mentally the Indians are least isolated from other Indians with whom they share the same world view, and next least from rural Ladinos whose world view is almost as primitive, while from the urban Ladinos they are mentally isolated almost completely first by a difference in language and second by one of social distance. Their relations with such civilized Ladinos are for the most part perfunctory: they are employees or customers. The priests are few and their nonceremonial contacts confined to people of like culture and status. The high government officials the Indians see only on business, and the kind of business is not usually conducive to camaraderie. The Indians, since their Spanish is poor or nonexistent, can profit little by stray conversation of educated people or by bits from the radios they hear in town. Since they cannot read, old newspapers or other reading matter are valued for wrapping purposes only, unless there are pictures. When and if effective education is given the Indians in substantial numbers, and they learn Spanish and become literate, acculturation to the civilized world view will probably go on apace; and then their world view will become of the kind that is more usually associated with the kind of social relations they have so long had.

A general implication to be drawn from the distinction made between the world view of a people and their social relations is that it might be profitable to distinguish two kinds of acculturation. In one kind, both our world view and our type of social relations are imposed on native peoples. In the other, only our world view is imposed on a people who have independently (or previously) developed an analogous kind of social relations. It seems likely that the effects of the contact might be more rapid in the first class of instances, since the imposition of our kind of economic and social system seems to result in rapid breakdown of all aspects of native culture. It may also be that in the second class of instances, where only our world view is substituted for that of the native, there does not result the shaking-to-foundations of societies and cultures that occurs in places like Polynesia.

NOTES

1. Antonio Batres Juareguí, *Vicios del lenguaje y provincialismos de Guatemala*, Guatemala, p. 91.

2. Chester Lloyd Jones, *Guatemala, Past and Present*, Minneapolis, University of Minnesota Press, p. 269. Jones has digested many of the published sources on the history of Guatemala and has briefly summarized conclusions.

3. Manuel Cobos Batres, *Carrera*, 1° cuaderno, Liberia Renacimiento, Guatemala, 1935, pp. 12 ff., cited in Jones, *ibid*.

4. Jones (*op. cit.*, p. 272) says that "those who take on Ladino dress and activities become Ladinos even though of Indian blood" and adds in a footnote (p. 395) that "Precedents of this sort were created by law even in the colonial period. A law of October 13, 1876 expressly authorized such changes." It may be added that change from Indian to Ladino ways, especially in language and costume, appears to be encouraged rather than discouraged by both the government and Ladino opinion. What little anti-Indian prejudice there is among Ladinos is expressed in depreciation less of Indian blood and character than of Indian "backwardness."

5. This statement is based chiefly on field experience, but it is borne out by the census records. If very many Indians were passing into the Ladino class,

the rate of increase of the Ladino population would probably be considerably higher than that of the Indian. But the rates of geometric increase per 1,000 from 1893 to 1921 were calculated by Shattuck (*A Medical Survey of the Republic of Guatemala*, Carnegie Institution of Washington Publication 499, Washington, 1938, p. 11) as 13.5 for Ladinos and 13.7 for Indians. Nor can the possibility that the rate of natural increase is greater among Indians be allowed, for Shattuck (*op. cit.*, p. 13) calculates the natural increase rate per 1,000 population as 22.5 among Ladinos and 21.9 among Indians. Unless, therefore, it be supposed that many Ladinos pass into the Indian group (contrary to observation) the conclusion is inescapable that Indians have not been becoming Ladinos.

6. Sol Tax, "The Municipios of the Midwestern Highlands of Guatemala," *American Anthropologist*, 1937, XXXIX, 430, 432.

7. *Ibid.*, pp. 433 ff.

8. F. W. McBryde has described economic specialization and the market system in *The Native Economy of Western Guatemala*, thesis, University of California, Berkeley, 1940.

9. R. Linton, *The Study of Man*, New York, 1936, pp. 282–283.

10. Described in Robert Redfield, "Primitive Merchants of Guatemala," *Quarterly Journal of Inter-American Relations*, 1939, I, 48–49.

11. *Ibid.*, pp. 53–54.

12. *Ibid.*, p. 54.

13. *Ibid.*

14. *Ibid.*, pp. 55–56.

15. Cf. my "Culture and Civilization in Guatemalan Societies," *The Scientific Monthly*, May 1939, p. 467.

16. "Culture Changes in Yucatan," *American Anthropologist*, 1934, XXXVI, 57–69.

17. *Ibid.*

18. Tax, "Culture and Civilization in Guatemalan Societies," *op. cit.*, p. 467.

19. Redfield, "Primitive Merchants of Guatemala," *op. cit.*, p. 55.

20. Franz Boas, *The Mind of Primitive Man*, New York, The Macmillan Company, 1929, pp. 197 ff.

Ethos Components in Modern Latin American Culture

JOHN GILLIN

Culture, both as a concept and as reality, touches so many facets of meaning in the minds of its students (cf. Kroeber and Kluckhohn 1952; Bidney 1953) that one sometimes despairs of being able to reach common understanding, even with other professional cultural anthropologists, to say nothing of more casual observers. The hazards of agreement are considerably greater when one ventures statements about an important area of the modern world whose spokesmen are not only genial and *simpáticos* but also highly literate and intelligent. The hurdles of linguistic and national boundaries in such a case are of a sort that appeals more to sporting blood than to scientific caution.

In this piece I shall make no attempt to present a comprehensive picture of the total Modern Latin American Culture, but shall focus primarily on a limited number of components of the ethos, which is taken to mean the constellation of acquired drives or motivations that are characteristic of the culture, plus the goals, both explicit and implicit,

---

Reprinted from *American Anthropologist*, 1955, LVII, 488–500, by permission of the author and publisher. This article is based in part upon researches made possible by a grant from the Carnegie Corporation of New York, to which grateful acknowledgment is made.

toward which cultural activities are directed or upon which high value is placed. Included in this concept, then, for present purposes are also concepts that various writers have called "themes," "implicit premises," "values," "controlling patterns," "mental patterns," and so on.

First, it is legitimate to ask if there is a common pattern of customs, institutions, and ethos that characterizes modern Latin American society as a whole and that may be properly considered a culture. Are there certain cultural uniformities that regularly recur throughout the area and that distinguish the behavior and attitudes of the people from those of other areas? I myself have not hesitated to answer this question in the affirmative in the sense that the existence of Modern Latin American Culture is at least a tenable and researchable hypothesis (Gillin 1947a:-151–154; 1947b; 1948a; 1949; 1953). The Committee on Latin America of the National Research Council in 1948 published in the *American Anthropologist* and in *Acta Americana* a plan for coordinated research into this problem. The Foreign Service Institute of the State Department gives courses on "Latin American Culture and Personality" for U. S. representatives going to that region. An increasing number of North American anthropological field workers are producing evidence which supports the hypothesis. For example, Foster (1951:316–317) writes,

> In spite of large Indian population segments in the New World, and of large areas of Indian influence in non-Indian culture, contemporary Hispanic American culture cannot be described as Indian any more than it can be described as Spanish. It is a new, distinctive culture, with roots deep in two separate historical traditions, but with a unique and valid ethos of its own.

Wagley, if I interpret his writings correctly, sees the national culture of Brazil as a special and somewhat unique variety within the general pattern of Latin American culture.

> Many . . . cultural institutions and elements are common to all Latin American cultures, and, in a sense, are characteristic of Brazil. Yet, the national culture of Brazil is clearly distinguishable from other Latin cultures [1948:461].

Certain writers, however, see no common framework of culture. For example, James (1950:767), concentrating on the regional human geography of Latin America, says, "The word 'Latin' applied to America describes no common culture. . . ." This, I believe, is a perfectly natural conclusion if one concentrates primarily on those aspects of culture involved mainly with adaptation to the environment. I would be the first to admit that the Latin American area exhibits many subcultures of regional type, and that these are mutually distinguishable principally with respect to such features as house type, costume, modes of transport, techniques of exploitation, and other items of material culture. Likewise, one must recognize a distinction betweeen urban and rural phases of the culture. And, finally, we must not neglect to distinguish special subcultures related to various classes and social categories. Such subcultures and phases might be regarded, in terms of the old apothegm, as the trees. It is my contention, however, that the trees collectively constitute a forest which has some general characteristics that characterize or permeate all or almost all of the trees. It is quite necessary for full understanding to study both the forest and the trees, but one cannot overlook either. In this article attention will be given only to certain characteristics of the general pattern. Space is not available here to deal with special features of the Brazilian as distinguished from the Hispanic American variety, or of the various subcultures and phases.

Numerous Latin American writers assert an underlying unity in Modern Latin American Culture. A few quotations may be taken more or less at random. Among the most forceful statements of this sort are those of Luis Alberto Sánchez. "Between the countries of Latin America," he writes, "there are as many differences as between the provinces that make up the United States, but fewer than those between the nations of Europe" (1944:10). "In comparison with Latin American uniformity of culture, the 'unity of Europe' would hardly rise to the threshold of a remote hypothesis" (1944:17). "When one thinks of the visible interest with which foreign powers underline repeatedly and emphatically our differences either in order to convert them into cracks in the continental unity, or in order to maintain the supremacy of one part of the hemisphere over the other, one cannot avoid bitter suspicions" (1944:10). Somewhat similar ideas are expressed by José Vasconcelos. "In the tacit conspiracy against the recognition of our ethical and cultural unity," he says, "are writers, capitalists, and soldiers of imperialism. Cultivated Europe has been accustomed to judge us and treat us as the dispersed remains of a shipwreck" (n.d.:17). "We must recognize that we are only one of two peoples and cultures which share the new world, and our job is to search for the means whereby these two cultures [North American and Latin American] instead of wasting themselves in conflict, can put themselves in agreement and collaborate toward progress" (Vasconcelos n.d.:18). Zum Felde, while differing in some points of view, likewise affirms a modern culture of Latin America, although he is concerned with its further independent development. "Our virtues have not achieved their own expression in concrete cultural forms. That which is our own is not yet formulated and that which we have formulated is not our own" (1943:36). Alvarado García speaks of the modern culture as ". . . the constructive and creative synthesis of Europe and America, of Spaniards and Indians . . . a spiritual symbiosis which is still in full evolution" (1952). Picón Salas submits that the historical point of view was much too narrow "when, from the local standpoint or on the basis of elementary formulas of primitive caudillos we wished to understand our true historic problem which was that of the metamorphosis which European institutions experienced here, the struggle to found the state and modern culture on the medieval remains of the *coloniaje*" (1951:332–333). And he goes on to demonstrate that essentially the same historico-cultural problems were faced in all the nations of Latin America. "The differences come, not from differences in historical situation, but from the temperaments of the actors" (1951: 335–336). Basadre writes that, "Central America and South America belong, as do North America, South Africa, Australia and New Zealand to the 'World West' they form, together with Brazil, an Iberic-Criollo-Indian zone" (1951:356). Finally, we need mention only that intellectual and spiritual "declaration of independence" for Latin America published by José Enrique Rodó in 1900 under the name of *Ariel*. Attacking mainly the positivism and utilitarianism which he perceived in United States culture, and which had been proclaimed as the modern ideal for Latin Americans by the Argentine writers Sarmiento and Alberdi, Rodó exalted what he saw as the true values of an integral Latin American culture. Although I am inclined to agree with Zum Felde (1943:98 ff.) that Rodó unconsciously or otherwise took over some of his basic ideas from the French philosopher Renan and therefore did not fully epitomize the independent Latin American culture values, his book and his sentiments have had a strong influence throughout the area up to the present time. Even if ". . . the most advanced nuclei of the continent have now passed the adolescent state of Arielismo . . . Rodó did express a type of choice which we Latin Americans have made concerning culture and, in that sense, he was a precursor" (Zum Felde 1943:107–108).

I do not necessarily agree with all the points of view expressed in the various works of the foregoing writers, but have quoted a few of their words as a small sample of a very wide self-consciousness concerning Latin American culture as an independent reality, which one finds in the writings of modern Latin Americans.

If one had the space to document approximately, if not exhaustively, some of the basic patterns, or (to use the sociologists' favorite term) trends, in Latin American culture, of what would he treat? For present purposes I would deal with the following basic "components of the ethos" in Modern Latin American Culture: (1) the underlying common concept of the individual and the individual's culturally respected objectives; (2) the concept of man in society, human beings in a hierarchical organization of social stratification and the purposes of such; (3) the transcendental or idealistic view of the world, coexistent with the Latin American concept of reality—and what men are supposed to do about it; and (4) the patterns derivative from such basic premises, if you will, in political life, economic affairs, and spiritual posture. The latter points would have to be discussed in terms of the discrepancy between valued goals and achievement. In the end we might have an equation which would at least describe, and perhaps in part explain, the frustrations and dissatisfactions of Latin Americans as we see them in the world of today.

Since the [*American Anthropologist*] is the organ of a North American . . . association, it may be as well to begin as follows. Both North Americans and Latin Americans place high value upon *individuality* (other words may, of course, be used). Yet, I believe that it can be demonstrated that although cognate words may be used in Spanish, Portuguese, and English, the Latin American notion of the value of the individual differs radically from that current in the North American culture. To put it as succinctly as possible, each person is valuable because of a unique inner quality or worth he possesses. The United States credo, on the other hand, holds (at least ideally) that the individual merits respect because he has the right to be considered "just as good as the next person," or at least because he has the right to "an equal chance" or opportunity with other persons. In other words, in the United States the average individual is seen in terms of his *equality* with others—equality, either of right or opportunity. In Latin American culture, however, the individual is valued precisely because he is not exactly "like" anyone else. He is special and unique. This creed may not always be honored toward social inferiors. But it can be shown, I believe, that almost all persons in superordinate positions, whose statuses involve human relations and who expect to hold them longer than momentarily on any other basis than naked force, do follow the culture pattern of at least ostensibly respecting the inner uniqueness of others, even subordinates. This inner quality is often spoken of as the "soul" (*almo, ánima*), which Latin Americans are not at all loath to discuss at great length.

The historical origins of this concept of the soul cannot fully be explored here. No doubt the Roman Catholic view of the soul as elaborated in medieval Spain contributed at the time of the Conquest and after. Likewise native concepts of the soul, as manifested in beliefs and ceremonies (which persist in the modern culture) concerned with "guardian spirits," "soul loss" (*espanto, susto,* and the like), and various types of magic workable upon the inner spirit of the person, are all involved in the modern concept (Gillin 1948b). As Waldo Frank (1932) has written, "The Spaniard believed in his own person. The most tangible reality in his world was his individual soul. . . ." An Ecuadorian writer, Benítez, holds that in the New World the Spanish conquerors exaggerated the concept of individual worth because they were "marginal men." These men were "nobodies who wanted to be somebody." In the new lands they conquered they made themselves *hidalgos*—"sons of someone" (*hijos d'algo*). Each person had to insist that he was distinctive, because he had no ascribed distinction (Benítez 1950:53–54, and *passim*). Perhaps the present-day almost universal usage of *distinguido* in polite Latin American speech (as contrasted with Spain) is a reflection of this attitude; certainly it is commonly applied in polite discourse to persons who can lay little or no claim to being "distinguished" in the sense of having received social recognition for their accomplishments; in English it is perhaps better translated as "distinctive," i.e., the person referred to is *distinct* from others simply by virtue of being himself.

Whatever the origins of this deeply imbedded mental pattern regarding the soul, in the modern culture it has now lost much of its purely religious connotation and has become largely a secular notion. One of its expressions is ubiquitous in *la dignidad de la persona,* which cannot be fully translated to English by the literal rendering of "the dignity of the person." This concept would seem to be as important in Brazil as in Spanish America, as shown by the statement in a recent study concerning "dignity, which the Brazilians cherish almost as much as their Spanish-speaking kin" (Allen 1951, with comment by Ruth Landes). On the basis of much time spent discussing this concept with Latin Americans of all social classes and of examining its use in literature, I believe I am correct in saying the *dignidad de la persona* refers to the inner integrity or worth which every person is supposed to have originally and which he is supposed to guard jealously. It should not be confused with dignity of social position or dignity of office. The latter concepts are fully recognized and strongly motivating in Latin American culture, but belong to another category of mental patterns.

A few corollary cultural aspects of *dignidad de la persona* and the general high value put upon the individual soul may be mentioned. Every person is supposed to defend his inner integrity to the utmost of his ability, and a person who submits abjectly and without emotion to slurs upon it is usually regarded as much "lower" than one who merely breaks the laws established by society. Thus, words or actions that are interpreted as *insults* to the individual's soul are highly explosive; they evoke emotional reactions which to the average North American seem to be sometimes exaggerated and "unrealistic." These emotional reactions may be manifested, depending upon circumstances, in verbal or physical violence, or in sullen resentment, refusal to cooperate, and sub rosa seeking for "revenge." Conversely, both American Spanish and Portuguese contain elaborate patterns of *ceremonial politeness* that are in constant use between all but closest friends and kinsmen, and one function of which is apparently to guarantee avoidance of insult in the sense just discussed. (Brazilians, although motivated by *dignidad,* are said to be less touchy in this respect than Spanish Americans, less given, as Wagley [1948] puts it, to "saving face.") I should add, however, that I do not regard this matter exactly as "saving face"; "face" in English idiom refers to "externals." In Latin America, *dignidad* is an "internal" matter, the "external" aspects of which are incidentals. One of the subtleties outsiders often have difficulty with is that these ceremonial precautions are not necessary when reference is made merely to clearly understood and commonly recognized social position. For example, it is no insult to his *dignidad* to address a waiter or a common laborer as *mozo*, although, except in the case of old family retainers and master–servant relationships of long standing, you will get better service if you use certain polite forms.

The *macho* (literally, the "male") is a highly valued ideal in Latin American culture. In a sense it corresponds to an ideal type of male social personality. Yet, regardless of social position, the *macho* is admired. The cultural concept involves sexual prowess, action orientation (including verbal action), and various other components. But, a "real *macho*" is one who is sure of himself, cognizant of his own inner worth, and willing to bet everything on such self-confidence. There can be no question about his *dignidad*. The *macho* may express his own inner convictions by overt action, as in the case of bandits and "revolutionary" military leaders, or he may do so verbally, as in the case of a leading intellectual, lawyer, or politician. From this it is but a short step to the *caudillo* ("leader"), whose existence is so much maligned by observers of Latin American culture. As Williamson (1949) has observed, a man is not commonly either elected or acclaimed to office because he represents the socio-economico-political positions of his followers, but because he embodies in his personality those inner qualities that they themselves feel that they possess and which they would like to manifest, had they but the talent to do so, in their own actions. To be sure, the *caudillo* may have facility in verbalizing and actually implementing certain social, economic, and political aspirations of his followers, but these rationalistic qualities are secondary in the emotions of his followers to what can only be described as their identification with his soul aspirations. It is true, of course, that some of the same charismatic qualities are attached to certain leaders in North America, but the record shows that over the long run, in contrast to Latin America, North American followers or constituents are more motivated by rational or, at least, pragmatic judgments concerning their leaders, considered both in prospect and on the basis of performance. Both the *macho* and the *caudillo* (who, among other attributes, should also be a *macho*) may be considered as social personality types in the Latin American culture, which, although they may be deplored by outsiders (including intellectual commentators of Latin America itself), nevertheless must be recognized in any objective analysis of the less obvious aspects of the cultural whole.

The controlling concept of the soul is, I believe, logically and emotionally connected with the pattern of *personalism* in Latin American life. A more extended analysis of this matter would doubtless involve an analysis of security, psycho-socially considered, as a product or precipitate of the operation and practice of the culture. Nevertheless, on the level we are discussing here, I believe that it is correct to assert that the pattern prescribes that for the modern Latin American only those persons with whom he is in personal, that is, intimate, relationships can be expected to have with him a reciprocal appreciation of his soul. On the psychological level, this means that only with such persons can he feel secure. Now, in Latin American culture there are three pathways or patterns whereby one may establish intimate-friendship relations with other persons in this sense: (1) kinship, including both consanguineal and affinal (the latter somewhat weaker than the former); (2) ceremonial friendship or "kinship," which so far as the *compadrazgo* is concerned is actually a formalized or institutionalized form of friendship (see Mintz and Wolf (1950); also Foster (1951), who points out that the *compadrazgo*, although practically everywhere important in Latin America, has comparatively little significance from this point of view in Spain); (3) and "mere pure friendship" *(mera pura amistad)* which in many cases is established between individuals who understand each other's souls, but who do not think of imposing on each other by invoking the relationship of *compadrazgo*. In the latter case, once the relationship is established, the persons involved address each other in the "*tu*" form (*vos*, in some parts) and enjoy certain joking privileges with each other not permitted to those in a more formal relationship. Friendship, or the intimate personal connection, is the essential of interpersonal relations in the Latin American culture. And my impression is that the most intimate form of friendship is that which is institutionalized in the *compadrazgo*.

The Chilean sociologist Schwartzmann (1950) holds that the fundamental characteristic of Latin Americans is the sentiment of inner value (*ensimismamiento*, which also has connotations of introversion as well as self-containment), but it seems to me that he, at least in the first volume of his work, does not give due credit to the ties of intimacy which, to my mind, constitute one of the fundamental characteristics of the Latin American, and which, I submit, are logically and emotionally founded on the underlying concept of the soul. In Latin America, only persons united by ties of kinship, *compadrazgo*, and real friendship can trust one another. Something like this is, of course, true in all societies. Yet the impersonal confidence which, say, a buyer has toward a salesman of a large established corporation in the United States is not yet part of the pattern in Latin America. There, you have to know him as an individual and to understand his "soul" really to have confidence in him. The Spanish expression *hombre de confianza* does not necessarily imply equality of social position or of opportunity. It does, however, not only imply, but require, a mutual understanding and appreciation of one another's inner worth and, at least with respect to certain goals, commonality of interests. I have employed quite a few *hombres de confianza,* and, once we understood one another, there was never any doubt between us. Perhaps I am overdrawing or exaggerating this aspect of the individual soul, but let it be openly and freely discussed.

Thus it is commonly recognized that even the average man in Latin America has not only the right but the obligation to fulfil himself, that is, to try to realize the aspirations his inner integrity demands. He may do this vicariously by following some *caudillo* or other leader with whom he has identified himself. He may try to do it directly by his own action, without rising to the eminence of leader, by choosing one or more of a dozen different patterns available to him—violence, intrigue, gossip, passive resistance, and so forth. Obviously, the individual thus culturally motivated and directed is not by any means to be equated with the "citizen of democracy" as this phrase is understood in United States culture. The individual, in short, is, in the phrasing of Latin American culture, accorded the right to follow his individual, unique goals. This is one reason why the *forms* of democracy, which in all Latin America have been borrowed, either from the United States or from the French Revolution, seem to have little control over the actual political behavior of the real Latin Americans. The concept of individuality is different in the several systems involved, a fact which some North American political scientists, at least, with their emphasis on formal documentation, seem to have been unable to grasp. The special individuality of the Latin American can be and is organized in various ways, the discrepancy between such organized action and the constitutional forms is loudly discussed on the verbal level, and events seem to continue about as they have for the last 125 years. One may expect, provided the appeals of various nondemocratic forms, particularly communism, do not take hold, that a specifically Latin American form of democracy will eventually develop. It is my belief that all partisans of democracy (as opposed to totalitarian forms of government) should attempt to understand this Latin American cultural situation and aid its development in the democratic direction, even if the Latin American forms do *not* represent a "package export" of the United States variety of democracy.

Now we come to what many North Americans consider extremely paradoxical in Latin American culture, namely, its acceptance of social inequality. This pattern, like others, may of course change. But, as of the present, the peculiarly Latin American mental pattern or premise of individual worth is in fact involved in a cultural configuration that recognizes and accepts the *social* inequality of human beings. Latin American societies are *stratified* societies, and there is no question about this among most members of the populace, whether urban or rural. Every person realizes that, from the point of view of social structure, he is *not* equal with everyone else, either in position or opportunity. With the advent of European and North American ideas of democracy and of Marxian notions of the eventual dictatorship of the proletariat, this fact is now resented in some quarters, but, culturally speaking, it is, I think, still almost universally accepted as a fact. The "typical informant" (used as a substitute for "average man") will readily admit that there are social categories above or below him. Yet, he, as an individual with a soul in his inner consciousness or unconsciousness, does not have to pay too much attention to the unfair distribution of rights and privileges which the social system imposes upon him. There has recently been considerable concern among certain intellectuals respecting the rather feeble development to date of the Latin American middle classes (Pan American Union series 1950–51). With this concern, I might say, I am glad to associate myself. Yet, I feel that an objective appraisal of the situation must take into account, as of 1955, the still-persisting cultural pattern that accords the so-called middle classes a marginal and, in many cases, no more than an imaginary or ideal position in Latin American social structure. The progressive development of the Modern Latin American Culture will, I believe, eventuate in the full recognition of the middle classes, but, as of now, one has to admit that such full recognition is not universally accorded. One result of this is that members of the so-called middle classes strive, not to identify with the middle class, but rather to identify either with the proletarian intellectuals or with the upper classes.

However, although the class situation (including the caste position of tribal or communal Indians) is universally recognized, it seems that precision regarding the structure is not at present an established part of the pattern. I made a small inquiry in three Latin American countries (one Middle American, two west coast South American) regarding the extant social classes. My informants in this investigation involved three secretaries (one in each of the countries, each one of whom considered herself "upper middle"), eighteen intellectuals, twenty-four workers *(obreros)*, thirty-six *empleados* ("white-collar workers"), and sixteen landowners and industrialists. The question in essence was, "What social classes are there here?" (meaning, "in this country"). The answers varied from two to as many as seventeen. In each case I asked the informants to specify and to describe in detail the differences between the classes. The details must be given in another publication, but the points of interest for this article are that: *(a)* social classes, or at least positions, are universally recognized; but *(b)* the precise details of the class structure are rather vague to its participants. My conclusion, on the basis of this and other investigations, is that all participants in Latin American culture are (1) very class- or social-position-conscious; and (2) likewise conscious of the possibilities of mobility. To put it in other words, everyone is aware that he is born to a certain social position which is one of the facts of life, but that at the same time he can perhaps improve his position. For it is clearly a part of Latin American culturally controlled thinking that one can work up in the social system. And there are numerous examples of national presidents and less prominent *caudillos* who have done just that. To be sure, one seldom wins recognition as a member of the universally recognized top layer without birth or marriage connections with an old family, but it is well known that persons *can* win prominence without this. No one pretends (as is ideally the case in the United States) that the son of a common laborer has an equal chance with the son of an old *hacendado* family. Yet it is evident—and according to the pattern—that boys and girls with a poor start in life can in certain cases, at least, make the grade, if they really have the soul to do so. Consider, for example, the present or recent presidents in Latin America. None of them came from old upper-class families. It is true that Galo Plaza (president of Ecuador, 1948–52) was the scion of a prominent, landowning family. But it was well known that his father started life as a *montuvio* on the coast, who by valor and intelligence became a military leader and president of the republic, and eventually married into an old established family of the Sierra (highland region). Thus, according to the Latin American pattern, one may rise in the social scale if he has the soul to do so; but at the same time one recognizes and accepts, at least for the time being, his position in society. He has no right to expect more. Strange as it may seem to a North American, the acceptance of the social order as given is not, for Latin Americans, inconsistent with the concept of individuality as they conceive it. At one and the same time, therefore, the average Latin American is motivated to maintain the established order and also to take advantage of it for his own personal ends with the help of his friends, including kinsmen of various types previously mentioned.

Next we must consider the component of the ethos that some philosophers and commentators call the idealistic or transcendental world view. On the most mundane level, I believe that it must be admitted that Latin Americans on the whole are not primarily motivated by pragmatic, materialistic, or utilitarian considerations. This does not mean that they are not *capable* of learning or practicing patterns whose goals are utilitarian. For example, U. S. corporations and Point IV officials have proved that Latin Americans are quite able to learn and to follow the routines of modern mechanics, industrialization, scientific agriculture, and so forth. They learn the routines, but they are not primarily *interested* in or attracted by the underlying premises involved. It is true that all Latin Americans, except the millionaires, complain of their poverty and hard lot. But words and perhaps concepts have a higher value than things. The pragmatic, empirical investigation of premises and of data is not congenial, or highly motivating, to the Latin American, as of the present. We must be clear that in stating this we do not make value judgments. Who is to say that the North American practical point of view is more valuable than that of the Latin Americans, who are primarily interested in spiritual values? Yet this is one very fundamental point which, in my opinion, Point IV and similar programs planned to aid the underdeveloped regions of Latin America have missed. And it is very understandable.

The United States was colonized by refugees, shall we say, from the Old World who were essentially homogeneous in their desire for liberty, i.e., negation of autocratic or authoritarian power, whether of a political, religious, or economic nature. Except for Maryland, the Thirteen Colonies were mainly Protestant and principally of a nonconformist type, at that. Likewise, among the people there were no marked or socially recognized differences in social status (except perhaps in Virginia and a few other places in the South). Thus, when they won their independence from Great Britain, the former North American colonists were not confronted with problems of a spiritual or social or economic nature. If anyone did not like his position in these respects, he could move west and seek his fortune on the frontier. A safety valve was thus available for discontents of a spiritual-social-economic nature. But two problems *did* confront the North Americans, namely, the physical conquest of a virgin continent and the development of industry. The North Americans developed (to oversimplify) two successful formulas for the solution of these problems: hard work and technical ingenuity. These formulas seemed to succeed: the North Americans conquered their continent and they developed the most productive industry in the modern world. It is not surprising, then, that these precepts should become imbedded in their culture and that they should be projected upon peoples of foreign culture. In essence, the so-called foreign aid programs applied to Latin America, at least, seem to rest on the following implicit reasoning: "If we give the Latin Americans our technical know-how, and if they will just work as hard as we did, they will enjoy the materialistic benefits these things provided for us." Most of our aid programs to Latin America involve the transmission of technology, whether in agriculture, education, public health, engineering, military planning, medicine, or what-not. It is just possible that technology and pragmatism alone do not ring a bell in the Latin American culture.

If the present interpretation of the Modern Latin American Culture is correct, some of the basic (if not literally expressed) goals of the culture are (among others): realization of the potentialities of the individual soul; personal adaptation to and/or manipulation of an established hierarchical social structure; and satisfying contact with something beyond this life, or mundane existence. Obviously, for people conditioned to such a culture, the pragmatic and technological approaches do not, in themselves, constitute what might be called a first-order appeal. In terms of the Latin American culture, they must be combined with something more.

What is this "something more," something beyond the practical affairs of everyday life? "It," in precise definition, varies from one region and from one social class and from one school of philosophy to another, but it has more or less general manifestations throughout Latin American societies.

One of these manifestations is the almost universal preoccupation with death. Not only are funerals, their anniversaries, All Souls' Day, and the like, very elaborately celebrated, but the living tend to dote upon inevitable death with a certain sweet sadness (*tristeza*). This is connected with the theme of the importance of the soul, whose essence outlives the body. Ruben Reina and I, in making an incomplete content analysis of Latin American poems and works of fiction, have found the theme of death in such interpretative works to be about twice as frequent as in (what we hope is) a comparable selection of United States literary efforts.

Conversely, the Latin American pattern, as is well known, places great emphasis on fiestas and other forms of merrymaking. Such affairs involve drinking, dancing, gambling, fireworks—and on the whole may be regarded as distinctly "dionysiac." Numerous observers have remarked on the apparent lack (in the strict orthodox, Christian sense) of spiritual aspects in such celebrations. Yet, it seems to me that such patterns provide the way whereby the Latin American transcends the world of everyday affairs and grasps, even though momentarily, for something more. A careful psycho-socio-cultural analysis would doubtless demonstrate that the fiesta complex is often a culturally patterned outlet for the frustrations imposed upon the individual by the overall system.

Another possible aspect of this theme is the great value given to words and their manipulation, as in argument, compared to the comparatively low rating accorded to the empirical investigation of premises and data. Every visitor to Latin America, who goes with a working knowledge of the languages, has been astounded by the enormous verbal facility of his hosts. Even in published scientific works in the social sciences (except archeology and physical anthropology), the North American reader is often treated to a virtuosity of argumentation, phraseology, and theory to which he can only weakly and perhaps discourteously reply by asking, "Where are the facts?" It is all very well, and probably true, to say that these performances are the result of a system of education that lays great stress on rote learning and the development of verbal facility. But it is perhaps closer to the mark to point out that such a system of education is merely the instrument of an approved culture pattern, the instrument whereby some individuals may become more felicitous than others in reaching the culturally desired goal. For I believe that it is still generally true in Modern Latin American Culture that the Word is more valued than the Thing (in the sense of empirical reality). Again, I must warn against implied value judgments. Perhaps the Latin Americans are right. Who is to say? Not I, in this article, at least. But I will say this, that the Latin American search for something beyond the self, something above the world of crass, everyday reality, deserves recognition in its own right and also in the interest of good international relations. The yearning for the idea, the concept, the word, the creative interpretation, is, for me, a definite component of the Latin American ethos. Both the goals and the means or instruments to their realization are highly valued, in various ways, among Latin Americans of all social stations (except perhaps tribal or communally organized Indians), and, I think, the United States' "practical planners" and "cultural experts" alike would be well advised to take them into account.

REFERENCES CITED

Allen, William H.
1951 "Problems encountered in teaching Brazilian students," *Human Organization* 10:4:21–25.

Alvarado García, Ernesto
1952 "El Significado de la Cultura Hispano-américana," *Anales, Sociedad de Geografía e Historia de Guatemala* 24:257–261, Guatemala.

Basadre, Jorge
1951 "Notas Sobre la Experiencia Histórica Peruana," in *Ensayos sobre la Historia del Nuevo Mundo,* Instituto Panamericano de Geografía e Historia, Mexico, 31.

Benítez, Leopoldo
1950 *Ecuador: Drama y Paradoja,* Fondo de Cultura Económica, Mexico.

Bidney, David
1953 *Theoretical Anthropology,* New York, Columbia University Press.

Foster, George M.
1951 "Report on an Ethnological Reconnaissance of Spain," *American Anthropologist* 53:311–325.

Frank, Waldo
1932 *América Hispana,* Buenos Aires, Espasa Calpe.

Gillin, John
1947a *Moche: A Peruvian Coastal Community,* Smithsonian Institu-

tion, Institute of Social Anthropology, Publication 3. Washington, D.C.

1947b "Modern Latin American Culture," *Social Forces* 25:243–248.

1948a "The Culture Area of Latin America in the Modern World," *América Indígena* 8:31–43, Mexico.

1948b "Magical Fright," *Psychiatry* 11:387–400.

1949 "Mestizo-America," in Ralph Linton, ed., *Most of the World*, pp. 156–211, New York, Columbia University Press.

1953 "Latin America," in *Approaches to Community Development*, Phillips Ruopp, ed., pp. 331–334, The Hague, W. Van Hoeve.

James, Preston E.

1950 *Latin America*, Rev. ed., New York, Odyssey Press.

Kroeber, Alfred L. and Clyde Kluckhohn

1952 *Culture: A Critical Review of Concepts and Definitions*, Peabody Museum of Harvard University Papers 47, no. 1, Cambridge.

Mintz, Sidney W. and Eric R. Wolf

1950 "An Analysis of Ritual Co-parenthood (*Compadrazgo*)," *Southwestern Journal of Anthropology* 6:341–368.

Pan American Union

1950–51 *Materiales para el estudio de la clase media en la América Latina*, Tomos 1–6, Publicaciones de la Oficina de Ciencias Sociales, Unión Panamericana, Washington, D.C. (Mimeographed).

Picón Salas, Mariano

1951 "Unidad y Nacionalismo en la Historia de Hispano-América, in *Ensayos sobre la Historia del Nuevo Mundo*, Instituto Panamericano de Geografía e Historia, Mexico, 31.

Rodó, José Enrique

1900 *Ariél*, Montevideo, Dornaleche y Reyes.

Sánchez, Luis Alberto

1944 *Existe América Latina?*, Fondo de Cultura Económica, Mexico.

Schwartzmann, Félix

1950 *El Sentido de lo Humano en América: Un Ensayo en Antropología Filosófica*, Tomo I. Santiago, Universidad de Chile.

Vasconcelos, José

n.d. *Indología: Una Interpretación de la Cultura Ibero-Americana*, Barcelona, Agencia Mundial de Librería.

Wagley, Charles

1948 "Regionalism and Cultural Unity in Brazil," *Social Forces* 26:457–464.

Williamson, René de Visme

1949 *Culture and Policy: The United States and the Hispanic World*, Knoxville, University of Tennessee Press.

Zum Felde, Alberto

1943 *El Problema de la Cultura Americana*, Buenos Aires, Losada.

The Criollo *Outlook in the Mestizo Culture of Coastal Peru*

OZZIE G. SIMMONS

This paper is concerned with identifying and analyzing one of the key patterns of mestizo culture, particularly with reference to Lima, in relation to selected aspects of mestizo culture and social structure in coastal Peru. The discussion presents this pattern, here termed the *criollo* (Creole) outlook, as it is defined and participated in by the mestizo; delineates the popular stereotype of the *criollo* "ideal personality"; and points out some of the major functions of the *criollo* outlook, principally in the ordering of class and ethnic relations.

I

The outstanding attempt to identify common denominators in mestizo culture is that represented by John Gillin's concept of "Creole culture" (1947a, 1947b, and 1949), which is a tentative delineation not only of the culture of the Peruvian mestizo but of the way of life of

Reprinted from *American Anthropologist,* 1955, LVII, 107-117, by permission of the author and publisher. Read at the 1953 meetings of the American Anthropological Association in Tucson, Arizona. The materials on which this paper is based were obtained during the writer's residence in Peru as field representative of the Smithsonian Institution's Institute of Social Anthropology from 1949 to 1952. The writer wishes to thank Jorge C. Muelle and Luís Alberto Sánchez for their aid in clarifying his thinking on *criollismo,* and Benjamin D. Paul for reading the original manuscript.

mestizos in twelve other Latin American countries as well. Although Gillin's proposition that the "Creole" cultures of Latin America are characterized by a common general framework that distinguishes them from North American culture may be readily conceded, the writer accepts Tschopik's (1948) criticism that the identifying criteria used by Gillin are too general to distinguish one national Latin American culture from another, and are only partially useful in differentiating mestizo from recent Indian culture within Peru itself. The writer also follows Tschopik in objecting to Gillin's use of the term "Creole" for designating the "non-Indian," "mixed" culture of Peru,[1] but is not in accord with the reasons Tschopik offers for his objections. According to Tschopik (1948:255–256),

> . . . "criollo" (or Creole), as a cultural term, should be reserved more properly for a way of life which is vastly different from that of the Mestizos, or of the Indians . . . "criollo" . . . designates a post-Colonial Spanish way of life which, fundamentally, is rooted in neither archaic Iberian nor in indigenous Peruvian culture. It derives rather from the later eighteenth- and nineteenth-century Spanish culture, and is tinged with strong French influences. . . . This Spanish derived and oriented criollo culture is preserved today as the class culture of the old-guard aristocrats of such cities as Lima and Arequipa, and, to an even greater extent, of Trujillo, Piura, and Tacna . . . it is today exclusively a class culture, and is nowhere shared by all the members of any community. . . . In Lima and Arequipa, it is usually called "*alta sociedad*" ("high society"), while in Cuzco it is known as "*jailé*" (from English "high life").

Tschopik is technically and historically correct in this description of the origins of upper-class Peruvian culture, and in designating its original carriers as the true *criollos,* i.e., "the Peruvian-born descendants of Spaniards." However, in his insistence on reserving the term *criollo* for this purpose, he obscures the important development that the *criollo* concept has undergone in quite another context, and does violence to its meaning as it is at present used by the Peruvians themselves.

This discussion is not concerned with terminology as such, and no quarrel is intended with either Gillin's general description of contemporary Latin American culture or Tschopik's description of upper-class culture. However, the writer does object to Gillin's use of the term *criollo* to embrace Peruvian mestizo culture as a whole, and to Tschopik's restriction of its use to refer to the upper-class way of life. In coastal Peru today, the term *criollo* is used popularly to designate a set of patterns that represent an integral part of mestizo culture, but these patterns do not begin to exhaust the content of mestizo culture, and in Lima, at least, the majority of those oriented to the *criollo* outlook are to be found in the lower and middle class rather than, paradoxically enough, the upper class Tschopik refers to. This *criollo* outlook has as yet received no systematic treatment from North America students of Peruvian culture.

As reflected in popular usage, there is a wide range of variation in the meanings attached to the principal classificatory terms *cholo*, *indígena* (Indian), and *criollo*, but only their most common implications, with relation to each other, can be indicated here. The term *cholo* is the equivalent of mestizo, which term is rarely used in Peru. In the biological sense, the term *cholo* has been used to distinguish the "mixed blood" of Spanish and Indian descent from the other principal "racial" types and mixtures in Peru, such as the *indígena*, the Negro, and the *zambo* (Negro-Indian or Negro-mestizo mixture). Although this biological significance still lurks in the background, the terms *cholo* and *indígena* are at present used principally by Peruvians to distinguish between the two main variants in Peruvian culture, the mestizo and Indian. The term *criollo*, which originally referred to purity of strain, now has only cultural connotations, and refers to one variant of the mestizo, or *cholo*, culture. Tschopik (1948:253) has pointed out that:

> . . . the ways in which Peruvians classify themselves vary from one region to the next, and there is no general agreement as to what comprises Indian culture . . . what characterizes "Indian culture" . . . in one region of Peru symbolizes "Mestizo culture" . . . in another.

The only consistency to be discerned is that in the use of the terms *cholo* and *indígena* to refer to cultural differences, but the bases of the distinction may vary greatly depending on the particular local context. In some places, such as the highland regions of Cuzco and the Callejón de Huaylas, the term *cholo* is reserved for those "Indians" who are rapidly acculturating to the mestizo culture group but have not yet "arrived." The term *cholo* may have depreciatory or complimentary connotations, also depending on the context. In other Latin American countries it is used to refer to all Peruvians, sometimes in a depreciatory way, just as *roto* is used to refer loosely to Chileans, *cuico* to Bolivians, *mono* to Ecuadorians, and *gaucho* to Argentinians (Raygada 1936:190–191). In Lima, there is an upper-class tendency to equate *cholo* with *indígena*, and the former was traditionally associated with servant status, the domestic servant being referred to as the *cholo* or *chola*. Among mestizos themselves, however, it is usually used as a form of address expressive of friendliness and affection.

II

In Peru, the term *criollo*, purged of biological connotations, has come to refer to a set of related idea and action patterns that express a cultural outlook to which mestizos are oriented in differential degrees. As an adjective, *criollo* is associated only with the *cholo*, the Negro, or the *zambo*, but never with the *indígena*. A *cholo* may be classified as more or less *criollo*, depending on the degree of his orientation to the *criollo* outlook, but an *indígena* (i.e., as defined by the mestizo) is considered far removed from *criollismo* (the *criollo* "way of life"). From the point of view of those oriented to the *criollo* outlook, *criollismo* is esoteric as regards the *indígena*, and potentially exoteric as regards the *cholo* group in general. The term *criollo* may be used in a nationalistic, an ethnic, a status, or a regional sense, but all of these are related manifestations, on different levels, of the *criollo* outlook.

The essence of this outlook is its explicit affirmation of the uniqueness and originality of the mestizo culture. Those Peruvian writers who have been moved to attempt an explanation of *criollismo* usually refer to it as the *criollo* "spirit," "way of life," or "soul" (Gálvez 1947; Mejía Baca 1937; Portal 1912), and regard it as a sort of elusive *weltanschauung* that cannot in itself be concretely defined, but which stamps mestizo culture and mestizo personality with a particular identity and integrity of their own. *Criollismo* is the mestizo's answer to the painful question of who and what he is, his assertion that his "way of life" is a positive creation of his own rather than a casual European-indigenous mixture. "Legitimate," "true," or "pure" *criollo* are the terms ordinarily employed to classify those idea and action patterns that are thought to have a strictly local development, a Peruvian development, and to be most characteristic of the *criollo* outlook. However, this provides no barrier to culture borrowing since *criollismo* is capable of appropriating any element of foreign origin and "reworking" it in the *criollo* mold, just as any foreigner who acculturates enough to display evident orientations to *criollo* symbols and to participate meaningfully in *criollo* patterns is hailed as becoming "creolized."

The symbols of *criollismo* are most prominently to be found in the mestizo patterns of diet, drinking, dancing, music, humor, fiesta celebration, and leisure-time activities in general. The *criollo* outlook also finds its expression in other aspects of culture and social structure, such as courtship and the concept of romantic love, and the performance of political and occupational roles. Moreover, it defines a characteristic personality appropriate to and compatible with the *criollo* mode of participation in all these patterns. Lima has been traditionally considered, by both its own inhabitants and those of the provinces, as the source and pulse of *criollismo* (cf. Gálvez 1947:*passim*; Matto de Turner 1895:125 ff.; Portal 1912:38; Raygada 1936:175–76; Vega 1936:90–91). Consequently, the sketch of *criollo* patterns that follows depicts these in the forms they have typically assumed in Lima.

Among the most explicit and pervasive symbols of *criollismo* are various dishes, usually seasoned generously with hot peppers, that are prepared in a manner different from foreign or other Peruvian dishes; the classic *marinera*, a highly stylized song and dance form, and of more recent development the *vals criollo,* a waltz of European origin made over in the *criollo* mold; and the *jarana*, a type of fiesta of extended duration, either public or private, that is characterized by much drinking, merrymaking, dancing, and generally uninhibited behavior. At the *jarana,* the food served will be *criollo,* the music and dancing will be solely *marinera* (for which a box drum and a harp or guitar are considered indispensable) and *vals criollo*, and the liquor drunk will be *pisco* (grape brandy) and *chicha* (corn beer), also prominent symbols of *criollismo*. The *jarana,* which in the Spanish tradition simply meant a revelry or carousal, has taken on special connotations in Peru, and purportedly is the most complete expression of the grace, ingenuity, and *picardía* (roguishness) that are believed to be peculiarly *criollo* attributes. The dancing of the *marinera*, which depicts the courting of the female by the male, and the improvisation of lyrics for the *marinera* tunes, provide ample opportunity for the display of these attributes, and for indulging the *criollo* penchant for dramatic spectacle and affective release. Similarly, the coastal Peruvian versions of bullfighting and cockfighting express these same attributes, and are considered typically *criollo* pursuits. More recently, automobile racing and soccer have been "made over" in the *criollo* mold, and have been added to the *criollo* "sports" of spectator participation.[2]

The manifestation of *criollismo* in aspects of culture and social structure other than leisure-time activities is best considered in relation to the popular stereotype of *criollo* personality. The *criollo* personality type is ideally depicted as characterized by a quick and brilliant mentality, a facile creative talent, and a profound sense of humor. The mestizo who is *criollo*-oriented is supposed to display these in an easy mastery and elaboration of the song, dance, and literary forms, graceful adeptness and dexterity in the performance of the *criollo* "sports" and other pursuits, consummate skill in repartee, and exceptional cleverness in turning a situation to his own advantage. *Viveza* (shrewdness), *ingenio* (ingenuity), and *picardía* (roguishness) are qualities consistently attributed to the mestizo who is thought to be very *criollo,* as is the ability to *palabrear,* to be very good at verbal suasion. Popular appreciation of these qualities and abilities reaches its high point when their display involves "getting away" with something, or when they are employed to gain some desired end with the least possible effort. This supplies the "roguish" touch that is considered a principal hallmark of *criollismo*. Outwitting or overcoming an opponent through astute trickery, whether it be on the soccer field or in a political campaign, is an example of the *criollo* talent at work, just as the bullfighter or trainer of fighting cocks, e.g., who triumphs through sheer skill, in a dramatic way against great odds, is hailed as very *criollo*. This genius for scoring a decisive success in a dramatic way is summed up in the phrase *malicia criolla* (*malicia* may be roughly translated as surpassing shrewdness), which is an indispensable attribute of the "legitimate" *criollo*.

In the local literature on *criollismo* (see, e.g., Gálvez 1947; Mejía Baca 1937; Portal 1912), and in conversations with Peruvian colleagues on the subject, much emphasis is placed on *engaño* (guilefulness) as a characteristic attribute of the *criollo*, who is described, more often than not, as devoting his talents to beguilement in some form or other. "*Criollo* politics" is a synonym for political chicanery, and to seek a political appointment where there is opportunity for *buscas* (graft and bribes) is considered typically *criollo* (see Gamarra 1911 and 1921, and Portal 1912:197–207 for portrayals of the *criollo* politician). In the occupational sphere, there is the *comechado* (literally, one who eats lying down), who can, through one artifice or another, draw salary by obtaining a sinecure in the state bureaucracy or, more rarely, in private enterprise, or who can get by successfully with only a minimum expenditure of effort on the job. In courtship, the *criollo* is traditionally depicted as the expert lover, always falling in and out of love, and captivating the opposite sex by his smooth verbal facility (Mejía Baca 1937:92). Described, in a recent newspaper editorial, as a "national institution" are the *gorreros* ("gate-crashers"), who are "members of that historic, roguish, and most *criollo* sect that eat without paying, smoke without buying cigarettes, attend the cinema without buying admission, travel without tickets, and clothe themselves without tailor bills" (*La Prensa*, December 20, 1952).

There is an ambivalence to be detected in the evaluations of such distinctive *criollo* characteristics as shrewdness, roguishness, and guilefulness made by those who have written extensively on *criollismo*. Pride and admiration predominate, but there are occasional laments to the effect that these are aspects of *criollismo* that are detrimental to the "progress" of Peru. Those who lament, however, will, in the next breath, betray their deep attraction to these *criollo* ways. To give one recent example, an editorial in Lima's *La Prensa* (December 29, 1952) concerned with the inroads into the municipal budget made by *comechados* on the payroll of the city-owned bus lines says that they represent an "onerous institution for the State and for that part of the public that pays its bills and taxes," but the writer goes on to say that this is an "institution that in its essence bears that seed of roguishness that is the grace of our way of life." It may be expected that where high valuation is placed on "getting away" with something and turning a situation to one's own advantage, whether it be in play or in earnest, there will be little mutual trust and confidence. This is reflected in the constant protestations that he is a "person of confidence," an assurance that the *criollo* feels called upon to offer in those dealings with his fellows where trust is a necessary condition.

No attempt can be made here to delineate the mestizo values implicit in *criollismo,* but it should be evident that they differ significantly from those that prevail in a culture profoundly influenced by the "Protestant Ethic," such as our own. It is significant that popular attempts to define the uniqueness of mestizo culture through its *criollo* "way of life" are directed primarily toward those aspects of cultural and institutional life that are concerned with the use of leisure and largely ignore what the mestizo regards as the grim business of getting a living. Where *criollismo* does take note of the latter, it prescribes techniques for getting around work or at least making it as palatable as possible. The mestizo is not averse to work, and can work hard and long when there is no other alternative, but he is far from feeling the ethical obligation to his occupation that Weber summed up in his concept of a "calling."

III

Some of the patterns considered characteristic of the *criollo* outlook have been in process of development in coastal Peru since colonial times, while others can only be traced as far back as the nineteenth century, when they were borrowed from the "Spanish derived and oriented *criollo* culture" that Tschopik (1948:255) calls "true" *criollo,* or were developed independently of this. Although most of the patterns described here are derived from the Spanish culture of both the colonial and post-colonial periods, a few, such as the major part of the diet and the drinking of *chicha,* are derived from the indigenous culture.

For present purposes, the question of Spanish or Indian derivation is less relevant than that of class origin.[3] References to the *jarana* in Peruvian literature, both past and contemporary, consistently identify it as the fiesta pattern of the lower class (the terms traditionally employed to designate the lower class are *gente del pueblo* and *gente de medio pelo,* which are still current today), although it apparently attracted, in a peripheral way, many of the scions of upper-class families in the latter nineteenth century (Gálvez 1947:54–55, 58). Writing about early nineteenth-century Lima, Tschudi (1865:103–107) states that *pisco* and *chicha* are largely imbibed by the "lower classes and the people of color." Of other prominent patterns associated with the *jarana,* the *marinera,* originally called the *zamacueca,* appeared in Lima around 1823, although analogous picaresque dance forms of European origin were borrowed as early as the beginning of the seventeenth century. Vega (1936) amasses considerable evidence to show that the *marinera,* or *zamacueca,* was originally embraced by both the "illustrious" and lower classes, but by mid-nineteenth century was "taboo" in "high society" as being "plebeian," and remained highly popular only with the lower class. The fact that its subsequent development was significantly contributed to by the Negro and *zambo* (Raygada 1936:175) undoubtedly reinforced its lower-class identifications.

Cockfighting was traditionally embraced by both lower and upper classes, and as late as the beginning of this century "men of all social hierarchies" mingled indiscriminately at the cockfights (Portal 1912: 86–87). Few members of the upper class are to be seen at the cockfights held in Lima today, however. Bullfighting too has always drawn its adherents from all classes (Tschudi 1865:108–110; Matto de Turner 1895:241), as it does today, but the upper-class conception of bullfighting reflects this group's predominantly Hispanophile orientations, while the lower-class approach is considerably removed from the association of bullfighting with its Flamencan antecedents so assiduously cultivated by the upper class. The high valuation placed on shrewdness and ingenuity is now characteristic of only the lower and the emerging middle classes, but seems to have received its initial stimulus from romanticization of an upper-class "type" of the nineteenth century, the *mozomalo*, and later the *mataperros*, described as young bachelors of "aristocratic" family, who "assiduously concurred at the *jaranas de medio pelo*, in which they excelled for their witticisms, their gracefulness, and the facility with which they improvised a couplet and danced a *resbalosa* [an early picaresque dance]" (Gálvez 1947:53–54).

Literary awareness of *criollismo* in the sense in which it has been discussed here was born with the *costumbristas*, the republican writers of the mid-nineteenth century, such as Felipe Pardo, Manuel A. Segura and later Ricardo Palma, who initiated the search for the unique in Peruvian culture and found it in the folk culture of Lima, in the "typical" and "picturesque" customs of the city's lower-class *mestizos* and *zambos*. This quest for the "typical" in mestizo culture has been carried over into the present century by writers such as Portal, Gálvez, Mejía Baca and Belaúnde. Their writings, and those of others cited in this paper, indicate that most of the patterns popularly defined at present as *criollo* have been traditionally associated with the lower class, although some of them are borrowed from the "true" *criollo* upper-class culture whose members subsequently abandoned these patterns.

The descendants of the "true" *criollos*, who still dominate Peru's upper class in Lima and the coastal cities of Arequipa, Piura, and Trujillo, have shied away from any identification with the *criollismo* of the lower class and the emerging middle class. They look upon themselves as the heirs of the Spanish tradition in Peruvian culture, as the guardians and conservers of that tradition, and as those who have accomplished whatever has been done for Peru, in spite of the *jarana* orientations of the masses. To their Hispanicism they have assimilated much of the cosmopolitan way of life of New York and Paris, and they have felt little attraction for the patterns of the *criollo* outlook, in contrast to the prestige they carry for the lower and middle classes. The close identification of the *criollo* patterns with the lower class is reflected in the widespread practice of labeling an upper-class person who participates in any of these patterns as *huachafo* (see Schwab 1942 on the etymology and contemporary meaning of this Peruvianism), i.e., as deviating from expected class behavior and failing to maintain his "proper station," just as the lower-class individual who rejects the *criollo* patterns or imitates upper-class ways is also ridiculed as *huachafo*. In such upper-class strongholds as Lima's Club Nacional, the music is contemporary European and American rather than *vals criollo* or *marinera*, the cuisine is French or other European, and whiskey is served rather than *pisco* or *chicha*. In view of his aversion for the popular *criollo* patterns and their concomitant valuation of shrewdness and astuteness, the upper-class individual would consider it offensive rather than complimentary if he were praised as very *criollo*.

Recently, to the extent that they have become motivated by the search for *Peruanidad*, for a national culture, the upper class has selected a few *criollo* elements, such as the *marinera*, *pisco*, certain items of dress, and the native food, as national symbols which they emphasize as Peruvian rather than *criollo*, but even these are regarded as having traditional and quaintly folkloric value rather than as being an integral part of the upper-class way of life. The upper-class Peruvian still tends to think of himself as a *blanco* (white), to play down the *cholo* or mestizo element in Peruvian culture, and to minimize as much as possible the Indian element. The persistence of the upper-class penchant for Hispanicism and avoidance of identification with popular *criollismo* can only be understood in relation to this upper-class desire to maintain and reinforce its social distance from the rest of the populace. Where there are nationalistic objections to an outright affinity for Hispanicism, the upper class will emphasize its "Peruvianism" so as to sidestep any connection with popular *criollismo*, which, for many lower- and middle-class persons, is closely bound up with nationalism.

If orientation to Hispanicism has served the upper class in its attempts to keep itself free of identification with the *cholo* and popular *criollismo*, the latter has in the same way served the mestizo with regard to the *indígena* and as a source of prestige within the mestizo group itself. Orientation to and manifestation of *criollismo* are generally regarded as the strategic criteria for distinguishing the "mestizo" from the "Indian," and to a lesser extent, the *costeño* (coastal inhabitant) from the *serrano* (highlander). The extensive immigration of highlanders, oriented in varying degrees to indigenous culture, to Lima and other coastal cities has provided a powerful impetus for urban mestizos to re-emphasize their *criollismo* as a reaction to the *indígena* invasion (cf. Simmons 1952). Although some evidence of *criollismo* may be found among the mestizo components of local cultures in the highlands, its principal locus is to be found in the mestizo cultures of the coast, and as has been indicated, it is most closely and consistently identified with the mestizo culture of Lima.

Outside of Lima, in the smaller coastal mestizo communities that form part of the culture area dominated by Lima, the principal adherents of *criollismo* are not the lower and middle (where it exists at all) classes but the upper class. The members of this provincial upper class enhance their status in the rural community by imitation of the way of life of the capital, and for them this means orientation to *criollismo*, which they regard as the acme in "urban sophistication." There are small upper-class groups in cities such as Arequipa, Trujillo, and Piura who have always participated in the "true" Spanish-oriented *criollo* culture carried by Lima's upper class, but the upper-class way of life in the smaller coastal communities, as studied by the writer and other investigators (unpublished research), bears little resemblance to the "true" *criollo* culture as briefly described by the writer and by Tschopik, and as depicted in some detail by Tschudi (1865) in the nineteenth century and Tristán (1946) and Diéz Canseco (1934) in the present century. Since they know little, and understand less, of the culture of Lima's upper class, the provincial upper class turns to *criollismo* in aspiring to the "urban" way of life. Thus, while *criollismo* is associated with only lower- and middle-class status in Lima, it is a mark of upper-class status in the rural mestizo communities.

IV

This discussion has been concerned principally with describing the *criollo* outlook in Peruvian mestizo culture as representing the mestizo's attempt to establish and affirm his cultural identity. *Criollismo* finds its fullest expression in mestizo organization of, and mode of participation in, leisure-time activities, but its manifestations in various other aspects of mestizo culture and social structure, particularly social class, have been briefly indicated. It is possible that the study of *criollismo* in relation to other sociocultural aspects, such as the family, ceremonial kinship, religion, authority, and so on would yield findings consistent with those presented here.

The mestizo's preoccupation with identifying his way of life as peculiarly his own can be better appreciated when viewed in the historical perspective of his traditionally marginal position between the Spanish "criollo" culture on the one hand and the indigenous culture on the other. However, *criollismo* is not to be regarded simply as a historical curiosity evolved by a marginal group, but as playing an important contemporary role in ordering the mestizo's relationships with other ethnic groups and within his own group as well. It is a source of, and at the same time reflects, nationalistic orientations; it provides criteria for differentiating the mestizo, according to his own point of view, most sharply from the *indígena;* and it is a source of prestige for determining relative status in the hierarchical structure that characterizes the mestizo group itself. With regard to the latter, it has been shown that possession of the attributes of *criollismo* carries prestige within the lower and petty middle classes of Lima, and that in provincial mestizo communities orientation to *criollismo* is a mark of upper-class status.

It may be said, therefore, that class, as well as various other aspects of culture and social structure in the coastal mestizo communities of the sort that have thus far been the object of the anthropologist's study, can be fully understood only with reference to the structure of the regional sociocultural context in which these communities function, and within this context, Lima and the *criollismo* of Lima play an important role. The definitive assessment of the role of *criollismo,* in Peru and other Latin American countries, as an integrating symbol or set of symbols for mestizo culture, with its wide range of diversity, must await more comprehensive study than has been attempted thus far. This paper has been offered as a first approximation toward the assessment of that role, and as a contribution to the quest for common denominators in mestizo culture.

NOTES

1. In his most recent writing, Gillin refers to mestizo culture as "Modern Latin American culture" when describing it for Latin America as a whole, but still calls it "Creole culture" when considering Peru (1949:166–167).

2. Consider the following remarks from an article in Lima's principal newspaper: "When Peruvian *futbol* [soccer] was born, it was introduced rapidly in all the stadia, taking on at the same time the *criollo* version of a sport that arrived with a set of phlegmatic rules [a reference to the British manner of playing it]. Here it assumed the rhythm of faith, vibrated like a night of *jarana,* picaresque and joyous, and was kindled with passion in the multiple cry of the masses. That is why its play is accompanied by popular euphoria, which each Sunday [when the most important games are played] seeks a message of glory and promise. That is why our *futbol* has its virtues, its norms, and also its heroes" (*El Comercio,* October 30, 1952). The *criollo* attributes expressed in bullfighting, cockfighting, and automobile racing are extolled in a similar way.

3. The analysis of *criollo* patterns for the purpose of sorting out their Spanish or indigenous origins would be of doubtful value in any event, since we are dealing here largely with culture elements that are products of Spanish-Indian fusion and unique to mestizo culture. Therefore, they cannot be meaningfully reduced into Spanish and Indian components.

REFERENCES CITED

Belaúnde, Victor Andrés
1945 *La realidad nacional,* Lima, Peru.
Diéz Canseco, José
1934 *Duque,* Santiago, Chile.
Gálvez, José
1947 *Una Lima que se va,* Lima, Peru.
Gamarra, Abelardo M. (pseud. El Tunante)
1911 *Rasgos de pluma,* Lima, Peru.
1921 *Cien años de vida perdularia,* Lima, Peru.
Gillin, John
1947a *Moche: A Peruvian Coastal Community,* Smithsonian Institution, Institute of Social Anthropology, Publication 3, Washington, D.C.
1947b "Modern Latin American Culture," *Social Forces* 25:243–248.
1949 "Mestizo America," in *Most of the World,* Ralph Linton, ed., pp. 156–211, New York, Columbia University Press.
Matto de Turner, Clorinda
1895 *Herencia,* Lima, Peru.
1948 *Aves sin nido,* Cuzco, Peru.
Mejía Baca, José
1937 *Aspectos criollos,* Lima, Peru.
Palma, Ricardo
1952 *Tradiciones peruanas,* Madrid, Aguilar.
Portal, Ismael
1912 *Lima de ayer y hoy,* Lima, Peru.
Raygada, Carlos
1936 "Panorama musical del Perú," in *Boletín Latino-Americano de Música,* Curt Lange, ed., 2:169–214, Lima, Peru.
Schwab, Federico
1942 "Lo huachafo como fenómeno social," *Peruanidad* 2:400–403, Lima, Peru.
Segura, Manuel Ascensio
1885 *Artículos, poesías y comédias,* Lima, Peru.
Simmons, Ozzie G.
1952 "El uso de los conceptos de aculturación y asimilación en

el estudio del cambio cultural en el Perú," *Perú Indígena* 2:40–45, Lima, Peru.

Tristán, Flora
1946 *Peregrinaciones de una paria,* Lima, Peru.

Tschopik, Harry, Jr.
1948 "On the Concept of Creole Culture in Peru," *Transactions of the New York Academy of Sciences* 10:252–261.

Tschudi, J. J. von
1865 *Travels in Peru,* New York, Wiley and Putnam.

Vega, Carlos
1936 *Danzas y canciones argentinas,* Buenos Aires.

On the Concept of Social Race in the Americas

CHARLES WAGLEY

The present paper is concerned with a limited aspect of race relations in the Americas, namely, with the systems of classification of people into "social races" that have been used in the past and are used today in our American societies. The term "social race" is used because these groups or categories are socially, not biologically, defined in all of our American societies, although the terms by which they are labeled may have originally referred to biological characteristics (Wagley 1952:14). Such terms as "Negro," "white," "Indian," or "mulatto" do not have genetic meanings in most of our American societies; they may in one society be classifications based on real or imaginary physical characteristics; in another they may refer more to criteria of social status such as education, wealth, language, and even custom; while in still another they may indicate near or distant ancestry. Thus, a man with identical physical characteristics might be classed as a mulatto in Brazil, a Negro in the United States, and perhaps a mestizo in Mexico. In this paper, the point of view is taken that the way people are classified in such social races in a multiracial society tells us in itself much about the relations between such groups. More specifically, the criteria for defining social races differ from

---

Reprinted from *Actas del 33 Congreso Internacional de Americanistas,* 1959, San José: Lehmann, Tomo I, pp. 403–417, by permission of the author and publisher.

region to region in the Americas. In one region *ancestry* is stressed, in another region *sociocultural* criteria are emphasized, and in still another, *physical appearance* is the primary basis for classifying people according to social race. This produces in each of these regions a different number of social races and different structural arrangements for race relations. The different ways that each region conceives social races reflects the relations between people of diverse biological and cultural origin within a larger society.

To understand how these different classifications of social race came about and the different functions they have played in the various nations, it will be helpful to look at some of the simple and relatively well-known facts regarding the formation of the populations of our American nations. All of our American nations are multi-racial in some degree. Biologically speaking the population of the New World has been formed by three racial stocks—the Amerindian of Mongoloid derivation, the African Negroids, and the European Caucasoids. Each of these three racial stocks has contributed in different proportions in the various regions of the Americas. The Amerindian predominated in the highland countries from Mexico south to Chile; the Negro formed numerically the most important element of the population in the lowland region from southern United States, into the Caribbean, and on the South American mainland south into Brazil; Caucasoids have contributed in greatest numbers in the northern- and southern-most extremes of our continents, namely, in Canada and northern United States and in Uruguay, Argentina, and Chile. Yet, everywhere the three racial stocks have contributed in some degree to the contemporary populations.

Likewise, throughout the Americas, the process of intermixture between the three racial stocks began early—almost at once after the arrival in the New World of the Europeans and their African slaves. In the highland countries, the Spanish *conquistadores* mated freely with Indian women and by the end of the sixteenth century, people of mixed Spanish-Indian ancestry were relatively numerous throughout the highland countries. Furthermore, in Mexico and also in other highland countries, a considerable number of African slaves were imported to work in the mines and on the plantations; the majority of these Africans were males and they too mated with Indian women. Their offspring added to the racially mixed population and further complicated the types of mixtures present in colonial society.

Likewise, in the tropical and semi-tropical regions of the Americas, a similar process of race mixture began soon after 1500. At first, the Spanish, Portuguese and even the English mated with Indian women. But since the Indian population was sparse as compared to the highlands and since many tribes were soon decimated as the result of contact with Europeans, such unions were not numerous and did not in general produce a large European-Indian mixed population as it did in the highlands. Still, in certain areas of the lowlands European-Indian populations were important; in Brazil, the *mamelucos*, the children of Portuguese fathers and Indian mothers, became relatively numerous in the late sixteenth century and in Paraguay where the Spanish *conquistadores* lived as the owners of veritable harems of Indian women, a mixed European-Indian group soon became the most important element of the colonial population. But, throughout most of the tropical lowland region, the formation of a mixed population comparable to that in the highlands awaited the arrival of the flood of African slaves.

From the middle of the sixteenth century until the end of the eighteenth century, this region received literally millions of Negroes, mainly from West Africa. The story of miscegenation of the European slave owners with their female slaves is so well known that it need not be documented here. Such unions were probably most frequent in Brazil and in the West Indies between Spanish, Portuguese, and French males and Negro women. This has been attributed, particularly in the case of the Portuguese, to a lack of prejudice—even considerable attraction—toward women of darker hues (cf. Freyre 1946:4). But, the men from these Latin countries were not alone in being attracted to Negro women. The Dutch and the English also mated frequently with Negroid women. Although the laws and social pressure against miscegenation were stronger in the English colonies (and later in the United States) than in the colonies of other European powers, there is no doubt that miscegenation was almost as frequent. This is attested by the large mulatto population which took form in the British Islands and in southern United States. By 1850, for example, about one twelfth of the slave population of the United States and over a third of the "free" Negroes were said to be of mixed Negro-Caucasoid ancestry (Frazier 1949:67).

Miscegenation took place also on a large scale even in those regions which are today predominantly European. In Canada during the eighteenth and early nineteenth centuries, the so-called *metís*, the offspring of French fur traders and Indian women, outnumbered Europeans in western Canada. In Argentina, mestizos (Indian-Europeans) greatly outnumbered people of European ancestry until after the middle of the nineteenth century. In both Uruguay and in Argentina, there were an appreciable number of mulattoes and Negroes during the first half of the eighteenth century.[1] There have been numerous "explanations" for the disappearance of these people of Negroid ancestry and the large number of mestizos in Argentina and Uruguay; an example is the explanation that they were killed off in various wars.[2] But it should be obvious that they were almost totally physically assimilated by the great wave of European immigrants of the late nineteenth and early twentieth centuries.

Throughout the Americas, the process of miscegenation between Caucasoids, Amerindians, and Negroes produced hybrid populations. It also produced a complicated social hierarchy in which racial appearance or ancestry was perhaps the most important criterion of rank. At first, this social-racial hierarchy was simple. Everywhere the European whites dominated by force the American Indians and/or the African slaves. In the social hierarchy the European whites were on top and the Indian and African were on the bottom. Caucasoid physical features were symbolic of membership in the "superior" social group, and Amerindian and Negroid physical features were symbolic of membership in the "inferior" groups. But within a generation, the process of miscegenation produced groups who were intermediate not only in their physical appearance but also in social status. During the early colonial period, it was usual to attempt to describe such people in terms of their mixed ancestry, their intermediate physical appearance, and their intermediate social position. In order to account for these groups of mixed ancestry, and the intermediate social status accruing to them, it was necessary to develop a profusion of categories of social race, especially in those regions where intermixture of the component racial stocks was greatest.

In Brazil, in addition to the *brancos* (whites), *indios* or *indígenas* (Indians), and *pretos,* there were *mamelucos* (Indian-Portuguese), mulattoes (Portuguese-Negro), *cafusos* (Negro-Indian), *cabras* (Portuguese-mulatto) as well as terms for other mixtures (cf. Ramos 1944:205). For Mexico, Aguirre Beltrán has brought together a series of systems of classification of social race or, in other terms, the system of *castas* that took form in the seventeenth century; in each of these systems a long series of ancestral types and degrees of intermixture, each with its relative position in accordance with "closeness" to full Spanish ancestry, are listed. Thus, in the system described by Aguirre Beltrán (1940:166–172), there are in addition to *bermejos* (i.e., whites or Spaniards) and *indios* (Indians); *negros* (Negroes) divided into two categories; mulattoes, divided into seven categories; and mestizos, divided into five categories. Although these were color categories, they also were based upon other anatomical characteristics such as hair, lips, and nose. Ancestry was often specified; a mulatto *morisco,* for example, was specifically "the offspring of a Spaniard and a *mulata*" (*ibid.*:167). Likewise, throughout the Caribbean region there was a proliferation of social-racial categories based primarily on skin color but also upon ancestry. Perhaps the most elaborate of these is the system ascribed to Haiti in the eighteenth century by Moreau de Saint Méry (1797, Tome I, pp. 68–88). Saint Méry explained the system by attributing to all men 128 parts (almost like genes). Thus, a *blanc* (white) has 128 parts white, a *négre* (Negro) 128 parts black, and the offspring a *mulâtre* (mulatto) 64 parts white and 64 parts black. In addition, he listed also *sacatra* (8 to 23 parts white), *griffe* (24 to 39 parts white); *marabou* (40 to 48); *quateron* (71 to 100); *métif* (101 to 112); *mamelouc* (113 to 120); *quateronné* (121 to 124) and finally a *sang-mêlé* (125 to 127) (*ibid.*:86).[3]

Even within the southern United States, the slaves were often differentiated according to such ancestral types as mulatto, quadroon (one quarter Negro ancestry), octoroon (one-eighth Negro ancestry) and "mustie" (near white). Although still slaves, these people of intermediate ancestry were considered by their owners to be more intelligent, brought higher prices in the slave market, and received preferred occupation on the plantations. Furthermore, they were more often freed (sometimes by their white fathers), and the "free Negroes," who were relatively numerous, especially in Charleston and in New Orleans, were mainly of mixed ancestry (Frazier 1949:76 ff).

Everywhere in the Americas, these early systems of classification of people emphasized ancestry as well as physical appearance as their dominant criteria. They also represented a preoccupation with the intermediate social position of such groups between the dominant Caucasoids and the Negro slaves and the subjugated American Indians. But for several reasons, such elaborate systems of classification soon became unworkable and impossible to maintain. First, they could not possibly be extended in complexity to account for all possible mixtures. As mating took place not only between whites, Indians, and Negroes but also between individuals of the growing variety of race mixtures, the number of categories theoretically had to be amplified. According to one system reported for Mexico, the type called *Ahi-te-Estas* illustrates the absurd lengths such classifications could be extended. The *Ahi-te-Estas* was a person born of one *coyote-mestizo* and one mulatto parent. A *coyote-mestizo*, in turn, was a person born of one *chamizo* and one Indian parent and a *chamizo* was the offspring of one *coyote* and one mulatto (Whetten 1948:51–52). Obviously, as mixture between the various types continued, such systems became even theoretically impossible to maintain.

Second, while most of the systems described ancestry, they also implied either explicitly or implicitly that individuals of a given category would share in general a similar phenotypical appearance; that is a person who was a mulatto of one white and one Negro parent would have a physical type intermediate between Caucasoid and Negroid. This was roughly so, as long as it involved mating between individuals of two distinct racial stocks. But, as soon as the situation involved the mating between the intermediate types themselves, physical appearance no longer was so indicative of ancestry. Not all individuals, even offspring of the same parents, who had three white ancestors and one Negro ancestor, for example, had a similar phenotype. The genetic process of transmission of physical characteristics does not work like the combination of chemical elements. Rather the genes of the parents sort themselves out quite distinctly in the different progeny. It was perfectly possible, therefore, to have two individuals both of whom were by the criteria of ancestry *moriscos* (i.e., one Spanish and one mulatto parent according to the same complex scheme mentioned above for Mexico) but who by the criteria of physical appearance could be placed in different categories. If one were dark in skin color, he would be a mulatto (one Spanish and one mulatto parent); the other lighter in skin color might be an *albino* (one Spanish and one *morisco*).

But perhaps the most important reason that such complex schemes were destined to fall out of use was the fact that sociocultural criteria were not only implied by a term for a category but soon came into play in placing an individual in such groups. In the sixteenth century, the terms *gaupuchin*, *criollo*, Negro, and Indian in Mexico described with relative certainty not only a physical type but also the occupation, wealth, education, and language of a group. Similarly *preto* (Negro) in Brazil in the early period implied slave status and *branco* the status of a free man. But soon throughout the Americas, in greater or lesser degree, a conflict began to develop between classification of an individual by either ancestry or physical appearance and these social and cultural criteria. Thus, soon there was the anomaly of those individuals who were in terms of ancestry and/or physical appearance Indians and mestizos but who were in terms of language, dress, education, wealth, and other social and cultural characteristics Spanish "whites." Or, there were free people of Negroid ancestry and physical appearance who by sociocultural criteria should be mulattoes or even whites. Clearly a Spanish-speaking individual who was wealthy could not be classed with the people living in an isolated and primitive village despite his Amerindian physical appearance and ancestry nor could a black professor be classed with the black workers on a plantation. Social and cultural criteria became entangled with criteria of ancestry and phenotypical appearance, further complicating and confusing these systems of classifying people by social race.

During the nineteenth century, and to a certain extent as a reaction to the idealistic creeds of the new American republics, there was a trend everywhere of resolving this conflict between the classification of people simultaneously by physical appearance, ancestry, and sociocultural status. The conflict became especially acute as abolition came in the regions with a large slave population and as social and economic mobility increased the number of people who were Negro, mulatto, Indian, mestizo, or other intermediate types in physical appearance but "white" in accordance with social and cultural status. Everywhere there seems to have been a simplification of the systems of classification of people by social race. Numerous intermediate types based primarily upon ancestry and color disappeared from official usage, but not entirely from the popular vocabulary in many regions and countries. In Spanish America all of the intermediate types of the so-called *castas* fell out of general use and such broad categories as mestizo, Ladino, and *cholo* came to be used. In Brazil, at least such terms as *pardo* (literally "brown") and *caboclo* (meaning any lower class rural person of mixed ancestry) supplanted the more elaborate terms once used for intermediate types. In the United States, although mulatto was used on several occasions as a category in taking the census, the terms for various degrees of Negro-white ancestry disappeared from general usage. But more important a basic difference, perhaps already apparent in the earlier periods, appeared between the different regions and countries in the Americas as to the criteria used in classifying people by social race. And, this difference in criteria has continued into the twentieth century to set the frame of reference for "race relations" in the different regions. This difference consists of making use of, or even of placing greater weight upon, one of the three sets of criteria for classification mentioned above, namely, *ancestry, physical appearance,* or *sociocultural status.*

Broadly speaking the United States stands apart from most of Latin America in making use of ancestry almost exclusively in defining who is a Negro and who is a white. Curiously, during slavery more weight had been given to social and cultural criteria; despite the fact that many slaves were of obvious mixed ancestry, it was their legal condition that placed them in a slave category. And, during slavery a relatively large group of free people of color had taken form who stressed their intermediate brown color and their intermediate social position between the slaves and the whites. But, by the late nineteenth century, there was a decided shift in the criteria used to classify people as to social race and the possibility of a social race of mulattoes, intermediate in physical appearance and social position, was precluded. The dominant whites were able to establish a rule of descent based upon ancestry which states that anyone who has a known Negro ancestor is a Negro. This rule became a law in many southern states. Thus, the system of classification of people by social race was reduced to a twofold castelike system of "Negroes" and "whites." Not even the fair-skinned individual with Caucasoid features with a remote Negro ancestor can be classed as a "white," although thoroughly adapted in occupation, education, social graces, and economic position to middle- or upper-class status. This did not prevent a large number of such people, however, from "passing" as whites (i.e., assuming the status of a white by migrating to a locality where one's ancestry is unknown); and it did not prevent the "Negroes" themselves from making use of the other criteria of physical appearance and social and cultural status in determining rank within their own "caste."

The formation of this system of two "castelike" social races was, of course, the reflection of, and a result of, the pattern of relations between Negroes and whites that took form after abolition. It provided a structure favorable to a system of segregation. With but two groups vis-à-vis each other, without intermediate groups, segregation in schools, housing, public conveyances, restaurants, and other public meeting places was feasible. The difficulties of segregation under another system of classification of people by social race is brought home strikingly if we allow ourselves to imagine the complexities of segregation, if the intermediate position of mulattoes, quadroons, and octoroons were recognized nowadays in the United States. If segregation on the basis of but two social races is considered costly to the nation, then it would have been prohibitive to provide at least parallel facilities for four or five separate social racial groups. In the United States, by emphasizing ancestry combined with a rule of descent, a system of two castelike social races with little mobility between the groups has been amenable to segregation and productive of tension.

In the region of the Americas which consists of Mexico and Guatemala (and this probably also applies to Ecuador, Peru, and Bolivia which have large Indian populations) the classification of people by social race took another form in the nineteenth and twentieth centuries. In this region the emphasis has been placed mainly on the criteria of social and cultural status, almost to the point of ignoring the criterion of physical appearance. Furthermore, except within certain local communities, ancestry as a criterion for membership in a social race has little or no importance. In each of these countries, there continues to be a relatively numerous segment of the population classified as *indígenas* or Indians, an intermediate social race called mestizos in Mexico and Ladino in Guatemala, and finally a social race which we might call the whites. The difficulty in distinguishing between Indian and mestizo (or Ladino) on any basis except social and cultural criteria such as language, custom, community membership, costume, and self-identification is well known and need not be restated here. It is enough to say that physical appearance seldom serves as a criterion to classify a person in one of these two groups. Similarly, although a highly educated man in the city might have Indian-mestizo physical features, it would be difficult to classify him as mestizo or Ladino. The answer to this lack of emphasis upon physical appearance as a criterion for classifying individuals as to social race is that there is an almost imperceptible gradation of physical appearance from Amerindian to Caucasoid running from the Indians to the whites. This is the result, of course, of a high frequency of miscegenation between Indians and Europeans in the colonial period and, as we shall see, from continued biological intermixture even today.

Yet, something must be said concerning the importance given to ancestry as a criterion for social racial classification in Mexico and Guatemala. It is probably true that in these countries (and in the other Indian countries) ancestry still is an important criterion for membership in the group of "aristocratic families" who claim "pure" European descent, sometimes conveniently forgetting an Indian ancestor in colonial times. Yet such "aristocratic families" form but a small segment of the "whites." But ancestry as a criterion is also important in some regions of Mexico and Guatemala where in local communities it is applied with a force that is reminiscent of the United States. In the region of southeastern Guatemala, in the northwestern highlands of the same country, in highland Chiapas, and perhaps in other local regions where relations between Indians and non-Indians are tense, it is virtually impossible for an Indian *within his own community* to overcome the criterion of ancestry and to become a mestizo or Ladino on the basis of social and cultural criteria. This creates a twofold castelike situation similar to that in the United States (Tumin 1952; Gillin 1951). But there is a vast difference between the two situations. Lacking emphasis upon physical appearance as a criterion for social race, it is easier to "pass"; and it is always possible for an Indian who leaves his home community and who acquires the social and cultural criteria of a mestizo or Ladino to lose his identification as an Indian and to be accepted as a Ladino or mestizo. Furthermore, the emphasis upon ancestry producing a castelike structure is far from universal within these nations. In other regions of Guatemala, for example, it is possible for, at least, the offspring of a man of known Indian ancestry who acquires Ladino culture to be classed as a Ladino; and in Mexico, Beals speaks of whole Tarascan communities which "may gradually shift through time from being Indian to being regarded as mestizo" (Beals 1955:9–22). There could be no clearer witness to the emphasis upon sociocultural criteria to the almost total exclusion of the criteria of both physical appearance and ancestry than the fact that *a whole community may change its social race presumably without a change in physical type.*

Like the castelike system of the United States, the system of social race of Mexico and Guatemala reflects the kind of relationship that has taken form between the various groups. Indians are looked down upon and discriminated against by non-Indians. But contrary to the situation of the Negro in the United States, they are not being identified by the indelible criteria of physical appearance nor are they placed in the "inferior" group by ancestry. There is then a greater possibility for individual, and even whole community, mobility from Indian to mestizo. Furthermore, while the system of social race of the United States actually perpetuates itself, the system of Mexico and Guatemala seems to contain in itself the seeds of its own destruction. Miscegenation between Negro and white in the United States only adds to the numbers of the Negro group. In Mexico, intermarriage between Indian and mestizo, mestizo and white, or Indian and white generally adds to the mestizo group. The offspring of such unions are generally raised within the mestizo culture and thus become mestizos. And, this system promotes continued racial intermixture; an individual who is an Indian in physical appearance but classed as a mestizo on the basis of social and cultural criteria will most probably mate with a mestizo and his or her offspring will be raised as such. At least, theoretically, it is only a question of time until such populations may be entirely classed as mestizo by social race and social differentiation will be entirely in terms of socioeconomic classes.

Finally, in Brazil and in the Caribbean region of the Americas the system of classification of people by social race has taken still another turn. In this region, emphasis has been placed upon physical appearance rather than ancestry or social and cultural criteria.[4] In this region of the Americas there are no striking cultural contrasts comparable to that between Indians and non-Indians in Mexico and Guatemala. There are religious beliefs and rituals of African origin in some localities, such as Haiti and northern Brazil. And, in some parts of the Caribbean a Creole language, partially derived from Africa, is spoken by peasants. These cultural and linguistic traits are often identified with the Negro, but they are hardly limited to those classed as Negroes, being shared by a wide variety of people regardless of social race. The criteria of ancestry seems only to be important in the Caribbean and Brazil, as in Mexico and Guatemala, among those segments of the population who seek to prove the purity of their European derived lineage. For the large mass of people, ancestry seldom acts to place an individual in a particular social race. But the indelible mark of physical appearance, with the higher prestige accruing to Caucasoid features and the lowest to Negroid features, remains as an important set of criteria by which to classify people in social races. Throughout this whole region, such features as color, shape of lips, hair texture, and shape of nose are closely analyzed in order to place an individual in the proper social race.

But in populations such as those of Brazil and the Caribbean where mixture between the racial stocks has been so extensive, there is a tremendous variety in physical appearance. Although such terms as mulatto, "people of color," and *pardo* (literally "brown") are used to describe a wide range of physical types, intermediate between Negro and white, in popular usage, there are a numerous set of more precise terms describing people of intermediate social races. In one Brazilian community, for example, with a highly variegated population Hutchinson lists eight categories and several subcategories descriptive of people of Negro and mixed Negro-white descent. In this one community individuals are classified as: (1) *preto*, Negro or dark; (2) *cabra* (female *cabrocha*), lighter in skin color than *preto,* hair less kinky, and facial features less Negroid; (3) *cabo verde,* dark skin color but straight hair, thin lips, and narrow nose; (4) *escuro,* literally a "dark man" but meaning dark skin with some Caucasoid features—generally used for an individual who does not quite fit the three above categories; (5) *mulato,* yellowish skin color, kinky to curly hair, thin to thick lips, narrow to wide nose—subtypes are light and "dark" mulatto; (6) *pardo,* "brown," a classification most often used officially for census and the like, but sometimes applied in common parlance for individuals who "are closer to the white than a light mulatto"; (7) *sarará,* light skin, reddish-blond but kinky hair, and Negroid facial features; and (8) *moreno,* literally brunette—"excellent" fair skin, dark curly hair, features—much more Caucasoid than Negroid (Hutchinson 1957:120). Similar systems of multiple categories have been reported for other Brazilian communities by Harris (1956:119 ff.), Nogueira (1955a:460), Pierson (1942:135–136), Zimmerman (1952) and Wagley (1953). Although none has as many category terms as that described by Hutchinson, all contain from four to seven category terms.

Likewise, the societies of the Caribbean are characterized by the classification of people by a series of terms describing their social racial appearance and again, as in Brazil, such features as skin color, nose, lips, and hair textures are the diagnostic traits. In the French West Indies, for example, there are such terms as *béké* (white), *mulâtre clair* (or *blanc*), *mulâtre foncé* or *noir* (dark or black mulatto), *câpre* (straight hair but mulatto or Negroid features), *chabin* (rather dark skin but Caucasoid features and light-colored hair), *nègre* (Negro), and *congo* (very black with "bad" features) (Leiris 1955; Debrueil 1957). Similar systems of multiple categories of social race are reported by Henriques (1953) for Jamaica, by Steward and associates (1956) for Puerto Rico, and by Crowley (1951) for Trinidad, to cite but three examples.

What is distinctive about these Brazilian and Caribbean systems of social race is that they are actually a continuum from Caucasoid through the various degrees of mixed physical appearance to Negroid. They do not in themselves form social groups that interact vis-à-vis one another as do Indian and mestizo in Mexico, and Negro and white in the United States. They are a way of describing and classifying individuals according to physical appearance, but this is but one way that these societies classify people. The position of an individual in the hierarchy of social race combined with education, economic status, occupation, family connections, even manners and artistic abilities places one in his or her proper rank. Each of the categories of social race is divided by socioeconomic classes, although it must be said that the largest proportion of Negroes are in the lower classes and the majority of the upper class is white since educational and economic opportunities for mobility have not been generalized. Thus, neither Negroes, mulattoes, *pardos,* whites or any other social race acts as a group nor attempts to improve their situation as a group. This situation is thus less conducive to discrimination and segregation on the basis of social race. Yet given the presence of relatively rigid socioeconomic classes deriving out of the colonial period, class discrimination and segregation often functions in a manner superficially similar to "racial" discrimination and segregation.

In addition, these Brazilian and Caribbean system of social race provide a situation favorable to individual mobility. An individual does not "pass" from Indian to mestizo nor from Negro to white. Rather by means of improving his education, financial position, and other qualities capable of modification within a lifetime, he may move up in the class structure while still remaining "low" in the hierarchy of social race. People politely try to ignore such an individual's disability of personal appearance. There is then a noted tendency in such societies to "lighten the skin" of individuals who have the other qualifications for high rank, except personal appearance or social race. Thus, a man who is dark in skin color and who has Negroid features but who is a well-placed engineer or physician, for example, may be classed as a *moreno* or a *pardo* rather than as a "dark mulatto" or "Negro." Thus, even physical appearance is often perceived subjectively, distorted by other criteria. Only a sense of the ridiculous prevents Brazilians from carrying out literally their traditional statement: "A rich Negro is a white man and a poor white man is a Negro," and in some degree this applies to the Caribbean as well.

Each of these systems of classifying people by social race produces a very different structural situation for "race relations." Each defines social races in different terms. In Mexico and Guatemala (and elsewhere in the Indian countries) an "Indian" is defined in sociocultural terms. In the United States, a Negro is defined in terms of ancestry alone. In the Caribbean and in Brazil, social racial types are defined on the basis of physical appearance as modified in their perception by the total social status of the individual. These different definitions of social race have different consequences and thus so-called "race problems" are different problems in each of the three regions. In the United States, the definition of the Negro in terms of ancestry has created two castelike social races and the race problem of the United States consists of the struggle of the Negroes as a group to achieve equality of opportunity vis-à-vis the whites. But, even if equality of opportunity is achieved by the Negroes in the United States, the continued presence of the two self-perpetuating castelike social races will provide a situation highly conducive to continued competition and conflict. In Mexico and Guatemala, it might be said that there are also two self-conscious groups —Indians and non-Indians—and that the Indians act to improve their position as a group vis-à-vis the non-Indians. Yet, by defining Indian in cultural terms, the way is always left open for individuals and whole communities to transform themselves from Indians into non-Indians. In the Caribbean and in Brazil, the situation is highly permissive to individual mobility. Social races do not form self-conscious groups and "race relations" do not take the form of interaction between "racial" groups. Despite low position in the hierarchy of social races, individuals may improve their total position in society by achievement in other ways. Yet, rigid barriers of socioeconomic classes operated to reduce the mobility of all people of low socioeconomic status; the "race problem" of this region is to a large extent a problem of socioeconomic classes.

Yet, in all of our American societies classifications of social race, however defined, remain as a basis for formal or informal social, economic, and even legal discrimination and often as the basis of prejudice against whole groups. In view of the extensive miscegenation between people of all three major racial stocks and between the various intermediate types and especially in view of the criteria used to define these social races, it is clear that nowhere do such categories as mulatto, Negro, Indian, mestizo and even white have genetic validity. But, in the course of our American experience such racial terms have become entangled with social and cultural meanings and they remain as symbols out of the past of slavery, peonage, and cultural differences to plague a large segment of our American people.

NOTES

1. According to the estimate of the Argentine sociologist Ingeneiros (cited in Taylor 1948:56), the Argentine population in 1869 contained 350,000 whites, 1,315,000 mestizos, 120,000 mulattoes, 3,000 Indians, and 15,000 Negroes. It was essentially a mixed population.

2. This argument is again brought to life in a recent book, *La vida rural uruguaya,* by Daniel D. Vidart (Montevideo, 1955), p. 57.

3. Aguirre Beltrán gives examples of a series of "erudite" classifications which were set down in the early nineteenth century in New Spain which are as complex as that given by Moreau de Saint Méry. According to Aguirre Beltrán, these systems "fortunately never were carried into practice" (1940: 175). Like the "theoretical" system of Moreau de Saint Méry, they do, however, indicate the growing complexity of attempting to take into account the various types of intermixture.

4. In two brilliant essays (1955b and 1957) the Brazilian sociologist Oracy

Nogueira has examined the different consequences between "prejudice of color" (*marca* or *côr*) in Brazil and "prejudice of origin" in the United States. In my terms, this distinction is between the criterion of physical appearance (Brazil and the Caribbean) and ancestry (United States). I have drawn heavily in this from these two essays but I have attempted to stress the structural consequences of the use of these different criterion rather than their consequences in the type of prejudice.

REFERENCES CITED

Aguirre Beltrán, Gonzalo
1940 *La Población Negra de México, 1519–1810*, Mexico, D.F., Ediciones Fuente cultural.

Beals, Ralph
1955 "Indian-Mestizo-White Relations in Spanish America," in *Race Relations in World Perspective*, Andrew W. Lind, ed., pp. 412–432, Honolulu, University of Hawaii Press.

Crowley, Daniel J.
1957 "Plural and Differential Acculturation in Trinidad," *American Anthropologist* 59:5:817–824.

Frazier, E. Franklin
1949 *The Negro in the United States*, New York, Macmillan.

Freyre, Gilberto
1946 *The Masters and the Slaves (Casa grande e senzala)*, New York, Alfred A. Knopf.

Gillin, John
1951 *The Culture of Security in San Carlos*, Middle American Research Institute Publication 16, New Orleans, Tulane University.

Harris, Marvin
1956 *Town and Country in Brazil*, New York, Columbia University Press.

Henriques, Fernando
1953 *Family and Colour in Jamaica*, London, Eyre and Spottiswood Co.

Hutchinson, Harry
1957 *Village and Plantation Life in Northeastern Brazil*, Seattle, University of Washington Press.

Leiris, Michel
1955 *Contacts de civilisations en Martinique et Guadeloupe*, Paris, UNESCO.

Moreau de Saint Méry
1797 *Description topographique . . . de l'isle Saint-Dominique*, Tome I, Philadelphia.

Nogueira, Oracy

1955a "Relações Raciais no municipio de Itapetinga," in *Relações raciais entre negroes e brancos em São Paulo,* Fernandes and Bastide São Paulo, eds., pp. 362–554.

1955 "Preconceito Racial de Marca e Preconceito Racial de Origem," *Annais do XXXVI Congr. Internacional de Americanistas,* São Paulo, pp. 409–434.

1957 "Côr da pele a classe social," Seminar on Plantation Systems in the New World, San Juan, Puerto Rico (Mimeo).

Pierson, Donald

1942 *Negroes in Brazil: A Study of Race Contact at Bahía,* Chicago, University of Chicago Press.

Ramos, Arthur

1944 *Las poblaciones del Brasil,* Mexico, Fondo de Cultura Económica.

Smith, T. Lynn

1954 *Brazil: People and Institutions,* rev. ed., Baton Rouge, Louisiana State University Press.

Steward, Julian *et al.*

1956 *The People of Puerto Rico,* Urbana, University of Illinois Press.

Taylor, Carl

1948 *Rural Life in Argentina,* Baton Rouge, Louisiana State University Press.

Tumin, Melvin M.

1952 *Caste in a Peasant Society,* Princeton, N.J., Princeton University Press.

Vidart, Daniel D.

1955 *La vida rural uruguaya,* Montevideo, Department de Sociología Rural, Pub. # 1.

Wagley, Charles

1953 *Amazon Town: A Study of Man in the Tropics,* New York, Macmillan.

Wagley, Charles (ed.)

1952 *Race and Class in Rural Brazil,* Paris, UNESCO.

Whetten, Nathan

1948 *Rural Mexico,* Chicago, University of Chicago Press.

Zimmerman, Ben

1952 "Race Relations in the Arid Sertão," in *Race and Class in Rural Brazil,* Charles Wagley, ed., pp. 82–115, Paris, UNESCO.

Mental Health and Migration to Cities: A Peruvian Case

WILLIAM P. MANGIN

Large-scale internal migration in Peru is not a new phenomenon. Kubler[1] and others have commented on migration in Inca and colonial times. Migration from the provinces to Lima is of long standing and has largely accounted for the growth of the city. García Frías[2] pointed out the extent of migration in and out of Lima in 1940, and the most casual observer in Lima today can note the large numbers of migrants arriving daily from the provinces. The migrants include people from all social classes, all types of settlements, and all regions, and are found in all sections of Lima. The few white upper-class migrants from the large haciendas and towns of the provinces are generally quite familiar with Lima and Lima culture before they migrate and therefore have little difficulty in adjusting. In many cases they are quite involved in extended families which maintain Lima residences as well as provincial ones. The small kinship-oriented upper class of Peru controls the vast majority of the wealth of the country but is relatively unimportant in

Reprinted from *Annals of New York Academy of Sciences,* 1960, LXXXIV, Art. 17, 911–917, by permission of the author and publisher. The investigation reported in this paper was supported by a research grant from the National Institute of Mental Health, Public Health Service, Bethesda, Md. The research in Peru was conducted from 1957 to 1959.

terms of migration. Another group that, until the last few years, figured somewhat less in migration than others is the conservative Indian group,[3,4] that is, the people characterized by Quechua speaking, coca chewing, trial marriage, remnants of patrilineal ancestry, and homespun Indian clothing, and who generally migrate to a provincial city, a mine, or a hacienda for a number of years, even a generation, before coming to Lima.

The bulk of the migrants are mestizos, *cholos* (progressive Indians who have left Indian communities and are participating in national Peruvian culture, generally a one-generation transitional group), and those who, for lack of a better term, I shall call modern provincial Peruvians. The *cholos* are mostly bilingual mountaineers, but so are many of the mestizos and the modern Peruvians. As Simmons noted[5] there are two ideal types in Peru, the coastal-urban-Creole (or modern Peruvian) and the mountain-rural-Indian, but there is considerable intermixture of the categories in actual fact. The dominant high-status culture pattern in Lima is certainly the urban, modern Peruvian.

Some current (and ancient) writings in social science would lead us to expect that the low-status migrants whose culture differs most from that of the dominant group will suffer severe stress and exhibit disorganized and maladaptive behavior supposedly characteristic of people in the trans-culturation situation.[6] The problem is enormously complex and has been studied only minimally but my own four-year study in Peru does not support this expectation. The important factors in the adjustment of migrants to Lima seem to have relatively little to do with migration as such. Many are faced with the necessity of learning new patterns in a short time, but my data indicate that they do so in a manner characteristic of their response to problems in the mountains. Drastic changes in personality were not found among the respondents, and changes in the degree and nature of social participation seemed to be largely within the control of the individual; that is, a man who desires either more or less contact with kinsmen and/or *paisanos* can usually arrange it either way. A man who wants the primary-group relationships of a small community in Lima can usually satisfy this want even as a man who desires to escape from precisely these relationships can usually escape. It is also possible for a man to cut himself off completely from contacts with his home locality, or to participate intensely with people from that locality in Lima and stay in almost daily contact with the actual home town through seeing visitors and making visits.[7] The most important "migration" in Peru, in terms of culture change, is not the move from the provinces to Lima but the socio-psychological change from a conservative Indian cultural group to modern Peruvian national culture. This may or may not be accompanied by geographical relocation.

For many people migration is a response to a change in level of aspiration; for others it is a continuation of some early aspiration; for still others it is forced by economic or political conditions. For some it reflects hope, for others despair. There are migrants who try to carry their mountain cultural patterns over into Lima, and among them are those who succeed and those who fail. There are also those who try to change markedly, usually in the direction of modern Peruvian culture and social class mobility, and among them there are those who succeed and those who fail. Actually most people fall somewhere in between. The largest numerical group, those who preserve a semblance of mountain culture in Lima, appears to be only a one- or two-generation category, since most of the individuals involved do not want their children to remain in the same condition. They are in fact markedly and unrealistically upwardly mobile for their children while maintaining low levels of aspiration for themselves.[8] One place to study most types of migrants from the mountains to Lima that satisfies the anthropological bias for community studies and has the practical advantage of localizing informants is the "clandestine urbanization," or squatter settlement, called a *barriada*. After residing in Lima for some time many of the migrants discover the *barriadas* that ring Lima on the hillsides and river banks. The backgrounds of the residents vary tremendously, but one *barriada* does not seem very different from another.

Barriadas are located on state, municipal, or church lands in or near the city. They were originally formed by some sort of an organized invasion and each has a formal association and is considered a community by the residents.

At its worst a *barriada* is a crowded, helter-skelter hodge-podge of inadequate straw houses with no water supply and no provision for sewage disposal; parts of many are like this. Most do have a rough plan, and most inhabitants convert their original houses to more substantial structures as soon as they can. Construction activity, usually involving family, neighbors, and friends, is a constant feature of *barriada* life and, although water and sewage usually remain critical problems, a livable situation is reached with respect to them.

In a 1956 census Matos Mar of the University of San Marcos showed a population of approximately 120,000 in fifty-six *barriadas* of Lima-Callao.[9] In 1958, a somewhat less carefully taken census of roughly the same area showed a population of 276,600 in 129 *barriadas*. The latest official census[10] figure for Lima-Callao is 592,347, taken from the 1940 census. The calculated population for 1957 for Lima-Callao is 1,260,729.[11] Granting considerable leeway for error in all the figures, it would seem that from 10 to 20 per cent of the population of Lima lives in *barriadas*.

Lima is changing rapidly, as are the *barriadas*, and it is difficult to compile a list of characteristics that will apply to all *barriadas* or to any one *barriada* over a period of time. It is possible, however, to describe an ideal type of *barriada* and indicate the direction of change. There is variation between *barriadas*, of course, but their histories are remarkably similar.

A typical *barriada*, allowing for a few months' settling period, exhibits the following characteristics:

1. The overwhelming majority of the adults are provincial-born, and the majority of these are from the mountains. They are usually young people with children; there are few adolescents or aged.

2. Few residents have come to the *barriada* directly from the province, but have resided for some time in Lima.

3. The residents are all "owners" of the lots and the straw-mat houses they themselves have constructed. In some cases there has been land speculation from the beginning, but generally speculators have been rare among the original settlers. There are no units that are not dwellings, and the usual household group is the nuclear family. In many cases the association will allow only nuclear families and married couples to build.

4. There is a feeling of separateness from the city, a feeling of being under attack, which is reinforced by the lack of municipal services and protection and by unfavorable public attitudes toward *barriadas*.

5. There is a relatively high degree of integration and "belongingness," and considerable pride in achievement and satisfaction with home ownership.

6. The *barriada* associations (such as Fathers of Families of Mariscal Castilla, Defenders of Mirones, and Home Owners of Santa Clara de Bella Luz) consist of self-appointed groups, usually the leaders and organizers of the original settlements, and leadership is based chiefly on the personality of the members plus kinship and regional loyalty.

The direction of change for each of the above items seems to be as follows:

1. The percentage of provincial-born goes down as more children are born in a *barriada*. The heads of new families, both those who construct new homes and those who replace moving families, continue to be provincial-born, and many people come from the provinces to reside in the new house of a relative.

2. More people come directly to the *barriadas* from the provinces, often upon the advice and with the assistance of relatives and kinsmen.

3. Renting becomes more frequent, and many individuals sell, lease, or lend their houses, almost always without having clear title. The number of boarders goes up as does the number of extra people in the household. The open conflicts over lot ownership characteristic of the early period give way to litigation before the *barriada* association or in the

police stations and courts. Many open stores or bars in houses and some public buildings (school, assembly hall, office for association, movie) are constructed. A half-finished chapel is a common sight. Most houses are gradually converted to cement and brick. The nuclear family is augmented by relatives of various degrees of closeness; desertion by husbands is common enough to make the woman-children household a frequently encountered phenomenon.

4. Generally the feeling of separateness lessens and services increase, but there is considerable variation on this point. In many cases, where there has been no continued pressure for the land from outsiders or where the inhabitants have successfully resisted such pressure, the area gradually becomes "urbanized" and blends into the city, as in the case of Zarumilla and parts of Fray Martin de Porres and Mirones. The electric company serves the area, branch banks and stores appear, movies are opened, bus lines operate, priests come, and finally the government recognizes the existence of the *barriada* for more than tax collection by appointing schoolteachers and, in one case, even appointing two mounted police to patrol an area of five square miles and 20,000 people.

5. Belongingness and integration tend to be replaced by co-residence. The original settlers are swallowed up by the growing population, and some of them move out. The need for unity in defense against outside threats to the *barriada* lessens, and internal tensions increase. Many more people rent, and many of the older inhabitants, who were pleased with their situation at first, begin to complain of the surroundings, quarrel with their neighbors, and comment unfavorably on new arrivals ("too many brute-Indians," "too many brute-Negroes," and "too many bad people"). Many individuals also develop new, or reinforce old, relationships with outsiders on the basis of such ties as kinship, region, occupation, and politics.

6. The association takes on a more political character and, even though personality and regionalism continue to be important in the local elections, national politics and national issues play a larger part. The original leaders often move out (in which case they may or may not continue to exert influence) or, following a time-honored Peruvian tradition, a reform faction accuses them of stealing money and they, in turn, can choose to fight, flee, or sulk. As the *barriada* becomes more a part of Lima the association usually loses power.

For most of the migrants the *barriada* represents a definite improvement in terms of housing and general income, and Lima represents an improvement over the semi-feudal life of the mountain Indian, *cholo*, or lower-class mestizo.

There is very little violence, prostitution, homosexuality, or gang behavior in *barriadas*. Petty thievery is endemic throughout Lima, but *barriadas* seem somewhat safer than most neighborhoods in this respect, perhaps because there is less to steal.

In collaboration with Humberto Rotondo, a psychiatrist from the Ministry of Health, and José Matos Mar, an anthropologist from the University of San Marcos, a study of one *barriada* was carried out during 1958 and 1959. In addition to traditional anthropological methods such as observation, conversation, and participation, we administered five questionnaires, including the Cornell Medical Index, to a selected sample of 65 of the 600 families. In 1959 I also assisted Walter Slote, a psychoanalyst, in the collection of Rorschach and partial TAT records from an arbitrarily chosen group of residents.

The material has yet to be systematically analyzed but, in regard to pathological behavior, it does not seem to be directly related to migration. The high percentage of "yes" answers on the Cornell Medical Index indicating the presence of neurotic and psychotic symptoms does not seem very different from the percentage on records of mountain residents from Huancavelica and Puno. In fact my own work and that of Wellin[12] indicate that a general preoccupation with illness (real and imagined), panic reaction to illness, and a belief in the relatedness of personal responsibility to illness through witchcraft and taboo violation seem characteristic of both Indian and mestizo culture throughout Peru.

Rotondo's interviewers administered a modified inventory of symptoms of childhood behavior problems to mothers in the sample, and they found a very high frequency of fear of the dark and bed-wetting in children up to the age of twelve.[13] At my suggestion some local disease categories were added to the list (such as evil eye, fright, and bewitchment), and most of the symptoms of illness such as vomiting, diarrhea, and fever were classified by the mothers into these categories, which are also the common diseases of children outside of Lima.

Rotondo has noted, in another study,[14] the incidence of respondents who, although in precarious situations economically and socially, felt themselves to be objects of envy. This is also true in the *barriada* we studied. Assuming a certain amount of projection, it would seem that there is considerable envy of those whose dependency needs are satisfied. I encountered this phenomenon frequently in my work in the mountains of Ancash.

Another characteristic we noted in the *barriada* that is also commonly noted throughout Peru is relatively severe depression. Descriptive words such as "depressed," "sad," and "pitiful" occur with great frequency in our interviews and field notes. The humble, passive, tranquil, modest individual described by many informants as the ideal personality type is not strong and forbearing but rather frightened and ineffective.

Another set of phenomena that have their mountain counterparts but are more extreme in Lima and are more Creole or mestizo than Indian are the following ambivalent attitudes about marriage and the family:

1. A large number of men and women, both in and out of the sample, say that marriage is desirable and to be sought, but at the same time say that the bachelor has more possibilities than the married man and "My failure was caused by marrying too young." This is also illustrated by frequent contradictory statements about spouses in the same interview; for example, "My husband is a good man with me and with the children"; "If my husband hadn't abandoned us when I had epilepsy I would have recovered faster"; and "He has been a disillusion for me."

2. Many respondents express open ambivalence about children, which is quite rare in the mountains. "My happiness is with my children"; "My children are a burden to me"; "My children will take care of me when I am old—I can call on them for anything"; "I am disenchanted with my children—they care only for themselves"; "I am happy only in my home with my wife and children"; and "I am unable to progress because of too many children."

3. A common contradiction that may not be as contradictory as it first appears is that in which one encounters verbalizations about happiness and enjoyment only with wife and children from the very same men who habitually beat their wives and children. Violence toward wife and children is the most frequently encountered form of violence in Peru and, in many cases, there was no hint of it in the questionnaires. This was one of the many occasions where the questionnaires became valuable only in conjunction with the observational data of the anthropologist.

4. Although fathers are quite indulgent and loving towards sons during the first six or seven years, avoidance and tension are common in the relationship from that time on. Fathers often assert their authority verbally and physically, but the children generally side with the mother; the father's intimate relationships tend to be with male peers and with his own sisters and, to a lesser extent, his brothers.

The perception of the mother seems to be represented by two extremes: the good mother and the bad mother. One image is the nurturing, comforting mother one can depend upon for support and counsel; the other is the mother who says, "Go out and succeed" but who also communicates in other ways that the child had better not leave or he will be a social and moral failure. Abandonment by the parents, especially by the mother, is one of the most commonly encountered themes in the *barriada* data and in Peruvian folklore. The search for someone to depend upon is carried on in many situations, constantly ending in disillusionment.

One informant, a thirty-year-old mestizo married man with two children, who migrated from the mountains of Ancash to Lima and was unemployed at the time of the interview, expressed a view of his plight that in addition to being poetic, is a prototype of the socio-psychological situation of many lower-class Peruvians. The following story, a combination of Hansel and Gretel, a Peruvian folktale,[15] and the informant's own projections, was given as a response to the blank TAT card. Among other things it brings out the theme of abandonment by the parents and disillusion in other substitute authority figures.

"These are monsters, very ancient things. The monster had power because he was from God—against human beings. There was a married couple in a place where there was nothing to eat—a poor family. They had two children, a little girl and a little boy. The parents went far away to look for food. They found only one piece of bread for themselves at night. The children were waiting for their parents. When the parents arrived the children woke up asking them for bread. Not finding any food for themselves, the parents decided to throw the children off a precipice far away. The mother said it was better to kill them; the father said it was not better. They decided not to kill the children there but to put them in a bag and to take them to the precipice. They left them hanging in the air by a rope over the precipice. During the day the children cried for help. Hearing this, a condor came and took them, carrying them down to the ground. The children got out of the bag and started to walk. The condor flew away, scared. The children walked alone to an unknown place. The little girl was ten and the boy only five. The girl spoke perfectly and could walk. During that whole day they found only one kernel of corn, which somebody had thrown out; they divided it in two and ate. In that lonely place they cried in the night for their mother and father. A high voice answered their call. A little while later the monster presented himself to the children and took them to his cave. Then the monster spoke. He said, 'Who are you and from where did you come?' The children said they had lost their parents, and the monster said, 'I'll take care of you.' The monster put rocks in a pot and boiled them as though they were potatoes, but the children couldn't eat them because they were rocks. The monster began to eat the rocks as though they were stewed potatoes, trying to show them how to eat, but they couldn't eat them. He said, 'If you can't eat these potatoes, I'm going to eat you.' While the monster was asleep in his cave, the children escaped. The children, fleeing, found a wooden cross, and they said, 'Sir, save us from this danger, we've lost our parents.' They heard the monster coming. They went to hide under the cross, and when they hid under the cross there was no monster. They heard a voice from the sky that said, 'My children, come up.' Looking up they saw nothing but a rope ladder. They went up the ladder to the sky—into space. Then the monster came and asked the cross to put the ladder down so he could follow the children. The cross did, and he started up the ladder after the children. The monster said, 'Just as you have God, I also have God, and when I catch you I'll eat you.' But on the ladder the monster was climbing there were two rats and they were tearing the rope ladder. The monster said to them, 'Brothers, don't destroy my ladder, I have to destroy my prisoners.' The rats answered, 'For a bad person there is no ladder to God.' Then they tore through the ladder, and the monster fell to the ground, landing on the edge of a hill. His blood splashed all over one tremendous hill and on to others; the hill he landed on exploded like a bomb. The story ends now. Whenever anybody calls, the hills answer or, better said, they echo. When somebody calls, he thinks it is a person answering, but it is not a person."

NOTES

1. Kubler, G., *The Indian Caste of Peru, 1785 to 1940: A Population Study Based upon Tax Records and Census Reports,* Smithsonian Institution, Institute of Social Anthropology, Publication 14, 1952.
2. García Frías, R., "Intensidad absoluta y relativa de la emigración provinciana al Departamento de Lima," *Estadística Peruana,* 1947, V, 54–66.
3. Beals, Ralph L., "Social Stratification in Latin America," *American Journal of Sociology,* 1953, LVIII, 327–339.
4. Mangin, William P., "Estratificación social en el Callejón de Huaylas," *Revista del Museo Nacional,* 1955, XXIV, Lima.
5. Simmons, Ozzie G., "El uso de los conceptos de aculturación y asimilación en el estudio del cambio cultural en el Perú," *Peru Indígena,* 1952, II, 40–45.
6. Fried, J., "Acculturation and Mental Health among Migrants in Peru," in M. K. Opler, ed., *Culture and Mental Health,* New York, Macmillan, 1959.
7. Mangin, William P., "The Role of Regional Associations in the Adaptation of Rural Population in Peru," *Sociologus,* 1959, IX, 23–36, Berlin.
8. Mangin, William P., "Conflictos culturales y salud mental," paper presented at the Second Latin American Congress for Mental Health, 1959, Lima.
9. Matos Mar, José, *Censo de las barriadas de Lima,* 1956. (Manuscript.)
10. *Censo Nacional de Población del Perú,* Ministerio de Hacienda, 1940, Lima.
11. *Estadística peruana,* Ministerio de Hacienda, 1958, Lima.
12. Wellin, Edward, "Water Boiling in a Peruvian Town," in B. Paul,

ed., *Health, Culture, and Community*, New York, Russell Sage Foundation, 1955.

13. Gildea, M., H. R. Domke, I. N. Mensh, A. D. Buchmueller, J. C. Glidewell, and M. B. Kantor, "Community Mental Health Research: Findings after Three Years," *American Journal of Psychiatry*, 1958, CXIV, 970–976.

14. Rotondo, Humberto, *et al.*, *Estudios de psiquiatría social en áreas urbanas y rurales*, Mendocita, 1959. (Mimeo.)

15. Arguedas, J. M. and F. Izquierdo Rios, *Mitos, leyendas, y cuentos peruanos*, Ministry of Education, Lima, 1947. (See the story "El Achiguée," pp. 130–134, for similar themes.)

A Selected Bibliography

The following bibliography is intended as a guide to beginning students. Although authors from several disciplines are represented, there is a strong emphasis on anthropological perspectives. Space limitations disallow the inclusion of references to numerous excellent articles in periodicals, but a list of research aids and bibliographies will help the student gain familiarity with this sizeable and significant part of the literature.

Books marked with * are available in paperback editions. Those marked (*) are available in both Spanish and English; the original is cited.

Research Aids and Bibliographies

American Geographical Society. *Current Geographical Publications* (10 issues yearly, since 1938).

Baldus, Herbert
1954 *Bibliografía crítica de etnología brasileira,* São Paulo, Comissão do IV centenário da cidade de São Paulo.

"Bibliographie Americaniste," *Journal de la Société des Américanistes de Paris,* Paris (annually since 1919).

Butler, Ruth L., ed.
1950 *Guide to the Hispanic American Historical Review, 1918–1945,* Duke University Press, Durham, N.C.

Carroll, Thomas F.
1962 *Land Tenure and Land Reform in Latin America: A Selective Annotated Bibliography*, preliminary edition, Inter-American Development Bank, Washington, D.C.

Center of Latin American Studies, University of California, Los Angeles *Statistical Abstract of Latin America* (annually since 1955).

Ewald, Robert
1956 *Bibliografía comentada sobre antropología social, 1900–1955*, Seminario de Integración Social Guatemalteca, Guatemala.

German Parra, Manuel and Wigberto Jiménez Moreno
1954 *Bibliografía indigenista de México y Centroamérica (1850–1950)*, Memorias del Instituto Nacional Indigenista, Vol. IV, Mexico.

Gibson, Charles, with E. V. Niemeyer
1958 *Guide to the Hispanic American Historical Review, 1946–1955*, Duke University Press, Durham, N.C.

Gibson, G. D.
1960 "A Bibliography of Anthropological Bibliographies: The Americas," *Current Anthropology* 1:61–75

Handbook of Latin American Studies, University of Florida Press, Gainesville (annually since 1935).

Instituto Indigenista Interamericano
1961 *Guide to the Indian Population of America*, Special Issue of the *Boletín Indigenista*, 170–266, Mexico.

Inter-American Review of Bibliography, Pan American Union, Washington, D.C. (quarterly since January 1951).

International Congress of Americanists. *Proceedings* (issued every two years at location of Congress).

Kidder, Frederick E. and Allen Bushong
1963 *Theses on Panamerican Topics*, 4th ed., Pan American Union, Washington, D.C.

O'Leary, Timothy J., ed.
1963 *Ethnographic Bibliography of South America*, Human Relations Area Files, New Haven.

Pan American Institute of Geography and History. *Boletín Bibliográfico de Antropología Americana*, Mexico (annually since 1937).

Sanchez, George I. and Howard Putnam
1959 *Materials Relating to the Education of Spanish Speaking People in the United States: An Annotated Bibliography*, Latin American Studies 17, University of Texas, Austin.

XXXV Congreso Internacional de Americanistas
1962 *Bibliografía antropológica: trabajos publicados en México, 1955–1962*, Mexico, Comité organizador.

Trujillo Ferrari, Alfonso
1956 "Las ciencias sociales en Perú durante los últimos quince años" *Ciencias Sociales* 7:38:101–157, Washington, D.C.

(Portuguese version originally appeared in São Paulo in *Sociologia*, Vol. 16, no. 2, pp. 36–106, 1954).

Zimmerman, Irene
1961 A *Guide to Latin American Periodicals: Humanities and Social Sciences*, Kallman, Gainesville, Fla.

Monograph Series

GENERAL

Ibero-Americana, University of California, Berkeley and Los Angeles.

Latin American Monographs, University of Florida, Gainesville.

Monographs of the Department of Social Affairs of the Pan American Union, Washington, D.C.

Monographs of the Institute of Latin American Studies, The University of Texas, Austin.

Publications of the Centro Latinoamericano de Investigaciones en Ciencias Sociales, Rio de Janeiro.

Publications of the Institute of Social Anthropology, Smithsonian Institution, Washington, D.C. (No longer issued.)

Foreign Area Studies Division, Special Operations Research Office, *Special Warfare Area Handbook*, and *U.S. Army Area Handbook* Series, Washington, D.C. (Issued so far are volumes on Bolivia, Colombia, Cuba, and Panama.)

MIDDLE AMERICA

Acta Antropológica, Mexico.

Estudios de Cultura Maya, Mexico.

Estudios de Cultura Nahuatl, Mexico.

Memorias del Instituto Nacional Indigenista, Mexico.

Notes on Middle American Archaeology and Ethnology, Carnegie Institution of Washington.

Publications and *Informes* of the Instituto Geográfico de Costa Rica, San José.

Publications of the Middle American Research Institute, Tulane University, New Orleans.

Publicaciones del Seminario de Integración Social Guatemalteca, Guatemala.

SOUTH AMERICA

Brasiliana. Companhia Editora Nacional, São Paulo. Coleção *Corpo e Alma do Brasil*, Difusão Européia do Livro, São Paulo.

Monografías Andinas, Lima.

Monografías Sociológicas, Bogotá.

Monographs issued by Plan Regional para el Desarrollo del Sur del Perú, Lima.

Publications of the Instituto de Sociología, University of Chile, Santiago.

Serie Monográfica del Plan Nacional de Integración de la Población Aborígena, Lima.

Serie Monografías Ethnológicas, Universidad Nacional Mayor de San Marcos, Lima.

Textos Brasileiros de Instituto Superior de Estudos Brasileiros, Rio de Janeiro.

Travaux de l'Institut français d'études andines, Paris.

General Sources

American Anthropologist

1955 57:3, June 1955 (special issue devoted to Latin America, edited by Sidney W. Mintz).

American Assembly

*1959 *The United States and Latin America,* Columbia University Press, New York.

Burr, Robert N., ed.

1961 "Latin America's Nationalistic Revolutions," *Annals of the American Academy of Political and Social Science,* Vol. 334, Philadelphia.

Council on Foreign Relations

*1960 *Social Change in Latin America Today,* Harper, New York.

Crevenna, Theo., ed.

1951 *Materiales para el estudio de la clase media en la América Latina,* 5 vols., Pan American Union, Washington, D.C. (Mimeographed.)

Davis, Kingsley, ed.

1958 "It's a Crowding Hemisphere: Population Changes in the Americas," *Annals of the American Academy of Political and Social Science,* Vol. 316, Philadelphia.

Foster, George M.

1960 *Culture and Conquest: America's Spanish Heritage,* Viking Fund Publication in Anthropology 27, New York.

Gillin, John

1949 "Mestizo America," in Ralph Linton, ed., *Most of the World,* Columbia University Press, New York.

*Hanke, Lewis

1959 *Modern Latin America: Continent in Ferment,* 2 vols., Van Nostrand, New York.

Hauser, Philip M., ed.

1961 *Urbanization in Latin America,* UNESCO, New York.

*Hirschman, A. O., ed.

1961 *Latin American Issues: Essays and Comments,* Twentieth Century Fund, New York.

International Labor Organization

1953 *Indigenous Peoples,* Geneva. (*)

1957 *The Landless Farmer in Latin America,* Geneva.

James, Preston E.

1959 *Latin America,* 3d rev. ed., Odyssey Press, New York.

Johnson, John J., ed.

1964 *Continuity and Change in Latin America,* Social Science Research Council, New York.

*Leonard, Olen E. and Charles P. Loomis, eds.
1953 *Readings in Latin American Social Organization and Institutions,* Michigan State College Press, East Lansing.
*Lieuwen, Edwin
1960 *Arms and Politics in Latin America,* Praeger, New York.
Mecham, J. Lloyd
1934 *Church and State in Latin America,* University of North Carolina Press, Chapel Hill.
*Pan American Union
1959 *Plantation Systems of the New World,* Social Science Monograph 7, Washington, D.C.
Parsons, Kenneth H., Raymond J. Penn, and Philip M. Raup
1956 *Land Tenure,* University of Wisconsin Press, Madison.
Pike, Frederick B., ed.
1959 *Freedom and Reform in Latin America,* Notre Dame University Press, Notre Dame, Ind.
Platt, R. S.
1942 *Latin America: Countrysides and United Regions,* McGraw-Hill, New York.
*Poblete Troncoso, Moisés and Ben G. Burnett
1960 *The Rise of the Latin American Labor Movement,* Bookman Associates, New York.
Rosenblatt, Angel
1954 *La población indígena y el mestizaje en América,* Editorial Nove, Buenos Aires.
Silvert, Kalman H.
1961 *Reaction and Revolution in Latin America,* Hauser Press, New Orleans.
Steward, Julian, ed.
1946–1950 *Handbook of South American Indians,* 6 vols., Bureau of American Ethnology Bulletin 143, Washington, D.C.
Steward, Julian and Louis C. Faron
1959 *The Native Peoples of South America,* McGraw-Hill, New York.
Tax, Sol, ed.
1952 *Acculturation in the Americas,* University of Chicago Press, Chicago.
de Vries, Egbert, José Medina Echavarria and Benjamin Higgins
1963 *Social Aspects of Economic Development in Latin America,* 2 vols., UNESCO.

Area Studies

THE UNITED STATES

Berle, Beatrice Bishop
1958 *Eighty Puerto Rican Families in New York City: Health and Disease Studied in Context,* Columbia University Press, New York.

Burma, John
1954 *Spanish-speaking Groups in the United States,* Duke University Press, Durham, N.C.

Clark, Margaret
1959 *Health in the Mexican-American Culture:* A *Community Study,* University of California Press, Berkeley and Los Angeles.

Edmonson, Munro S.
1957 *Los Manitos, A Study of Institutional Values.* Middle American Research Institute Publication 23, pp. 1–72, Tulane University, New Orleans.

Kibbe, Pauline R.
1946 *Latin Americans in Texas,* University of New Mexico School of Inter-American Affairs, Inter-American Series Studies 3, Albuquerque.

Kluckhohn, Florence
1961 "The Spanish Americans of Atrisco," in F. Kluckhohn and F. Strodtbeck, eds., *Variations in Value Orientation,* Row, Peterson Co., Evanston, Ill.

Leonard, Olen E. and Charles P. Loomis
1941 *Culture of a Contemporary Rural Community: El Cerrito, New Mexico,* U. S. Dept. of Agriculture, Rural Life Studies, no. 1, Washington, D.C.

Mills, Charles Wright, Clarence Senior, and Rose Goldsen
1950 *The Puerto Rican Journey,* Harper, New York.

Padilla, Elena
1958 *Up from Puerto Rico,* Columbia University Press, New York.

Rubel, Arthur J.
In Press *Across the Tracks: Mexican Americans in a Texas City,* University of Texas Press, Austin.

Saunders, Lyle
1954 *Cultural Differences and Medical Care: The Case of the Spanish-speaking People of the Southwest,* Russell Sage Foundation, New York.

MIDDLE AMERICA
(MEXICO, CENTRAL AMERICA, AND PANAMA)

Adams, Richard N.
1957 *Culture Surveys of Panama-Nicaragua-Guatemala-Honduras-El Salvador,* Pan American Sanitary Bureau, Scientific Publication 33, Washington, D.C.

Tax, Sol, ed.
1952 *Heritage of Conquest,* Free Press, Glencoe, Ill.

Wauchope, Robert, ed.
1964– *Handbook of Middle American Indians* (14 vols. to be published), University of Texas Press, Austin. Robert C. West, ed., Vol. I, *Natural Environment and Early Cultures.*

Wolf, Eric R.
*1959 *Sons of the Shaking Earth,* University of Chicago Press, Chicago.

MEXICO

Aguirre Beltrán, Gonzalo
*1953 *Formas de gobierno indígena,* Imprenta Universitaria, Mexico.
1957 *Cuijla, un pueblo negro,* Fondo de Cultura Económica, Mexico.

Bailey, Helen Miller
1958 *Santa Cruz of the Etla Hills,* University of Florida Press, Gainesville.

Beals, Ralph L.
1945 *Ethnology of the Western Mixe,* University of California Publications in American Archaeology and Ethnology, Vol. 42, Berkeley.
1946 *Cherán: A Sierra Tarascan Village,* Smithsonian Institution, Institute of Social Anthropology Publication 2, Washington, D.C.

Bennett, Wendell C. and Robert M. Zingg
1935 *The Tarahumara, an Indian tribe of Northern Mexico,* University of Chicago Press, Chicago.

Brand, Donald
1951 *Quiroga, A Mexican Municipio,* Smithsonian Institution, Institute of Social Anthropology Publication 11, Washington, D.C.

Covarrubias, Miguel
1946 *Mexico South: The Isthmus of Tehuantepec,* Knopf, New York.

De la Fuente, Julio
1948 "Cambios socio-culturales en México," *Acta Antropológica* 3:4, Mexico.
1949 *Yalalag; una villa zapoteca serrana,* Museo Nacional de Antropología, Serie Científica, no. 1, Mexico.

Diaz Guerrero, Rogelio
1961 *Estudios de psicología del Mexicano,* Mexico.

Foster, George M.
1948 *Empire's Children: The People of Tzintzuntzan,* Smithsonian Institution, Institute of Social Anthropology Publication 6, Washington, D.C.

Gamio, Manuel
1922 *La población del Valle de Teotihuacán,* Dirección de Talleres Gráficos, Mexico.

Guiteras-Holmes, Calixta
1952 *Sayula,* Sociedad Mexicana de Geografía y Estadística, Mexico.
1961 *Perils of the Soul: The World View of a Tzotzil Indian,* Free Press, Glencoe, Ill.

Hancock, Richard H.
1959 *The Role of the Bracero in the Economic and Cultural Dynamics of Mexico: A Case Study of Chihuahua,* Stanford University Press, Stanford.

Iturriaga, José E.
1951 *La estructura social y cultural de México,* Mexico, Fondo de Cultura Económica.

Kelly, Isabel
1965 *Folk Practices in North Mexico,* Latin American Monographs, No. 2, Institute of Latin American Studies, The University of Texas, Austin.

Kelly, Isabel and Angel Palerm
1952 *The Tajin Totonac, Part I: History, Subsistence, Shelter, and Technology,* Smithsonian Institution, Institute of Social Anthropology Publication 13, Washington, D.C.

Leslie, Charles
1960 *Now We Are Civilized: A Study of the World View of the Zapotec Indians of Mitla, Oaxaca,* Wayne State University Press, Detroit.

Lewis, Oscar
*1951 *Life in a Mexican Village: Tepoztlán Restudied,* University of Illinois Press, Urbana.*
*1959 *Five Families: Mexican Case Studies in the Culture of Poverty,* Basic Books, New York. (*)
*1961 *The Children of Sanchez,* Random House, New York.

Madsen, William
1960 *The Virgin's Children: Life in an Aztec Village Today,* Unisity of Texas Press, Austin.

Malinowski, Bronislaw and Julio de la Fuente
1957 "La economía de un sistema de mercados en México," *Acta Antropológica, Época* 2, Vol. 1, no. 2, Mexico.

Parsons, Elsie Clews
1936 *Mitla, Town of the Souls,* University of Chicago Press, Chicago.

Pozas, Ricardo
*1948 "Juan Perez Jolote: biografía de un Tzotzil," *Acta Antropológica* 3:3, Mexico. (In English: *Juan the Chamula,* University of California Press, 1962.)
1959 *Chamula: un pueblo indio de los altos de Chiapas,* Memorias del Instituto Nacional Indigenista, Vol. 8, Mexico.

Redfield, Robert
1930 *Tepotzlán: A Mexican Village,* University of Chicago Press, Chicago.
1941 *The Folk Culture of Yucatan,* University of Chicago Press, Chicago.
*1950 *The Village That Chose Progress,* University of Chicago Press, Chicago.

Redfield, Robert and Alfonso Villa Rojas
*1934 *Chan Kom: A Maya Village,* Carnegie Institution of Washington Publication 448, Washington, D.C. (reprinted by University of Chicago Press).

Spicer, Edward H.
1954 *Potam: A Yaqui Village in Sonora,* American Anthropological Association, Memoir 77.

Taylor, Paul S.
1933 "A Spanish American Community: Arandas in Jalisco, Mexico," *Ibero-Americana,* no. 4, Mexico.

Villa Rojas, Alfonso
1945 *The Maya of East Central Quintana Roo,* Carnegie Institution of Washington Publication 559, Washington, D.C.

West, Robert C.
1948 *Cultural Geography of the Modern Tarascan Area,* Smithsonian Institution, Institute of Social Anthropology Publication 7, Washington, D.C.

Whetten, Nathan
1948 *Rural Mexico,* University of Chicago Press, Chicago.

Whiteford, Andrew H.
*1960 *Two Cities of Latin America: A Comparative Description of Social Classes,* Logan Museum Publications in Anthropology no. 9, Beloit, Wis.

Zantwijk, R. A. M. van
1960 *Los indígenas de Milpas Altas,* Instituto Real de los Tropicos, Sección de Antropología Cultural y Física, no. 64, Amsterdam.

GUATEMALA

Adams, Richard N., ed.
1957 *Political Changes in Guatemalan Indian Communities,* Middle American Research Institute Publication 24, pp. 1–54, Tulane University, New Orleans.
*1960 "Social Change in Guatemala and U. S. Policy," in *Social Change in Latin America Today,* Harper, New York.

Arriola, J. L., ed.
1956 *Integración social en Guatemala,* Seminario de Integración Social Guatemalteca, Guatemala.

Bunzel, Ruth
1952 *Chichicastenango: A Guatemalan Village,* University of Washington Press, Seattle.

Gillin, John
1951 *The Culture of Security in San Carlos,* Middle American Research Institute Publication 16, Tulane University, New Orleans. (*)

La Farge, Oliver
1947 *Santa Eulalia: The Religion of a Cuchumatan Indian Town,* University of Chicago Press, Chicago.

McBryde, F. Webster
1945 *Cultural and Historical Geography of Southwest Guatemala,* Smithsonian Institution, Institute of Social Anthropology Publication 4, Washington, D.C.

Monteforte Toledo, Mario
1959 *Guatemala: monografía sociológica,* Imprenta Universitaria, Mexico.

Nash, Manning
1958 *Machine Age Maya,* American Anthropological Association Memoir 87.

Reina, Ruben E.
1960 *Chinautla, a Guatemalan Indian Community: A Study in the Relationship of Community Culture and National Change,* Middle American Research Institute, Tulane University, New Orleans. (*)

Tax, Sol
1953 *Penny Capitalism: A Guatemalan Indian Economy,* Smithsonian Institution, Institute of Social Anthropology Publication 16, Washington, D.C. (*)

Tumin, Melvin M.
1952 *Caste in Peasant Society,* Princeton University Press, Princeton, N.J.

Valladares, Leon A.
1957 *El hombre y el maíz: etnografía y etnopsicología de Colotenango,* Guatemala.

Wagley, Charles
1941 *The Economics of a Guatemalan Village,* American Anthropological Association Memoir 58. (*)
1950 *Social and Religious Life of a Guatemalan Community,* American Anthropological Association Memoir 71. (*)

Whetten, Nathan
1961 *Guatemala: The Land and the People,* Yale University Press, New Haven.

Wisdom, Charles
1940 *The Chorti Indians of Guatemala,* University of Chicago Press, Chicago. (*)

EL SALVADOR

Baron Castro, Rodolfo
1942 *La población de El Salvador,* Instituto de Gonzalo Fernández de Oviedo, Madrid.

Marroquin, Alejandro D.
1959 *Panchimalco: investigación sociológica,* Editorial Universitaria, San Salvador.

COSTA RICA

Biesanz, John and Mavis Biesanz
1945 *Costa Rican Life,* Columbia University Press, New York.

Loomis, Charles P., *et al.*
1953 *Turrialba: Social Systems and Social Change,* Free Press, Glencoe, Ill.

Sandner, Gerhard
1961 *Agrarkolonisation in Costa Rica,* Schriften des geographischen Instituts der Universität Kiel, Band XIX, Heft 3.

Sariola, Sakari
1954 *Análisis socio-económico del Barrio Sagrada Familia, área recien urbanizada de San José, Costa Rica,* Escuela Superior de Administración Pública, San José.
1954 *Social Class and Social Mobility in a Costa Rican Town,* Inter-American Institute of Agricultural Science, Turrialba.

PANAMA

Biesanz, John and Mavis Biesanz
1955 *The People of Panama,* Columbia University Press, New York.

Guzman, Louis E.
1956 *Farming and Farmlands in Panama,* University of Chicago, Department of Geography, Research Papers, no. 44, Chicago.

Hooper, Ofelia
1945 *Aspectos de la vida social rural de Panamá,* Bulletin of the Institute of Social and Economic Research, Vol. 2, no. 3, pp. 67–315, Panama.

VENEZUELA

Buitrón, Anibal
n.d. *Causas y efectos del éxodo rural en Venezuela,* Pan American Union, Washington, D.C.

Corsejo de Bienestar Rural
n.d. *Problemas economicos y sociales de los Andes venezolanos,* Caracas.

Hill, George W.
1960 *Central Tacarigua: estudio sociológico,* Corporación Venezolana de Fomento, Caracas.
1961 *El estado Sucre: sus recursos humanos,* Universidad Central de Venezuela, Ediciones de la Biblioteca, Caracas.

Hill, George W., José A. Silva Michelena, and Ruth Oliver de Hill
1960 *La vida rural en Venezuela,* Ministerio de Agricultura y Cría, Caracas.

Lieuwen, Edwin
1961 *Venezuela,* Oxford University Press, New York.

Silva Michelena, José A., ed.
1960 *Aspectos socio-económicos, socio-métricos, culturales y socio-psicológicos de Cumaripa,* Caracas.

COLOMBIA

Crist, Raymond F.
1952 *The Cauca Valley, Colombia: Land Tenure and Land Use,* University of Florida Press, Gainesville.

Fals-Borda, Orlando
1955 *Peasant Society in the Colombian Andes: A Sociological Study of Saució,* University of Florida Press, Gainesville. (*)
1957 *El hombre y la tierra en Boyacá,* Editorial Antares, Bogotá.

Gutiérrez de Pineda, Virginia
1958 *El país rural colombiano,* Revista Colombiana de Antropología 7:1–126.

Guzman, German, Orlando Fals-Borda, and Eduardo Umaña Luna
1962 *La Violencia en Colombia,* Universidad Nacional, Facultad de Sociología, Monografías Sociológicas, no. 121, Bogota.

Parsons, James J.
1949 "Antioquia: Colonization in Western Colombia," *Ibero Americana,* 32, Mexico. (*)

Reichel-Dolmatoff, Gerardo and Alicia Reichel-Dolmatoff
1961 *The People of Aritama: The Cultural Personality of a Colombian Mestizo Village,* University of Chicago Press, Chicago.

Savage, Charles
1964 *Social Reorganization in a Factory in the Andes,* Monograph No. 7, Society for Applied Anthropology.

Smith, T. Lynn, Justo Rodríguez Díaz, and Luis Roberto García
1945 *Tabio: A Study in Rural Social Organization,* U.S. Department of Agriculture, Office of Foreign Agricultural Relations, Washington, D.C.

West, Robert C.
1957 *The Pacific Lowlands of Colombia,* University of Louisiana Press, Baton Rouge.

Whiteford, Andrew H.
*1960 *Two Cities of Latin America: A Comparative Description of Social Classes,* Logan Museum Publications in Anthropology, no. 9, Beloit, Wis. (*)

ECUADOR

Cisneros Cisneros, César
1948 *Demografía y estadística sobre el indio ecuatoriano,* Talleres Gráficos Nacionales, Quito.

Collier, John and Anibal Buitrón
1949 *The Awakening Valley,* University of Chicago Press, Chicago.

Ferndon, Edwin N., Jr.
1950 *Studies in Ecuadorian Geography,* Monographs of the School of American Research, no. 15, pp. 1–86, Santa Fe, N.M.

Leonard, Olen E.
1947 *Pichilinque: A Study of Rural Life in Coastal Ecuador*, U.S. Department of Agriculture, Office of Foreign Agricultural Relations, Washington, D.C.

Parsons, Elsie Clews
1945 *Peguche: A Study of Andean Indians*, University of Chicago Press, Chicago.

Rubio Orbe, Gonzalo
1956 *Punyaro: estudio de antropología social y cultural de una comunidad indígena y mestizo*, Casa de Cultura Ecuatoriana, Quito.

PERU

Adams, Richard N.
1959 *A Community in the Andes: Problems and Progress in Muquiyauyo*, University of Washington Press, Seattle.

Bourricaud, François
1962 *Changements à Puno: étude de sociologie andine*, Université de Paris, Travaux et mémoires de l'Institut des Hautes Etudes de l'Amérique latine, 11, Paris.

Castro Pozo, Hildebrando
1924 *Nuestra comunidad indígena*, El Lucero, Lima.

Escobar, Gabriel
1960 *La estructura política rural del Departamento de Puno*, Cuzco.

Ford, Thomas R.
1955 *Man and Land in Peru*, University of Florida Press, Gainesville.

Gillin, John
1947 *Moche: A Peruvian Coastal Community*, Smithsonian Institution, Institute of Social Anthropology Publication 3, Washington, D.C.

Hammel, Eugene A.
1962 *Wealth, Authority and Prestige in the Ica Valley, Peru*, University of New Mexico Publications in Anthropology, no. 10, Albuquerque.

Holmberg, Allan R.
1960 "Changing Community Attitudes and Values in Peru," in *Social Change in Latin America Today*, Harper, New York.

Matos Mar, José, *et al.*
1958 *Las actuales comunidades de indígenas: Huarochiri en 1955*, Universidad Nacional Mayor de San Marcos, Serie Monografías Etnográficas, Vol. 1, Lima.

Mishkin, Bernard
1946 "The Contemporary Quechua," in Julian Steward, ed., *Handbook of South American Indians*, Vol. II, Bureau of American Ethnology Bulletin 143, Washington, D.C.

Nuñez del Prado, Oscar
1952 *La vida y la muerte en Chinchero,* Talleres Gráficas "La Economía," Cuzco.

Sáenz, Moisés
1933 *Sobre el indio peruano y su incorporación al medio nacional,* Secretaria de Educación Pública, Mexico.

Stein, William
1961 *Hualcan: Life in the Highlands of Peru,* Cornell University Press, Ithaca, N.Y.

Tschopik, Harry
1947 *Highland Communities of Central Peru,* Smithsonian Institution, Institute of Social Anthropology Publication 5, Washington, D.C.
1951 *The Aymara of Chucuito, Peru. I: Magic,* Anthropological Papers of the American Museum of Natural History, Vol. 44, Pt. 2, New York.

BOLIVIA

Heath, Dwight B., *et al.*
(forthcoming) *Land Reform and Social Revolution in Bolivia,* University of Wisconsin Press, Madison.

La Barre, Weston
1948 *The Aymara Indians of the Lake Titicaca Plateau, Bolivia,* American Anthropological Association Memoir 68.

Leonard, Olen E.
1948 *Canton Chullpas: A Socio-economic Study in the Cochabamba Valley of Bolivia,* U.S. Department of Agriculture, Foreign Agricultural Report 27, Washington, D.C.
1952 *Bolivia: Land, Peoples, and Institutions,* Scarecrow Press, Washington, D.C.

Osborne, Harold
1955 *Bolivia: A Land Divided,* 3rd rev. ed., Royal Institute of International Affairs, London and New York.

Patch, Richard
1960 "Bolivia: U.S. Assistance in a Revolutionary Setting," in *Social Change in Latin America Today,* Harper, New York. (*)

CHILE

Baraona, Rafael, *et al.*
1961 *Valle del Putaendo: estudio de estructura agraria,* Universidad de Chile, Instituto de Geografía, Santiago.

Borde, Jean y Maria Gongora
1956 *Evolución de la propiedad rural en el Valle de Puanque,* Universidad de Chile, Instituto de Sociología, Santiago.

Butland, Gilbert J.
1957 *The Human Geography of Southern Chile*, Institute of British Geographers, Publication 24, London.

Faron, Louis C.
1961 *Mapuche Social Structure*, University of Illinois Studies in Anthropology, no. 1, Urbana.

Lambert, Charles J.
1952 *Sweet Waters, a Chilean Farm*, Chatto and Windus, London.

McBride, George M.
1936 *Chile: Land and Society*, American Geographical Society, Research Series 19, New York.

Mostny, Grete, Fidel Jeldes, Raúl González, and F. Oberhausen
1954 *Peine: un pueblo atacameño*, Universidad de Chile, Instituto de Geografía, Publication 4, Santiago.

PARAGUAY

Krause, Annemarie Elizabeth
1952 *Mennonite Settlement in the Paraguayan Chaco*, University of Chicago, Department of Geography, Research Papers, no. 25, Chicago.

Raine, Philip
1956 *Paraguay*, Rutgers University Press, New Brunswick, N.J.

Reh, Emma
1946 *Paraguayan Rural Life: Survey of Food Problems*, Institute of Inter-American Affairs, Washington, D.C.

Service, Elman R. and Helen S. Service
1954 *Tobatí: Paraguayan Town*, University of Chicago Press, Chicago.

ARGENTINA

Cochran, Thomas C., and Ruben E. Reina
1962 *Entrepreneurship in Argentine Culture*, University of Pennsylvania Press, Philadelphia.

Fillol, Thomas
1961 *Social Factors in Economic Development: The Argentine Case*, M.I.T. Press, Cambridge, Mass.

Germani, Gino
1962 *Política y sociedad en una época de transición de la sociedad tradicional a la sociedad de masas*, Paidós, Buenos Aires.

Taylor, Carl
1948 *Rural Life in Argentina*, Louisiana State University Press, Baton Rouge.

BRAZIL

Azevedo, Fernando de
1950 *Brazilian Culture: An Introduction to the Study of Culture in Brazil*, W. R. Crawford, trans., Macmillan, New York.

Blondel, Jean
1957 *As condições da vida política no Estado da Paraíba* (Traducão e notas de Alcântara Nogueira), Fundação Getúlio Vargas, Rio de Janeiro.

Cardoso, Fernando Henrique and Octavio Ianni
1960 *Côr e mobilidade social em Florianópolis,* Brasiliana, Vol. 307, Companhia Editora Nacional, São Paulo.

Diegues Junior, Manuel
1960 *Regiões culturais do Brasil,* Centro Brasileiro de Pesquisas Educacionais, Rio de Janeiro.

Freyre, Gilberto
*1946 *The Masters and the Slaves* (translated from *Casa Grande e Senzala*), Knopf, New York.
1959 *New World in the Tropics: The Culture of Modern Brazil,* Knopf, New York.

Hack, H.
1959 *Dutch Group Settlement in Brazil,* Royal Tropical Institute, no. 132, Department of Cultural and Physical Anthropology, no. 61, Amsterdam.

Harris, Marvin
1956 *Town and Country in Brazil,* Columbia University Press, New York.

Hutchinson, Bertram, *et al.*
1960 *Mobilidade e trabalho: um estudio na cidade de São Paulo,* Centro Brasileiro de Pesquisas Educacionais, Rio de Janeiro.

Hutchinson, Harry W.
1957 *Village and Plantation Life in Northeastern Brazil,* University of Washington Press, Seattle.

Morse, Richard M.
1958 *From Community to Metropolis: A Biography of São Paulo, Brazil,* University of Florida Press, Gainesville.

Oberg, Kalervo
1957 *Toledo: A Municipio on the Western Frontier of the State of Parana,* USOM/Brazil, Rio de Janiero.

Pierson, Donald
1942 *Negroes in Brazil: A Study of Race Contact at Bahía,* University of Chicago Press, Chicago.
1951 *Cruz das Almas: A Brazilian Village,* Smithsonian Institution, Institute of Social Anthropology Publication 12, Washington, D.C.

Ramos, Arthur
1937 *The Negro in Brazil,* Associated Publishers, Washington, D.C.

Schurz, William
1961 *Brazil, the Infinite Country,* Dutton, New York.

Smith, T. Lynn
1954 *Brazil: People and Institutions,* rev. ed., Louisiana State University Press, Baton Rouge.

Smith, T. Lynn and Alexander Marchant, eds.
1951 *Brazil, Portrait of Half a Continent,* Dryden Press, New York.
Wagley, Charles, ed.
1952 *Race and Class in Rural Brazil,* UNESCO, Paris.
*1953 *Amazon Town: A Study of Man in the Tropics,* Macmillan, New York.
1963 *An Introduction to Brazil,* Columbia University Press, New York.
Willems, Emilio
1947 *Cunha: tradição e transição em uma cultura rural do Brasil,* Secretario da Agricultura do Estado de São Paulo, São Paulo.
1961 *Uma villa brasileira; tradição e transição* Difusão Européia do Livro, São Paulo.
Willems, Emilio and Giocondo Mussolini
1952 *Buzios Island: A Caicara Community in Southern Brazil,* University of Washington Press, Seattle.

THE CARIBBEAN

Keur, Dorothy L. and Vera Rubin, eds.
1960 *Social and Cultural Pluralism in the Caribbean,* Annals of the New York Academy of Science, Vol. 83, Art. 5, pp. 761–916, New York.
Mintz, Sidney W., ed.
1960 *Papers in Caribbean Anthropology,* Yale University Publications in Anthropology, nos. 57–64, New Haven.
Rubin, Vera, ed.
1960 *Caribbean Studies: A Symposium,* University of Washington Press, Seattle.
Smith, M. G.
1962 *West Indian Family Structure,* University of Washington Press, Seattle.

CUBA

Nelson, Lowry
1950 *Rural Cuba,* University of Minnesota Press, Minneapolis.
Ortiz Fernández, Fernando
1947 *Cuban Counterpoint,* Knopf, New York.

HAITI

De Young, Maurice
1958 *Man and Land in the Haitian Economy,* Latin American Monographs, no. 3, University of Florida Press, Gainesville.
Herskovits, Melville J.
1937 *Life in a Haitian Valley,* Knopf, New York.
Leyburn, James G.
1941 *The Haitian People,* Yale University Press, New Haven.

Métraux, Alfred
1951 *Making a Living in the Marbial Valley (Haiti)*, UNESCO Occasional Paper in Education, no. 10, Paris.
1960 *Haiti: Black Peasants and Voodoo* (translated by P. Lengyel), Universal Books, New York.

JAMAICA

Beckwith, Martha Warren
1929 *Black Roadways: A Study of Jamaica Folk-Life,* University of North Carolina Press, Chapel Hill.

Blake, Judith
1961 *Family Structure in Jamaica, the Social Context of Reproduction,* Free Press, Glencoe, Ill.

Clarke, Edith
1957 *My Mother Who Fathered Me: A Study of the Family in Three Selected Communities in Jamaica,* G. Allen and Unwin, London.

Henriques, Fernando
1953 *Family and Colour in Jamaica,* Eyre and Spottiswoode, London.

Kerr, Madeline
1952 *Personality and Conflict in Jamaica,* Liverpool University Press, Liverpool.

Roberts, George W.
1957 *The Population of Jamaica: An Analysis of Its Structure and Growth,* Cambridge University Press, Cambridge.

PUERTO RICO

Hatt, Paul K.
1952 *Backgrounds of Human Fertility in Puerto Rico,* Princeton University Press, Princeton, N.J.

Hill, Reuben, *et al.*
1959 *The Family and Population Control: A Puerto Rican Experiment in Social Change,* University of North Carolina Press, Chapel Hill.

Landy, David
1959 *Tropical Childhood: Cultural Transmission and Learning in a Rural Puerto Rican Village,* University of North Carolina Press, Chapel Hill.

Mintz, Sidney W.
1960 *Worker in the Cane: A Puerto Rican Life History,* Yale University Press, New Haven.

Steward, Julian, *et al.*
1956 *The People of Puerto Rico,* University of Illinois Press, Urbana.

Tumin, Melvin M. and Arnold Feldman
1961 *Social Class and Social Change in Puerto Rico,* Princeton University Press, Princeton, N.J.

TRINIDAD

Herskovits, Melville J. and Francis S. Herskovits
1947 *Trinidad Village,* Knopf, New York.
Klass, Morton
1961 *East Indians in Trinidad,* Columbia University Press, New York.
Niehoff, Arthur and Juanita Niehoff
1960 *East Indians in the West Indies,* Milwaukee Public Museum Publications in Anthropology, no. 6, Milwaukee, Wis.

THE GUIANAS

Herskovits, Melville J.
1934 *Rebel Destiny: Among the Bush Negroes of Dutch Guiana,* Lippincott, New York.
Kahn, Morton C.
1931 *Djuka, the Bush Negroes of Dutch Guiana,* Viking Press, New York.
Smith, Raymond T.
1956 *The Negro Family in British Guiana,* Routledge and Kegan Paul, London and Jamaica.

THE LESSER ANTILLES

Keur, John and Dorothy L. Keur
1960 *Windward Children: A Study in the Human Ecology of Three Dutch Windward Islands in the Caribbean,* Humanities Press, New York.
Smith, M. G.
1962 *Kinship and Community in Carriacou,* Yale University Press, New Haven.

Index

THE EDITORS

RICHARD N. ADAMS, Professor of Anthropology, Chairman of the Department of Anthropology and Assistant Director, Institute of Latin American Studies, The University of Texas, received his A.B. from the University of Michigan and his M.A. and Ph.D. from Yale. He was an ethnologist for the Smithsonian Institution, served with the World Health Organization, and has taught at Michigan State University and the University of California, Berkeley. His work in Latin America has specialized in the Andean region and Central America. He is author of *A Community in the Andes, The Problems and Progress in Muquiyauyo* (1959), *Culture Surveys of Panama–Nicaragua–Guatemala–El Salvador–Honduras* (1957); and he is the co-author of *U.S. University Programs in Latin America* (1960) and *Social Change in Latin America Today* (1962).

DWIGHT B. HEATH is Associate Professor of Anthropology at Brown University, and Associate Director of Peace Corps-Studyman Project in Bolivia. He was graduated from Harvard and received his doctorate from Yale. He has done extensive anthropological field work in Mexico, Guatemala, the southwestern United States, and especially in Bolivia, where he has served as research anthropologist and consultant to Peace Corps, Research Institute for the Study of Man, Land Tenure Center, and Special Operations Research Office. He is author of *Mourt's Relation: A Journal of the Pilgrims at Plymouth* (1962), and co-author of *Land Reform and Social Revolution in Bolivia* (forthcoming).

CONTRIBUTORS

THALES DE AZEVEDO, Professor of Anthropology and Ethnography, University of Bahia.

RALPH L. BEALS, Professor of Anthropology, University of California, Los Angeles.

CHARLES J. ERASMUS, Professor of Anthropology, University of California at Santa Barbara.

GINO GERMANI, Full Professor of Sociology, and Director, Institute of Sociology, University of Buenos Aires.

JOHN GILLIN, Research Professor of Anthropology, University of Pittsburgh.

DANIEL GOLDRICH, Associate Professor of Political Science,

and Research Associate, Institute for Community Studies, University of Oregon.

SIDNEY M. GREENFIELD, Assistant Professor of Anthropology, University of Wisconsin, Milwaukee.

MARVIN HARRIS, Professor of Anthropology, Columbia University.

GEORGE W. HILL, Visiting Professor, Land Tenure Center, University of Wisconsin.

RUTH OLIVER DE HILL, friend and colleague to George W. Hill.

BERNICE A. KAPLAN, Assistant Professor of Sociology and Anthropology, Wayne State University.

JOHN H. KUNKEL, Assistant Professor of Sociology, Arizona State University.

ANTHONY LEEDS, Associate Professor of Anthropology, University of Texas.

OSCAR LEWIS, Professor of Anthropology, University of Illinois.

WILLIAM P. MANGIN, Professor of Anthropology, Syracuse University.

SIDNEY W. MINTZ, Professor of Anthropology, Yale University.

SANFORD A. MOSK, late Professor of Economics, University of California, Berkeley.

OSCAR NÚÑEZ DEL PRADO, Professor of Anthropology, University of Cuzco.

ROBERT REDFIELD, late Robert M. Hutchins Distinguished Service Professor of Anthropology, University of Chicago.

ELMAN R. SERVICE, Professor of Anthropology, University of Michigan.

HELEN S. SERVICE, friend and colleague to Elman R. Service.

JOSE A. SILVA M., Professor of Sociology, Central University of Venezuela.

OZZIE G. SIMMONS, Professor of Sociology, and Director, Institute of Behavioral Science, University of Colorado. Senior Faculty Associate in Research, Florence Heller Graduate School for Advanced Studies in Social Welfare, Brandeis University.

JULIAN STEWARD, Research Professor of Anthropology, University of Illinois.

ARNOLD STRICKON, Assistant Professor of Anthropology, Brandeis University.

SOL TAX, Professor of Anthropology, University of Chicago.

MARIO C. VÁZQUEZ V., Field Director, Peru-Cornell Project, Vicos, Peru.

CHARLES WAGLEY, Professor of Anthropology, and Director, Latin American Institute, Columbia University.

ERIC R. WOLF, Professor of Anthropology, University of Michigan.

A NOTE ON THE TYPE

The text of this book is set in Electra, a typeface designed by W(illiam) A(ddison) Dwiggins for the Mergenthaler Linotype Company and first made available in 1935. Electra cannot be classified as either "modern" or "old style." It is not based on any historical model, and hence does not echo any particular period or style of type design. It avoids the extreme contrast between "thick" and "thin" elements that marks most modern faces, and is without eccentricities which catch the eye and interfere with reading. In general, Electra is a simple, readable typeface which attempts to give a feeling of fluidity, power, and speed.

W. A. Dwiggins (1880–1956) was born in Martinsville, Ohio, and studied art in Chicago. In 1904 he moved to Hingham, Massachusetts, where he built a solid reputation as a designer of advertisements and as a calligrapher. He began an association with the Mergenthaler Linotype Company in 1929, and over the next twenty-seven years designed a number of book types, of which Metro, Electra, and Caledonia have been used very widely. In 1930 Dwiggins became interested in marionettes, and through the years made many important contributions to the art of puppetry and the design of marionettes.